Doctors and slaves

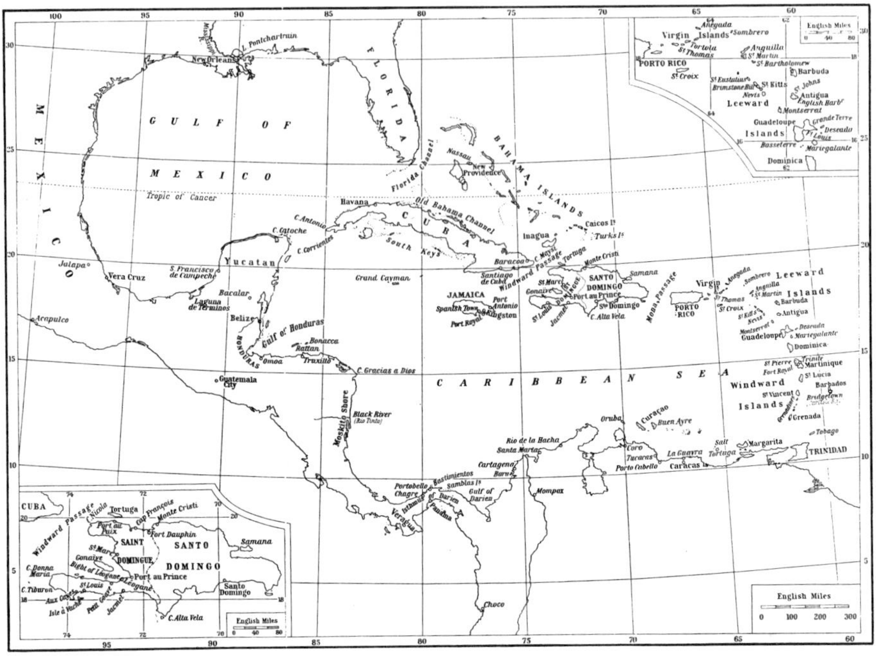

The West Indies about 1750. From Richard Pares, *War and Trade in the West Indies 1739–1763* (Oxford: Clarendon Press, 1936).

Doctors and Slaves

A medical and demographic history of slavery in the British West Indies, 1680–1834

RICHARD B. SHERIDAN

University of Kansas

The right of the University of Cambridge to print and sell all manner of books was granted by Henry VIII in 1534. The University has printed and published continuously since 1584.

CAMBRIDGE UNIVERSITY PRESS

Cambridge

London New York New Rochelle

Melbourne Sydney

Published by the Press Syndicate of the University of Cambridge
The Pitt Building, Trumpington Street, Cambridge CB2 1RP
32 East 57th Street, New York, NY 10022, USA
10 Stamford Road, Oakleigh, Melbourne 3166, Australia

First published 1985

Printed in the United States of America

Library of Congress Cataloging in Publication Data

Sheridan, Richard B., 1918–

Doctors and slaves.

Bibliography: p.

Includes index.

1. Medicine – West Indies, British – History – 17th century. 2. Medicine – West Indies, British – History – 18th century. 3. Medicine – West Indies, British – History – 19th century. 4. Slaves – Diseases – West Indies, British – History. 5. Slaves – Medical care – West Indies, British – History. 6. Slavery – West Indies, British – History. I. Title. [DNLM: 1. Blacks – history – West Indies. 2. History of Medicine, 17th Cent. – West Indies. 3. History of Medicine, 18th Cent. – West Indies. 4. History of Medicine, 19th Cent. – West Indies. WZ 70 DW5 S5d]
R475.W47S48 1985 362.1'0880625 84-9600
ISBN 0 521 25965 7

To Audrey, Richard, and Margaret

Contents

Tables and figures

Tables

Figures

Preface

In writing this book I have investigated facets of slave life that affected their health and well-being, such as culture shock, diet, work loads, punishment, housing, clothing, sanitation, and occupational hazards. I have looked at the demographic experience of the slaves, their birthrates, death rates, sex ratios, longevity, and, above all, their failure to increase their population by natural means. I have looked at the principal diseases of the slaves, contemporary and modern theories of disease causation or etiology, and methods of treatment and their efficacy. I have looked at problems of natality and infant and child care. I have investigated the state of medical science and art in Europe and Africa; the education of doctors, midwives, nurses, and apothecaries; the nature of plantation medical practice; and the quality of health care. Because of its size and economic and political importance, Jamaica has been given central attention in this study; however, other British Sugar Colonies have been investigated to the extent that demographic and medical records permit.

My approach to slave medicine and demography has been influenced by the environmental and ecology movements of recent decades. *Ecology* is a term used in the biological sciences to describe a total system of interrelated populations of different species; it is the study of the relationship of plants and animals to their environment, of the relationship of plants and animals to one another, and of the influence of humans on the ecosystem. Human ecology is the study of the relationships between humans and the innumerable factors in their environment. Medical ecology is concerned with epidemics and the environmental basis of disease. *Environment* may be defined as the sum of the external forces or conditions that act on an organism or community of organisms. Environmental factors that may place people's health in jeopardy consist of those of a physical-chemical or inorganic nature, those that are biological or organic, and sociocultural factors. Knowledge of ecological and environmental relationships is a prerequisite to understanding infectious disease, its distribution and control. More broadly, each civilization has its own pattern of diseases determined by its climate, customs, technology, and living standards. The health of people who live in tropical regions has often been in great jeopardy owing to the warm and damp conditions that make parasitic infestation a common hazard and provide a stimulating environment for the growth of such pathogens as bacteria, fungi, protozoa, and viruses, as well as the insect and other vectors that help to support the life cycles of these pathogens.

What I hope to demonstrate in this study is that the world system advocated by European politicians and economists in the age of mercantilism, colonization, and chattel slavery needs to be reexamined in the light of environmental and ecological insights and impacts. The world system called for occupational and regional specialization and division of labor and the exchange of metropolitan goods and services for the primary products of colonies and dependencies – all contained within closely regulated and relatively self-sufficient imperial systems. In this schema plantation colonies were ideal colonies. By employing African slaves to grow tobacco, sugar, indigo, and rice, among other staples, the plantation colonies were little or no drain on the labor force of the mother country. It was believed that, compared with free and bonded white labor, African slaves were cheaper inasmuch as the cost of their initial purchase and transport to the colonies was low, they were more docile and tractable, they could be directed to perform combined labor for extended periods of time, they were less costly to maintain, and, to some extent at least, they reproduced themselves. Moreover, plantation production multiplied the wealth of the metropolis. Merchants and manufacturers were encouraged to invest in the production of such plantation inputs and transportation equipment as ships, hardware, and foodstuffs; to invest in sugar refineries and textile mills, which used the output of the export industry; and to engage in commercial and financial transactions, which were commonly lucrative but risky.

Caribbean Sugar Colonies were viewed by mercantile politicians and economists as ideal plantation colonies. Not only did they produce the most valuable and widely consumed tropical agricultural commodity of all the European colonies, but this commodity was also produced under near-monoculture conditions. Colonials produced what they did not consume and consumed what they did not produce. Resources such as land, slave labor, European capital, and technology were concentrated on sugar production to such an extent that most other types of agricultural and nonagricultural production were eliminated. A great dependency thus developed for European goods and services, African slaves, North American foodstuffs and building materials, and livestock and other products from the neighboring Spanish colonies. Specialization, division of labor, and the exchange of surplus goods and services thus made the Caribbean sugar plantation a most profitable and prized possession in the age of mercantilism.

The story I attempt to tell in this study is that of the opposite face of materialist success and riches – namely, the catastrophic health and welfare costs of slavery and dependency, in short, the "curse of slavery and monoculture." Monocropping not only drained fertility from the soil, but it also violated the laws of species diversity, which give natural ecosystems the rich mixture of plant and animal species that is necessary for a state of equilibrium. The natural environment was under constant human interference. Motivated by greed and avarice, they disrupted the ecological equilibrium by using their scientific and technological knowledge for private gain. By growing sugarcane on a monocultural scale, humans caused the natural predators of the cane to multiply owing to their increased food supply. Not only were crops and animals faced with destruction by pests and disease, but humans themselves were exposed to the same fate. The concentration of people, plants, and animals in lowland tropical areas suited to cane sugar production opened a Pandora's box of debilitating and lethal pathogens and their vectors to prey on the black and white inhabitants. Thus the curse of a slavery monoculture offset the great wealth derived from the Sugar Colonies.

Although the first principle of an ecosystem is that everything depends on everything else, historical analysis calls for a dissection of problems into their component parts or topics and an explanation of how these topics are interrelated. Moreover, a historical monograph requires a common theme to hold the topics together and underline coherence and continuity. In this study the overriding problem is to explain why, apart from new recruits from Africa, the slave population on West Indies sugar plantations suffered attrition because the deaths exceeded the births. The common theme or main thread in the story of slave medicine and demography I will attempt to tell is the pervasive and significant impact of environmental and economic factors on the health and well-being of the slaves. Although innumerable factors – medical, demographic, environmental, and economic – impinged on the health of slaves, special attention will be given to environmental and economic factors. I will seek to weigh the relative importance of such microeconomic and environmental factors as work loads, diet, clothing, and housing, and such macroeconomic and environmental factors as the disease environments and epidemiology. Subordinate themes include the nature and impact of the two medical cultures – one African and the other European; the origins and credentials of European doctors who practiced in the West Indies; common diseases, their causes and treatment; the quality of health care; preventive medicine with special reference to smallpox inoculation and vaccination; and the care of pregnant women, infant and child care, and the pediatrics of slavery.

Although the medical and demographic aspects of slavery in the British West Indies have attracted some scholars, no comprehensive study of these topics has hitherto been undertaken. In 1968 Philip D. Curtin published a pathbreaking article, "Epidemiology and the Slave Trade," in *Political Science Quarterly*, which was followed a year later by his *The Atlantic Slave Trade: A Census*. Demographic aspects of slavery have been investigated by George W. Roberts, *The Population of Jamaica* (1957); Barry W. Higman, *Slave Population and Economy in Jamaica, 1807–1834* (1976); Michael Craton, *Searching for the Invisible Man: Slaves and Plantation Life in Jamaica* (1978); and David Lowenthal, "The Population of Barbados," *Social and Economic Studies* (1957). The contrasting demographic experience of the slaves in the United States has been investigated by Robert W. Fogel and Stanley L. Engerman in *Time on the Cross: The Economics of American Negro Slavery* (1974), and Engerman subsequently published "Some Economic and Demographic Comparisons of Slavery in the United States and the British West Indies" in *The Economic History Review* (1976). Medical histories of slavery have been published in recent years by Craton, *Searching for the Invisible Man*; Todd L. Savitt, *Medicine and Slavery: The Diseases and Health Care of Blacks in Antebellum Virginia* (1978); and Kenneth F. Kiple and Virginia Himmelsteib King, *Another Dimension to the Black Diaspora: Diet, Disease, and Racism* (1981).

This study is based on archival materials in three countries and a critical analysis of the printed sources, including the British Parliamentary papers and the journals of the Assembly of Jamaica. By bringing together materials from a wide range of medical, demographic, and economic sources, I hope that fresh light will be cast on the history of slavery in the British West Indies. Furthermore, it is hoped that this investigation will stimulate other scholars to pursue the subject in greater depth.

Acknowledgments

My research for this study has been undertaken at archives and libraries in the United States, the United Kingdom, and Jamaica. Also I have presented papers at historical conferences that bear on this study. In 1970, at the invitation of George C. Rogers, Jr., and James A. Rawley, I presented a paper on aspects of slave economics and demography at a conference at Columbia, South Carolina. This paper was later revised and published in *The American Historical Review*. At the invitation of Stanley L. Engerman and Eugene D. Genovese, I presented a paper on mortality and the medical treatment of slaves at a conference at the University of Rochester in 1972. In 1978, at the invitation of Svend Erik Green-Pedersen, I presented a paper on slave demography and the Atlantic slave trade at a conference at the University of Aarhus, Denmark. I wish to express my thanks for these invitations.

After some exploratory searches at the libraries at the University of Kansas, I made a short visit to the National Library of Medicine at Bethesda, Maryland. There I read printed works on the medical treatment of slaves in the British West Indies and the United States. I am grateful for the advice and assistance given me there by John B. Blake and James H. Cassedy. In 1973 the grant I had applied for was approved. This publication has been supported in part by the National Institutes of Health Grant LM 01539 from the National Library of Medicine. For this support I am most grateful. It enabled me to continue my research in the archives and libraries of the United Kingdom for six months and to engage in further work on this project at the University of the West Indies and the University of Kansas.

Several months of research in the archives and libraries of Edinburgh and Glasgow made me familiar with the Scots doctors who went to the West Indies and the West Indians who studied medicine at Edinburgh, Glasgow, and Aberdeen. The manuscript and printed literature shed light on the socioeconomic origins of the doctors; the nature of their education, training, and medical practice; and their motives for migrating to the West Indies. For their constructive advice and assistance, I wish to thank S. G. Checkland,

George Shepperson, John Imrie, Charles P. Finlayson, Thomas I. Rae, A. H. B. Masson, and Anand C. Chitnis.

After searching the Scottish records, I turned to medical and demographic materials in county record offices and universities in England and Wales. My search for collections of plantation manuscripts was motivated by a desire to discover "neutral" data that were generated in the day-to-day conduct of plantations. The collections of plantation papers include the John Gladstone Papers at Hawarden in North Wales, Senhouse Papers at Carlisle, Tharp Papers at Cambridge, Thistlewood Papers at Lincoln, Tudway Papers at Taunton, Gale-Morant Papers at Exeter, and Barham Papers at the Bodleian Library, Oxford. Among many others who helped me, I am indebted to Walter Minchinton and Stephen Fisher at Exeter, David Richardson at Hull, and Ivor P. Collis at Taunton. In London various manuscript and printed materials were searched at the Public Record Office, British Library, Library of the Royal College of Surgeons, and the Wellcome Library of Medical History.

In the summers of 1974 and 1977 I visited Jamaica. There I collected primary and secondary materials at the library of the University of the West Indies, the West India Reference Library, and the Jamaica Archives. Also I talked with people who are knowledgeable in fields related to my research, visited certain plantation districts, and viewed the ruins of slave hospitals. For their generous hospitality, encouragement, and assistance, I am indebted to Michael T. Ashcroft, Clinton V. Black, Douglas Hall, Barry W. Higman, Kenneth E. Ingram, and Carmen Latty.

Among the numerous people who have encouraged and helped me are Leslie R. C. Agnew, David Ashauer, Ruth Bjorgaard, Michael Craton, Deborah Dandridge, Marilyn Dechir, Arthur Drayton, John Duffy, Robert W. Fogel, David W. Galenson, David Barry Gaspar, Dennis Glasco, Jacob Gordon, Jack P. Greene, Ruth Haag, Jerome S. Handler, Bernice Jackson, Chantel Jones, Jeffrey P. Koplan, Merlin MacFarlane, Roderick A. McDonald, Alexandra Mason, Sidney W. Mintz, James A. Rawley, and Eleanor Von Ende. To the University of Kansas I am indebted for the grant of a sabbatical semester. To all the librarians and others who have assisted me, I express my sincere gratitude. Among my colleagues I am indebted to John T. Alexander, Richard S. Howey, Ronald R. Olsen, Jerry Stannard, Charles Stansifer, Thomas J. Weiss, and L. R. Lind, who encouraged me to undertake this project. Most particularly I am grateful to my wife, Audrey, who has lived through the ordeal of writing this book and given me her usual wise counsel and cheerful support; to Michael T. Ashcroft, who undertook to educate an aging economic historian in the mysteries of tropical medicine; and to Robert P. Hudson, Barry W. Higman, Stanley L. Engerman, and Richard A. Lobdell, who have influenced my thinking considerably and given me helpful suggestions for individual chapters. Also, I wish to thank the anonymous readers of my manuscript for their constructive criticisms. What I have written is, however, solely my responsibility.

Parts of this study have appeared in *The Economic History Review, The American Historical Review, Agricultural History, The William and Mary Quarterly*, and the *International Journal of African Historical Studies*. I am grateful to each of these journals for permission to reproduce some of the material from those articles here. Chapter 4 is taken to a large extent from my article, "The Guinea Surgeons on the Middle Passage: The Provision of Medical Services in the British Slave Trade," *International Journal of African Historical Studies*, Vol. 14, No. 4 (1981), pp. 601–25. Chapters 2 and 11 are taken, in part, from my chapter in the following book: Stanley L. Engerman and Eugene D. Genovese, eds., *Race and Slavery in the Western Hemisphere: Quantitative Studies*, copyright © 1975 by The Center for Advanced Study in the Behavioral Sciences, Stanford, California; "Mortality and the Medical Treatment of Slaves in the British West Indies," by Richard B. Sheridan, reprinted by permission of Princeton University Press.

Manuscript collections that have been used extensively in this study are as follows: the Letter Books of Dr. Walter Tullideph of Antigua and Scotland: I am indebted to the late Sir Herbert Ogilvy for permission to quote extracts from these letters; the Martin Papers in the British Library: I am indebted to the heirs of Sir Francis Davies for permission to quote extracts from these papers; J. Johnson MS., Beinecke Lesser Antilles Collection, the Burke Library, Hamilton College, Clinton, New York: I am indebted to Mr. Frank K. Lorenz for permission to quote extracts from this journal; the Papers of Sir John Gladstone, Flintshire Record Office, Hawarden, North Wales: I am indebted to Sir William Gladstone for permission to quote extracts from these papers; Tudway Papers, Somerset Record Office, Taunton, England: I am indebted to Mr. D. C. Tudway Quilter for permission to quote extracts from these papers; Barham Papers, Bodleian Library, Oxford: I am indebted to Lord Clarendon for permission to quote extracts from these papers; Penrhyn MSS., University College of North Wales, Bangor, Wales: I am indebted to Lady Janet Douglas Pennant for permission to quote extracts from these papers; Senhouse Papers, Carlisle Record Office, Carlisle, England: I am indebted to Mr. B. C. Jones for permission to quote extracts from these papers; the Diary of Dr. Jonathan Troup, The University of Aberdeen Library, Aberdeen, Scotland: I am indebted to Mr. Colin A. McLaren for permission to quote extracts from this diary; Gale-Morant Papers, University of Exeter Library, Exeter, England: I am indebted to Mr. D. W. Evans for permission to quote extracts from these papers; Journals of Thomas Thistlewood, Lincolnshire Archives Office, Lincoln, England: I am indebted to Lord and Lady Monson for permission to quote extracts from these journals; Chisholm Papers, National Library of Scotland, Edinburgh: I am indebted to Dr. Thomas I. Rae for permission to quote extracts from these papers; Cochrane MSS., Balfour-Melville Papers, and the Letter Books of the Cargen Trustees, Scottish Record Office, Edinburgh: I am indebted to Mr. James D. Galbraith for permission to quote extracts from these papers.

Richard B. Sheridan

Lawrence, Kansas
August 1984

1

The disease environments and epidemiology

> He [the adventurous physician] establishes for his guide some fanciful theory...of mechanical powers, of chemical agency, of stimuli, or irritability...or some other ingenious dream, which lets him into all nature's secrets at short hand. On the principle which he thus assumes, he forms his table of nosology...and extends his curative treatment...I have lived myself to see the disciples of Hoffman, Boerhaave, Stahl, Cullen, and Brown succeed one another like the shifting figures of a magic lantern...The patient, treated on the fashionable theory, sometimes gets well in spite of the medicine.
>
> Thomas Jefferson, 1807[1]

This introductory chapter surveys the sources of our knowledge of population in the West Indies; the physical, social, and disease environments of the region; and interactions with other disease environments. Accordingly, we investigate the rise of the South Atlantic System with special reference to the spread of infectious disease through the movement of people and their microorganisms, the expansion of slave-grown sugar and other agricultural staples, the killer diseases of malaria and yellow fever, and the findings of the Army Medical Board's Report. Later sections of the chapter focus on medical writings that sought to advance rational conceptual schemes of disease causation, prevention, control, or eradication. Major emphasis is placed on the nature and incidence of slave diseases and injuries.

The rise of the South Atlantic System

In his call for a new approach to the broad patterns of Atlantic history, Philip Curtin contends that "the social and economic development on the tropical shores of the Atlantic was a single process, regardless of the theoretically self-contained empires of mercantilist Europe." In this "South Atlantic System," which consisted of complex patterns of production and trade, the plantation was the central institution from the late sixteenth century to the early nineteenth. Plantations were worked by slave labor from tropical Africa, but directed by Europeans. Their purpose was to enrich their owners and contribute to the economic self-sufficiency of mercantile nations by producing tropical staples for European consumption.

Before the beginning of the Columbian age, the isolation of lands and peoples resulted in different patterns of immunity to disease. Three disease environments, each created by different circumstances of physical environment and isolation, interacted in the South Atlantic System: Europe and North Africa taken together, tropical Africa, and the American tropics. Curtin says that "Europe and North Africa were in the belt of intense intercommunication stretching from the north Atlantic to China. Most diseases of the temperate Afro-Eurasian land mass were already endemic there, and the Europeans had a wide range of immunities to match. They lacked, however, the diseases and the immunities of the Old World tropics."[2]

Because of less intense intercommunication, the disease environments of tropical Africa were more diverse than those of Europe. Old World temperate as well as tropical diseases were common in tropical Africa, but owing to the relative isolation of each community, it was "unlikely that any single African people had an endemic assortment that covered the whole range of diseases and strains of diseases available in the sub-Saharan region." Africans who were captured and taken from the interior to the coast to be sold as slaves were likely to be exposed to diseases for which they lacked immunity. Whether they were immune or not, Africans who suffered the fatigue of long marches, poor diet, and incarceration in disease-ridden barracoons awaiting the arrival of slave ships no doubt had a higher death rate than those who escaped the Atlantic slave trade. Dr. Mungo Park observed the Mandingo at close range during his exploration of the interior of Africa. Notwithstanding that longevity was uncommon among them, it appeared to Park that they had few diseases. "Their simple diet, and active way of life, preserve them from many of those disorders which embitter the days of luxury and idleness," he wrote. Although he estimated that the slaves in Africa outnumbered the free people by three to one, Park said that custom had established certain rules with regard to the treatment of slaves that it was thought dishonorable to violate. "Thus," he wrote, "the domestic slaves, or such as are born in a man's own house, are treated with more lenity than those which are purchased with money."[3] The economist Thomas Robert Malthus concluded from his perusal of the writings on Africa and the slave trade that, notwithstanding the constant emigration, loss of life from incessant wars, and the checks to increase from vice and other causes, the population of Africa was "continually pressing against the limits of the means of subsistence."[4]

As Curtin points out, it was widely believed that certain races had inborn qualities of strength and weakness fitting them for specific "climates." Indeed, this became an accepted "fact" and a cornerstone of pseudo-scientific racism. Although this racist explanation has been contradicted, there is some truth in the judgment of generations of planters in the American tropics that African slaves were somehow much better workers than any other group. The planters were wrong to attribute black superiority to inborn qualities, but their judgment finds some support from studies of the epidemiology of migration. "People die from disease," writes Curtin, "not from climate, and the world contains many different disease environments, each with a range of viruses and bacteria that differ in varying degrees from those found elsewhere. Physical environment and climate obviously play a role, but epidemiological differences exist even where physical environment is the same."[5]

Human beings are biological entities who affect and, in turn, are affected by other organisms. Good health implies that the complex organism is functioning correctly and in harmony with its environment, whereas disease implies that something is wrong. A pathogen is any agent that causes disease, especially microorganisms or microparasites such as viruses, bacteria, protozoa, or fungus. In their search for food in human tissues, microparasites may provoke acute diseases that kill their human host. On the other hand, the pathogen may provoke strong immunity reactions within the host's body that kill them off instead. Human beings, both individually and collectively, exhibit widely varying levels of susceptibility and/or immunity to infections. People who inhabit isolated disease environments are highly susceptible to exotic diseases brought in by people from other disease environments. The most significant immunities are acquired, not inherited. An individual who is attacked by disease may produce the required antibodies, or he or she may, as in the case of smallpox vaccination, be given the antibodies directly. Children are generally more vulnerable to diseases than adults, yet they often experience infectious diseases in a mild form and acquire immunity that protects them in later life.[6]

A major force in history has been the spread of infectious disease through the movement of people and their microorganisms. Dramatic movements have occurred among refugees, pilgrims, nomads, migrant laborers, armies, and others. They have moved from place to place, taking with them their own patterns of disease, acquiring new diseases, and disseminating their own diseases to others. Migration of people and their microbes upsets the equilibrium between the host population's pattern of immunity and its range of diseases. Most vulnerable to invaders are peoples who have long been isolated from other disease environments.[7]

Macroparasites, according to William H. McNeill, include not only such predatory animals as wolves and lions, but also humans insofar as they resort to cannibalism, plunder, rape, imperial conquest, and extraction of surplus value from serfs, slaves, and wage workers. West Indian slaves were obviously exploited in the sense that their labor power was used by their masters without giving a just or equivalent return. Slaves and their progeny were legally mere property, capable of being bought and sold, deprived of education, valued primarily as work units, subject to arbitrary punishment, often stinted in their rations of food, and at times forced into prostitution and crime. Although it will be our task in future chapters to delineate the nature and extent of slave exploitation, it will suffice here to observe that a recent study finds that the profits of British sugar planting averaged about 10 percent from 1650 to 1834. This rate of profit compares well with those made elsewhere in the British Empire.[8]

Columbus not only "discovered" America but he also set in motion an exchange of native life forms that permanently disrupted the delicate balance of the world ecosystem. This "Columbian exchange," as Alfred W. Crosby, Jr., describes it, involved both microparasites and macroparasites. In the latter category were the three-masted, gunned sailing ship; land forces equipped with cavalry units, artillery, and firearms; and the motives, capital, and organizational skills to direct these forces in a predatory direction. Religion supplied the pretext and gold the motive for European expansion, while technological progress provided the means, according to Carlo M. Cipolla. Although the Europeans learned to master the energy of the wind and gunpowder, which enabled them to discover new continents and new trade routes, they were highly susceptible to the tropical fevers of Asia and Africa. On the other hand, conditions were more favorable to the European invaders of the New World. Here the disease environment was less hostile to Europeans, at the same time that the Amerindians were technologically very primitive and highly susceptible to European infectious diseases and the spread of deadly epidemics. The Columbian exchange not only involved macroparasites and microparasites, but also included domesticated plants and animals, which Crosby contends have enriched nutrition and contributed to the rapid growth of population on a global scale.[9]

From a condition of general healthfulness when the Europeans first came, the Amerindian population suffered a series of disease shocks that depopulated some areas and left others too devastated for the people to resist conquest by invaders. Explanations of the healthfulness of the Indians focus on the isolation of the New World. It is suggested that the people who crossed the land bridge between Siberia and Alaska carried few diseases with them, that cold killed the germs, that the elimination of people who suffered from debilitating diseases resulted in the survival of the fittest, and that, apart from Mexico and Peru, the population was not dense enough to sustain human-to-human disease chains of infection indefinitely. The consequence, as Crosby observes, was that the Amerindians "lived, died, and bred alone for generation after generation, developing unique cultures and working out tolerances for a limited, native American selection of pathological micro-life."[10]

Once the human-to-human disease chains were established across the Atlantic, the nonimmune Amerindians died by the millions. Just as geographical isolation had tended to create a crude kind of mutual toleration between human host and parasite, now the migration of Europeans and their diseases was the chief cause of epidemics. The Arawak economy of the Greater Antilles had supported a large population with ample leisure in pre-Columbian times. In a few decades it was destroyed with drastic consequences to the people.[11]

The importance of the West Indies

The Columbian exchange had worldwide repercussions. The destruction of the Arawaks and the migration of Spaniards from the Caribbean islands to the mainland set in motion European rivalry for some of the best agricultural land in the tropical world. The demand for alternative sources of labor led first to white immigrants and indentured servants, who were later replaced by black workers on island after island. African slaves are estimated to have constituted 80 percent of the population of Jamaica by the 1690s; of Barbados and Antigua by 1707; and of St. Kitts, Nevis, and Montserrat by 1729. "The spread of the slave plantation," writes D. A. Farnie, "raised the price of food hitherto produced by white farmers. Thereby it opened up markets in the West Indies for foodstuffs from the 'bread colonies' of the mainland and for the refuse fish of Newfoundland as well as for the tobacco of Rhode Island and the cotton piece goods of Lancashire. Thus it stimulated trade between the islands and the mainland and reinforced the seaboard unity of the plantation colonies."[12]

Factors that influenced the disease environment of the West Indies included the size, density, geographical origin, and mobility of the population and the physical environment and its modification by European and African cultural influences. In his *Treatise on the Wealth, Power, and Resources of the British Empire* (1814), Patrick Colquhoun included a lengthy chapter on the West Indies in which he sought to measure and analyze the population, production, trade, and other features of the economy and society. The data in the author's "copious statistical tables" centered on the year 1812. In that year there were fourteen British colonies in the West Indies, including Bermuda, the Bahamas, and Honduras, which were valued at £100 million sterling. Moreover, there were fourteen conquered colonies (six French, five Dutch, three Danish), which were valued at £75.2 million sterling. The estimated annual production, including the food raised and consumed by the population, amounted to £18.5 million sterling for the British colonies and £10.2 million for the conquered colonies. The estimated value of exports amounted to £11.2 million sterling for the British and £5.8 million for the conquered colonies; the imports amounted to £7.6 million and £3.3 million sterling, respectively, for the British and conquered colonies. The shipping used in the trade to and from the British colonies was estimated at about 600 ships, averaging 300 tons, and employing 16,000 sailors.[13]

Colquhoun asserted that no country in the world exported as large a proportion of the produce of the soil as did the British West India colonies. The exports were almost wholly confined to sugar, rum, and molasses. Exceptions to this generalization were the islands of Jamaica, Dominica, and Grenada, where coffee plantations had been established, and Grenada and several other islands where cotton was cultivated. Other minor staples were cacao, tobacco, pimento, arrowroot, sarsaparilla, ginger, castor oil, tamarinds, and dye woods; the articles of human subsistence included Indian corn, Guinea corn, sweet potatoes, yams, plantains, and breadfruit. Blacks outnumbered whites to such an extent that the consumption of food was limited chiefly to "the negro labourers and the people of colour, who, with the exception of salt fish and a small quantity of Irish provisions, are fed almost exclusively on plantains, yams, and other vegetable food raised at no great expence, which are better liked, and which have been found more wholesome and nourishing than the flour of wheat or Indian corn."[14]

Table 1.1 shows the area, population, and estimated value of exports of the twelve British West India colonies in 1812. Omitted from this group are the three nonsugar colonies of Bermuda, the Bahamas, and Honduras, whereas the conquered colony of British Guiana (Demerara, Essequibo, and Berbice) has been included. It is remarkable that of the total population of 863,999, black slaves numbered 771, 096, or nearly 90 percent. The white population of 61,224 constituted 7.1 percent of the total, and free persons of color, 31,679, or 3.6 percent. Jamaica stands out as the most prominent colony, containing nearly one-third of the free persons of color, nearly one-half of the white and black populations, and three-fifths of the value of exports. Ranked by the number of slaves, Jamaica was first with 350,000, followed by British Guiana with 95,000, and Barbados with slightly less than 60,000. Three colonies – Antigua, Grenada, and St. Kitts – had 30,000 to 40,000 slaves; three others – St. Vincent, Dominica, and Trinidad – had 20,000 to 30,000. Nevis had 15,000 slaves, and Montserrat and the Virgin Islands each had 10,000.

To Colquhoun the most prominent feature of his table was the great disparity between the whites on the one hand, and the free coloreds and black slaves on the other, which was in the ratio of 1 to 13. He conceded that the number of Europeans in the colonies fluctuated widely and could be only estimated. Nevertheless, the disparity in numbers between free and slave, white and black, constituted a threat to public order and racial subordination. The disparity was much greater in some of the smaller islands,

Table 1.1 *British West India colonies: area, population, and value of exports, 1812*

Colony	Area in thousands of acres[a]	Population: White persons	Free persons of color	Black slaves	Estimated value of exports
Jamaica	2,724	30,000	10,000	350,000	£7,269,661
British Guiana[b]	1,100[c]	5,000	3,100	95,000	1,569,990
Barbados	106	15,000	3,000	59,506	548,803
Antigua	60	3,200	1,400	36,000	492,220
Grenada	80	800	1,600	32,603	565,782
St. Kitts	44	1,200	500	30,000	436,528
St. Vincent	104	1,280	1,170	27,156	516,001
Dominica	186	800	1,500	24,000	258,858
Trinidad	1,527	2,700	8,559	21,831	384,117
Nevis	21	500	250	15,000	217,682
Montserrat	21	444	200	10,000	104,720
Virgin Islands	21	300	400	10,000	94,122
Total	5,994	61,224	31,679	771,096	£12,458,484

[a]These areas diverge more or less from those based on modern surveys.
[b]British Guiana, consisting of Demerara, Essequibo, and Berbice, was a conquered colony in 1812. It was ceded by Holland to Great Britain in 1814.
[c]Cultivated acres only.
Source: Patrick Colquhoun, *A Treatise on the Wealth, Power, and Resources of the British Empire* (London, 1814), Table 9, pp. 378–81.

he said, "making in some instances *one* to *twenty*, and in others *one* to *thirty*. These islands cannot be considered secure, unless protected at the expence of a more considerable military force, and at a greater pecuniary sacrifice than ought to be made by the parent state."[15]

Table 1.1 shows that the population was roughly proportional to the land area in the smaller islands, but much less so in the larger islands and mainland colony. Colquhoun's table shows the cultivated and uncultivated acres in each colony except British Guiana where cultivated acres only are shown. High ratios of cultivated to total acreage are shown in the small islands of the Lesser Antilles, which had been settled in the seventeenth century. Barbados, the most densely populated island in the Caribbean region, had almost all its land – 95.3 percent – in cultivation. The four Leeward Islands of Antigua, St. Kitts, Montserrat, and Nevis were also settled in the seventeenth century. Here the percentage of cultivated to total acreage was 70.3. Less sparsely settled and of limited suitability for plantation agriculture were the British Virgin Islands of Tortola, Spanish Town, Jost Van Dyke, and others, where 57.1 percent of the land was cultivated. The islands of Grenada, St. Vincent, and Dominica in the Windward group were acquired by conquest in the 1750s and ceded by France to Great Britain in 1763. Because of their late settlement, mountainous terrain, and other factors, the percentage of cultivated to total acreage in these islands was 50.3. Jamaica, though first settled by the English after its conquest from Spain in 1655, contained much mountainous and savanna land unfit for cultivation; in 1812, according to Colquhoun's statistics, 29.7 percent of the land was cultivated. Trinidad, which the British conquered from Spain in 1797, was only partly developed by 1812, when only 1.8 percent of the land was cultivated. Finally, agricultural development in the continental colony of British Guiana was very circumscribed, being limited to lands along the seacoast and navigable rivers.[16]

Also shown in Table 1.1 is the estimated value of the exports from each of the West Indian colonies, of which about 94 percent of the total of £12.5 million was shipped to the United Kingdom. The annual value of export production per slave ranged from £9.3 in Barbados and £9.4 in the Virgin Islands to £19.0 in St. Vincent and £20.8 in Jamaica. The average of the twelve colonies was £14.5.

John Foster Barham, an absentee planter from Jamaica and member of Parliament, published a pamphlet in 1824 in which he proposed a plan for abolishing slavery in the British colonies. In an effort to ascertain what he regarded as fair compensation to slave owners, he compiled statistics and made crude calculations of the cost of rearing and maintaining slaves, the value of their production, their allocation to different occupations and units of production, and the aggregate profits of the slave colonies. He estimated that there were considerably more than 1,500 sugar works in all the colonies. Table 1.2 is Barham's summary table showing the allocation of slaves to agricultural and nonagricultural occupations, and the division of the former group into sugar slaves and other agricultural slaves. It is significant that Barham calculated that three-quarters of all the slaves in the West India colonies were attached to sugar plantations, where the disease environment was generally unfavorable to both the black and white inhabitants. It should be noted, however, that the ratio of sugar slaves to all slaves varied from island to island. In Jamaica, where coffee production and livestock ranching were of considerable importance, sugar slaves amounted to 49.5 percent of all slaves in 1832.[17]

Table 1.2. *Summary of slave employment in the British West Indies, 1824*

Employment	Number of slaves	Percent of total
Sugar slaves	600,000	75.0
Other agricultural slaves	111,000	13.9
Total agricultural slaves	711,000	88.9
Nonagricultural slaves	89,000	11.1
Total slaves	800,000	100.0

Source: J. F. Barham, *Considerations on the Abolition of Negro Slavery* (London, 1824), pp. 79–83.

Malaria and yellow fever

As Richard Harrison Shryock observed, the coming of the Europeans and Africans meant that "the colonies served as a melting pot for diseases as well as for human populations. Europeans, Africans, and Indians engaged in a free exchange of their respective infections. And in the whole sinister process Indians were the greatest sufferers."[18] Whereas the Indians were either exterminated or sought refuge in areas remote from white contacts, the Europeans and Africans who came to the lowland tropical areas of the New World faced the probability of abbreviated life-spans. Mortality in the Sugar Colonies was frightfully high for whites and blacks alike in the seventeenth century, according to Richard S. Dunn. "Englishmen who moved to the Caribbean shortened their life expectance significantly. . . For the blacks the situation was if anything worse. Negroes imported to the sugar islands died much faster than they were born. West Indian slave masters soon gave up trying to keep their Negroes alive long enough to breed up a new generation and instead routinely bought replacement slaves year in and year out."[19]

Two of the world's great killer diseases – malaria and yellow fever – are thought to have been carried from Africa to the New World via the slave trade. Malaria, which was also called intermittent and/or remittent fever, is an infectious febrile disease caused by protozoan parasites known as plasmodia, which are transmitted by the bites of infected mosquitoes of the genus *Anopheles*. The disease is characterized by attacks of chills, fever, and sweating, and frequent nausea, vomiting, and severe headache. These attacks may occur daily (quotidian), every other day (tertian), or with an interval of three days (quartan). Of the three major types of malarial parasites, one (*Plasmodium falciparum*) tends to cause death; the other two (*Plasmodium vivax* and *Plasmodium malariae*) are more benign and self-limiting. Until recent decades malaria was one of the world's greatest killers, and when it did not kill it reduced its victims to a listless and debilitated state. People who live in areas where the man–mosquito malarial cycle is intense undergo genetic adaptation that confers a high degree of immunity. The genes produce sickle-shaped red corpuscles in malaria victims at a high frequency, and such cells are less hospitable to the malarial plasmodium than normal red blood cells. Children who inherit both the sickle-cell trait and the anemia that often accompanies it usually die in childhood. They inherit sickle-cell anemia only when each parent contributes a gene for sickling. Those who inherit the sickle-cell trait without anemia, however, acquire some immunity to malaria. Studies have shown that a group of people who continue to be infected with malaria in the same proportion will, over a period of generations, have more people who experience a mild form of the disease and fewer of them will die.[20]

Though it has been argued by some medical historians that malaria was indigenous to the Americas, more evidence points to Africa as the homeland from whence this mosquito-borne disease was transmitted to the New World via the slave trade. Studies have shown that whereas the Amerindian populations lacked the genetic traits associated with tolerance of malarial infection, Africans exhibit such tolerance to a significant extent. Moreover, wild monkeys of the New World lacked the immunity to malaria that was characteristic of their counterparts in Africa. P. M. Ashburn, among others, contends that the most certain large introduction of malaria "came with African slaves, who, as unwilling emigrants, and partly immunized subjects of the disease, were all potential or actual carriers of it." He also contends that malaria contributed to the depopulation of lowland tropical areas formerly inhabited by Amerindians, thus opening these areas to European-dominated plantation agriculture, which drew on the labor reservoir of Africa over four centuries.[21]

Yellow fever is like malaria in that it depends for its survival on stagnant water and mosquitoes. But unlike malaria it has had a more limited geographical distribution and on a global scale has accounted for fewer deaths. Nevertheless, as Ashburn points out, yellow fever has excited more attention and interest than its African cousin because of its high morbidity and mortality among nonimmune people; the large and spectacular part it has played in military, colonial, and commercial history; and the fact that its etiology and epidemiology were long unknown. Classical yellow fever is an urban disease characterized by acute infection caused by a virus transmitted by mosquitoes of the genus *Aedes aegypti*. It is marked by headache, backache, high fever, general lassitude, nausea, and jaundice resulting from the necrosis of the liver. Mortality is generally high, running from a tenth to a half of those infected. The disease is of short duration; cases that terminate in death occur within ten days. Infected persons younger than fourteen usually escape death, and women survive the disease better than men. As with malaria, blacks contracted yellow fever less frequently than whites and experienced it in a milder form. Similarly, blacks had a high degree of immunity to this disease and rarely died from it.[22]

The origin or "cradle" of yellow fever, like malaria, has been disputed by authorities. Several medical historians have argued that yellow fever originated in America, citing early Spanish authors who told of men who contracted severe fevers and whose skin became yellow before they died. Also in support of this argument is the fact that yellow fever was definitely and well described in America almost a century and a quarter earlier than in Africa. But advocates of the African origin of the disease point out that the west coast of Africa was the "white man's grave" chiefly because of malaria, dysentery, and liver abscesses, and that yellow fever was probably masked by these more deadly diseases. Then, too, it is argued that not enough whites were congregated in one place to provide material for a real epidemic, at the same time that the blacks were either relatively immune to yellow fever or absolutely immune because of attacks in childhood. In a recent article, James D. Goodyear strengthens the case for the African origin of yellow fever and its transmission to the Americas by slaves. He finds that well-identified outbreaks of yellow fever occurred in five separate Caribbean locales between 1635 and 1655, and that these outbreaks were closely associated with sugarcane cultivation, milling, refining, or shipping, and also the presence of African slaves. The sugar industry provided sufficient non-immune people, stagnant water, and *Aedes aegypti* mosquitoes, which are especially attracted to sweet fluids. These ecological conditions, Goodyear argues, lend support to his hypothesis "that the sugar industry from the seventeenth century through the nineteenth century had a marked impact on the epidemiology and history of yellow fever."[23]

The Army Medical Board's Report

In October 1835, the British secretary at war initiated an inquiry into "the extent and causes of the sickness and mortality among the troops in the West Indies, with the view of founding thereon such measures as might appear likely to diminish the great loss of life annually experienced in those colonies." Alexander M. Tulloch, captain, 45th Regiment, and Henry Marshall, deputy inspector general of hospitals, were appointed to search the voluminous historical records accumulated by the Army Medical Board since 1816 and report their findings to the secretary at war. In particular, they sought to discover how the health of the troops was affected by their "diet, duty, and employment, the state of the barrack and hospital accommodation, the topography of the station, the nature of the soil, the climate, the productions of the colony, &c." From the various sources they proceeded to show "the sickness, mortality, and prevailing diseases among the troops in the West Indies, from 1817 to 1834." In subsequent years similar reports were submitted on the experience of British troops in the United Kingdom, Mediterranean, British North America, West Africa, Cape of Good Hope, Ceylon, and other British colonies. "The investigations of Tulloch and Marshall," writes George Roberts, "constitute the most comprehensive attempt ever made to present an overall picture of health and mortality in the British West Indies."[24]

Mortality ranged widely among British troops sent to different parts of the Empire, according to the reports submitted by Tulloch and Marshall. Owing to the relatively crowded and unsanitary conditions of barrack life, the rate increased from 11.5 per thousand per year to 15.3 per thousand for civilians who were recruited and remained in Britain. Troops sent to stations in temperate climates fared better on average than those sent to the tropics. Mortality ranged from 12 to 22 per thousand in such geographically remote but relatively temperate regions as South Africa, Nova Scotia, Canada, and Gibraltar. The strikingly different experience in the tropical world can be separated into three broad regions of increasing mortality, writes Curtin: "Around the Indian Ocean, mortality rates ranged from 30 to 75 per thousand. In the American tropics, the rate rose to a level between 85 and 138 per thousand. Finally, West Africa showed a disastrous mortality range from 483 to 668 per thousand mean strength per annum."[25]

Whereas the military establishments in West Africa consisted of a handful of posts extending from Gambia on the north to the Gold Coast on the south and east, the more numerous West Indian garrisons extended from the Bahamas to British Guiana in a north to south direction, and from Barbados on the east to Honduras on the west. These scattered garrisons formed four military commands – the Windward and Leeward, Jamaica, the Bahamas, and Honduras. The commands in the Bahamas and Honduras were outside the slave–sugar complex, which is the focus of this study; Jamaica had only a small detachment of one of the black regiments and its medical data base is too small and unreliable for an adequate analysis of the disease environment.

The troops in the Windward and Leeward Command were employed in garrisoning various islands and possessions extending from 6° to 17° north latitude, and 56° to 63° west longitude, and including that portion of the South American continent called British Guiana, with the islands of Trinidad, Tobago, Grenada, St. Vincent, Barbados, St. Lucia, Dominica, Antigua with Montserrat, and St. Kitts with Nevis and Tortola. Although they had a common tropical lowland ecology and a conspicuous sea orientation, these garrisons varied considerably in climate, soils, vegetation, and land forms.[26] The troops attached to the garrisons of the Windward and Leeward Command consisted of several regiments of the line, about four companies of artillery, one West India regiment composed of blacks, and a body of black military laborers. The black troops, which had numbered as many as 5,900 during the Napoleonic Wars, had been gradually reduced to 1,188 in 1836. The white troops had been employed since the war in routine garrison and regimental duty, except during occasional insurrection movements among the slaves, which obliged them to take the field. The military laborers were generally employed on the public works and heavy fatigue duties, and the black troops took such of the guards as were most likely to prove prejudicial to the health of the whites.[27]

The report compares the white and black troops with respect to hospital admissions and deaths from 1817 to 1836. It shows that whereas the number of deaths among white troops in the West Indies was only about one-sixth that of such troops in West Africa (78.5 per thousand compared with 483 per thousand), the black troops in the West Indies had a death rate that was a third greater than for similar troops in West Africa (40 per thousand compared with 30 per thousand). Compared with white troops in the United Kingdom, those in the Windward and Leeward Command were admitted to the hospital about twice as often. However, in the United Kingdom one in twenty-four of the cases proved fatal, compared with one death out of every sixty-seven cases in the West Indies. Owing to the improved disease environment for the military forces in the Windward and Leeward Command, the mortality was considerably less for both the white and black troops in the two decades following the war than it had been in the years from 1803 to 1816. Fevers were the principal cause of sickness and mortality among the white troops, constituting considerably more than a third of the admissions and about a half of all the deaths. Malaria caused about 90 percent of the deaths from fevers; yellow fever and typhus accounted for the other 10 percent. Though much less lethal than the fevers of West Africa (36.9 per thousand compared with 410.2 per thousand), the fevers of the West Indies took a heavier toll than those among troops in the United Kingdom. Admissions were ten times greater, and the deaths twenty-five times as numerous.[28]

Next to fevers, diseases of the stomach and bowels caused much sickness and mortality. "The principal source of this mortality is chronic dysentery," wrote Tulloch and Marshall, "of which one case in five proves fatal, and unfortunately a very great proportion of the cases of acute dysentery and diarrhoea, however slight in their commencement, by frequent recurrence ultimately terminate in this form of the disease. Every time the patient is admitted into the hospital it assumes a more intense and unmanageable character, till after several partial recoveries and relapses, he ultimately sinks under it."[29]

Other diseases were considerably less severe. Diseases of the lungs consisted chiefly of acute and chronic catarrh, diseases of the brain were attributed chiefly to the "brain fever of drunkards," dropsies were attributed to a certain extent to the prevalence of fevers, and diseases of the liver, though not assigned a cause, were said to occasion about five times more mortality than among troops in the United Kingdom. High admissions but few deaths occurred among troops who were plagued with abscesses, ulcers, wounds, and injuries.[30]

The black troops and pioneers in the Windward and Leeward Command consisted chiefly of former slaves who had been born in Africa. In the years from 1817 to 1836, an average of 820 of these troops had been admitted to the hospital annually and 40 had died. By contrast, the report said that there was probably no country where troops composed of the indigenous inhabitants were subject to a higher mortality than 15 per thousand of mean strength annually. The deleterious effect of migrating from one disease environment to the other was explained in the following words:

> It is by no means extraordinary that African troops should suffer as well as the whites from the climate of the West Indies, seeing that they are for the most part natives of the interior of Africa, of which the climate is probably very different; and it is well known that though the indigenous races of tropical as well as temperate climates are peculiarly fitted by nature for inhabiting and peopling the respective portions of the globe wherein they or their forefathers were born, the effects of a transition to any other is in general productive of a great increase in the scale of mortality.

That the black troops were better "seasoned" to the climate of the West Indies in the period of the report than in the previous years from 1803 to 1816 is indicated by the average mortality of 64 per thousand in the earlier period, or half again as much as in the subsequent twenty-year period.[31]

Ranked first among the principal diseases of the black troops were diseases of the lungs. As many as two-fifths of all the deaths among these troops arose from this class of diseases, and more died annually from it alone in the Windward and Leeward Command than among the same number of troops in the United Kingdom from all diseases taken together. Diseases of the stomach and bowels – chiefly dysentery – ranked second in deaths per thousand. Next came fevers, which accounted for about one-fifth of admissions to the hospital but less than one-eighth of the deaths. However, deaths by fevers were nearly double the number among the black troops of

West Africa. Smallpox, an eruptive fever, took the lives of ninety black soldiers. It was principally confined to Trinidad and St. Lucia, where it appeared in an epidemic form in 1819 among both the black troops and the civilian population. However, smallpox never prevailed to any extent in the other years or at any of the other stations. Blacks died less than whites from diseases of the brain, in part because they consumed less alcohol. Deaths from dropsies occurred at the same rate among blacks and whites. Diseases of the liver were said to affect black troops only slightly. Moreover, the report said that black troops were much less affected by venereal diseases than the whites, presumably because most of them were married men.[32]

The general summary of the report noted that although the climate of each colony affected the constitution of the black troops in a different way, throughout the whole command diseases of the lungs and the bowels were generally the most fatal. Furthermore, it was found that the mortality in all the islands except Antigua, Grenada, and Tobago was higher among the black troops than in the male slave population. On average, the annual mortality of the black troops and pioneers was 40 per thousand as compared with 30 per thousand for the male slave population. Tulloch and Marshall found this comparison the more remarkable because the mortality of the slave population was calculated for males of all ages, including old men and infants, the sick and healthy, whereas that of the troops was calculated for persons in the prime of life only. They speculated that the troops were subject to some deteriorating influence from which the male slave population was exempt.[33] There are good reasons for believing that the male slave mortality is underestimated in the report, however. Black troops and pioneers were said to have been recruited through purchase from the "best conditioned slaves" in Jamaica and presumably the other islands; black troops and pioneers were never completely under the medical supervision of the army so their sickness and death were underreported. Moreover, Roberts finds that for British Guiana – "the only colony for which a reasonably detailed picture is available" – the slave death rate between 1820 and 1832 was 44 per thousand. Thus it would appear that Tulloch and Marshall's comparison of the death rates of slaves and black military personnel in the West Indies is invalid.[34]

This apparent defect notwithstanding, what is most significant about the Army Medical Board's Reports is the disparity they reveal about deaths from fevers among white and black troops. In the Sierra Leone Command in West Africa, 756 out of a total of 2,600 white troops died of fevers (or 410 per thousand) in an eighteen-year period, whereas deaths from fevers among the black troops numbered only 18 out of 405 (or 2.4 per thousand). In the Windward and Leeward Command, deaths from fevers among the white troops numbered 3,195 out of a total of 62,163 (or 36.9 per thousand) in a twenty-year period, whereas deaths from fevers among the black troops were 190 out of a total of 6,856 (or 4.6 per thousand). Because of their immunity to malaria and yellow fever, black regiments were recruited and dispatched to parts of the British Empire where European troops had been plagued with tropical diseases.[35]

The Army Medical Board's Reports, though breaking new ground in their systematic presentation of data on troop morbidity and mortality, were published after the emancipation of the slaves in the British Empire. Thus they appeared too late to have any influence on the practice of slave medicine, but they do have value for this study because of the insights they afford into the epidemiology of hot climates. In the remainder of this chapter we explore this branch of medicine as it is exemplified in the writings of doctors who had intimate knowledge of the West Indies in the age of slavery.

Early works on epidemiology

Epidemiology may be defined as the study of the distribution and determinants of diseases and injuries in human populations. It is concerned with the causes, natural history, and interrelationships of disease. It seeks to advance rational conceptual schemes of causation of diseases with a view toward their prevention, control, or eradication. Whereas the basis of clinical research is the observation of individual patients, epidemiology is concerned with the occurrence of disease in an aggregation of individuals who make up a group or population. Epidemiologists study the spread of infectious diseases in terms of the human host; the agents of disease, which are usually microorganisms; and the physical, biological, and social environment. The physical environment includes such geographical features of a place as climate, altitude, and soil composition; the biological environment includes the vectors that transmit diseases, such as flies and mosquitoes, plants and animals, and such reservoirs of infection as other human beings; and the social environment embraces the overall economic and political organization of a society and the institutions and customs that are related to health. Because it is concerned with the distribution of diseases in populations or groups, epidemiology draws on demography to supply information on age, sex, race, geographical distribution, and occupation. Originally the word *epidemic* was applied to an explosive, acute outbreak of disease; however, the time period of epidemics is no longer confined to a few weeks or months. Historically, epidemiology arose out of the great epidemic diseases such as plague, smallpox, and cholera, which occurred in periodic waves associated with high mortality. Its scope has now expanded to include all diseases that affect populations, if such diseases are studied as group phenomena. Although the term *endemic* implies the habitual presence of a disease or agent of disease within a given area, many endemic diseases rapidly become epidemic if environmental or host influences change in a way that favors transmission. Historians of epidemiology seek to trace the evolution of our ideas of disease causation. They analyze the primary and secondary factors and the theories that have been advanced to evaluate these factors.[36]

As the father of clinical medicine as well as the first true epidemiologist, Hippocrates believed that the universe was made up of four elements: earth, air, water, and fire. In the human body these correspond to cold, dry, moist, and hot humors. Blood is hot and moist; phlegm is cold and moist; yellow bile is hot and dry; black bile is cold and dry. Health comes from proper balance among these four humors or body fluids, whereas disease results from one humor getting the upper hand. If excessive, the disease could be treated by depletion (bleeding, purging, sweating); if deficient, the patient could be aided by restoring the humors through proper diet and drugs. Hippocrates focused on restoring balance to the system of his patient rather than treating specific diseases. In his famous essay "On Airs, Waters and Places," Hippocrates remarked on how the health of a given community was affected by the seasons of the year, the winds, whether hot or cold, the waters the inhabitants used, the characteristics of the place they lived, and their mode of life.[37]

According to Charles Winslow, "five different sorts of causes of epidemic diseases have been invoked ever since the days of the Hippocratic writings: (1) the wrath of the gods, (2) the general epidemic constitution of the atmosphere, (3) local miasmatic conditions due to climate, season and organic decomposition, (4) contagion, and (5) variations in individuals vital resistance." The first of these factors has been discarded by serious students since the Middle Ages, and the fifth was a vague assumption to explain exceptional cases. "A study of theories of epidemiology from Hippocrates to Pasteur centers, therefore, about the relative emphasis laid upon epidemic constitution of the atmosphere, local miasms, and contagion."[38]

European doctors came to the West Indies to treat white settlers, military, naval, and government personnel, and black slaves. The cultural baggage they brought with them included conventional dress and dietary habits, knowledge of European medical theories and practices, and preconceived attitudes toward peoples of different races, religion, and national origin. They came to tropical islands that had markedly different patterns of climate and weather, exotic flora and fauna, and people of dark skin pigmentation whose languages, customs, and diseases were often strange and foreboding. Some of the doctors wrote treatises or essays that described the new physical, social, and disease environments with a view toward preventing disease and making known different modes of treatment. Because relatively few doctors came to the West Indies in the seventeenth and early eighteenth centuries and the white inhabitants were numerous in relation to the African slaves, the doctors were chiefly engaged in treating ailing whites. Moreover, the doctors tended to follow closely the medical theories and practices that were popular in Europe.

The growth of plantation agriculture and slavery altered the balance between white and black medicine. More and more planters became concerned that the number of slave deaths tended to exceed slave births and that, at times, the price of slaves rose in relation to that of sugar and other slave-grown commodities. They hired white doctors to visit their plantations on a contract basis to treat ailing blacks. Some of these doctors published works setting forth the nature and incidence of slave diseases and injuries, suggesting rules for the management of slaves in health and for their treatment in illness. Faced with numerous diseases that were indigenous to Africa, they found it expedient to depart from the canons of European pathology and epidemiology and propound theories of disease causation and cures based on empirical studies. In this effort they were aided by a knowledge of African folk medicine and local plants that possessed medicinal properties. In particular, European doctors directed attention to the need for preventive measures to enhance the life chances of slaves. These measures included the provision of better diet, clothing, housing, and sanitation; the tempering of work loads and punishment; and better treatment of pregnant women, mothers, and children. Moreover, attention was directed to the differences between Africans and Europeans with respect to resistance and susceptibility to various diseases.

The remaining portion of this chapter is devoted to some European doctors who practiced in the West Indies and wrote essays in which they described the physical, biological, social, and disease environments of the islands. It will be of special interest to see how these doctors viewed the new disease environment and sought to analyze and interpret it with the concepts and theories of European medical science, to learn how and to what extent they modified their views as they confronted diseases that were alien to their European background, and to trace the evolution of their ideas of disease causation. The doctors whose works are treated fall roughly into two groups. Members of the first group wrote chiefly about problems that Europeans encountered in adapting to a tropical environment, the diseases they contracted, their ideas of disease causation, and their modification with special reference to the five different causes of epidemic disease. Those in the second group wrote chiefly about the health problems and diseases of African slaves. They faced the difficult problems of understanding and treating people of an alien culture and disease environment, who entered the islands as chattel slaves and continued, with few exceptions, as bondsmen generation after generation in a plantation economy and society that exploited their labor power, often to the point of impaired health and premature death.

Thomas Trapham, Jr., was a doctor who lived in Jamaica from 1673 to 1702 and contributed to the life of the island as an author, planter, politician, and physician. His father was surgeon general to the Parliamentary forces and "body surgeon" to Oliver Cromwell. After receiving his M.A. at Oxford, Trapham attended Leyden University in the Netherlands and obtained his M.D. at Caen in France in 1664. He is best known for his *Discourse of the State of Health in the Island of Jamaica* (1679). His 149-page *Discourse* was the first English book on tropical medicine.[39]

Following Hippocrates, his revered master, Trapham sought to show how the health of the people was influenced by "the Air, the Place, and the Water: The Customs and Manners of Living; &c." He wrote of the healthy, "very nitrous" air, the climate and weather, the "Woods, Plants, Seeds, Fruits," the economic and social life of the people – all with an eye to the effects of environmental factors on human health. Trapham traveled with a party from the south to the north side of Jamaica. In the parish of St. Thomas in the Vale he visited a sugar plantation and saw herds of livestock grazing on the large savannas. "Notwithstanding its surrounding Mountains and great ascending Fogs," he wrote, this parish "hath hitherto been reputed a wholesome and healthy place, greatly planted and almost crowded with the greatest settlements." On the other hand, he wrote that when Henry Morgan and his men returned from their buccaneering raid on Panama, "they brought with them an high if not pestilential Fever, of which many dyed throughout the Country."[40]

Trapham claimed that the diseases of Jamaica fell far short of the number of afflictions suffered by the inhabitants of England. There were no smallpox (or only very rarely when it was brought with the slaves from Africa), no scurvy, and no depopulating plague. Consumption was infrequent, and venereal diseases assumed a milder form than in Europe. The "morbisick affections" that usually and chiefly infested Jamaica were diarrhea, dysentery, fevers, dropsy, worms, venereal diseases, yaws, and the dry bellyache. Dysentery or bloody flux was said to proceed either from a "colliquation of humors" or through a "sluggish thickness of blood." Fevers were chiefly intermittent or malarial, of which the most common form was the tertian, or what Trapham described as "the every other daies Fever and Ague." The dry bellyache, or colic, which afflicted its victims with an "exquisite pain," produced the same effects as did the "lead works of Derby" on the cattle exposed to its fumes. Although Trapham does not directly attribute this disease to lead poisoning, the association became evident many years later from the drinking of rum made in stills with lead or pewter coils.[41]

Racist views were expressed in explaining the origin of two of the principal diseases. Trapham described the yaws as a "seminal taint" that first corrupted the "spermatick parts" and then spread to other parts of the body. He said the disease originated in Africa from "the unnatural mixture of humane with brutal seed." Since bestiality was "a sin against the principles of our Being," the "polluted Yawes" was the divine punishment meted out to transgressors. Syphilis, the other principal disease, was "the corrupted seminals in the Blacks and Indians from whence it may well be propagated under the present appearance of the Pox." Because of their sexual trangressions, the blacks had been condemned to slavery, while the Indians were too weak to defend their lands against the invading Spaniards. Having cohabited with the Indians and contracted syphilis, the Spaniards themselves were morally and physically unfit to rule their vast American conquests. It remained for the English to "separate the pure from the impure, the Gold from the dross, [and] enjoy the West *Indies* without its native diseases."[42]

Trapham, like all doctors of his time, had an erroneous understanding of etiology, writes M. T. Ashcroft. "Most diseases, he believes, are caused by factors such as sudden chilling, exposure to night airs, and intemperance, and are influenced by changes in the lunar cycle. His treatment included the use of emetics, cathartics, venesection, mercurials, and various herbal remedies, which, when not positively injurious, would have been ineffectual." Trapham, however, was less drastic in his treatment than were many later Jamaican physicians. He writes, "For my great Master tells me, Nature is the curer of all her diseases, the Physitian is but the observing Minister to suggest her necessaries and remove impediments." He recommended warm baths, moderate exercise, and a diet containing large amounts of cocoa to preserve health.[43]

Trapham's *Discourse* gives some insight into the health problems faced by Europeans who settled in the West Indies. From the standpoint of etiology and epidemiology, he sought to apply the theories of Hippocrates and his disciples to the disease environment of tropical America. The work displays the author's curiosity about the new diseases he encountered and his attempt to assimilate them into the corpus of European medicine. Unlike the practitioners of heroic medicine who scorned the healing powers of nature and sought to conquer their patients' diseases by bleeding, purging, blistering, vomiting, and sweating, Trapham was more inclined to use gentle remedies in an effort to aid the healing powers of nature. Apart from his concern with yaws and other diseases that were brought to Jamaica from Africa, Trapham expressed little interest in the harsh conditions that prevailed among the growing body of African slaves in Jamaica.

Sir Hans Sloane (1660-1753) is the best known European doctor who practiced in the West Indies in the age of slavery. Born in Ireland of Scottish parents and educated in England and France, he lived most of his life in

London as a physician and collector. As a young man he became a protégé of Thomas Sydenham, who introduced him to practice by recommending him to his patients when he was disabled by gout. Sydenham, whose fame lay in the systematic study of the symptoms he observed in his patients, told Sloane he "must go to the bedside, it is there alone you can learn disease."[44]

Sloane, however, was not yet ready to settle into practice as a London physician. During his student days in France he had developed a keen interest in the study of plants, both as a science in itself and as a source of pharmacological remedies. Opportunity to further such study was afforded by the offer he received to go to Jamaica as physician to the Duke of Albemarle and his family, the Duke having been appointed the island's governor. Sloane, who accepted the offer with alacrity, was later to write in the preface to his *Natural History of Jamaica*, "This Voyage seem'd likewise to promise to be useful to me, as a Physician; many of the Antient and best Physicians having travell'd to the Places whence their Drugs were brought to inform themselves concerning them."[45]

Arriving in Jamaica in December 1687, Sloane lost little time in commencing his search for new plants for use as drugs or food. He wrote: "I was resolved to go to the North-side of the Island, and visit the Mountains between it and the South side, to see what they brought forth. Wherefore I got some Gentlemen of the Country, one who drew in *Crayons*, a very good Guide, and a sure-footed Horse, and set out." His collecting effort was so successful that when he returned to England, he brought about 800 plants, most of which were new, together with the drawings to illustrate his book. One reason for writing his *Natural History*, he said, was "to teach the Inhabitants of the Parts where these Plants grow, their several Uses, which I have endeavour'd to do, by the best Informations I could get from Books, and the Inhabitants, either Europeans, Indians or Blacks."[46] Although Sloane was interested primarily in cures and remedies, he did make known certain opinions concerning the differences between the diseases of Jamaica and Europe and their causes. He was told that the diseases of Jamaica were all different from what they were in Europe. This made him very uneasy lest by ignorance he should kill instead of cure. After treating many patients, however, he said he never saw a disease in Jamaica that he had not met with in Europe, excepting one or two.[47]

Sloane, like his mentor Sydenham, had no difficulty in abandoning ancient authorities when experiments demonstrated that their theories were in error. One case in point was the Peruvian or Jesuits' bark or quinine used in the treatment of malaria or ague. When the old theory of "humors" could not explain the experimental fact that quinine reduced temperature in fever, Sloane wrote to a friend, "A poor Indian who first taught the cure of an Ague, of which the Lady of the Count of Chincon was sick, overthrew with one simple Medicine, without any Preparation, all the *Hypotheses* and Theories of Agues, which were supported by some Scores not to say Hundreds of Volumes."[48]

A large part of Sloane's introduction to his *Natural History* is an account of the diseases he observed in Jamaica and his methods of cure. He includes descriptions of leprosy, madness, worms, venereals, diarrheas, dysentery, yaws, melancholia, and intermittent fever or malaria. Malaria was very epidemic all over the island during the rainy season, he said, and generally very violent. It also occurred frequently near marshes. This fever and the extravagant drinking of rum were said to cause dropsies.

Although his medical practice was confined largely to white people, Sloane gives some attention to sick blacks and such prevalent black diseases as leprosy, worms, and yaws. He held erroneous or questionable ideas concerning yaws, which he says was propagated by ordinary conversation, by trampling with bare feet on the spittle of those affected with it, and mostly by copulation. As we shall see in Chapter 3, Sloane had a low opinion of the folk medicine of the blacks. On one occasion he derisively called attention to one Hercules, a lusty black overseer and doctor famous for curing gonorrheas, "who was so far from being able by Specifics to cure that Disease, that he was very ill of it himself."[49] In his descriptive account of the slaves and their manner of living, Sloane was a more acute observer than Trapham. He wrote on such topics as slave family life, diet, provision grounds or gardens, clothing, housing, work loads, punishment, personal hygiene, and medical ideas and practices. That he felt any more horror of slavery than was common among men of his age is highly improbable. In fact, he described without any sign of disgust the revolting punishments that planters and overseers meted out to the slaves of Jamaica. Sloane himself came to own a large gang of slaves after his marriage to a sugar heiress of Jamaica. Sloane left Jamaica on 16 March 1688/9 and lived the remainder of his distinguished life in London.[50]

William Hillary, M.D. (d. 1763), practiced medicine in Barbados from 1747 to May 1758 and wrote one of the best known early treatises on Caribbean diseases. He was a student of Hermann Boerhaave at Leyden, where he graduated M.D. in 1722. He practiced at Ripon and removed to Bath in 1734. Hillary's *Observations on the Changes of the Air, and the Concomitant Epidemical Diseases of Barbadoes* was first published in London in 1759; the second edition, 360 pages long, was published in London in 1766. It was reprinted in Philadelphia in 1811, with a dedication and notes by Benjamin Rush, M.D. As a pupil of the celebrated Boerhaave, Hillary was said to have learned the necessary connection of theory with experience in the practice of medicine.[51]

In the first part of his *Epidemical Diseases*, Hillary studies the most material changes of the air and weather. For six years he kept meticulous daily records of the temperature and pressure of the air and the quantities of rain that fell in each month and year. Likewise, he recorded the variations of the concomitant epidemical diseases he observed in his practice, with a view toward ascertaining "how these diseases were either influenced, caused, or changed, by those variations of the weather. . . as also such variations, either in the method of curing those diseases, or such alternations in the medicines given, as I found were necessary, and the success they had; all which I have endeavoured carefully to relate." Hillary expressed hope that his book would be generally useful to mankind and especially to the medical practitioners and inhabitants of Barbados.[52]

Hillary, on a month-by-month basis, summarizes the weather of Barbados and the concomitant diseases. Generally speaking, the early months of the year were cool, pleasant, dry, and healthful. However, January, February, and March witnessed the spread of such inflammatory and respiratory ailments as coughs, quinsys, catarrhs, pleurisies, ophthalmies, inflammatory fever, and slow nervous fever. From the cool and dry weather of the early months, the season from April to June continued generally dry with scattered showers and a warming trend. Inflammatory diseases were most acute during the dry and warm season in April and May. Late May and June saw occasional epidemics stemming from alterations in both temperature and moisture. Accompanying the heavier rains of June were numerous cases of diarrhea and dysentery.[53]

Generally warmer weather with frequent rain showers characterized July, August, and September. When rain fell, diarrheas appeared and dysentery became more frequent. Dysenteries that were frequent in July and August became epidemic all over the island among both whites and blacks in September 1756. Between the showers there were clear and hot periods when the inhabitants of Barbados were susceptible to inflammatory diseases and the continued remitting fever. In July 1754 the pertussis or whooping cough seized many children in Bridgetown and other parts of the island, while in September 1755 arthritics suffered much from the "gouty humour."[54]

During the last quarter of the year the generally wet and cool weather was accompanied by diarrheas, dysenteries, and fevers. Many more fevers were reported, including "an irregular, ingeminated, intermitting, quotidian fever," "putrid, bilious, or yellow fever," "depuratory fever," and a "continued slow fever of a synochus kind." Intervals of dry and warm weather were linked to a higher incidence of inflammatory fever, catarrhal fever or influenza, pleurisy, pneumonia, quinsy, and ophthalmia. Asthmatics and consumptive patients were said to have suffered much from catarrhal fever, which proved fatal to some of them. As in former periods, children frequently fell victim to whooping cough.

December, which was generally drier and cooler than the preceding months, marked a transition in the disease environment. Upon the coming of dry weather in December 1752, Hillary wrote that "the dysenteries which were frequent and epidemical all over the island in the three last months, now totally ceased and disappeared." Inflammatory diseases were also very few, but they increased toward the end of the month, when many people were seized with catarrhs.[55]

Contrary to the view expressed by Sir Hans Sloane, Hillary contended that most of the diseases he encountered in Barbados were peculiar to the West Indies and seldom or never seen in the colder countries of Europe. In his inquiries into the nature and causes of these diseases, however, he relied chiefly on European medical concepts, etiology, and epidemiology, especially the writings of Hippocrates, Boerhaave, Sydenham, and John Huxham. Intermitting fever or malaria was very rarely seen in Barbados, he said, unless it was introduced from neighboring islands that were less cultivated and not yet cleared of their woods. Like other medical writers, Hillary classified malaria as an intermittent fever of miasmatic origin. Lacking scientific knowledge of etiology and epidemiology, his classification of fevers was imperfect and his analysis unsystematic.[56]

Though it is chiefly concerned with the diseases of Europeans in the West Indies, Hillary's *Epidemical Diseases* gives some attention to diseases of African origin and the medical ecology of black slaves in Barbados. From his wide reading in the literature of European and Arabic medicine, he gleaned interesting facts about the origin, nature, and treatment of such African and Arabic diseases as leprosy, yaws, ophthalmia, elephantiasis, and the Guinea worm. The yaws, which he said were indigenous to Africa and Arabia, "seldom fail to attack the negroes in Africa, at one time or other in their life-time, but most frequently the children and young people; and that they very rarely or never have it a second time, if they have been perfectly cured the first time, either in their own native country by their negro doctors, or after they arrive here." The yaws were said to be very infectious to those who handled or cohabited with its victims. As concomitant causes of dysentery, he listed "their too freely eating the herbs, roots, and fruits of the earth," and their being "too much exposed to the inclemencies of the weather, and hard labour in the fields, and some of them ill-cloathed; all which jointly contribute to cause this disease."[57]

The fever books

Colonial wars and the expansion of settlements in tropical regions involved increasing numbers of Europeans and led to greater concern with the causes and cure of diseases peculiar to such climates. Several works on the diseases of Europeans in the tropics were based on experiences during the Seven Years' War (1756–63). Foremost among the authors of such works was James Lind (1716–94), who graduated M.D. at Edinburgh and was a surgeon in the navy on the coast of Guinea as well as in the West Indies, Mediterranean, and Channel. He is best known for *A Treatise on the Scurvy* (1754), in which he recommended the use of lemon juice for the prevention of that disease. In 1768 Lind published *An Essay on Diseases Incidental to Europeans in Hot Climates*, of which five editions appeared during his life, a sixth in 1808, and also French and German translations. Lind observed that whereas few persons visited either the East or West Indies for pleasure, thousands left England every year to settle in those regions or serve in the military garrisons. The purpose of his book was to ascertain the comparative degrees of health that Europeans enjoyed in hot countries, "to point out the most effectual Means of obviating the malignant effects of the Climate, and to give the proper Treatment of the Diseases, to which in each, they are most exposed."[58]

Lind described and compared the disease environments of territories within and outside of the expanded British Empire. He noted that whereas some climates were healthy and favorable to European constitutions, most countries beyond the limits of Europe that had been frequented by Europeans had unfortunately proved very unhealthy to them. The most certain signs or "proofs" of an unhealthy country were as follows: (1) sudden and great alterations in the air at sunset from intolerable heat to a chilling cold (this radical alteration in temperature occurred chiefly in areas of unhealthy, swampy soil where, after sunset, the vapors emitted made the air raw, damp, and chilling); (2) thick noisome fogs arising chiefly after sunset from the valleys and particularly from mud, slime, and other impurities; (3) numerous swarms of flies, gnats, and other insects that were attracted to stagnated air and places covered with trees; (4) places where all butchers' meat quickly rotted and became full of maggots; and (5) areas with a certain sandy soil that had been found injurious to health.[59]

Europeans in wet tropical regions fell victim chiefly to what Lind described as "fevers and fluxes." He defined a fever as "an indisposition of the body attended, commonly with an increase of its heat, a thirst, often with a headach[e], but more frequently with a remarkable quickness of the pulse; or at least a great change from its natural state; accompanied, for the most part, with various other symptoms of distress, which in a few days terminate, either in a recovery, a remission, or in death." Lind classified fevers into intermitting, remitting, and continual. "An intermitting fever," he writes, "is supposed to leave the patient perfectly free, from all symptoms of the fever, during the absence or intermission." These fevers were called quotidian or tertian as they renewed their attacks every day or every other day, respectively. The immediate cause of intermitting fever or malaria was the soil and air of the place. However, the more remote causes that disposed the constitution to receive a hurtful impression of a bad air included lying in a damp room, neglecting to put on dry clothes immediately after being wet by rain, and the like. Lind said that "a remitting fever is supposed to have irregular or imperfect intermissions; and a continual fever to have no perceptible intermissions." All three of these fevers were said to be bilious "if the bile, either pure or mixed, be copiously or frequently evacuated, by vomit or stool."[60]

Lind observed that most tropical countries have, properly speaking, only two seasons, the wet and the dry. The wet season, which commonly lasted about four months, was one of sickness, whereas the dry season was for many months as healthy and pleasant as in any part of the world. Europeans on the coast of Guinea were highly susceptible to fevers propagated by the vapors exhaled from putrid stagnant water. The weight Lind gives to the miasmatic theory is underscored by his belief that if a tract of land in Africa was as perfectly freed from trees, shrubs, marshes, and the like as was the island of Barbados, the air would be rendered equally healthy and pleasant.[61]

If the disease environment of Barbados was benign, the same could not be said of other islands in the West Indies. Lind asserted that fevers and fluxes were fatal to Europeans in the sugar islands, but the disease called yellow fever was particularly destructive to them. Fevers and fluxes generally proceeded "from the intense heat and from a peculiar unhealthfulness of the air, though sometimes perhaps they may be brought on by a gross habit of body, excessive drinking of spirituous liquors, or being overheated in the sun." Like the advice given by Hippocrates, Lind urged whites to escape from bad air. He told of elevated and temperate situations in Jamaica and other islands that were clear of woods, shrubs, or stagnant water and where Europeans enjoyed good health during all seasons of the year.[62]

Lind made only passing mention of the slave trade and slavery. He thought it intolerable that Europeans should suffer heavy fatalities from cutting down woods and clearing the ground from trees. "If the purchasing of negroes on the coast of Guinea can be justified," he writes, "it must be from the absolute necessity of employing them in such services as this is. It does not seem consistent with British humanity, to assign such employments to a regiment of gallant soldiers, or to a company of brave seamen."[63]

Whereas Lind's book was based chiefly on his experiences during the Seven Years' War, other doctor-authors were motivated by their service in the War of American Independence and the wars of the French Revolution and the Napoleonic War. One of these doctor-authors was Robert Jackson, M.D. (1750–1827). He wrote on the causes, course, consequences, and cure of contagious fevers. He displayed a speculative and analytical turn of mind, examining the various theories and principles then extant and observing that "the theories which physicians hold concerning the nature of diseases influence practice directly or indirectly." He considered endemic fever to be essentially one disease that took a variety of forms – inflammatory, putrid, nervous, bilious, simple, complicated, mild, and malignant. Jackson attributed the forms of fevers to variations in the constitution or temperament of the patient. He distinguished six different temperaments bearing the formidable names of sanguine, phlegmatic, serous, gangrenous, phlegmaticliquescent, and serous-liquescent.[64]

Jackson claims to have opened new ground in his study of contagious fevers. He emphasized the diversity of such diseases, calling on the physician to consider the case before he wrote the prescription. He was a pioneer in recommending cold bathing as a remedy for fevers. "When we read Jackson's book," writes Lester S. King, "we appreciate his earnest strivings. Clearly, febrile disease took different forms. Clearly, some factor or factors must be responsible for these differences. But what? From time to time we see a flash of insight which helped to illumine the confusion."[65]

Colin Chisholm, M.D., F.R.S. (d. 1825), wrote extensively on fevers and other tropical diseases. He classified the diseases of the West Indies into those influenced by the seasons and those that were not. Diseases not influenced by the seasons included elephantiasis, the glandular disease, hydrocephalus, yaws, putrid and ulcerous sore throat, mortification of the fingers and toes, chronic aphthae, leprosy, tetanus, and occasionally hydrophobia. Compared with the seasonal diseases, they were "not less tremendous in their consequences, although much longer protracted in their course." Endemic diseases were either bilious or inflammatory as the seasons were hot and wet or cool and dry. During the winter and spring, northerly winds sometimes brought an uncommon and disagreeable chilliness, but the atmosphere was less moist than at other times of the year. Under these conditions "pleurisies, often attended with fever, catarrhal fevers, rheumatic fevers, ophthalmias, inflammatory angina, erysipelas, chronic rheumatism, and the guinea worm, in certain situations, are the most common epidemics."[66]

Like Sydenham and others, Chisholm adhered to a humoral-climatic and miasmatic theory of medicine. In explaining that all inflammations were disorganizations of the structure of the blood, whereby a disunion of its constituent parts took place, he confessed that this old theory was "the least objectionable, the most rational, and that by which all the phenomena of inflammation can be most readily explained."[67] Although Chisholm's theories were all wrong, Lester King says he tried to merge contemporary scientific data into medical thinking and was on the path of progress.[68]

Slave medical manuals

Medical manuals for the treatment of ailing blacks differed from those intended for Europeans in hot climates. Whereas the latter were concerned largely with fevers that took a proportionately higher toll of Europeans than Afro-West Indians, the former covered a wide range of diseases, accidents, and minor ailments to which the slaves were prone. The medical manuals for whites drew heavily on European authorities for their etiology and epidemiology and were fairly evenly balanced between causes and cures, but those for slaves were less dependent on European authorities and emphasized treatment and cures more than symptoms and causes. Whereas Europeans in the tropics were chiefly adult men and the medical manuals were directed to their disorders, the slave population consisted of adults and children of both sexes and the manuals were accordingly directed to the needs of males and females of different ages and blacks who were either African-born or Creoles. Whereas Europeans in the tropics were prone to overeat, overdrink, overdress, and neglect exercise, slaves were often underfed, underclothed, overworked, and harshly punished. Doctors who were in intimate contact with slaves realized that medical treatment was futile if their patients were undernourished or otherwise debilitated. In their medical manuals they urged planters and overseers to improve the management of their slaves.

James Grainger, M.D. (1721?–66), was the first doctor to write a medical manual for the treatment of slaves in the British West Indies. He was born of Scots parents, probably at Dunse in Berwickshire. He studied medicine at Edinburgh University for three years, served as army surgeon during the Scottish rebellion of 1745 and in Holland during the Seven Years' War, and returned to Edinburgh and graduated M.D. in 1753. He then settled in London where he practiced medicine and wrote poetry that brought him to the attention of the leading literary men of his time. He also became acquainted with absentee proprietors from the island of St. Christopher or St. Kitts. In 1759 he went to St. Kitts as tutor to the heir of a sugar estate. There he married a sugar heiress, practiced medicine, studied botany, and wrote a poem, *The Sugar Cane*, which was published in 1764 with copious notes. He expanded these notes into *An Essay on the More Common West-India Diseases; and the Remedies which that Country itself produces: To which are added, Some Hints on the Management, &c., of Negroes. By a Physician in the West Indies* (London, 1764). A second edition "With Practical Notes, and a Linnaean Index, by William Wright, M.D., F.R.S.," was published in Edinburgh in 1802 (see Figure 1.1). Grainger died at St. Kitts on 16 December 1766, a victim of a fever.[69]

Coming to St. Kitts soon after the Seven Years' War, Grainger found a lively economy and society. Slave imports from Africa increased markedly

AN

ESSAY

ON THE MORE COMMON

WEST-INDIA DISEASES;

AND THE

REMEDIES WHICH THAT COUNTRY ITSELF PRODUCES:

TO WHICH ARE ADDED,

SOME HINTS

ON THE

MANAGEMENT, &c. OF NEGROES.

By JAMES GRAINGER, M.D.

THE SECOND EDITION.

WITH PRACTICAL NOTES, AND A LINNÆAN INDEX,

By WILLIAM WRIGHT, M.D. F.R.S.
PHYSICIAN TO HIS MAJESTY'S FORCES.

Nulla in re, proprius accedunt homines ad Deos, quam salutem hominibus dando. CICERO.

EDINBURGH:
PRINTED FOR MUNDELL & SON, AND LONGMAN & REES, LONDON.

1802.

Figure 1.1. Title page of Dr. James Grainger's "Essay on West India Diseases."

after the moribund war period, plantation slavery expanded to neighboring islands ceded to Great Britain, and slave prices rose as demand outpaced supply. Yet in this expanding slave society Grainger found it a "matter of astonishment... that among the many valuable medical tracts which of late years have been offered to the public, no one has been purposely written on the method of seasoning new Negroes, and the treatment of Negroes when sick." To Grainger it was a "melancholy truth, that hundreds of these useful people are yearly sacrificed to mistakes in these two capital points." To correct these defects, he wrote his *Essay* to enable those who were entrusted with the management of blacks to treat them in a more scientific manner. At the same time he said that his ninety-eight-page *Essay* was "wholly divested of the parade of learning, being purposely written with as much shortness as was consistent with perspicuity." Grainger's *Essay* was principally intended for the owners and managers of slaves in the Sugar Colonies. In the "Advertisement" to the second edition, William Wright said he knew physicians and surgeons who had profited much from Grainger's *Essay* "both in the knowledge of the diseases of the Negroes, and of the indigenous remedies."[70]

Part I of Grainger's *Essay* supplies information on the physical and social characteristics of different African peoples and advice on their purchase and treatment during the period of acclimatization or seasoning. Newly imported slaves required much care since they often arrived in a debilitated condition and were liable to contract diseases that were troublesome to cure and sometimes fatal. Part II begins with a discussion of the costs and benefits of newly purchased or "saltwater" slaves as compared with Creoles or those born on the island. Grainger believed the advantage lay with the Creoles, who were generally healthier but also more expensive than Africans. Readers of the *Essay* were cautioned that "too great care cannot be taken either of the Negresses when pregnant, and in the month, or of their infants when born." Part II also treats the diseases to which the blacks were most often exposed and points out medicines of local origin for treating these diseases. The author explains that since the plantations were often far from medical assistance, he had given explicit directions for preparing and administering medicines. Thus he hoped that many valuable lives would be saved, "a circumstance not less profitable to the owner, than pleasing to humanity."[71]

Following his instructions for the treatment of infants, Grainger takes up the ailments and diseases that afflicted both blacks and whites. He said that worms killed more people in the West Indies than all other diseases with the exception of dysentery. The remote causes of worms were the warm climate, the great use of vegetable food, and humidity. The immediate cause, he said, was relaxation. Although worms were more fatal in the torrid zone than fevers, these too proved more deadly there than in Europe. In a footnote to Grainger's discussion of fevers, William Wright asserted that white people in the West Indies were susceptible to remitting fevers, whereas the fever of blacks was inflammatory. Grainger wrote that dysentery or flux was often produced by corrupted bile, sudden suppression of perspiration, and too great indulgence in eating watery crude vegetables. Lest dangerous relapses occur, blacks who had recovered from a flux should not return too soon to hard labor. Other diseases that occurred more or less frequently and acutely among both blacks and whites were diarrhea, tetanus, dropsy, cholera morbus, malignant sore throat, and hepatitis.[72]

In part III of his *Essay*, Grainger is concerned with the management and diseases of black slaves. He notes that although white people in the West Indies were not exempted from leprosy, the blacks were most subject to this dreadful calamity. He doubted whether leprosy was infectious, but it was prudent to remove the distempered from the sound. Grainger attributed leprosy to such superficial causes as being overheated and getting too suddenly cool. Closely related to leprosy was the "joint evil," which was confined to blacks and often resulted in the loss of the victims' toes. Yaws was a disease that luckily attacked the blacks but once and was said to be both tedious and difficult to cure. Nyctalopia or night blindness is failed or imperfect vision at night or in dim light, with good vision only on bright days. It was not common in the Leeward Islands and the only victims that Grainger saw were among slaves brought from Africa. The Guinea worm also came with the slaves from Africa. It was said to have been a tedious, but not a dangerous disease. Ruptures, though not confined to the blacks, were more frequent among them owing to sprains and overexercise. Similarly, blacks were more frequently afflicted with burns and ulcers than were whites.[73]

"But it is not enough to take care of Negroes when they are sick," wrote Grainger; "they should also be well clothed and regularly fed." Thus begins part IV of the *Essay*, where the author makes some observations on the food, clothing, and punishment of slaves, the "sick houses" or hospitals in which they were confined, and the medicines every plantation owner should have sent annually from England. Though Grainger himself owned slaves, he found it shocking to philanthropy that human beings were made to act from motives of fear only. Were they instructed in the practical principles of Christianity, he asserted, they would be rendered much better servants and thus be treated less severely.[74]

Grainger's short *Essay* was the first of its kind in the West Indies. It was directed chiefly to slave diseases and their cure, taking into account the characteristics of different African peoples, the vicissitudes of the Middle Passage, the seasoning, and environmental conditions conducive to accidents, debility, and endemic and epidemic disease. The *Essay* is infused with a spirit of understanding and compassion for the lot of the blacks, at the same time that its chief purpose was to render real service to medical practitioners and owners and managers of slaves.

By far the most comprehensive and widely known medical manual for slaves was written by a doctor-planter who preferred to remain anonymous. He revealed certain facts about his life, however, and we learn from other sources that he was Dr. David Collins who resided on the island of St. Vincent. He wrote that his education was originally professional and that during more than twenty years in the West Indies he had directed a large gang of slaves whose health and productivity he successfully preserved. From a contemporary authority we learn that Dr. Collins was an eminent medical practitioner and an able and experienced planter who raised an ample fortune by his skill and assiduity in the management of his own sugar estate. In 1803 Collins published his *Practical Rules for the Management and Medical Treatment of Negro Slaves, in the Sugar Colonies. By a Professional Planter* (see Figure 1.2). It was reprinted in London in 1811 and reprinted again in Freeport, New York, in 1971. Notwithstanding his professions of humanity, Collins was motivated chiefly by a desire to render slavery more efficient and profitable, to reduce morbidity and mortality at the same time that efforts were made to increase natality. Above all, measures should be taken to increase the slave population by natural means and thus obviate the need for new recruits from Africa.[75]

Thus Collins's book, which was originally written to instruct his manager, was later offered to the public in an enlarged form to assist planters and medical practitioners in the management and medical treatment of slaves. He expressed hope that it would be highly useful to exhibit a series of rules deduced from experience. Consistent with his belief that slaves who were well cared for were less prone to morbidity and mortality than those who were treated harshly, Collins in the first half of his 395-page book lays down rules that would tend to preserve blacks when in health. He was primarily concerned to keep the laboring slaves in a state of health consistent with the profitable production of plantation staples. After pointing out that domestic slaves were as healthful and prolific and lived as long as any other class of people in the West Indies, Collins asserted that

> the greater destruction of field negroes, and their consequent decrease, doth not proceed either from the insalubrity of the climate to African constitutions, or to any defect in the organisation of their stamina, but from the vice of regimen, and the operation of causes, which may be successfully resisted by means within the power of every Planter to employ compatibly with his interest.[76]

Collins then proceeds in nine chapters to lay down rules for correcting "the vice of regimen." In the first chapter he compares the labor of free

PRACTICAL RULES

FOR THE

MANAGEMENT

AND

MEDICAL TREATMENT

OF

NEGRO SLAVES,

IN THE

SUGAR COLONIES.

By a PROFESSIONAL PLANTER.

London:

PRINTED BY J. BARFIELD, WARDOUR-STREET, SOHO,
PRINTER TO HIS ROYAL HIGHNESS THE PRINCE REGENT,
FOR
VERNOR, HOOD, AND SHARP, IN THE POULTRY; AND
HATCHARD, PICCADILLY.

1811.

Figure 1.2. Title page of Dr. David Collins's "Practical Rules for the Medical Treatment of Slaves."

men and slaves on West India plantations and delivers some observations on black slaves. The second chapter treats the seasoning of slaves newly imported and lays down rules intended to obviate the fatal consequences attendant on their change of climate and habits. The diet of slaves is taken up in chapter three. Collins said he was persuaded that the planters had been "more reprehensible in that respect than on most others; and that there remains still much to be mended in that branch of negro economy." Rules with regard to clothing and lodging the slaves are laid down in chapters four and five, respectively. "The sixth chapter treats on a subject of very great consequence," he wrote, "that of the breeding of negroes; which appears to have been less understood, and worse attended to, than any other part of West-Indian management." The eighth chapter treats their discipline, which, he advised, should be regular though not severe. Finally, brief attention is given in chapter nine to the subject of religion. That the principles of blacks were susceptible to improvement by religion was evident, Collins declared, from the experience of the French sugar colonies, where the slaves were said to be "incomparably better disposed than our own."[77]

Having discussed the management of slaves in health in part I of his book, Collins turns in part II to the diseases of blacks and their treatment in sickness. Here he ranges widely from such minor ailments as ringworm and the itch to the great killer, dysentery. He observed that whereas the disorders of blacks did not differ much from those of whites in their qualities, they did differ markedly in their severity. Blacks had much greater tolerance of heat than whites, they were less prone to succumb to fevers, but they were more vulnerable to bowel complaints than whites. Moreover, the different types of scrofula and leprosy attacked the blacks with some frequency, though rarely the whites. The yaws also, which frequently proved fatal to the blacks, was seldom encountered among the whites.[78]

Like James Lind, Collins asserted that fevers and fluxes were the chief killers of whites and blacks in the West Indies. Although the blacks were as subject to "feverish affections" as the whites, they seldom died of them as did the whites. Collins divided the fevers of blacks into three classes: the simple, the intermittent, and the inflammatory. The first two classes of fevers were attended with little danger, but the third was more threatening. Inflammatory fevers were common in December, January, and February. If they did not kill in a few days, as they sometimes did, their victims might become consumptive and die after many months and sometimes years of indisposition.[79]

Bowel complaints were more fatal to blacks than to whites. "The seat of the greater part of negro disorders," wrote Collins, "from a variety of causes dependent upon their food, their clothing, lodgings, and exposure to the weather, is in their bowels." Colic or bellyache, which made up two-thirds of the stomach complaints of plantation slaves, arose from wind created by eating unripe roots and fruit or from the juice of the sugarcane. Diarrhea was a common disorder among the blacks when the air grew colder and the perspiration less abundant. It arose from eating unripe canes, yams, Indian corn, or any other unripe vegetable. Dysentery or bloody flux was said to be a very common disorder among the blacks and by far the most fatal disorder on plantations. Consistent with the humoral-climatic and miasmatic theory of epidemiology, Collins asserted that dysenteries proved more or less violent "as the situation is dry and healthy, or low, swampy, and unhealthful." Since dysentery was highly infectious, every means should be adopted to keep the infected apart from the sound.[80]

Collins wrote extensively on other infectious and noninfectious diseases. The yaws attacked blacks at all ages, but chiefly infants who were "the most sensible of impressions from the virulent humour of this disease," which not unfrequently killed them. Because the yaws were communicated by contact, its victims should be isolated from those who had escaped the disease. Leprosy baffled all the efforts of art, leaving the poor victims both odious to themselves and intolerable to others. Dropsy, though occurring more frequently, was much less fatal in the West Indies than in Europe. It proceeded most commonly from a relaxation, and often from an obstruction of perspiration. Finally, "mal d'estomac" or dirt eating was a very common disorder among blacks in the West Indies. Collins attributed this disease to "a mean and unsubstantial diet" and to "any great depression of mind" that the blacks labored under from the rigorous treatment of their masters.[81]

Dr. Collins compressed his twenty years of experience as a planter and doctor in the West Indies into a single volume. As a planter, he wrote of the harsh and precarious lives of slaves as they labored in the fields and sugar factories, came home bone weary at the end of the day to cook and eat their meager rations, slept fitfully on plank beds in wattled and daubed huts half exposed to the elements, and possibly found consolation in fiery new rum or the religions of Africa or Europe. As a doctor, Collins wrote of the diseases and distempers of blacks, their incidence, symptoms, causes, progress, and cures. More than any other doctor-author, he showed how slave disorders were related, either directly or indirectly, to work loads, diet, clothing, lodging, punishment, and exposure to the weather. Calling attention to the fact that he had lost very few of his own slaves, Collins urged his fellow planters to heed his practical rules for the management and medical treatment of their black bondsmen. That he was pragmatic and motivated by a spirit of enlightened self-interest is evident from reading his book. "It may be laid down as a principle, susceptible of the clearest demonstration," he wrote, "that every benefit conferred on the slaves, whether in food, or clothing, or rest, must ultimately terminate in the interest of the owner."[82]

John Williamson, M.D., was the author of a two-volume work that combined his own experiences as a medical practitioner with features of earlier works on West Indian medicine. He received a diploma from the Royal College of Physicians at Edinburgh and served for a time as surgeon to a Scottish regiment. Williamson came to Jamaica in 1798 and practiced medicine there until 1812 when he returned to England. The medical journal he kept in Jamaica, together with other papers, was prepared for the press and published in 1817 under the title, *Medical and Miscellaneous Observations, Relative to the West India Islands*.[83] Most of Williamson's book consists of his edited and abbreviated journal or medical memorandums. The journal began with his departure from London to Portsmouth to take passage to Jamaica on 27 May 1798 and ends 17 May 1812 upon his return to London. He made entries on the climate and weather; customs and manners of the people; their occupations, diseases, and accidents; plantation medical practice; the island's medical profession; and suggestions to ameliorate the condition of the slaves, provide better health services, and encourage family life and reproduction. Upon his arrival at Jamaica he began to write monthly medical memorandums. "Where minute details of cases were desirable," he wrote, "they were collected at the patient's bed-side. As he proceeded in this plan, it was found that these notes proved of essential service in practice; and his zeal increased as he proceeded." In fact, his zeal led him to urge young practitioners to keep similar records as "a source of satisfactory reflection, which the importance of their duties, and conscientious fulfilment, can only inspire."[84]

As with Dr. Hillary of Barbados, Williamson introduced each month's report with a short detail of the weather. He sought to discover what diseases the inhabitants were predisposed to at different seasons of the year and ascertain any possible patterns. Williamson subscribed to the humoral-climatic and miasmatic theory of disease causation as did so many doctors of his time. He associated good health with dry weather and the vigorous growth of vegetation. On the other hand, the decomposition of vegetable matter in combination with inclement weather and sudden alterations of temperature was believed to contribute to high morbidity and mortality. For example, in November 1799, at a time of heavy rainfall and north winds, Williamson wrote:

> In a country where immense masses of vegetable matter are constantly perishing, we cannot help thinking that, in such a process, our atmosphere is so infected, to a certain degree, as to prove a source of many of those diseases peculiar to what is termed the fall of the year, including the months of October, November, December, and January.

September 1810 was a month of acute distress when "the extreme heat, oppressive nature of the atmosphere, heavy and continued rains, state of perishing animal and vegetable matter, combined to produce many sources of disease, such as fever, dysentery, cholera, ophthalmia, eruptive diseases, and fevers in children, attended by fits."[85]

Closely associated with seasonal patterns of weather and disease were behavior patterns characteristic of slave life on West Indian plantations. Williamson was highly critical of the slaves for exposing themselves to noxious night air while attending dances and engaging in other leisure activities. He deplored the Christmas holidays for affording "an irrational indulgence to negroes in the excessive use of spiritous liquors" and "the full gratification of their passions." Pleurisy, among other diseases, was attributed to the excesses of the holiday season. At other times of the year pneumonia and pleurisy were accounted for "by the unseasonable hours which negroes keep, night visiting, and intemperance." Besides their leisure activities, slaves contracted colds and fevers when they were forced to work in wet clothes. Despite the heavy labor demanded at crop time, it was contended that this was a healthy time for the slaves because they received extra rations of cane juice and molasses. Williamson recorded instances of illness caused by scarcity of foodstuffs and the eating of unripe food.[86]

Williamson in the course of his practice became aware of differences between European and African inhabitants of Jamaica in their susceptibility and resistance to certain diseases. He found that attacks of fever were seldom severe among blacks, nor did they run any regular course insofar as his plantation practice enabled him to judge. Differences were also apparent in the incidence of epidemic catarrh or influenza. Whites were not severely liable to it at times when it had a destructive influence among the blacks.[87]

The greater part of Volume II of Williamson's *Medical Observations* is devoted to essays on medical and religious subjects. He wrote on epidemic influenza, yaws, vaccination against smallpox, medical practice on estates and plantations, the medical profession, care of black women and children, and the mal d'estomac or stomach evil. He attributed the stomach evil or dirt eating to despondency resulting from Obeah or witchcraft. The more general sources of this disease were said to be an unfavorable climate, indifferent food, and imperfect clothing. One essay proposed to establish Christianity among the slaves, while another criticized certain Methodist missionaries in the West Indies. We shall return to Williamson's interesting and revealing *Medical Observations* in future chapters.[88]

James Thomson, M.D. (d. 1822), practiced medicine in Jamaica and wrote a small book on the diseases of blacks. His career is significant for at least two reasons. First, it was linked closely to that of other doctor-authors, and second, he was the only Jamaican who wrote a medical manual concerned exclusively with the diseases of slaves. Thomson may have been born in Jamaica or lived there as a youth. He received his M.D. degree from the

Edinburgh Medical School in 1813. After practice in London he settled in Jamaica as a medical practitioner and had a large plantation practice at the time of his death in 1822. Thomson drew on his education and experience to write *A Treatise on the Diseases of Negroes, As they Occur in the Island of Jamaica* (1820). It was dedicated to Dr. John Quier, who was the friend and medical partner of Thomson's father. Thomson wrote in the introduction to his 168-page *Treatise* that during his medical studies at the University of Edinburgh he was strongly advised by his friend, Dr. William Wright, "formerly high in the medical department of this island, if my situation in life ever led me to the West-Indies, to institute enquiries into the nature of the disorders to which the negroes are liable, as affording a subject rich with materials." Thomson's purpose in writing his book was "to enable the planter to afford relief with more confidence and success when medical assistance is not at hand, and where it often, I am sorry to say, is not worth having."[89]

Like the other doctors we have sketched, Thomson was highly conscious of differences in the incidence of disease among whites and blacks. He noted that although the blacks frequently had irregular attacks of fever during the fall when north winds began to prevail, they were speedily cured by a few doses of bark and bitterwood. Thomson took special interest in the constitutional or hereditary disorders of blacks, which no medical authorities that he knew of had attempted to explain. Africans were more likely to contract leprosy, elephantiasis, and yaws than were Europeans. He believed that leprosy had its origin "in climate, predisposition in the patient's constitution, peculiarity of diet, or probably in all." Thomson took issue with a Jamaican doctor who wrote that yaws had a bestial origin. He also disagreed with those who affirmed that yaws could be propagated only by actual contact. "When the air is highly impregnated with the disease miasmata," he wrote, "actual contact is not required. On many estates I have known it spread in a singularly rapid manner, and attack negroes who, from their dread of it, had avoided every possible medium of communication."[90]

Thomson was influenced by both old and new theories of medicine. Among the new theories was that of "vitalism," developed by George Ernst Stahl (1660–1737), Friedrich Hoffmann (1660–1742), Hermann Boerhaave (1668–1738), William Cullen (1710–90), and John Brown (1735–88). "Toward mid-century," writes Richard Shryock with reference to the eighteenth century, "the humoral pathology was partly replaced by theories about nervous and vascular tensions." Cullen, whose influence spread widely throughout Europe and the American and West Indian colonies, declared that fever was "a spasm of the extreme arteries" induced by the state of the brain. John Brown, a pupil of Cullen, went back to the vitalists and used the concept of excitability, whose seat was in the nervous system, as the basis of his teachings.[91] That Thomson was influenced by vitalist theories is evident from a close reading of his *Treatise*. He described in great detail the "low nervous fever," which was at times fatal to blacks. Everyone in a weak, relaxed habit of body was said to be susceptible to this fever. Most vulnerable were women who had produced many children and young women who labored under great mental agitation before menstruation had been established. On another occasion Thomson was baffled by the seemingly best directed efforts to conquer a fatal epidemic of influenza. Those who explained the epidemic according to traditional theory were dismissed with words of ironic intent. "As an apology for ignorance," he wrote, "most say it depends on an *epidemic constitution* of the atmosphere, and when you ask what that means, they gravely tell you an *epidemic constitution* of the atmosphere, and there they very wisely leave you to your medications." Thomson said he opened between forty and fifty bodies of blacks who died of influenza. He claimed that the information he obtained from these dissections proved that "the effects of irritation on such delicate organs are rapid and extensive, and put at defiance any feeble relief that may result from the remedies we oppose to them." The facts he uncovered proved to his satisfaction that the origin of the disease resided in the nervous system itself. He was thus enabled "to prosecute a plan of treatment with much more success."[92]

Thomson's career is remarkable in other respects. Among the doctors already described, none displayed a keener interest in scientific questions than he did. We have seen that he dissected the bodies of slaves to ascertain the cause of influenza. Moreover, he dissected the cadavers of blacks and whites in "a series of experiments regarding the differences of anatomical structure, observable in the European and negro, but particularly those of the skin." Though he could find no satisfactory cause of black pigmentation in Afro-West Indians, he found it intriguing that "some ingenious men have affirmed that our *first* parents were black, and that the European complexion is a degenerated state." Thomson's interest in blacks was not confined to their physiological differences from whites. He found their social and cultural life to be equally attractive. He criticized whites who said they could not distinguish between blacks, "seeing they all have woolly hair, and are of an uniform complexion," by asserting that they had been brought to Jamaica from the most diversified regions of Africa. Indeed, they exhibited "modifications in stature, complexion, and moral qualities, that equal in every respect those acknowledged to exist amongst the inhabitants of the European continent." Having studied black culture himself, Thomson urged his fellow doctors to acquire intimate knowledge of the domestic arrangements of their patients. Most intriguing to Thomson was the folk medicine of the blacks. He deplored the fact that very little was known of the real nature and virtues of indigenous medicinal substances. To correct this deficiency, he devoted a substantial part of his *Treatise* to "Some Observations and Experiments on the Medicinal Plants of Jamaica." Like James Grainger, William Wright, and others, James Thomson ranks high among the European doctors in the West Indies who sought to meld what they regarded as the best elements of African and European cultures into a Creole society.[93]

Conclusion

In this chapter on disease environments and epidemiology, we have seen that Columbus set in motion an exchange of peoples, plants, animals, and microbes that had worldwide repercussions. Not only were Europeans accompanied to the New World by invisible microparasites, but these conquerors and colonists were themselves macroparasites who, with superior technology and organization, plundered and destroyed Amerindian cultures. They then proceeded to build a South Atlantic System in which the slave-manned plantation was the centerpiece. Why these plantations were established in the West Indies rather than West Africa has puzzled historians. Part of the answer is that had the choice gone to West Africa, plantation slaves would be more prone to escape and return to their home villages than slaves who were transported overseas. Moreover, compared with the West Indies, West Africa had more densely populated coastal areas, thus making land acquisition more difficult, and it was generally less well endowed with natural port facilities and favorable patterns of winds and currents for sailing vessels.

Perhaps more of the answer lies in the epidemiology of the South Atlantic System. It has been noted that the world contains many different disease environments and that a major force in history has been the spread of infectious diseases through the movement of people and their microorganisms. Long before the dramatic findings of the Army Medical Board's Report were published, it was common knowledge that West Africa was the "white man's grave" to a much greater extent than the West Indies. Compared to Europeans who lacked immunity to malaria and yellow fever, native Africans lived in areas where the man–mosquito–malarial cycle was intense enough to cause genetic adaptation that conferred a high degree of immunity. It can be argued that, given these diverse patterns of immunity and vulnerability to tropical diseases, Europeans chose to locate plantations in the West Indies where their own health risks were less severe. They then came to depend more and more on the labor reservoir in West Africa. Adding masses of Africans to the Europeans and surviving Amerindians made the Sugar Colonies a melting pot for diseases from Europe, Africa, and the New World. Though the newly imported Africans were highly immune to malaria and yellow fever, they succumbed to other diseases during the difficult period of acclimatization or seasoning. Thus was set in motion the vicious circle of the number of deaths exceeding births and the need for more recruits from Africa just to keep up the plantation labor force.

Jefferson, as we have seen, said that patients sometimes got well in spite of their treatment by doctors who subscribed to fashionable theories. Logan Clendening, M.D., says that the writings of great medical theorists of past centuries reminds the reader of the gibe that medicine is a "succession of forgotten theories."[94] This is perhaps too pessimistic a view. Proponents of the miasmatic doctrine, though wrong to postulate putrid exhalations or tiny particles that floated in the air and were not visible, did urge the cleanup of marshes and the disposal of animal and human wastes, thus putting practical stress on sanitary measures that limited the spread of infectious disease. One ancient theory that was not forgotten because it proved highly successful in the decades after this study was contagion. Charles Winslow explains why the development of the concept of contagion was so slow to be adopted by physicians. "Until the theory of inanimate contagion was replaced by a theory of living germs," he writes, "and until to that theory were added the concepts of long-distance transmission by water and food supplies and, above all, of human and animal carriers – the hypothesis of contagion simply would not work."[95]

Moreover, it can be argued that some progress was made in understanding the nature and causes of illness and accidents among the slaves on West Indian plantations. Although the European theories of epidemiology and therapy are now generally held in ill repute, enlightened doctors in the age of slavery realized that even therapeutically beneficial treatment was futile if their patients were undernourished or otherwise debilitated. We have seen that several doctor-authors became skeptical of the conventional wisdom of European medicine and developed theories of disease causation and cures based on empirical studies and knowledge of African folk medicine. Even if their remedies were ineffectual, they did not kill like the methods and medicines of the practitioners of heroic medicine. Above all, the doctor-authors who wrote slave medical manuals stressed the need to enhance the life chances of slaves by means of better diet, clothing, housing, and sanitation; the tempering of work loads and punishment; and better treatment of pregnant women, mothers, and children. Whether or not the insights, cautions, and advice of these few leaders of the profession were heeded by the general run of practitioners is a question we will seek to answer, in part, in the following chapter, which looks at the medical profession in the Sugar Colonies.

2

The medical profession

This is a superb country [Jamaica] for physicians; a customary fee is a doubloon (5*l*. 6*s*. 8*d*. currency), and the inhabitants are all sick in their turn; for there are very few who escape a seasoning; and a great proportion die, or to use the metaphor of Aesculapius, "go the grand tour." A physician is certainly interested in saving your life, for there is no trifling here: Nature hurries to a crisis, and many a patient is in a state of dissolution before death.

Cynric R. Williams, 1823[1]

Given the harsh disease environment and the heavy investment in slave laborers in the Sugar Colonies, it was expected that the planters would employ physicians and surgeons to supply medical services to the blacks. In this chapter our attention is first centered on the recruitment of white doctors and efforts to upgrade the medical profession. After a brief survey of medicine in Cuba and North America, we look at the doctors who held diplomas from European medical schools and especially the doctor-scientists and authors. The conclusion attempts to assess the strengths and weaknesses of the white medical profession from the standpoint of their black patients.

Recruitment of doctors

Increasing the number and quality of medical practitioners was a concern to inhabitants and governments from the foundation of colonies. New settlements needed physicians and surgeons not only to treat diseases imported from Europe and Africa but also to cope with diseases that were indigenous to the New World. Almost all newcomers came down with fevers and other ailments, with large numbers dying during the difficult period of acclimatization or seasoning. The health of Europeans and Africans in the New World tropics was imperiled on all sides. Besides endemic and epidemic disease, newcomers were vulnerable to exposure to the elements, teeming insect life, poisonous flora and fauna, accidents, corporal punishment, and warfare. Despite the great demand for medical services, early settlements attracted few white doctors, and those who came administered chiefly to the European elite. Except for those with acute illnesses, slaves were indifferently supplied with medical services. In fact, much mischief was done by medical men of bold pretension and little knowledge and skill. Near the end of the eighteenth century medical services to slaves were extended under the twin pressures of rising slave prices and humanitarian and political agitation to prohibit the Atlantic slave trade. This was the period of the coming of some well-educated professional men, including several doctor-scientists and authors of treatises on the medical treatment of slaves. The Sugar Colonies remained backward in the creation of medical schools, professional societies, and the publication of learned journals, however. Plantation medicine attracted growing numbers of doctors whose qualifications varied widely and who were seldom required to meet strict licensing standards.

Even if there were few restraints on the medical profession, it was no easy matter to attract qualified practitioners. European physicians and surgeons who went abroad had a wide choice of services and locations, including the army and navy, East India Company, Royal African Company, South Sea Company, Guinea trade, and colonies in North America and the West Indies. Outfitting costs for private practitioners in the colonies were generally higher than the outlays needed for surgeons attached to naval and military units and chartered companies operating in overseas areas. Newly arrived doctors in the colonies had difficulty gaining acceptance among colleagues and inhabitants, although this was less difficult if a young man had proper professional credentials and letters of introduction from men of influence.

The correspondence of brother doctors from 1714 to 1743 reveals some of the problems of emigrating and establishing a medical practice in the colonies. All the letters were written by Dr. John Cochrane to his brother William Cochrane, doctor of medicine at Edinburgh. Writing from London on 11 September 1714, Dr. Cochrane said he had accidentally met a young surgeon going to Guinea who had been in Jamaica. Cochrane made a bargain with him, paying four pounds for his "instruments, chest and medicines and bed cloaths. . . which is the cheapest way I could furnish myself."[2] Three months later Cochrane wrote that he was going surgeon's mate on a Guinea voyage. He hoped the voyage would turn to good account, for he had a "promise of recommendations to Gentlemen living upon the Island which I rely more upon than those to L[or]d Archibald [Hamilton, Governor of Jamaica]." He added, "no body and especially Surgeons in Jamaica are respected unless they go handsome in their Cloaths – this is not vanity but meer Necessity."[3]

Cochrane became thoroughly soured on the prospects of a career at sea, "considering how long I may be here [London] after a ship comes home out of business and what necessaries I'll want everie voyage besides a great many inconveniences I be under the time the Ship is abroad." His hopes were buoyed by the proposal he received from Mr. Lawrence, a London apothecary, "to go over to Jamaica in order to be copartner w[it]h a Surgeon there and hath offer'd to give me Credit for 100£ worth of medicines for 12 months upon security without paying interest." Mr. Lawrence was described as "a very discreet Gentleman." He was said to be "ye making of Dr Cockburn in Jamaica and gave him Credit when he went over who was not worth 10£ in he world and now has made about 5 or 6 thousand pounds."[4]

After 1715 there is a gap of twenty years in the Cochrane correspondence. In the meantime Dr. Cochrane had become established as a medical practitioner at Kingston, Jamaica. His practice was apparently remunerative, for in a letter he wrote to his brother in Edinburgh on 24 June 1735, he enclosed a bill of exchange on a London merchant for £500 to defray the cost of redeeming the estate of "Roughsoile being a place upon which you have set your heart so much."[5] Two years later, after learning that his brother's bad health was due to the cold climate, Dr. Cochrane proposed that he come to Jamaica. Lack of funds should be no obstacle, for the Kingston doctor offered "to share allways half of my penny and for a further encouragement I must tell you that at this time we much want a good Physician here."[6] The Edinburgh doctor did not act on his brother's proposal, for the latter wrote to the former in December 1743 that he was enclosing a bill of exchange for £35 "design'd to defray the Charges of Doctors degrees which you mention you could purchase for me."[7]

The demand for doctors, though increasing in the long run, moved up and down as wars alternated with peace and the prices of slaves and sugar fluctuated. Tobias Smollett was a surgeon's mate on a naval vessel at the abortive siege of Cartagena in 1741. The sick and wounded overtaxed the medical resources on ship and shore, especially at Jamaica where emergency hospitals were erected. Roderick Random, Smollett's fictional counterpart, hoped to return to his native Scotland in a short time when the admiral's surgeon came on board. The latter told Random and another surgeon's mate that, owing to the great scarcity of surgeons in the West Indies, "he was commanded to detain one mate out of every great ship that was bound for England." Random, to his great disappointment, was detained in Jamaica. After his patients were recovering, he was sumptuously entertained by planters on their rural estates. On one occasion Random accidentally met a former surgeon's mate of his acquaintance who had been recommended to a gentleman of fortune with whom he lived "in quality of surgeon and overseer to his plantation."[8]

Doctors who were difficult to recruit for private practice in the colonies in wartime were generally in surplus at the conclusion of a European war. One case in point is William Wright, who was a surgeon's mate attached to naval units in the West Indies during the Seven Years' War. At the conclusion of the war in 1763 he returned to Scotland, where he obtained his M.D. degree. Supplied with his diploma and letters of introduction, he sailed from

London to Jamaica in December 1763. Upon his arrival on the island in March 1764, "he found to his mortification that the supply of medical practitioners in Jamaica, was, from the same causes which left him unprovided, quite as much above the level of demand, as he had found it in Great Britain; insomuch, that individuals whom he had known acting as surgeons in the navy, he found serving under indentures at the rate of £40 a-year."[9] Several years after Dr. Wright came to Jamaica, the widow of a doctor who had practiced in the island wrote concerning her son who wished to follow in his father's footsteps. She warned that if he intended to settle in Jamaica, the medical profession would "not afford him bread."[10]

Private practitioners were frequently in short supply during the American War of Independence and the long wars of the French Revolution and the Napoleonic Wars. Writing from Dominica in January 1810, a plantation attorney informed an absentee proprietor in England that since the death of a Dr. Raney the previous September "there has been no Medical Person in this neighbourhood to attend the sick nor is there any to be had in the country to undertake the duty." Having requested two absentees in England to engage a doctor without success, the attorney appealed to an absentee of Scottish origin whom he supposed "would be more likely of engaging a person qualified for that purpose about Edinburgh." The late Dr. Raney was said to have had an income of £700 to £800 per year, which the attorney thought should be matched by a doctor of character and ability.[11]

Again, as after earlier wars, doctors came to the West Indies in great numbers after Waterloo. In Jamaica this influx was commented upon by Sir Jacob Adolphus, M.D., deputy inspector of hospitals. In March 1820 he replied to the query of a Dr. Forbes, "With respect to the procuring a situation for a young medical man, it might a few years ago have been done with great facility, but at the present moment nothing can be more difficult. The profession in the Island is overstocked, and the peace by depriving so many of occupation, who during the state of war had been attached to the Army has rendered our brethren *mere drugs* in the Market."[12]

Important factors in increasing the number of doctors in the West Indies were rising slave prices and humanitarian and political agitation to prohibit the Atlantic slave trade. Planters who had been indifferent to the medical needs of their slaves when they could replace them with low-cost recruits from Africa were alarmed at the rapid price increase in the late eighteenth century and made efforts to provide better health services. More compelling was the agitation to prohibit the slave trade. Partly as a matter of self-interest, partly to counter their anti-slavery critics, planter-governments adopted amelioration measures that included provision for the health care of slaves. The Assembly of Jamaica, for example, enacted a "New Consolidated Act" or "Code Noir" in December 1788. It required the doctor or surgeon who had the care of the slaves on every plantation, pen, or other settlement to submit a report annually to the justices or vestry of all slaves who died, "with the causes of such deaths, to the best of his knowledge, judgment, and belief, under the penalty of twenty pounds for every neglect."[13] Similar laws were enacted in the other Sugar Colonies, so that for the first time it became necessary for every owner of slaves attached to plantations, pens, or other settlements to employ a doctor or surgeon.

The number of medical practitioners in the West Indies increased irregularly in the long run, although individual islands may have had periods of declining numbers. In Antigua there were twenty-two doctors in 1731, at a time when a roster was drawn up to assign medical men to militia units. Another roster for 1780 lists fifteen doctors in Antigua, although it is not certain whether it includes the young doctors who were employed as medical assistants.[14] Barbados is thought to have had more doctors in proportion to its population than any other island, but no complete roster has been discovered. Seventeen doctors are listed as subscribers to Poyer's *History of Barbados* (1808), of whom five are M.D.s.[15] In a subsequent chapter it will be shown that Grenada had twenty-five doctors who certified the deaths of slaves in 1820, and eighteen in 1830.[16] Twenty-three surgeons and assistant surgeons were attached to militia units in St. Vincent in 1787.[17] For Jamaica *The Medical Register for the Year 1780* gives the names, degrees, towns and parishes of residence, and publications of seventy-four doctors, of whom ten are M.D.s. Four years later the names, residences, and degrees of fifty-nine doctors, of whom nine are M.D.s, are printed as subscribers to Dr. Thomas Dancer's *Short Dissertation on the Jamaica Bath Waters*.[18] Though no names are listed, a parish-by-parish census revealed that there were 200 legally authorized medical practitioners in Jamaica on 1 September 1833.[19] In conclusion, it may not be too wide of the mark to estimate the total number of European doctors in the British West Indies at more than 400 on the eve of slave emancipation in 1834.

Medical gentlemen and quacks

If the medical profession of Jamaica was typical, West Indian practitioners ranged widely in training, experience, and character. "Those persons who pursue the practice of healing art in Jamaica are of various grades," wrote Dr. John Williamson, "from the apothecary's boy to men of the greatest eminence and worth."[20] Charles Leslie, who lived in Jamaica before 1740, said that physicians there of any note generally made fine estates. On the other hand, the island "was quite crowded with raw unexperienced Youths, who imagine this the properest Place for a Settlement; and when they come over, are generally set to prescribe to a parcel of Negroes in some Country-plantations. Their Numbers make but dull Business for most of them; and in the Towns there are generally one or two eminent Men who have the Employment, and soon get to be rich."[21] William Beckford, the planter-historian, contended that the better practitioners in Jamaica had received a regular education and made surgery and physic their study and profession. They were "as intelligent and skilful, as patient and humane, as are to be met with, among professors of this useful and respectable class, in any other country."[22] If Bryan Edwards, another planter-historian, is to be believed, the quality of practice had improved by the latter part of the eighteenth century. He maintained that planters had become intolerant of "illiterate pretenders in medicine" and sought for and encouraged "young men of skill and science."[23]

Early nineteenth-century writers either were laudatory or had mixed feelings about the state of the profession. The historian Robert Renny may have indulged in hyperbole when he asserted, "In no colony in the world, are medical practitioners to be found, better educated, more attentive, more humane, or more worthy of respect, than those of Jamaica."[24] While conceding that Jamaica had doctors of the greatest eminence and worth, Dr. John Williamson was persuaded "that few, if any, countries suffer so severely as Jamaica, owing to the admission of persons to practice medicine, surgery, &c. among them, who have no competent pretensions."[25] John Stewart, the planter-author, admitted that some medical men in Jamaica were not the most competent that could be desired. "Dispensing with the customary formalities of college lectures, hospital attendance, and diplomas," he wrote, "they set up as healers of disorders, with no other pretensions than having served a few years of apprenticeship to an apothecary, or performed one or two voyages on board of an African trader as assistant *surgeon*." On the other hand, Stewart knew of "many able practitioners in the island, though very few of them are regularly-bred physicians. A practitioner here unites the functions of physician, surgeon, and apothecary; he prescribes, performs operations, and compounds his own medicines."[26] The Reverend John Barry, Methodist missionary to the slaves of Jamaica, gave evidence to the select committee of the House of Lords in 1832. He believed that the physicians of Jamaica did not rank among "those who would be considered clever at Home, and there are some whose principal Subsistence depends upon their Appointment to Properties. With regard to Character, they stand on a Par with the Generality of the People of Jamaica, and live in the same State."[27]

In his *History of Jamaica*, Edward Long presents "the history of a Jamaica Quack" for the amusement of his readers. Mr. Apozem, the son of a house carpenter in London, was apprenticed at the age of fifteen to an apothecary of mean circumstances and little business. Four years later the apothecary died by inadvertently swallowing one of his nauseous compositions, leaving Apozem only partly trained for his profession. Through his father's friendship with the captain of a Guinea trader, the young man was taken on as surgeon. In Africa they took on 300 slaves and sailed for the Jamaica market. Apozem's first great exploit, writes Long, was to greatly diminish the number of slaves and sailors on board. Upon learning of the appalling mortality, the merchant to whom the surviving slaves were consigned "soon found means to engage Mr. Apozem in the service of an honest planter who dealt with him; and who, conceiving the highest opinion of Mr. Apozem's skill and knowledge, from the many encomiums that were lavishly given both by the captain and merchant, stipulated so handsome a salary, that Apozem quitted the sea without the smallest hesitation." Within six or eight months Mr. Apozem had extended his practice to other families and plantations and was "continually upon the high-trot, riding post, and spreading depopulation far and wide. His principal instruments of death were mercury and *opium*, ever mistakenly applied, and injudiciously combined." To faster accumulate wealth he compounded "rotten and sophisticated" drugs that generally made a profit of 1,000 percent when sold at retail. "The sale of these poisons formed the most gainful part of his business; though he was, occasionally, a physician, apothecary, surgeon, man-midwife, dentist, phlebotomist, farrier, &c." The amazing Dr. Apozem "professed every branch, knew as much of one as of another, understood none: and, thus accoutred, he was ready at all calls, and engaged in the cure of distempers, whose names he had never heard before."[28]

Efforts to upgrade the profession

Long had a serious motive for writing his history of a Jamaica quack. He regarded it as the highest reproach, even an impiety, that a tribe of Apozems could overrun and depopulate a colony, "preying on the purses and lives of innocent men, with an impudence, ignorance, and rapacity that is unparalleled." He urged the legislature of Jamaica to "take vigorous and effective measures, for excluding all those from commencing physicians, who do not bring with them authentic and sufficient credentials, certifying their qualifications for so arduous a business."[29] About a generation later Dr. Williamson revived Long's campaign for a law to require doctors to be licensed. Williamson thought it would be the wisest policy to secure well-educated doctors and to shut out improper persons. Professional men who intended to practice in the West Indies should, in his judgment, have at least one of the following qualifications: "a surgeon's certificate from the London, Dublin, Edinburgh, or Glasgow Colleges; qualifications in practise of midwifery;

and of having served for a certain time to an apothecary, or an apprenticeship to a surgeon-apothecary." Williamson believed the legislature "should pass an act to prevent the admission of unqualified persons to the practice of medicine, surgery, pharmacy, &c. within the respective islands."[30]

Trinidad was the first British colony in the West Indies to require medical practitioners to be licensed. Actually, Spanish licensing laws continued on the statute books after the British conquest of 1797, although these laws were allowed to become dead letters. Upon learning that many persons were practicing medicine without the necessary license, Governor Ralph Woodford issued a proclamation on 20 December 1814 reestablishing the medical board and licensing law. Consisting of four members appointed by the governor, the board was charged with examining credentials, issuing licenses to qualified medical men, and regulating the sale of medicines and drugs. The proclamation required all practitioners of medicine and surgery and sellers of medicines and drugs to appear before the medical board to register their "names, quality, and profession respectively" and to "produce any permission, licence or authority by virtue of which such person or persons now practise Physic or Surgery or vend any Medicines or Drugs in this Island under the penalty of FIVE HUNDRED DOLLARS, and being from thenceforth prohibited from practising Physic or Surgery, or vending any Medicines or Drugs within the said Island." One clause permitted medical men who could not produce proper credentials to be licensed after passing an examination; another required shops that sold medicines and drugs to be inspected at least four times a year and be licensed.[31]

That the medical board was ineffective in upgrading the medical profession of Trinidad was the contention of the author of an address of 1824. The address was written by a spokesman of the colored people of Trinidad and submitted to Earl Bathurst, principal secretary of state for the colonies. The author complained that the medical board asked candidates for practice a few trifling questions on subjects readily learned from the most common books. What was worse, racial discrimination led the board to admit a white man to practice after a perfunctory examination. "His immaculate colour will prove indubitably his acquaintance with all the arts and mysteries of medicine." On the other hand, if a well-qualified colored man approached the board, it was "a thousand to one but objections will be started to him." The upshot was that "raw apprentices, and journeymen apothecaries" were licensed to experiment on the bodies of their patients "with no other recommendation than the most brazen effrontery."[32]

Though unsigned, the address was probably written by John Baptiste Philip, M.D., a leading spokesman for the colored community of Trinidad. Philip was probably born on the island. His mulatto parents were said to be blessed with the advantages of fortune but excluded from the highest offices and liberal professions. They resolved to spare no pains in developing the talents of their son. Young Philip was sent to England where he impressed his schoolmaster as a quick learner. He matriculated at the medical school at the University of Edinburgh in 1812 and received his M.D. degree in 1815. He then traveled on the Continent and attended medical lectures at Leyden and Montpellier. Upon returning to Trinidad in 1816, Philip took up the crusade against mulatto discrimination. Though his superior professional talents gained him a potentially lucrative medical practice, he devoted much time to leading the free colored movement for equal rights. He wrote a well-known book entitled *Free Mulatto* and led a delegation to the Colonial Office to represent the grievances of his people. Following his death on 29 July 1829, he was eulogized as a man who sacrificed self-interest and comfort for the welfare of his fellow citizens. Today Dr. Philip ranks among the patriots of Trinidad.[33]

Jamaica did not obtain a licensing law until near the end of the slavery era. On 21 November 1826 the Assembly received a petition from John Smith, doctor of medicine and member of the Royal College of Surgeons of London, who was a practitioner in the city and parish of Kingston. Smith's petition called for the establishment of a medical or anatomical school and a medical board "for the purpose of examining the credentials of medical gentlemen arriving in this island, and giving certificates of qualification." After the reading of the petition, a motion was made "that a committee be appointed to inquire into the present state of the medical profession throughout this island, and to report what may be expedient to prevent abuses arising from ignorant pretenders practising medicine and surgery." The committee was chaired by Sir Michael B. Clare, M.D. On 9 December 1826 he presented to the assembly a "bill for regulating the practice of physic and surgery in the island of Jamaica." After the bill was passed by the Assembly it was carried to the council and for some unknown reason was not approved by the governor in council.[34]

A project to revive the medical licensing bill was initiated in 1830. It apparently began with a series of five letters to *The Kingston Chronicle and City Advertiser* signed by "L.L.L." The author railed against "the noisy and impudent Quack, whose education probably consisted in being taught how to use the pestle and mortar, and whose knowledge does not proceed beyond the names of some medicines, and a few hard words, which he frequently misapplies." To increase the respectability of the medical profession, the author proposed to establish a college of physicians and surgeons. It would be charged with regulating the profession throughout the island and establishing a medical library and an employment exchange for medical assistants who were properly qualified.[35] Again, highly respected members of the medical profession urged the Assembly to enact a licensing law. Accordingly, an

"Act for regulating the Practice of Physic and Surgery, and for establishing a College of Physicians and Surgeons in this Island" was put in force on 18 October 1833. The act was a disappointment to one critic, who wrote that it contained clauses "by which every quack, those who can hardly read or write, are not only placed on the same footing, and secured in the same privileges, as those who have been regularly educated, and in possession of a diploma from some recognized college, but even of the fellows of the Jamaica College themselves." If the critic was right, it was fortunate that the act was disallowed by the Privy Council, allegedly because it infringed on the prerogative ceded to the colleges in Great Britain.[36]

Only Trinidad and Jamaica among the West India islands are known to have had licensing laws. Because these laws were apparently ineffective in keeping out quacks, however, it may be asked whether the profession might not have been upgraded by establishing medical colleges in the West Indies. Such an institution was proposed by two Jamaicans. Edward Long believed that besides proper licensing laws, the practice of medicine would be established on a proper footing in Jamaica by "the erection of a college, endowed with a library, lectures on physiology, pathology, anatomy, botany, and the *materia medica*; with licensed inspectors of apothecaries shops and drugs."[37] In his petition of 1826, Dr. John Smith said "that in consequence of there being no medical or anatomical schools in this island a variety of diseases, peculiar to warm climates, are unknown to any practitioner here, till after long experience." He believed that "a knowledge of these diseases might be most advantageously obtained by establishing a faculty or school of medicine, with competent teachers, for educating pupils for general practitioners in medicine." Smith said he had provided at great expense the equipment to establish an anatomical lecture room and offered to supply the Assembly with testimonials of his competency to conduct such a school from the Royal College of Surgeons of London. To Smith's disappointment, the committee of the Assembly reported that the establishment of an anatomical school was impracticable.[38]

Although Dr. Smith's plan for a medical college in Jamaica came late in the slavery era and gained no support from the planter-dominated Assembly, Codrington College in Barbados had begun more than a century earlier and was amply endowed by its benefactor. Christopher Codrington was a planter-governor who acquired a fortune in Barbados and the Leeward Islands. In his will of 1710 he devised two plantations in Barbados and part of the island of Barbuda to the Society for the Propagation of the Gospel. The society was charged with instructing the slaves in the Christian religion and establishing a college in Barbados. Codrington's will said the professors and scholars "shall be obliged to study and practice physic and chirurgery, as well as divinity; that by the apparent usefulness of the former to all mankind, they may both endear themselves to the people, and have the better opportunities of doing good to men's souls, whilst they are taking care of their bodies." Several men came from England to teach the scholars "Divinity, Physick, and Chirurgery." But for many years the level of instruction was that of an English grammar school, there were few scholars, difficulty was encountered in attracting and holding qualified professors, and the income of the plantations fell off because of bad management, wars, and hurricanes. Not until 1828 were resolutions adopted by the governing board of the college to appoint a medical professor to give lectures in medicine and surgery. Given the late start in establishing medical education at the university level, it is doubtful whether Codrington College made any contribution to the medical treatment of slaves in the West Indies.[39]

Medicine in Cuba and North America

Although the Spaniards in the New World boasted of their medical schools and licensure laws, medical education remained backward prior to the "medical revolution" of the late eighteenth and early nineteenth centuries, and measures to confine medicine to licensed practitioners were seldom effective. The Spaniards in the Americas founded ten major universities and fifteen minor ones, of which two were in Santo Domingo and one in Cuba. Medical education, however, was long held back by conservative forces, and a reform movement did not establish a foothold until near the end of the eighteenth century. Moreover, charlatanry flourished despite repeated efforts to enforce minimum standards of professional education and competence. Centralized control of the medical profession began in 1570 with the creation in the great colonial cities of the *Protomedicato General* as a court and board of medical examiners. Consisting of leading doctors, these courts and boards were charged with examining and licensing candidates for the medical profession, stopping unlicensed doctors, inspecting the medicines dispensed by pharmacists, and reporting to Spanish officials the data gathered on indigenous "herbs, trees, plants, and medicinal seeds, as well as the use and quantity of the medicaments, methods of growing them, information on the species, and whether they grew in dry or humid climate."[40]

Cuban medicine during the long era of slavery was a mixture of elements. The formal or official occupational categories, according to Ross Danielson, were barber, bleeder, dentist, surgeon, pharmacist, and physician, plus such less formal categories as midwife, bonesetter, and herniotomist. "The trappings of the physician were more likely to include one or two classical medical treatises, some knowledge of Latin, and a formal scholastic education rather than simple apprenticeship." Havana probably had only six or seven legitimate physicians before 1600; perhaps fifty, mostly Spanish, came to Cuba in the seventeenth century. By the end of the eighteenth century Cuba had an estimated 100 physicians. After 1728 all Cuban practitioners fell under the authority of the *Protomedicato*, which was established in Havana, but wide scope was given to informal and extralegal practice because of the few formally trained doctors and the unenforced professional codes. Many Cubans turned to native herb healers whose "influence on the folk practice of medicine was eventually eclipsed by, and mixed with, that of the African practitioners."[41]

The University of Havana was founded in 1734 and organized under the authority of the Franciscan order. It was divided into three schools: theology, law, and medicine. Danielson says that the university had only marginal influence over the actual practice of medicine. Its medical scholasticism consisted of "a Galenic metaphysics of vital fluids, bleeding techniques, balsams, and purgatives." Few medical students were attracted to the university, and most of Cuba's licensed physicians came from Europe despite the university's exclusive authority to validate foreign diplomas. Danielson attributes much of the improvement in Cuban medicine to the talent and leadership of one man, Tomás Romay y Chacón, M.D. (1764–1849).

> The thrust of Romay's work in medical education was to secularize medicine. First, medicine was removed from a hierarchy of medical priesthood and sacred texts; second, medicine and health became subjects to analyze in ways common to such prosaic matters as agriculture and economics; and third, medicine became something that could be learned and applied by ordinary men, using ordinary abilities, without the use of mysterious words, manners, or secret potents. These changes were of course incomplete and did not immediately produce great medicine.

As the "high priest" of Cuban medicine, Romay championed smallpox vaccination, which was administered to whites and blacks alike with mixed success. He worked for pharmaceutical regulations, hospital construction, and, as a member of the *Protomedicato*, "training in practical anatomy and clinical medicine as prerequisites for licensure in medicine."[42]

As in Cuba, medical practitioners in the British North American colonies were a mixed lot. At one end of the spectrum there were folk practitioners and quacks, at the other gentlemen physicians who usually had university degrees and practiced among the upper classes. Between these extremes were surgeons, apothecaries, clergymen, planters, housewives, overseers, midwives, sectaries, and others who ranged widely in their medical knowledge and skill. Most colonials apparently dosed themselves and consulted practitioners only when alarmed. Colonial medical practitioners fell into three main groups: regular diploma-holding physicians, regular non–diploma-holding practitioners, and irregular practitioners. There were an estimated 3,500 established practitioners in the colonies on the eve of the American Revolution. Of these, not more than 400 had received any formal training, and of the latter only about half (or barely more than 5 percent of the total) held degrees. By far the most medical practitioners acquired their training through apprenticeship or self-education; in rural areas and small towns they commonly combined the functions of physician, apothecary, and surgeon by prescribing and selling drugs and engaging in surgery.[43]

Quacks and charlatans were said to abound in the American colonies like the locusts in Egypt. The reason for this, as John Duffy explains, was that because medicine could not prevent, cure, or alleviate many of the disorders troubling patients, the public frequently turned to anyone who promised relief. Quack medicine shaded imperceptibly into useful alternative approaches to regular medicine so that no clear-cut distinctions can be made. "Between the remedies of the household and the standard treatments of the physician stood 'irregular' medicine," writes Todd L. Savitt. Irregular medicine, consisting of folk healers and such medical sectaries as the Thomsonians and homeopaths, challenged conventional medicine and gained enthusiastic proponents among a sizable minority of planters and other inhabitants of Virginia and other colonies and states.[44]

In an effort to extirpate quacks and pretenders and upgrade the medical profession, measures were taken to license physicians. The Provincial Assembly of New York, with strong support from prominent physicians, passed the first colonial licensure law in 1760. Assisted by reputable physicians, government officials in that colony were charged with examining and licensing physicians. New Jersey followed New York with a similar licensure law in 1772. Both these laws proved useless, however, because they failed to provide procedures and personnel for enforcement. After the American Revolution most of the older states passed licensure laws, but authority was divided among state boards of examiners, medical schools, and medical societies. Again, there were few penalties for noncompliance. On the other hand, all attempts to pass licensure laws were rejected by the legislatures in the new states that were admitted to the union, so that by the 1850s it was only a mild exaggeration to say that everyone was allowed to practice medicine.[45]

Despite the failure to enact enforceable licensing laws, diploma-holding physicians increased both absolutely and relatively. Very few such physicians emigrated from Europe to the colonies, but growing numbers of Americans went to European medical schools to prepare for professional careers upon their return. It was chiefly to Leyden, Edinburgh, and London that American medical students migrated after about 1730 in search of real professional training. Here they not only were taught medical science and its application by such masters as Boerhaave, Cullen, Monro, Smellie, and Pott, but they also came into contact with an integrated medical culture consisting of medical colleges, professional guilds, societies, publications, and hospitals.[46]

Just as the Edinburgh Medical School was in many ways an offshoot of the University of Leyden, so the first American medical school at the College of Philadelphia was planned by colonial students at the University of Edinburgh. Established in 1765, it brought to America the Continental-Scottish tradition of a university college and was an immediate success. Three years later the King's College Medical School was organized in New York, and in 1782 Harvard College established a medical school. Though they met with considerable difficulty, these three schools managed to survive the war years. By 1800 there were four medical colleges in the United States, with Dartmouth College having established such a school in 1798.[47]

Like their counterparts in the North, students from the southern colonies who aspired to become physicians migrated to Leyden, Edinburgh, and London. After about 1800, however, they began to go to Philadelphia and New York for their professional education. Meanwhile, the growth of local and state medical societies promoted a corresponding growth of professional consciousness in southern cities, leading to agitation for the establishment of local medical colleges. Not only would such institutions contribute to the growing demands for cultural independence from the North, but also medical teaching and practice could be adapted to the belief in inherent biological differences between the races. Accordingly, medical colleges were established in a number of southern universities and cities. "While medical schools had been slow in appearing during the first thirty years of the new nation's history," writes Duffy, "their numbers increased rapidly after 1810. No less than twenty-six were founded between 1810 and 1840, and another forty-seven between 1840 and 1875."[48]

Diploma holders from Europe

Lacking medical schools of their own, West Indians sought doctors who were educated at the leading medical schools in Europe and North America. Few highly qualified doctors came until the latter part of the eighteenth century, and those who did come treated the white inhabitants chiefly. During most of the slavery era the slaves either cared for themselves or were treated by apothecaries and surgeons who had been trained by apprenticeship and by hospital instruction but rarely held degrees. Doctors came to the West Indies with a wide variety of credentials. University graduates with M.D. degrees came from Europe and the British Isles. European universities that sent their medical graduates to the British West Indies included Leyden,

Rheims, Montpellier, Caen, and probably Paris. Medical graduates came from the universities of Oxford and Cambridge in England; Dublin in Ireland; and Glasgow, St. Andrews, Aberdeen, and Edinburgh in Scotland. Other medical doctors may have come to the West Indies from the colleges at Philadelphia, New York, and Boston in North America. Besides the holders of M.D. degrees, physicians and surgeons came with diplomas or as fellows or licentiates from the Royal College of Physicians of London, Glasgow, and Edinburgh; the Royal College of Surgeons of England and Edinburgh; and Surgeons' Hall in London.

During the first half of the eighteenth century, Leyden was the chief resort of West Indians who aspired to eminence in the medical profession. Founded in 1574, the University of Leyden became the foremost center for medical education in Europe. Its success was based on its famous professors, its patient-centered or clinical method of instruction, and its policy of admitting students of all religions, including Catholics and Jews, to matriculation. Foremost among its professors was Hermann Boerhaave (1668–1738), who is regarded as the greatest physician of modern times. His fame spread far and wide for his clinical ability and skill as a chemist, botanist, and anatomist, which he synthesized in his brilliant lectures and books.[49]

The period from 1713 to 1830 saw the matriculation of thirty-five West Indians at the University of Leyden, of whom nineteen matriculated before 1760. Of the thirty-five, nine came from Barbados, eight each from Antigua and Jamaica, five from St. Kitts, two from Tortola, and one each from Nevis, Montserrat, and Demerara. Twenty-two of the West Indians received M.D. degrees from Leyden, three went on to take M.D.s from the University of Edinburgh, one received his M.D. from the University of Rheims, one received an M.D. degree from Cambridge University, and eight did not graduate. Those who are known to have returned to their native islands to practice medicine are James Athill, M.D., Antigua; George Leonard Blyden, M.D., Tortola; George Crump, M.D., Antigua; John Dunbar, M.D., Antigua; Fortunatus Dwarris, M.D., Jamaica; Matthew Gregory, M.D., Jamaica; Thomas Jarvis, M.D., Antigua; John Kirton, M.D., Barbados; John McQuistin, Jamaica; Matthew Mills, M.D., St. Kitts; and John Coakley Lettsom, M.D., Tortola. William Beckford, who inherited a great fortune in Jamaica and later became lord mayor of London, studied medicine for a time at Leyden. Besides the twelve West Indians who returned home after their studies at Leyden to practice medicine, there were eighteen young men from the British Isles who matriculated and/or graduated from the University of Leyden who went to the West Indies to practice medicine.[50]

Edinburgh followed Leyden as the center of medical education. "The torch of learning which had been lit in Greece had passed to Salerno," writes Dr. Douglas Guthrie, "then to Montpellier and Padua, then to Leyden, and early in the eighteenth century it was handed to Edinburgh, which then became the centre of medical learning."[51] There was much coming and going between Edinburgh and Leyden. In fact, the four leading Fellows of the College of Physicians who were appointed professors at the establishment of the Edinburgh Medical School in 1726 had studied at Leyden under Boerhaave. Under the leadership of the first Alexander Monro and William Cullen, the medical school attracted students from the British Isles and overseas dependencies and countries near and far. By the late eighteenth century Edinburgh had acquired an international reputation as a center for medical education. As Dr. Anand C. Chitnis explains its success, "Edinburgh was the first city in Britain which could claim all the following features – a University medical school, Royal College of Physicians and Surgeons, many private lectures and extensive hospital and dispensary facilities."[52]

In his *Guide for Gentlemen Studying Medicine at the University of Edinburgh* (1792), J. Johnson wrote that, except for botany, the medical lectures commenced on the last Wednesday of October and were concluded at the end of April, and the fee for attending each course was three guineas. Johnson listed the lecture courses given annually and the lecturers as follows: anatomy, Dr. Alexander Monro; botany, Dr. Daniel Rutherford; chemistry, Dr. Joseph Black; institutions or theory of medicine, Dr. Andrew Duncan; materia medica, Dr. Francis Home; midwifery, Dr. Alexander Hamilton; and practice of medicine, Dr. James Gregory. Readers of Johnson's *Guide* learned how the lecture courses were organized, how to take notes, what books and syllabuses should be studied, and what idiosyncracies of the lecturers were noteworthy. Dr. Home, for example, was said to divide his course into two parts: "the first comprehending the history, qualities, doses, &c. of all the animal, vegetable, and mineral substances which are used occasionally in the prevention or cure of diseases. In the second part, he treats of pharmacy or the manner of preparing all the various medicines for the purposes of practice." Every medical student was advised to take Dr. Hamilton's course of lectures, which was "calculated to exhibit a complete scientific view of the diseases of women and children."[53] Dr. Chitnis writes that "Edinburgh's method of teaching increasingly came to emphasize observation and experiment. Duncan's method of teaching included lectures, experiments, exhibitions of specimens and plates, and the introduction of pharmaceutical trials." Prior to 1824, the M.D. course lasted three years. Students were expected to attend courses in anatomy, surgery, materia medica, pharmacy, the theory and practice of medicine, clinical medicine, midwifery, chemistry, and botany. Two of the following short courses were also required: practical anatomy, natural history, medical jurisprudence, clinical surgery, and military surgery. Candidates for the M.D. degree at Edinburgh were required to write a dissertation on some medical subject, be examined by a faculty committee, and defend the dissertation in a public meeting – all these proceedings to be conducted in Latin. Furthermore, all dissertations were printed, as is illustrated by the title page of one written by a West Indian in Figure 2.1.[54]

Edinburgh came to rival every other medical school in Europe within about forty years of its founding. According to John Morgan, M.D., himself an Edinburgh graduate and founder of the medical school at the College of Philadelphia, there was "a great resort of medical students at the university of Edinburgh, as well from Great-Britain, Ireland, and the West-Indies, as from the Continents of Europe and America." These young men brought considerable advantages to the university and city and, in return, carried "the fame of their learning and their professors to every quarter of the globe."[55] No less than 2,792 doctors of medicine graduated from Edinburgh University from 1776 to 1826, and even more spent some time in medical study there. British colonials who matriculated at Edinburgh increased from an annual average of thirty-six in 1811–15, to forty-six in 1816–20, and to fifty-one in 1821–5. On the other hand, colonials who earned M.D. degrees increased irregularly from an annual average of four in 1791–5 to ten in 1821–5. The cosmopolitan character of the students is illustrated by Professor James Gregory's class list for his practice of physic class from 1785 to 1790. "The average attendance was 215, including 91 from Scotland, 55 from England, 35 from Ireland and twelve each from the West Indies and America. The others came from Portugal, Brazil, France, Italy, Germany, Switzerland, Geneva and Flanders, and included East Indians of English extraction."[56]

Table 2.1 shows that almost 500 West Indians came to Edinburgh to study medicine in 1744–1830. A little more than half of these West Indians (54 percent) matriculated but did not graduate. Jamaicans made up nearly half the medical students in this category. Lagging far behind Jamaica were Barbados, Antigua, St. Kitts, and Dominica, which sent from twelve to thirty-nine students who studied medicine but did not graduate. Jamaicans accounted for nearly two-fifths of the Edinburgh graduates in medicine, followed by Barbados with one-fifth, and the three islands of Antigua, St. Kitts, and St. Croix, each with 7–9 percent. None of the other twelve islands had more than five medical graduates in 1744–1830.[57]

Table 2.2 shows the number of Edinburgh medical graduates who came from Jamaica, Barbados, Antigua, St. Kitts, and St. Croix and the decades in which they graduated. The 187 graduates from these five islands accounted for 86 percent of all graduates from the West Indies. There were thirty-two graduates in 1744–90, or 17 percent of all graduates from the five leading islands. The numbers increased greatly after the 1780s; in fact, more than four-fifths of the graduations took place in the period 1790–

DISSERTATIO MEDICA

INAUGURALIS,

DE

VARIOLIS

QUAM,

ANNUENTE SUMMO NUMINE,

Ex Auctoritate Reverendi admodum Viri,

D. GULIELMI ROBERTSON, S. T. P.

ACADEMIÆ EDINBURGENÆ Praefecti;

NEC NON

Ampliſſimi SENATUS ACADEMICI conſenſu.

Et nobiliſſimae FACULTATIS MEDICÆ decreto,

PRO GRADU DOCTORIS,

SUMMISQUE IN MEDICINA HONORIBUS AC PRIVILEGIIS

RITE ET LEGITIME CONSEQUENDIS;

Eruditorum examini ſubjicit

GULIELMUS MACDOUGALL,

AB INSULA ST CROIX IN INDIA OCCIDENTALI,

Societ. Reg. Med. Praeſes Annuus.

Soc. Nat. Studioſ. Praeſidarius;

Nec non,

Soc. Reg. Phyſ. Sod. Honor.

Ad diem 12. Septembris, hora locoque ſolitis.

EDINBURGI:

Apud BALFOUR et SMELLIE,

Academiae Typographos.

M DCC XCI

Figure 2.1. Title page of Edinburgh University medical dissertation. By permission of Dr. J. T. D. Hall, Sub-Librarian, Special Collections, Edinburgh University Library, Edinburgh.

Table 2.1. *West Indians who studied medicine at the University of Edinburgh, 1744–1830*

Colony	Matriculated[a]	Graduated	Total
Jamaica	123	85	208
Barbados	39	47	86
Antigua	19	20	39
St. Kitts	14	19	33
St. Croix	9	16	25
Dominica	12	4	16
St. Vincent	9	5	14
Demerara	7	2	9
Trinidad	6	3	9
West Indies	4	5	9
Nevis	4	4	8
Montserrat	3	4	7
Grenada	4	2	6
Berbice	1	3	4
Tortola	2	0	2
Tobago	2	0	2
St. Lucia	1	0	1
Total	259	219	478

[a]Since the West Indians who entered the University of Edinburgh were frequently temporary residents of Great Britain at the time of matriculation, the figures in this column are likely to be understated.

Source: Medical Matriculation Albums, 1740–1830, University of Edinburgh Library; *List of Graduates in Medicine in the University of Edinburgh, From MDCCV to MDCCCLXVI* (Edinburgh: printed by Neill & Company, 1867), pp. 2–89.

1830. Most remarkable was the increased number of graduates from Jamaica, amounting to eighty of the 156 graduates in 1791–1830. In the same period there were forty graduates from Barbados, sixteen from St. Croix, eleven from Antigua, and eight from St. Kitts.[58]

West Indians who studied medicine at Edinburgh were with few exceptions white men who came from professional, mercantile, and especially planter families. Genealogical and other records show that their fathers were planters, merchants, government officials, military officers, lawyers, doctors, and an occasional skilled craftsman. It is not unusual to find records of families

Table 2.2. *University of Edinburgh medical graduates who came from Jamaica, Barbados, Antigua, St. Kitts, and St. Croix, 1744–1830*

Years	Jamaica	Barbados	Antigua	St. Kitts	St. Croix	Total
1744–50	0	0	1	1	0	2
1751–60	1	1	0	1	0	3
1761–70	0	1	0	2	0	3
1771–80	2	4	4	5	0	15
1781–90	2	1	4	2	0	9
1791–1800	17	6	3	0	2	28
1801–10	12	12	5	5	2	36
1811–20	22	12	3	2	7	46
1821–30	29	10	0	1	5	45
Total	85	47	20	19	16	187

Source: List of Graduates in Medicine in the University of Edinburgh, From MDCCV to MDCCCLXVI (Edinburgh: printed by Neill & Company, 1867), pp. 2–89.

with two or more doctors who were related as brothers, father and son, or uncle and nephew.[59]

One case in point concerns the uncle and brother of James Stephen, the barrister and antislavery leader. William Stephen, the younger brother of Stephen's father, was "bred to surgery and physic" in Scotland. He settled as a medical practitioner in St. Kitts and continued there until his death in about 1781. He was a bachelor. After his mother's death, Stephen's brother William went to St. Kitts to live with his uncle. He gained the confidence of his uncle who resolved to educate him as a surgeon and physician so that he could serve as his assistant and ultimate successor. Accordingly, uncle William sent his nephew to Aberdeen, recommending him "to the special care of his old friends, Doctors Livingstone and Robertson of that place, the most eminent Physicians and Surgeons there, who had the sole charge of the Aberdeen Infirmary and had no rivals to Medical reputation in the whole North of Scotland." After three years of apprenticeship at Aberdeen, brother William was to take his degree at the University of Edinburgh, which would be "the best means of qualifying himself for practice in the West Indies, where, as in the North of Scotland, Physic, Surgery, Pharmacy, and all the other branches of the healing art are united in the same practitioner." Unfortunately, uncle William died before the plans for his nephew were completed, and brother William had to leave Edinburgh before he graduated and return to St. Kitts to succeed to his uncle's medical practice.[60]

Doctor-scientists and authors

Among the university graduates were doctors who combined the practice of medicine and surgery with scientific investigation and the publication of books concerned with tropical medicine and natural history. Scientifically oriented doctors made collections of flora and fauna, corresponded with eminent scientists in Europe and North America, wrote papers for the journals of learned societies, established and directed botanical gardens and mineral water baths, and published medical works on diseases that afflicted white and black people in the tropical environment of the West Indies. The following brief career sketches of the leading doctor-scientists will afford some understanding of their contributions to natural science and medicine. Whether or not these contributions had any marked effect on the day-to-day practice of slave medicine is a question we will return to later in this chapter.

Writing in 1789, Benjamin Moseley, M.D., Fellow of the Royal College of Physicians of London and practitioner in Jamaica, observed that the resident practitioners in the West Indies were "people of more science, and of better education than they were in the time of those I have mentioned." Nevertheless, he deplored the fact that medical science was backward, chiefly because the "acquirement of wealth" had been the principal goal of "the adventurers in physic in the West-Indies since their first settlement." Furthermore, he deplored the medical tracts written by doctors who, after a short stay in the islands, brought home materials for a book or a new method of treating diseases. Only by "long residence, great practice, and observation" was it possible to write a book that contained anything useful. It was Moseley's view that "*Barbados* has ever borne the palm of West Indian medical literature." Jamaica, on the other hand, was "greatly in arrears, though it has long been, and is at present, numerously supplied with many well-informed and judicious practitioners."[61]

Except for a treatise written by a doctor in the Royal Navy in 1672,[62] no medical or natural history publications were written by the doctors or scientists of Barbados until the eighteenth century. Dr. Richard Towne, a local practitioner, published a treatise on West Indian diseases in 1726. Towne's purpose was to "lay down in a plain and intelligible manner the genuine and distinguishing Types of such Distempers as are most frequent and remarkable in the Island of *Barbadoes*, annexing a Method of Cure which I have experienced to be most effectual through a Course of seven Years Practice." Another important motive was to assist "such *Practitioners* as have been bred up in the Island, and have never had the Advantage of passing thro[ugh] a regular Course of Studies, or enjoying an Academical Education."[63] Dr. Henry Warren, another practitioner in Barbados, published in 1741 a treatise on the symptoms and treatment of yellow fever, together with other diseases and cures.[64]

Two Barbadians published works on natural history and medicine in the 1750s. The Reverend Griffith Hughes, rector of St. Lucy's Parish, described the island's flora and fauna in his natural history, which also contains information on plant use for medicinal, dietary, and other purposes.[65] As mentioned, William Hillary, M.D., practiced in the island for six years, during which time he kept careful records of medical cases and the weather.[66]

Civil and military doctors published works in later decades. William Sandiford, M.D., gave an account of an epidemic that raged in Barbados for three months in 1770.[67] James Hendy, a military doctor, published an essay on the glandular disease of Barbados,[68] which was criticized by John Rollo, an army medical doctor stationed in Barbados.[69] In the 1790s, J. Bell published a book on tropical medicine with special reference to British soldiers in the West Indies.[70] Colin Chisholm, M.D., F.R.S., was mentioned briefly in Chapter 1. Together with Dr. J. Clark and others, he published an account of the yellow fever that killed British soldiers in the great epidemic of 1793–6.[71] James Dottin Maycock, M.D., professor of medicine at Codrington College, published a book on the flora of Barbados that criticized the floral descriptions and taxonomy given by Rev. Griffith Hughes.[72] James Grainger, M.D., had an extensive medical practice among the slaves and also wrote an essay on West Indian diseases and remedies.[73]

John Coakley Lettsom, M.D., F.R.S. (1744–1815), was an eminent Quaker physician and philanthropist. He was born on the island of Little Jost Van Dykes in the British Virgin Islands. As a young man he lived in England with relatives and studied medicine.[74] In 1767 he sailed to Tortola to get money to finish his medical education. He refused one source of money, for his Quaker antislavery scruples impelled him to free the ten slaves he inherited from his father's estate. Lettsom then turned with great zeal to the practice of medicine on Tortola and neighboring islands. He wrote that he often saw fifty to a hundred people before breakfast. Indeed, in only six months his practice yielded the surprising sum of nearly £2,000.[75]

Lettsom studied at the Edinburgh Medical School and the University of Leyden, where he took his M.D. degree in 1769. He succeeded to the London practice of John Fothergill, M.D., and at the height of his career earned £12,000 in a single year. He founded the Medical Society of London and the Royal Sea Bathing Hospital and was active in the Royal Humane Society and prison reform. From Dr. Fothergill he acquired a keen interest in natural science. The botanical garden at his country villa at Camberwell included specimens from remote lands and climates. One of his numerous books was *The Naturalist's and Traveller's Companion* (1772). He also published *Reflections on the General Treatment and Cure of Fevers* (1772), which drew on his medical experience in the West Indies.[76] As a vigorous supporter of causes and a controversial figure, Lettsom made enemies and did not escape the satirists, who wrote of him:

I, John Lettsom,
Blisters, bleeds and sweats 'em.
If after that they please to die,
I, John Lettsom

In his *Medical Advice to the Inhabitants of Warm Climates* (London, 1790), Dr. Robert Thomas combined useful hints to preserve the health and prevent sickness among white people with observations on the management and medical treatment of blacks. Thomas resided for nine years on the island of Nevis and had more than 3,000 slaves annually under his care as a surgeon. He advised planters on the proper management of newly imported slaves and the care of lying-in women and infants. His book treats each of the common diseases separately under four headings: causes, symptoms, prognostic, and treatment.[77]

As emphasized in Chapter 1, the first book concerned exclusively with slave medicine was Dr. David Collins's *Practical Rules for the Management and Medical Treatment of Negro Slaves in the Sugar Colonies* (1803).[78]

At least two British doctors published works on the natural history and medicine of the Guianas. Edward Bancroft, M.D., F.R.S. (1744–1821), practiced medicine in Dutch Guiana from 1763. After he moved to England he published a natural history of that colony in 1769.[79] John Hancock, M.D., practiced medicine in British Guiana from 1804 to 1828. In the preface of his *Observations on . . . British Guiana* (1835), he said he acquired some knowledge of the botany of "a country most rich in medicinal plants, and of some peculiar practices followed with great success by the inland tribes, in the cure of diseases."[80]

Jamaican doctor-scientists and authors

For more than two centuries after its conquest by Cromwell's forces, Jamaica with its magnificent flora was a magnet for amateur and professional botanists. Numbered among these collectors were men who became eminent natural scientists and medical doctors. Some of the doctor-scientists took a special interest in discovering plants that had medicinal properties. They encouraged the planter-dominated government to establish botanical gardens and support schemes to introduce and propagate useful plants. Moreover, they assumed the leadership in establishing public baths at mineral water sites. These activities, together with the publication of books on tropical medicine, were intended to benefit chiefly the white inhabitants and military forces stationed on the island. Not until the early nineteenth century did the doctor-scientists of Jamaica begin to publish works that were concerned primarily with the disease environment and medical treatment of slaves.

Dr. Henry Stubbe, physician to the island of Jamaica in 1662–5, was the first English doctor to investigate the climate, soil, natural history, and diseases peculiar to that island and their remedies. He published two papers on these subjects in the *Philosophical Transactions of the Royal Society*.[81]

Thomas Trapham, M.D., as noted in Chapter 1, was the first English doctor in the West Indies to publish a book on tropical medicine. Although he made no systematic effort to collect and classify medicinal plants, Trapham made use in his practice of such local plants as tamarinds, aloes, physic nut, cinnamon bark, cassia fistula, and China root. Like other doctors of his time, he believed that for every disease there was a natural remedy close at hand. Indeed, "through the overflowing bounty of the great healer of us all. . . a balm for every Sore" had been given that was "neer at hand" and "both easie and cheap."[82]

Foremost among the doctor-scientists in the West Indies was Sir Hans Sloane, M.D., F.R.S. (1660–1753). During his long life Sloane received many honors, including his appointment as first physician to George II and his election as president of the Royal Society. He is best known for his great collection of natural history specimens, manuscripts, and books, which became the first collection of the British Museum.[83]

Dr. Henry Barham, F.R.S. (d. 1721), a friend and associate of Sloane, made significant contributions to the natural history of Jamaica. At the age of fourteen he left the surgeon to whom he was apprenticed to become a surgeon's mate and later master surgeon on vessels of the Royal Navy. He settled in Jamaica about 1680 and became established in a lucrative medical practice. He was highly regarded by Sloane, with whom he conducted an extensive correspondence, for his minute knowledge of the flora and fauna of Jamaica. Barham's *Hortus Americanus: containing an Account of the Trees, Shrubs and other Vegetable Productions, of South America and the West-India Islands, and particularly of the Island of Jamaica; interspersed with many curious and useful observations, respecting their uses in Medicine, Diet and Mechanics* was published at Kingston, Jamaica, in 1794. It was attributed erroneously to Henry Barham, Jr., M.D., a physician in Jamaica.[84]

Eight other doctor-scientists and one clergyman-scientist made collections of flora and fauna and published works on the natural history of Jamaica. William Houstoun, M.D., F.R.S. (d. 1733), matriculated at Leyden in 1727 and received his M.D. from St. Andrews in 1732. His botanical manuscripts and drawings of plants that he collected in Jamaica, Cuba, Venezuela, and Central America are in the Department of Botany of the British Museum.

He died in Jamaica in 1733.[85] Dr. Anthony Robinson (d. 1768) was a physician and naturalist who made extensive collections of the plant and animal life of Jamaica. His large portfolio of botanical drawings is also in the Department of Botany of the British Museum.[86] Patrick Browne, M.D. (1720–90), matriculated at Leyden and received his medical degree at Rheims in 1742. He spent some time in Antigua and Jamaica. His *Civil and Natural History of Jamaica* (London, 1756) was based on his studies of the geology, botany, and natural history of the island.[87] Arthur Broughton, M.D. (d. 1796), graduated at Edinburgh in 1779. He practiced medicine at Bristol and was elected physician to the infirmary there. In 1783 he went to Jamaica on a leave of absence but never returned, dying at Kingston in 1796. He is best known for his *Hortus Eastensis, or a catalogue of exotic plants in the garden of Hinton East, Esq. in the mountains of Liguanea at the time of his decease* (Kingston, 1792).[88] The Reverend John Lindsay, D.D., made over 200 drawings of the natural history of Jamaica, and Dr. John Lindsay, surgeon and assistant to the island botanist, left manuscripts that are deposited in the Edinburgh University Library and the Royal Society and also contributed papers printed in the *Transactions of the Linnaean Society*.[89] F. Macfadyen, M.D., made extensive botanical collections and published *The Flora of Jamaica*, etc., in two volumes in 1837 and 1850.[90] The careers of William Wright and Thomas Dancer will be sketched later in this chapter.

Submitting a statement to a committee of the Privy Council in 1789 was John Quier (1738–1822), practitioner in physic and surgery in Jamaica. He said he had studied surgery in London and physic at Leyden and served as assistant surgeon in military hospitals in the former war. For more than twenty-one years he had practiced in Jamaica, where he had 4,000 to 5,000 slaves constantly under his care. Quier claimed that he reduced infant deaths from tetanus or lockjaw. He was a pioneer in inoculation for smallpox and is said to have preceded European doctors by more than a century in the diagnosis of measles. Quier was the principal author of *Letters and essays on the small-pox and inoculation, the measles, the dry belly-ache, the yellow and remitting, and intermitting fevers of the West Indies*, etc. (London, 1778). Quier had a long and distinguished career. He testified on 17 November 1815 that he had been a magistrate for thirty years and had practiced physic and surgery in Jamaica "for upwards of forty-eight years, formerly very extensively, but for the last twenty years he has declined extensive practice, and only attends a few properties in the neighbourhood of his own plantation."[91]

William Wright, M.D., F.R.S., F.R.C.P. Edinburgh (1735–1819), was an eminent doctor-scientist in Jamaica and Scotland. He was born in the village of Crieff, Perthshire, Scotland, where he attended grammar school. At the age of seventeen he was apprenticed to a surgeon at Falkirk, and in 1756 entered the Edinburgh Medical School. Two years later he was licensed at

Surgeon's Hall, London, and then he served as surgeon's mate on several men-of-war as well as in military hospitals in the West Indies. At the end of the Seven Years' War he left the navy and obtained a M.D. degree from St. Andrews University.[92]

Wright then went to Jamaica where he practiced medicine and acquired a sugar plantation. He said his practice was undertaken to advance medical science. He was a close observer of nature and was said to have pried with a curious eye into her most secret recesses. He claimed that his remedies, though few, were efficacious. One of Wright's colleagues in Jamaica wrote that "his contributions to the improvement of his profession, and generally to literature, should be long remembered by the faculty and the public of that country in particular, who have so essentially derived advantage from his labours." Much of Dr. Wright's fame rested on his natural history collections and the scientific papers he published. For many years he collected plants in Jamaica, supplying specimens to the Royal Gardens at Kew and the botanical gardens in Liverpool and Glasgow.[93]

Thomas Dancer, M.D. (1755?–1811), was the most versatile of the doctor-scientists, serving as director of public institutions and publishing works on the medicine, botanical gardens, and mineral springs of Jamaica. The son of an English farmer of moderate circumstances, Dancer was enabled to further his education with money bequeathed by his uncle.[94] He went to Jamaica in 1773 to practice medicine. Six years later he went as physician on the expedition that captured Fort San Juan from the Spaniards in Central America. Upon his return to Jamaica he published an account of the expedition. In 1781 he was appointed physician to the Bath of St. Thomas the Apostle in Jamaica, serving in that capacity until 1795 when he went to England for his health. Upon his return to Jamaica he was appointed island botanist and remained at the botanical garden at Bath until 1799, when he moved to Kingston to become a private practitioner. He relinquished the post of island botanist in 1802 but held it again from 1805 until his death. Dancer was elected physician to the Kingston Hospital but claimed that he was unlawfully hindered from serving in that capacity.[95] He was a man of strong likes and dislikes and had an irascible temper. Among his enemies was Dr. David Grant, a Kingston doctor. In one exchange with Dr. Grant, Dancer said that although he did not mean to deprecate a college degree, he believed it must be admitted that such a degree did not confer sense. He contended that an apothecary who had the learning and skill of a physician was to all intents and purposes a physician, and that properly speaking there were few apothecaries in Jamaica.[96]

Dr. Dancer's scientific and medical efforts were directed to ascertaining the curative quality of the mineral water bath, obtaining exotic specimens for the botanical garden, and publishing a medical manual for use by families and on plantations. He published *A Short Dissertation on the Jamaica Bath Waters* (Kingston, 1784), which he claimed were useful for that "loathsome distemper of negroes, the yaws." Two of Dancer's works, both published in Jamaica, concerned the botanical garden at Bath: *A Catalogue of plants, exotic and indigenous, in the Botannical Garden* (1792) and *Some observations respecting the Botanical Garden* (1804). Upon Captain Bligh's arrival in 1793, "a nursery was immediately established" and "few of the bread-fruits were placed in the botanic garden under the care of Dr. Dancer." Dancer is best known for *The Medical Assistant, or Jamaica Practise of Physic: Designed chiefly for the use of Families and Plantations* (Kingston, 1801), which went through three editions and has been used by Jamaicans in the present century. It describes the common diseases of Jamaica with remedies. The appendix contains formulas for compounding medicines and a list of "simples" or healing herbs found in the island.[97]

Two Jamaican doctor-authors engaged in a pamphlet war that led to violent confrontation and death. John Williams, M.D., a Kingston practitioner, published *An essay on the bilious or yellow fever of Jamaica* (1750). This essay was criticized "line by line, sometimes unnecessarily rudely" by Parker Bennet, M.D., also a Kingston doctor, in a pamphlet entitled, *An enquiry into the late essay on the bilious fever.* Exploding in anger, Williams replied in a pamphlet that was answered, in turn, by Bennet in an equally abusive pamphlet. The upshot was that personal vilification reached a point at which the opposing doctors resorted to fists, swords, and pistols and the bloody murder of both antagonists. All these pamphlets were published together in London in 1752 and sold for two shillings. M. T. Ashcroft, M.D., who has documented this fatal medical controversy, says that Williams's pamphlet of 1750 was the first medical book to be published in Jamaica.[98]

Five other doctors with experience in Jamaica published works on fevers and especially the yellow fever, and two others wrote on the yaws. John Hunter, superintendent of military hospitals in Jamaica, published *Observations on the diseases of the army in Jamaica and on the best means of preserving the health of Europeans in that climate* (London, 1788). Robert Jackson, M.D., who was mentioned in Chapter 1, published *A Treatise on the fevers of Jamaica* (London, 1791), and *An Outline of the history and cure of fever, endemic and contagious; more expressly. . .the yellow fever of the West Indies* (Edinburgh, 1808). William Lempriere, apothecary to His Majesty's Forces, published *Practical Observations on the Diseases of the Army in Jamaica, As they occurred between the Years 1792 and 1797* (2 vols., London, 1799). David Grant, M.D. (d. 1818), was a leading practitioner who had a bitter quarrel with Dr. Dancer. He published an *Essay on the yellow fever of Jamaica* (Kingston, ca. 1804). Edward Nathaniel Bancroft, M.D. (1772–1842), was the son of Edward Bancroft, M.D., of Guiana. He became deputy inspector of army hospitals in Jamaica and wrote an essay on yellow fever and other diseases of the West Indies.[99] The two local practitioners who wrote on the yaws were J. F. Nembhard, *A Treatise on the nature and cure of yaws* (Kingston, 1793), which was a standard work on almost every plantation; and James Maxwell, M.D., *Observations on Yaws*, etc. (London, 1839). Maxwell, who was formerly surgeon to the Anotto Bay Marine Hospital in Jamaica, also published an article, "Pathological Inquiry into the Nature of Cachexia Africana [or dirt eating]," which was published in the second volume of *The Jamaica Physical Journal* in 1835.[100]

Doctors Moseley and Williamson published works that have been indispensable for writing this and other chapters. Benjamin Moseley, M.D. and diploma, Royal College of Physicians of London (1742–1819), was born in Essex in 1742. He studied medicine in London, Paris, and Leyden and received his M.D. degree from St. Andrews in 1784. In 1768 he settled as a medical practitioner in Jamaica and grew rich from his fees. He returned to England and in 1788 was appointed physician to the royal hospital at Chelsea. His first publication was *Observations on the Dysentery of the West Indies, with a new and successful Method of treating it* (Jamaica, 1780, reprinted in London 1781). His most important work was *A Treatise on Tropical Diseases and on the Climate of the West Indies* (London, 1787).[101] The career of John Williamson, M.D., was sketched in Chapter 1. His medical practice among the slaves is treated in Chapter 11.

The remarkable career of James Thomson, M.D. (d. 1822), was also discussed in Chapter 1. Not only did he display a keen interest in the scientific questions of his time, but he was also one of a very few doctors who made an effort to learn from the folk wisdom of the blacks. As a doctor who treated slaves in Jamaica, and as a scientist who diligently carried on the work begun by Doctors Quier and Wright, he observed the relationship between medicinal plants and the slave doctors and doctresses who collected, prepared, and prescribed them to black patients. He urged white doctors to gain the confidence of their black patients. It is of interest that the books by Doctors Collins and Thompson were read by slave owners in Virginia, where they were the only books in English that described the specific medical treatment of blacks for individual diseases.[102]

Conclusion

In these concluding remarks we will attempt to assess the strengths and weaknesses of the white medical profession in the Sugar Colonies. If we confine our assessment to the doctor-scientists and authors, it appears that they generally combined the practice of medicine and surgery with scientific investigations and the publication of treatises on tropical medicine and natural history. Among other things, they made collections of flora and fauna, corresponded with eminent scientists, wrote papers for learned journals, and established and directed botanical gardens and mineral water baths. Generally speaking, they made an effort to learn from the folk wisdom of the blacks, studied their herbal remedies, and searched out indigenous plants that had medicinal properties. Moreover, they became more knowledgeable about how the health of slaves was affected by such problems as malnutrition, fatigue, poor sanitation, and lack of proper clothing and shelter. They urged planters and overseers to provide sick and ailing slaves with hospitals serviced by black medical attendants, and pregnant women, mothers, and children with lying-in wards, midwives, nurses, and child care centers.

These positive developments were probably outweighed by those that had a negative impact. Medical practitioners in the West Indies were not unlike their counterparts in Europe and North America in adhering to the humoral-climatic and miasmatic theories of medicine. Largely because of these theories, they were likely to resort to such harmful practices as bloodletting, purging, vomiting, blistering, and sweating. We shall see in Chapter 12 that overdosing with opium, mercury, and antimony was particularly destructive to the slaves. Overdosing was encouraged because the sale of medicines imported from Europe made up a large part of the average doctor's income. The harsh fact is that European medicine could do little to prevent, cure, or alleviate many disorders of blacks. In this confused situation quacks such as Dr. Apozem thrived by concocting rotten and sophisticated drugs that spread depopulation far and wide.

Planters came under pressure from rising slave prices and the antislavery movement in England in the late eighteenth century, leading to laws to improve the health services delivered to slaves. Data on medical graduates from the universities of Leyden and Edinburgh, together with the career sketches of doctor-scientists, support the belief of contemporaries that the profession was upgraded. Yet it may be asked whether the slaves benefited in any material way from these improvements. Edward Long argued that since American diseases differed in many respects from those of Europe, they required a different *materia medica* consisting of native productions of the country to which the diseases were endemic. He asserted that the medicinal virtues of the Jamaican plants were little known to any practitioners, who found it less trouble "to find a medicine in the next drawer, or gallipot, than ramble into the woods for it, or enter upon a laborious course of experiments. And, in truth, very few here understand any thing of botany, or chemistry."[103] Unlike the United Kingdom and the United States, the British West Indies failed to develop a medical culture of professional schools, hospitals, societies, and journals. Medical science was backward to a large extent because doctors came to the colonies to acquire wealth from professional and planting pursuits in the hope of returning home after a few years to become members of the landed gentry. The medical way to get rich quick was to cater to the health needs of white planters and merchants. Dr. Collins thought it extraordinary that none of the "many gentlemen of professional abilities in the West Indies. . . had devoted their pens very particularly to the subject of negro disorders." Those who had written well on the diseases of the climate had laid down rules that were "much more applicable to the condition of the whites, who have all the advantages of good nursing, lodging, and medical attendance, than to that of our slaves, who possess none of them, at least, in an equal degree."[104] Although Doctors Grainger, Collins, Dancer, Williamson, and Thomson wrote manuals to guide planters in the medical treatment of slaves, it is doubtful whether these and other medical works made any substantial contribution to the improved health of the blacks.

One important reason for the limited attention given to the health care and reproduction of slaves in the British West Indies was access to the labor reservoir in West and Central Africa during the century and a half prior to the closure of the Atlantic slave trade in 1808. Africa was the chief source not only of labor but also of certain diseases and their remedies. In the following chapter we will investigate African religious and medical beliefs and practices and their transmission and adaptation to the slave societies of the British Caribbean colonies.

3

African and Afro-West Indian medicine

> I had intended to have given you some account of the medical plants of this island [Jamaica], especially of those whose medical properties are known to the negroes; but I find it would be impossible to enumerate them even in any reasonable limits. I am, however, so thoroughly persuaded that a variety of very valuable plants are known to the negroes, whose medical uses we are unacquainted with, that I think any person who would undertake an account of the popular medicine of the negroes, would bring to light much information serviceable to medical science.
>
> R. R. Madden, M.D., 1835[1]

In this chapter we examine the medical culture of West Africa, the extent to which it was carried by the slaves to the West Indian colonies, and how it was modified and, in part, suppressed when it came into contact with the white medical establishment on sugar plantations. Separate sections focus on the treatment of yaws, the slave medical attendants on plantations, and the role of women in Afro-West Indian medicine.

The two medical cultures: Africa

Two medical cultures – one African, one European – have dominated the British Caribbean territories during the past three centuries. African medicine, which combined mystical beliefs and rituals with herbal remedies and poisonous substances, was brought to the New World by the slaves. Telling the story of African folk medicine in the colonies is difficult. White colonials were so convinced of their cultural superiority that they dismissed African medicine or "white magic" as mere superstition. On the other hand, they could not ignore the African's "black magic," which included the use of poisons and other means to throw off the shackles of bondage. The upshot was a preoccupation with the malevolent side of African medicine and ignorance and neglect of the day-to-day practice of herb medicine.

Bringing the two cultures together in an uneasy alliance were economic and humanitarian pressures to improve the demographic performance of the slaves attached to plantations. More and more plantations had slave hospitals. Here the white doctor's orders and prescriptions were administered to patients by black and colored doctors, doctresses, nurses, cooks, midwives, and nursery attendants. These assistants and attendants played an indispensable role in providing medical services to the slaves. They mediated between the white establishment and the generally more numerous sick and ailing slaves on the plantations. In part, their power and influence were enhanced by the close ties they maintained with patients and their families, which contrasted with the widespread fear and distrust of white doctors and their medicines by the slaves. In part, the black attendants gained power and influence because their herbal remedies occasionally contained effective drugs, and even if ineffectual, they seldom harmed the patient. African medicine was most effective in the treatment of diseases endemic to tropical regions. When such diseases were also infectious by direct contact and resulted in ugly ulcers and even permanent disfigurement, the victims were isolated and treated almost exclusively by black attendants. This was the case with the African disease called yaws, which will be treated at some length in this chapter.

The "cultural baggage" African slaves brought to the New World included beliefs about the right relationships between man and man and between humans and the gods. West African religions were remarkable for their uniformity of supernatural beliefs. The main features of these religions, according to Orlando Patterson, "are the beliefs in a supreme being too remote to be active in the ordinary affairs of man; the worship of a pantheon of gods which are usually non-human spirits associated with natural forces; ancestor worship; and the belief in the use of charms and fetishes."[2] Disease was attributed to a harmful spirit or supernatural agency. A special caste of magicians or physicians claimed to control the supernatural powers vested in the gods of healing on the one hand and the demons of disease on the other. These medicine men often combined the offices of physician, priest, and magician.[3]

Thomas M. Winterbottom, M.D., who practiced in the colony of Sierra Leone, observed that among the native Africans, the effects of medicine were so much blended with magical ceremonies and incantations that it was often difficult to discover on which they chiefly relied for success. He found that "the practice of medicine and the art of making greegrees and fetiches, in other words amulets, to resist the effects of witchcraft, or the malicious attempts of evil spirits, is generally the province of the same person." Although the Africans believed that every dangerous disease was caused by witchcraft or poison, they readily admitted that sickness might occur independently of these causes. Africans were not unlike Europeans, however, who were said to have great faith in amulets, especially when hung round the necks of children, to protect them from convulsions in teething and to cure worms, whooping cough, and other diseases.[4]

Medical knowledge and practice were not confined to medicine men. On the contrary, knowledge of herbal medicine was widely diffused; there were both male and female doctors as well as general practitioners and specialists in such fields as midwifery, bonesetting, and the treatment of rare diseases. By trial and error, remedies were discovered for common ailments that had therapeutic value and were handed down from father to son, or from the midwife to the daughters of the tribe. George Way Harley writes that the treatment of the most common diseases closely approached the rational medicine of Western culture. On the other hand, religious or magical elements were concentrated around the largely inexplicable crises of life – birth, puberty, war, and death. An African who was ill would first consult an old woman who knew all the common remedies and many unusual ones, including poisons. If she could not cure the illness, the patient turned to a medicine man who might also be a priest. He prescribed remedies and procedures of a more magical nature, seeking to exorcise the "witch" who caused the disease. When the medicine man failed, the patient sought help from a diviner. He would seek out the person among the sick person's acquaintances who had cast the spell and press him or her to confess and remove the spell. If the patient died, the survivors would resort to the diviner who would catch the one guilty of witchcraft by using the poison ordeal. Thus, there was a progressive appeal to the mysterious forces of the unknown as the disease became more serious and culminated in death.[5]

Women played a more important role in African medicine than their counterparts in Western countries. Girls of the Mano tribe in Liberia learned to make simple herbal remedies for common ailments as part of the curriculum of the initiation school. A woman doctor commonly combined the functions of midwife, gynecologist, pediatrician, general practitioner, as well as surgeon when the girls were circumcised. "Both as midwife and as an expert in treating children's diseases," writes Harley, "she occupies a field scarcely touched by the professional medicine man." Men of the medical guild, though familiar with common remedies for such things as intestinal disorders, gonorrhea, rheumatism, ulcers, and trauma, were more often called on to treat special disorders like leprosy, abscess of the liver, smallpox, tumors, and sleeping sickness. Male doctors were more familiar with magical and hypnotic or psychotherapeutic measures than their female counterparts. According to Harley, male and female doctors of the Mano tribe used medicines and remedies in various ways:

> They may be administered by mouth as hot or cold infusions, either alone or cooked with food. Some are chewed but not swallowed . . . Many remedies in various forms are rubbed on the skin, sometimes with massage. Poultices are sometimes used. Local heat is applied in various ways. Mud baths, sweat baths, and hot medicated baths are common.

> Fumes are inhaled for headache. Splints are applied to fractures. A tourniquet is tied above a snake bite. Small incisions are made over abscesses and counter-irritants applied. Mixtures thought to develop immunity are licked off the finger in small amounts daily. A hot bath in the evening is almost a ritual for men. Women bathe in the streams where they wash their clothes. After the bath a soothing mixture of clay and aromatic herbs is rubbed on, or a bit of fine oil is rubbed into the skin.

In brief, African medicine made use of many rational remedies applied internally and externally. Surgery was limited to bonesetting, and bloodletting was limited to small, shallow incisions.[6]

Africans made a distinction between "good" and "bad" medicine men. The bad medicine man or woman, who was also called a sorcerer or witch, hurt people through his or her knowledge of witchcraft. Harley defines a witch as "one who has some control over the crises of life and death, or the knowledge of the controlled use of some substance, drug, or poison, capable of producing an unusual effect, either good or evil." M. J. Field defines witchcraft as "a bad medicine directed destructively against other people, but its distinctive feature is that there is no palpable apparatus connected with it, no rites, ceremonies, incantations, or invocations that the witch has to perform." Witchcraft is also defined as the art of perverted medicine. A fetish may be defined as an object that is the potential dwelling place of a spirit or spirits capable of controlling the powers of evil or black magic for personal ends. African medicine thus embodied the principles of good and evil; the good medicine man used a combination of herbs and white magic for good purposes, whereas the bad medicine man or sorcerer used poisons and black magic to hurt and destroy people.[7]

On the basis of his researches into Asante (Ghana) nonreligious medical practices in the nineteenth century, D. Maier finds that both preventive and curative measures were taken by native medical practitioners. Laxatives, abortants, sedatives, and antidiarrheals used by Asante herbalists were usually effective for the symptoms. He finds that illness was in many cases approached as a physical disorder to be combated at first with physical means before resorting to religious or magical cures. He contends that herbs as well as elementary surgical methods implied a crude conception of cause that was not the same as, although not mutually exclusive of, a belief that the supernatural and spirits determined one's health and illness.[8]

Lending support to Maier's generalizations are the writings of European travelers in West Africa in the era of the Atlantic slave trade. Preventive measures included the provision of cloacae or toilets. During his visit to the city of Kumase in 1817, T. E. Bowdich reported:

> What surprised me most...was the discovery that every house had its cloacae besides the common ones for the lower orders without the town. They were generally situated under a small archway in the most retired angle of the building, but not unfrequently upstairs, within a separate room like a small closet where the large hollow pillar also assists to support the upper story: the holes are of small circumference, but dug to a surprising depth, and boiling water is daily poured down, which effectually prevents the least offence.[9]

Other preventive measures included street cleaning and the removal and burning of rubbish and offal from houses, frequent baths, and variolation or inoculation against smallpox.[10]

That there was a considerable body of knowledge regarding the use of herbal and vegetable remedies was the contention of William Bosman, who visited the coast of Africa in the early eighteenth century. "The chief Medicaments here in use," he wrote, "are first and more especially Limon or Lime-Juice, Malaget, otherwise called The Grains of Paradise, or the Cardamon, the Roots, Branches and Bumms of Trees, about thirty several sorts of green Herbs, which are impregnated with an extraordinary Sanative Virtue." Bosman maintained that the remedies were effective. The green herbs, which were the principal remedy used by the blacks, were of "such wonderful Efficacy, that 'tis much to be deplored that no European Physician has yet applied himself to the discovery of their Nature and Virtue."[11] H. Tedlie, a European doctor who practiced in West Africa, recorded thirty-seven different plants used for medicinal purposes by Asantees, of which approximately 30 percent were used for various digestive difficulties and another 20 percent for skin problems. Other Europeans told of herbal remedies for ophthalmia, fevers, and dysentery and of techniques for extracting Guinea worms, various surgical practices, and bonesetting.[12] According to Edward Long, the Jamaican planter-historian, "the chief medicaments among the Negroes are lime juice, cardamons, the roots, branches, leaves, bark, and gums of trees, and about thirty different herbs. The latter have been experienced in many cases wonderfully powerful, and have subdued diseases incident to their climate, which have foiled the art of European surgeons at the factories.[13]

When he studied the Azande of the southern Sudan in the early twentieth century, Sir Edward Evans-Pritchard found that medicines consisted of any object in which mystical power was supposed to reside and that was used in magic rites. Medicines were used to prevent or cause rainfall; to ensure the fruitfulness of food plants; to ensure success in hunting, fishing, and collecting; to thwart the malevolent spells of witches and sorcerers; to make for success in love affairs; and to treat physical and mental disorders. Training novices to perform magical rituals and to identify and use medicinal plants under the tutelage of medicine men was an educational process that Evans-Pritchard sought to understand despite the secrecy and taboos associated with magic and medicine. "Magic must be bought like any other property," he writes, "and the really significant part of initiation is the slow transference of knowledge about plants from teacher to pupil in exchange for a long string of fees." Indeed, the Azande were said to know about hundreds of different plants that yielded drugs.[14]

Although Evans-Pritchard had little faith in the therapeutic value of Azande drugs, the findings of recent research in Africa south of the Sahara are more positive. Among these developments is the launching of the *Journal of Ethno-Pharmacology*, an interdisciplinary journal devoted to bioscientific research on indigenous drugs. It publishes research papers concerned with the biological activities and the active substances of plants and animals used in the traditional medicine of past and present cultures. One issue of the journal contains a world survey on medicinal plants and herbs. One contributor underscores the fact that plants are the principal means of therapy in traditional medicine and that this type of medicine has the very important task of healing 75 to 80 percent of the world's population. Other contributors report on the knowledge of medicinal plants in Africa today. This knowledge, which resides with the medicine men of Africa, has from time to time been released and documented in scientific literature. For example, in his work with the traditional healers in Ghana, one investigator "has proven the efficacy of certain medicinal plants in the treatment of guinea-worms, some skin diseases, diabetes mellitus, and bronchial asthma."[15]

The two medical cultures: West Indies

Caribbean plantation slaves were affected by African medicine in various ways. The impact was no doubt greater during the century and a half of the legal slave trade when Africans often outnumbered Creoles on plantations than it was after the trade was prohibited in 1807. Given the prevailing antinatalist policy of the planters and the limited number of white doctors available to treat black patients, wide scope was given for African medical ideas and practices to penetrate the slave community – however, not without concerted efforts by the whites to extirpate witchcraft and especially the use of poison. As in Africa, folk medicine in the West Indies was divided between good and bad medicine men, although there was some blurring of these divisions. As in Africa, folk medicine in the West Indies made extensive use of herbal and other remedies, which were transmitted by oral tradition from one generation to another. As in Africa, folk medicine in the West Indies made use of charms, spells, fetishes, incantations, and poison. As in Africa, women played an important role in West Indian folk medicine. It is ironic that the planters contributed indirectly to the perpetuation of African folk medicine by long refusing to provide their slaves with European education and religious training.[16]

Bad medicine in the West Indies was called Obeah, which is thought to have come from the West African word *obeye* meaning a spiritual being or minor god. Patterson says that "Obeah was essentially a type of sorcery which largely involved harming others at the request of clients, by the use of charms, poisons, and shadow catching. It was an individual practice, performed by a professional who was paid by his clients."[17] Obeah men were at the same time revered, abhored, and consulted by the slaves. According to the evidence submitted to a committee of the Privy Council by three leading Jamaicans, blacks resorted to these oracles with the most implicit faith "for the Cure of Disorders, the obtaining of Revenge for Injuries or Insults, the conciliation of Favour, the Discovery and Punishment of the Thief or the Adulterer, and the Prediction of future Events." Slaves went to Obeah men to get drugs and poisons that were maliciously administered to overseers, masters, and livestock. Obeah practitioners were, with few exceptions, Africans who were the oldest and most crafty men and women, somewhat harsh and diabolical, with knowledge of medicinal and poisonous plants that gave them power over the weak and credulous.[18] "It is the unique power of the Obeah Man to control the spirit world which is the source of his extraordinary influence in the Negro community," writes Martha Beckwith. "The Obeah Man first persuades a man that someone is 'working obeah' upon him, and then he offers to 'take it off' for a consideration."[19]

Because they challenged the white domination of black slaves, Obeah men were harshly repressed. Obeah men challenged the white minority by their use of witchcraft and sorcery to gain ascendancy over the slaves, by their skillful use of poisons, and by the part they played in slave rebellions. In his *History of the Island of Dominica*, Thomas Atwood wrote that the Obeah people were "very artful in their way, and have a great ascendancy over the other negroes, whom they persuade that they are able to do miracles by means of their art; and very often get good sums of money for their imaginary charms." Moreover, Atwood claimed that many white people had been poisoned under the persuasion of these Obeah men.[20] According to Patterson, Obeah men played a key role in insurrection plots, administering oaths of secrecy and distributing fetishes that were claimed to give the insurgents immunity to the bullets fired from the guns of the whites.[21] After Obeah men were discovered to be implicated in the Jamaican slave rebellion of 1760, the white legislature enacted that "any Negro or other Slave, who shall pretend to any supernatural Power, and be detected in making use of any Blood, Feathers, Parrots Beaks, Dogs Teeth, Alligators Teeth, broken

Bottles, Grave Dirt, Rum, Egg-shells or any other Materials relative to the Practice of Obeah or Witchcraft, in order to delude and impose on the Minds of others, shall upon conviction thereof, before two Magistrates and three Freeholders, suffer Death or Transportation."[22]

A great many slaves were reportedly hanged for Obeah crimes in the twenty years after the act of 1760. Thereafter, as Edward Brathwaite points out, the public leadership of a large mass of the slaves shifted from Obeah people to black preachers with the influx of American Baptist slaves or freedmen into Jamaica as a result of the American Revolution. Nevertheless, Obeah people continue to this day to exert an influence even among middle-class West Indians.[23]

Myalism is a religious sect of African origin that is in many ways the antithesis of Obeah. Though the origin of the word *Myalism* is not known, the religion is thought to have begun in Jamaica in a secret society composed of men who claimed invulnerability to weapons and power even to raise the dead. Whereas Obeah is secret and malicious, Myalism is beneficent in its purpose and practiced in the open. Although Myalism is generally regarded as the opposite of Obeah, the latter word is sometimes used in a generic sense to include the former. Myalism, according to Patterson, "was obviously a form of anti-witchcraft and anti-sorcery. The most important difference from Obeah, was the fact that it was not an individual practice between practitioner and client, but was organized more as a kind of cult with a unique ritual dance." What is most distinctive about Myalism from the standpoint of the present study is that its practitioners understood the medicinal value of certain plants and built up a body of knowledge of herb medicine that was of real service in curing the sick. In fact, many Myal doctors worked in the plantation hospitals during the slavery era.[24]

Twentieth-century studies have added to previous knowledge of medicinal plants in the West Indies and especially Jamaica. In 1922 and 1924 Martha Beckwith secured the names of 136 plants used for medicinal purposes among the black peasantry, with the method of preparation and the use to which each was put. In 1929 Morris Steggerda collected forty-one plants to which the Jamaicans attributed medicinal properties. In the early 1950s, G. F. Asprey and Phyllis Thornton conducted a monumental study of the use of local plants for medicinal remedies in Jamaica. In their four-part article more than 160 species of plants distributed through sixty-two plant families are dealt with in detail. Although in many cases the claims made for the plants remain to be substantiated, the claims made for some of the plants may occasionally be justified. The authors make some attempt to record uses in other areas of the Caribbean and in Africa as perhaps showing a relationship with Jamaican practices.[25]

The survival of African religions and folk medicine in Trinidad has been documented by George E. Simpson. He tells of the Shango cult, an Afro-Trinidadian syncretistic cult whose beliefs and practices are derived from Yoruban traditions from southwestern Nigeria and from Catholicism. Named for the Yoruban god of thunder, the Shango in Trinidad have cult centers and leaders, ritual songs and dances, specific African names, and a wide range of plant and other materials used in healing and conjuring. Ordinary illnesses are attributed by the Shango to "natural" causes and can be dealt with by either healers or medical doctors. Other diseases, as well as many accidents, are said to be caused by "powers" or evil spirits. Virtually every Shango leader engages in healing, working generally on a part-time basis and basing his charges on the nature of the illness and the ability of the client to pay. Simpson lists some 260 materials used in healing and conjuring, classified into leaves, grasses, barks, flowers, roots, seeds, pods, fruits, oils and perfumes, other drugs, miscellaneous, and accessories. Practitioners are familiar with remedies for the whole range of human ills, both physical and emotional, and most of them will undertake to cure any complaint. Twenty-eight remedies are prescribed without rituals; those that include rituals are "bad" ulcers and driving out evil spirits. Although folk medicine had lost some ground in the decade preceding 1962, Simpson predicted it would continue for some time to be functional in the lives of many lower-income Trinidadians.[26]

Folk medicine

Though most Europeans in the West Indies dismissed African medicine as mere superstition and its practitioners as charlatans, a number of doctors took an interest in herbal remedies and a few made some effort to incorporate them into their professional practice or home remedies. Generally speaking, these doctors were among the select few who had a university education, they were eager students of tropical flora and especially medicinal plants, and they wrote scientific papers and books on natural history and medicine.

Foremost among these doctor-scientists was Sir Hans Sloane. He was a close student of African and Amerindian herbal medicine during his residence in Jamaica. The blacks, he observed, used "very few decoctions of Herbs, no distillations, nor infusions, but usually take the Herbs in substance. For instance in a Clap, they grind the roots of Fingrigo and Lime tree between two stones and stir them with Lime juice till it be pretty thick and so make the patient take it evening and morning for some time." For cold, fever or numbness, "they boil Bay leaves, Wild Sage, etc., in water in one of their Pots, when boiled they tye a Fasiculus of these plants together, and by putting that into the Decoction sprinkle their Bodies all over with it as fast as they can, they being naked."[27] Besides simples, blacks used the lancet to remove blood from the nose to relieve headaches. "They thrust up the Lancet into the tip of the nose, after tying a Ligature about the Neck, and some drops of Blood follow, whence they think themselves relieved in Colds, with Hoarseness and stuffed Noses." They cupped with calabashes the pained parts of the body. Clay was mixed with water and placed over affected parts of the body and exposed to warm sun. Ailing blacks bathed frequently in water mixed with aromatic and medicinal substances. Sloane was skeptical of the "many such Indian and Black Doctors, who pretend, and are supposed to understand and cure several distempers." He concluded from what he could see of their practice that "they do not perform what they pretend, unless in the vertues of some few Simples. Their ignorance of anatomy, Disease, Method, &c. renders even that knowledge of the Vertues of Herbs, not only useless, but even sometimes hurtful to those who imploy them."[28] Sloane's criticisms should be judged from the standpoint of contemporary European medicine, which consisted primarily of bleeding, cupping, purgatives, emetics, and the use of opium and mercury, which are said to have killed more patients than they cured.

More favorable opinions of folk medicine were expressed by other writers. James Knight, a leading Jamaican, said that the black doctors seldom revealed their nostrums or method of practice, "though some of our Practitioners have now and then got out of them the use and Virtue of many Simples, that were unknown to them or any physician in England. And I am of Opinion, that many Secrets in the Art of Physick, may be obtained from the Negro Doctors, were proper Methods taken, which I think is not below our Physicians to Enquire into, as it may be of great Service to themselves, as well as mankind."[29] Charles Spooner, colonial agent for St. Kitts and Grenada, testified that the Obeah people sometimes used their knowledge of plants for beneficial purposes. He noted that "from their skill in simples, and the virtues of plants, they sometimes operate extraordinary cures in diseases which have baffled the skill of regular practitioners, and more especially in foul sores and ulcers. I have myself made use of their skill for the last with great success."[30]

Building on the work of Sloane, Henry Barham, and Patrick Browne was William Wright, M.D., who practiced many years in Jamaica and sought to advance the knowledge of natural history and medical science. Much of Wright's fame rested on his natural history collections and scientific papers. He collected some 760 plants, which he described according to the system of Linnaeus. In a paper he read before the Philosophical Society of Edinburgh on 6 August 1778, he said he had spent all his spare hours examining the plants of Jamaica. "In this delightful walk of science, I discovered and ascertained many hundreds of new plants which had escaped the diligence of former botanists."[31]

As we have described, James Thomson, M.D., treated slaves in Jamaica and studied natural history and medicine. He observed closely the relationship between medicinal plants and the slave doctors and doctresses who collected, prepared, and prescribed them. He wrote that it was the serious duty of every planter to provide a proper black person to superintend the management of the sick. Thomson candidly acknowledged that the effects of his most labored prescriptions had often been superseded by the persevering administration of the black doctors' most simple remedies. He wrote at length of his and other doctors' experiments with the medicinal plants of Jamaica, and he recommended that as many as twenty-eight varieties be kept on every plantation.[32]

"Western medical science," writes Frantz Fanon, "being part of the oppressive system, has always provoked in the native an ambivalent attitude."[33] In contrast with metropolitan society, where the attitude of a sick person in the presence of a medical practitioner is confidence, the doctor–patient relationship in a colonial society is characterized by misunderstanding, mistrust, and fear. Few white doctors were as perceptive as Dr. Thomson, who observed, "The intimate union of medicine and magic in the minds of the African is worthy the consideration of those interested in their welfare, as it exerts the most serious influence in our success in relieving their disorders, particularly those of the chronic description." Thomson urged the medical practitioners on every plantation to gain the confidence of those entrusted to their care, going so far as to gratify their patients' wishes when they did not materially interfere with the actual state of the disease.[34]

That Thomson's advice was seldom heeded is suggested by accounts of ailing blacks spurning the advice of white doctors and seeking out their own healers. As a case in point, Matthew Gregory Lewis told of a poor creature named Bessie who was afflicted with coco bays, a disease akin to leprosy. When she appealed to him for medicine, he asked, "Had not the doctor seen her?" "Oh, yes! Dr. Goodwin; but the white doctor could do her no good. She wanted to go to a black doctor, named Ormond, who belonged to a neighbouring gentleman." Lewis told Bessie that she could go to Ormond if he understood her particular disease better than others but not if he pretended to cure by charms or spells or anything but medicine. Upon inquiry, Lewis learned "that Bessie's black doctor is really nothing more than a professor of medicine as to this particular disease; and I have ordered her to be sent to him in the mountains immediately."[35]

Yaws and its treatment

Ailing slaves were customarily confined to plantation hospitals where they were attended by black nurses under the supervision of white doctors, proprietors, or overseers. An exception to this practice occurred in the treatment of yaws or frambesia. White doctors were repulsed by yaws patients, whose bodies were often covered with disgusting ulcerous eruptions. Because yaws was contagious by physical contact, it was customary to remove its victims to a remote corner of the plantation and confine them to a yaws hut and yard surrounded by a stockade under the direction of an old female slave. Here there was freedom to treat yaws patients with African remedies. Ironically, certain white doctors came to acknowledge that African remedies were more efficacious than those of European origin. Since newly arrived slaves from Africa were often infected with yaws, the incidence of this disease depended in part on the ratio of African to Creole slaves. The closing of the African trade, together with the stricter isolation of yaws patients and the use of African remedies, probably led to the decline of yaws in the decades preceding emancipation.

Yaws is a contagious disease characterized by skin eruptions and an indefinite incubation period, followed usually by fever, rheumatic-like pains, and the appearance of sores that generally develop into foul and fungous tubercules and ulcers. Yaws is caused by a spirochete, a minute organism that is indistinguishable from that of syphilis when viewed through a microscope, but different in its other properties. The disease is found throughout the tropics, including Africa, the East Indies, the Pacific islands, South and Central America, and the West Indies. It is highly contagious, being transmitted directly by skin contact and perhaps indirectly by insects and the viruses from previous yaws patients that impregnate the floors and walls of dirty houses. The spread of yaws is facilitated by overcrowding, filthy habits, unsanitary conditions, and high temperature. Although modern studies show that no age is exempt, approximately two-thirds of the yaws cases occur before puberty; about three males appear to be infected to every one female. Moreover, modern studies show that the disease is prevalent in areas of high rainfall, except where there is a pervious limestone formation and ample vegetation.[36]

Yaws lasts for weeks or months or even years, depending on general health, hygiene, and treatment. It was believed that slaves who were well clothed and fed and lived under favorable hygienic conditions had every chance of going through the disease in a few weeks or months without suffering, but otherwise they suffered physical disfigurement, ostracism, pain, and misery for more than two years. The course of the disease may be divided into three stages: primary, secondary, and tertiary. Pains in the joints and limbs, resembling rheumatism, were followed by small skin eruptions, which soon increased and became protuberant pimples. During the first stage there appears a primary sore, called the "mother yaw," which persists, unless treated, for months. In the secondary stage, which may last for several years, the yaws infection spreads and sores break out on various parts of the body. The sores become ill-disposed lesions or ulcers, which discharge a thick viscid matter that forms an ugly scab around the edges of the excrescence. Prolonged cases of yaws are characterized by successive crops of eruptions. In the tertiary stage, the bones of the face may be destroyed, resulting in terrible disfigurement known as gangosa. Yaws on the soles of the feet and palms of the hand, called "crab yaws" by the slaves, was particularly difficult and painful. Because these parts were callous from walking barefooted or from labor, they became swollen, inflamed, and painful, and unless skillfully treated, continued troublesome for years. Unless the patient is exposed to secondary infections and other diseases, yaws eventually runs its course and has a spontaneous cure. Moreover, yaws patients are relatively immune to the disease after the secondary stage subsides (see Figure 3.1).[37]

Some doctors called attention to the appalling suffering and loss of labor resulting from yaws and the need for better treatment of yaws patients. "The havock this terrible disorder annually makes amongst Negroes in the West Indies is truly deplorable," wrote Dr. Wright, "and merits the attention of the Statesman, the Planter, and Physician. It may not be in our power to prevent the spreading of this disorder amongst the Negroes, but humanity and sound policy call aloud on us to alleviate the sufferings and distresses of this class of mankind, when they are so unfortunate as to be infected with this cruel malady."[38] Dr. Williamson maintained that improvement in the political economy of the West Indies, together with the amelioration of slavery, would surely produce a corresponding improvement of, if not remove entirely, that loathsome disease. He believed that "by exercising the means of comfort and cure, we will blot out one of the remaining causes for imputation against both of these."[39]

For the most part, however, white doctors neglected to treat yaws patients unless they contracted other diseases that were too serious to neglect. When Dr. Williamson went to Jamaica in 1798, he found neglected or ill-treated yaws patients who suffered from bone aches, decrepitude, and other effects of the disease. He visited the yaws houses frequently on different properties, trying to get some of them put under the regular direction of a medical practitioner. He wrote in his *Medical Memorandums* of August 1799 that

> the yawy negroes on estates seemed to me to be in a very neglected state. In the progress of disease, that maintenance was not afforded them which, for curative objects, should be liberally dispensed. A dis-

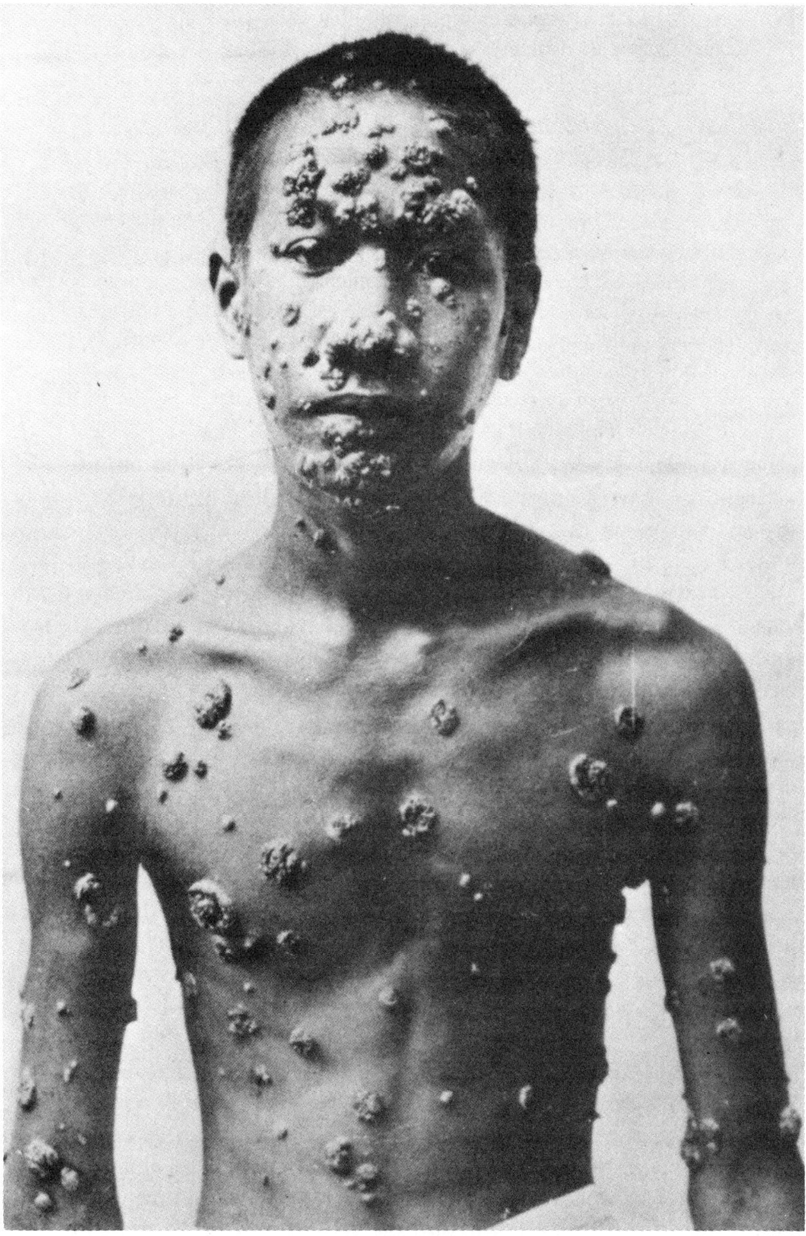

Figure 3.1. Yaws or frambesia at the secondary stage.

> ease, in itself injurious to the constitution, is aggravated from such causes; whereas, if nature were supported by fit diet, clothing, cleanliness, and comfortable housing, she would work her own cure in most cases.
>
> An immense deal of labour is thus lost to the proprietor; but this is not all; for, owing to patched-up cures, premature disappearance of the yawy eruption, disease lies lurking in the system. Bone-aches attack the unfortunate negro; the master loses a valuable servant; and this servant drags on a miserable existence.
>
> To obviate such manifest mismanagement an establishment, properly regulated, should be provided on every estate, under the occasional direction of the medical gentleman who attends the estate or plantation.
>
> In the formation of a house for yawy patients, it ought to be situated near the banks of a rivulet, that they may have it in their power to wash their bodies while the water is tepid after noon-day.[40]

Dr. Williamson admitted that his efforts to cure yaws did not work and he eventually gave them up. He attributed his failure to the fact that yaws was so contagious that white people naturally felt a horror of exposing themselves to the risk of infection. He advised doctors who visited the yaws house "to have some covering over the face and to protect them against the consequences which might follow from a fly, having yaws fluid on it, alighting on and inoculating any part about the eyes, nose, lips, ears, &c. as these parts are obviously more readily susceptible to infection."[41] According to Dr. Wright, white doctors did not have the immediate charge of blacks who had yaws unless some other acute disease, such as fever or dysentery, intervened. Both Dr. Wright and Dr. James Maxwell emphasized the fear of contracting the disease. "The extremely loathsome and contagious nature of this affection," wrote Maxwell, "and the disgrace and ruin which would be the consequence to any respectable white person contracting it, deter most medical men from making themselves conversant with this interesting disease. There have been instances of distressing acts of suicide committed by genteel young men, who had been accidentally infected, to escape the overwhelming obloquy which is associated with a European labouring under Yaws."[42]

Besides the fear of contagion, white doctors had little knowledge of yaws because they were unable or unwilling to investigate the folk remedies used by the blacks. White doctors generally considered yaws to be beyond their province, and its treatment was consigned to the blacks almost by tacit consent. Dr. Maxwell was exceptional. From the blacks he learned that yaws ought to be left to nature without any other interference than the local application of some simple vegetable dressing. He believed the African method of treatment was infinitely preferable to the widespread use of mercury by white doctors. Although mercury temporarily repelled the eruption of yaws, it was in his opinion an exceedingly dangerous and destructive medicine. He therefore insisted upon the total abolition of mercury in the treatment of yaws.[43] Dr. William Hillary of Barbados said that the blacks had found, by long observation and experience, a method of curing yaws "with the caustic juices of certain escarotic plants externally applied, and giving the juice or decoction of others internally." With this method of treatment, which they kept secret from white people but preserved among themselves by tradition, they sometimes performed notable cures.[44]

The treatment of yaws by black doctors and doctresses attracted the attention of certain planters. James Knight wrote that even though the physicians and surgeons of Jamaica seemingly cured the yaws, it generally broke out again. On the other hand, Knight knew of some black doctors who had made "very Surprising Cures, and particularly one belonging to Mr. Dawkins of Clarendon." Their method of practice was to make a hot bath with several sorts of herbs and simples or to use fomentations. Knight wrote that the black doctors very seldom prescribed anything to be taken inwardly, "which probably is one Reason that attaches their own Colour so much to them, and makes them have so little Confidence in our Physicians and Surgeons."[45] Writing seventy years later, John Stewart said that the blacks of Jamaica were "acquainted with the use of many simples for the cure of certain disorders – as yaws, ulcers, bone-ache, &c.; and the care and management of negroes afflicted with these disorders is generally confided to an elderly negro woman who professes a knowledge of this branch of physic."[46]

A. J. Alexander, a young planter of Grenada, told of the success his black doctor had in the treatment of yaws in letters written to Professor Joseph Black, his former teacher of chemistry at the University of Edinburgh. When Alexander returned to Grenada he found thirty-two patients in the yaws hospital. He said the medicine chiefly used was mercury in different forms, which often destroyed the patients' constitutions. The sad plight of his yaws patients motivated Alexander to try an experiment. He found an old slave on his property who understood the African method of treating yaws and let him have his way. Alexander put one group of patients under the care and direction of the surgeon on his estate, and another group under the black doctor. "The Negro Method," he wrote, "is making them stand in a Cask where there is a little fire in a pot & sweating them powerfully in it twice a day, giving them decoctions of 2 Woods in this Country called Bois Royale & Boix Fer & applying an Ointment of Lime Juice & Rust of Iron to their Sores." The result of the experiment was that the black doctor's patients were well in a fortnight, but not one of the white doctor's patients was apparently better. The latter patients were then turned over to the black doctor who cured them in a very short time.[47]

West Indian blacks reportedly continued the African practice of inoculating their children with yaws. Bryan Edwards was informed by a black woman who came from a village near Anamaboo "that the natives on the Gold Coast give their children the *yaws* (a frightful disorder) *by inoculation*." According to Dr. Maxwell, many black mothers inoculated their children a little before they were weaned while they were in good health. He said he had daily opportunities of observing the mild nature of the disease when a healthy child contracted yaws.[48]

Because of their highly contagious and repulsive disease, yaws victims were isolated from other slaves. During most of the slave era there appears to have been no regular method of treating yaws, and its victims were expected to let the disease run its course. Dr. Benjamin Moseley wrote that the victims were banished to some lonely place by the seaside to bathe or to the mountains where they could watch provision grounds. Here the afflicted slave had "a cold damp, smoky hut for his habitation; snakes and lizards for his companions; crude, viscid food, and bad water his only support; and shunned as a leper; – he usually sunk from the land of the living."[49] Contrasted with Dr. Moseley's dismal account is Dr. Wright's optimistic version of the treatment of yaws patients on every well-regulated estate in Jamaica. The yaws house was erected in a cool and healthy place, the patients had plenty of good food and clothes, and they were cared for by a "careful and discreet matron."[50] Yaws patients were confined to the care of some elderly black woman who acted in the double capacity of doctor and nurse, according to Gilbert Mathison, the planter-author. "Her practice is generally very simple," he wrote, "consisting of cold ablutions, which are performed by soaking the ulcerated part in cold water for a considerable space of time, and of the application of the leaves of some astringent plants, in the form of a vegetable poultice, to the surface of the ulcers." Yaws children were kept in a separate house; Mathison declared they should not be removed on any pretense to a distant part of the estate or be less attended than children in the nursery.[51]

Yaws, which was endemic on the coast of Africa, grew to epidemic proportions on the crowded Guinea vessels that transported slaves to the Sugar Colonies. The disease was spread not only to uninfected slaves on the Middle Passage, but also to Creole slaves in the colonies. The incidence of yaws receded first in the small sugar islands of long settlement. This was the case with Barbados, Antigua, and St. Kitts, among others, where the slave trade was reduced to a trickle before the end of the eighteenth century; all the available land was cultivated or taken up by settlers, so that all the slaves were under the supervision of their white masters. By putting an end to one important source of contagion, the closing of the Atlantic slave trade after 1807 contributed to the declining incidence of yaws. Yet the disease lingered on, especially in the mountainous islands with heavy rainfall where yaws was often spread by runaway slaves who found food, shelter, and a hiding place in the virgin forests.[52] On the basis of his research in Jamaica and other Caribbean territories, M. T. Ashcroft, M.D., believes that owing chiefly to the use of penicillin, yaws transmission today is probably at an end.[53]

Slave medical attendants

Due in part to the difficult relationship between white doctors and black patients and in part to the decision to economize on providing medical services to slaves, planters commonly built slave hospitals or hothouses (apart from the yaws hospital) that combined features of infirmaries and prisons, and staffed them with black and colored attendants who were in daily contact with the slave patients. The hospital staff varied in number and quality from plantation to plantation, depending on such factors as the number of slaves in the labor force, the size of the hospital, and the proprietor's or manager's willingness to train and employ slaves and an occasional freedman as medical attendants. The staff on a large plantation might consist of a black doctor or doctress, a hospital assistant, several sick nurses, hospital cooks, a midwife and nurse or nurses in the lying-in ward, children's attendants, and a yaw's hut attendant. On the other hand, small plantations or inadequately staffed large plantations might have only one or two attendants on full-time duty in a jerry-built hospital. The recruitment, training, duties, and performance of these different black medical attendants will be investigated in the remaining sections of this chapter; the physical and organizational aspects of the slave hospitals will be taken up in Chapter 10.

Superintending the day-to-day management of the sick on a typical plantation was the responsibility of the black doctor or doctress. According to Dr. Thomson, it was the serious duty of every planter to provide a person for this responsibility who was above all prejudice and superstition and who commanded the implicit respect and confidence of the slaves.[54] Though the selection and training of black doctors were generally local decisions, they occasionally involved absentee proprietors. One such proprietor who had also been a medical practitioner in Jamaica was Dr. James Chisholme. On one occasion he wrote to his plantation manager to "endeavour to make a Doctor of Chamba Tom, as I think will make a good one, and I think we are likely to want such a character."[55] Besides a white doctor, Dr. Collins of St. Vincent said it was proper for a planter "to have a sensible negro man instructed in bleeding, and in the drawing of teeth, in the spreading of plasters, and the dressing of sores, in weighing and compounding of common drugs, which will save you a great deal of trouble, though you should be qualified to do these things yourself." The fledgling dentist could learn the extraction of teeth by observing an experienced practitioner "and by practising on the jaw of some dead animal, first freed from the covering, and afterwards with the skin and flesh on, before he proceeds to operate on the living subject."[56]

According to Alexander Barclay, a pro-planter writer, every estate had a "hospital doctor" and a sick nurse; "the former is an intelligent man (most commonly of colour) who, acting for years under the direction of the white doctor, acquires a sufficient knowledge of common complaints of the negroes, to be capable of administering some simple medicines in cases of slight indisposition."[57] Black doctors, not unlike noncommissioned officers in military units, were sometimes better qualified than their certified white superiors. George Pinckard, M.D., a distinguished British physician, said it was an unhappy truth that some of the white doctors in Barbados were "only pre-eminent in ignorance" and in learning and manners not far above the slaves. Indeed, they were "more illiterate than you can believe, and the very *negro doctors*, of the estates too justly vie with them in medical knowledge."[58]

Sick nurses often combined supervisory, professional, and menial duties as they labored long hours in the slave hospitals. Among other things, they administered the medicines, provided food and other comforts, and kept the hospital and the patients clean. "Negro sick nurses acquire a surprizing skill in the cure of ordinary diseases," wrote the Reverend James Ramsay, "and often conquer disorders that have baffled an host of regulars."[59] Both white and black nurses served in the Codrington plantation hospitals in Barbados. Black nurses performed such duties as administering the "castor oil, green tar, biscuits, rice, chocolate, port and other items that were bought for the patients."[60] Black doctors and nurses were presumably superintended by the master or manager, who saw that the medicines were given according to the written directions from the white doctor.[61]

It was not unknown for certain devoted and capable nurses to be singled out for praise. Nancy was one of the hospital nurses on Cornwall estate in Jamaica and also the housekeeper of Matthew Gregory Lewis's plantation attorney. Lewis wrote that the attorney was unjust in saying that Nancy was of no use to the estate, "for she is perpetually in the hospital, nurses the children, can bleed, and mix up medicines, and (as I am assured) she is of more service to the sick than all the doctors."[62]

Nurses were appointed to care for the children while their mothers labored at their assigned tasks. Laurel-Hill plantation in Trinidad was very well off in this respect, according to Mrs. A. C. Carmichael, the proprietor's wife. "Patience was really patient," she wrote, "both by name and nature; and many a merry song and dance, she sang and danced to the 'little niggers,' as she called them; and when one or two began first to walk, she was as proud as possible to exhibit them, and all the little tricks she had taught them."[63]

That infirm and superannuated men and women were usually selected by planters as hospital and childrens' doctors and nurses was deplorable to certain white doctors. Richard Madden, M.D., was asked by a select committee of the House of Commons in 1836, "Who are the persons who are usually selected as hothouse doctors?" He replied, "They are generally infirm negroes, generally selected for being persons incapable of working in the field, and being thought superior in intelligence to the generality of negroes." Madden went on to say that hothouse doctors were appointed by attorneys and overseers and worked directly under the supervision of white doctors without receiving anything more than some additional allowances.[64] Black nurses, according to Dr. Collins, commonly lacked the strength and character to command the respect of the sick and to insure their obedience. Nursing was of such importance that the best black woman in the gang was not too good for the office, Collins believed. "Pains should be taken to instruct her in the use of the simples of the country, which she will soon acquire; the dressing of sores, and the doses of different purges and vomits." Having acquired such skills, the woman would be employed infinitely more advantageously as a nurse than as a fieldworker or in any other occupation.[65]

Data for analyzing the black medical personnel who belonged to one of the wealthiest planters of Jamaica are given in the personal property inventories of the ten properties owned by the late John Tharp. Table 3.1 gives the names, age, country or place of birth, occupation, physical condition, and value in Jamaican currency of the black medical attendants on the Tharp properties in April 1805.

Of the fifty-one black medical attendants on the Tharp properties, thirty-four were female and seventeen male. Ages ranged from 24 to 65, with the average or mean being 36.8 and the median 46. Female attendants averaged 49.4 years; male attendants 36.8. That the attendants were considerably older than all slaves is revealed by Table 3.2, which compares the fifty-one medical slaves on ten Tharp properties with all the slaves on Good Hope estate, where the mean age was 29.3 and the median 30.0.

Table 3.1 shows that there were twenty-eight Creole attendants compared with twenty-three Africans (eleven Eboe, four Coromantee, two Nago, two Chamba, and one each of Mandingo, Banda, Congo, and Moco). Superintending the hospitals were nine hothouse doctors (or doctor men) who ranged in age from 24 to 45. Although the hothouse doctors had a high average value of £154 Jamaican currency, all but three of them were weak, ruptured, or had bad sores; the one male hospital assistant was lame. Compared with the hothouse doctors, the nine female hothouse attendants or

Table 3.1. *Medical slaves on the estates of John Tharp in Jamaica, 24 April 1805*

Name	Age	Country	Occupation	Condition	Value
Good Hope estate (total of 484 slaves)					
Esther	61	Eboe	Nursing children	Weak	£ 10
Betty	52	Nago	Hospital cook	Able	40
Barbara	43	Banda	Hospital cook	Weak	70
Peggy	48	Creole	Midwife	Weak	30
Betty	46	Creole	Attending children	Weak	100
Cuba	52	Creole	Attending yaws children	Weak	5
Sontoo	51	Chamba	Nursing children	Weak	0
Diana	49	Creole	Nursing children	Weak	10
George	24	Creole	Doctor man	Weak	240
Luna	35	Creole	Nursing children	Weak	5
Covey estate (total of 438 slaves)					
Patty	60	Creole	Midwife	Weak	20
Casar	45	Creole	Hothouse doctor	Weak	70
Rachael	40	Creole	Hothouse attendant	Able	180
Samson	58	Creole	Hothouse attendant	Lost a leg	20
Bess	58	Creole	Attending yaws children	Elephantiasis	20
Celia	30	Creole	Hothouse cook	Elephantiasis	50
Lettice	33	Creole	Hothouse cook	Weak	90
Wales estate (total of 349 slaves)					
Will	25	Creole	Hothouse doctor	Able	250
Potosi estate (total of 293 slaves)					
Tower	32	Creole	Hothouse doctor	Able	180
Jenny	34	Eboe	Midwife	Able	140
Lansquenet estate (total of 403 slaves)					
William	30	Creole	Hothouse doctor man	Able	180
Lewis	35	Creole	Hothouse assistant	Lame	40
Dick	35	Creole	Yaws children attendant	Ruptured	100
Prue	50	Creole	Midwife	Weak	50
Rachel	50	Creole	Hothouse attendant	Healthy	100
Nanny	65	Creole	Hothouse attendant	Weak	70
Abigail	40	Eboe	Hothouse cook	Weak	20
Nelly	65	Eboe	Attending children	Weak	30
Sukey	60	Eboe	Attending children	Weak	30
Nanny	55	Coromantee	Attending yaws children	Weak	100

Table 3.1. (cont) *Medical slaves on the estates of John Tharp in Jamaica, 24 April 1805*

Pantre Pant estate (total of 412 slaves)					
Rodney	34	Coromantee	Doctor man	Ruptured	150
Hercules	39	Creole	Hothouse attendant	Ulcerated leg	50
Gift	48	Creole	Attending yaws negroes	Weak	100
Jonny	49	Coromantee	Hothouse cook	Weak	30
Princess	39	Eboe	Hothouse attendant	Weak	30
Nancy	49	Creole	Children's nurse	Weak	70
Merrywood estate (total of 221 slaves)					
Gift	27	Eboe	Hothouse man	Bad sores	120
Rosanna	60	Creole	Hothouse woman	Weak	70
Stella	55	Creole	Midwife	Weak	0
Chloe	56	Nago	Cook for children	Incurable sores	0
Kitty	60	Congo	Cook for children	Weak	0
Windsor penn (total of 214 slaves)					
Chance	45	Moco	Hothouse doctor	Weak	100
Billy	30	Creole	Hothouse attendant	Bad sores	100
Bess	50	Eboe	Children's cook	Weak	40
Nancy	58	Eboe	Attending yaws negroes	Weak	10
Top Hill penn (total of 67 slaves)					
Handfull	38	Creole	Attending hothouse	Weak	150
Nanny	48	Eboe	Attending children	Weak	40
Jenny	46	Mandingo	Nurse for children	Swelled knees	50
Chippenham Park penn (total of 109 slaves)					
Tom	32	Chamba	Hothouse man	Ruptured	100
Bell	30	Eboe	Midwife	Insane	0
Princess	50	Coromantee	Midwife	Weak	30

Source: Jamaica Archives, Spanish Town, *Inventorys*, Vol. 104, ff. 33–74, Personal Property Inventory of the Estate of John Tharp in the Parishes of Trelawny and Saint Ann, Jamaica, 24 April 1805.

nurses were older (ranging from 30 to 65 years), less healthy (only one was able), and lower valued (average £85 11s. Jamaican currency). Six women served as hospital cooks, ranging in age from 30 to 50; all but one were weak or had elephantiasis, and they were valued at an average of £50.

Presiding at the birth of infants and caring for the children were twenty-five (approximately half) of the attendants on the Tharp properties. Of the seven midwives who ranged in age from 30 to 60 and whose average value

Table 3.2. *Age distribution of slave medical attendants and all slaves on Good Hope estate*

Age	Medical slaves on all Tharp properties (%)	All slaves on Good Hope estate (%)
0–39	35.3	69.8
40–60	58.8	26.1
Over 60	5.9	4.1

Source: Same as for Table 3.1; Michael Craton, "Jamaican Slave Mortality: Fresh Light from Worthy Park, Longville and the Tharp Estates," *The Journal of Caribbean History*, Vol. 3 (November 1971), p. 7.

was £38 17*s*., only one was physically able or healthy. Five were weak and one insane. Ten women nursed or attended the children. They ranged in age from 35 to 65, all but one was weak and that one had swelled knees, and they averaged £34 10*s*. Three other women, aged 50, 54, and 60, served as children's cooks. Two of these cooks were weak and the other had incurable sores. One was valued at £40; the other two were *not* valued. Finally, there were four women and two men who attended yaws children or yaws adults. They ranged in age from 35 to 58, were weak or otherwise indisposed, and averaged nearly £55.

By far the most medical attendants on the Tharp properties were in poor physical condition and valued at less than the average of all plantation slaves. Only seven were listed as able or healthy: three were hothouse doctors, two were nurses or hothouse attendants, and one was a midwife. Their values ranged from £40 to £250, and averaged £178 7*s*. Forty-four attendants were superannuated, weak, or afflicted with various disorders, and their average value was only £55. This compares with the average value of all fifty-one medical slaves of £68 8*s*; seventeen males, £116 10*s*.; thirty-four females, £44 8*s*.; and all 2,990 slaves on the Tharp properties, £98 – all in Jamaican currency. Although it seems incongruous that Good Hope estate had ten attendants for 484 slaves while Wales estate had only one hothouse doctor for 349 slaves, the large hospital on Good Hope estate was intended to serve the medical needs of the slaves on all the Tharp properties.

The planter Thomas Roughley called the black medical attendants on a plantation "a most fearful fraternity, who in the course of the year, may do a great deal of good, or promote and establish an infinite number of disorders."[66] Though it will be shown in Chapter 10 that slave hospitals increased in number, size, and furnishings, there is little evidence of improvement in the skill and physical condition of the black attendants. For example, Dr. Williamson complained of the crude and unhygienic practices of midwives, which he saw as being "barbarous," "cruel," and "ignorant." No action was taken, however, to implement his proposal that the government of Jamaica should establish two or three lying-in hospitals in different parts of the island "at which a professional gentleman ought to instruct a certain number of women from estates to take care of those in childbed."[67] After reviewing a large body of evidence, Dr. Lucille Mair concludes that "it was clearly the accepted policy to give to aging women or young women in frail health who could not labour in the fields, the responsibility of preparing food for the working gang, and for attending mothers, infants, and sick slaves. As a consequence the health needs of the women, children, and patients receiving such services could only be inadequately met."[68]

Whereas we have some knowledge of the blacks who were attached to plantation hospitals and other medical facilities, very little is known about blacks who treated themselves, their families, and friends. Women medical practitioners or lay healers played a key role in dispensing herbal remedies in West Africa. Though few records are extant, it is reasonable to assume that this folk tradition survived the Middle Passage and that black women served as folk healers and nurses in the islands apart from the plantation establishment. One body of indirect evidence consists of modern studies of medicinal plants that are common to Africa and the West Indies, of which some are known to have been brought to the islands in the era of the Atlantic slave trade. About 60 out of 160 species of medicinal plants in Jamaica are known to have been or continue to be used in Africa. For example, Jamaica senna, which is used as a cathartic, is stated to have been introduced into the island by a slave. Kola or bissy nut, which is used in Jamaica for stomach pains, was brought to the island from the Guinea coast. Groundnuts, or peanuts, were often given as food to slaves on voyages from Africa. In Jamaica these nuts were crushed and applied in the form of a poultice to reduce inflammations caused by venomous stings of bees, scorpions, and wasps.[69]

Women have continued to play an important role in Caribbean folk medicine into the twentieth century. Indeed, the heritage of African folk medicine may survive to this day in the balm yard of Mother Rita Forbes of Pedro Plains in the parish of St. Elizabeth, Jamaica. Mother Rita is only two generations removed from slavery; she learned her craft from her mother, Mammy Forbes, who, in turn, was instructed by her mother who was a slave. Mammy Forbes, who died in 1930, was described by Martha Beckwith as "an honest religious mystic who has intuitive skill in diagnosis, knows her herbals, and does not seek to defraud people by means of obeah."[70]

Herbalists or "weedwomen" of the U.S. Virgin Islands were active as late as the 1950s. These women collected, prepared, sold, and prescribed drug plants, which they collected from gardens, fields, and woods and brought to the weekly peasant markets. The weedwoman was widely known throughout the community for her skill and was looked upon with much respect and admiration. In their study of these weedwomen, A. J. Oakes and M. P. Morris list fifty-nine plants that were used by Virgin Islanders as home remedies. In St. Croix they became acquainted with two elderly sisters whose knowledge of medicinal plants was handed down from their mother who was a weedwoman during the Danish ownership of the Virgin Islands. Two others came to St. Croix from the neighboring British islands, bringing with them practices that were strikingly similar to those of the native Virgin Island weedwomen. The authors conclude that although the weedwoman has made valuable contributions to her society, she continued to do so only in areas where the physician was unavailable.[71]

Conclusion

Comparison of black folk medicine in the British West Indies and in the American South reveals some interesting similarities. Both regions had dual systems of health care – that is, treatment of ailing slaves by white doctors, planters, and overseers on the one hand, and self-treatment by blacks on the other hand. Slaves in both regions demonstrated deep hostility toward white doctors and tended to fall back on their own folk remedies. In both regions there were good and bad black medical practitioners. As Todd L. Savitt observes, the black practitioners in antebellum Virginia were "conjure doctors" who used trickery, violence, and poison against their masters and enemies, or they were "root doctors" who were empirics well versed in herb and root medicines made from local plants. As in the West Indies, laws were passed by American legislatures to prohibit the slaves, on pain of death, from administering medicines without the consent of their owners or patients. Notwithstanding these laws, blacks in both regions performed certain medical functions legally. Blacks in Virginia, for example, served as nurses, midwives, surgeons, physicians, and dentists. They dispensed not only white remedies but also, when not under the direct supervision of whites, folk remedies that were passed down privately from generation to generation.[72]

One apparent difference between the islands and the mainland was the tendency for the slaves in the antebellum South to care for their own health needs to a greater extent. Although the white-managed medical establishment on the typical sugar plantation was larger and more highly structured than that on the typical cotton plantation, it can nevertheless be argued that black self-care in the islands was as widespread as that on the mainland. The survival of balm yards and weedwomen in different parts of the West Indies suggests that informal practice was more widespread than the records indicate. It can also be argued that the psychological aspects of black medicine contributed more to the survival of the blacks than any therapeutic benefits that resulted from folk remedies. Black folk medicine made its greatest contribution, according to Eugene D. Genovese, "in its function as an agency for the transmission of black religious sensibility into a defense against the psychological assaults of slavery and racial oppression." In the words of W. E. B. Du Bois, the black doctor in the New World carried on the African tradition in his function as "the healer of the sick, the interpreter of the Unknown, the comforter of the sorrowing, the supernatural avenger of wrong, and the one who rudely but picturesquely expressed the longing, disappointment and resentment of a stolen and oppressed people."[73]

In the following chapter the discussion of African and Afro-West Indian medicine will help explain the disease problems encountered in the Atlantic slave trade, especially from the standpoint of the Guinea surgeons who served on British slave ships.

4

The Guinea surgeons

> A young man, who has no immediate prospect of settling in his profession, is often lured by fair promises to become a surgeon of a Guinea ship; but ere long the bright prospect vanishes, and he finds that he has been cruelly deceived, and deplores, when too late, his degrading situation. If he possesses sensibility, his feelings are constantly on the rack; if his constitution be weak, his health is ruined, and he narrowly escapes with life. His attention to the poor creatures under his care must be unremitted.
>
> Thomas Winterbottom, M.D., 1803[1]

This chapter focuses attention on the Guinea surgeons who treated sick slaves on British vessels engaged in the Atlantic slave trade. Early sections of the chapter are concerned with economic and demographic aspects of the slave trade and slavery, the dimensions of the trade, and West Africa's involvement in it. Questions are raised about the Guinea surgeons, their professional credentials, motivation, and especially the medical services they supplied to slaves. Later sections deal with mortality on the Middle Passage and efforts to reform the medical and other aspects of the trade.

"To buy or to breed"

The failure to produce a self-sustaining slave population was the most striking demographic peculiarity of the slave plantation societies of the Caribbean and other South Atlantic regions. Whereas the slave population of the southern mainland colonies of North America increased by natural means after the early eighteenth century, that of the West Indies had an excess of deaths over births that was made up for by new recruits from Africa. Even after the Atlantic slave trade to the British Caribbean colonies was prohibited in 1807, only the island of Barbados succeeded in increasing its slave population by natural means. Philip Curtin has compiled statistics showing that of all Africans who arrived in the New World during the period of the slave trade (1500–1870), the United States received about 6 percent. Robert Fogel and Stanley Engerman have estimated that the United States contained about one-quarter of the New World slave population in 1825. By contrast, the

British West Indies received 17 percent of all slave imports but had only about 10 percent of the black population in 1825.[2]

Slavery in the British Caribbean colonies falls into three periods with respect to the mix of demographic and economic factors. Early slavery dates from about 1640 with the beginning of the sugar industry in Barbados. It gave way in the late seventeenth and early eighteenth centuries to near-monoculture when slave conditions became harsher and there was more dependence on replacements and additions from Africa. The third stage of slave amelioration and abolition in the late eighteenth and early nineteenth centuries was characterized by outside pressure to encourage family life and reproduction in the effort to create a self-generating labor force in the islands.[3]

Early slavery was perhaps mild by comparison with the institution that developed subsequently. Since slaves represented a large capital investment, were permanent servants, and were few in comparison with white indentured servants, planters tended to assign them to light tasks and provide them with adequate food and other necessities. Richard Ligon, who was in Barbados from 1647 to 1650, wrote that the planters purchased as many female as male slaves, that family life and child rearing were encouraged, and that the slaves were well fed. Early Jamaica planters, according to Richard Blome, purchased as many women as men in order to increase their stock of slaves.[4] In his study of a seventeenth-century Jamaican sugar plantation, J. Harry Bennett finds it surprising that the proprietor did not lose a single slave during two years and eight months when he increased the number to fifty-five. He believes the slaves owed their survival chiefly to the unfinished state of the plantation. The proprietor "was building a stock of Negroes for future use in a fully equipped property; in the meantime the tasks of the slaves must have been comparatively light."[5]

With respect to the duration, exertion, and pace of work, sugar slaves were generally overworked in comparison with cotton, coffee, and tobacco slaves. Moreover, sugar slavery became more strenuous over time because cane lands had to be hoe plowed, planted, fertilized, and weeded more often. Hardships increased with the movement toward monoculture. Cane lands encroached upon pastures and woodlands, with the result that land for pasture and forage for livestock decreased. Planters were thus slow or unwilling to introduce animal-drawn plows and harrows, relying instead on the hoe culture of their slaves. Slaves in the smaller islands were often forced to pick grass for the estate animals. To economize on scarce livestock and pasture, slaves were also given the arduous task of carrying heavy baskets of dung from the feedlots to the cane pieces.[6]

Apart from the toll taken by the Middle Passage and seasoning, overworking and underfeeding were the leading causes of mortality. Richard Pares has written that "many colonies made no laws at all about the feeding of the slaves before the humanitarians forced them into it at the end of the eighteenth century; and even where there were laws, the standards which they enforced were pitiably low." To a considerable extent the slaves fed themselves from their provision grounds, which they cultivated after working hours and on weekends. Hurricanes and droughts frequently destroyed their crops, however, and at times the slaves died of starvation when imported supplies were not forthcoming.[7]

Probably the chief cause of the excess of deaths over births was the low cost of imported slaves. Since the planters generally considered it cheaper to buy new workers than to bear the cost of breeding and raising a slave to working age in the colony, they preferred to import more men than women. Not only did the birthrate decline, but the death rate may also have increased because of hard labor, cruel punishment, malnutrition, epidemics, and accidents. Most of the deaths occurred during the seasoning, for the mortality among new slaves for Africa was higher than that among Creoles or island-born blacks.[8]

The Atlantic slave trade

The Atlantic slave trade involved the maritime nations of Europe in the transfer of millions of black laborers from their homeland to the mines and plantations of the New World. The trade was launched by Portuguese mariners in the middle of the fifteenth century. Sporadic raiding parties in time gave way to the establishment of trading posts and the exchange of European goods for African slaves. Strategically located trading posts were transformed into massive forts and castles occupied by European traders and soldiers and served as concentration points for goods and slaves. Portugal's exclusive claim to the Guinea trade did not go unchallenged. The Dutch conquered much of the Portuguese empire in Africa, Brazil, and the spice islands in the seventeenth century. They carried slaves and European goods to the infant Caribbean colonies established by the French, English, and Danes. In time the maritime nations of northern Europe threw off their dependence on Dutch middleman and began a course of empire building that called for chartered companies to supply slaves to their New World plantations. In the age of mercantilism the Guinea coast and the Middle Passage figured largely in international war and trade. Even after revolutionary wars and humanitarian movements had curtailed certain branches of the slave trade, Africans continued to be transported to Cuba, Puerto Rico, and Brazil until about 1870.

Modern estimates of the number of Africans imported into New World territories during more than four centuries of the trade range from 3.5 million to 25 million. Philip Curtin has surveyed the literature on the slave trade

Table 4.1. *Estimated slave imports into the British Caribbean colonies*

Jamaica	747,500
Barbados	387,000
Leeward Islands	346,000
St. Vincent, St. Lucia, Tobago, and Dominica	70,100
Grenada	67,000
Trinidad	22,400
Other British Caribbean colonies	25,000
Total	1,665,000

Source: Philip D. Curtin, *The Atlantic Slave Trade: A Census* (Madison: University of Wisconsin Press, 1969), p. 268.

and used statistical methods not only to approximate total numbers but also to differentiate among centuries, sources of supply, European trading countries, and receiving colonies and countries. Curtin's estimate of total slave imports into the Americas from 1451 to 1870 is 9,566,100.[9] Curtin's estimate has undergone substantial upward revision, however, by the research of J. E. Inikori, J. F. Ade Ajayi, Robert Stein, David Eltis, and James A. Rawley, whose estimates range from 11.3 to 15.4 million slaves imported into the New World. For the British Caribbean colonies, Rawley has raised Curtin's estimate of 1,665,000 to 2,443,000. On the other hand, Paul E. Lovejoy contends that Curtin's initial tabulation was remarkably accurate.[10]

According to Curtin's estimate, only 2.9 percent of the slaves arrived from 1451 to 1600. The percentage increased to 14.0 from 1601 to 1700, to 63.3 from 1701 to 1810, and then declined to 19.8 from 1811 to 1870. The British Caribbean colonies took a total of 1,665,000 slaves, or 17.4 percent, and ranked second among the eight regions and countries of import. Brazil ranked first with an estimated total of 3,646,800 slaves.[11] Table 4.1 gives Curtin's estimates for the British Caribbean colonies.

Jamaica took 44.8 percent of the African slaves who were imported legally into the British Caribbean colonies. Table 4.2, which is based on data compiled by the author and differs somewhat from those presented by Curtin, shows that total imports amounted to 911,696, reexports to 193,288, and retained imports to 630,408. The percentage retained ranged from 58.6 in the first quarter of the eighteenth century to 88.0 from 1801 to 1808; the average was 69.1. During the eighteenth century imports and retained imports were highest in the last quarter, whereas reexports were highest in the second quarter when the South Sea Company made Jamaica its chief base for supplying the Spanish colonies with slaves under the Asiento agreement of 1713. An annual average of thirteen vessels brought human cargoes to

Table 4.2. *Jamaica's slave trade, 1655–1808*[a]

Years	Number imported	Number exported	Number retained	Percent retained
1655–1701[b]	88,000	n.d.	n.d.	
1702–25	120,788	50,001	70,787	58.6
1726–50	182,071	59,395	122,676	67.4
1751–75	194,867	27,571	167,296	85.9
1776–1800[c]	262,949	48,750	214,199	81.5
1801–8	63,021	7,571	55,450	88.0
Total	911,696	193,288	630,408	69.1[d]

[a]Data for 1702–1808 are taken chiefly from the records kept to assess the duties levied on slaves imported into and exported from Jamaica. They are lower-bound figures, since numerous slaves were reportedly smuggled into and out of Jamaica to avoid the duties.
[b]Estimate.
[c]No data for 1788.
[d]For 1702–1808. The trade was prohibited after March 1, 1808.
Source: Period 1655–1701: R. B. LePage, "An Historical Introduction to Jamaican Creole," in R. B. LePage, ed., *Jamaican Creole* (London, 1960), pp. 69–76, 80.

Period 1702–75: Public Record Office, London, *C.O.* 137/38, Hh 3, 4: appendix to a memorial from Stephen Fuller, agent for Jamaica, to the Board of Trade, January 30, 1788. Two other copies of this report with some variance in the numbers imported and exported can be found in the Long Papers in the British Library; see British Library, *Add. MS.* 12,435, ff. 27–30.

Period 1776–87: British Library, *Add. MS.* 12,435, ff. 37–39; the Papers of Edward Long of Jamaica and England.

Period 1789–98: *British Parliamentary Papers*, 1803/4, Vol. X, p. 175–39G, report of David Innes, naval officer at Kingston, Jamaica, November 14, 1799; Enclosure No. 13 to the Earl of Balcarres's letter of March 22, 1800.

Period 1799–1800: *British Parliamentary Papers*, 1801/2, Vol. IV, No. 653, pp. 50–51, Abstract of the Slave Imports and Exports of the British West Indies.

Period 1801–8: *Journals of the Assembly of Jamaica*, Vol. XII, November 23, 1815, p. 825.

Jamaica in the first decade of the century; the figure increased irregularly to thirty-five in the last five years of the century.[12]

Comparing Tables 4.2 and 4.3, we see that the slave population of Jamaica increased by less than the increase in retained slave imports. In fact, some 575,000 new laborers were needed during the eighteenth century to increase the population by about 250,000.

Bryan Edwards, the Jamaican planter-historian, sought to determine the origin and character of the slaves brought to the West Indies from the African

Table 4.3. *Jamaica's slave population and slave imports, selected years, 1703–1800*

Year	Estimated slave population	Net slave imports (annual average)	Net imports as a percent of population
1703	45,000	2,660	5.9
1730	75,000	5,500	7.3
1750	115,000	4,960	4.3
1775	200,000	10,500	5.3
1800	300,000	11,400	3.8

Source: Same as for Table 3.2; R. B. LePage, ed., *Jamaican Creole* (London: Macmillan, 1960), p. 74; George Roberts, *The Population of Jamaica* (Cambridge: Cambridge University Press, 1957), pp. 36–8.

coast between Senegambia in the northwest and Angola in the southeast. These peoples included the Mandingoes, the Koromantyns, the Pawpaws and Nagoes, the Eboes and Mocoes, and slaves from the Congo and Angola. The Mandingoes, who came from Senegambia and the Windward Coast, were mainly Mohammedans. They prided themselves on their literacy and were, in Edwards's opinion, gentle of disposition but much given to theft and "not well adapted for hard labour." The Koromantyn, or Gold Coast natives, were firm of body and mind, ferocious, brave, stubborn, and capable fieldworkers under managers they respected. From the "slave coast" between the Volta and Lagos rivers came the Pawpaws and Nagoes. Edwards said they were "unquestionable the most docile and best-disposed Slaves that are imported from any part of Africa." The Eboes and Mocoes came from the Bight of Benin. They were described as timid and prone to suicide. The blacks from the Congo and Angola were fitter for domestic service than for field labor; they also became expert mechanics. These, of course, are the crude and not unbiased characterizations of a leading planter-historian. Modern studies show how the origins of the slaves changed over time.[13]

West Africa and the slave trade

As Eric Williams points out in his brilliant essay, *Capitalism and Slavery*, the slave trade to the British Caribbean colonies was part of the larger British trade, which in large measure conformed to a triangle. British manufacturers, foodstuffs, liquor, and other goods were shipped to West Africa where they were bartered primarily for slaves and secondarily for gold dust, ivory, dying woods, gums, and drugs. Foodstuffs, water, and wood fuel were taken on board with the slaves who were carried on the second leg of the triangle, known as the Middle Passage, chiefly to the West Indies and to a lesser degree the North American colonies. On the third leg of the triangle the slaves were exchanged for sugar, coffee, rice, indigo, tobacco, and dying woods, which were transported back to the home port. After about 1760, however, the slavers commonly returned from the West Indies in ballast or with a quickly gathered cargo, carrying the proceeds to the slave sales largely in the form of sterling bills of exchange.[14]

Though profits were at times handsome and even exorbitant, risk and uncertainty plagued the merchants and mariners engaged in the triangle trade. One analysis of the factors making for success was done by John Atkins, a surgeon in the royal navy:

> The success of a Voyage depends first on the well sorting, and on the well timing of a Cargo. Secondly, in a knowledge of the places of Trade, what, and how much may be expected every where. Thirdly, in dramming well with English Spirits, and conforming to the Humours of the Negroes. Fourthly, in timely furnishing proper Food for the Slaves. Fifthly, in Dispatch; and Lastly, the good Order and Management of Slaves when on board.[15]

The cargoes sent to Africa, wrote Edward Long, the Jamaican planter-historian, consisted of "a great variety of woolen goods; a cheap sort of fire-arms from Birmingham, Sheffield, and other places; powder, bullets, iron bars, copper bars, brass pans, malt spirits, tallow, tobacco-pipes, Manchester goods, glass beads." Also included were "some particular kind of linens, ironmongery and cutlery ware; certain toys, some East India goods, but, in the main, with very little that is not of British growth, or manufacture."[16] Missing from Long's list are the casks of rum and brandy to be dispensed as gifts or bribes to important persons, horse beans and other foodstuffs to feed the crew and slaves, potable water, medicines, wines, and special foods for the sick. One study shows that in the 1790s the average voyage time from England to the coast of Africa was 85.6 days.[17]

The best sources for the study of the British slave trade are the reports of the Privy Council and the committee of the House of Commons of 1789–91, which grew out of the agitation of the Society for the Abolition of the African Slave Trade.[18] These committees interrogated individuals who were concerned in or had knowledge of the slave trade and colonial slavery. Included among them were masters and mates of slave vessels, medical doctors who treated slaves on ship and shore, slave merchants and factors, colonial officials, military officers, planters, and clergymen. Among other things, these individuals were interrogated about the size or tonnage of slave ships, the manner of fitting up the ships, provisions and medicines that were taken on board, the means by which the slaves were procured in Africa, the treatment of slaves on the Middle Passage, slave mortality and its causes, and the manner of selling the slaves in the West Indies.[19]

The Privy Council committee heard much testimony concerning the methods by which slaves were obtained in Africa, or "the general manner of making slaves." Sir George Young of the Royal Navy made inquiries during his stay on the coast and ventured to rank the methods as follows:

> First, as Prisoners of War, and these, he thinks, are the greatest Number. Secondly, such as are supposed to have been guilty of Crimes. Thirdly, those who are panyared, which is the Country Term for kidnapping, or seizing by Force or Treachery. Fourthly, such as are seized by the Kings, and sold when they are in want of European Commodities.[20]

Mungo Park, the great African explorer, estimated that the slaves in Africa nearly outnumbered the free people by three to one. The greater number were domestic slaves who were treated more leniently than those who were purchased with money. The master's authority over these slaves extended only to reasonable correction. The sale of domestic slaves was generally restricted to those condemned for crimes, although the master was permitted to sell one or more of his domestics to purchase provisions for his family if it was threatened by famine, and in the case of the master's insolvency, his slaves were likely to be sold for the payment of his debts.[21]

Park divided the slaves who were brought from the interior of Africa into two distinct classes; "*first*, such as were slaves from their birth, having been born of enslaved mothers; *secondly*, such as were born free, but who afterwards, by whatever means, become slaves." Those of the first description were by far the more numerous. He said that slaves of the second description generally became so by one of the following causes: captivity, famine, insolvency, and crimes. By the established custom of Africa, a free person became a slave by being taken in war. Park affirmed that war was, of all others, the most productive source of slaves. As for famine, he observed that there were many instances of free people voluntarily surrendering their liberty to save their lives during famines. Moreover, parents of large families who were exposed to absolute want frequently sold some of their children to purchase provisions for the rest. Creditors not only had a claim on the property of debtors, "but even the insolvent himself, is sold to satisfy the lawful demands of his creditors." Finally, free men and women who were convicted of such crimes as murder, robbery, adultery, and witchcraft were generally sold into slavery. Park described slaves in the Gambia as follows:

> Most of these unfortunate victims are brought to the coast in periodical caravans; many of them from very remote inland countries...On their

> arrival at the coast, if no immediate opportunity offers of selling them to advantage, they are distributed among the neighbouring village, until a slave-ship arrives, or until they can be sold to black traders, who sometimes purchase on speculation. In the meanwhile, the poor wretches are kept constantly fettered, two and two of them being chained together, and employed in the labours of the field; and, I am sorry to add, are very scantily fed, as well as harshly treated.[22]

John Atkins described two methods of trade on the coast of Africa: factory trade and boat trade. A factory was a storehouse where a permanent supply of European goods was kept on hand to exchange for slaves, a barracoon was a stockade or prison for slaves awaiting sale to European slavers, and a trade castle or fort combined the features of the factory and barracoon. Furthermore, the trade castle or fort was guarded by European troops and was frequently under the control of a chartered company. Factories, barracoons, and forts were places of considerable trade, wrote Atkins, "keeping always a number of Slaves against those demands of the Interlopers, who, they are sensible, want dispatch, and therefore make them pay a higher Price for it than any where on the whole Coast." Other ships brought two or three boats with them, and while the mates went away in them with goods to exchange for slaves, local traders brought slaves on board to negotiate their sale to the captain. By these and other methods, the time for trading was shortened, since delays resulted in sickness and mortality among the slaves and crew and heavy charges for wages, food, and medical attendance. Liquor played no small role in the success of a slaving voyage because the black traders, it was said, never cared to do business with dry lips.[23]

Slavers seldom completed their business on the coast in less than four or five weeks and they were sometimes delayed for a year or longer. The study referred to shows that British ships were on the coast for an average of 114.2 days in the 1790s.[24] Occasionally, a full cargo of slaves could be obained at one trading fort or factory, but more often the vessel called at several trading centers to exchange European goods for slaves, gold, ivory, gums, and rare woods. The captains of slave vessels were aided by Africans and mulattoes, who acted as middlemen and translators in dealing with African leaders. Both sides drove hard bargains, which generally included presents of liquor or goods to the African heads. Both firearms and strong drink were vital commodities in the slave trade. Indeed, Walter Rodney has written that "African rulers found themselves selling slaves to get guns to catch slaves to buy more guns. This can be described as a 'vicious circle.' "[25]

More male slaves were purchased than females. Planters generally preferred to purchase young men who were capable of sustained field labor rather than females who were periodically idled by pregnancy and child care. In Africa, fewer females than males were offered for sale by black

Table 4.4. *Male and female slave imports, Jamaica, 1764–74, 1779–84*

	Males	Females	Total
Total of 121 cargoes	25,893	15,732	41,625
Percent of total	62.2	37.8	100.0

Source: British Parliamentary Papers, Vol. XXVI, 1789, No. 646a, Part III, Jamaica Appendix: "Report of the Lords of the Committee for Trade and Plantations on the Slave Trade."

traders. This was because it was customary for men to have several wives and women were highly valued as cultivators of the soil. Moreover, women were less likely to run away and commit crimes, which were punishable by enslavement and sale.[26] The number of males and females imported and sold by four Jamaican slave merchants, as shown in the Privy Council report, is shown in Table 4.4. The marked dominance of both males and adults is underscored by the statistics compiled by Herbert S. Klein. From a sample of 49,884 slaves imported into Jamaica in 149 ships from 1791 to 1798, he calculates that 57.5 percent were men, 35.5 percent women, 4.3 percent boys, and 2.7 percent girls.[27]

Modern scholarship sheds light on the observations made by Europeans who visited West Africa in the period of the slave trade. Not only have the cargoes sent from England to West Africa been examined, but also it has been shown how Africans, in their capacity as consumers of imported trade goods, affected relationships with Europeans.[28] Firearms and liquor had the malevolent effect of destroying and enslaving Africans. In his investigation of the import of firearms into West Africa, J. E. Inikori finds that between 283,000 and 397,000 guns were imported per year, and there was a strong connection betweeen guns and the acquisition of slaves.[29]

The exchange of European and American goods for slaves, gold, ivory, and other African commodities involved large numbers of middlemen who maintained trading posts, bought and sold goods, granted credit, arranged transport and storage, and performed other functions. Numerous studies have added to our understanding of such topics as the patterns of slave marketing, commercial and financial organization, transport, and the activities of middlemen.[30]

As to the methods of "making slaves," one recent study of the delivery of slaves from the central Sudan to the Bight of Benin finds that slaves were acquired chiefly by capture, as payment of tribute, by purchase, and by chiefs who made free gifts of slaves to favorites who eventually sold some of them. Because of their economic usefulness, a large proportion of the slaves from the central Sudan were retained within the forest zone and not taken to the European slave merchants on the coast.[31] Another study calls attention to the records of interviews conducted in the 1850s by a European linguist among slaves released and brought to Sierra Leone. Of those interviewed, 34 percent said they had been taken in war, 30 percent had been kidnapped, 11 percent admitted to having been sold after being condemned by judicial process, 7 percent were sold by relatives and superiors, and 18 percent gave no specific cause of enslavement.[32]

Among the topics of some controversy among researchers of Africa are the origins of slavery, the scope and nature of indigenous systems of slavery, the role of female slaves, and the impact of the Atlantic slave trade on economy and society of West Africa. Since it is not directly relevant to our study, we will pass over the question of slavery origins. Indigenous or "domestic" slavery has attracted the attention of both anthropologists and historians. Some maintain that African societies were receptive to all opportunities for bringing outsiders into their midst as dependents and retainers, and that most of the acquired outsiders fell between the extremes of Africans who were captured or bought for sale as chattels and those whose descendants functioned as quasi-kinsmen as well as units of productive labor. Igor Kopytoff and Suzanne Miers see the roots of African servile institutions "in the need for wives and children, the wish to enlarge one's kin group, and the desire to have clients, dependents, servants, and retainers."[33] A study by Jack Goody shows that women captives in Africa were usually kept by their captors for reproduction and labor. To a large extent they became the mates, and specifically the legitimate sexual partners, of free men. Thus, far fewer females than males were offered for sale and they generally commanded higher prices.[34]

Studies by modern historians that minimize the impact of the slave trade on the people of West Africa have given way to more recent studies that take a more critical look at this impact.[35] In their cost–benefit analysis of the West African economy, Henry A. Gemery and Jan S. Hogendorn find that "even under the most favorable assumptions the eighteenth-century Atlantic slave trade subjected West Africa to long-term economic losses even if the enormous social costs of the trade are not considered." They contend that the welfare of West African society as a whole deteriorated during its centuries-long involvement in the trade.[36] Among other losses, countless numbers of captives failed to survive the shock of imprisonment, malnutrition, and epidemic disease that was their fate during long marches in slave coffles and confinement in crowded and filthy coastal barracoons awaiting the arrival of slavers.[37]

The Guinea surgeons

Guinea is the European name of a portion of the west coast of Africa, extending from Sierra Leone to Benin. Guinea surgeons treated sick and ailing slaves under conditions that were abominable by any standard. They were intimately involved with the miserable wretches who were crowded together in dark, hot, and stinking compartments. What manner of medical men braved the hazards of a Guinea voyage? What compensation could they expect? What education and training did they receive? How were they recruited? What duties did they perform before sailing on the first and second legs of the triangle voyage? What diseases were prevalent among the slaves on the Middle Passage? How were these diseases treated and with what effect? What medical measures were taken to reduce the mortality of slaves on the Middle Passage? Was the decline in mortality the result of increased government regulation or other factors? How important was pre-embarkation and post-debarkation mortality in relation to mortality on the Middle Passage? Government reports and other printed and manuscript materials will be drawn upon in an effort to answer these questions.

Nautical medicine developed as a specialty in the age of maritime discovery, colonial expansion, and international trade. Ship design changed to accommodate heavy artillery, which constricted the living quarters of seamen, immigrants, and slaves. Such innovations as the Portuguese caravel, mariner's compass, and astrolabe made possible long voyages to remote islands and continents. Problems of food preservation led to an overdependence on salted meat, which, in turn, resulted in the sea diseases of scurvy, fevers, and fluxes or dysentery. Europeans not only "discovered" new lands and peoples, but they also encountered strange and frightening diseases. On most long voyages Europeans did not encounter exotic disease environments until they reached their destination. If they sailed to North America they ran little risk of contracting diseases from the Indians who were thinly dispersed over the continent. But the Atlantic slave trade combined the above-mentioned elements of congestion, dietary imbalance, and multiple disease environment in a potentially lethal mixture. The trade was unique in linking the three disease environments of Northern Europe, Africa south of the Sahara, and the West Indies.[38]

Surgeons in the Guinea trade were motivated primarily by economic gain and secondarily by humanitarian concerns. This was underscored by Thomas Aubrey, M.D., who in 1729 published a little book, *The Sea Surgeon, or the Guinea Man's Vade Mecum*, which was written for the use of young surgeons in the Guinea trade. Surgeons were admonished to preserve the slaves committed to their care.

> The more you preserve of them for the Plantations the more Profit you will have, and also the greater Reputation and Wages another voyage. Besides it's a Case of Conscience to be careful of them as the White Men. For although they are Heathens yet have they a rational Soul as

well as us, and God knows whether it may not more tollerable for them in the latter Day than for many who profess themselves Christians.[39]

Since the compensation of Guinea surgeons varied according to the number of slaves delivered alive in the colonies, surgeons had an interest in the financial outcome of ventures, which in large measure depended on the health of slaves. Surgeons were generally supplied by owners with medicines and surgical instruments. They commonly received a monthly salary plus several perquisites. Captain James Fraser, who commanded several ships from Bristol in the African trade, testified in 1790 that the surgeon was paid "head money" of one shilling for each slave who was sold, and also the right to the proceeds from "privilege slaves." The latter perquisite, which also went to the first mate, consisted of two slaves, one male and one female, "allowed them in consideration for their care and trouble in the management of Slaves on board the ship."[40] Further incentives were incorporated in Dolben's Act of 1788, by which surgeons received a premium of £50 if mortality on the Middle Passage did not exceed 2 percent, or £25 if losses did not exceed 3 percent.[41]

Surgeon John Tebay's income and expenses, including cash paid for his coffin and funeral fees, have been extracted from the list of expenses of the ship *Lottery* of 1798 as follows:[42]

Case of medicines	£22 15*s.* 10*d.*
Surgeon's instruments	3 10*s.* 0*d.*
To John Tebay, Surgeon, pay	6 guineas a month
To John Tebay, Surgeon, for his privilidge of 2 slaves on an average of £92.2.3¼	184 4*s.* 6½*d.*
Funeral fees for Dr. Tebay	5 15*s.* 5*d.*
Cash paid for coffin for ditto	14 0*s.* 0*d.*

Surgeon Tebay's fatal experience – he died before he was eligible for the head money – was common enough to have served as a deterrent to others. The prospect of gain appears to have more than offset the estimation of risk and uncertainty, however, especially when alternatives were closed to surgeons.

Demand and supply factors influenced the recruitment of surgeons. Dr. Falconbridge stated that "surgeons employed in the Guinea trade are generally driven to engage in so disagreeable an employ by the confined state of their finances."[43] Guinea surgeons were in short supply during war time when the navy made large demands on available personnel; conversely, supply mushroomed at the onset of peace. When Archibald Dalzel was mustered out to the navy at London in 1763, he wrote to his brother in Scotland of the great number of surgeons and surgeon's mates who had been applying for places since the peace was concluded. Lacking money and experience, he ruled out practicing medicine in Scotland and England, or going as a surgeon to West India or straits ships. "Guinea is the only place that I have a probability of raising myself in. It is to be sure very warm there, but as to the unwholesomeness of it, I am inclined to believe it is far from being so great as some represent."[44]

Generally the prospective surgeon or physician was apprenticed to a practitioner for several years before rounding off his training at a hospital or university. Tobias Smollett, the novelist, served his apprenticeship as apothecary and surgeon before becoming a naval surgeon. Roderick Random, his fictional counterpart, applied to Surgeon Launcelot Crab who needed an apprentice. Random told him that he understood a little pharmacy and had studied surgery with great pleasure and application when he lived with Mr. Potion. Crab ridiculed the idea that surgery could be studied. He underscored the practical side of medical education when he demanded, "Can you bleed and give a clyster, spread a plaster, and prepare a potion?"[45]

Surgeons were commissioned after examination at Surgeons' Hall in London. When Random appeared there the first question put to him was, "Where was you born?" To which he answered, "In Scotland." "In Scotland," said the examiner, "I know that very well; we have scarce any other countrymen to examine here; you Scotchmen have overspread us of late as the locusts did Egypt." When the examiner learned that the term of Random's apprenticeship was only three years, he fell into a violent passion and swore that it was a shame and a scandal to send raw boys into the world as surgeons, pointing out that every apprentice in England was bound to seven years at least. After he satisfied his examiners, Random received his qualification sealed up and took it to the Navy Office, where he applied for a commission as surgeon's third mate on a man-of-war.[46]

The British slave trade attracted some surgeons of high qualification and talent, even if the overall level of professional attainment may have been low. Surgeons in the Royal Navy who participated in the trade included Thomas Trotter, M.D., Robert Jackson, M.D., James Arnold, Isaac Wilson, Ecroide Claxton, and Archibald Dalzel. Dalzel was, among other things, director of the British fort at Whydah, governor of Cape Coast Castle on the Gold Coast, and author of *The History of Dahomy* (1793). Although his business ventures seldom met with success, he surpassed most of the eighteenth-century slave traders and Guinea surgeons in intellectual training.[47] Isaac Wilson testified in 1790 that he was educated at Trinity College, Dublin, at Edinburgh, and Glasgow, and had been examined and qualified by the surgeons of London at Surgeons' Hall. He was principal surgeon of the ship *Elizabeth*, which carried 602 slaves, out of which 155 were lost during the voyage.[48] Mungo Park returned to England from his exploration of the interior of Africa by way of the West Indies, serving as surgeon on a North American slaver.[49]

Thomas Trotter, M.D. (1760–1832), was one of the most distinguished naval surgeons of his time. He joined the navy as surgeon's mate in 1779 at the age of nineteen. At the end of the War of American Independence in 1783, he sailed from Liverpool as surgeon of the ship *Brooke*. During a stay of about ten months on the coast of Africa a cargo of more than 600 slaves was taken on board, and on the Middle Passage to Jamaica about seventy were lost. Trotter made only this one slave voyage, an experience he recalled with profound distaste. In 1786 he published his *Observations on Scurvy* and two years later took his medical degree at Edinburgh. He rose to the post of physician of the fleet. In 1802 he retired to private practice at Newcastle upon Tyne, where he died in 1832.[50]

Surgeons testified on behalf of both pro- and antislavery organizations at the investigations of 1789–91. In support of the African merchants were Archibald Dalzel and John Anderson, who was a surgeon before he became master in command of slave ships. Other surgeons were marshaled as witnesses by Thomas Clarkson, leader of the Society for the Suppression of the Slave Trade. These were Alexander Falconbridge, Thomas Trotter, Isaac Wilson, Ecroide Claxton, and James Arnold. Arnold was a naval surgeon before he served as surgeon's mate on the slave ship *Alexander* in 1783. On the next voyage he joined the *Little Pearl*. In 1787, when he was about to sail on a third voyage, he met Clarkson at Bristol and agreed to keep a personal diary of the voyage, which Clarkson later used in his crusade against the slave trade.[51]

Foremost among the medical supporters of the Antislavery Society was Alexander Falconbridge. After his medical training at Bristol and London he made four slave voyages between 1780 and 1787. Returning to Bristol in 1787 he met Thomas Clarkson, who was later to write, "I can hardly say how precious I considered the facts with which Mr. Falconbridge has furnished me from his own experience, relative to the different branches of this commerce."[52] The two men traveled to Liverpool to collect more facts on the slave trade. In London they worked together to plan the submission of evidence to government bodies. Falconbridge wrote that on his last slave voyage he became convinced that it was "an unnatural, iniquitous and villainous trade and I could not reconcile it to my conscience." His *Account of the Slave Trade*, of which 3,000 copies were printed, was described by Dr. John Lettsom, a leading London physician who was born in the West Indies, as "a sensible, well-written publication against the Slave Trade."[53]

Duties on the coast

Though no clear line of responsibility was established, Guinea surgeons had certain duties to perform at the port of embarkation. Dr. Aubrey urged surgeons to speak boldly to the owners and captains for adequate supplies of food, medicines, brandy, and tobacco and pipes, saying that it was much better for the owners to incur extra expenses of one hundred pounds than to lose more than half their slaves, "since the Death of a very few will be upwards of the Money out of their way." Before going on board the surgeon should encourage the owners to direct the captain, "and that in your Presence, to leave the Management of the Slaves wholly to your Care in all respects, according as you find it necessary to feed and physick them." Aubrey warned the surgeon not to begin a voyage without such authority, since his reputation depended on his success in preserving the health of the slaves. He should "nourish them well, deal kindly with them, and divert them often with Drum, Dancing, &c. in order to dissipate the sorrowfull Thoughts of quitting their own native Country, Friends, and Relations."[54]

Of course, practice frequently fell short of precept. Food, medicines, and other supplies for the Middle Passage sometimes ran out. The welfare of the slaves suffered in other ways when masters and surgeons quarreled and worked at cross-purposes. One surgeon wrote from the coast of Africa to the ship's owner in Bristol that the apothecary had fitted out his medicine chest in a "most scandalous Manner, his Tartar Emetic and many more of his Medicines are worth nothing. If I had not provided myself with a little quantity of my own I should have been in a poor situation."[55] The same surgeon also quarreled with his captain over the management of slaves. From Kingston, Jamaica, he wrote to the owner in Bristol: "I am certain I did more than my Duty as Surgeon on Board; should I ever sail out again to Africa, I will have my own instructions from a Merch[an]t and have nothing to do with a Capt[ain]. They are a set of overbearing men."[56] Captains, in return, complained of incompetent and unruly surgeons; one captain wrote that his surgeon was too fond of liquor to expect any good of him.[57]

Dr. Trotter was interrogated at some length by the committee of the House of Commons regarding the differences he had with Captain Clement Noble of the *Brooke*. In reply to the question, "Did he ever complain to you of your inattention towards the Slaves?" Trotter replied, "He certainly very frequently accused me of ignorance in my profession." Trotter said he was thwarted by the captain in exercising his profession, particularly with regard to the medicines he prescribed for slaves who had fluxes, "and in violent bursts of anger he swore they fell victims to my medicines." The scurvy broke out among the slaves before they left the coast of Africa. Trotter urged his captain to lay in a stock of limes and oranges, but his opinion was treated with contempt. Many slaves died of scurvy, and many more were tainted with this disease when the ship arrived at Antigua where quantities of limes and oranges were taken on board for the voyage to Jamaica. Even the rapid recovery of the slaves failed to convince the captain, who attributed every misfortune to "the machinations of the doctor and devil."[58]

The physical inspection of slaves offered for sale occupied the surgeon during the stay on the coast. Surgeons and captains were instructed to be very careful in their choice of slaves. They should purchase only merchantable slaves who were free from sickness, distempers, ruptures, and loss of limbs. Aubrey held it absolutely necessary that surgeons inspect all slaves before they were bought, and especially those with venereal diseases and ulcers. Slaves hid their imperfections, he said, fearing that they would be punished or starved if they were rejected by potential buyers.[59] Among those rejected, wrote Falconbridge, were slaves with bad eyes or teeth, those who were "lame, or weak in the joints, or distorted in the back, or of a slender make, or are narrow in the chest."[60] Arnold explained that "the slaves are examined to see if they are physically fit, have healthy eyes, good teeth, stand over four feet high, and if men, are not ruptured; if females, have not 'fallen breasts.' "[61]

Surgeons were also occupied during the stay on the coast with caring for slaves taken on board and advising their masters to purchase additional supplies of food and water. Surgeons, especially those who were new to the trade, were often baffled by diseases they were unable to diagnose and treat and by slaves who refused to eat or take medicine. The captain of one Bristol slaver wrote to the owner from Bonny Island that one woman who had been sent ashore to recover from an illness was now mending fast.

> When we have trusty persons with whom we can lodge a sick slave I think it is the best method, for our surgeons are so little acquainted with their modes of life & their habits which are so extremely different from ours & the effect of their food which appears from what I can learn to be almost entirely vegetable, that either not understanding how these circumstances operate upon the constitution or not considering them they scarcely ever treat them with propriety.[62]

Similarly, Aubrey wrote that it was necessary to become acquainted with the nature, constitution, and accustomed manner of living of Africans, so as to better qualify the Guinea surgeons for preserving their health and restoring them when afflicted.[63]

Few men could have met with more misery on the coast than did William Chancellor, surgeon of the sloop *Wolf,* which sailed from New York in September 1749 for Africa. Darold D. Wax writes that he "experienced nearly all that a slaving voyage to Africa had to offer: disputes with his captain, slaves who were sick and frequently died, a serious slave mutiny, and bloody encounters with foreigners, all stretched over more than a year of slaving on the coast." The *Wolf* took on 135 slaves during the fourteen-month stay on the coast. Sixty died or were traded before the sloop departed for New York.[64]

Diseases and their treatment

Although a few slavers made the Middle Passage without the death of a single slave, all had sick slaves to be cared for and many were at times pesthouses in which epidemics raged beyond the capacity of the surgeon to cure. It was the duty of the surgeon to go below every morning to ascertain the health and welfare of the slaves. Those found to be sick were generally removed to a separate apartment, called the hospital or sick berth, where they were cared for by the surgeon and his assistants. According to the testimony of Captain John Anderson, himself a former Guinea surgeon, there was always a surgeon on board. If the men were sick they were immediately taken out of their shackles, "and the Surgeon attends them, who administers every Relief by Medicine or otherwise – the same Care is taken of the Women when they are sick."[65] Robert Norris, a captain of slave ships, testified that there was always a surgeon and sometimes two. Particular attention was given to the slaves' diet as well as the medicines the surgeon had laid in for the voyage. Sick slaves were said to have been supplied with wine, sago, and fresh stock.[66] Less favorable was the testimony of Alexander Falconbridge, who said that sick slaves had nothing to lie upon but bare planks. They suffered exceedingly from friction sores, especially those who were emaciated. In fact, he had seen the prominent parts of their bones about the shoulder blades and knees bare; "if I have put any kind of plaister or bandage on them, they generally remove them, and apply them to other purposes."[67]

Since every Guinea ship was the meeting place of geographically remote disease environments, it is not surprising that their human cargoes became breeding grounds for diseases that originated in Africa, Europe, and the Americas. Included among the long list of diseases and ailments suffered on the Middle Passage were dysentery, diarrhea, ophthalmia, malaria, smallpox, yellow fever, scurvy, measles, typhoid fever, hookworm, tapeworm, sleeping sickness, trypanosomiasis, yaws, syphilis, leprosy, and elephantiasis. Slaves also suffered from friction sores, ulcers, and injuries and wounds resulting from accidents, fights, and whippings.[68] Causes advanced by contemporaries to explain the diseases of slaves included those of a miasmatic nature, malnutrition, congestion, heat, and melancholia. Various medical measures were taken to reduce slave mortality on the Middle Passage, of which the most successful were perhaps inoculation for smallpox and the use of citrus fruits and other antiscorbutics for scurvy. Alexander Bryson, M.D., director general of the Navy Medical Service who served for nine years in ships on the coast of Africa, ventured to rank the diseases. "The diseases from which negro slaves suffer most severely on board of the vessels destined for their transportation, are dysentery, fever, small-pox, ophthalmia, and diarrhoea; the first two are by far the more generally destructive and it not unfrequently happens that they acquire such virulence, as to carry off a fourth or even a third of the whole cargo in the short period of a few weeks."[69]

Dysentery, or the bloody flux, is the inflammation of the mucous membrane and glands of the large intestine and is attended by gripping pains and the discharge of blood and mucus. Though known in Europe and Africa from antiquity, dysentery became an important killer during the eighteenth century with European expansion into tropical regions and the rapid growth of the slave trade. In his description of the coasts of South Guinea, John Barbot wrote in 1732: "The Bloody-flux is also common, and sweeps away multitudes of the Blacks after they have lost all their blood. They fancy this distemper is given by witches and sorcerers called here *Sovah-Monou*. The Quojas Negroes affirm, they never knew of the bloody-flux till it was brought from Sierra Leone in the year 1626, eight months after the Dutch admiral Laun had left that place."[70] Epidemics of bacillary dysentery broke out among slaves in the barracoons on the African coast and on the slave ships. On crowded ships it was, with the exception perhaps of smallpox, the most revolting disease. "The effluvium which issues from her decks, or rather prisons," wrote Bryson, "is peculiar and sickening by any conception, and is generally perceptible at a great distance to leeward."[71] Although it is not known whether amebic dysentery existed in America before the coming of the Spaniards, it is certain that this infection was carried to the New World by African slaves.[72]

Included among the great number of human cargoes that were decimated by dysentery was that of the *Hannibal*, which weighed 450 tons, was commanded by Thomas Phillips, and sailed from London to Africa in 1693 in the service of the Royal African Company. European goods were exchanged for "elephants teeth, gold, and Negro slaves" at various trading centers along the coast until 700 slaves (480 men and 220 women), together with provisions, wood, and water, were loaded. From its departure from Africa on 27 July until its arrival at Barbados on 25 August, sickness and mortality took a dreadful toll, amounting to 14 seamen and 320 blacks. Few of the victims of smallpox died. "But what the small-pox spar'd," wrote Phillips, "the flux swept off, to our great regret, after all our pains and care to give them their messes in due order and season, keeping their lodgings as clean and sweet as possible, and enduring so much misery and stench so long among a parcel of creatures nastier than swine; and after all our expectations to be defeated by their mortality."[73]

Confinement and melancholia were causes of dysentery, according to two surgeons who testified in 1789 and 1790. Captain John Anderson said the disease the blacks were chiefly subject to on board ship was the flux. They contracted the flux more readily than the sailors, and male slaves more readily than females. In imputing the disease to confinement, Anderson observed that the women, who were not confined, were less subject to the flux than men.[74] Dr. Isaac Wilson was of the opinion that melancholia was the primary cause of death of a large proportion of the 155 slaves who died on the ship *Elizabeth*. Slaves who exhibited no symptoms of melancholia responded well to medicines. On the other hand, those who said they wished to die and refused sustenance became debilitated and died of the flux. Wilson explained the causal relationship as follows: "The symptoms of melancholy are lowness of spirits and despondency; refusing their proper nourishment still increases these symptoms; at length the stomach gets weak, and incapable of digesting their food: Fluxes and dysenteries ensue; and, from the weak and debilitated state of the patient, it soon carries him off."[75]

Alexander Falconbridge thought that the principal causes of dysentery were "a diseased mind, sudden transitions from heat to cold, breathing a putrid atmosphere, wallowing in their own excrement, and being shackled together." He could not conceive any situation so dreadful and disgusting as a bad epidemic of dysentery. The deck was said to be covered with blood and mucus, and the stench and foul air were intolerable. Falconbridge testified that he never could recover a single slave who had severe dysentery, nor did he believe the whole college of physicians, if they were there, could be of the least service, for he believed that a disease could not be cured while the cause remained.[76]

Even when medicines were reputedly effective they were difficult to administer to recalcitrant and debilitated slaves. James Morley, gunner on the ship *Medway*, testified that he had seen surgeon's mates, on giving the slaves medicines, force the pannikin between their teeth and throw it over them so that not half of it had gone into their mouths. This was done, he said, "when the poor wretches have been wallowing or sitting in their blood or excrement, hardly having life; and this with blows with the cat; damning them for being sulky Black b———."[77]

Confusion regarding the kinds of fevers and their causes led to faulty diagnosis and treatment by Guinea surgeons. The fatal consequences were underscored by Dr. Aubrey:

> Abundance of these poor Creatures are lost on Board Ships to the great prejudice of the Owners and Scandal of the Surgeon, Merely thro' the Surgeon's Ignorance, because he knows not what they are afflicted with, but supposing it to be a Fever, bleeds and purges, or vomits them, and so casts them into an incurable *Diarrhoea*, and in a very few Days they become a Feast for some hungry Shark.[78]

From a comparatively mild disease, smallpox became the most lethal illness, especially among the young, from the late seventeenth to the early nineteenth century. Introduced into the Americas by Spaniards and Africans, smallpox devastated the Indians of the Greater Antilles and New Spain. Outbreaks of smallpox in the barracoons of West Africa and on the Guinea ships struck terror into whites and blacks alike, and there are instances of victims of the disease being quarantined in longboats towed by slavers. According to John Barbot,

> the distempers of the *Blacks*, are the venereal disease, megrin or head-aches, bloody-fluxes, fevers, which they called *Abrobra*, cholicks, pains in the stomach; the small-pox, which makes the greatest havock among them, as does also that strange disease of the worms.[79]

Dr. Aubrey wrote that Africans were "subject to the Measles and Small-pox, as well as white People, and they they are commonly seized with great Heaviness and Pain in the Head and Back, a gentle Fever, and Vomiting or Nauseas."[80]

Treatment of smallpox ranged from the use of tar-water to inoculation and vaccination. Bishop George Berkeley, the philosopher, advocated the use of tar-water for a variety of illnesses and ailments. He told of a Liverpool vessel on which 170 slaves were seized by smallpox. Only one died who refused to drink tar-water, and the remaining 169 recovered by drinking it. This wonderful fact, he said, was attested to by the solemn affidavit of the ship's captain.[81] If the efficacy of tar-water strains one's credulity, no such doubt attaches to the practice of inoculation and vaccination in reducing the incidence of smallpox among slaves. Contrary to common belief, Africans practiced inoculation or variolating for smallpox before its adoption by Europeans and Americans. Mungo Park was assured on the authority of a European doctor who practiced in the Gambia that the blacks there practiced inoculation. According to Thomas Winterbottom, M.D., physician to the colony of Sierra Leone, "inoculation has been frequently practised to a considerable extent on board of slave vessels, and though no instance has fallen under my observation, it has always proved successful."[82] Jamaican newspapers frequently advertised the sale of slave cargoes that had been inoculated for smallpox. For example, the following notice appeared in *The Daily Advertiser* of Kingston, Jamaica, on 9 July 1793.[83]

For Sale
On Wednesday the 17th Instant
120
Choice Young Eboe Negroes
Imported in the Ship Will
Capt. John Ward from Calabar
Lindo & Lake
N.B. The Negroes have been inoculated on the Coast and are perfectly recovered from the Small Pox.

Ophthalmia, which is a contagious inflammation of the eye that may result in blindness, was carried from Africa to the West Indies by the slave trade. Guinea surgeon John Atkins wrote that "Whydah Slaves are more subject to Small-Pox and sore Eyes; other parts to a sleepy Distemper, and to Windward, Exomphalos's [sic]"[84] Dr. Winterbottom described several African remedies for ophthalmia, the principal one being the juice of a pear-shaped fruit called pan-a-pánnee by the Timmanee people and tontáy by the Soosoos.[85] Dr. James Grainger, who practiced in the island of St. Kitts, told of a disease called "night blindness" that was brought from Africa and that he claimed could be cured with a mixture of bark, orange peel, and old rum.[86] It is of interest that the Liverpool Institute for the Blind was the conception of Edward Rushton, who partially lost his sight aboard a Guinea ship while treating slaves afflicted with malignant ophthalmia.[87]

Dietary restriction and imbalance on the Guinea vessels were major causes of diarrhea, according to Dr. Aubrey. Free Africans took their meals at irregular intervals, he said. They ate an abundance of palm oil and pepper with flesh or fish, roasted plantains and ears of corn, perhaps ate a few dates, and drank either water or palm wine. When they were taken on board as slaves, however, only two meals a day were provided, their rations of palm oil and pepper were very limited, and too much salt for their taste was applied to the coarse provisions carried from Europe. The upshot was refusal to eat, loss of appetite, harsh punishment, sickness, and not infrequently death.[88] Dr. Falconbridge stressed the importance of diet when he wrote that "almost the only means by which the surgeon can render himself useful to the slaves, is, by seeing that their food is properly cooked and distributed among them."[89]

Yaws and worms were other diseases that afflicted slaves in the barracoons and on the Guinea ships. Yaws, or frambesia, is a venereally related disease that may be acquired during childhood by direct contact. Highly infective ulcers and papules appear on the body, persist for months, and are difficult to cure. The slave trade was the means by which yaws was carried from the African rain forest to the islands in the West Indies. Dr. Aubrey wrote of the "yaws flux," which was "the mortal Disease that cuts off three parts in four of the Negroes, that are commonly lost on Board ships."[90] Worms of the intestines were common among Africans and frequently caused diseases, especially among children. According to Dr. Winterbottom, the slaves who were brought to the coast by the Foolas to be sold were always infested with tapeworms; "This probably arises from the very scanty and wretched diet which they are fed in the *path*, as they term the journey, and which, from the distance they are brought inland, often lasts for many weeks, at the same time that their strength is further reduced by the heavy loads they are obliged to carry."[91]

Preserving the health of seamen and slaves

Drawing on the experience gained on the long voyages undertaken by Captain Cook and Admiral Anson, Archibald Dalzel submitted to the committee of the Privy Council a list of proposed regulations for preserving the health of seamen and slaves in the African trade. He called for some respectable body of men to be vested with authority to inspect all ships, "taking Care that they be provided with a sufficient Quantity of wholesome Provisions, Water Casks, Antiscorbutics, and other Medicines." To insure an adequate supply of water, every ship should carry a still to convert saltwater into freshwater. Moreover,

> let a Book, containing in a concise Manner, the Observations of Dr. Lind, Captain Cook, and other ingenious Men on the Distillation of Sea Water, the Treatment of the Scurvy, and other Disorders incident to seafaring People, with Directions for cleaning and ventilating the Ships, and every other necessary Information, concerning the Health of the Crew, be published by the Inspectors, and delivered to the Surgeon, or other Person performing his Duty, and let every such Person be obliged, on the Ship's Return, to produce a Journal to the Inspectors, communicating such of his Remarks as he may deem beneficial to Society.

Dalzel regarded these regulations as necessary to disseminate knowledge, prevent avarice, and preserve human lives.[92]

Although Dalzel's proposed regulations were not translated into law, Dolben's Act of 1788 provided that every slaver should carry a trained surgeon and that masters and surgeons be granted premiums for limiting the mortality of slaves on the Middle Passage. Moreover, every surgeon was required to keep a "regular and true journal" in which he recorded the number of slaves on his vessel, the deaths of slaves and seamen during the voyage, and the causes thereof. Surgeons were required to deliver their journals to the collector or other officer at the first British port where the vessel arrived after leaving Africa and swear to the truth of such a journal. Furthermore, it was provided that copies of the journal should be transmitted to the commissioners of the customs in London.[93]

British Parliamentary Papers contain extracts from five journals of surgeons employed on ships that sailed to the coast of Africa and carried slaves to the port of Roseau in the island of Dominica. Slave purchases ranged from 154 to 374 per vessel, and mortality from 3 to 25. Altogether, 1,190 slaves were purchased, of whom 63 (or 5.3 percent) died on board the five slave ships.[94] Extracts from the journal of Joseph Buckham, surgeon of the ship *James*, are shown in Table 4.5.

Dolben's Act required all Guinea surgeons to be examined and certified by the Company of Surgeons of London. Surgeons at Edinburgh challenged the London Company by securing an amending act of 1789, by which a Guinea surgeon was to produce "a Certificate of his having passed his examination at Surgeons' Hall or at some publick or County Hospital or at the Royal College of Surgeons of Edinburgh."[95] Although few Guinea surgeons were examined at Edinburgh, the case was different at Liverpool. Candidates examined at the Liverpool Infirmary from 1789 to 1807 numbered 634, of whom 151 were failed. "An attempt was obviously made to maintain a high quality," writes E. N. Chamberlain.[96]

Records show that a total of 1,283 ships left from the ports of London, Bristol, and Liverpool for Africa from 1795 to 1804 and that they were legally allowed to carry 389,863 slaves. If each ship carried one surgeon, the numbers ranged annually from 79 in 1795 to 160 in 1798 (average 128), while the numbers of slaves legally allowed per surgeon ranged from 251 in 1804 to 356 in 1798 (average 305).[97]

Mortality on the Middle Passage

Although considerable evidence points to the decline of slave mortality on British vessels on the Middle Passage, it is not clear whether this was due primarily to the regulatory laws. Sample mortality statistics show a significant decline in mortality from the late seventeenth century to the late eighteenth and early nineteenth centuries. The records of the Royal African Company show a marked decline in loss during transit of 23.5 percent in 1680–8 to an average of 10 percent in 1734. Roger Anstey has calculated a mean mortality of 8.5 percent from a large random sample spanning the years from 1769 to 1787. Samples for subsequent years show that the rate declined steadily from 9.5 percent in 1791 to 2.7 in 1795, and averaged 4.0 percent during the last decade of the lawful trade.[98] Other national carriers, including the French, Dutch, and Danish, experienced similar declines in mortality on the Middle Passage, although there is no reason to believe that they matched the reduction achieved by the British from the early 1790s onward.[99]

Table 4.5. *A surgeon's journal of slave mortality: "An account of all the Slaves that died on Board the Ship* James, *Mathew Morley, Master, from Africa from the 4th November 1788 to the 8th February 1789"*

Date		Sex	Of what disorder
1788, November	4	One man	Inflammation of the liver
	29	One man	Of a dysentery
December	18	One woman	Suddenly
1789, January	1	One man	Of a dysentery
	3	One woman	Ditto
	6	One woman	Of a lethargy
	15	One boy	Of a dysentery
	16	One man boy	Ditto
	17	One girl	Ditto
	18	One man	Ditto
	19	One boy	Ditto
	28	One boy	Ditto
	31	One woman	Sulkiness
February	3	One man boy	Of lethargy
	8	One man	Of a dysentery
	70 men above 4 feet 4 inches		
	23 men boys under 4 feet 4 inches		
	15 women girls under 4 feet 4 inches		
	46 women above 4 feet 4 inches		
	154 total slaves		

(signed) Joseph Buckham,
Surgeon of the Ship *James*

Sworn before me this 25th Febr[uar]y 1789
N. A. Blake, Coll[ecto]r
Rouseau, Dominica

Source: Accounts and Papers (Parliamentary Papers), 1789, XXIX (632), p. 3, "Extracts of Guinea Surgeons' Journals, 16th June 1789."

Mortality varied among major African slave-providing areas. A specialized study concerns 301 British slavers that transported a total of 101,676 blacks to the West Indies in 1791–7. Nearly three-fifths of these blacks were carried to Jamaica, followed by Grenada and St. Vincent with nearly one-tenth each. The remaining one-fifth or more went to Barbados, Dominica, Cuba, Trinidad, Tobago, Martinique, St. Croix, and Demerara. Average mortality ranged from 2.75 percent for Gold Coast slaves to 10.56 percent for those from the Bight of Biafra. The overall average is 5.65 percent. Mortality ranged between 2 and 3 percent for slaves from the Gold Coast and Senegambia; between 3 and 4 percent for those from the Windward Coast, Congo-Angola, and Sierra Leone; and between 4 and 5 percent for those from the Bight of Benin. The abnormally high rate for slaves from the Bight of Biafra will be commented on presently.[100]

In introducing his regulation bill, Sir William Dolben asserted that putrid disorders and fatal disease resulted from the slaves being crowded together on slavers "like herrings in a barrel." Whereas some modern authorities support Dolben's view that "tight packing" was a major cause of mortality on the Middle Passage,[101] others, on the basis of statistical analysis, have failed to find any close relationship between crowding and mortality. According to Herbert S. Klein, "the studies of the English, French, and Portuguese trades agree in that they all show no signifigant correlation between slave mortality and the number of slaves carried." He admits, however, that most of the material for such analysis is still fragmentary. Furthermore, he admits that even the reduced rates that prevailed toward the end of the eighteenth century would have amounted to a mortality crisis if they had occurred among sedentary peasant populations in the same time.[102] Further research on this subject will need to take account of epidemiological factors, which were certainly encouraged by unhygienic conditions and overcrowding (see Figure 4.1).

Factors other than tight packing seem to have played a significant part in the decline of slave mortality. These included the changes in trading practices that reduced the time the slavers were detained on the coast of Africa, and improvements in ship design and construction that reduced sailing time on the Middle Passage.[103] Recent scholarship has focused attention on the conditions in African slave trading centers and supply areas as causes of mortality. Morbidity and mortality resulted from crop failures and other causes of dietary deficiency, adverse disease environments, wars, debility resulting from long journeys from the interior to the coast, long waiting times in barracoons and on shipboard before sailing, and supply and demand pressures in local slave markets. One study shows that the Dutch West India Company had a pre-embarkation loss of 3 to 5 percent.[104]

Why the slaves from the Bight of Biafra had the highest mortality is not easy to explain until further research is undertaken. To cite one contemporary opinion, James Jones, a leading Bristol slave trader, wrote from West Africa that the people at Bonny and New Calabar near the Bight of Biafra commonly ate yams and a little fish. He said he never sent ships to those areas because the people there were "Sickly, and the Slaves inferior to any other, very Weakly and liable to great Mortality."[105] Klein suggests that local crop and disease conditions both along the coast and in the catchment areas for slaves

Figure 4.1. Sectional view of slaver, used by Wilberforce in his campaign. In Wilberforce House, Hull birthplace of William Wilberforce. By permission of Mr. John Bradshaw, Curator of Museums and Art Galleries, Hull.

strongly influenced the ultimate mortality pattern on the Middle Passage. Moreover, he suggests that conditions in Africa influenced even the different rates of what has been called "seasoning" mortality or early adjustment to local epidemiological conditions in the West Indies.[106]

It will be our task in Chapter 5 to analyze the seasoning mortality, but it is appropriate here to call attention to a study of slaves who died within a short time after their arrival in the West Indies. In its report of 12 November 1788, a committee of the Assembly of Jamaica sought to demonstrate that the net natural decrease in the slave population of that island did not arise from the causes assigned in the petitions presented to the House of Commons – namely, neglect, excessive labor, or other maltreatment – "but from other Causes not imputable to us, and which the People of Great Britain do not seem to comprehend." The principal causes of the loss of slaves, according to the committee, were: "First, the Disproportion between the Sexes in the annual Importation from Africa. Second, the Loss of new Negroes on, or soon after their Arrival, from epidemic Diseases brought from Africa, or contracted in the Voyage." From statistics compiled by the committee it was demonstrated that the ratio of male to female imports was five to three, and that 4.6 percent of the imported slaves perished in Kingston Harbor before the day of sale. It was also explained that the slave population had declined because of reexports, desertion, manumission, famine following hurricanes and droughts, and the high rate of infant mortality from lockjaw or tetanus.[107]

Conclusion

From the evidence presented in this chapter it can be argued that Parliamentary regulation and advances in medical science and practice played some part in the decline of mortality on the Middle Passage. Noteworthy advances in medical science included the use of citrus fruits to combat scurvy, inoculation against smallpox, and Peruvian bark or cinchona for malaria. Moreover, the quality of medical services may have improved as a consequence of laws that required the examination and certification of Guinea surgeons on slave vessels. Although laws were enacted to reduce congestion and improve ventilation, it is doubtful whether they were of much help in checking the spread of communicable diseases on slave ships. Most serious, perhaps, was the lack of legislation to enforce minimum standards for food and drink on the Middle Passage.

Yet, apart from their efforts to improve dietary and sanitary standards and reduce the incidence of scurvy, smallpox, and malaria, the Guinea surgeons probably could not do much to preserve the health of slaves on the Middle Passage. They had no control over the conditions under which the slaves were captured, transported, and cared for while awaiting shipment from Africa. Countless millions of Africans died from warfare, malnutrition, and disease between the time of capture and the time of embarkation. Others were so debilitated that, even if they survived the crossing to the West Indies, they were unable to cope with the hazards of the new disease environment and plantation labor demands. It was not only the quantitative but also the qualitative loss to Africa that was appalling. "The massive loss to the African labour force was made more critical because it was composed of able-bodied young men and young women," writes Walter Rodney. "Slave buyers preferred their victims between the ages of 15 and 35, and preferably in the early twenties; the sex ratio being about two men to one woman."[108] In the end, the greatest contribution to Africa and the Africans was made by Dr. Falconbridge and other like-minded Guinea surgeons whose critical testimony convinced the British Parliament that the Atlantic slave trade must be abolished.

5

Slaves and plantations

Whatever property exists, or has ever existed in the Colonies, is the direct fruit of the labour of the slaves. That this labour has never received its due Compensation is matter of absolute certainty. Slaves still bear, and have always borne, a high price in the Colonies. Why is it that a man finds it worth his while to purchase a labourer? The answer plainly is, because his labour is worth more than the cost of the maintenance he is to receive. The price paid is a fair criterion of the amount of the wages which have been kept back, and of the loss sustained by the labourer.

Lord Goderich, 1831[1]

This is the first of two chapters concerned with the physical and social environments in which most of the Afro-West Indians lived during the slavery era. This chapter focuses on the sugar plantation and on how newly imported Africans were treated, how the slaves were clothed and housed, how they were assigned to labor groups and tasks, and how they were affected by the system of absentee proprietorship. Chapter 6 is concerned chiefly with the labor, diet, and punishment of slaves.

The sugar plantation

Caribbean plantation economies and societies were remarkable for their production of wealth and notorious for their treatment of slave laborers. "From the perspective of post-Roman European history," writes Sidney W. Mintz, "the plantation was an absolutely unprecedented social, economic and political institution, and by no means simply an innovation in the organization of agriculture."[2] The plantation stemmed from the growing demand of Europeans for a wider range of foodstuffs and raw materials, the large-scale production of which was only feasible in humid tropical and semitropical regions with open resources. The New World plantation represented a combination of African labor, European technology and management, Asiatic and American plants, European animal husbandry, and American soil and climate. Root crops were grown alongside tree crops and cereals; animal husbandry was combined with tillage; and animate sources of energy, such as plants, domesticated animals, and black slaves, were combined with inanimate energy captured by windmills, water wheels, and sailing vessels. Plantations were at once ecosystems, farming and industrial systems, economic systems, and social systems. The plantation was truly an innovation in the Schumpeterian sense.[3] It established new trade routes and shipping lanes, shifted millions of African hoe cultivators from one side of the Atlantic to the other, determined the movement and direction of capital, induced the growth of temperate-zone colonies to supply intermediate products, produced a class of noveau riche planters and merchants, and became a prize in the contest for power and plenty among the mercantile nations of Europe.[4]

The typical sugar plantation was a big business establishment in comparison with contemporary units of industrial and agricultural organization in Europe. It was both farm and factory; it combined the growing of sugarcane with the manufacture of raw sugar and the distilling of molasses into rum. The Reverend Hope Masterton Waddell, Scottish missionary in Jamaica near the end of slavery, wrote that a sugar estate in good order was a fine sight. The canes presented an appearance of utmost luxuriance, and the pastures with their beautiful trees seemed like English parks. The sugar works comprised an extensive range of buildings:

> There were the overseer's house and stores, with the barracks for book-keepers, carpenter, and mason; the mill-house, boiling-house, cooling-house, and still-house; the carpenters', coopers', and blacksmiths' shops, and extensive trash-houses. A little way off stood the hospital or "hot-house;" and on a rising ground overlooking all, the Great House or proprietor's mansion, flanked by the "negro houses" or slave village; these last being buried in cocoa-nut, orange, mango, and avocado-pear trees [see Figure 5.1].[5]

Waddell noted, however, that appearances were misleading, for the typical sugar plantation was neither the home of contented workers nor at the time he wrote a profitable unit of production. Cheerful and willing labor was not to be found. The proprietors or island nobility was for the most part absent. Plantation attorneys, some with many estates under their care, formed the squirearchy of the island. Waddell wrote that every plantation had its own overseer, "who has 'book-keepers,' carpenter, and mason under him. From the attorney down all were unmarried, yet all had families. A married lady was rarely seen. Some planters had not seen one since they left home."[6]

The Europeans who were attached to sugar plantations – largely, white men – were organized into a hierarchy. In the absence of the proprietor, the attorney oversaw the plantation. Among other things, he ordered the plantation supplies, purchased slaves, and superintended the shipment of sugar and rum. He carried out the instructions of his employer, hired and

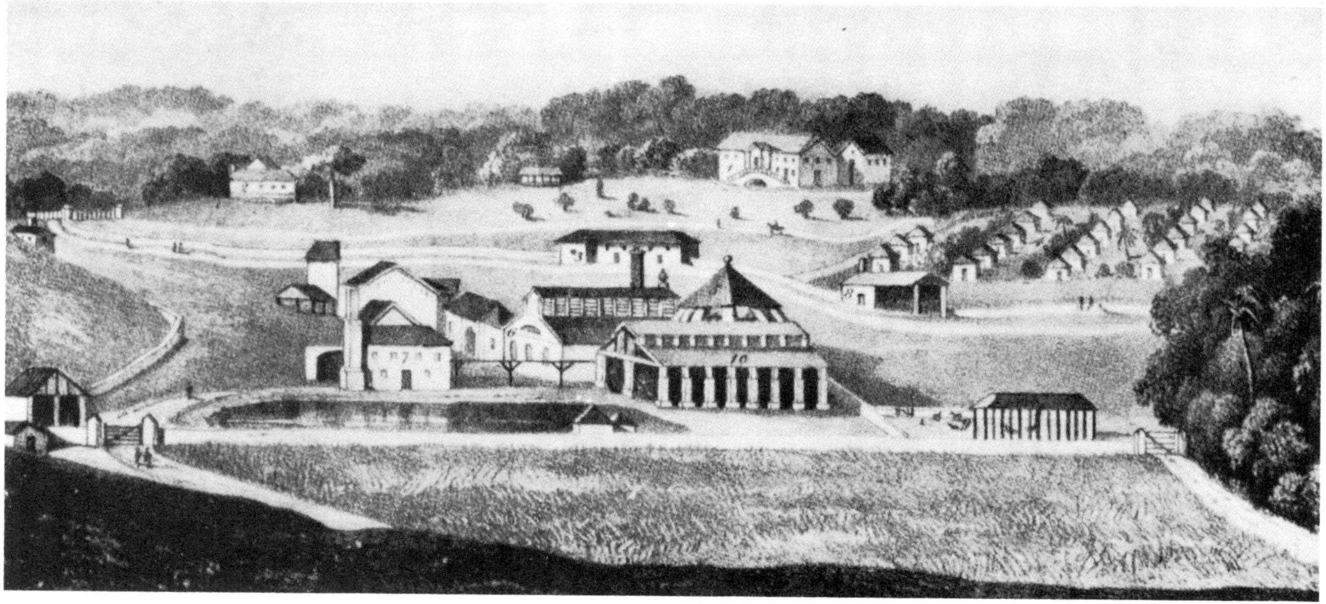

Figure 5.1. View of Roehampton estate, Jamaica. The slave hospital is in the background, far left. By permission of Professor Orlando Patterson, as reproduced in his *The Sociology of Slavery* (Jamaica: Sangster's Book Stores Ltd., 1973), frontispiece.

fired the overseers, inspected the plantation records, and reported on the general conduct and performance of the plantation.[7] Underneath the proprietor or attorney was the overseer or manager. On a day-to-day basis he superintended the planting and manufacturing concerns of the plantation. He directed the slaves in their tasks and had the responsibility of supplying them with food, clothing, shelter, and medical services. White bookkeepers were in the middle rank, being under the overseers or managers and immediately above the black drivers. They attended gangs of slaves in the field, and superintended the manufacture of sugar and rum in the boiling and distilling houses. White artisans who were assisted and not infrequently supplanted by their mulatto and black apprentices consisted of carpenters, millwrights, wheelwrights, masons, coopers, ropemakers, and distillers. Medical services were provided by white doctors, who were assisted by black doctors, doctresses, nurses, and midwives.[8]

Plantations used a plentiful supply of low-productivity labor, which was mobilized under the close supervision of white managers to yield substantial profit to the proprietors. Both the Amerindians and Europeans were unable or unwilling to perform disciplined work voluntarily for low wages. "As a result," writes Jay R. Mandle, "nonmarket methods of allocation and control became essential in order to carry out profitable production in large volume. Force was required to supply the manpower the plantations required, and continued coercion was needed after the workers arrived on the plantations to ensure that the goals of the plantations were achieved." In particular, force was used to motivate the workers to work and to prevent them from leaving the plantations. Each plantation was, in effect, both an authoritarian political institution and a profit-making business. Planters and their agents wielded extra-economic authority to maintain a sufficient supply of workers to ensure profitable production.[9]

Elsa Goveia uses the term *slave society* to refer to the whole community based on slavery, including masters and freedmen as well as slaves. In this society the white minority successfully imposed its claims to superior status on the overwhelming black majority of the population, who were generally immobilized without hope of escape in the lowest ranks of the social structure.[10]

Treatment of slaves

Failure to make clear what is meant by the treatment of slaves in New World plantation societies has led to much waste of time, effort, and good temper, according to Eugene D. Genovese. He says we ought to distinguish carefully the three different meanings of the word *treatment* if we are to judge the relative severity of different slave systems. One meaning is the slave's condition of life, including family security, opportunities for an independent social and religious life, and other cultural opportunities. The slave's access to freedom and citizenship by the practice of manumission is the second meaning. The third meaning, which is the one used in this study, is the day-to-day living conditions, including "such essentially measurable items as quantity and quality of food, clothing, housing, length of the working day, and the general conditions of labor."[11]

The purchase of slaves was an annual charge for a plantation. It was motivated by the need to replace slaves who had died or to expand the labor force to augment production and profit. The number of slaves purchased at any one time depended on such factors as their availability and price, the creditworthiness of the purchaser, and available supplies of food, clothing, housing, and other facilities. Purchases also varied according to such seasonal factors as local crop and disease conditions and the time of arrival of slave vessels. There was marked seasonality in the arrival of Jamaica-bound African slaves, according to Herbert S. Klein. Imports were greatest during the late fall, winter, and early spring, or November through March. Klein attributes this seasonal pattern to such factors as Atlantic winds and currents, African crop and weather patterns, and American work demands based on harvest cycles.[12]

Planters were advised to purchase slaves in limited numbers and of the proper age and sex. Dr. David Collins noted that it was usual for purchasers to prefer males to females from many motives, "but principally from their being less subject to indisposition, and from the variety of services on a plantation, which are not to be executed but by masculine vigour."[13] Similarly, the preference for males was explained by William Beckford in terms of the imbalance of work assignments. "A negro man is purchased either for a trade, or the cultivation and different processes of the cane," he wrote; "the occupations of the women are only two, the house, with its several departments, and the supposed indulgences, or the field with its exaggerated labours." Beckford thought that too many old slaves were brought to the islands. In his opinion, those who were twelve to sixteen years old were most advantageous to purchasers, "since young slaves had fewer regrets" than those who had "been forced from the endearing ties of wife and children, and under the painful anticipations of their future wretchedness and want."[14]

Seasoning imported slaves

It was tragic that the slaves were transferred from the pestilential disease environment of the Guinea vessels to disease-ridden ports to await the day of sale. Sanitary arrangements were said to be unknown in the port of

Kingston, where most of the slaves entering Jamaica landed; "dunghills abounded, and from these the ruts in the streets and lanes were filled up after every heavy rain. In the early morning negro slaves might be seen bearing open tubs from the various dwellings, and emptying their indescribable contents into the sea."[15] A close reading of the Journals of the Assembly of Jamaica reveals that few attempts were made to inspect and quarantine ships that entered Jamaica with slaves infected with smallpox and other contagious diseases.[16] Kingston, Jamaica, and presumably other British West Indian ports lagged far behind Cartagena and other Spanish ports where slaves and slaving vessels underwent thorough health inspections. Moreover, instead of being quartered in the towns of Spanish America, new slaves were kept on outlying farms and restored to health before they were sold.[17]

Moving imported Africans from the disease environments of ships to those of ports and plantations was highly destructive to life and labor, yet the demand for unskilled labor was at times so great that little preparation was made for the reception of new slaves. Planters were torn between the need to immediately augment their labor force by the purchase of new slaves and the need to extend the life and improve the quality of their investment in human capital by the assignment of light tasks and measures of health care known as the "seasoning." They were tempted to resort to the former expedient because they were commonly supplied with slaves at the time they were wanted and in the numbers needed. Moreover, long credit was commonly granted.[18]

Losses during the seasoning made a heavy drain on the newly imported slaves of even the best managed plantations. Charles Leslie wrote in 1740 that almost half the newly imported slaves died in the seasoning, and several decades later Edward Long admitted that one-fourth of the newcomers were likely to die during the first eighteen months of the seasoning.[19] Writing in 1790, William Beckford said, "Let a purchaser of new Negroes be ever so successful in seasoning them, he does not think that he will be able with the most unremitting attention, and even with a superfluity of food, to preserve and domesticate, in three years, one out of four, who shall turn out a really industrious and efficient Slave."[20] That the seasoning mortality could be of horrendous magnitude is underscored by the experience of the Codrington plantations in Barbados, where, from 1741 to 1746, 43 percent of all imported slaves died within three years of their arrival on the island.[21] Two doctors in Jamaica attributed the high mortality among the recently imported slaves to the many "disorders" they brought with them from Africa, "the bad Habit of Body these People have contracted from the long Confinement, bad Food, and improper Treatment in the Voyage."[22]

Apart from putting new slaves under the supervision of older seasoned slaves from their own country, little attention was given to the seasoning of new recruits from Africa until the advent of the antislavery movement. Writing in 1764, Dr. James Grainger of the island of St. Kitts found it astonishing that, among the many valuable medical tracts that had been published in recent years, not one had been "purposely written on the method of seasoning new Negroes, and the treatment of Negroes when sick." In his *Essay on West-India Diseases*, Grainger laid down rules for the feeding, clothing, housing, medical treatment, and labor of new slaves. He cautioned that no African could be seasoned to the climate of the West Indies until he had resided there "at least a twelvemonth." Above all, he warned against requiring new slaves to perform heavy field labor. "To put a hoe in the hands of a new Negroe, and to oblige him to work with a seasoned gang, is to murder that Negroe," Grainger exclaimed. He went on to say, "The African must be familiarised to labour by gentle degrees. This precept respects not only the aged, but even the young." New slaves should be properly clothed and supplied with food that was as similar as possible to their former diet in Africa. They should bathe frequently and anoint their bodies with palm oil. Care should be taken to restrain them from eating unripe fruit and vegetables. They should never be sent to mountain plantations where they were "very liable to catch cold, or fall into fluxes, which always prove troublesome to remove, and sometimes fatal." In general, Grainger thought it was not wrong to have new slaves blooded, but the quantity should never exceed six ounces. He recommended the administration of vomits of thistle seed, purges of castor oil, and, above all, "a decoction of worm-grass, clarified with lemon juice, or cow-itch sheathed with melasses" as remedies for worms.[23]

Dr. Collins devoted a chapter to the seasoning of blacks in his comprehensive planter's manual. In his judgment, six causes accounted for the death of nearly one-fourth of the new slaves within three or four years after their arrival. First, diseases contracted both before and during the voyage from Africa, such as dysentery, yaws, and Guinea worms, pursued the newcomers on shore and often proved fatal. Second, changes of climate, especially when the seasoning took place in cool mountain regions, sometimes led to fatal cases of fluxes and dropsies. Third, food could produce unfavorable effects on new slaves when it was defective in quality, deficient in quantity, or differed from dietary patterns in Africa. Fourth, labor was said to be "the most frequent cause of the mortality of new negroes, some of whom have never experienced any considerable portion of it in their own country, and none in the manner in which they are obliged to work in ours." Fifth, severity in the form of harsh rebukes, threats, and chastisements created disgust and terror, leading some slaves to resort to suicide, which was the sixth cause of mortality during the seasoning. Conceding that much less attention was bestowed upon new slaves than they deserved and required,

Collins laid down rules to correct existing practices. His goal was not only to extend the lives of newly imported Africans but also to gradually train them to habits of labor and obedience.[24]

William Beckford criticized the prevailing methods of seasoning new slaves. His own plan included such features as a thorough medical inspection, placing newcomers in a dormitory prepared for their reception, and providing ample supplies of wholesome food, clothing, and medicine. Light labor should continue for at least one year. As soon as a new slave learned to cultivate his own provision ground he should be helped to build a house, encouraged to establish a family, and by degrees initiated into the labors of the cane field.[25]

Most planter-authors defended the slave trade while seeking to mitigate its effects, but Clement Caines of St. Kitts was the unusual planter who called for the immediate abolition of the trade in human chattels. "Though few died in their passage from Africa," he wrote, "multitudes die in consequence of it." It was during the passage that "the seeds of debility and despondence, of sickness, and of death" were sown among them and never afterward eradicated. Caines went so far as to declare that it was useless to supply new slaves with an abundance of food, to introduce them gradually to labor, and to guard against their sickness. It was useless to try to reconcile them to their lot. "The melancholy and despondence cannot be rooted out," he believed. "They pine and droop, linger rather than live, and shortly sink into the grave." Caines said he fully believed that a whole generation of imported Africans was swept away in less than "a fourth part of the age of man" after their arrival in "this land of exile, toil, and scarcity." Caines described what modern scholars term "culture shock," or the general feeling of despondency that pervaded the African-born slaves who, upon arrival in the West Indies, often showed a spirit of desperation and sought to commit suicide.[26]

Clothing and housing

Planters realized that slaves were vulnerable to a host of diseases, and the more enlightened among them sought to minimize the risks by maintaining adequate standards of diet, clothing, housing, and medical care. These standards, however, insofar as they applied to clothing and housing, were low in comparison with those of northern latitudes where protective measures were essential to counteract the rigors of the climate. Dr. Collins found fault with the conventional wisdom that gave low priority to the need for clothing and shelter. Although the heat and cold of the tropical zone were by no means severe, he said, they were "sufficiently so in the circumstances of wind and moisture, to demand a better occasional safeguard for the human body, than what nature has provided for its protection." Blacks were particularly sensitive to cold and suffered under a very moderate degree of it. They were observed to "crawl out of their huts in the morning, torpid and shivering, and incapable of exertion, until warmed and invigorated by the influence of the ascending sun." Fluxes and other diseases frequently resulted from sleeping in wet clothes and from the lack of bed covering. Dr. Collins observed, "Fluxes are more common, as well as more fatal, in the mountains than in the low lands, in the cold and rainy months, than when the air is warmer and drier."[27]

Enlightened planters, both resident and absentee, linked the health of their slaves to how they were fed, clothed, and housed. For example, Nathaniel Phillips, an absentee from Jamaica, wrote to his overseer: "The fatal disorder which attacked the Negroes last fall was truly alarming. Dry Houses, warm clothing and wholesome ripe food bid fairest to prevent these dreadful calamities. I am satisfied you did your best, as well as the doctor."[28]

Clothes were of vital importance to slaves newly arrived from Africa who were highly vulnerable to the change of climate. The change was particularly felt by those who arrived early in the year, as most of them did. In Jamaica the buyer was said to have clothed his newly acquired subjects with a coarse German linen called Osnaburg, and provided them also with hats, handkerchiefs, and knives. Dr. Collins said that new slaves should be supplied with caps, jackets, blankets, and petticoats or trousers, according to the sex. If proper dresses and trousers were not ready, the slaves should be furnished with warm blankets at any rate. Supplying the new slaves with clothing had two benefits; it counteracted the effect of the climate, and it was "some gratification to their minds, which are pleased at being clothed."[29]

From the late seventeenth century onward, planter governments enacted slave laws that included clauses establishing minimum standards of food and clothing. These laws were amended under the pressure of antislavery propaganda, although such amendments were largely window dressing because the acts were almost impossible to enforce. Whereas the Consolidated Slave Law of Jamaica (1788) provided that the justices of the peace and vestry of each parish should determine what constituted "proper and sufficient clothing," the slave laws of other islands commonly itemized the clothing allowance. For example, by the act passed in November 1788 in Grenada

> a Proprietor is to allow Annually to each Man Slave above Fifteen Years old, a Suit of Cloaths, consisting of a Hat, Jacket, Shirt (or in lieu of a Jacket an additional Shirt), Trowsers, and Blankets; to every Female Slave above Thirteen Years old, a Suit of Cloaths, consisting of a Hat, Jacket, Shift (or in lieu of a Jacket an additional Shift), Petticoat, and Blanket; and to every Child above Eight Years old, a Hat, Shift, or Shirt.

Any proprietor who failed to provide such clothing was to forfeit £20.[30]

That the slave codes did little to improve clothing standards may be surmised from the observations of contemporary writers. Dr. George Pinckard said the clothing issue in Barbados consisted of a shirt and a pair of breeches, or only the latter, for the men, and a single petticoat for the women. The slaves received no bedding or bedclothes. In fact, they usually slept on a hard plank in the clothing of the day, or, if enterprising, they made a crude mattress of dried plantain leaves.[31] Robert Renny contended that the coarse and scanty covering provided by the Jamaican slave law was too sparingly allotted to the slaves by the proprietors; in many instances two years passed before new clothing was issued.[32]

Generally speaking, slaves suffered from inadequate clothing and footwear. They were unable to change from wet to dry garments and were thus prone to contract colds and fevers. Moreover, they often suffered from insufficient clothing and bedding in the colder seasons of the year and in mountainous regions. Apart from privileged slaves and domestics, blacks were seldom issued shoes and stockings. They frequently cut and bruised their bare feet and legs as they engaged in hazardous work and play. When these abrasions were neglected, ugly sores and ulcers developed, which might culminate in gangrene and death if the diseased limb was not speedily amputated.[33]

Plantation slaves generally lived in a village close to the sugar works and great house, usually near a river or spring to give access to water, in houses largely of their own construction, and in "family" units of two or three or more, or, if unattached males or females, in groups held together by common tribal origins or as shipmates on the Middle Passage. In his *Essay on Plantership*, Samuel Martin wrote that besides plenty of wholesome food, the strength and longevity of blacks depended on their master choosing

> airy, dry situations for their houses, and to observe frequently that they be kept clean, in good repair and perfectly water-tight; for nastiness, and the inclemencies of weather, generate the most malignant diseases. If these houses are situated also in regular order, and at due distances, the spaces may at once prevent general devastation by fire, and furnish plenty of fruits, and pot herbs, to please an unvitiated palate, and to purify the blood.[34]

Similarly, Dr. Collins suspected that next to hard labor and scant feeding, nothing contributed more to the disordering of blacks than bad lodging.[35]

Compared to Jamaica, where the typical plantation had sufficient land to permit the proper spacing of slave houses, such houses tended to be crowded together in the smaller sugar islands where intensive monoculture was practiced. Governor David Parry of Barbados attributed slave morbidity and mortality in part to unhygienic, congested living conditions.

> It is to be observed that the Negroes of a Plantation all live in little Towns, their Houses being so much nearer each other, and as it is found so impossible to give them a due sense of the Danger of Intercourse with the Sick, they are much more in the way of communicating a Disease one to the other than the lowest class of White Inhabitants, who are more cautious, and live all separate from each other, either as Tenants on detached Pieces of Land belonging to the Plantations, or as Occupiers of Little Parcels of Ground, appertaining to themselves.

Efforts to relocate their houses from "unwholesome situations" to "healthier Spots" met with resistance, for the slaves were said to be "superstitiously attached to the Burial Places of their Ancestors and Friends," which were frequently "under the Bed-places on which they sleep, an unwholesome and dangerous Practice, which they would think it the utmost Tyranny to alter."[36]

John Stewart, the Jamaica planter-author, described the construction, size, and furnishings of slave houses in that island:

> The houses of the slaves are in general comfortable. They are built of hard-wood posts, either boarded or wattled and plastered, and the roof formed of shingles (wood split and dressed into the shape of staves, and used as a substitute for them), or thatched with the leaves of the sugar cane, or the branches of the mountain cabbage (a species of the palm). This latter is of so durable a nature that it will last for thirty or forty years. The size of the house is generally from fifteen to twenty feet long, and from ten to fifteen wide. They contain a small hall, and one or two bed rooms, according to the size of the family. The furniture of this dwelling is a small table, two or three chairs or stools, a small cup board, furnished with a few articles of crockery-ware, some wooden bowls and calibashes [sic], a water-jar, a wooden mortar for pounding Indian corn, &c. and various other articles. The beds are seldom more than wooden frames spread with a mat and blanket.

Furthermore, Stewart said that adjoining each house was a spot of ground, commonly called the "kitchen garden," in which the householders grew vegetables and tree crops, raised poultry and pigs, and buried their dead.[37] Since none of the printed or manuscript literature refers to privies, it is likely that slaves had to "go a bush" for this function.

Modern researchers have used plantation records and archeological techniques to add to our understanding of slave housing and family life. On the two Codrington plantations in Barbados, according to J. Harry Bennett, shelter was regarded as the slaves' own problem; they used "cane trash, sticks, and perhaps a few pennies worth of rope yarn to aid in the thatching . . . to construct and reconstruct their precarious wooden huts in the yards designated for them." In emergencies, however, as after the severe hurricane of 1780, the management took direct responsibility for slave housing. Moreover, after 1775, the overseers gave some help in housing the more deserving or helpless slaves. These outlays were meager, though, amounting to less than six pounds for the erection or upkeep of about twenty-five huts between 1775 and 1793. Like other slaves, the Codrington blacks probably used planks for beds and gourds for dishes.[38] In their Barbadian research, Jerome S. Handler and Frederick W. Lange find that thatched, wattle-and-daub houses with packed dirt floors were the major type throughout the period of slavery. By the late eighteenth and early nineteenth centuries, however, slaves were increasingly housed in stone-walled dwellings with thatched or occasionally wood shingle roofs.[39]

On the two Jamaica sugar plantations and one cattle ranch belonging to Charles Rose Ellis (created Lord Seaford in 1826), Barry Higman finds that the slaves' houses were within 200 yards of the works or great house. He also finds that the mother-child tie was the strongest element in the creation and maintenance of households. Some households occupied more than one house. Higman thinks it is probable that these "multiple-house households formed tight units or 'yards,' with the houses set around a central open area." The reason for this was that grown sons who were establishing households tended to stay near their mothers, whereas daughters tended to move away. When a group of slaves was moved from one property to another, their new houses were described as "good; stone, shingled."[40]

That the typical slave in the West Indies was housed more poorly than his counterpart in the United States may be surmised by the research of Robert W. Fogel and Stanley L. Engerman. In the United States the slaves typically lived in cabins about eighteen by twenty feet, constructed usually of logs or wood, with floors that were usually planked and raised off the ground; chimneys were usually constructed of brick or stone, and it was quite common for children to sleep in lofts. Fogel and Engerman contend that whereas such housing was mean by modern standards, the houses of slaves compared well with the housing of free workers in the antebellum period.[41]

Although it appears that most of the slaves on West Indian plantations lived in single-family, wattle-and-daub houses with thatched roofs and dirt floors (see Figure 5.2), they were sometimes housed in barrack-like structures with several apartments. One Barbadian absentee owner instructed his attorney to construct such a building for the reception of newly purchased slaves. He wrote that a building forty feet long and twelve feet wide would conveniently lodge twenty-four slaves.[42]

Pro-planter authors supplied accounts of slave villages and houses that were lavish in their praise. For example, Matthew Gregory ("Monk") Lewis said he never witnessed on the stage a scene as picturesque as a slave village. After walking through his own village and visiting the houses of the drivers

Figure 5.2. Typical slave huts in Jamaica. From Adolphe Duperly and Son, *Picturesque Jamaica* (Kingston, Jamaica, ca., 1895), p. 67.

and other principal persons, he decided that if he were to choose according to his own taste, he would infinitely have preferred their habitations to his own. "Each house is surrounded by a separate garden, and the whole village is intersected by lanes, bordered with all kinds of sweet-smelling and flowering plants," he wrote.[43] Planter critics, on the other hand, found much to fault in the slave villages and houses. For example, the Reverend James M. Phillippo, Baptist missionary in Jamaica, noted that the villages were situated among groves of fruit trees that gave them a pleasing aspect when viewed from a distance,

> but on a nearer approach they were unsightly, and, owing to the offensive effluvia arising from quantities of decayed vegetable matter, far from healthy. The houses were thrown together without any pretence to order or arrangement; and, with a few exceptions, were wretched habitations. They consisted of posts put into the ground at the distance of about two feet asunder; the intermediate space being closed up with wattle, daubed over on the inside with mud. In some instances they were divided into two or three apartments, but thousands consisted of one room only This served the whole of the family for all domestic uses.[44]

According to Robert Renny, "The huts of the Negroes are truly wretched habitations, being barely sufficient to screen them from the inclemencies of the weather . . . The cottages are generally huddled together, and form a small village, destitute of beauty, order, or regularity."[45]

Contemporary statements regarding slave housing, clothing, diet, and punishment must be viewed skeptically because of their generally partisan nature. The report of J. Johnson can be assumed to be free of bias, however, because of the circumstances under which it was written. Johnson was employed by James Adam Gordon, an absentee proprietor living in England, to inspect and submit a report on the management of Gordon's six properties in the islands of St. Kitts, Antigua, and St. Vincent. Whereas the absence of comments on slave clothing on most of the properties he visited suggest that Johnson met with no serious problems, one property was exceptional. Johnson was shocked by the nakedness of the slaves on Fairhill and Brebner sugar plantation in St. Vincent. When he asked the plantation attorney to explain this condition, he was told that the slaves preferred being naked, that rain in the island rotted their clothes much sooner than the time for the annual supply to come around, and that slaves might occasionally sell their clothes. Not satisfied with this explanation, Johnson assembled the slaves and required those who had complaints to come forward one at a time and tell him their grievances. All but one of the twenty-five slaves who came forward complained that they did not receive their full allowances of clothing and provisions, and eight complained of ill treatment by punishment. Although Johnson was unable to verify the specific complaints before his departure for England, he was nevertheless severely critical of the management of this plantation.[46]

Johnson reported on the state of slave housing on three of the four sugar plantations that belonged to James Adam Gordon. On the property in St. Vincent, he found the slave houses in "very indifferent order." Several of the slaves complained that their houses had been burned down or were in a delapidated state from age and that they were allowed neither time nor materials to either replace or repair them.[47] On Lavington plantation in Antigua the slave houses were well situated and had initially been laid out at proper distances from each other. To accommodate the growing population, however, other huts had been built in the intervening spaces with no regard for order or security from fire, and the slaves had become very confined and consequently unhealthy. The housing problem was most acute on Sanderson's plantation in Antigua, where many slaves complained that they had long lived with their relatives for want of houses of their own.[48] Because slave houses were constructed of highly combustible and fragile materials and were close to one another as well as to outdoor cooking fires, storms and fires took a heavy toll of these structures. We shall see in Chapter

6 that hurricanes and severe storms from time to time swept away slave villages and left their inhabitants destitute of shelter and locally grown provisions.

As with other aspects of slave treatment, Dr. Collins not only diagnosed the problems of slave housing but also recommended practical reforms. He wrote that in the erection of slave houses, there should be three objectives: the preservation of the health of the slaves, their preservation from storms and hurricanes, and their security from fire. In siting the slave village, too low an elevation would result in the accumulation of stagnant water and exposure of the slaves to fluxes, whereas too high an elevation would expose the houses to the wind, resulting in roofs being carried away and fire spreading. The houses should not be too distant from the great house, "so that the proprietor, or his manager, may at all times have an eye to his gang, to be informed of their proceedings, to permit and encourage innocent mirth, but to suppress turbulent contentions." An interval of about thirty feet should be allowed between every house, and they should be ranged in equidistant lines for free air to circulate. Floors should be raised six or eight inches above the ground and kept dry at all times. The risk of fire should be reduced by plastering the insides of houses, and fire engines should be provided to fight fires. Stone "hurricane houses" should be built large enough to accommodate all the villagers and their belongings in times of emergency. Since the typical slave was fully occupied in plantation labor and in obtaining and cooking his or her food, no time remained to erect or repair houses. It was thus incumbent on their masters to supply building materials and order tradesmen to build and repair the houses.[49]

The work force

Given the manifold tasks to be performed, the seasonal nature of labor, the combination of field labor with the manufacture of raw sugar and rum, and the large number of slaves on a typical sugar plantation, elaborate specialization and division of labor developed. Field operations, which went on almost all the time, consisted of preparing the land, manuring, planting, and weeding; whereas the harvesting and manufacture of sugar and rum, which went on for less than half the year, consisted of cutting, crushing, boiling, curing, and distilling. Most of the labor force was committed to relatively unskilled and repetitive agricultural labor, but a sizable group of slaves was engaged in supervisory, craft, and paraprofessional occupations that required specialized knowledge and conferred elite status.[50]

Some idea of the degree of specialization and division of labor is afforded by an analysis of the slave work force on Worthy Park estate, a large, integrated sugar plantation in Jamaica. The work force, which averaged 446 in 1787–1838, was broken down into four divisions with the following numbers of slaves and percentages of total slaves: slave elite, 13 (2.91 percent); lower elite, 46 (10.31 percent); laborers, 284 (63.69 percent); and unproductive 103 (23.09 percent). In each division there were one or more categories, for a total of twenty categories. The slave elite consisted of head people and drivers; the lower elite consisted of domestics, hospital attendants, factory craftsmen, and other craftsmen; the laborers were factory laborers, stock workers, nonfactory and nonfield workers, first gang, second gang, third gang, fourth gang, and field laborers, and miscellaneous or unspecified; the unproductive slaves consisted of watchmen, miscellaneous unemployed (including sick), aged, young (under six years), women with six children, runaways, and manumitted.[51] Slaves who, because of age, disease, physical defects, or perverseness of temper, could not be adapted to field labor were not allowed to remain idle. On the contrary, they were trained as tradesmen, watchmen, hospital nurses, stockkeepers, or other occupations in accordance with their qualities and talents.[52]

Table 5.1 shows the distribution of labor on Latium estate in Jamaica during the last two years of slavery.[53] Table 5.2 shows the "Journal of the Work and Transactions of Parham New Work plantation in Antigua, the property of John Paine Tudway, during the week 7–12 March 1825. It would appear that sugar was manufactured during this week, with the possible exception of Wednesday, 9 March.[54]

Gang labor in Antigua was described as follows by John Luffman on 3 October 1787:

> The negroes are turned out at sunrise, and employed in gangs from twenty to sixty, or upwards, under the inspection of white overseers, generally poor Scotch lads, who, by their assiduity and industry, frequently became masters of the plantations, to which they came out as indentured servants; subordinate to these overseers are drivers, commonly called dog-drivers, who are mostly black or mulatto fellows, of the worst dispositions; these men are furnished with whips, which, while on duty, they are obliged, on pain of severe punishment, to have with them, and are authorized to use, wherever they see the least relaxation from labour; nor is it a consideration with them, whether it proceeds from idleness or inability, paying, at the same time, little or no respect to age or sex.

Luffman went on to say that at the end of field labor at sunset, the slaves were occupied for about an hour in picking bundles of grass for the cattle that belonged to the plantation.[55]

Authors of planter manuals cautioned masters to proportion the labor of slaves according to their age, sex, and strength, and treat them with kindness

Table 5.1. *Distribution of labor on Latium sugar plantation in Jamaica, 1832, 1833*

	1832		1833	
Agricultural workers				
First gang	135		131	
Second gang	60		60	
Third gang	34		33	
Fourth gang	27		27	
Caring for livestock	16		17	
Various jobs	19		17	
Grass cutters	15		17	
Watchmen	24		25	
Total agricultural workers		330		327
Mechanics, etc.				
Domestics	15		15	
Carpenters	9		9	
Coopers	10		8	
Masons	7		7	
Smiths	1		1	
Total mechanics, etc.		42		40
Total slaves who work		372		367
Nonworking slaves				
Diseased	4		3	
Invalids	12		16	
Women with six children or upward	7		6	
Servants at great house	14		13	
Young children	45		46	
Total nonworking slaves		82		84
Total slaves on plantation		454		451

Source: Extracts from tables compiled by Henry Hunter, attorney of Latium estate, Jamaica, and printed as an appendix in Joseph Sturge and Thomas Harvey, *The West Indies in 1837 Being the Journal of a Visit to Antigua, Montserrat, Dominica, St. Lucia, Barbados, and Jamaica* (London: Frank Cass, 1968), p. lxxvii.

and good nature. These principles were not sufficiently attended to, according to Dr. Collins. He said it was customary to divide the slaves on a given plantation into two parts: adults and children. The consequence of this was "either that the weaker negroes must retard the progress of the stronger ones, or your drivers, insensible of the cause of their backwardness, or not weighing it properly, will incessantly urge them, either with stripes or threats, to keep up with the others; by which means they are overwrought, and compelled to resort to the sick-house."[56]

Table 5.2. *Journal of Parham New Work sugar plantation in Antigua for the week 7–12 March 1825*

Occupations, etc.	Mon. 7	Tues. 8	Wed. 9	Thurs. 10	Fri. 11	Sat. 12
Field workers						
First class	37	38	56	38	38	38
Second class	19	19	27	19	19	19
About the works	24	24	0	24	24	24
Carters and ploughmen	6	6	4	6	6	6
Mule boys and plough boys	2	2	2	2	2	2
Tradesmen and apprentices	15	15	15	15	15	15
Jobbing slaves						
Men	1	1	1	1	1	1
Old women loading carts with manure	7	7	7	7	7	7
House servants, cooks, and washers	6	6	6	6	6	6
Nurses and pregnant	23	23	23	23	23	23
Stockkeepers	2	2	2	2	2	2
Watchmen	4	4	4	4	4	4
Invalids and aged above 60 years of age	18	18	18	18	18	18
Sick	7	6	6	6	6	6
Laid up with yaws or sores	2	2	2	2	2	2
Children under 12 years	72	72	72	72	72	72
Midwives and seamstresses	2	2	2	2	2	2
Rangers, foremen, and attendants on the sick	5	5	5	5	5	5
Total slaves	252	252	252	252	252	252

Source: Journal of the Work and Transactions of Parham New Work plantation in Antigua, the property of John Paine Tudway of Wells, County Somerset, England, *Tudway Papers*, Somerset County Record Office, Taunton.

So that the weak should not work too much, nor the strong too little, Collins advised planters to divide their labor force into more sections or gangs. Newly purchased slaves should be initiated by degrees into field labor. They should not join the great gang until they matured and acquired sufficient bodily strength. Under normal conditions, children aged nine or ten were shifted from the grass gang to the weeding gang, where they remained until they were fourteen or fifteen when they were removed to the second gang. At maturity, they moved up to the first or great gang. Thus, as Collins pointed out, the planter obtained "a perpetual succession of recruits, gradually trained and habituated to labour, and fitted for every purpose whatever on the plantation."[57]

Management of absentees' estates

Black field slaves were the most poverty stricken and oppressed group in the islands, writes Elsa Goveia. "They worked under the discipline of the driving system, backed by the master's private powers of punishment and by the force of public laws made by the slaveowning class; and they were kept dependent on their masters for the barest necessities of life while their labour provided the white ruling class with the conspicuous wealth which strengthened their hold on the organization of the community." In short, the black field slave was truly the "muzzled ox" of West Indian society, whose life was one of unceasing toil, subjection, and deprivation.[58]

Contributing to the life of unceasing toil and deprivation was the system of management whereby great numbers of West Indian proprietors became absentees, leaving their slave plantations under the care of agents. Edward Long wrote in 1774 of the many property owners in Jamaica who had flocked to Great Britain and North America. He estimated that there were as many as 2,000 "annuitants and proprietors non-resident." In 1775, when there were reportedly 775 sugar estates in Jamaica, local records show that 234 of these estates were held by 180 absentee proprietors or by minors or incompetents. Absenteeism increased both absolutely and relatively; in 1832 the records show that as many as 540 of a total of 646 sugar estates were owned by absentees, minors, or incompetents.[59]

The management of absentees' estates progressed from informal arrangements with relatives and friends to more formal agreements with professional attorneys or managers. People of various descriptions and qualifications set themselves up as attorneys. Some were planters on their own account, whereas others were merchants, physicians, lawyers, and even clergymen. Some attorneys lived in the great house of the absentee and managed one or more contiguous estates. Others who had more extensive concerns were "followed about the country with a retinue of carriages, of servants, and of horses, which shake the ground as they thunder along; and when he arrives upon the plantation, the command goes forth, to catch and kill; the table is covered with profusion, and few are suffered to go empty, I had almost said sober, away."[60]

Attorneyships were eagerly sought after. The attorney drew a salary or a commission of 5 or 6 percent of the gross value of the produce of the plantation in his care. From this he had to make an allowance "to a person to keep the books of the property, and to do in his absence such business as the overseer, from a different line of occupation, is either incompetent to, or has not leisure to superintend."[61] If the legally allowed income was ample, the rewards were sometimes exorbitant because of the perquisites and opportunities for peculation and fraud. William Beckford called attention to the incompetence and dishonesty of certain attorneys, yet he noted that many of them were leaders in the community, "independent legislators, useful magistrates, and men of property; and who are besides attentive and just to the interest of their employers, and respectable both in public and private life."[62]

Slaves who were owned by absentee proprietors were reportedly less well cared for than their brothers and sisters who belonged to resident proprietors. Contributing to this were the divergent interests of absentees and their attorneys and managers. Whereas the former had a permanent interest in the preservation of their labor force, the latter had an interest only in their reputation. As Dr. Collins explained it,

> The character of a manager is generally deduced from the quantity of produce which he extracts from the estate, though the loss sustained by the mortality of the slaves, in consequence of his undue exertions, is sometimes considerable enough to exhaust the whole amount of its produce, notwithstanding it was as ample as the estate was capable of affording. In such cases, the credit of the crops is appropriated to those who direct the estates, whilst the destruction attending them is charged upon Providence. The public is generally very indulgent in that respect to residents: indeed, they form the public, and determine its voice.

Collins urged proprietors to judge the performance of their attorneys and managers by demographic rather than short-term economic considerations. He wrote that crops could be too large if obtained by the destruction of the labor force. Indeed, he argued that "the scarcity of deaths, and the number of births will afford much more certain indications of good management, than that of mere produce can do, unless that be far short of what might reasonably be expected from the season, the subject, and the power employed on its culture."[63]

Conclusion

A sugar plantation was a landed estate that specialized in the production of an agricultural staple for export; it used a plentiful supply of low-productivity labor under the authority of a planter or his agent. A major task in this chapter has been to analyze the problems encountered by African slaves in adapting to life on sugar plantations. Since they lacked immunity to local diseases and were often debilitated from long confinement, bad food, and improper treatment on the voyage, newly imported slaves died in great numbers from disease and despondency. It can be argued that although enlightened planters took measures to protect the health of newcomers during the seasoning, they were outnumbered by planters who, by purchasing new slaves to harvest crops and cope with other exigencies, condemned their bondsmen to an early grave.

Besides the problem of seasoning newcomers, this chapter has looked at the treatment of slaves in other respects. It has been argued that the standards of clothing and housing in the British Sugar Colonies were low in comparison with those of slaves in the United States, even making allowances for differences in climate. Authors of planter manuals and critics of slavery charged slave owners with neglecting clothing and housing. Slave houses were frequently thrown together with materials scavanged from the plantations; they were overcrowded, drafty, pest-ridden, and vulnerable to storms and fires. Standards varied, however, and some planters constructed slave houses of ample size and durability, taking precautions against fire and storm.

Whereas the authors of planter manuals cautioned masters to proportion the labor of slaves according to their age, sex, and strength, practice often fell far short of precept and the weak were forced to work too much while the strong worked below capacity. Notwithstanding the widespread failure to conform to the standards of their critics, sugar planters could not avoid dividing their labor force into gangs. Most slaves performed unskilled and repetitive agricultural labor in gangs that were roughly adapted to the difficulty of the tasks, but a sizable number was trained as artisans, supervisors, domestics, and paraprofessionals. Contributing to the life of unceasing toil and deprivation of the black field slaves was the system of absentee proprietorship, whereby the slave fell victim to the divergent interests of absentees and their attorneys and managers.

As Lord Goderich noted, the typical slave yielded an annual surplus over the cost of his or her maintenance and the amortization of his or her initial cost. Because the amount of the surplus depended in large measure on the physical exertion of slaves, their dietary needs, and punishment, it will be our task in Chapter 6 to investigate these critical areas and their effect on the health and well-being of the slaves.

6

Labor, diet, and punishment

> To expect the Slaves in general, worn down as very many of them are, by daily, and, in crop time, by nightly labor, to support themselves, by working on Sundays, in their own grounds; – to trust to the desultory, heartless exertions of such beings, to avert famine!, is, to say the least of it, extremely impolitic . . . Certainly the admission of foreign provisions, in consequence of tempest, drought, or other unavoidable calamities, should be no precedent to the planters to depend on a resource of which they often felt the inadequacy, even before there was any restraint on the American trades.
>
> William Dickson, 1814[1]

Our task in this chapter is to investigate in some detail the nature of the plantation labor system in its agricultural and industrial aspects and on a seasonal basis, and to describe and analyze the systems of supplying the workers with food and the adequacy of their diets. Furthermore, we investigate the nature and frequency of slave punishments and show how they were related to other forms of treatment.

Cane hole digging and night work

Writers on slavery differed about how long and hard the blacks worked. Philip Gibbes, an absentee planter of Barbados who sought to reform slavery, believed that the cultivation of sugarcane, from the insertion of the plants in the earth to the packing of the sugar in the cask, was a continuous process of hard labor.[2] Captain John Samuel Smith, a critic of the institution who had lived in Antigua, contended on the other hand that plantation work of itself was not hard. "It is the use of strength instead of contrivance:" he wrote, "it is the want of food, clothes, rest, and sleep, that wears slaves out. It is the drawing out of their tasks from early dawn to dusky night; it is the wandering three or four miles under the meridian sun to pick up their bundles of grass, that constitutes their hardships."[3]

The fact is that sugar slavery was more or less arduous and enervating, depending on such factors as the extent to which the slaves were driven by their masters, the tasks they performed, the hours of work, diet, and rest periods. The tasks varied greatly between the sugar harvest or "crop time"

Figure 6.1. Holing a cane piece on a plantation in Antigua. From William Clark, *Ten Views in the Island of Antigua* (London, 1823), reproduced by courtesy of Mr. David A. Jessop, Director, The West India Committee, London.

and the remainder of the year, or so-called dead season. During the dead season, which generally extended from May or June to December or January, the field slaves dug cane holes, made and carried dung, planted, replanted, weeded, and thinned the canes. Shortly before they were cut, the canes were stripped of their leaves or "trashed." Field slaves also cut and gathered wood and other fuel to stoke the furnace in the boiling house, gathered grass and other fodder for the livestock, and tended their kitchen gardens and provision grounds. Skilled slaves were kept busy maintaining and repairing buildings and equipment, making hogsheads and barrels, transporting supplies, tending livestock, ministering to the sick, exterminating rats, catching fish, and doing other tasks.

Cane hole digging was considered the most strenuous labor performed by field slaves (see Figure 6.1). Hoe-wielding blacks excavated holes approximately five feet square to a depth of five to twelve inches for the purpose of checking wind and water erosion, concentrating fertilizer, and sheltering infant cane plants from the trade winds and storms. James Ramsay, the antislavery leader who lived in St. Kitts, wrote that it was a common day's labor "for thirty grown slaves to dig with hoes, in a loose gravelly soil, an acre of ground, into holes of five feet by four, from about seven to twelve inches deep, leaving space between the rows equal at least to half the holes, untouched, to receive the mould." In his classic account of the "driving system," James Stephen, another antislavery leader who lived in St. Kitts, wrote that "in holeing a cane piece" for the reception of the cane plants "the slaves, of both sexes, from twenty, perhaps, to fourscore in number, are drawn out in a line, like troops on a parade, each with a hoe in his hand, and close to them in the rear is stationed, a driver, or several drivers, in number duly proportioned to that of the gang." Wielding a "long thick and strongly plaited whip, called a *cart whip*," the driver's task was to urge forward the holers and see that all in the line, "whether male or female, old or young, strong or feeble," worked as much as possible in equal time and with equal effect. "No breathing time, no resting on the hoe, no pause of languor, to be repaid by brisker exertion on return to work, can be allowed to individuals: All must work, or pause together," wrote Stephen (see Figure 6.1).[4]

Other contemporaries called attention to the deleterious effects of digging cane holes. A critic of slave management in Jamaica wrote:

> It is very customary for overseers to mix the weak and sickly negroes in the same gang with the stout and healthy, and to make them keep up their rows alike, and when any of these miserable, and probably half-starved wretches lag, to insist on their black deputies to cut and mangle their shrivelled skins, and torture them from morning till night, in like manner as if they were mules or oxen![5]

Testifying before a Parliamentary committee in 1832, William Taylor, a Jamaican plantation attorney, said that cane hole digging called for severe exertion and had a very bad effect on the female frame. It was the general feeling among overseers that the slave population increased on coffee plantations and cattle pens but decreased in the sugar districts. Taylor concluded that the decrease "was owing to the hard work on sugar estates, and chiefly owing to cane hole digging, because the other work is not so hard."[6]

Heavy applications of fertilizer were required to grow sugarcane. In Barbados the slaves reportedly carried baskets of manure on their heads, each weighing eighty pounds. One basketful was deposited in each cane hole, amounting to a total of sixty-four tons per acre. On her visit to St. Kitts, Janet Schaw saw everywhere large dunghills of compound manure. She observed a group of slaves, each with a basket, "which he carries up the hill filled with the manure and returns with a load of canes to the Mill. They go up at a trot, and return at a gallop, and did you not know the cruel necessity of this alertness, you would believe them the merriest people in the world."[7]

Picking grass and other fodder to feed livestock required little exertion but encroached on time the slaves normally regarded as their own. Grass picking was required of slaves in the small islands and parts of Jamaica

Figure 6.2. A mill yard on a plantation in Antigua. From William Clark, *Ten Views in the Island of Antigua* (London, 1823), reproduced by courtesy of Mr. David Jessop, Director, The West India Committee, London.

because the planters were so intent upon growing sugarcane that they lacked sufficient pastures and land in forage crops to support their livestock. Field slaves were often required to pick a bundle of grass within a limited time during the noon dinner break and again at the end of the day. In St. Kitts, according to Ramsay, they could be seen before sunset scattered over the land "like the Israelites in Egypt, to cull, blade by blade, from among the weeds, their scanty parcels of grass." If they were late or returned with less than the required amount "they were punished with a number of stripes, from four to ten. Some masters, under a fit of carefulness for their cattle, have gone as far as fifty stripes, which effectually disable the culprit for weeks." Ramsay considered grass picking "the greatest hardship that a slave endures, and the most frequent cause of his running away, or absenting himself from his work; which not only subjects him to frequent punishment, but actually renders him unprofitable, worthless, and deserving of punishment."[8]

The activity that characterized crop time was viewed by Michael Scott from shipboard as he approached Jamaica (see Figure 6.2). "The breeze-mill towers burst into light," he wrote in *Tom Cringle's Log*,

> and cattle-mills, with their cone-shaped roofs, and overseers' houses, and water-mills, with the white spray falling from the wheels, and sugar-works, with long pennants of white smoke streaming from the boiling-house chimneys seaward in the morning wind. Immediately after, gangs

> of negroes were seen at work; loaded waggons, with enormous teams of fourteen to twenty oxen dragging them, rolled along the roads; long strings of mules loaded with canes were threading the fields; drogging vessels were seen to shove out from every cove.[9]

By far the most slaves labored in the cane fields wielding long heavy "bills," "cutlasses," or "machettes." One at a time the ripened canes were cut close to the roots, stripped of the remaining leaves and cane tops, and then cut into shorter pieces to be tied into bundles. The bundles were carried to the mill by slaves, pack animals, or carts drawn by draft animals. At the mill, which was powered by wind, water, or draft animals, the canes were fed through the rollers, from whence the juice was conveyed to the cisterns and finally to the boiling house. Slaves called "boilers" skimmed off the impurities that rose to the surface of the boiling liquid, which was ladled from one copper basin to another until it became viscid enough to crystallize. Curing took place in a separate building where the brown mass was shoveled into hogsheads or earthenware pots and allowed to stand for several weeks while the molasses drained from the sugar. The molasses might be consumed on the plantation, sold at a local market, or distilled into rum. The final steps consisted of packing the sugar into hogsheads, which were transported by carts and wagons to the seaside where they were loaded onto droghers or lighters to be taken to the seagoing vessels anchored in the coves, bays, and harbors.[10]

The sugar harvest, extending from four to six months, combined the work of field and factory both day and night in what was a harsher labor regimen than in the satanic mills of the Industrial Revolution. The pace was accelerated and working hours extended to finish the crop before the May rains. Since greed and avarice induced the planters to grow more canes than they had the labor, power, or time to manage, there was a rush to harvest as much as possible, often to the physical impairment of the workers. The piling of night work on top of labor from sunrise to sunset can be explained by a combination of technical factors and greed. The technical factors were that the mills were small and inefficient by modern standards, more canes were cut on a given day than could be accommodated by the mills, and after they were cut the canes had to be manufactured into sugar in about forty-eight hours, otherwise they spoiled.

Crop time saw the able-bodied slaves working at their regular daytime tasks such as cutting canes and also performing night work in the mill house and boiling house. Evidence on the nature and extent of night work was given by several leading Jamaicans who testified before the Select Committee on the Extinction of Slavery in 1832. According to Robert Scott, "All the able people are divided into spells; upon some estates there are three spells, and upon others only two, according to the population; each of those spells is subdivided, so that one division of them take the work the first part of the night, and the other division the second part." Daytime labor extended over approximately twelve hours with a half-hour break for breakfast and two hours for dinner. Scott said that the spells generally came to work at eight o'clock at night and worked until midnight, at which time they were relieved by the second division of that spell who worked until they were relieved by the daytime factory workers at six the next morning. Upon leaving the boiling house at six, the slave went to the field and worked until sunset, with the exception of the time for breakfast and dinner. The slave would then have the night off, work all the following day in the field, after which he would work the eight to twelve night shift.[11]

As explained by James Beckford Wildman, the double spell was "the alternation of 12 [hours] out of 24, and 18 out of the 24 that the slave on the estate, who works from sunrise to sunset, goes to the boiling-house at 6, and continues till 12 on Monday night; he then goes off, performs his usual day's work on Tuesday, is all Tuesday night in bed, and then on Wednesday night, after his field labour, he comes on at 12 o'clock, and works 18 hours in that 24, so that is an alternation of 12 hours and 18 hours of every four-and-twenty during crop." Wildman testified that night work destroyed the lives of his slaves. It was particularly destructive to slaves who came to the mill after working in the field all day. They were sprayed with cane juice as they fed the mill, laid down to sleep in their wet clothes during slack intervals, contracted colds and pneumonia, and frequently died.[12] According to Gilbert Mathison, another Jamaica planter, all blacks were pressed into night work "to divide as much as possible the fatigues of the crop." Whereas the young, active people were said to have performed their duties "with cheerfulness and without injury," the elderly and weakly shrunk from such fatigues and suffered "most cruelly during a long protracted crop, under the pressure of these heavy duties."[13]

Planters frequently remarked on the healthfulness and cheerfulness of their slaves during crop time, despite the long hours of labor they required. This condition of well-being was attributed chiefly to the unrestricted quantities of cane juice the slaves were permitted to consume. Less optimistic was the report of the Reverend John Masterton Waddell, a Presbyterian missionary in Jamaica. He noted that the slaves were lively at the beginning of the crop and seemed to thrive on the sweet cane juice, of which they had a plentiful supply. "But 'ere the season closed they began to suffer, were fagged and sickly, from excessive toil and want of proper food." After working from sunrise to sunset in the field, the night workers never went to their houses, he said, "but threw themselves down to sleep in the trash-houses, to be near when called, huddled together regardless of sex or age."[14]

Robert W. Fogel contends that the development of a new, industrial labor discipline was a major technological innovation of the sugar planters. "This was at once their greatest technological achievement," he writes, "the foundation of their economic success, and the ugliest aspect of their system."[15] Not only did the discipline consist of combined and constant labor under a regimen of coercion, but it also extended the duration of labor beyond the traditional daylight hours. James Stephen, the antislavery leader, drew on Parliamentary reports to calculate the amount of slave labor on sugar plantations in comparison with that of agricultural laborers in England. He found that "the time of the slave-labour, to the time of the free-labour, is, on an average of the whole year, as sixteen, at least, to nine," and that the consequence of intense and excessive labor for the slaves was "exhaustion and weakness, sickness, and premature death."[16]

War and famine

Slaves needed ample supplies of nutritious food if they were to be physically capable of performing the labor their masters required. They needed carbohydrates and fats, which are the body's main sources of energy and heat; proteins for repairing the cells that are constantly broken down and repaired; and iron, calcium, vitamins, and other essential elements. Food requirements varied according to a slave's size, sex, and age. Moreover, they varied according to a slave's occupation and physical exertion. Workers engaged in heavy or sustained manual labor require higher-energy foods than those in less active or sedentary jobs. Sugar planters often took advantage of the dead season after the harvest to direct their slaves in the growing of food crops. Yet as the plantation frontier expanded and a greater proportion of land was planted in sugarcane, fewer acres remained for growing provisions and pasturing livestock. The upshot was an increased dependence on imported supplies of intermediate goods – that is, provisions, livestock, building materials, and containers.

West Indian sugar planters recognized two systems of feeding slaves: one at the expense of the master and the other by the labor of the slave. Under the former system, slaves might be fed imported foodstuffs, they might be required to grow food crops on their master's land as a regular part of plantation labor, they might be supplied with cash to purchase food, or they might depend on a combination of these methods for their sustenance. Planters not only directed slaves in the cultivation of food crops, but in some cases they also provided cooked food for slaves who were sick, indigent, or aged, and for mothers, infants, and older children. Slaves were fed by their own labor when they cultivated on their own time land that was not needed for the production of exportable staples. Generally speaking, the slave was allowed to plant what he wanted and was not supervised. He could specialize in any type of crop, raise poultry or swine, or produce handicrafts. Any surplus above the requirements of his family could be sold at market and the proceeds used to buy food, drink, clothing, or household furnishings.

Factors that influenced the degree to which the slaves were fed by imported or locally grown foodstuffs included access to low-cost, dependable supplies from abroad, availability of land capable of growing foodstuffs but considered submarginal for staple production, and the policies and practices of individual planters and imperial governments. To the extent that British Caribbean planters were economically rational, they were encouraged by the structure of the Atlantic economy and the mercantile system to concentrate their resources on sugar production, and to depend on imported African slaves, foodstuffs, milling equipment, building materials, and other items of fixed and variable capital. What was considered economically rational, however, could well be nutritionally irrational.

The sharp reduction of trade between the United States and the British West Indies during and after the American Revolution had far-reaching consequences. Before the revolution the resources of the Sugar Colonies had been concentrated on producing and exporting tropical staples to the extent that the islands were highly dependent on the continental colonies for equipment and supplies. Curtailment of trade set in motion a series of crises, resulting in efforts to expand alternative overseas sources of supply and markets and to diversify the island economies. Most critical was the problem of providing subsistence for the slaves, who had been supplied with largely North American foodstuffs before the revolution. Compounding the problem was an unprecedented series of hurricanes and tropical storms that denuded the islands of vegetation and left the inhabitants without reserves of locally grown foodstuffs.

Following a period of plentiful supplies and low prices at the outbreak of the war came scarcity and high prices, which induced the West Indians to seek alternative sources of foodstuffs. Although the planters devoted more land and labor to the cultivation of food crops, they were forced to rely chiefly on imports from Great Britain and Ireland, wartime captures, and trade with neutral territories in the Caribbean. An act of Parliament of December 1775 prohibited commercial intercourse with the rebellious colonies. One of its provisions allowed British merchants to trade with those continental colonies that remained loyal to the crown and with areas under the control of British troops. When this led to extensive illegal trade with the rebel colonies, efforts were made to restrict trade to areas under British control by means of licenses. After 1775 the only legal mainland trade was with Canada, Nova Scotia, East Florida, and West Florida. For a time the islanders received food and other supplies from American vessels that were seized in Caribbean waters. Other indirect sources of American supplies were the free ports of Caribbean islands held by Holland, Spain, France, and Denmark, and the Bahamas and Bermuda, which remained loyal to the crown.[17]

The increased cost of imported supplies, together with shipping losses to privateers, bore heavily upon the Barbadians. The council and assembly addressed the king in 1777, stating that "we have, Sir, near 80,000 black and 12,000 white people daily to support. Our ground provisions (the internal resource) have failed for want of seasonable rains; the stock of provisions on hand will not last many weeks; and we are without hope of future foreign resources."[18] The assembly reported to the crown on 14 April 1778 that the colony was "decayed and impoverished," credit had ceased, and trade was very low.[19] Governor Edward Hay wrote two months later that the inhabitants seemed despondent: "Their Credit lessens dayly; Creditors become Sollicitous to recover their Debts." A measure of relief was afforded by the arrival of six vessels from England early in 1778 with cargoes of flour, beans, and peas, accompanied by two more laden with fish.[20]

Unlike Barbados, which was largely foreign fed, Jamaica had ample land for the cultivation of foodstuffs and did supply a substantial part of its needs. Yet the profits from sugarcane had induced planters to neglect subsistence crops in peacetime when supplies from North America were forthcoming. At the beginning of the revolution the situation was less critical in Jamaica than it was in the eastern Caribbean, although severe scarcity had led to an embargo on the exportation of provisions for Jamaica by January 1776.[21]

A planned slave insurrection in July 1776, though discovered and savagely crushed, increased the troubles in Jamaica. Supplies of food became scarce because of drought, a state of martial law, and the need to feed additional troops. Many parts of the island were reported to be "labouring under the distresses of Famine" in October 1776.[22] The following July a plantation manager reported to an absentee proprietor that everything was extravagantly dear: "If the unfortunate war in America is not soon ended we shall suffer greatly. This Country Corn is now from 5/- to 12/6 and should *our own provision* fail we must starve of which we had a specimen last year."[23] The moderate to exorbitant increases in Jamaican prices of rice, Indian corn, and common flour are shown in Table 6.1.

The Leeward Islands were the most vulnerable of the British Sugar Colonies to embargo and war because of their close proximity to islands held by foreign nations, the extent to which sugar monoculture was practiced, their dependence on external food supplies, and frequent droughts. Word of the threatened embargo had reached Colonel Samuel Martin, an Antigua planter, by 6 July 1774, when he wrote his eldest son, a member of Parliament, "I suppose you have seen in the News Paper the several resolutions

Table 6.1. *Prices of foodstuffs in Jamaica*

Commodity	Before the war	During the war
Rice, per cwt.	13*s*. 9*d*. to 20*s*.	40*s*. to 80*s*.
Indian corn, per bu.	2*s*. 6*d*. to 6*s*. 3*d*.	6*s*. 8*d*. to 17*s*. 6*d*.
Common flour, per cwt.	15*s*. to 20*s*.	20*s*. to 50*s*.

Source: P.R.O. London, *C.O.* 137/85, report made in March 1785.

of the Boston people to starve the Sugar Colonies out of spite to great Britain. Most inhuman and unchristian resolutions!"[24] Martin was hard pressed to find ways to feed his more than 300 slaves. Hearing that the islands were to be "starved by the American resolutions," he wrote on 8 October 1774 that he had sent to Virginia for corn and lumber. On 13 July 1775 he reported that he was making all prudent provision possible "by planting black-eyed Peas, and Guinea Corn and by remittance of Rum to North Carolina for the purchase of Indian Corn." One month later he expressed his dread of famine to come when the North American ports were shut, necessitating greater recourse to provisions imported from England and Ireland and to locally grown supplies.[25]

The Tudway correspondence details the impact of embargoes and war on the slaves of Antigua. Clement Tudway, member of Parliament for Wells, owned more than 500 slaves on his two plantations in that island. He was informed by his plantation manager in March 1776 that

> it is necessary for You to send out a good many more Beans and Oats this Year than You have usually sent. If you will please to look back into your Accounts, You will find we have every Year expended a great deal of American Corn, to feed the Negroes and Stock, besides the Oats and Beans that have been sent from England, and in that proportion an additional quantity of both Beans and Oats will be wanted, and some of each must soon be sent, especially the Beans, or the Negroes must starve, unless reconciliation between Great Britain and her American Colonies should very soon take place, of which there does not at present seem to be any probability.

More ominous news arrived a few weeks later:

> This Island was never so much threaten'd with Famine as it now is, we can get nothing from North America, and the Weather is so dry that we can raise no kind of Provisions here. Pray God send us better times. I beg you will not forget to order out a supply of Oats and Beans as soon as possible, particularly the latter. You have more than five hundred Negroes to feed, who will eat your Cattle and Mules, if they have nothing else to eat, and cut my Throat, if I attempt to prevent them.[26]

Antigua was approaching famine in October 1777, when emergency measures were taken to import provisions from the French and Dutch islands. Some corn was harvested in Antigua. Yet despite these supplies, Tudway's plantation attorney estimated that "from 1000 to 1500 Negroes will be lost in consequence of this scarcity, many are already Dead and a great many so reduced it will scarcely be practicable to raise them, however, your Negroes are not in this unhappy situation, but always had a tolerable allowance of Provisions." By December 1778, not a bushel of grain could be bought in Antigua. Many people were "without any kind of Food for their Negroes, nor do we know from whence any is to be bought, St. Eustatius excepted, where there are only a few hundred Bushels of Beans, and a Gentleman is gone to purchase them . . . A great many Slaves have died for want of Food, and I am sure many more will die."[27]

Tragic conditions were again reported in September 1779. Tudway's plantation manager was very unhappy about the condition of the blacks. They were sick throughout the island, and mortality among them was higher than at any time in his memory. Tudway's own losses were shocking: "You have buried Seventeen Negroes since the 24th July, fifteen of whom you will find have died since my last Letter. You now have many Sick, some very ill, and God knows where our Losses in Slaves will End." Severe drought throughout the island dried up the ponds and made the import of water necessary. Food supplies became so critical that the blacks were allowed but one pint of horse beans a day. On 1 July 1779 the assembly of Antigua authorized the borrowing of £20,000 to be expended on provisions. Emergency supplies were needed to cope with the famine.[28]

Severe food shortages had become general throughout the Leeward Islands when Governor William Burt wrote to Lord George Germaine from St. Kitts in March 1778: "From the best information I have been able to collect, the Island of Antigua has lost about a thousand Negroes, Montserat near twelve Hundred, and some Whites – Nevis three to four Hundred, and This Island as many from the Want of Provisions." Burt begged for provisions: "Unless these Ships are sent, the Ground and Colonial Provisions will not half supply us; add to this, should there be a Hurricane God only knows what may be the Event."[29]

Hurricanes, wars, and famine

The weather had a determining influence on slave subsistence, particularly when trade was interrupted or uncertain. Jamaican slaves grew more food than their counterparts in the Lesser Antilles, but their needs were seldom fully met without imported supplies. Douglas Hall writes that the essential goods for immediate consumption can be arranged into three categories: "those produced and sold in the Island; those imported as substitutes for the first group; and those imports which were not or were not considered to be, substitutes for the first group." In the first group were such slave-grown provisions as yams, sweet potatoes, cassava, plantains, eddoes, corn on the cob, and fruit. The supply of these was greatly dependent on weather conditions. Imported substitutes included flour, cornmeal, bread, and salted or pickled beef or pork; the nonsubstitutes consisted of such items as salt fish, pickled fish, oil, soap, and candles.[30]

Beginning in 1780 a series of hurricanes and earthquakes struck the West Indies, exacerbating the crisis of slave subsistence. Jamaica was the first island to be devastated by hurricanes and earthquakes in 1780. First came the hurricane of 22 February, which damaged or destroyed more than forty vessels in Montego Bay and damaged plantations along the north coast. The second hurricane produced a tidal wave that destroyed the little seaport town of Savanna-la-Mar on 3 October. "This most dreadful Catastrophe," wrote Governor John Dalling to Lord Germaine, "was succeeded by the most dreadful Hurricane that was ever felt in this Country, with repeated Shocks of an Earthquake which has almost demolished every Building in the parishes of Westmoreland, Hanover, part of St. James's and some part as well of the Negroes."[31] The parishes of Westmoreland and Hanover were the principal victims, with somewhat less destruction in St. James and St. Elizabeth. In Westmoreland alone the loss was estimated at £700,000. More than a thousand lives were lost, buildings were leveled, and there was "not a tree, bush, or cane to be seen." The *Annual Register* reported that "a great number of the white inhabitants, and of necessity, a much greater of the negroes, perished during the course of the hurricane. The provisions were entirely destroyed; and the live stock escaped little better." The merchants of Kingston responded by supplying provisions, clothing, and other temporary relief amounting to £10,000.[32]

One week later, on 10 October, a hurricane struck Barbados. It engulfed the tiny island, leveling buildings, uprooting trees, destroying cane fields and plantain walks, and driving vessels onto the beaches. Devastation among the slaves and cattle was very great. Indeed, the losses sustained by the whole island, as recorded by the local government, amounted to 2,033 blacks and 6,606 head of cattle killed, and damage and destruction totaling £1,320,000.[33] The merchants of Bridgetown formed an association and appointed committees to bury the dead and distribute provisions and clothing. A petition was submitted to the British government detailing the calamity and appealing for relief. In consequence of this and other petitions, the House of Commons voted £80,000 to Barbados and £40,000 to Jamaica.[34]

Few islands escaped the hurricanes of 1780. Although no bad effects were reported in Antigua, many vessels were forced on shore at St. Kitts. In the Windwards damage was reported at St. Lucia, St. Vincent, Dominica, and Grenada. By far the greatest losses occurred at Martinique, where the deaths were estimated at over 9,000, and at St. Eustatius, where between 4,000 and 5,000 people perished.[35]

The Jamaica hurricane of 1 August 1781 struck only ten months after the great storm of the previous year. Governor Dalling reported that the effects were not so dreadful as those of the earlier hurricane, "yet in several parishes and more particularly those of Westmoreland and Hanover, the damage is very great, in the destruction of the Plantain Trees and Corn by which the Negroes are chiefly subsisted; – nor have the Shipping escaped."[36]

West Indians, who at the peace treaty of 1783 expected trade to resume on the prewar footing, were sorely disappointed. William Pitt's bill for liberal trade concessions to the United States was brushed aside. In its place were adopted two orders-in-council that represented a victory for the defenders of the navigation laws. By these orders West Indians were allowed to import all kinds of U.S. lumber, livestock, grain, vegetables, flour, and bread, and to export British-grown products to America in British ships. American vessels were excluded from the islands, as were American beef, pork, dairy products, and fish. Meanwhile the islanders were becoming restive. "The unsettled and confused state of Government in England for some time past, must be attended with very bad consequences to the whole Empire," wrote Main Swete Walrond from Antigua in April 1784. "We feel it much here, and especially in not yet having a free and open Trade with the Americans, which we were in hopes would have taken place soon after the War was over."[37]

Once again the starvation-prone islands were struck by nature's fury. From Kingston, Jamaica, came a report on 31 July 1784 that the dreadful hurricane of the previous night had been devastating beyond imagination. Most of the vessels in the harbor were either dismasted or driven on shore, and many lives were lost.[38] The lieutenant governor, by advice of his council, published a proclamation of 7 August permitting the free importation of provisions and lumber in foreign bottoms for four months. In consideration of the limited imports and high prices, the period was later extended to 31 January 1785, after which the slaves were said to have suffered extremely until the corn and ground provisions were harvested.[39]

The fifth hurricane that hit Jamaica on 27 August 1785 was more violent than the storm of the previous year, lasted longer, and did greater damage. Immense losses were reportedly sustained by the inhabitants, who had not recovered from the heavy injuries of the previous year. Fortunately, the island was well supplied with provisions, which sold at low prices. To prevent their exportation an embargo was laid on shipping for six weeks.[40] Jamaica was not the only sufferer. On 24 August a heavy gale did considerable damage on St. Kitts, Antigua, Nevis, and St. Eustatius. Letters from Antigua and other islands brought "melancholy accounts of the distresses of the inhabitants for want of corn and other provisions; the hurricanes, and a variety of other bad weather, having wasted almost their whole produce. If not allowed to trade with the Continent of America, a famine is apprehended."[41]

The sixth and last group of hurricanes ranged broadly across the Caribbean Sea. Early in August 1786, the southern coast of Hispaniola was almost laid waste by a violent storm. On 2 September, Barbados was thrown "into the utmost consternation" by a severe hurricane. Shipping losses were heavy in Carlisle Bay. The buildings on many estates were crushed; plantain walks, corn, cotton, and cane were damaged or destroyed; the slave houses were mostly blown away; and many of the inhabitants were killed. "In short, nothing can be represented more deplorable," wrote a Barbadian to the *Gentleman's Magazine.* Following the blow to Barbados came the hurricane of 10 September, which destroyed much of the plantations on Guadeloupe. Finally, a storm struck Jamaica on the night of 19 October, causing great destruction in many parts of the island.[42]

The number of slaves who died from causes directly or indirectly connected with trade embargoes, war, droughts, and hurricanes was a concern to island governments, planters, and humanitarians. In the hurricane of 1780, 2,033 Barbadian blacks were reported lost. William Dickson wrote that this list appeared to have been made up from the returns of the churchwardens "who had not the means of accuracy." He quoted higher figures from other sources, in particular the lists of "Negroes" used for the poll tax. According to this return, Barbados had 68,270 slaves in 1780 and only 63,248 in 1781, or a difference of 5,022, "*most* of them killed by the hurricane."[43]

Slave losses in Jamaica were estimated by a committee of the House of Assembly. The committee fixed the total deaths at 15,000 out of a slave population of about 256,000. "This Number we firmly believe to have perished of Famine, or of Diseases contracted by scanty and unwholesome Diet, between the latter End of 1780 and the Beginning of 1787."[44] This report was challenged by a Mr. Wynne, who was convinced by much inquiry that the stated loss of 15,000 slaves was low by several thousands. Besides the multitude of slaves who perished in the famine, which Wynne was convinced exceeded 21,000, he firmly believed "that far more were so broken down that they gradually pined away; but, as they died not during the scarcity, their death was attributed to fluxes, etc. not considering that these were induced by the preceding famine."[45] Hector McNeill, a Scotsman who was visiting Jamaica during the great storm of 1780, wrote that a European could form no just idea of a West India hurricane, far less of its dire effects. He maintained that "it was not the destruction of whole districts – the complete loss of produce – the ruin of stock, and the demolition of all kinds of works and buildings on each estate, that we are principally to consider." However dreadful, these consequences were small compared with other evils. "It is the total destruction of those provisions, which constitutes the support and existence of your Negroes – it is the inability, and impossibility of procuring other provisions in time to keep them alive – it is your sick without a hospital – your infirm without shelter; and it is the misery of beholding hundreds of wretched beings wasting around you, clamouring for food, and imploring that assistance which you cannot bestow." These were scenes, McNeill wrote, to awaken sensibility and make the moralist exclaim with indignation, "*cursed by your isles, and cursed your institutions*!"[46]

Many slaves died of malnutrition, often combined with common infections and epidemic disease. One health hazard that followed great storms was dysentery, which was attributed chiefly to the lack of potable water. Other losses were attributable to factors other than hurricanes. Dr. Samuel Athill said before the Lords' Committee of the Privy Council, which investigated the slave trade in 1789, that epidemics of various kinds frequently carried off so many slaves in Antigua and its sister islands that the loss could not be repaired for many years. He estimated that in 1779 nearly a fourth or fifth of the slaves in Antigua died of dysentery and that great numbers perished every year of the same cause. Great numbers were killed in 1782 by an epidemic of pleurisy, in 1783 by the measles, and in 1786 by the chin cough or whooping cough. Moreover, notwithstanding the attention given to the inoculation of blacks, considerable numbers died of smallpox.[47]

Pickled and salted fish

Slave subsistence was jeopardized on numerous occasions during the wars of the French Revolution and Napoleonic Wars, which lasted, with brief intermission, from 1793 to 1815. Fish imports were often in short supply. In a representation of 10 July 1805, the Jamaican Assembly informed the lieutenant governor that herring fishing on the coasts of the British Isles had failed for the past two seasons. Only one vessel had arrived in Kingston with salt fish since 21 May, and it was from the British North American colonies. The slaves, "being deprived of what they know to be absolutely necessary, and have been accustomed to consider their right," had become discontented, and there had "already been instances of gangs of negroes leaving the plantations, to complain to the civil magistrate of the usual allowance being withheld."[48]

The importance of fish in the slave diet was underscored by both friends and foes of the peculiar institution. A report of the Assembly of Jamaica in

December 1815 said that the food regularly distributed by the masters consisted principally of pickled and salted fish, which were not merely reckoned palatable by the blacks but were acknowledged "to be well calculated for seasoning and rendering both salutary and nourishing, the soups and mucilaginous and farinaceous dishes, which form the principal food of the negroes." Modern nutritionists recognize that fish not only are an important source of animal protein, but also contain amino acids. It is calculated that a 150-pound man needs 70 grams of protein per day.[49]

In an effort to refute William Wilberforce's contention that the slaves were starved of fish, the Assembly of Jamaica made an elaborate calculation that showed an allowance of thirty-eight barrels of fish per year for every hundred slaves in 1806. From other sources it can be shown that a barrel of herrings, the most common variety of fish issued to blacks, weighed 228 pounds and contained approximately 900 herrings. This reduces to slightly more than seven herrings, or 1.75 pounds of fish per week. Using a modern food conversion table, a herring a day contains only 19.6 grams of protein. In another calculation based on data extending over a century and a half, Richard Bean finds that each slave received slightly more than 1 pound of preserved fish per week, or 56.1 pounds per year. "If fish had been the slave population's only source of protein (but of course it was not)," writes Bean, "then slaves would have been receiving about one-sixth of the 1971–72 average daily United States' protein consumption."[50]

Numerous West Indians testified before Parliamentary committees that all adult slaves received regular allowances of six to ten fish per week, and children half rations. Other testimony casts doubt on these assertions, however. The Select Committee on Negro Apprenticeship in 1836 interrogated several Jamaicans about allowances and indulgences during the period of slavery. William Burge, agent for the island and its former attorney general, contended that the law required masters to supply their slaves with "ample and sufficient provisions," but there was no obligation to furnish them with particular articles. When asked by the committee whether he ever knew any case when the allowance of herrings was withheld, he replied: "Certainly, there are continual instances in which in consequence of the high price, herrings have been withheld, and there are as many estates in which herrings are not given, as those in which they are." Burge went on to contend that herrings and salt fish were considered an indulgence and not an allowance. He conceived that "the whole system of indulgences operated upon the negro population as a stimulus to good conduct, because they were withheld whenever their conduct was not good...that the allowances were not uniform as to the quantity given, nor uniform as to the times when they were given and withdrawn by the master."[51]

Although slaves raised poultry, swine, goats, and occasionally cows, it appears that most of their livestock was sold to the white inhabitants and transients. The fact that slaves were reported to have eaten vile and putrid meat suggests that they were starved of protein. The Reverend Robert Boucher Nicholls said that herrings and salt fish often arrived in Barbados in a putrid condition. Moreover, he testified that he had rarely known salt beef and pork to be given, except either upon the failure of other provisions or as a great indulgence in small quantities. John Terry, formerly an overseer in Grenada, testified that he had known slaves who were driven to satisfy their hunger by eating putrid carcasses. According to the Reverend James Phillippo, some Jamaican slaves were particular in their diet and scrupulously clean in its preparation, "but with others cane-rats, cats, putrid fish and even reptiles and animals in a state of decomposition, were their common food."[52] Later in this chapter it will be seen that the Christmas holiday was a time of feasting on foods with a high protein content.

It is misleading to think that only slaves were fed imported foodstuffs. A large proportion of food imports were consumed by the white inhabitants and transient traders, sailors, and soldiers. That imported foodstuffs were insufficient to supply physical needs is borne out by Richard Bean, who finds a pattern of almost unchanged per capita calorie imports from 1680 to 1816 of about 500 calories per person per day for Barbados and Jamaica. Since imports made up one-fifth to one-quarter of daily consumption requirements, it is not surprising that famines could occur when wars and embargoes cut off food imports and locally grown foodstuffs failed.[53]

Slave provision grounds

Since all the islands had land that could be cultivated but was unsuited to staple production and there were times when the slaves could be spared from plantation labor, it may be inquired whether land and labor could have been combined to grow foodstuffs as well as sugarcane, cotton, and coffee. The answer is, of course, affirmative, although the possibilities of growing food varied from plantation to plantation, island to island, season to season, and slave to slave.

Jamaica, with its comparatively large land area and mixture of coastal plains, interior valleys, and mountain areas, was considered ideal for combining staple production with the growing of foodstuffs. It developed a system of largely unsupervised food growing by slaves who were allotted small plots known as "yards," "house plots," or "kitchen gardens" near their huts and on the outskirts of plantations larger plots known as "provision grounds," "negro grounds," or "polinks." As described by John Stewart, a leading planter-author:

> Adjoining to the house is usually a small spot of ground, laid out into a sort of garden, and shaded by various fruit-trees. Here the family deposit their dead, to whose memory they invariably, if they can afford it, erect a rude tomb. Each slave has, besides this spot, a piece of ground (about half an acre) allotted to him as a provision ground. This is the principal means of his support; and so productive is the soil, where it is good and the seasons regular, that this spot will not only furnish him with sufficient food for his own consumption, but an overplus to carry to market. By means of this ground, and of the hogs and poultry which he may raise (most of which he sells), an industrious negro may not only support himself comfortably, but save something. If he has a family, an additional proportion of ground is allowed him, and all his children from five years upward assist him in his labours in some way or other. On the sugar plantations the slaves are not allowed to keep horses, cows, sheep or goats, and they are obliged to prevent their hogs from wandering over the estate.[54]

Stewart and other planter-historians and authors went to great lengths to praise the provision ground system and show how it benefited both the slaves and their masters. William Beckford contended that, if regularly planted, well cultivated, and kept clean of weeds, a quarter of an acre of land was fully sufficient to supply a moderate family and might enable the cultivator to market some surplus. Edward Long believed that the blacks not only fed themselves but also supplied the white inhabitants and transients with "all manner of provisions, fruits, fresh fish, milk, poultry and other small stock of all kinds."[55] According to Bryan Edwards, masters did not interfere with the little "peculium" acquired by their slaves. Moreover, the slaves were "permitted to dispose at their deaths of what little property they possess, and even to bequeath their grounds or gardens to such of their fellow slaves as they think proper." Indeed, it was Edwards's judgment that the provision ground system was "judicious and beneficial; producing a happy coalition of interests between the master and the slave."[56]

Modern historians of Jamaica find the origins of the peasantry in the slavery period when the blacks fed themselves to a large extent from their kitchen gardens and provision grounds and disposed of their surplus produce in local markets. It is contended that the provision ground system enabled slaves to have a better diet, a small income, and a feeling of proprietorship in land. These developments, it is argued, made the slaves less discontented, less likely to run away, and less prone to rebel.[57]

However true it may be that the Jamaican peasantry had its origins in the provision ground system, there remain questions concerning the performance of this system in the context of plantation slavery. Were the slaves given ample time away from plantation labor to cultivate their grounds? Did they have the will and energy to grow food for themselves? How great a distance separated the slave huts from outlying provision grounds, and how much time was needed to walk to and from these grounds and the markets where surplus produce was sold? Were the slaves allotted large enough plots of land of suitable quality to grow sufficient foodstuffs? Did they diversify crop production sufficiently to compensate for adverse weather and normal seasonal variations in growing conditions? Were adequate reserves set aside for a rainy day? Were adequate measures taken to prevent theft and pilfering and the trespass of livestock? Was the provision ground system adapted to the needs of aged, infirm, and young slaves?

The provision ground system came under regulation in Jamaica by the terms of the consolidated Slave Act of 1788 and subsequent amendments. Owners and masters were required to allot "a sufficient quantity of land for every slave;" however, owners and masters without land had to find "some other ways and means" equal to the value of 2*s*. 6*d*. per week for each slave. This currency equivalent was increased in subsequent acts. Masters or overseers were required to inspect the Negro grounds at least once a month "in order to see that the same are cultivated and kept up in a proper manner." Except during crop time, slaves were allowed one day in every fortnight to cultivate their provision grounds, exclusive of Sunday and the usual holidays at Christmas, Easter, and Whitsuntide. This clause was amended in 1801 to allow not less than twelve complete days in every year except during crop time, and in 1816 at least twenty-six days except during crop time. In both amendments the work days allowed to grow provisions were exclusive of Sundays and the usual holidays. In addition to the allotment of individual provision grounds, the act of 1788 required "all masters, owners, or possessors of plantations, pens, or other lands" to plant at least one acre of land for every four slaves. Four years later this clause was amended to require one acre for every ten slaves.[58]

Critics of slavery contended that the blacks had insufficient time and energy to grow, transport, and market their provisions. They contended that during the four to six months of crop time, Sunday was the only day the slaves were allowed to cultivate and keep in order their provision grounds, the only day they had to take their produce to market, and the only day they had to fetch from their grounds the plantains, yams, eddoes, and other produce to feed their families. William Taylor testified that many slaves spent Sundays in their grounds and going to market. He was firmly of the opinion that, if a slave were to devote every Sunday to repose, he could not maintain himself and his family by working the twenty-six days he was allowed by law. Moreover, Taylor told of slaves who cultivated their kitchen gardens during the dinner hour on weekdays. Benjamin McMahon knew of plantations where the laborers' provision grounds were "almost entirely neglected, from their being unable, after the toil and barbarity to which they had been subjected by their task-masters for six days out of the seven, to cultivate them." Testifying before the Select Committee of the House of Lords on Slavery, the Reverend John Barry said he believed that excess mortality was caused, in part, by harsh punishment, the "very late Hours at which the Negroes are obliged to labour in their Provision Grounds to support themselves and their Families, coupled with the long and tiresome Journies they have frequently to undergo in travelling to the Markets."[59]

Because Sunday labor cut into the time for religious worship, it is not surprising that the Nonconformist missionaries were the most vocal critics of the labor regimen, which occupied the slaves seven days a week during crop time. William Taylor said that during the months when Sunday was the only day the slaves had to work for themselves, he had heard the clergymen of the mission stations "complain that on those Sundays they could not get congregations generally." The Reverend Peter Duncan, who claimed to have had three or four thousand blacks in his congregation, was asked by the House of Commons select committee of 1832, "In your opinion was that attendance on their provision grounds on Sundays, necessary for the supply of the urgent wants of himself and his family, or was it for the purpose of raising such surplus produce as when sold, would command some of the conveniences and luxuries of life?" "I believe that it is indispensably necessary for the negroes to labour on Sunday;" he replied, "I never expected to see the negroes at any of our chapels oftener than once a month; and I have found that even in those parts of the country where their masters and owners were the most favourable, the attending Divine Service once a month is a pretty fair average of what the negroes could command."[60] The Reverend Thomas Cooper was engaged by Robert Hibbert, an absentee proprietor, to improve the condition of the slaves to his Georgia estate in Jamaica. Cooper wrote that one great obstacle to his success as a religious instructor was that the slaves had little or no time to attend. During the five months of the sugar harvest, Sunday was the only day the slaves had to work for themselves. He was allowed one afternoon every fortnight during crop time for religious worship and instruction, which gave him only ten or eleven times in the year to preach to the slaves. After remaining in this unsatisfactory state for more than three years, Cooper left Jamaica and returned to England.[61] From Demerara the Reverend John Smith wrote, complaining that

> the days of this week have passed away, and I have done almost nothing: the negroes are worked so hard they have no time to come to me... besides the smallness of the congregation, we are much annoyed... by the noise of the cattle-mill grinding coffee, and often by the flogging of the negroes.[62]

Reaching the provision grounds and markets from their villages frequently involved the slaves in hardships. In the infancy of a plantation the provision grounds were near the slave quarters and sugar works. However, the extension of a plantation made it necessary to open new grounds farther away and to get the slaves to cooperate in the change without disrupting their food supply. In Jamaica the distance from the provision grounds to the Sunday markets ranged from a few miles to as many as thirty-five. The Reverend John Barry testified that he knew slaves who traveled twenty-five or twenty-six miles to market. The slave would gather and pack his produce generally on a Saturday, travel overnight to arrive in time for the Sunday market, and be occupied the whole of Sunday returning home.[63]

The provision ground system can be faulted on other grounds as well. If not sufficiently guarded by watchmen, who were often said to be too old and feeble to function properly, the grounds might be pilfered by hungry slaves or damaged by trespassing livestock. Slaves who depended on their grounds for sustenance were seldom able or willing to provide adequate reserves. Although he favored the system in most respects, Bryan Edwards thought it a misfortune that the slaves trusted "more to plantain-groves, corn and other vegetables, that are liable to be destroyed by storms, than to what are called *ground provisions*; such as yams, eddoes, potatoes, cassada, and other esculent roots; all of which are out of the reach of hurricanes; but prudence is a term that has no place in the Negro-vocabulary." Edwards called attention with pride to the slave act of 1792, which required every proprietor of lands to properly cultivate ground provisions, one acre for every ten slaves, exclusive of the provision grounds allotted to the slaves.[64]

One planter who commented unfavorably on the provision ground system was Gilbert Mathison, who returned to Jamaica in August 1808 after an absence of nearly thirteen years. He complained of the onerous burden placed on slaves to feed themselves, the callous disregard shown by owners and managers to slaves who were unable to fend for themselves, and the lack of food reserves to tide the dependent population over the seasons of the year when their grounds were unproductive. The law that Edwards had praised as a precaution against famine resulting from hurricanes was found by Mathison, after an absence of such storms for many years, to be universally disregarded. Famine sometimes occurred in June, July, and August when, owing to the immature growth of food crops and dry weather, general scarcity prevailed throughout the island. It was tragic that the breadfruit that Captain Bligh had brought to Jamaica fifteen years earlier was cultivated chiefly as an ornamental tree and only secondarily as a fruit tree. "It is the duty of the Negro to feed himself;" wrote Mathison, "and it is his fault, it is said, if he does not take the necessary precautions against want; the system thus affording a plausible, though certainly an insufficient apology, for the supineness, amounting to wickedness, of the overseer, who, to say nothing of the common duties of humanity, ought to be prepared at all points and under every possible emergency, to preserve the valuable property confined to his care." Every adult male was expected to supply his family and himself by his own exertion. If the provision ground was neglected because of idleness, sickness, old age, or too large a family, the adult male was "not allowed to expect, nor, in point of fact, does he obtain, assistance from the stores of the plantation." This, notwithstanding many exceptions, was "the general practice from one end of the island to the other." Mathison concluded that the established system for the subsistence of plantation slaves was valuable, though imperfect, requiring vigilance and occasional relaxation.[65]

Calories and protein

The evidence suggests that the typical slave in Jamaica and most of the Lesser Antilles was poorly fed until emancipation in 1834. We have seen that the slaves of Jamaica and Barbados received approximately 500 calories per day from the imported food they consumed, and that in all likelihood their intake of animal protein was seriously deficient. In her economic history of Jamaica, Gisela Eisner estimates that the per capita consumption of ground provisions was 21.9 pounds per week in 1832, which amounts to a daily intake of 1,400 calories. Although the slaves grew cereal grains, vegetables, pulses, and fruits in addition to ground provisions, the vulnerability of these crops to hurricanes, storms, droughts, and predators made them a less reliable source of foodstuffs than ground provisions.[66]

Table 6.2 shows the legal minimum quantity of food provided to every slave confined to every workhouse or jail in Jamaica. If we convert these weekly rations to their daily calorie equivalents, we find that wheat flour contained 2,477 calories; plantains, 2,495; Indian corn, 2,865; and yams or cocoes, 3,810. Since a very small part of the slave population was incarcerated and it is likely that these inmates were better fed than those outside, it seems reasonable to infer that the typical slave in Jamaica received little more than 2,000 calories per day.[67] Similarly, Robert Dirks has drawn on data in the *House of Commons Accounts and Papers* for all the Sugar Colonies and finds that the average plantation allowance amounted to 1,500–2,000 calories and approximately 45 grams of protein per day.[68] These estimates are far less than the per capita intake of 3,340 calories in the developed market economies in 1972–4, but they may have approached the 2,180 calories in the developing market economies in 1972–4. They are also far less than the daily diet of the typical American slave on the eve of the Civil War, which, according to Professors Fogel and Engerman, amounted to 4,185 calories and exceeded the daily recom-

Table 6.2. *Weekly allowance of foodstuffs per slave in the Bahamas and Leeward Islands, and to workhouse slaves in Jamaica*

Bahamas	Jamaica	Leeward Islands
1 peck of unground Indian or Guinea corn	*Not less than*	9 pints of corn or beans
		or
	7 quarts of unground Guinea or Indian corn	8 pints of peas or wheat or rye flour or Indian corn meal
or		
21 pints of wheat flour	*or*	
	21 pints of the flour or meal of either	*or*
or		9 pints of oatmeal
7 quarts of rice		*or*
	or	7 pints of rice
or	21 pints of wheat flour	*or*
56 pounds of potatoes or yams		8 pints of cassava flour or farine
	or	
	56 full-grown plantains	*or*
		8 pounds of biscuit
	or	20 pounds of yams or potatoes
	56 pounds of cocoes or yams	*or*
		16 pounds of eddoes, tanias, or tyres
	and	
	7 herrings or shads	*or*
		30 pounds of plantains or bananas
	or	
	other salted provisions equal thereto	*and*
		1¼ pounds of herrings, shads, mackerel, or other salted provisions
		or
		double the quantity of fresh fish or other fresh provisions

Source: Bahamas: *Act of the Council and Assembly of the Bahamas*, 1797, quoted in James Stephen, *The Slavery of the British West India Colonies Delineated*, 2 vols. (London, 1824, 1830), Vol. I, p. 465.

Jamaica: *The Consolidated Slave Law of Jamaica*, 1788, reprinted in Bryan Edwards, *History of the British West Indies*, 2 vols. (Dublin, 1793), Vol. II, pp. 169–70. This food allowance was provided to every slave confined in every workhouse or jail in Jamaica.

Leeward Islands: *Laws of Antigua*, Vol. I, Leeward Islands Act No. 36, 1798, Clause I.

mended level of proteins by 110 percent, calcium by 20 percent, and iron by 230 percent. When it is considered that a well-fed worker consumes between 3,000 and 4,000 calories per day in moderate to exceptionally active labor, there are strong grounds for believing that the typical slave in Jamaica was underfed and overworked.[69]

Food rations, as shown in Table 6.2, were issued to the slaves of the Bahamas and the Leeward Islands by the acts of 1797 and 1798, respectively. The Bahamian act required that every slave should have, over and above the allowances shown in Table 6.2, a sufficient quantity of land as his or her proper ground. By the act of the Leeward Islands, "masters were allowed to distribute the total amount among their slaves at discretion, provided they gave the full ration to all sick or disabled slaves, and they were also permitted, in all except the Virgin Islands, to diminish the set allowance by one-fifth in crop time." Further diminution was permitted if the master declared on oath that an allotment of one acre of provision land was available for every ten slaves and they were given sufficient time to cultivate it.[70]

James Stephen compared the treatment of slaves in the Bahamas and Leeward Islands with respect to food allowances and provision grounds. Both groups of islands had legislated minimum weekly allowances of food and required masters to allot provision grounds to their slaves. From these laws Stephen discovered wide variation in the treatment of slaves. For example, the Leeward act called for a weekly allowance of nine pints of corn or beans (approximately 1,850 calories daily), whereas the Bahamian act called for one peck or sixteen pints of unground Indian or Guinea corn (approximately 3,275 calories daily). Taking into account the various substitutes for corn and beans, Stephen concluded that the subsistence of the Bahamian slave compared with that of the Leeward Islands slave was as fourteen to five, not allowing for the poultry and swine that the blacks in the Bahamas raised and consumed in ample quantities. Even wider discrepancies were shown with respect to allotments of provision grounds in the two groups of islands. Moreover, Stephen maintained that the Bahamian act had been fully conformed to by the slave owners of that colony, whereas the act of the Leeward Islands had been "notoriously and confessedly abortive." Because of heavy debts and low sugar prices, the Leeward Islands sugar planter was said to be very tempted "to be too sparing of provisions; for they cannot be supplied without augmenting his embarrassments." The fact that plantation agriculture failed to develop in the Bahamas by contrast with the Leeward Islands goes far to explain the dietary and demographic polarity.[71]

Owing to such factors as the irregular arrival of provision ships and variations in the production of local foodstuffs, food availability fluctuated from season to season even in the absence of hurricanes, droughts, and other irregular occurrences. Foodstuffs arrived irregularly from abroad, partly due to seasonal weather hazards, partly to different crop cycles in Europe and North America, and partly to the need to exchange such produce for sugar and rum, which also followed a cyclic pattern. Few ships ventured into Caribbean waters during the hurricane season from July to October when insurance rates were exorbitant. Locally grown foodstuffs were plentiful or scarce depending in part on seasonal growing patterns and labor force availability. Generally speaking, the sugar harvest from December or January to May and June was a season of relative food abundance. In part, this was due partly to the slaves being permitted to drink liberally of cane juice and chew newly cut canes, partly to the harvesting of ground provisions and the ripening of a wide variety of fruits, and partly to the arrival of many provision ships. On the other hand, the months of July through November saw few ships arrive with provisions, less local food was harvested from annual and perennial plants and trees, and little or no ripe cane juice was available. This was the season the slaves called the "hard time" or the "hungry season." According to Robert Dirks, "Slaves were victims of starvation on a consistent basis, stemming from the fact that no abatement in the demand for labor accompanied the seasonal decrease in the availability of locally produced foodstuffs."[72]

After long months of deprivation and hunger, slaves were surfeited with food and drink during the Christmas season. For one thing, such food crops as maize, yams, plantains, bananas, and sweet potatoes matured during December and January. Another nutritional increment came from cattle that were slaughtered, providing several pounds of meat to each adult black. Perhaps the largest increment of high-quality foodstuffs came from abroad. Ships and convoys carrying plantation supplies for the sugar harvest left ports in North America and Europe so as to arrive in the West Indies after the hurricane season and by the beginning of the Christmas holiday. According to Sir William Young, a prominent absentee planter, ships in the convoy that left Portsmouth and Cork should weigh anchor on 20 October.

> The importance of this fleet's arrival before Christmas-day carrying out the Irish beef and provisions for the annual treat of 500,000 negroes at that season, and freighted with their new clothing for the festivity, cannot, to any humane person, and who knows, as I do, the anxiety of each poor negro on the plantations for the timely arrival of his holiday comforts, be regarded lightly, or as not to be provided for.[73]

Table 6.3 shows the export of Irish provisions which were intended chiefly for consumption by the slaves.

Dr. John Williamson wrote that the "negro holiday" which continued

Table 6.3. *Exports of Irish provisions to the British Sugar Colonies, 1804–5*

	Quantity	Value
Beef	17,932 barrels	£71,726
Pork	15,220 barrels	60,880
Butter	29,146 firkins	72,865
Herrings	2,800 barrels	5,600

Source: Sir William Young, *The West-India Commonplace Book* (London, 1807), p. 98.

three days beginning on Christmas day, was the only period of unrestricted festivity the blacks enjoyed throughout the year.

> An abundant supply of beef, and every other article, is then liberally dealt out to them by the estate. When they have enjoyed themselves, they parade round the place with music peculiar to their country, dressed in a gay and fantastic manner. Their familiarities with the whites at this season are permitted; and they, with the negro men and the fair negresses, mix promiscuously in the dance.

Williamson went on to say that it was the highest mark of disrespect and contempt if the white overseer avoided having the dance at his house.[74]

That the sudden change from food scarcity and hunger to an abundance of nourishing food radically altered the behavior of the blacks is the contention of Robert Dirks. He finds that slaves who suffered persistent hunger and food scarcity were fatigued and wasted; they were inclined to be docile, tractable, and apathetic; and they were isolated and withdrawn from group social activity. On the other hand, food abundance contributed to such traits as vigorous physical activity, gregariousness, group solidarity, and aggressiveness, which made the Christmas holidays a time of not only feasting and dancing but also slave rebelliousness when the white militia was alerted to quell disturbances. From the standpoint of plantation agriculture, masters must have linked the feasting of the slaves at Christmas with the heavy labor demanded of them by the sugar harvest, which generally began soon after. The nutritional bonus that came from Christmas feasting was prolonged by free access to cane juice and ripened canes, but the bonus frequently turned into a deficit before the end of crop time. Hunger and destitution then stalked the blacks intermittently until the next Christmas holiday, when they were once again fattened for another harvest.[75]

Provisioning slaves in the eastern Caribbean

If any sugar island could claim to have fed its slaves adequately in the decades before emancipation it was, perhaps, Barbados. Paradoxically, the dietary improvement was achieved by means of less dependence on imported foodstuffs and without resort to the unsupervised labor of slaves on individually allotted provision grounds. The late J. Harry Bennett believed that the West Indies in general was converted to the idea of greater self-sufficiency in food production during the American Revolution. If this generalization may be questioned with respect to Jamaica and the Leeward Islands, it appears to be valid for Barbados. Beginning about 1760, certain Barbadian planters who were motivated by economic self-interest attempted to ameliorate the condition of their slaves in an effort to reduce mortality and encourage breeding. As part of this program, more land was planted in corn and ground provisions and more attention given to the raising of poultry and swine. Except for the hurricane of 1780, Barbados did not require any considerable supply of corn from abroad from 1777 to 1800, according to William Dickson. "After the closing of the African slave trade in 1808," writes Bennett, "the newly formed agricultural associations brought home the lesson that the planters could no longer afford to lose Negroes to famine. When trade with the United States was almost cut off during the Napoleonic Wars, the Barbadians were prepared for the emergency."[76]

In densely populated Barbados, where most of the land was suited to growing sugarcane, the planters allotted little land and allowed little time to their slaves to grow food crops for themselves. In his testimony of 1789, Governor David Parry said that few plantations allowed their slaves any set times to labor for themselves. Small portions of land were annexed to each slave house, but these house plots were not assigned as part of their subsistence. Parry said that most plantations had a "Field of Land called the Negro Ground, the Profits of which are taken to the Use of those who cultivate them, independently of the Allowance they receive from their Owners in common with other Slaves." Although each householder on the Codrington plantations had his own "patch of land," these house plots were very small and had little part in feeding the villagers. Instead of feeding themselves, the slaves could safely look to the Codrington managers to supply them with an abundance of fruits, vegetables, and salt fish, according to Bennett.[77]

The Barbadian system of supervised food production developed in response to the uncertainty and high cost of imported foodstuffs and the need to find a balance between cash crops, chiefly sugarcane, and other crops grown for animal forage and human consumption. This system, as perceived by two English visitors, was introduced after the natural fertility of the soil was lost by repeated cropping in sugarcane. By the substitution of other crops, particularly millet or Guinea corn, "a system of soiling and tethering cattle was introduced, which has not only been the means of retrieving the lands, but has, perhaps, made them more productive than ever." Animal manure was carefully husbanded and mixed with crop residues to supply the cane lands with organic matter. The Barbadians were said to have excelled in the management of both slaves and cattle. Their aim was to keep their slaves "in the highest working and breeding condition, in which they succeeded; and though ever reputed the severest disciplinarians, yet theirs was the only sugar colony where the population rapidly increased." According to Dr. John Davy, the Barbadians had three objectives in mind: "first, the production of as much sugar as possible for profit; secondly, the preserving a certain extent of land in pasture, for the support of live stock; and thirdly, the growing of 'ground provisions' consisting of roots and grain, the yam and sweet potato, the maize or Indian corn and others, some selected as rotation crops, some, especially the grain, for marketable produce, and in aid of forage." Judicious and prudent planters planted half of their estates in canes, with the other half reserved for pasture and provisions.[78]

Dr. Davy explained how the food crops were interplanted with sugarcane and forage crops. Owing to the rapidity of their growth, most of the provision crops were "intermediate ones, that is, capable of coming to maturity between the harvesting of one crop of canes and the planting of another." Sweet potatoes matured in three months and could be planted in any season. The yam, which was a more delicate plant than the sweet potato and required more careful tillage, matured in about four months. Indian corn and Guinea corn took more nutrients out of the soil than ground provisions and were generally planted after the canes were harvested; they matured in about three months. Davy wrote that one-fourth of each plantation was devoted to Guinea corn, which was the principal food of the slaves. If protected from insects, it could be kept many years.[79] Table 6.4, which Davy extracted from the minutes of the Agricultural Society of Barbados, shows how the land on one plantation was apportioned among canes, food crops, and forage crops.

The Barbadian system was explained by the plantation attorney of the Codrington plantations to one of his principals in England. He wrote that the system of feeding the slaves in the island differed from that in every other West India colony. In fact, the cultivation of provisions formed a considerable part of the system of management on every plantation. In raising provisions, "at least one-third of the labour of all the slaves on every estate is expended, producing a sufficient quantity of corn, yams, potatoes, &c. for the year's consumption, which is carefully stored, and afterwards dealt out to them in daily rations, and when the crop is short, an additional quantity is purchased." By contrast, he said it was the practice in the other colonies

Table 6.4. *Acres planted in cash, food, and forage crops on a sugar plantation in Barbados, 3 August 1811*

31	acres in first crop canes
31	acres in second crop canes
34	acres under preparation for the ensuing crop, in four fields, each 8½ acres, of which one is holed and planted with Indian corn on the banks, another is planted with red and white yams; the third will be holed immediately after the second crop canes now on it are reaped, and then planted on the banks with potatoes; the fourth is a Guinea grass field, which is to be destroyed in the month of November, and planted in the next spring
68	acres under Guinea corn; 16 acres of which are planted in seed to give suckers to plant 36 acres, and 16 acres are in second crop
24	acres under Guinea grass
1	acre under sour grass
2	acres under ocroes
5	acres under potatoes
3	acres holed for eddoes
8	acres under young pigeon peas
29	acres under tenements, yards, negro grounds, &c.
236	total acres
162	Negroes, 60 of which are effective laborers
17	slaves were added last year
70	head of livestock, consisting of 43 head of stake cattle, 5 horses, 7 mules, 6 cows, and 11 calves

Source: Minutes of the Agricultural Society of Barbados, 3 August 1811, quoted in John Davy, M.D., F.R.S., *The West Indies Before and Since Slave Emancipation, etc.* (London, 1854), pp. 130–1.

to allot a piece of ground to the slaves and allow them a portion of time to cultivate it and feed themselves. The Barbadian slaves were given daily allowances of provisions, molasses, rum, salt, and salt fish. To feed the 381 slaves on the Codrington estates, the annual average food crops cultivated consisted of 130 acres of Guinea corn, 30 acres of Indian corn, 30 acres of potatoes, 20 acres of peas, 15 acres of plantains, 12 acres of yams, 8 acres of eddoes, "besides pumpkins, ocroes, and other minor articles of food; in addition to which, every family has a small portion of ground about their house."[80]

Corn, chiefly Guinea corn or millet, was the staple food of the plantation slaves of Barbados. Adult working slaves on the Newton plantation, according to Handler and Lange, received an average of one and a half pints of corn daily. Privileged slaves, including drivers and senior tradesmen, often received more, whereas children, slaves "past labor," and women not working in the field received less. Salt fish was issued about once a fortnight, approximately one-half pound per working slave daily; at Christmas and another holiday special allowances doubled this amount. Working slaves also received a small ration of salt. Other foodstuffs, including yams, sweet potatoes, eddoes, and beans, were distributed, albeit less frequently. Moreover, each adult slave received a rough annual average of about four gallons of molasses. The Newton slaves supplemented their food allowances by consuming the small livestock, poultry, and food crops they raised on their house plots or had stolen. They also exchanged or sold their produce or stolen goods at the Sunday market. In addition to their allowance of "undressed provisions," the slaves were provided a cooked breakfast or noonday meal on some Barbadian plantations by the late eighteenth century.[81]

Compared with the plantations of Barbados and the Leeward Islands, those of the Windward Islands generally had more marginal land suited to the cultivation of food crops. At the same time provision grounds were less extensive in the Windwards than in Jamaica. The slaves in the Windward Islands were thus fed, in part, by their own labor; in part, by the assistance of their masters. According to one absentee planter, the provision grounds in St. Vincent and Grenada were so large and produced so much that it was not necessary to import large quantities of foodstuffs except in certain seasons of dry weather.[82]

Dr. David Collins of St. Vincent sought to convince his fellow planters that a well-fed slave could produce proportionally more sugar and other cash crops than one who was half-starved. A hungry slave who was reduced to the hard alternatives of either starving or stealing would, in his opinion, "embrace the latter only as the least evil of the two, and thus provide for his stomach, at the expense of his posterior." Instead of a scanty pittance of six or seven pints of flour or grain with as many salt herrings, Collins recommended a weekly allowance of no less than ten or twelve pints of flour or grain and three or four pounds of fish to each adult slave. Food that was issued in an undressed state was often poorly cooked because the slaves had little time or were careless in preparing their meals. To help correct this situation, Indian corn, horse beans, and peas should be ground into flour or bruised in a mill before they were issued to slaves. It was not only necessary to augment the allowances and see that they were properly dressed; it was also necessary to have a pot of prepared food to be served out at regular meals to the sick, the weak, the orphans, the improvident. If the slaves were expected to feed themselves by their own labor, it was not enough to assign them grounds to plant. The master should also see that they were as diligent in cultivating their provision grounds as they were in growing canes; "otherwise you will find them very much neglected, and your negroes as much at a loss for provisions, as if they had no ground at all." Slaves who could not be trusted to tend their grounds should be made to work together "on a piece assigned for the use of the pot-gang, under the care of a driver, who is to be responsible for the proper use of their time." Since the provision grounds varied in their yield, ample reserves should be accumulated to tide the slaves over the dry season and hurricane months.[83]

The French, according to Dr. Collins, were much celebrated for the good treatment of their slaves. They surpassed the British "in nothing so much as in the articles of feeding and clothing," he wrote. On the other hand, the French were said to have punished offenses with greater severity and worked their slaves harder than the British. By way of mitigation, Collins noted that offenses occurred rarely and the French slaves could work much harder because provisions were so abundantly supplied. That Collins made these invidious comparisons with little knowledge of French slavery may be surmised from the research of Professor Gabriel Debien. Debien finds that whereas the French plantations cultivated provisions for their slaves, it was more common to feed slaves cheaply by having them cultivate their own provision grounds. Food was distributed by the planters only in the last extremity. Food allowances, when made, were not always regular or abundant. Lacking in protein, the food and diet of the French slaves were often monotonous, insufficient, and badly supervised. In his important article on the feeding of slaves on the plantations in the French West Indies, Debien concludes that "bad food, and underfeeding, were the permanent scourge of the islands, and the greatest evil of slavery."[84]

The punishment of slaves

Slaves who resisted hard labor and food deprivation were punished severely. Resistance to the harsh conditions they suffered took many forms. Slaves resorted to malingering, destroying property, attacking white masters, poisoning, stealing, running away, committing suicide, burning houses and cane fields, and mass rebellion. Orlando Patterson says there were two basic forms of resistance to slavery: one passive, the other violent. Passive resistance included such actions as refusing to work, satire, running away, and committing suicide, whereas violent resistance consisted of individual violence and collective violence in the form of spontaneous revolts or organized mass rebellion.[85]

Stealing goods from their masters was a common complaint, and the main object of theft, as one might expect, was food. Dirks asserts that slaves stole chickens and eggs; they broke into storehouses and pilfered grain and flour;

they butchered their masters' cattle, horses, mules, and asses despite the death penalty for such exploits; and, according to one contemporary estimate, they stole 15 to 20 percent of the annual crop of sugar. Not only did they steal from their white masters, but hungry slaves also stole from other slaves to such an extent that watchmen had to be posted to guard the slave provision grounds.[86]

Numerous laws were passed by planter-dominated legislatures to deal with slave behavior that threatened public order and private property. Elsa Goveia has analyzed the slave laws of the British Sugar Colonies. She writes that the St. Kitts slave acts of 1711 and 1722 were typical of early slave laws of the Leeward Islands. "For the detection of runaways and thefts, Negro houses were to be regularly searched. All slaves guilty of running away, of theft, or of other crimes were to be punished by a slave court, consisting of two or more justices acting without a jury. Concealment of runaways was also punished." By the provisions of a Montserrat law of 1693, "Negroes found guilty of stealing anything of the value of 12*d.* or over were to suffer death. For stealing anything of less value the punishments inflicted were, for the first offence, whipping and the amputation of both ears; for the second offence, death. A Negro might be shot if found stealing provisions more than 40 feet away from the common path." This act did extend some protection to the slaves, however. To prevent thefts committed by hungry slaves, the law provided "that one acre of provisions must be planted for every eight slaves in the possession of a master, and the penalty of a fine of 1,000 pounds of sugar was inflicted for every six months' neglect of this regulation."[87]

Bryan Edwards said that fear was the leading principle upon which government was supported in slave societies. By fear he meant a sense of that "absolute coercive necessity" that superseded all questions of right and left no choice of action. Up to the time when organized humanitarian action began in the 1780s, writes Elsa Goveia, West Indian slave laws included relatively few protective clauses. The willful killing of a slave by a white man was seldom recognized as an act of homicide or murder. On the other hand, slaves were subject to the penalties of whipping, mutilation, and death for striking or insulting a white man. Although the evidence of slaves was not admitted for or against free persons, such evidence was admitted for or against other slaves. Since slaves were regarded by English law as a special kind of property, the owner of such property was given wide discretion in enforcing subordination and control.[88]

That harsh and cruel punishments were meted out to slaves before the 1780s cannot be denied. Though he believed they were exaggerated, the charges of inhuman and cruel treatment of blacks by whites could not be denied by James Knight, the Jamaican planter-historian. By way of extenuation, he called attention to the blacks' superiority in numbers and what he regarded as "the sullen, deceitfull, Refractory Temper of most of them; that some are Careless, others Treacherous or Idle, and apt to Run away." Because their master's interest depended on the care and diligence of his slaves, Knight was convinced of the absolute necessity of keeping a vigilant eye and a strict hand over them. The punishment usually inflicted on slaves was a severe whipping on the bare back. Knight admitted that such correction, though indispensably necessary, might be shocking to a tender mind. He believed that the common soldiers in Europe were punished with much greater severity than the slaves in Jamaica. Above all, Knight believed that the use and treatment of the blacks depended on the temper and discretion of the master.[89]

The Reverend James Ramsay criticized the planters who managed their slaves with the whip, bean stock, dungeon, and chains. Avarice, fear, and oppression ruled relations between master and slave. By making his slave a mere instrument of profit, the master believed his slave viewed him as his enemy and oppressor, upon which perception the master acted to oppress his slave in revenge. "It is a certain Fact," wrote Ramsay, "that generally speaking, in my Time, a Slave was not considered as an Object of Sympathy or deserving of regard. Every possible Exertion was forced out of him; no Exertion was rewarded; he was worked, managed, and whipped as a Brute; he was suspected and hated as a Rival, and treated as an Enemy." The use of the whip was to Janet Schaw "a circumstance of all others the most horrid." On her visit to St. Kitts she observed that every ten slaves had a driver who walked behind them, holding in his hand a short whip and a long one. "They are naked, male and female, down to the girdle, and you constantly observe where the application has been made," she wrote.[90]

Recalling his boyhood days in Barbados, the Reverend Robert Boucher Nicholls testified before the select committee of the House of Commons in 1790 that "the usual instruments were the throng whip, chains on the legs, irons on the neck, and confinement to what was called the dungeon." Enormous crimes called for "gibbeting alive in chains," but this method of punishment was rarely used. Nicholls was asked, "Is whipping so inflicted as to be a severe punishment?" He replied, "Undoubtedly so." To the question, "Do the marks of whipping long continue visible?" he replied, "I believe in some instances they remain for life, as I have seen Negroes carry them very visibly to old age; the punishment is with a thong whip, which cuts deep into the flesh."[91]

In British Guiana, where the slave population declined by 52,000 in the eleven years preceding 1832, the frightful mortality was accompanied by harsh punishment. "Punishments amounted in 1829 to over 20,000 a year," writes Eric Williams, "or one punishment annually for every third slave, totalling two million lashes. If the workers of Britain had been punished in the same proportion, wrote [James] Stephen, between six and seven million punishments would have been inflicted. British Guiana was a crown colony, where all the ameliorating measures of the abolitionists had been put into effect."[92]

Reacting to their critics, planter-governments enacted consolidated slave laws that were intended to afford their slaves greater protection and security. By the Jamaican acts of 1788 and 1792, persons convicted of mutilating or dismembering any slave or slaves were fined and imprisoned. It was made unlawful to punish ill-disposed slaves by fixing iron collars round their necks or loading their bodies with chains, irons, or weights. No slave could receive more than ten lashes at any one time and for one offense unless the owner or overseer should be present, and no more than thirty-nine lashes at one time and for one offense could be inflicted when the owner or overseer was present. Subsequent laws sought to extend the protection. By the act of 1826, the justice of the peace was instructed, upon receiving information of maltreatment or improper punishment, to immediately send for the slave and convey him to the workhouse for protection until the case could be legally and thoroughly investigated. No second punishment should take place under any circumstances until the "culprit" was entirely recovered. No slave should be sent to the workhouse for more than ten days, nor should he receive more than twenty lashes therein without an order from the justice of the peace. No collars were to be fixed on any slave without the sanction of the justice of the peace. Generally speaking, the Jamaican act of 1826 levied stiffer fines and prison sentences than did the previous slave codes.[93]

Individual planters are known to have moderated the punishment of their slaves. Matthew Gregory ("Monk") Lewis impressed upon the mind of the manager of his estate in Jamaica his extreme anxiety for the abolition of the cart whip, but there were individual plantations on which punishments were meted out incessantly. One such plantation, according to Benjamin McMahon, was Harmony Hall, where the miserable blacks assuaged their burdens in the following heartrending song: "Poor nega ... we flesh belongs only to whip, and we blood belongs to the ground – whip when we complain of hungry – whip when we no get to field before day – whip when we tired – whip when we look cross – whip when we laugh – whip when we complain of book-keeper to busha – whip when we go to hot-house sick – whip every Monday for dem have sore foot. Buckra give poor nega whip for medicine – whip for make him strong at work – whip for make him weak to go to hot-house – whip to make him leave hot-house and go to work, and whip to make him work more than his 'trength able ... Buckra make whip do every ting, but make life, and that it no able to do, but it make plenty dead."[94]

The testimony given by absentee planters before the select committee of

1832 casts doubt on claims that punishment was greatly mitigated. William Shand said that in the state that existed in Jamaica, it was very doubtful whether the slaves could be managed without the whip or some means such as a whip. When he was asked whether he considered it necessary to continue the flogging of women, he replied, "I think it is necessary to punish the women as well as the men, and in all low people that the women are fully as vicious as the men, often more so." Shand believed that agitation of the slavery question in England had excited the slaves to discontent and had made it necessary to continue the use of the whip.[95]

James Beckford Wildman, after testifying that the punishments inflicted on the slaves of Jamaica were "very cruel ones," went on to say that "the general system of flogging is to give them a certain number of stripes with a long whip, which inflicts a dreadful laceration, or a dreadful contusion; and then they follow up that by a very severe flogging with ebony switches, the ebony being a very strong wiry plant, with small leaves, like a myrtle leaf, and under every leaf a very sharp tough thorn, and then after that they rub them with brine." William Taylor, who had been Wildman's plantation attorney, said he had entered into an agreement to abolish the whip and manage the plantation on a moderate humane system. Unfortunately, Taylor was disappointed in his expectations. The following extract from a letter he wrote to Wildman was submitted in evidence: "By our system, we take away the motive that leads to labour on the neighboring estates; that is, the dread of the lash; and we cannot substitute that which makes the English labourer industrious, namely, the fear of want; for the law of Jamaica compels the slave proprietor to feed his slave, to clothe him, and to house him, whatever the conduct of the slave may be." Taylor said he had come to the conclusion that the only effectual remedy was emancipation.[96]

Conclusion

From this discussion it is evident that several stereotypical views of sugar slavery are in need of revision. The view that slave labor was per se low-productivity labor can be questioned. This was especially true of cane hole digging, where the workers were forced to wield their hoes in equal time and with equal effect irrespective of their sex, age, and strength. Slaves were also forced to plant, fertilize, weed, and cut canes, pick grass, and work night shifts in the mill house and boiling house. Indeed, one leading authority regards this new industrial labor discipline as a major technological innovation imposed by the sugar planters.

Slaves obviously needed an abundance of nutritious food to perform combined and constant labor on sugar plantations, but we have seen that, allowing for certain exceptions, the slaves were overworked and underfed. Here the "curse of monoculture" can be invoked, at least during the long years of international warfare in the Caribbean region. Having concentrated their resources on the production and sale of sugar and rum, the planters had come to depend on imported foodstuffs to feed their slaves. The embargoes and wars, however, together with an unprecedented series of hurricanes, exposed these foreign-fed islands to famine and death. When they turned to growing provisions locally, the planters found it difficult to cut back on cash crops that supported the Atlantic economy's superstructure of trade, shipping, and finance. Because of its greater land area, Jamaica was better situated to combine cash crops with subsistence crops, but questions have been raised regarding the Jamaican system of slave provision grounds and Sunday markets as a viable alternative to supervised local food production or dependence on imported foodstuffs. In fact, it has been argued, chiefly on the basis of testimony before Parliamentary committees, that the typical field slave in Jamaica had insufficient time and energy to grow, transport, and market his provisions, especially in crop time. The harsh fact is that slaves were consistently victims of starvation during the hungry season. On the other hand, the nutritional bonus supplied to plantation slaves during the Christmas holiday provided energy that helped to sustain them during the long and arduous sugar harvest. It can be further argued that the Barbadian planters achieved a rough balance among cash crops, animal forage crops, and the supervised food production by slaves for their own subsistence. Reserves of locally produced foodstuffs may have been sufficient to tide the slaves over the hungry season and thus contributed to the better demographic performance of the Barbadian slaves.

James Stephen wrote that the owners of West India estates in general believed that they could not effectively improve the condition of their slaves and preserve the large profits of their sugar plantations. Self-interest, he said, had by long experience discovered "the lowest degree of subsistence, and the highest degree of labour, generally consistent with the preservation of life, and the capacity of regular work." No doubt the greater number of adult slaves, given a small allowance of food, were able to work for their masters as well as feed themselves, albeit at a margin of subsistence that left them with little resistance against disease. The nonworking slaves in general, and the shirkers and troublemakers in particular, were often badly treated. The evidence suggests that when discipline was enforced by harsh punishment and the denial of food, a vicious circle was set in motion that frequently led to premature death. Dr. Collins knew of instances where the death of a slave, whether from starvation or stealing, was "set down as a positive benefit to the estate . . . the question being entirely overlooked, whether he might not have been re-established in his health, or reclaimed from his criminal course, by a more generous treatment."[97]

7

Morbidity and mortality

> All the numerous chronic diseases which arise from a scanty or an excess of vegetable diet, are common among the slaves in the West Indies. This evil, I have been well informed, cannot be remedied while slavery remains on its present footing; for very accurate calculations have made it evident, that the whole profit of a sugar estate, as it is now conducted, is saved from the necessary food and cloathing of the slaves.
>
> Benjamin Rush, M.D., 1788[1]

It is our task in this chapter to show how the patterns of morbidity and mortality were related to age, sex, occupation, and mode of life, as well as to the physical environment. We analyze the relationships between malnutrition and disease and how contemporary and modern authors have contributed to our understanding of these interrelationships. Separate sections are devoted to the diseases and disease patterns of infants, children, and adult slaves.

"Disorders peculiar to the Negroes"

Slave morbidity and mortality were the most vital and sensitive issues that confronted the West Indian planter class. Bryan Edwards admitted that the "grand and most plausible" accusation against the general conduct of the planters arose "from the necessity they find themselves under of having an annual recruit of slaves from Africa, to fill up the numbers that perish in the West Indies."[2] Until the abolition of the slave trade in 1808, planters attributed high morbidity and mortality chiefly to the influx of diseased Africans, whereas in the subsequent period they tended to blame the population failure on the poor hygiene and sexual promiscuity of the slaves. Abolitionists, on the other hand, held the planters responsible for the untimely death of their slaves from overwork, underfeeding, cruel punishment, and dirty living conditions. From the standpoint of this study it is fortunate that the contest between protagonists and antagonists of the peculiar institution in the British Caribbean yielded a wealth of demographical and medical information.

The immunity that resulted from the mutual adaptation between human host and infectious organisms broke down when people moved across the ocean from one disease environment to another. Unfamiliar diseases attacked newcomers who came to the West Indies from environments that provided no source of immunity. Writing in 1824, John Stewart, the Jamaica planter-author, said that it was

> not a little remarkable, that some of the diseases to which the white people in this island are subject seldom or never affect the negroes; while the former are totally exempt from the disorders peculiar to the negroes, unless communicated by infection. But there are diseases, also, which are common to both, as pulmonary complaints, liver disease, bowel disorders, dropsy, common intermittent fever, &c.

Stewart went on to say that malignant epidemic fever or yellow fever, "that dreadful scourge of the whites," did not attack the blacks.[3] The Reverend J. H. Buchner was told by a medical author of some celebrity in Jamaica that in a practice of twenty years he had known only two black men to die of yellow fever.[4] Dr. David Collins of St. Vincent said it was notorious that whereas more than nineteen out of twenty of the whites were killed by fevers, not one in a hundred blacks died of those disorders, though they were subject to feverish affections.[5] Modern medical science has demonstrated that yellow fever, like malaria, is a mosquito-borne illness. It was endemic along much of the coast of West Africa where the relatively mild form of the disease among infants and small children generally conferred immunity for life.[6]

Jamaican doctors who practiced among the slaves testified to the low incidence of malaria. Dr. John Williamson observed that remittent fever, though more common among domestics than field slaves, was very rare in the rural parish of St. Thomas in the Vale where he practiced.[7] Dr. James Thomson wrote from the same parish that although blacks frequently had irregular attacks of fever in the fall of the year when the north winds began to blow, they were "speedily cured by a few doses of bark and bitterwood combined." Dr. Curten, a physician at Rio Bueno on the north coast of Jamaica, in speaking of the blacks, was quoted as saying, "I have not met among them with a pure tertian intermittent in the whole of my practice, and those of forty years' experience mention it as a rare occurrence, confined in mulattoes and house-negroes."[8]

Besides the differential impact of malaria and yellow fever, there were black/white differences in tolerance to cold, hypertension, tuberculosis, hookworm, cystic fibrosis, and skin cancer. Todd Savitt writes that blacks have been shown to have a poorer adaptive response to cold exposure than do whites; on the other hand, there is little difference in heat tolerance when both races are equally active in the same environment over a period of time.[9]

The myth that blacks were better able than whites to stand the strain of hard labor in hot countries was long used to justify slavery.[10] Other studies have shown that hypertension or high blood pressure is more severe among blacks than other racial groups and that tuberculosis often manifests itself more violently in black than in white patients. On the other hand, Africans in the New World were much less susceptible than Caucasians to hookworms, cystic fibrosis, and skin cancer, among other diseases.[11] Dr. George Farquhar of Jamaica asserted that the blacks were susceptible to a much greater variety of diseases than the white inhabitants. They suffered from yaws, coco bays (a form of leprosy), elephantiasis, Guinea worms, ulcers, geophagy or dirt eating, and tetanus.[12] Fevers and fluxes were the principal disorders in the West Indies, according to Dr. Collins; fevers were the fatal diseases of the whites, and fluxes or bowel complaints proportionally more fatal to the blacks.[13]

Before 1808, the Atlantic slave trade affected slave morbidity and mortality in several ways. The influx of predominantly young adult and male slaves created a concentration of the population in the prime working-age bracket. Hector McNeill, a Jamaica planter, wrote in 1788 that "the common practice of purchasing a greater number of males than females [was] on account of the superior strength and labour of the men and their being much less liable to disease and confinement."[14] But comparative mortality suggests that female diseases were less lethal than those that afflicted males.[15]

Irrespective of sex, however, new African slaves had far higher mortality than seasoned Creoles. The Assembly of Jamaica reported in 1788 that the most general and prevailing causes of the natural decrease of the slave population of that island were, first, "the great Proportion of Deaths that happen among Negroes newly imported," and, second, "a loss which prevails among the Negro Infants that are born in the Country." Attached to the report was the examination of Dr. James Chisholme, of the parish of Clarendon, who said

> that a very great number of newly-imported Negroes are lost by Diseases, the predisposing Causes of which they bring to this Country along with them. Most new Negroes when first landed, are much subject to putrid Complaints, arising from a scorbutic Habit contracted during the Voyage, which frequently manifests itself soon after they are landed in putrid Dysenteries, or by foul Ulcers, tending strongly to Mortification. Many Negroes, while abroad, are afflicted with the most virulent venereal Complaints, others have the Yaws, some malignant Ulcers, all of which, when the Day of Sale draws near, are, by the Management of the Ship's Surgeon, dried up, and the morbid Matter repelled into the System, so that the Surface of the Skin shall appear clean and smooth for a Time, but which afterwards creates the most dreadful Complaints, too frequently baffling all Attempts to cure.[16]

Although losses in the seasoning varied in time and place, it is generally believed that one-third of the imported slaves died in their first three years in the West Indies.[17]

Sickness and accidents

When planters wrote that "the *general* treatment of the Negroes in the British West Indies is mild, temperate and indulgent," they were referring chiefly to sugar plantations that were large in acreage, labor force, and capital equipment, and accounted for nearly two-thirds of the total British Caribbean slave population.[18] Given a master who had many acres, ample capital, a staff of white managers, a white doctor, a slave hospital, and other facilities, it seems reasonable to argue that such an establishment would have a healthier and more contented labor force than that of planters with more limited resources. It is true that the slaves on some sugar plantations fared better than those on smaller properties; however, recent scholarship has demonstrated convincingly that the reverse was generally true. Barry Higman has analyzed the wealth of statistical data from Jamaica, using multiple regression analysis to weigh the variables that affected the slave demography of that island at the time of emancipation. He finds that mortality was highest on sugar plantations, particularly those of an apparently optimum size of 250 slaves. Conversely, the birthrate was lowest on the largest plantations, which experienced the greatest natural decrease of the slave population. Next highest in mortality were the coffee plantations, followed by cocoa, cotton, and pimento plantations, and cattle ranches or pens, then the towns, and finally the marginal subsistence agricultural units.[19]

Slave morbidity and mortality on sugar plantations were related both directly and indirectly to unhygienic conditions, accidents, suicide, punishment, diet, and work loads. Sugar plantations were generally regarded as health hazards by white Creoles. Since they were often close to the ports and shipping where Europeans and Africans intermingled, their inhabitants were vulnerable to communicable diseases. Plantations occupied relatively flat, lowland areas, which were often poorly drained and where stagnant water attracted disease-carrying mosquitos and flies. Since privies were seldom provided or used, slaves were likely to "go a bush" for nature's calls. Excrement and garbage were strewn around the slave quarters and attracted insects, rats, and vultures. Septic organisms were ingested by children who played in the grounds around the huts where fecal matter was abundant. Food and water supplies might be contaminated by the human, animal, and vegetable wastes that impregnated the soil with disease organisms.

Disease conditions were exacerbated by poorly constructed and poorly repaired slave houses. Dr. John Quier of Lluidas Vale, Jamaica, said that the occupants sometimes suffocated with heat and smoke; at other times, when the fires subsided at night, they suffered from the cold, damp air, which was admitted "through innumerable crevices and holes of the walls, which are seldom kept in proper repair." The sudden transition from heat to cold, by occasioning "peripneumonic fevers," was, in Quier's opinion, the most general cause of the death of newborn black infants in that part of the country where he practiced.[20]

As an agro-industrial establishment that combined the growing of canes with the manufacture of crude sugar, the typical sugar plantation confronted its workers with numerous hazards. Cuts and bruises from the careless use of edged tools, kicks from horses and mules, limbs crushed in moving machinery, burns and scalds from boiling cane juice, falls from high places, bolts of lightning and other acts of God – these and other accidents maimed and killed many slaves. Many limbs and some lives were lost feeding canes through the three-roller mill to extract the cane juice. Since the mill could not be stopped quickly, axes were kept within reach of the mill tenders to amputate fingers and hands before the whole body was drawn through and squeezed to atoms. Joseph Senhouse told of a terrible accident that occurred on the Farmer's plantation in Barbados in February 1799.

> Two Negroe Women, being Chained together, by way of punishment for some offence, were employed in returning the Trash in a Windmill, one of them unfortunately reaching too near the Rollers, her fingers were caught between them, and her Body was drawn thro[ugh] the Mill. The Iron Chain, being seized by the Rollers, was likewise drawn through & notwithstanding every effort was used, to stop the Mill, yet that was impossible to be done, before the other Female Negroe, was dragg'd so close to those Cylinders, that her Head was severed from her Body.[21]

An ingenious machine to prevent such dreadful accidents and save the labor of two blacks had recently been invented in Barbados, according to Senhouse. Known as a trashturner, it consisted of a square wooden box made circular on the inside and fixed to the back of the middle roller to direct the cane back through the mill to squeeze out the remaining juice.[22]

Dr. James Grainger wrote that there was nothing so common as burns and scalds, which were generally ill treated. Slaves who worked in the boiling house were apt to get scalded, especially when they were obliged to continue their labor at night.[23] Dr. John Williamson treated many slaves who were injured and killed by accidents and acts of God. In February 1799 he treated Neptune, aged about seventeen, on Williamsfield estate, who was kicked in the face by a powerful horse. In June of the same year he amputated a slave's hand, which had been "broken in pieces by getting between the mill rollers."

Several blacks were said to have perished in a storm in October 1799, and another slave was struck dead by lightning in the following May. In March 1801 he treated a woman who had her thighs and legs scalded by hot liquor in the boiling house. A year later he performed extensive surgery on a woman who "by carelessness, allowed her elbow to get in between the rollers in feeding the mill."[24]

Morbidity and mortality resulted from the cruel and barbarous punishment of slaves. Sir Hans Sloane, who saw slavery firsthand in Jamaica, wrote:

> The Punishments for Crimes of Slaves, are usually for Rebellions burning them, by nailing them down on the ground with crooked Sticks on every Limb, and then applying the Fire by degrees from the Feet and Hands, burning them gradually up to the Head, whereby their pains are extravagant.[25]

Crimes of a lesser nature were punished by "Gelding, or chopping off half of the Foot with an Ax," while for running away the slave was burdened with iron rings, chains, pottocks, and spurs.[26] Presumably with the concurrence of his employer, Thomas Thistlewood, the plantation overseer in Jamaica, made running away a capital offense. On 9 October 1751 he wrote in his journal that three runaways – Robin and two boys – had been captured. To deter others from running away, Robin was hung and beheaded and his head put on a pole "at ye Angle of ye Road in the home pasture."[27]

Unusually severe and often fatal punishments were reported even after the antislavery movement alerted the British public to the horrors of slavery. Captain Robert Ross, who resided in Jamaica from 1762 to 1786 as a bookkeeper, overseer, and property owner, gave evidence to the select committee of the House of Commons in 1790. He testified that he had known slaves who had received "two hundred lashes at a time, by the command of the overseer, for some crime for which the law would only have inflicted thirty-nine lashes." To the question, "Do you believe the punishments were ever so severe as to occasion the Negro's death?" Ross replied, "I do; because I have known Negroes that have been severely punished, which with bad care afterwards, was the occasion of their death, in many places."[28]

Morbidity, or the state or quality of being morbid or sick, included a wide range of ailments to which the blacks were susceptible. Plantation slaves suffered burns, bruises, cuts, and other accidents, which, if not fatal, left them blind, lame, disfigured, or with amputated limbs. Insect bites, if improperly treated, festered into sores and ulcers that were difficult to cure. Similarly, coughs and colds, if neglected, could develop into putrid sore throat, pleurisy, or pneumonia. It was generally believed that heat and cold, moisture and dampness, could all cause fevers and colds. A variety of ailments were attributed to noxious air or miasma – that is, the vapors and "putrid effluvia" or minute particles that emanated from moist and swampy soil, stagnant pools, and decayed vegetation. Moreover, the impact of the environment on morbidity and mortality was thought to vary from season to season with changes in temperature, prevailing winds, and growing or decaying vegetation.

The miasmatic theory was applied to the tropical environment by Dr. George Farquhar in his *Account of the Climate and Diseases of Jamaica*. He maintained that Jamaica, with its mountains and lowlands and variable winds and currents, had a diversity of climate that was perhaps unsurpassed by any country of the same extent in the world. The sea breeze set in from eight to nine o'clock in the morning. It increased as the sun approached the meridian and then gradually declined, to be succeeded by the land wind, which blew during the night from the mountains to the lowland in all directions. Diseases were said to be prevalent in the lowlands where the swamps and lagoons were exposed to the heat of the sun, but not in swampy lands where the action of the sun was shielded by high woods.[29]

The seasons were alternately healthy and sickly. During the prevalence of north winds and the dry atmosphere in the early months of the year, the whites as well as the blacks were particularly healthy, wrote Farquhar. In fact, he said it was not unusual to have the plantation hospitals shut up for many weeks in February and March. During the rainy season in May, pleurisies and other inflammatory diseases were very prevalent among the blacks. Sickness became general among both races during May and November when the extreme heat "concentrated the marshy miasmata" to produce malaria and other diseases. July, August, and September, the warmest months, were generally healthy; however, "those of a more relaxed habit" were "frequently affected with diarrhoea, and other bowel complaints, occasioned by an increased secretion of bile." August, September, and October formed what was called the "hurricane season." This was a rainy season when the north winds set in. The autumnal rains, which commenced sometimes at the end of September and at other times not until the middle of October, lasted longer and were more severe than those in May. "During the continuance of the rains," wrote Farquhar, "the negroes are particularly liable to inflammatory complaints of the lungs, and affections of the bowels." November was said to be the most sickly period of the year when the inhabitants of all descriptions, as well as strangers, suffered from the effects of the preceding rains.

The most healthy period of the year, according to Farquhar, was from the first of December until April. During this time "the cold north wind blows, the atmosphere is clear, and the effects of the autumnal rains having ceased, those, who have suffered from Indisposition during the month of November, begin to recover, and by March are entirely restored to health."[30]

Table 7.1. *Condition of the slaves belonging to Rose Hall sugar plantation, St. Thomas in the Vale, Jamaica, 31 December 1789*

Able and healthy	57
Healthy	42
Weak, healthy but weak, or very weak	22
Ulcers and sores	9
Sick	8
Invalids, all very old and weak	8
Useless or almost useless	4
In the yaws	4
Blind or almost blind	3
Bone ache	2
Ruptured	2
Other ailing or ineffective slaves, including one infant	7
No condition given, includes 6 slaves living off the plantation, and 2 who were recently purchased	12
Total slaves	180

Source: Celia M. King, "Introduction to The Papers of Davison, Newman & Co. Ltd. 1753–1897 in the Guildhall Library, London," in W. E. Minchinton, ed., *British Records Relating to America in Microform* (EP Microform Ltd., East Arsdley, Wakefield, Yorkshire, 1976), Appendix I, pp. 15–22.

Table 7.1 gives a "snapshot" picture of the health of the slaves on one sugar plantation in Jamaica. Of the 180 slaves on Rose Hall plantation on 31 December 1789, only ninety-nine (or 55 percent) were "able and healthy" or "healthy." On the other hand, those who were weak, afflicted with ulcers or sores, sick, invalid, blind, or otherwise physically impaired numbered sixty-nine (or 38.3 percent of the total). Whether the Rose Hall slaves were more or less sick and physically impaired than their counterparts on other plantations is difficult to say, given the paucity of data. Even if the general health of slaves improved over time, as some contemporary writers maintained, after the abolition of the Atlantic slave trade, a growing proportion of the population came to be young and old, and slaves in these age brackets were especially vulnerable to disease and death.

It is of interest that the Rose Hall slaves who were afflicted with ulcers and sores slightly outnumbered those who were sick. Though sores and ulcers contributed to the death of slaves, they more often crippled them or rendered them unfit for labor and not infrequently resulted in the amputation of limbs to arrest the spread of gangrene. Lacking adequate covering for their bodies, and especially their feet, slaves stepped on thorns, sharp rocks, or broken glass, had insects burrow into their skin or bite them, or bruised or cut their bodies. If neglected, an innocuous insect bite or cut could become infected and develop into an ugly sore or ulcer. Matthew Gregory Lewis said that the most general Negro infirmity appeared to be lameness.[31] On newly settled plantations, according to Dr. Collins, it was "not unusual to have a third, or half of the negroes, confined to the house by sores, or working in the fields with bandages about their legs, which indicate that they are fitter for the hospital than for labour; and thither they should be sent on the first appearance of a sore, however inconsiderable."[32]

Rather paradoxically, the labor and sometimes the life of a slave could be lost for want of a knife and the inclination to remove the eggs laid in human flesh by the tiny chigoe. The chigoe – also referred to by contemporaries as the chigre, chiga, jigger, or gigger – is a small species of flea found in the West Indies and South America. The female burrow beneath the skin of humans and causes itching and painful sores. These insects were said to thrive most in dry seasons and were always found in dust and ashes and among shavings. Blacks, who were apt to put their feet in ashes where the chigoes bred, had these insects burrow into not only their toes and heels but also their buttocks, hands, and elbows. There the female insect formed herself into a bag as large as a pea into which she deposited her eggs. If not removed by the delicate use of a small knife or needle, the bag broke and formed a terrible sore or ulcer.[33] The frequency with which infected toes were amputated is indicated by the experience of Dr. William Chisholme. Upon learning that he was being charged for the "Lancett & amputating the Negroes Toes," Chisholme informed his plantation attorney that during the time of his practice in Jamaica he "never thought of charging for taking off Toes, & neither of which ought to be allowed."[34]

Doctors and planters were concerned to prevent chigoe bites from degenerating into sores or ulcers. "All the young, as well as the new Negroes," wrote Dr. Grainger, "should have their feet and hands examined regularly once a week. For want of this precaution, Negroes often lose many a joint of their toes, &c. and so become less useful upon a plantation." Grainger went on to say that black women were very dexterous in picking out the chigoe with a pointed knife. He believed that a little snuff, mixed with a small quantity of verdigris was the best powder to put in the hole from whence the chigoe was extracted.[35]

Creole and seasoned slaves, according to Dr. Collins, suffered but little inconvenience from chigoes because they removed them before the egg sack broke. Many of the indolent, and particularly the newcomers, however, were soon crippled. Since the chigoe was averse to grease or oil, Dr. Collins recommended that the feet of blacks should be washed and greased every morning with a mixture of lamp oil and oil of turpentine. Preventive measures being uncertain, he recommended that for the extraction of chigoes, "your negroes should be furnished with small knives, called chigo-knives, which, by their breadth of point, are the best adapted to such a service."[36]

Todd Savitt says that for the slaves of Virginia, shoes were probably the most important article of clothing in terms of health and disease. Shoes provided protection against cuts, bruises, burns, punctures, and hookworm penetration, and also kept feet and toes warm in winter when frostbite threatened. Except for protection against cold, all these reasons for wearing shoes should have applied equally to Caribbean slaves. The select committee of the House of Lords was much concerned about shoes in its investigation of West Indian slavery. John Baillie, a leading planter and attorney of Jamaica, was asked by the committee whether shoes would be useful to the field slaves or the slaves in general. He answered in the negative, giving such reasons as the slaves' objection to wearing shoes and the high cost of outfitting a gang of blacks. Costs were said to be exorbitantly high because of wear and tear and the need for frequent replacement, and the racist argument that a shoemaker would need to measure every slave's feet because "the Formation of a Negro's Foot is totally different from that of a White Person." Baillie was asked by the committee if disorders in the feet arose from the blacks coming into contact with the prickly pear and other hard substances. Although he admitted that this might happen, he categorically denied that shoes would be of any use in preventing sores and ulcers from chigoes. When asked whether shoes were ever provided by the master, Baillie said he had supplied three pair: "Two for the Rangers and another for a Brown Man on the Property; but I never saw a Field Negro with a Shoe on."[37]

Patterns of mortality

Barry Higman has analyzed the demographic experience of the slave population of the British Caribbean in the period 1807–34, drawing chiefly on the slave registration returns, which begin generally in 1817 and continue until emancipation in 1834. From the data in the triennial and annual returns he has calculated some basic demographic indexes for the sixteen British Caribbean colonies. Table 7.2 shows the indexes for Barbados, Antigua, Trinidad, Demerara, and Jamaica, which together accounted for 556,000 (or three-fourths) of the total population of about 750,000 slaves in the first registration period. Perhaps 20 to 25 percent of the births and deaths went unrecorded when the latter followed quickly on the former within the three-year registration periods. Since the numbers of unrecorded births and deaths varied from colony to colony, the indexes shown in the table are calculated from the original returns.[38]

Higman finds that the Sugar Colonies can be divided into three major

Table 7.2. *Some basic demographic indexes, 1816–32: Barbados, Antigua, Trinidad, Demerara, and Jamaica*

	Total slave population	Males per 100 females	Births per 1,000	Deaths per 1,000	Natural increase per 1,000
Barbados					
1817–20	77,919	86.1	31.7	28.3	3.4
1820–23	78,581	86.5	34.9	28.5	6.4
1823–26	79,684	84.9	40.2	28.1	12.1
1826–29	81,227	85.1	38.0	28.0	10.0
1829–32	81,701	85.8	40.7	30.6	10.1
Antigua					
1817–21	31,627	87.4	18.5	22.8	–4.3
1821–24	30,650	87.9	27.1	27.6	–0.5
1824–27	30.077	88.8	25.5	25.2	0.3
Trinidad					
1816–19	24,541	125.1	19.3	37.6	–18.3
1819–22	23,463	126.5	21.2	34.5	–13.3
1822–25	23,920	124.0	22.8	24.5	–1.7
1825–28	24,114	117.1	18.0	25.5	–7.5
Demerara					
1817–20	77,622	128.7	20.9	30.3	–9.4
1820–23	76,177	124.4	19.7	31.5	–11.8
1823–26	73,180	120.5	20.5	34.8	–14.3
1826–29	70,425	116.9	22.2	27.1	–4.9
1829–32	67,512	112.6	20.2	34.7	–13.5
Jamaica					
1817–20	344,266	99.7	23.6	24.3	–0.7
1820–23	339,318	98.7	22.8	25.9	–3.1
1823–26	333,686	97.4	23.0	25.1	–2.1
1826–29	326,770	96.5	22.2	25.6	–3.4
1829–32	317,649	95.5	23.2	28.0	–4.8

Source: Calculated from *Parliamentary Papers*, 1833, 26 (530), pp. 473–7; ibid., 1835, 51, by Barry W. Higman, in "The Slave Populations of the British Caribbean: Some Nineteenth Century Variations," in Samuel Proctor, ed., *Eighteenth-Century Florida and the Caribbean* (Gainesville: University Presses of Florida, 1976), Appendix, pp. 67–70.

groups on the basis of crude estimates of the rate of natural population increase or decrease. The first group (Bahamas, Barbados, Montserrat, St. Christopher, Antigua, Nevis, Virgin Islands, St. Lucia) was characterized by a tendency toward natural increase, but only the Bahamas and Barbados managed to maintain a positive natural increase throughout the period 1816–34. The second group (Trinidad, Demerara, Berbice, St. Vincent, Grenada, Tobago) experienced heavy though lessening natural decreases, and the third group (Jamaica and Dominica) had light though deteriorating decreases. The colonies in the first group had all been settled in the seventeenth century, those in the second in the late eighteenth century, and those in the third had a wide range of settlement dates.[39]

The premature aging and short life expectancy of slaves in Jamaica and British Guiana are demonstrated by modern demographic research. Higman finds that, excluding infants, the most common age of death of Jamaican slaves on the eve of emancipation was between thirty and forty. There were significant differences between Africans and Creoles, however. Even lower figures held in British Guiana, where, according to George Roberts, the average length of life was less than twenty-three years in 1820–32. He concludes from his analysis of the data in the slave registration returns that the age structure and severe mortality resulted in a rapidly wasting population.[40]

Philip Curtin has argued that the Sugar Colonies tended to have a regular demographic history. Because of the high ratio of imported to Creole slaves and the marked differences in the mortality of these two groups, the early colonies are said to have had high rates of natural decrease. As a given colony developed economically, however, the slave population began to grow less rapidly and recruits from Africa made up a diminishing proportion of the total population. Furthermore, the sex ratio became more balanced, with a presumed positive influence on the birthrate. Eventually, as in the case of Barbados by 1810, births came to equal and subsequently to exceed deaths. Although Curtin's model of demographic development is useful for understanding the experience of the British Caribbean territories in broad outline, Higman finds that his untested assumption that the Creole section of the slave population would grow naturally does not conform to the experience of certain plantations and parishes in Jamaica.[41]

Figures 7.1 and 7.2 are population pyramids that show the age structure of the slaves on York sugar plantation in Trelawny Parish, Jamaica, in 1778 and 1829, respectively. During this fifty-year period the number of slaves on this plantation declined from 485 to 303 (or by 37.1 percent). In 1778 there were 123 males per hundred females; in 1829 this ratio had fallen to 80 per hundred as women tended to outlive men and the recruitment of male slaves from Africa became unlawful after 1808. The age pyramids show that the dependency ratio increased. In 1778 young and old slaves numbered

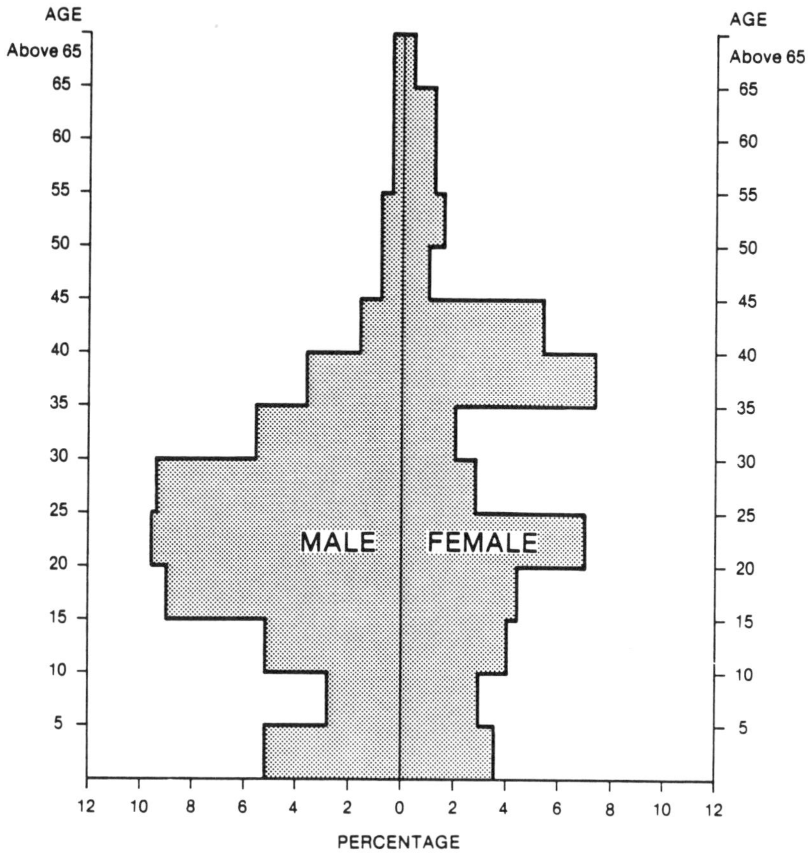

Figure 7.1. Population pyramid, York plantation, Jamaica, 1778. From List of Slaves on York Estate, Jamaica, 1 January 1778, *Gale-Morant Papers*, 3/c, University of Exeter Library.

156 and comprised 32.2 percent of all slaves. Of these 156 slaves, 113 were fourteen or younger (or 23.3 percent of all slaves), and 43 were forty-five years and older (or 8.9 percent of all slaves). In 1829, on the other hand, young and old slaves numbered 156 (or 51.5 percent of all slaves). Of these 156 slaves, 82 (or 27.1 percent of all slaves) were fourteen or younger, and 74 (or 24.4 percent of all slaves) were forty-five years and older.

Abolition of the Atlantic slave trade in 1808, together with the excess of deaths over births, frustrated the planters in their efforts to have most of their slaves in the prime working age group of fifteen to forty-four years. Figures 7.1 and 7.2 show a marked change in the ratio of prime workers to all slaves on York plantation. In 1778 there were 329 slaves (or 67.8 percent

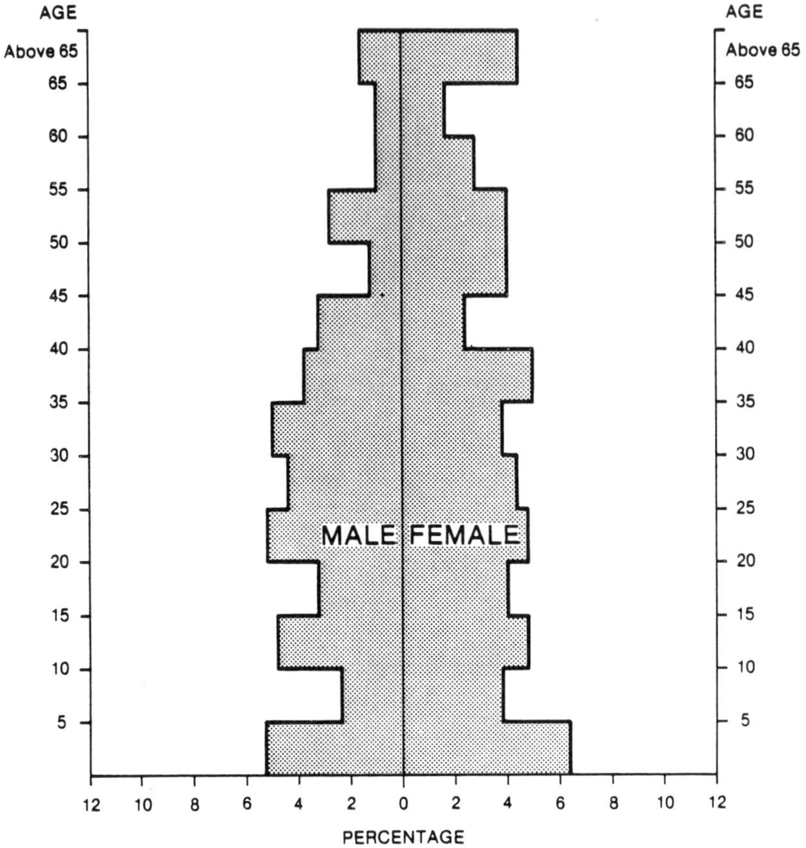

Figure 7.2. Population pyramid, York plantation, Jamaica, 1829. From List of Slaves on York Estate, Jamaica, 1 January 1829, *Gale-Morant Papers*, 3/d/3, University of Exeter Library.

of all slaves) in the prime age group, but in 1829 there was only 147 such slaves (or 48.5 percent of all slaves). The African-Creole ratio also changed significantly. Of the 485 slaves in 1778, 241 (or 49.7 percent) were born in Africa. Of these 241 Africans, 150 were men, 85 women, and 6 children under fifteen years. Moreover, 235 Africans (150 men and 85 women) were in the prime working age group. In fact, they made up 71.4 percent of the 329 slaves in this category in 1778. Although the birthplaces of the slaves on York plantation are omitted on the 1829 list, the demographic data and analysis of Higman and Craton point to a significant increase in the ratio of Creoles to Africans and of females to males after abolition of the slave trade.[42]

Table 7.3. *Slave death rate in Grenada: frequency distribution by size of slaveholding, 1817*

Frequency	No. of slaves[a]	Deaths reported	Deaths per thousand
11–50	2,594	49	18.9
51–100	3,180	92	28.9
101–200	10,491	406	38.7
201–300	5,664	221	39.0
301–407	1,795	53	29.5
Total	23,724	821	34.6

[a]Omitted from this frequency distribution are all slaveholdings less than ten, and all slaves in the town of St. George. The 23,724 slaves in table constituted 86.1 percent of all slaves (27,565) in Grenada in 1817.
Source: P.R.O. London, *Treasury* 71/264 (1817), Grenada Slave Registration, Increase and Decrease.

The economic and demographic experience of Grenada and the Grenadines is of interest for several reasons. Although sugar became the dominant staple of the island of Grenada itself, some of the outlying islands continued to grow cotton, spices, and other minor staples. The slave population of this group of islands declined from 27,565 in 1817 to 23,604 in 1831, while the number of males per hundred females declined from 95.2 to 93.9. The crude birthrate per thousand ranged from 16.3 to 30.7, while the crude death rate ranged from 26.6 to 43.2. It is significant that, overall, the population of Grenada and its appendages experienced a natural decrease in twelve of the fifteen years from 1817 to 1831. Table 7.3 shows that for approximately 85 percent of the population in 1817, there were 34.6 deaths per thousand. On a frequency distribution, however, deaths per thousand increased from 18.9 on holdings of 11 to 50 slaves, to a peak of 39.0 on those of 201 to 300 slaves, after which they declined to 29.5 on those of 301 to 407 slaves. What this means is that slaveholdings that were economically optimal for sugar production had high mortality. These findings are consistent with those Higman has calculated for the rural parishes of Jamaica.[43]

By contrast with the main island of Grenada, where sugar was the dominant staple, cotton continued to be grown on some of the smaller islands on the chain known as the Grenadines. Here, according to a contemporary historian, the increase of the slaves was very great. He attributed this increase "to the light work on cotton estates, the abundance of fish which they obtain with little trouble, and a compulsory sobriety, from the increased difficulty of obtaining rum."[44]

In contrast with the slavery experience of the United States, the slaves in the British Sugar Colonies never achieved positive natural increase with the lone exception of the island of Barbados. In his comparative study of slavery in the two regions, Stanley Engerman finds that in about 1830 the crude birthrates in the United States and Jamaica were about 50 and 23 per thousand, respectively, and the death rates 20–30 and 26 per thousand, respectively. Engerman's results suggest "that the mortality experience of creoles in the islands may not have differed as markedly from that in the United States as did the fertility rates, despite the general presumption of quite high tropical mortality rates and the apparent existence of somewhat higher mortality." He points out, however, that the mortality experience of Caribbean slaves differed significantly in the period before the end of the slave trade.[45]

Malnutrition and diseases of infants and children

Slave diseases and deaths were related to age, sex, country of origin, weather and climate, hygienic conditions, diet, punishment, occupation, and conditions of labor. For the individual slave the ability to resist disease organisms was, in part, a function of age and sex. Slave infants and children were highly susceptible to certain infectious diseases, to which, if they survived, they became immune. They suffered and died from tetanus, bowel disorders, putrid sore throat, colic, whooping cough, measles, smallpox, yaws, worms, and marasmus, among other diseases. Adults, both men and women, were susceptible to the respiratory diseases of pleurisy, influenza, and pneumonia. They contracted the intestinal disorders of diarrhea, dysentery, and dry bellyache; were plagued by a variety of worms; and had their bodies disfigured and made miserable by ugly sores, yaws, elephantiasis, and leprosy. Women had gynecological disorders that included menstrual difficulties and complications of pregnancy and childbirth. Slaves tended to age and die prematurely, suffering from such troubles as rheumatism, boneache, ruptures, incurable diseases, and often indigence and neglect.

Trismus nascentium is tetanus of young infants caused by infection of the navel. Known as infant tetanus, lockjaw, or "jaw fall," it was perhaps the greatest killer among all ages of blacks in the West Indies in the eighteenth century. Infants were frequently attacked by this deadly disease within nine or ten days of their birth. Benjamin Moseley, M.D., of Jamaica believed that death by infant tetanus was the greatest drawback in the slave population. In fact, he asserted that the mortality of native blacks from this disease was "far more detrimental to estates in the course of time, than all other casualties put together."[46] According to Dr. George Farquhar, another Jamaican practitioner, there was such dreadful havoc from infant tetanus that "one-half of those born in the course of the year, are not unfrequently carried off, although I do not remember an instance of it occurring in a white child."[47] Barry Higman has estimated that, owing chiefly to tetanus, as many as 25 percent of births went unrecorded in Jamaica because deaths occurred in the first few days.[48]

Children under ten years old suffered other fatal diseases. The yaws killed many of them, according to Dr. John Quier. He went on to say that worm complaints were more frequent in Jamaica than in England, "and the same epidemical Diseases which are incident to Children in Europe, viz. the small Pox, Measles, and Whooping Cough, are equally common in Negro Children here, and in a severer Degree."[49] Dr. Castles of Grenada believed that much pain was occasioned by the teeth making their way through the gums and that convulsions and fatal fevers often resulted from dentition. Moreover, he maintained that worms in children were more common in the West Indies than in England, owing to "their vegetable diet, great part of which is used in a crude state, particularly fruits, which they have in greater plenty than the lower sort of people in this country [England]."[50] Worm fever was the most fatal complaint among children under ten years, according to Barclay. It was produced, he said, by eating fruit and drinking the juice of the sugarcane.[51] A plantation manager in Antigua believed that the diseases of children "proceed in a great measure from Worms, which too often baffle the prescriptions of the Doctor, & the care & attention of the Nurses."[52]

Today it is generally recognized in the West Indies that the triad of malnutrition, gastroenteritis, and respiratory tract infections are largely responsible for deaths of children younger than five.[53] A similar but more fatal disease environment confronted slave infants and children. Inadequate nutrition of mothers not only impaired their reproductive ability but also resulted in the malnutrition and death of their babies, especially if the latter were inadequately fed after birth. Marasmus and hookworm were two important killers of infants and children that were related to malnutrition. "The improperly regulated way of feeding children, by which they are kept puny and unhealthy, subjects them more severely to the effects of [w]hooping-cough, or any other incidental disease," wrote Dr. Williamson. Finding that whooping cough did not prove as destructive to healthy children, he concluded that "to mismanagement in diet, exercise, and clothing, may be imputed its destructive consequences."[54] Higman has found that deaths attributed to "swellings," "bloated," or "dirt eating" tended to affect younger slaves most often. "Since they were distinguished from dropsy and mal d'estomac [or dirt eating]," he writes, "these causes of death probably comprehended the deficiency diseases and anemias resulting from malnutrition."[55] These and other diseases and disorders of infants and children and pregnant and lactating women will be treated in greater depth in Chapter 8.

The planters' contention that their slaves were always adequately fed was disputed by evidence that the supply of food was frequently insufficient or of poor quality and that dietary deficiency, together with bad sanitation, harsh punishment, and hard labor, undermined the health of the blacks.[56] Modern studies have shown that nutrition is not merely a question of foods and calories in correct proportions, but that small quantities of hitherto unknown substances, or vitamins, are necessary to life. Moreover, studies have shown that a diet rich in carbohydrates but poor in animal proteins, minerals, and vitamins can lead to bone deformation and pulmonary and intestinal diseases. James Lind's discovery that the deficiency disease of scurvy could be prevented by the adequate use of fresh fruits or lemon juice was a milestone in the conquest of tropical diseases. It is perhaps true that malnutrition and gastroenteritis were two of the most important health problems of the slaves, and that infants and young children were extremely vulnerable to these problems. Generally speaking, there was a close relationship between diarrhea and other infectious diseases on the one hand and malnutrition on the other.

White doctors and planters had a rudimentary understanding of the relationship between malnutrition and disease. The relationship between salt fish, the chief source of animal protein, and the diseases of slaves were commented on by several writers. James Knight thought that, besides the common diseases, the blacks of Jamaica were troubled with some disorders that were probably due to their own manner of living. In particular, he condemned their custom of seasoning salted provisions with so much salt and pepper that no one could touch it but themselves.[57] At a time when imported supplies of salted provisions were curtailed by the conflict between Great Britain and the United States, the Assembly of Jamaica called on the governor to remedy the situation, asserting that "salted provisions are the chief corrective of the vegetable diet of the negroes, and a want of them inevitably brings on dysentery and disorders of that class, which, whenever prevalent, never fail to carry off great numbers."[58]

The prevalence of bowel complaints among children and sick adults on a plantation in Trinidad was blamed by the attorney on the salt fish and esculent roots, which he believed produced indigestion and acidity. To correct this disorder, the manager was ordered to supply these blacks, at both breakfast and supper, with "*Cocoa* made as it is on board of ships which is much more nourishing than their present diet and will be beneficial rather than injurious to their stomachs." It struck the attorney as extraordinary that "a thing so nourishing & wholesome and cheap and growing on the very spot should not have before been used."[59]

The modern sciences of nutrition and medicine have added to our understanding of the relationship between malnutrition and disease. Malnutrition can be divided into overnutrition or obesity, which is a problem in rich countries, and undernutrition, which is the overriding problem in poor countries. Undernutrition is a manifestation of poverty that has deep roots. Poverty, among other things, means scarce and poor-quality food, inadequate housing and clothing, poor water supply, lack of sanitary facilities and habits, bad customs, and limited health services. Undernutrition deprives millions of people of the health they need to lead happy and productive lives. Moreover, it interacts with infectious disease as both cause and effect. As Nevin S. Scrimshaw points out, "Malnutrition and infection interact synergistically so that the combined effect is more than the sum of the two separately." Thus, nutritional deficiencies generally decrease the capacity of people to resist the occurrence and consequences of infection, whereas most infections cause anorexia or the loss of appetite for food and decrease the intake of food.[60]

Young children and pregnant and lactating women in tropical countries suffer a disproportion of the disease and misery. Small children are especially vulnerable to severe undernutrition because they need about twice as much protein and energy in relation to overall body weight as adults require. Pregnant and nursing mothers also need extra food. Newborn babies in the tropics are susceptible to infections that may lead to septicemia or tetanus. Infants during the first year of life suffer infections of the respiratory tract (especially pneumonia), diarrhea, and nutritional marasmus. Those in the one to four age range are vulnerable to protein-calorie malnutrition (especially kwashiorkor), diarrhea, intestinal worms, tuberculosis, anemia, measles, and whooping cough. Children from five to fifteen do not have the high mortality found in younger groups; however, their health may be impaired by moderate malnutrition, infectious diseases such as measles, intestinal worms, attacks of malaria, and skin diseases. Derrick B. Jelliffe, M.D., says that "the 'Big Three' childhood ailments are usually malnutrition, diarrheal disease, and pneumonia. Following behind these come the remainder of the 'Top Ten' – tuberculosis, malaria, certain infectious fevers of childhood (notably measles and whooping cough), intestinal worms, accidents and infections of the new born." It is generally believed that children at the weaning stage are the most vulnerable.[61]

Recent findings by anthropologists, historians, and researchers in social medicine make it possible to forge certain links between the undernutrition and nutrition-deficient diseases of British West Indian slaves who lived two to three centuries ago and their free black descendants in the twentieth century. Slave skeletal remains from a burial ground in Barbados have been analyzed by anthropologists Jerome S. Handler and Robert S. Corruccini. They have analyzed ninety-four sets of teeth of slaves on the Newton plantation, which has produced sugar for more than three centuries. Using techniques developed by recent advances in dental morphology, Handler and Corruccini have derived data that, together with extensive historical documentation, are revealing with respect to dental problems, demographic characteristics, growth and maturation, diseases, infections, and nutritional crises and starvation. Especially revealing are the growth arrest lines on teeth, which point to periodic episodes of extreme dietary deficiency or starvation as well as severe diseases such as dysentery, measles, and smallpox. The skeletal mortality data suggest that the slaves on Newton plantation had an average life expectancy at birth of twenty-nine years.[62]

Comparative historical data on the height of slaves point to different levels of nutrition and other indicators that relate body growth to socioeconomic status. Data on the height of slaves in Trinidad have been compared with that of American slaves by Fogel and Engerman and Gerald C. Friedman. Fogel and Engerman find that "the mean terminal height of African-born slaves in Trinidad was just 60.5 inches or 1.0 inches shorter than Trinidad creoles, who in turn were 1.2 inches shorter than the U.S. slaves." These data suggest that the Trinidad diet was probably superior to the African diet but not as good as the U.S. slave diet, and that Trinidad slaves experienced moderate but not severe relative malnutrition. Higman corroborates and refines the findings of Fogel and Engerman and concludes that U.S. slaves were significantly taller than Afro-Caribbean slaves and that this contrast was greater for males than females. Higman makes the important point that differences in energy expenditure need to be taken into account in assessing the adequacy of the slave diet; the arduous labor regimen on Caribbean sugar plantations was unmatched by any other type of slavery in the plantation economies and societies of the Americas.[63]

That the pattern of growth differences among nineteenth-century slave populations was similar to that of their twentieth-century descendants is suggested by modern anthropometric studies. Dr. Michael T. Ashcroft and his colleagues have undertaken community surveys of children in different Commonwealth Caribbean territories to compare the influence of ethnic origin and environment, including nutrition, on anthropometric measurements used to assess nutritional status. To test the hypothesis that the retarded growth of children stems chiefly from protein-calorie deficiency, selected groups of children have been measured for heights and weights and the results compared with international standards. Certain Caribbean countries afford an excellent locus for such studies because people of different races live side-by-side under the same conditions, making it possible to ascertain the relative importance of ethnic origin and nutrition on body size. Genetic differences in weight and height between African, European, and Asiatic school children have been calculated and adjustments made to single out the importance of environmental factors, including health, nutrition, and maternal care, in influencing the growth of infants and children.[64]

The anthropometric studies were undertaken by Ashcroft and his colleagues in the 1960s and 1970s and concern mainly the heights and weights of school children. They extend from Bermuda on the north to Guyana on the south and include the intervening islands in the Lesser Antilles. On an east-west axis they extend from Barbados to Jamaica. In Kingston, Jamaica, surveys of pupils who attend fee-paying schools catering to the middle class revealed that Africans and Afro-Europeans were similar in height and weight to the Europeans. However, other surveys found that children who live in rural areas of Jamaica and those who attend government (non-fee-paying) schools in Kingston were smaller than preparatory school children. Ashcroft and his colleagues say that "the smaller size of children living in rural areas than of preparatory schoolchildren of the same race is almost certainly due to socio-economic rather than geographical reasons."[65] Guyanese primary school children of predominantly African origin differed little in mean heights and weights from those of the same racial origin in most other parts of the West Indies.[66] In the Leeward Islands it was found that boys and girls of African descent in Anguilla were heavier and taller than those in Nevis and St. Kitts. It is of interest that, unlike Nevis and St. Kitts, Anguilla has never had a plantation economy, although most of its inhabitants are descendants of slaves.[67]

Similarly, colored children in Bermuda are substantially taller and heavier than their counterparts in Guyana, Barbados, St. Kitts, Nevis, and Jamaica. Moreover, although the white school children of Bermuda are slightly heavier than their colored classmates, no consistent difference is shown in the mean height of these two groups. It is significant in these island comparisons that in the slavery era the Bermudian economy was based largely on trading and seafaring in contrast to the sugar plantations of the islands to the south, that the diseases of Bermuda are characteristic of temperate climates rather than of the tropics, and that today the socioeconomic condition of both white (mainly Caucasian) and colored (mainly African origin) people of Bermuda is good, if not equal.[68]

The relationship between malnutrition and disease among slave children in the antebellum South has been investigated in recent years by Kenneth F. Kiple and Virginia H. Kiple. They begin their article by calling attention to differing biological heritages that dictated different nutritional requirements and disease susceptibilities. Africans who came to the New World involuntarily brought with them the sickling trait and a tendency toward sickle-cell anemia, a high degree of lactose intolerance that made them prone to gastorintestinal complaints when they drank bovine milk, and a reduced capability to synthesize vitamin D because of their black pigmentation. As slaves on southern plantations, they were supplied with a core diet of fat pork and cornmeal, which interfered with bodily absorption of calcium and magnesium, lacked high-quality protein, and provided inadequate supplies of iron and vitamins B, C, and D.[69]

Slave infants and children in the antebellum South suffered markedly from the combined effects of their biological heritage and the diet of fat pork and cornmeal. Kiple and Kiple say that the practice of weaning plantation infants to a diet high in carbohydrates and low in proteins should have resulted in a fairly high incidence of protein-calorie malnutrition. From census and other data they find symptoms that point to a high incidence of the deficiency diseases of kwashiorkor and marasmus. Deficiencies of calcium, magnesium, and vitamin D resulted in the often fatal children's disease called tetany, which contemporary physicians referred to as "convulsions," "teething," and "tetanus." Nutritional deficiencies contributed to the high incidence of blindness, lameness, deformed bones, skin lesions, and dental problems. Moreover, nutritional deficiencies played a part in the infant and child diseases associated with worms and what was variously called *cachexia africana*, geophagy, pica, and dirt eating. (These two diseases will be discussed later in this chapter.) Kiple and Kiple's conclusion is that there was high slave child, and particularly slave infant, mortality relative to their white antebellum counterparts.[70]

In another article the Kiples have turned to the role played by deficiency diseases in preventing most Caribbean slave populations from sustaining a natural rate of growth. They emphasize the importance of the African biological heritage and the peculiarities of the Caribbean slave diet. Since proportionately more Caribbean slaves were born in Africa than were the slaves in North America, it is significant that the former suffered a more radical change in dietary habits during the period called the seasoning. As with their counterparts in North America, Caribbean slaves had diets that were low in calcium, deficient in vitamins A and B_1, and lacking in bovine milk. Unlike their counterparts, their diet was high in vitamin C and low in fat content. Whereas their low-fat/high-carbohydrate diet required much thiamine or vitamin B_1, it is highly doubtful that Caribbean slaves received sufficient thiamine. Because of these and other deficiencies, Caribbean slaves suffered from eye afflictions, dirt eating or mal d'estomac, beriberi, edema or dropsy, and infant tetanus. Whereas the Kiples maintain that Caribbean slaves were supplied with most of the basic nutrients, other studies point to a high incidence of protein-calorie malnutrition, particularly among infants and children.[71]

Diseases of children and adults

Although malnutrition was a major cause of slave diseases, the complex interrelationship between people and disease in a tropical environment was influenced by other factors. The climate directly affected the distribution of disease by providing parasitic agents or their vectors with suitable habitats. Although parasites are by no means confined to tropical and subtropical areas, they are, in general, more commonly found there than elsewhere in the world. Parasites play a large part in propagating diseases of the stomach and intestines, which are generally more common in the tropics than in temperate lands. The climate favors the rapid decomposition of food as well as the growth of harmful parasites. Because of poor standards of cleanliness and hygiene, infections may be conveyed by dust, flies, water, milk, fruit, and in many other ways. In the West Indies, the disease environment was exacerbated by the spread of European peoples and technology, improvements in communication, and the growth of trade and commerce. Island communities came to bear the brunt of infectious disease as they became densely populated with peoples from different disease environments who had different patterns of immunity and susceptibility and who had extensive links with the outside world.

Slave children and adults, whether male or female, African or Creole, suffered a variety of diseases connected with the respiratory tract, stomach, intestines, cardiovascular system, and nervous system. These and other disease categories were influenced, in turn, by diet, work loads, punishment, sanitation, climate, and other environmental factors. Higman's research shows that "slaves in the 20–44 age-group, who experienced the lowest mortality levels, died most often from dropsy, dysentery and consumption (the last probably concealing tuberculosis)." Moreover, he finds that they also suffered particularly from pleurisy, leprosy, venereal disease, and liver complaints, which were probably related to dysentery.[72] Dysentery and influenza were often epidemic. In Nevis, according to Dr. Robert Thomas, fluxes became very general every year during the rainy months "and were fatal to a great many full-grown Negroes, especially to those of weakly constitutions."[73] Dr. William Sells, who practiced in the parish of Clarendon in Jamaica, testified that a very destructive influenza epidemic raged in the district where he practiced in 1811, 1812, and 1813, "which proved fatal in above one hundred cases in his practice, at that time consisting of little more than three thousand slaves; those who fell victims to it were almost unexceptionably in the prime of life."[74]

Table 7.4 shows the major causes of death in selected years of all slaves in Grenada and British Guiana, slaves attached to Worthy Park plantation, and all inhabitants of the parish of St. Catherine's (Spanish Town), Jamaica.

Table 7.4. *Comparative causes of slave deaths: Grenada, 1830–1; British Guiana, 1829–32; Worthy Park, Jamaica, 1792–1838; and all deaths St. Catherine's (Spanish Town), Jamaica, 1774–8*

Causes of death	Grenada slaves, 1830–1	British Guiana slaves, 1829–32	Worthy Park slaves, 1792–1838	St. Catherine's (Spanish Town) slaves, 1774–8
Old age, debility	20.0%	19.1%	22.2%	3.6%
Dysentery, flux	4.8	12.0	8.7	9.3
Dropsy	10.0	9.2	9.5	3.4
Pulmonary diseases	8.0	9.2	11.4	5.7
Fevers (including measles, smallpox)	6.3	8.1	9.2	39.9
Yaws, ulcers	2.1	6.1	9.5	6.1
Inflammations, etc.	1.2	4.4	2.0	3.8
Gastrointestinal	9.1	4.3	6.0[a]	3.8
Dirt eating	4.1	4.3	—	—
Accidents	1.6	4.2	4.3	1.6
Leprosy	2.0	3.8	0.5	—
Convulsions	2.6	3.7	3.8	6.3
Lockjaw	3.0	2.6	0.5	0.8
Syphilis	—	1.0	—	1.1
Whooping cough	7.7	—	—	—
Cachexy	2.3	—	—	—
Marasmus	2.0	—	—	—
Others and unknown	13.2	8.0	12.4	14.6
	100.0%	100.0%	100.0%	100.0%
Total deaths	1,907	7,016	401	472

[a]Includes deaths from dirt eating.
Source: Adapted from a table in Michael Craton's "Death, Disease and Medicine on Jamaican Slave Plantations; the Example of Worthy Park, 1767–1838," *Histoire Sociale – Social History*, Vol. IX, No. 18 (November 1976), p. 245; Public Record Office, London, *Treasury* 71/314 (1830), 71/316 (1831), Grenada Slave Registration Books; George W. Roberts, *The Population of Jamaica* (Cambridge: Cambridge University Press, 1957), p. 175; Island Record Office, Jamaica, *St. Catherine's Copy Register, Causes of Death*, Vol. I.

Only rough approximations are possible because of problems of classifying and interpreting the data on causes of death in the returns of registration of slaves and private plantation records. The percentage of deaths from tetanus or lockjaw is no doubt understated because deaths that occurred in the first few days of life from this cause often went unrecorded. If infant tetanus accounted for as much as 20 percent of total mortality, this cause of death would rank with old age and debility in Table 7.4 as the leading cause of death. The tabulated causes of death are remarkably consistent among Grenada, British Guiana, and Worthy Park plantation. Indeed, Michael Craton contends "that there were health characteristics common and peculiar to sugar plantations wherever they were found within the Caribbean region." On the other hand, he finds that the disease patterns of West Indian towns, such as Spanish Town, Jamaica, differed markedly from those of sugar plantations. Unfortunately, the urban/plantation comparison is confused because of the inability to separate the mortality of white urban dwellers from their black and colored counterparts. Higman finds that approximately 8 percent of the slaves of Jamaica lived in towns, of which half resided in Kingston. Town slaves, who were to a large extent Creoles and coloreds, experienced natural increase over most of the period from 1817 to 1832; they were generally more skilled and more mobile than their brothers and sisters on plantations.[75]

Dysentery, or bloody flux, plague the slaves on the Middle Passage and frequently after their arrival in the colonies. It was believed to have been by far the most fatal of all slave diseases, with as many dying of it as of all other diseases combined. Two major forms of dysentery – bacillary and amoebic – are pathological conditions of the intestines that give rise to a discharge of blood and mucus. Both are transmitted from contaminated feces to the alimentary canal by means of flies, dirty hands, and contaminated food and water. Amoebic dysentery is caused by *Entamoeba histolytica*, a disease-producing amoeba that, when ingested, invades the intestinal wall and draws its nourishment from the red blood corpuscles and body tissue cells. Bacillary dysentery is caused by a unicellular organism or bacillus of the genus *Shigella*, which invades the bowels and causes a discharge of blood and mucus. Flies spread the *Shigellae*, which breed in excreta, decaying vegetation, and other organic filth. The infection, as a rule, spreads rapidly from person to person. Epidemics are more intense and frequent in countries where the spread of the disease is facilitated by unsanitary habits and primitive conditions. In the tropics and subtropics bacillary dysentery generally occurs more frequently than the amoebic type. It has a fairly definite seasonal pattern, being more prevalent during the rainy season and for a short time thereafter. If not controlled, bacillary dysentery can reach epidemic proportions, resulting in intestinal hemmorhage, dehydration, perforation of the bowels, liver abscess, peritonitis, and death.[76]

Dysentery attracted the attention of contemporary medical writers who sought to describe its symptoms, ascertain its causes, and prescribe remedies. Dr. Grainger, who distinguished between the flux that was watery with blood and the one that was bilious with blood and excrement, said that both types were equally difficult to cure and equally dangerous unless medicines were applied early. He recommended bleeding the patient if the flux was accompanied by fever. Vomits and purges were required "to expel the peccant humours." To promote perspiration and prevent patients from getting up in the night, Grainger recommended the administration of twenty drops of laudanum mixed with half a pint of sage tea. Dr. Collins, who sought to distinguish between diarrhea and dysentery, said that the latter existed when "together with a fever, you find the negro has great pain and gripes, that he goes frequently to the pan, and discharges little or nothing when there." As soon as the disorder was diagnosed to be dysentery, the doctor should be expeditious in his efforts "to remove it by evacuants, such as bleeding, purging, puking, and sweating, sometimes all of them in succession." If the violence of the symptoms increased, Collins thought it necessary to supply the bowels with an artificial slimy coating instead of a natural one by injecting with a clyster "half a pint of pretty thick starch, to which forty drops of laudanum have been added." To Dr. Moseley, author of a work on dysentery, the disease was regarded as a fever of the intestines caused by obstructed perspiration. Although he did not dispute the auxiliary aid that was occasionally supplied by "aromatics, wax, suet, soap, lime-water, calomel, verious purgatives, and even various astringents," he recommended "the use of SUDORFICS, that I mean, a careful, continued course of them, to keep up a SWEAT, in extent proportional to the violence of the disease."[77]

Dropsy, or edema, is a morbid accumulation of a serous or watery fluid in the body that impedes the functions of life. If the body fluids accumulate in the cavity of the abdomen, it is called ascites; if in the chest, hydrothorax; if in the cranium, hydrocephalus; and if in the cellular membrane, anasarca. Richard Bright, M.D. (1789–1858), said that one great cause of dropsical effusion was obstructed circulation caused by diseases of the heart. He distinguished between cardiac dropsy and renal dropsy or "Bright's disease," which he associated with an organic disease and a change in the structure of the kidney and the accumulation of urine in body cavities. Bright's discoveries were published in the late 1820s and 1830s and probably had no effect on medical practice in the West Indies.[78]

Dropsical patients exhibited symptoms that West Indian medical writers sought to explain by means of the humoral doctrine. Dr. Richard Towne attributed the high incidence of dropsy to the extraordinary heat and humidity, which rendered the fibers of the body more lax, abated the vigor of the circulation, increased the viscidity of the blood, and decreased perspiration. He believed that an immoderate use of strong spirituous liquors too often led to dropsy. As with Towne, Dr. Grainger maintained that because heat and moisture debilitated the solids and broke the tone of the blood, all ages and sexes were susceptible to watery complaints. If the swelling was considerable and the bowels were sound, the patient should be tapped and future accumulations of fluid prevented by aloetic purges and bitters. Among other remedies, Grainger noted that dropsy had "sometimes been cured by gunpowder taken with cow-piss."[79]

Dropsy has been associated with debility resulting from hard labor and malnutrition. Prolonged labor in the heat of the boiling house brought on dropsy in a situation Dr. Collins regarded as the most unhealthy of any to which the slaves were exposed. Planters were warned to relieve their black boilers when they showed any swelling in the legs and face. The diseases of the field slaves were for the most part those of debility, according to James Stephen. It incensed him to find that deaths were attributed to dropsy, diarrhea, and other diseases and so entered in the plantation bills of mortality when the predisposing weakness was induced by the driving whip. In a modern study of a Jamaica plantation, Richard Dunn writes, "By the manager's own reckoning, 11 percent of the slaves died 'bloated' or from 'dropsy.' These vague terms covered a wide range of bodily swellings, undoubtedly caused in many cases by protein and vitamin deficiencies."[80]

Purging, or relieving the bowels by evacuation, was the chief means of treating dropsy. "Weak ones [purges] will not succeed," asserted Dr. Collins, "they must be such as are of a strong and active power." He recommended a bolus made of the powders of jalap and gum gamboge, which would "generally purge the belly very sharply, and reduce its size by a large discharge of water which it procures with the stools." If the water was not discharged after three or four purges, it should be drawn off mechanically by tapping, after which care should be directed "to restore the strength of the patient, by good diet, wine, and steel medicines."[81]

William Withering's discovery of digitalis, or foxglove, as a remedy for dropsy was one of the great medical contributions of the eighteenth century. Dr. Williamson of Jamaica first used digitalis to treat a patient with ascites in November 1803. He was disappointed to find that all its unpleasant symptoms were brought on without subduing the disease. By the middle of the following year, however, he recorded that digitalis had been used with considerable success. Dr. Thomson, whose experience was similar to that of Dr. Williamson, wrote that digitalis could lose its peculiar virtue in a warm climate and urged doctors and planters to have it sent from England in small, well-secured bottles.[82]

"The disorders that are most fatal among the slaves are pleurisies and other affections of the lungs, inflammation of the bowels, dysenteries, and influenza," wrote John Stewart of Jamaica. Included among the respiratory or pulmonary complaints were colds, bronchitis, influenza, pneumonia, pleurisy, inflammation of the tonsils, or quinsy, and tuberculosis. Contemporaries used such terms as "complaints of the chest," "epidemic catarrh," "endemic catarrhal pneumonia," "serious catarrhal and pneumonic symptoms," "inflammatory sore throat," "ulcerated sore throat," "putrid sore throat," "epidemic pleurisy," and "pleurisy or pneumonic inflammation." If the experience of antebellum Virginia is a guide, pleurisy, which is technically an inflammation of the lining of the lungs with or without an accumulation of fluid in the pleural cavity, was defined loosely to include any otherwise unidentifiable disease that caused sharp chest pains and respiratory symptoms. Despite the confusion of terms, West Indian doctors and planters recognized that respiratory maladies struck most often in the colder and wetter months of the year, that they usually occurred in epidemics, and that they were frequently fatal.[83]

Pneumonia, which may take various forms, is an inflammation of the lungs caused by various bacteria and viruses. Minor infections of the respiratory tract caused by colds, chilling of the body, and debilitation precede the invasion of *pneumococci*, the tiny organisms that are inhaled from outside. Pneumonia is most prevalent in temperate climates but may occur anywhere. Young adults suffer from it most commonly. Pleurisy and pneumonia swept through plantations from time to time with mortal consequences. Upon beginning his practice in November 1798, Dr. Williamson observed that "complaints of the chest, constituting pneumonic inflammation, are there [Jamaica], as in other countries, of a very alarming nature. The disease is rapid in its progress; its treatment, by plentiful bleeding, and other remedies, is to be early resorted to; and we generally, as in this month, succeed in practice." That doctors were less successful at other times is evident from other entries in Williamson's journal. In December 1807, for example, he noted that "an epidemic pleurisy had made dreadful and destructive progress among the negroes." As with Williamson, Dr. Thomson of Jamaica recommended heavy bleeding followed by a strong purge in cases of pleurisy. Thomson drew on the humoral-climatic and miasmatic theories of medicine in his account of pleurisy, observing that "this acute disease attacks those of a robust, plethoric habit of body, and of the sanguine temperament. Hence it is more frequently met with in men than women, in those seasons when sudden alternations of the weather prevail, and their duties lead them to be exposed to the night air."[84]

Influenza is an acute viral infection of the nasopharynx and respiratory tract that occurs in epidemic and pandemic forms. On a global scale, particularly virulent influenza pandemics have alternated at irregular intervals with milder outbursts of the disease. Influenza is often accompanied by severe catarrh, fever, headache, loss of taste and appetite, pains all over the body, depressed spirits, and general debility. In the West Indies it was most fatal and distressing to children and old people or those with weak and relaxed habits. Dr. Williamson wrote a lengthy account of an epidemic catarrh or influenza that extended over a large part of Europe and was carried by seamen to Port Royal, Jamaica, in April 1802. The disease spread rapidly to Kingston and then from plantation to plantation in the rural parishes with great loss of life. It did not disappear until the following July. Williamson wrote of another influenza epidemic that spread to the interior parishes from Kingston in December 1807. It reached Spanish Town, some thirteen miles from Kingston, on about 14 December. By early January of the following year Williamson and his partner saw many cases and ones with additional malignant symptoms. In the rural parishes the epidemic made dreadful and destructive progress among the blacks before it subsided in early February. We have mentioned that a very destructive epidemic raged in the district where Dr. Sells practiced in 1811, 1812, and 1813. Writing in 1823, John Stewart said he knew of influenza epidemics that carried off a tenth of the population of some estates, while few escaped considerable loss.[85]

Whooping cough, or pertussis, is an infectious disease that has its basis in respiratory catarrh and at times killed many slaves. After an incubation period of about two weeks the catarrhal stage begins with slight fever, sneezing, runny nose, and a dry cough. This is followed in a week or two by the paroxysmal stage that lasts for three or four weeks with prolonged crowing or whooping respiration and frequently induces vomiting. The second stage is followed by a decline. The disease is much more prevalent in cold weather and is very contagious. Although whooping cough occurs most frequently in children, it is not limited to that age group. Together with measles, chicken pox, and mumps, it attacked adult slaves who had never had it in Africa. Kenneth F. Kiple and Virginia Himmelsteib King note that because of malnutrition, black children were more likely to contract whooping cough than white children, and thousands of them died from worms, diphtheria, and whooping cough in the antebellum South as well as in the West Indies. In Chapter 8 we will see that the great whooping cough epidemic of 1830–1 in Grenada accounted for 147 deaths (or 7.7 percent of all deaths).[86]

It was noted that blacks differed from whites in having a high degree of immunity to malaria and yellow or putrid fever. On the other hand, they contracted a wide variety of fevers and were perhaps as susceptible as the whites to measles, typhoid fever, and smallpox, which is discussed in Chapter 9. As Dr. Collins explained their nature and incidence,

> fevers are, at least, as frequent as any other complaints among the negroes. On certain occasions, not less than a tenth part of your gang will be in the sick-house from that cause. But, though frequent, and sometimes severe enough, yet they rarely kill; and when they do kill, it is not that class of them which proves so fatal among the whites, namely, the putrid fever, by which the mischief is effected.[87]

Collins divided the fevers of blacks into three classes: simple, intermittent, and inflammatory. Simple fevers, which were most prevalent, attacked with moderate symptoms. Though nature would effect a cure, planters and doctors were advised to admit the patient to the hospital and administer an infusion of lemon grass and essence of antimony to satisfy the patient that his welfare was not neglected. For persons who had had three or four attacks of intermittent fever, Collins recommended that a decoction of quassia, or bitter ash, be administered for three or four days and, if the fever returned, a decoction of Peruvian bark. Inflammatory fever of the lungs, which was not uncommon in the winter, was sometimes fatal in a few days and could linger for many months and sometimes years, terminating in consumption.[88]

Although measles affects chiefly the young in developed countries, in the slave society of the West Indies it attacked both young and old and at times took a heavy toll of life. One epidemic struck an interior parish of Jamaica in December 1770 and continued for three months. The doctor who reported the epidemic said that he seldom had fewer than 150 blacks with the measles at a time, and that those on whom the epidemic exerted its greatest fury were the most hale, strong, and valuable.[89]

As noted in Chapter 3, the ulcerous and highly contagious skin disease known as yaws reached epidemic proportions on the crowded Guinea ships and spread to Creole slaves in the colonies. Although yaws continued to disable and kill slaves, there is some reason to believe that its incidence diminished somewhat after the closing of the slave trade. After observing that yaws and coco bays were diseases of African origin, John Stewart of Jamaica wrote that "since the abolition of the slave-trade, they have become less common; indeed on some plantations they are altogether unknown; and it is probable that in a few years they will totally disappear." The incidence of yaws may also have decreased because of improved hygiene and the more general practice of isolating the victims of this disease in specially constructed huts where they were placed under the care of their own people. Furthermore, there is some evidence that white doctors became aware that their methods of treating yaws with mercury were often more destructive than the disease itself. Dr. Grainger deplored the many evil consequences that resulted when the yaws had been mismanaged, such "as bone-achs, nocturnal pains, inveterate ulcers with caries, ulcerated throats, and erosions of the cartilages of the nose."[90]

Although by no means confined to the tropics and subtropics, worms are most prevalent in warm climates with poor sanitation. The many varieties of worms have a basic life pattern. People harbor adult worms, of which the females produce eggs. With few exceptions, these eggs pass outside the body by the oral or anal route, but mainly by the latter mixed with feces. Larvae hatch from the eggs, which are deposited in the soil. The larvae of certain varieties of worms penetrate the skin from contact with the soil or through the bite of an insect. The eggs and larvae of other varieties are ingested in food and drink. Careless defecation habits seed the soil with viable eggs that hatch into larvae. Children and adults may ingest the larvae when they eat unwashed vegetables with dirty hands. The larvae then grow to mature worms in the body and begin anew the cycle of reproduction. Worms interfere with the digestion and absorption of nutrients in the body. Slaves in the antebellum South who harbored these parasites suffered from a lack of protein, iron, and vitamins A, B_{12}, and C.[91]

Dr. Williamson attributed many of the diseases of Jamaica to worms of the ascarides, teres, and taenia kinds. Although the teres variety has not been identified, the roundworm, or *Ascaris lumbricoides*, was a common affliction, as was the tapeworm, or *Taenia solium*. Adult roundworms live free and unattached in the small intestine and feed chiefly on semidigested food. Children readily contract the disease when they play in soil polluted with feces. When adult ascarids migrate from the small intestine to other organs, hemorrhaging and edema in the lungs can result. Moreover, a heavy burden of worms can result in protein malnutrition, particularly in growing children on a poor diet.[92]

The adult tapeworm, or *Taenia solium*, also inhabits the small intestine, where it is attached to the intestinal wall. It is flat and white, resembling a narrow tape. The tapeworm was "the worst and most dangerous species of worms," according to Dr. Collins.

> It is frequently many yards in length, occupying almost the whole course of the guts. It is the most difficult to be destroyed, and the most easy to be regenerated, as it possesses the power of producing itself, whilst there is a single joint remaining behind.

Collins said the tapeworm caused acute pains in the bowels and stomach and great anxiety and oppression about the heart.[93]

Slaves also hosted Guinea worms and hookworms. The Guinea worm, or *Dracunculus medinensis*, is a long thin nematode a meter or more long that inhabits the subcutaneous human tissues. The fully mature female comes to the surface of the skin and discharges her larvae externally. The method of extracting the Guinea worm is the same today as it was in slave days. When it broke through the skin, it was carefully removed by a black doctor who wound it around a small piece of cloth or wood. Only a certain length could be removed before the worm resisted, so it was necessary to continue the operation day after day. All was lost if the worm broke, since the portion left in the body continued to grow and caused an abscess.[94]

Doctors and planters administered many anthelmintic drugs or vermifuges to expel intestinal worms. Dr. Grainger admitted that he had tried "an infinite variety of medicines" against worms, but they had proved less effective than he could wish. He favored remedies that were indigenous to the tropics rather than those of European origin. These included aloes, ipecacuanha, stinking weed, cowitch, worm grass, and the bark of the mountain cabbage tree. Grainger noted that the juice of the aloe claimed preeminence as a purgative, that the juice of the wild ipecacuanha operated with violence "both up and down" as an antidote to worms, and that cowitch with molasses and the clarified juice of worm grass was more dependable. Dr. Collins regarded the down of cowitch pods as a very excellent vermifuge that could be used with just expectations of success. Dr. Williamson recommended cowitch as "a remedy of singular efficacy, acting on mechanical principles, by carrying numbers of spiculae along the stomach and intestines, which bring the worms in contact with them, either destroying or discharging them by stool."[95]

One variety of worm infection was known by its clinical symptoms, although neither the eggs nor the worms could be readily seen in stools. This was the *Necator americanus*, or hookworm, which was introduced into the Americas by black slaves from Africa. Unlike the other worm parasites that enter their host through the mouth, the tiny hookworm penetrates through the skin to small blood vessels. Barefooted slaves were vulnerable to hookworm invasion. Occupying the small intestines, hookworms may be present in enormous numbers. There is reason to believe that 500 to 1,000 worms must be present for at least six months to produce well-marked *ankylostomiasis*, or hookworm disease. Because hookworms are anemia-producing parasites themselves, the disease is exacerbated among people who eat coarse, bulky, nonnutritious food. Victims of hookworm disease exhibit such symptoms as an enormous appetite, extreme lethargy, generalized swelling, and retarded mental, physical, and, among children, sexual growth.[96]

Hookworm disease has been linked to what is variously called pica, geophagy, mal d'estomac, cachexia africana, stomach evil, and dirt eating. Pica was widely prevalent, frequently destructive, and one of the most obstinate and troublesome disorders that afflicted the blacks. It disabled slaves for a considerable time, sometimes years, and often terminated in dropsy. Earth eaters not only were common on almost every plantation in Jamaica, said John Stewart, but this strange propensity or craving was as common among children as among grown blacks. Dr. Thomas Dancer wrote that dirt eating prevailed more in wet than in dry parishes and that it sometimes killed half or more of the slaves on a plantation. Newly imported slaves were especially likely to eat clay, according to several contemporaries, from motives of self-destruction and a belief that after death they would return home to Africa. But Dr. James Maxwell contended that he had seen enough of dirt eating to convince him that it continued to operate as a powerful depopulating cause after the abolition of the slave trade. The disease therefore deserved "the deepest consideration, not only of medical men, but of all who are interested in the welfare of the negro-race."[97]

Though the symptoms of pica were readily apparent, the causes of this unnatural craving perplexed doctors and planters. Blacks who ate dirt or clay were habitually sick, complaining of stomach pains and shortness of breath. They became bloated, with discolored skin, a feeble pulse, nausea, vomiting, diarrhea, lassitude, and general depression and debility. Dr. Williamson said that although he had seen afflicted blacks lead an "unmeaning and slothful existence" for one or two years without hope of recovery, the disease more frequently terminated fatally in two or three months. Whereas whole gangs of newly imported slaves resorted to dirt eating with the most fatal consequences prior to 1808, in the subsequent period, according to Dr. Thomson, the disease more frequently originated "from melancholy, revenge, obeah, dissatisfaction, unhealthy climate." Thomson believed that the most frequent cause of adult addiction to dirt eating was "the temporary relief given to the melancholy, attendant on the idea of their being under the influence of witchcraft." To Dr. Maxwell, who made a pathological inquiry into the nature of pica, the causes were (1) long-continued lactation and improper nursing, (2) an idiopathic affection from imitation, (3) diseases inducing a bad habit of body, (4) mental disquietude, and (5) nonnutritious and indigestible food.[98]

Just as the etiology of pica or dirt eating perplexed doctors who treated slaves, so are modern authorities puzzled by the practice, which continues today in many parts of the world. Kiple and King have investigated the three schools of thought on the subject. They reject the theory that pica was a response to hookworm infection by pointing to studies that demonstrate that blacks have an immunity to the ravages of hookworm. Advocates of the cultural theory contend that pica was a habit acquired in Africa and brought to the New World by the slaves. The practice was handed down from generation to generation, chiefly because it was both pleasurable and habit forming. The third theory is that nutritional deficiencies play an extremely important part in the etiology of pica. Kiple and King find support for their nutritional thesis in several modern studies. In his important article, "Geophagy in Africa and in the United States: A Culture-Nutrition Hypothesis," John M. Hunter has mobilized an impressive body of evidence to support his thesis "that geophagy is a cultural institution that has evolved through stages as a behavioral response to the physiological imperative," that such imperative is manifested in "deficiencies of essential mineral nutrients, which are both diet and disease related," particularly during the stress of pregnancy and lactation.[99]

Pica was linked to malnutrition by several contemporary authors, although they did not always consider this link of paramount importance. Although he admitted that a deficiency of food and hard labor could bring on the disease of dirt eating, Dr. Dancer believed that dissatisfaction or discontent of the mind was the necessary and sufficient cause. Dissatisfaction arose, he said, from such sources as "a change of master, attorney, overseer, or driver – the dispossessing them of their grounds or habitations – shifting their residence, particularly from the lowlands to the mountains – but, perhaps, *obeah*, or the terror of witchcraft, is a much more frequent cause than any." Similarly, Dr. Collins noted that whereas "a mean diet" was commonly a cause of the disorder among blacks, other causes induced a laxity of the solids in the body. Dr. Williamson went the furthest in attributing pica to environmental factors when he wrote that "an unfavourable climate, indifferent food, and imperfect clothing, in a part of the country adverse to the preservation of their health, are more generally the sources of the disease."[100]

Slaves who were victims of the pica habit devoured a variety of substances. In Jamaica the favorite species was called *aboo* earth, or clammy marl, which tasted sweet and dissolved easily in the mouth. But "ill-disposed, idle slaves" who were bent on self-destruction promiscuously ingested "strong calcerous earths, common mould, and what they pick from the walls." Dr. Thomson knew blacks who, by selecting highly absorbent earth, continued to eat this foreign substance for a long time without any visible injury to their health. On the other hand, he said the variety called "streaked clay," which contained a mixture of red and white earth, was the most speedily fatal.[101]

Treating the pica craving with any degree of success had to be done at an early stage of development. According to Dr. Maxwell, it was in the first stage, "where the digestive organs are inordinately excited from incessant irritation," that an easy cure could be effected if the patient refrained from eating dirt. In the second stage, however, when morbid action had set in, the disease assumed an inveterate form and became more intractable. In the third stage, it generally proved fatal from the destruction of body parts essential to life. Medicines that were administered to victims of this disease included such emetics and purges as ipecacuanha, castor oil, lignum quassia, calomel, sulfate of iron, capsicum, and cow's urine. More than medicine was needed, however, as Dr. Williamson pointed out when he wrote that nothing could probably prevent a disposition to dirt eating in young people "but early detection, and adopting a plan of treatment, with regard to medicine, diet, exercise, cleanliness, and improved clothing, which admits of no delay whatever." Such an enlightened course of treatment was improbable. John Stewart, for example, criticized the many whites and even some blacks who treated "this wretched craving, not as a disease, but as a *crime*." Dr. Thomson believed that if those who died of dirt eating were buried in a separate burial ground as a warning to others, it would have more beneficial effects than all medical prescriptions. One ingenious but harsh invention to prevent dirt eating was a metal face mask or mouthpiece secured by a padlock (see Figure 7.3). Another scheme was to establish a floating hospital for those addicted to eating earth. Shipboard life was said to have the advantages of improved diet, change of air, and distance from substances improper for eating.[102]

Conclusion

In previous chapters we have looked at the macro disease environment and epidemiology of the South Atlantic System, the role played by the Atlantic slave trade as a disease vector, and the micro environment of the sugar plantation with its brutal labor system and poor dietary standards. This chapter attempts to link these environmental and economic factors to patterns of morbidity and mortality as well as to specific diseases with special reference to nutrition-deficient diseases. We have drawn on contemporary and modern authorities to show how the patterns of morbidity and mortality were related to such variables as age, sex, occupation, and mode of life; we have singled out the diseases that were transmitted through the slave trade; we have shown how infectious and parasitic diseases were associated with work loads, fatigue, food intake, housing, clothing, punishment, and sanitation; and we have been concerned with the nature and incidence of slave diseases connected with the respiratory tract, stomach, intestines, cardiovascular system, and nervous system. Epidemiologists have demonstrated that large populations are needed to maintain such human infections as measles, smallpox, whooping cough, and influenza. It seems evident that the growth of the slave population and its concentration in plantation villages close to one another created a suitable micro environment for the propagation of infectious disease. To this was added the plantations' proximity to port cities and other shipping points, which exposed their inhabitants to infectious disease from abroad.

Although he exaggerated, Dr. Benjamin Rush was probably not too wide

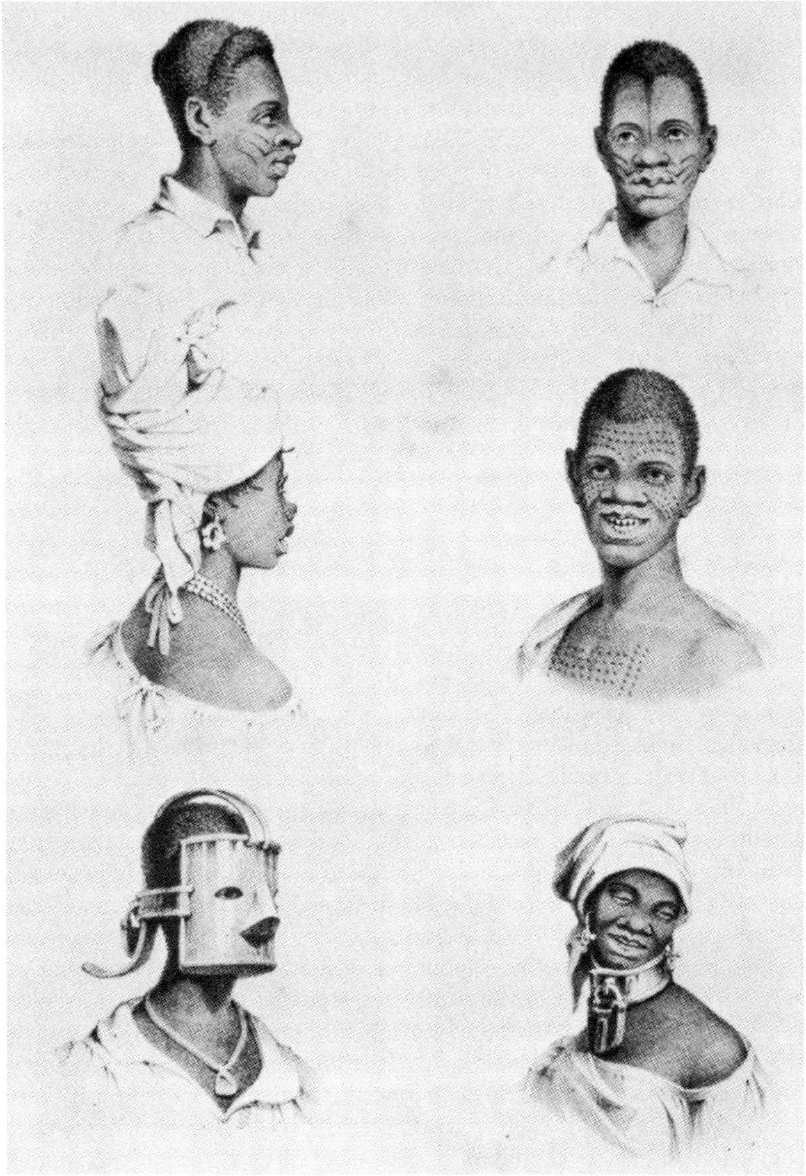

Figure 7.3. Slaves in Jamaica, showing tribal markings, female headdress, iron collar, and metal mask to prevent pica or "dirt eating." From Bridgen's "West India Sketches," reproduced in Terence Brady and Evan Jones, *The Fight Against Slavery* (New York: W. W. Norton, 1975), p. 116. By permission of The Royal Commonwealth Society, London.

of the mark when he wrote that West Indian slaves suffered all the numerous chronic diseases that arose from a scanty diet or one with an excess of vegetables. Other doctor-authors found links between malnutrition and various slave diseases. These links were, of course, based largely on symptoms and reasoning that was impressionistic and lacking in scientific rigor. Fortunately, we have been able to proceed beyond these impressionistic links by drawing on the literature of the modern sciences of nutrition and medicine. These sciences show, among other things, that nutritional deficiencies generally reduce the capacity of people to resist the occurrence and consequences of infection, and that the most vulnerable groups are infants and young children and pregnant and lactating women.

Our analysis in this chapter has also benefited from modern studies of West Indian slaves and their descendants that have been undertaken by anthropologists, historians, and researchers in social medicine. By studying slave skeletal remains, by analyzing data on the height of slaves, and by measuring the heights and weights of school children in the 1960s and 1970s, researchers have delineated different patterns of physical growth among people of different ethnic origins, rural and urban residence, and low and high socioeconomic status. Indeed, these studies point unmistakably to undernutrition as the chief factor retarding the physical growth of the British West Indian slaves who lived some two to three centuries ago and their free black descendants in the twentieth century. Above all, it was the sugar plantation – its physical environment and living and working conditions – that was inimical to the health of slaves.

8

The problem of reproduction

> If you are anxious to increase the population of your estate by the breeding of your negroes, as every man must now be, both from a better informed sense of his duty, and the extremely increased price of African negroes, you will bestow somewhat more attention to your women during their pregnancy, than they have usually received; for, to the ordinary diseases, to which they are at that time subject, equally as at any other, they have some peculiar to that state, which are superadded.
>
> Dr. David Collins, 1803[1]

From our concern with morbidity and mortality in Chapter 7 we turn now to problems associated with slave reproduction. The diseases and disorders of infants and children and pregnant and lactating women are treated in greater depth, as are the pro-natal policies and practices of planters and the difficulty of reconciling these policies to an economy and society that had long regarded women as primarily work units rather than breeding units.

Patterns of reproduction

Despite the great natural fecundity of the African race, the female slaves in the British West Indies were less fertile than their sisters in Africa and North America. Both contemporary and modern writers have sought to explain the basic differences of slave demography in terms of the cultural and psychological shock of enslavement, the survival of African mating and child-rearing customs, pro- and anti-natalist policies of slaveholders, disease environments, conditions of labor and livelihood, and economic factors related to the Atlantic slave trade and plantation slavery. Generally speaking, the pro-natalist policies that were adopted in the infancy of the sugar industry gave way to anti-natalist policies as the industry expanded and became more capital and labor intensive. Though conditions and policies varied in time and space, pro-natalist policies gained prominence again later in the eighteenth century and became mandatory after abolition of the slave trade in 1808. In spite of concerted efforts to encourage reproduction, however, the slave population of all the Sugar Colonies except Barbados continued to decline until emancipation in 1834.

Family life and reproduction were encouraged by the early sugar planters for at least three reasons: to augment the labor force, to improve slave morale, and to minimize breaches of discipline. According to Richard Ligon, Barbadian planters purchased an equal number of male and female slaves, "for, if they have more Men than Women, the men who are unmarried will come to their Masters, and complain, that they cannot live without Wives, and desire him, they may have Wives." Planters did not deny their privileged slaves two or three wives, but no woman slave was allowed more than one husband. The men were very jealous and considered it a great injury if another man made the least courtship of their wives. When the wife was in child bed, her husband called in a neighbor to help with the delivery. When the child was born the midwife made a little fire near the mother's feet, "and that serves instead of Possets, Broaths, and Caudles." In a fortnight the mother was back at work with her "pickaninny" on her back. "If the Overseer be discreet," wrote Ligon, "she is suffer'd to rest her self a little more than ordinary; but if not, she is compelled to do as others do. Times they have of suckling their Children in the fields, and refreshing themselves; and good reason, for they carry burthens on their backs; and yet work too."[2]

Family life and reproduction in Jamaica were the subjects of brief commentary by Dr. Hans Sloane. He said that every black had his wife and was very much concerned if she proved adulterous. "The care of the Masters and Overseers about their [slaves'] Wives," wrote Sloane, "is what keeps their Plantations chiefly in good order, whence they ever buy Wives in proportion to their Men, lest the Men should wander to neighbouring Plantations, and neglect to serve them." The black women were said to be fruitful. They returned to their work in the field about a week after giving birth with their little ones tied to their backs. "Their Children call'd *Piganinnies* or rather *Pequenos Ninnos*, go naked till they are fit to be put to clean the Paths, bring Fire-wood to the Kitchen, &c. when a Boy Overseer, with his Wand or white Rod, is set over them as their Task-Master."[3] Ligon and Sloane suggest that the early sugar planters did little more than purchase wives for their men, assuming that family life and procreation would follow naturally. They no doubt underestimated the psychological and cultural shock that their bondsmen suffered from being transplanted from Africa to the New World, and the adverse effects of this experience on stable sexual unions and reproduction.

Slave fertility declined and infant mortality increased during the expansion of the sugar industry because of such factors as unbalanced sex ratios, the industrial discipline of gang slavery, disease, despondency, and malnutrition. Patterns of reproduction were adversely affected by the general feeling of despondency that pervaded the African-born slaves and frequently led to suicide. Indeed, high fertility became unacceptable to both masters and slaves. Female slaves who came to be regarded more as "work units" than as "breeding units" avoided childbirth if possible, and children born under these conditions frequently died of neglect.[4] Morgan Godwyn, the Anglican clergyman who served in Barbados before 1680, wrote that "the *Pickininnies*, or young *Negro*-Children, except only the hardiest, wanting a due attendance and care of them, do most of them perish in their *Infancy*. Their *Mothers* continual labour in the Field, not admitting a necessary care or regard of them."[5]

The fertility potential was reduced by the high ratio of men to women. Slave cargoes came to consist of at least three males to two females, and on some plantations there were as many as five men to one woman. Around 1700, when the females represented about 40 percent of the population, the live birthrate in Jamaica has been estimated by Michael Craton at less than fifteen per thousand of the total slave population.[6]

The writings of two prominent Jamaicans were exceptional in the planter literature of the time in expressing concern about the great waste of slave life and the need to understand the causes in order to remedy the evils that impeded or frustrated the natural effects of procreation. According to Governor Edward Trelawny of Jamaica, "what chiefly contributes to their being so few Children among the *English* Negroes is the Practice of the Wenches in procuring Abortions. As they lie with both Colours, and do not know which the Child may prove of, to disoblige neither, they stifle it in Birth." Trelawny fancied that the "Negro Ladies would yield better, and at least keep up the present Stock" if "a little Linnen, or other Necessaries, were given to every Wench that was brought to Bed, and all the barren ones whipt upon a certain Day every Year."[7] Edward Long, the planter-historian, wrote that the women did not breed in Jamaica as they did in Africa. This was due in part to the high ratio of men to women and the "unseasonable" work requirements. Other reasons for the low birthrate were the alleged promiscuous sexual habits, venereal disease, obstructions that made childbearing difficult, the unskillful management of black midwives, and the taking of "specifics to cause abortion." Infant mortality was alarmingly high. Worms were extremely fatal to children; others frequently perished within nine or ten days of their birth from tetanus or lockjaw. Infants also died because they were not kept sufficiently warm, or they were given rum "an aliment of hard digestion."[8]

Much of the decrease of the slave population was due to the lack of care of women in pregnancy and childbirth and inattention to the rearing of children. During the era of the slave trade planters were warned of the risk of purchasing newly imported females. Because of their scanty clothing and other reasons, they were said to have incurable obstructions of the menses, which produced barrenness and many disorders.[9] Hard labor and inadequate nutrition further impaired female reproductive development after they were seasoned to work on the plantations.[10] Dr. Grainger compared the reproductive experience of black and white women in the islands, pointing out that "fewer Negresses die in child-bed, or of its consequences (not one in three hundred) than white women; but the children of the latter are less liable to perish within the month than those of the Blacks."[11] Dr. Jonathan Troup was told by a colleague in Dominica that "he had delivered 10 Children all in one year by instruments, all died but saved all Mothers except one. Many of the women had their Children dead, others had parts of Pelvis too narrow tho' the Mother had successfull Labours before."[12]

Lucille Mathurin Mair has drawn on the plantation records of Jamaica to ascertain the health of slave women. She finds that out of a total of 604 women on the Clarendon estates of William Beckford in 1780, 188 (or 31 percent) were "in various stages of physical malaise indicated either by the specific ailment, or variously labeled as 'sickly,' 'weakly,' 'infirm,' 'distempered,' or 'invalid.' In addition 30 women were listed simply as either 'superannuated' or 'useless.' " Of the 274 young adults – that is, women between the ages of fifteen and fifty who would normally be in the prime of life, as many as 78 (or 28 percent) were in poor shape. Similarly, of the 284 field women, who were presumably the healthiest and most physically fit women on the estates, 65 (or 22 percent) were physically below par.[13] "The majority of unwell women had no diagnosed disease," writes Dr. Mair. "The condition was referred to in 11 instances as 'distempered,' and in 119 instances as 'infirm' or 'weakly,' which suggests the general debility associated with, among other things, excessive exertion, or poor care."[14]

Debate on the population failure

Beginning in the 1770s, the slave trade and slavery came under attack from religious and humanitarian reformers in the British Empire. Probably the most telling blows were struck by certain men who had had direct contact with the peculiar institution. One of these reformers was the Reverend James Ramsay, an Anglican clergyman in the island of St. Kitts. In 1784 he published his *Essay on the Treatment and Conversion of African Slaves in the British Sugar Colonies*. Ramsay called on his own experience to castigate the planters for their harsh and unfeeling treatment of their black chattels. He wrote that he could not pass over in silence the usual treatment of pregnant women and nursing mothers. Planters were said to be fond of placing every black who could wield a hoe in the field gang. Pregnant women were often kept at this work during the last month of pregnancy and hence suffered many miscarriages. Some managers were unfeeling enough to express their joy at this event "because the woman, on recovery, having no child to care for, will have no pretence for indulgence." Those who avoided miscarriage "must be delivered in a dark, damp, smoky hut, perhaps without a rag in which to wrap her child, except the manager has a wife to sympathize with her wants." Lying-in women were allowed three, or in some plantations four, weeks for recovery. "She then takes the field with her child, and hoe or bill. The infant is placed in the furrow, near her, generally exposed naked, or almost naked, to the sun and rain, on a kid skin, or such rags as she can procure." Ramsay said that nursing mothers were occasionally given an extra allowance of food, but in general no other attention was paid to their condition except to excuse them from picking grass.[15]

West Indian planters and merchants were incensed by Ramsay's scathing criticisms. Their spokesman was James Tobin, formerly a planter in St. Kitts and Nevis and at the time of the controversy a Bristol sugar merchant. In his *Cursory Remarks Upon the Reverend Mr. Ramsay's Essay . . .*," Tobin accused Ramsay of dealing in rash assertions, gross misrepresentations, and virulent invectives. He wrote that he had seldom "(perhaps, I might say never)" seen a woman who was visible advanced in her pregnancy engaged in work that was the least laborious. On most large plantations there was a hospital in which one apartment was for the reception of lying-in women. Two suits of baby clothes were provided for each infant. The mother had a nurse to attend her and also a woman to suckle her child until she was able to do it herself. "A lying-in woman is always allowed a month, and more if necessary," Tobin maintained. "She never comes to work, as long as she suckles her child, till an hour or more after the other slaves; she picks no grass either at noon or night, and quits the field, in the evening, another hour before the rest." Although Tobin agreed with Ramsay that infants were taken to the field by their mothers, he pointed out that there was always an "elderly careful woman" to attend the suckling children when their mothers were employed and that a shelter was provided to protect them from the elements. Other indulgences included a full allowance of food given to each child as soon as its mother thought fit to wean it.[16]

Ramsay and Tobin not only continued their pamphlet debate but also testified before the Privy Council committee and the select committee of the House of Commons to investigate the slave trade. Ramsay repeated his assertion that not the least regard was paid to the breeding of slaves unless the manager's wife took a personal interest in the pregnant and lying-in women.[17] Tobin maintained that the cultivation of the sugar estates could not be kept up by a labor force that depended on a common course of propagation; thus the regular importation of slaves from Africa was necessary. He stated nine reasons for this opinion: (1) the importation of a greater number of males than females; (2) premature and promiscuous intercourse between the sexes; (3) the great variety of venereal complaints that were common to both sexes; (4) the custom among the young women of procuring abortions; (5) the many disorders the women were subject to in consequence of their irregularities; (6) the black women's custom of suckling their children a long time; (7) the premature debility of the men by an immoderate use of spirituous liquors; (8) the little care that too many black women took of their children; and (9) the many disorders to which black children were peculiarly subject, "such as fluxes, worms, and the fevers incident thereto, the tetanus or locked jaw, and what the French call mal d'estomac, vulgarly called eating of dirt."[18]

Tobin and other planters and their supporters who testified before the committees of the Privy Council and the House of Commons contended that the population failure was largely beyond their power to overcome. Tobin said that the sex ratio was unbalanced because the natives on the coast of Africa were universally polygamists and therefore unwilling to part with their women. He also explained that young female slaves procured abortions to preserve themselves as long as they were able.[19] Dr. John Castles of Grenada testified that

> the Negro women are not so prolific as the women in this country, which I apprehend to be owing to excessive and promiscuous intercourse with the other sex, and that commenced at a very early period; from this cause, they do not in general breed till a pretty advanced age, when they are not so much of objects of desire with the men; therefore a great part of the most proper time for the propagation of the species is totally lost.[20]

Dr. Robert Thomas of Nevis called attention to the number of chronic diseases to which the women of warm climates were more subject than those of colder climates, "such as obstructions of the menstrual discharge (the whites), and a falling of the womb, which prevents an impregnation."[21] Thomas Norbury Kerby of Antigua believed that many children died from the inattention of the mothers, who were apt to consider young children an encumbrance and a great barrier to their nocturnal meetings and dances. Kerby also contended that infants were lost because black women were partial to their own unskilled midwives and refused the attendance of white doctors in difficult childbirths.[22]

Although the planters contended that they encouraged their slaves to reproduce by means of various indulgences and professional care, their critics gave much contrary testimony to the committees of the Privy Council and House of Commons. Governor William Matthew of Grenada said that the principal causes that appeared to impede the increase were "the little Attention paid to the Cultivation of Religion and Morality among the Slaves, a Want of Laws to induce or compel Marriage or Pairing, consequently the early and promiscuous Commerce of the Sexes, Venereal Disorders, and the immoderate Use of Rum by the Men."[23] Henry Coor, who had been a millwright in Jamaica for fifteen years, said that he had often heard the overseers of plantations that belonged to absentee proprietors say that they would far rather the black children should die than live.[24] Dr. Robert Jackson, who had practiced in Jamaica, did not suppose that slave mothers were naturally deficient in parental affection, "but hard usage, and the idea of raising children to be subject to cruel treatment, often renders them indifferent, or even gives them the desire, that their offspring may fail; I have heard them wish that their children were dead, or that they had not borne them, rather than be obliged to witness their daily punishments."[25]

"To multiply and rear the human species"

Though it was no doubt rare, some planters encouraged reproduction during the middle of the eighteenth century. Upon his departure for England in 1754, Richard Beckford drew up detailed instructions for his plantation attorneys in Jamaica. He deplored the many "accidents" that had happened to lying-in women and to infants after their birth, which he attributed chiefly to the "badness" of their houses and their being turned out to work too soon. Accordingly, he left instructions that special care should be taken that there be "fit & Warm houses for ye Reception of ye Women under those Circumstances, and ye Mothers must not be Permitted to leave their houses 'till a reasonable Time after their delivery, and whilst their Children continue at the Breast their Labour ought to be Slight & Easy and Victuals allow'd them by ye Overseer."[26]

Some Barbadian planters were moving toward the amelioration of slavery before the outbreak of the American Revolution. The wartime disruption of the African slave trade may have induced more of them to improve the lot of their slaves and encourage them to breed.[27] Philip Gibbes, an absentee proprietor of that island, claimed that his *Instructions for the Treatment of Negroes* were taken from letters he wrote to his plantation manager before the American Revolution and that he was not motivated to defend the planters against their critics in the antislavery movement.[28] Besides monetary rewards, every woman on his plantation who had a child was exempted from labor one-half day per month, and each additional child increased the exemption to a maximum of one-half day per week for four children. Gibbes gave detailed instructions for the encouragement of family life and religion, the treatment of pregnant women, and the care of infants and children. In his slave hospital, proper rooms were said to be allotted for pregnant women to lie in, special food was prepared for mothers and children, and the latter were cared for in a nursery and playground. That economic self-interest was uppermost in Gibbes's mind is revealed by his instruction that "the common instruments of husbandry, made of a small size, may be given to them [slave children] as play things."[29]

In the face of growing criticism from British antislavery leaders, colonial legislatures sought to put their peculiar institution in a good light by enacting slave codes that, among other things, encouraged breeding. By the Jamaican Act of 1788, every slave who was born on a plantation, pen, or other settlement entitled the overseer to receive twenty shillings from the owner or proprietor, who, in turn, received a tax remission of the same amount. Four years later an expanded slave code was drawn up. It provided for overseers to receive three pounds for each newly born slave that represented an increase in the slave population of a plantation. To give further encouragement "to the encrease and protection of Negro infants," every female slave who had six children living was "exempted from hard labour in the field or otherwise," and the owner was exempted from all taxes for such female slave.[30]

That the Consolidated Slave Act of 1792 did not go far enough to encourage breeding is evident from the suggestions and queries that the ministry in Whitehall transmitted in a dispatch to the lieutenant governor of Jamaica in 1799. Masters were encouraged to bestow marks of distinction and pecuniary rewards on slave parents who had reared children and also on midwives who were particularly successful. It was asked whether pregnant women should not be exempted from field labor from six weeks to two months before delivery, and from all labor except taking care of their infants for the same time after delivery. "To multiply and rear the human species," said the dispatch, "there must be a marriage or something to that effect; a contract of this kind is absolutely necessary: At the time of delivery, the mother can only take care of the child, and requires the aid and assistance of the father to take care of herself." To restrain promiscuous intercourse and inculcate morality, the British government urged the legislature of Jamaica to establish the Christian religion and the institution of marriage among the slaves.[31]

Although certain planters are known to have adopted the measures recommended by the British government, formal legislative action was put off for more than a quarter of a century, and even then the new law went only part way and was refused Royal assent.[32] The Jamaican slave code of 1826 provided that all slaves were to be instructed in the Christian religion and the marriages of slaves were to be solemnized without fee or reward. Slaves who were sold could not be separated from their families. Moreover, the exemption from labor was extended to mothers who had six adopted children, and female slaves were protected against rape.[33] Although the provision for slave marriages seems highly significant, it was, in fact, largely ineffective, according to George Roberts. This was because the ceremony was performed only if the couple had the permission of their owner or owners, and if the clergy of the parish was satisfied that the couple had proper knowledge of the nature and obligations of such a contract. It is also doubtful whether the few clergy in Jamaica at the time would have undertaken such a burdensome task without receiving additional compensation.[34]

Gilbert Mathison was a Jamaican proprietor who returned to the island immediately following the abolition of the African slave trade. Although he admitted that the condition of the plantation slaves had improved during his absence of thirteen years, he was motivated to write a tract in which he pointed out the defects in the prevailing system of management and recommended suitable remedies. Mathison was alarmed by the loss of infants from tetanus or lockjaw, which he attributed to lack of care and sanitation in the cutting of the navel string. This important operation was generally performed by an old and infirm slave woman who was considered unfit for any other work. He found that the prevailing practice among the African "grandies" was "to confine the infant to the same clothes, without change, for the first nine days, during which time its fate is usually decided." Furthermore, he found that there were very few plantations with separate apartments for lying-in women. Mathison believed that if every plantation was provided with a proper lying-in apartment and a well-instructed midwife to care for mothers and their babies, lockjaw would no longer be a check to population in the West India islands. Every plantation should also have a nursery for children who had been weaned but were not yet old enough for work. He believed that it was only by collecting the children together that the overseer could ascertain whether they were suitably fed and properly attended to in other respects. "As cleanliness is of some value in preventing disease," Mathison wrote, "it would be proper to appoint suitable attendants to wash and free them [children] from vermin at stated periods."[35]

Pro-natalist policies frustrated

Absentee planters in Great Britain, especially those who were active in public affairs, were highly vulnerable to antislavery propaganda and likely to support measures for ameliorating slavery. Indicative of such support are the letters written by attorneys and managers to absentees that comment on policies and programs to encourage breeding and reduce mortality among children and adults.

Richard Pennant, the first Lord Penrhyn, was one absentee whose pronatalist policies are reflected in the letters he received from Jamaica. One letter was written in January 1805 by Rowland William Fearon, Penrhyn's recently appointed plantation attorney. Fearon reported that he saw dreadful inattention and culpable conduct by the overseers and carelessness by the midwives in the management of pregnant women. It appeared to him that they discouraged rather than encouraged the breeding women. Fearon said he soon put an end to that evil: "I have adopted My Lord the same mode of management on your Estates as I have on my own and have derived very great advantages, which is, as soon as I see a woman slave Pregnant, she ceases from the hardest labour of the Field, and put to light work . . ." To encourage the midwives to perform their duty with attention and ability, "every Child she brings me one Month old, as a reward, I give her 6/8 and the Mother of the infant 3/4 to buy the Stranger a Fowl to commence its little Stock in life; These are small trifles, they operate strongly in the minds of these people, and feel confident that they have the regard and affection of their Master."[36]

Fearon's tenure was too short to ascertain the results of his policy, but letters from other attorneys and overseers indicate that Lord Penrhyn expected them to ease the condition of his slaves. In commenting on the passage of the abolition bill, Samuel Jeffries wrote: "The Planters must now adopt measures to be satisfied with less produce and make the Negroes more easy. I have recommended that the Men should be worked by themselves and do the most laborious work; and the Women that labour which is more easy, by that means it is probably more Children will be raised."[37]

David Ewart, who was Jeffries's successor, wrote in August 1807, "I have always, My Lord, given great encouragement to Breeding, without reference to the late measure of the abolition, and I hold out several little rewards to the Women, which few others do. Your Lordship will observe a dozen suits of Baby Linen written for in the List of Supplies, after their arrival every Child will have one given to it." Each mother brought her one-month-old infant to Ewart and he gave her "two dollars in Money, with some other little things for the Child. I also give the Grandee, or Midwife, two dollars, for in this Country I have observed that a good deal depends upon her attention & good will."[38]

After Lord Penrhyn's death, his heir was informed in October 1814 by John Shand, a leading attorney, that although the decrease in the number of Penrhyn's slaves was not great, he much regretted "that the balance does not turn the other way and that we cannot boast of a regular increase, however small." Shand pointed out by way of extenuation, "Your people are worked moderately, have abundance of food, and are treated with care and kindness. I think that they ought to keep up their numbers even altho' the general population of the island should fall off."[39]

Whereas the Penrhyn plantations were in the central and western parishes of Jamaica, that of Jacob Franks was in the easternmost parish. In September 1810 Franks, an absentee who lived near London, was informed by the attorney of his Duckenfield Hall estate that the black women were not breeding. The attorney suspected that "a worthless old woman" and her son who was a driver had frightened the pregnant women, and that this had caused the frequent miscarriages. The poor demographic performance of this estate was not atypical, for the attorney observed: "Almost all the estates in the parish have fallen off in numbers, since the abolition of the slave trade, & three years experience has fully convinced us here, if indeed that has been at all previously necessary, that the black population cannot be kept up, without importations from Africa. The habits of the negroes themselves, are against the natural population increasing as it might otherwise do."[40]

Mathew Gregory ("Monk") Lewis, who inherited two Jamaican estates, visited them twice in the years after abolition of the slave trade with a view toward ameliorating the condition of his slaves. His journal indicates that he devoted much time and effort to lightening the labor of pregnant women, supplying them with nourishing food, having them attended by white doctors and black midwives and nurses, and providing special care for the nursing mothers and their infants. In January 1816 he wrote that he "gave the *graundee* [midwife] and the mothers a dollar each, and told them, that for the future they might claim the same sum, in addition to their usual allowance of clothes and provisions, for every infant which should be brought to the overseer alive and well on the fourteenth day." He also gave each mother a scarlet girdle to which was affixed a silver medal for each child. The bemedaled girdle was to be worn at feasts and on holidays when it would entitle the mother to "marks of peculiar respect and attention." To accommodate the pregnant women, Lewis built a new lying-in hospital on his Cornwall sugar estate.[41]

After launching these and other reforms, Lewis was disappointed to find on his second visit in January 1818 that "among upwards of three hundred and thirty negroes, and with a greater number of females than men, in spite of all indulgences and inducements, not more than twelve or thirteen children have been added annually to the lists of the births." On the other hand, more of his slaves had been sick and several of his most valuable workers had died, so that the total had decreased rather than increased since his last visit. Several months later Lewis noted that his slaves were "all well clothed and well fed, contented in mind, even by their own account, overworked at no time, and when upon the breeding list are exempted from labour of every kind." Yet, in spite of such care he was discouraged to find that there were only eight women on the breeding list out of more than 150 females. "I really believe that the negresses can produce children at pleasure;" Lewis declared, "and where they are barren, it is just as hens will frequently not lay eggs on shipboard, because they do not like their situation."[42]

Joseph Foster Barham was a third-generation absentee proprietor and member of Parliament who received letters from the attorneys of his two sugar plantations in Jamaica. In April 1809 John R. Webb wrote to Barham that it was particularly on sugar estates "that the Increase falls so much short of the Decrease of Slaves." The predominant cause, in his judgment, was the "general intercourse between the sexes." The blacks could not be induced to stay at home. They liked to travel at night, "forming attachments with females in other Properties [which] exposes them to many complaints." In June of the same year Webb wrote that he was "truly sorry that so few Children should be born on your Property, it is really as unpleasant to me as it is unprofitable to you, every inducement that can be devised has been held out to encourage them to this desirable end, & even the Law of the Island has made a provision that in case a female has six Children living she is exempted from any kind of work."[43]

"Agreeble to your request," Webb wrote to Barham in September 1810, "I have communicated to the Overseer your sentiments of encouragement for his Attention to the raising of Children on the property but I am of opinion, with all due submission to you; that if the greatest part of the premium you desire me to allow was to be given to the women who raise their Children to be a year old it would have a better effect . . . " Writing about a year later, Webb said: "It is certainly as you observe painful to see this gradual decrease without knowing what cause this arises from – to assign a cause I am at a loss, no local one existing at Mesopotamia [estate] that I can attribute this to – and I will venture to pronounce there are no Slaves in the Parish, perhaps Island, better supplied with Clothing, Provision grounds and sufficient days allowed them for the improvement of such ground." Webb said he was acquainted with some plantations where the slaves increased or kept up their number, "but that many, by far the greater proportion are on the reverse side – how or what may be the ultimate consequence time only will discover."[44]

Further encouragement to child rearing was reported in a letter of September 1812. This was a plan transmitted by Barham to Webb "of allowing those mothers who are deserving to keep a Cow or two for the benefit of themselves and children – this can be done by my purchasing a Heifer for each instead of giving them money, this I have suggested to them with which they are very well pleased." Webb also reported that he had indulged the mothers by having the stone wall rebuilt around their houses so they could raise hogs. Despite these and other indulgences, the Barham slaves failed to increase. In a letter of October 1812, Webb and his fellow attorney freely acknowledged that they had "not been fortunate in keeping up the number" of slaves. They conscientiously assured Barham, however, "that the Women's not breeding is neither oweing to their being hard worked or in any respect badly treated, there are no Negroes in the Parish of Westmoreland more indulged, better fed or better clothed."[45]

In a modern study of Barham's Mesopotamia plantation in Jamaica and John Tayloe's Mount Airy plantation in Virginia, Richard S. Dunn presents not only valuable data but also an analysis of why the demographic performance of the workers on these two plantations was markedly different. In 1799 to 1818, there were 124 births and 233 deaths on Mesopotamia. During this period 60 slaves were purchased and 6 others manumitted, so that the population declined from 364 in 1799 to 309 in 1818. Mount Airy, on the other hand, had 247 births and 128 deaths from 1809 to 1828; the slight decline from 384 to 362 is explained by a massive exodus and relocation on another plantation of approximately 177 slaves.[46]

Dunn's analysis focuses on the low fertility of the Mesopotamia black women. He dismisses such commonly cited reasons as the adverse sex and age ratios and the presence of African-born women with African child rearing habits. Compared with their counterparts on Mount Airy, the black women on Mesopotamia performed more debilitating labor, received less adequate nutrition, which is thought to have impaired their reproductive development, and were more likely to be exploited sexually by white overseers and bookkeepers. Their absentee owner, despite his humanity and expressed concern for their welfare, was unable to translate his good intentions into a community of blacks who were capable of reproducing themselves.[47]

The victimization of black youngsters

Given the little time that slave mothers were allowed to care for infants and children, the lack of sanitary facilities, population density, poor diet, and rudimentary medical services, it is not surprising that black youngsters fell victim to numerous ailments and diseases, of which many proved fatal. Three prominent Jamaicans testified before the committee of the Privy Council that if they could get over lockjaw, smallpox, measles, yaws, and worm diseases, more black children of that island would be reared. Testifying before the same committee was Dr. John Quier, a leading physician and surgeon of Jamaica. He believed that more children under ten died in that island than in England, and that there were some disorders to which the children were more susceptible than adults. Furthermore, Quier observed

> that the Yaws, a disease originally African, occasion Numbers of them to perish: That Worm Complaints are more frequent here than in England; and the same epidemical Diseases which are incident to Chil-

> dren in Europe, viz. the Small Pox, Measles, and Whooping Cough, are equally common in Negro Children here, and in a severer Degree.[48]

John Stewart, a Jamaica planter, said that black infants were susceptible to sore throats, whooping cough, convulsion fits, and other diseases. "The [w]hooping-cough is an epidemic complaint among the children here," he wrote, "and frequently carries off great numbers."[49]

The poor diet of black children was linked to worms by several contemporaries. Governor David Parry of Barbados testified that Negro mothers were too often inclined to load the stomachs of their children with improper food, which led to a relaxed state of the system and worms. From this cause numbers perished, and principally those under six years old. Robert Hibbert, a Jamaica planter, wrote that after the children were weaned they should be inspected daily by the overseer, "for they are subject to worms, and obstructions, from eating crude unripe fruits, which if not corrected by medicine and diet prove fatal." The Tudway plantation manager in Antigua thought that the diseases of children resulted in a great measure from worms, which too often baffled the prescriptions of the doctor and the care and attention of the nurses.[50]

Although they vary widely in quality, the slave registration records at the Public Record Office in London contain data for the systematic analysis of births and deaths. By far the most complete records are those for the island of Grenada. They contain, among other things, the name of each slave, his or her sex, age, occupation, owner, and "manner of death," and the name of the doctor who certified the death. Table 8.1 shows the ten leading causes of death in 1820 and 1830 for children who were ten years of age and younger. It is of interest that nine of the ten causes of death were common to both years, although they appear in a different order. Only pica or mal d'estomac and teething appear on only one list. Whooping cough was by far the greatest killer of children in 1830, when it made a devastating sweep of the island. It killed week-old babies and teenage children, with a heavy concentration of deaths in the one month to five year range. On some plantations whooping cough appears to have killed most of the children. Mount Rich estate, with a total of 286 slaves, had eleven births and twenty-eight deaths in 1830, of whom fifteen died of whooping cough from six days to thirteen years of age.[51]

Not included in Table 8.1 are the children ten and under whose "manner of death" was not among the top ten. In 1820 there were sixty-one such children (total deaths, 195), and in 1830 there were an additional ninety-four child deaths (total, 382). Many children died of dysentery or flux, diarrhea, itch, thrush, atrophy, yaws, inflammation of the lungs, catarrhal fever, consumption, apoplexy, chicken pox, and cachexia (which denotes a

Table 8.1. *Grenada children's "manner of death," 1820 and 1830: the ten leading causes, ages ten years and younger*

1820		1830	
Fever	24	Whooping cough	128
Tetanus or lockjaw	20	Worms	31
Whooping cough	17	Tetanus or lockjaw	24
Convulsions	14	Fever	22
Dropsy	12	Convulsions	17
Marasmus	12	Bowel complaint	15
Worms	12	Dropsy	14
Debility	9	Teething	14
Bowel complaint	8	Marasmus	12
Hookworm or mal d'estomac	6	Debility	11
Total	134	Total	288

Source: Public Record Office, London, *Treasury* 71/274 (1820), and T71/313 (1830), Grenada Slave Registration, Increase and Decrease.

state of constitutional disorder), malnutrition, and general ill health. Children's lives were also cut short by suffocation, drowning, burns, falls, and other accidents. Doctors were no doubt perplexed to know which cause to assign to many of the deaths that occurred. In the years of epidemics, like 1830, two causes were frequently assigned to a given death, presumably because the contagious disease killed many children who were already weakened by other diseases that it was thought necessary to record. Thus we find "hooping cough and itch," "hooping cough and fever," "hooping cough and thrush," "hooping cough and yaws." Marasmus, or the wasting away of the body, especially that of a baby, without apparent cause, was occasionally combined with worms.[52]

If we compare the accounts of children's diseases given as testimony before the committees investigating the slave trade with the manners of death shown in Table 8.1, several differences are worth our notice. Smallpox, measles, and yaws are said to have been big killers earlier but are missing from Table 8.1; tetanus or lockjaw is included in the records of both periods, but it apparently killed many more children earlier. Mr. John Spooner, agent for St. Kitts and Grenada, estimated that lockjaw killed nearly half the children of all blacks, whether slave or free.[53] When Henry Hew Dalrymple, a Grenada proprietor, was asked by the select committee of the House of Commons, "Was the tetanus or locked-jaw very fatal to the Negro infants in the island of Grenada, so far as you had an opportunity of knowing?" he replied, "It

Table 8.2. *Births and deaths of children in Grenada, 1820 and 1830*

	1820	1830
Total slave population, December 31	26,899	23,878
Total births	513	734
Total deaths, all ages	841	909
Children who died in one month or less	24	42
Children who died in one month or less as a percentage of total births	4.7	5.7
Children who died in one year or less	93	183
Children who died in one year or less as a percentage of total births	18.1	24.9
Children who died at age ten or under	195	382
Children who died at age ten or under as a percentage of total deaths	23.2	42.0

Source: P.R.O. London, T71/274 (1820), and T71/313 (1830), Grenada Slave Registration, Increase and Decrease.

was very fatal to them." Dr. John Castles practiced medicine in Grenada for more than twenty years and treated 1,200 to 1,500 slaves annually besides those on his own plantation. He said that tetanus or lockjaw was so fatal that slave mothers were very anxious until the infant survived to the ninth day. To the question, "What proportion of the Children which are born die within the month?" Castles replied, "On the estates which I attended, taken collectively, I think about one-third part of the children died within the month – on my own estates I lost more than that proportion." When he was asked what proportion of the black children who were born reached the age of puberty, he answered, "In my opinion not one-third – on my own estate I lost more."[54]

Table 8.2 shows that despite the rise in child mortality from 1820 to 1830, the children who died in one month or less was far less than the "one-third part" given in testimony by Dr. Castles. They made up between 4 and 6 percent of total births, respectively. This percentage may be too low, however, because there is some evidence that babies who died during the first nine days of their lives were not always registered. Substantially less than Castle's estimate of one-third were the children who died in one year or less. Children who died in ten years or less made up 23.2 percent of total deaths in 1820. This figure rose to 42.0 percent in 1830, due chiefly to the whooping cough epidemic. Actually, the death rate in 1830 was unusually high. Barry Higman has calculated the deaths per thousand for Grenada in 1817 to 1831. They rose from 32.7 in 1817 to 43.2 in 1819, after which they declined irregularly to a low of 26.6 in 1822. From 1823 to 1829 the deaths per thousand ranged between 27 and 33, and then rose to 41.0 in 1830 and 39.3 in 1831.[55]

Tetanus or lockjaw is caused by the bacillus of tetanus and results in spasms and muscular rigidity. During the period of slavery in the West Indies the first symptom was an uneasiness of the infant and a refusal to take the breast. In a few hours the jaw closed, a general spasm took place, and the body and limbs became quite straight. Infants were seldom attacked after the ninth day, but they might linger on until the fourteenth. Immediately before death a general relaxation set in and the lower jaw fell on the breast, thence called "jaw fall" by the blacks.[56]

Contemporary accounts indicate varying degrees of uncertainty regarding the causes of lockjaw. The Council and Assembly of St. Kitts said that the disease seemed in great measure peculiar to black infants; "many Reasons have been assigned, such as local Situation, Intemperance, and Irregularities of the Mother, Closeness, Dampness, and Smokiness of their Houses, &c. still none of these Reasons are satisfactory or consonant to Experience."[57] Dr. Adam Anderson of Jamaica testified that in his opinion one-fourth of the black infants perished of lockjaw before they had lived nine days. From a number of inquiries he could find no evidence of the disease occurring among infants in Great Britain and West Africa. He imputed the cause "to the Irritation of the putrid Matter generated at the separation of the umbilical Chord, previous to the Separation, which generally happens from the fifth to the Seventh Day." Anderson also stated that the disorder might proceed from the infant being exposed to cold air and from the meconium (or accumulated feces) not being properly carried off, but that these causes occurred very seldom.[58]

Today medical science has shown that the natural habitat of the tetanus bacillus is the soil, and especially richly manured soil. It was unfortunate for the slaves on sugar plantations that they lived close to livestock pens for making compost, and they labored in highly manured cane fields. This was an environment probably without equal for generating one of the deadliest poisons known to humans. Slave mothers and babies were also unfortunate in the generally poor care they received from their masters, midwives, and doctors. Dr. James Chisholme of Jamaica said that after the umbilical cord had fallen off, the raw part, after being slightly covered with lint or rags, was bound round with a coarse cloth. The cloth, which was soaked with urine in a few hours, was not removed before infection set in and resulted in spasms.[59]

If the accounts of doctors and planters are to be believed, some success was achieved in coping with infant and childhood diseases. One measure for the prevention of lockjaw was to plunge the infant into a tub of water and to repeat the quick immersion and withdrawal called "dipping" every other day. Dr. Collins of St. Vincent recommended this treatment most warmly, not only from his own practice of thirty years, "but also from that of many others, whom I have known in the West Indies, and the immemorial usage of many tribes in savage life, from whom the hint was probably first derived."[60] "Monk" Lewis, the Jamaican planter, wrote that he had been "positively assured that the custom of plunging negro infants, immediately upon their being born, into a tub of cold water, infallibly preserved them from the danger of tetanus."[61] The pro-planter author Alexander Barclay believed that because of a better system of management, deaths from tetanus had become rare. "The change of management," he wrote, "consisted in keeping the lying-in room more open, and having no fire in it; dipping the infants in water, and washing them once or twice a day: covering them more closely, and paying more attention to keep them dry."[62] James Maxwell, M.D., found from his perusal of a wide range of sources, including plantation records, that over a period of years the "depopulating influence of infantile tetanus" amounted to 25 percent of all the black children who were born. Subsequent to his study, however, Maxwell found that infant mortality had declined because of improved hygiene connected with the cutting and covering of the umbilical cord. He wrote that the directions he gave to midwives were "so plain and so easily understood, that since their adoption in my practice, infantile tetanus may be said to have disappeared."[63] Infant tetanus still occurs in the West Indies but is not common now, except perhaps in Haiti.[64] Though specific remedies may be regarded with skepticism, the circulation of popular medical and planter manuals calling for the construction of lying-in apartments, improvement of midwifery, communal feeding of children, vaccination of infants and children against smallpox, and better hygiene may have led to some abatement of the harsh conditions that prevailed, but not on a widespread basis.[65]

Black women as "work units" and "breeding units"

Together with high infant and child mortality, the low fertility of slave women explains in large measure the limited success of the pro-natalist policies in the British West Indies. Before 1808 the abolitionists had argued that closure of the Atlantic slave trade would force the planters to adopt amelioration measures aimed chiefly at raising fertility and otherwise encouraging the slaves to reproduce. It was contended that women who had been regarded as work units would now have to be treated largely as breeding units. In the absence of improved technology and organization, this would have entailed some diminution in the female labor force and, in consequence, plantation production and profits. It would have also called for a positive response by

Table 8.3. *Female field workers on York plantation, Jamaica, 1778, 1782, 1820, and 1829*

	1778	1782	1820	1829
Total slaves	485	451	388	303
Total working slaves	440	397	278	219
Total female workers	192	169	123	112
Female workers as a percentage of all working slaves	43.6	42.6	44.2	51.1
Total field workers	267	234	185	107
Total female field workers	147	138	111	67
Female field workers as a percentage of all female workers	76.6	81.7	90.2	59.8
Female field workers as a percentage of all field workers	55.1	59.0	60.0	62.6

Source: Lists of Slaves on York Estate, Jamaica, 1 January 1778, 9 May 1782, 1 January 1820, 1 January 1829, *Gale-Morant Papers*, 3/c, 3/c/1, 2/c/14, 3/d/3, University of Exeter Library.

females in the childbearing years of their lives. Partly because such a positive response was seldom forthcoming, and partly because planters were not willing or able to sacrifice present for future gains to alter the structure of their labor force, amelioration measures met with little or no success. Slave women generally outlived their male counterparts, which became more and more apparent after the closure of the Atlantic slave trade. As the number of male plantation slaves declined in relation to female slaves, a larger proportion of them was needed to serve as subordinate managers and skilled craftsmen, and fewer of them remained as field workers. Conversely, the female plantation slaves came to make up a larger proportion of the field gangs, which was inimical to their role as breeding units.[66]

The female labor experience of York sugar plantation in Jamaica is perhaps typical of many such plantations in that island. Table 8.3 shows an overall decline from 485 slaves in 1778 to 303 in 1829 (or 37.1 percent) and of working slaves from 440 to 219 (or 50.2 percent). Total female workers declined more slowly from 192 to 112, so that working females as a percentage of all working slaves increased from 43.6 to 51.1. For Jamaica as a whole, the precentage of female slaves to all slaves increased from approximately 44.0 in 1790 to 50.9 in 1829 (see Table 8.4).[67] It is remarkable that the number of female field workers on York plantation declined from 147 to 67 (or 54.4 percent) from 1778 to 1829, and that as a percentage of all female workers those engaged in field work increased from 76.6 to 90.2 from 1778 to 1820, and then declined to 59.8 in 1829. While the number

Table 8.4. *Increase, decrease, and total population of slaves, Jamaica, 1790–1829*

Year	Males	Females	Total	Increase by birth		Decrease by death	
				Males	Females	Males	Females
1790	140,000	110,000	250,000	—	—	—	—
1817	173,319	172,831	346,150	—	—	—	—
1820	170,466	171,916	342,382	12,201	12,145	13,425	11,681
1823	166,595	169,658	336,253	11,685	11,564	14,030	12,321
1826	162,726	168,393	331,119	11,604	11,422	13,520	11,650
1829	158,254	164,167	322,421	10,986	10,742	13,435	11,702

Source: Bryan Edwards, *History of the British West Indies* (Dublin, 1793), Vol. I, pp. 218–19; Vol. II, p. 135; *British Parliamentry Papers*, 1833 (539), Slave Registration Returns, Jamaica, as printed in Orlando Patterson, *The Sociology of Slavery* (London, 1967), p. 98.

of female field workers was cut by more than half, the number of male field workers declined even more, so that female field workers as a percentage of all field workers increased from 55.1 in 1778 to 62.6 in 1829.[68]

Other studies have data and findings that tend to support the experience of the female field workers on York plantation. On Worthy Park estate, the overall percentage of women rose from 46 to 60, whereas their percentage of the field labor force increased almost proportionately – from 54 in the 1790s to more than 65 throughout the 1830s. In 1832, 71 percent of the 185 females on the estate were field laborers, but only 55 percent of the 130 males were so employed. Because men virtually monopolized the elite jobs of drivers, headmen, craftsmen, and specialized occupations, women were relegated to unskilled, strenuous field labor. Dr. Lucille Mathurin Mair believes that even before 1820 when men outnumbered women in the slave population, "women nevertheless outnumbered men in the most menial and least versatile tasks on the plantation."[69]

The conflict between female labor and population growth was understood by contemporaries as having two sides. One was the physical damage that hard labor imposed on pregnant women; the other was the inability of hard-working mothers to care for their children. Edward Long said he could not deny "that those Negroes breed the best, whose labour is least, or easiest. Thus the domestic Negroes have more children, in proportion, than those on [livestock] penns; and the latter, than those who are employed on sugar-plantations." Long constructed a table to demonstrate the inverse relationship between the annual production of sugar in hogsheads and the growth of the slave population on plantations. He contended that if the number of hogsheads exceeded, or even equaled, the whole aggregate of slaves employed on a plantation, "but few children will be brought up on such estate, whatever number may be born; for the mothers will not have sufficient time to take due care of them; and, if they are put under charge of some elderly woman, or nurse, as the custom is in many places, it cannot be supposed that they meet with the same tenderness as might be expected from their parent."[70]

William Taylor testified to the low fertility and high mortality of Jamaican sugar plantations and the adverse effect of hard female labor on fertility. Taylor, who had managed three sugar plantations with about 700 slaves, testified before the Select Committee on the Extinction of Slavery in 1832. He believed that the decrease in the slave population was materially affected by the nature of the employment and particularly the severity of work by the women. Women fieldworkers were expected to dig holes for planting canes and at harvest to cut canes and work a night shift in the boiling house. Taylor singled out two of these tasks for special mention, pointing out that

> the cane hole digging is a work that calls for very severe exertion, and that I think must have a very bad effect upon the female frame; cane hold digging and night work I considered to be partly the causes of the diminution of the population. On coffee plantations there is neither night work nor cane hole digging, and I have always understood that they increase more than they do on sugar estates.

Taylor also believed that the whipping of pregnant women frequently destroyed the children they were carrying. He was emphatic in denying that women who were known to be pregnant were ever worked at cane hole digging or flogged. It was in the early stage of pregnancy, when the woman's condition was unknown, that miscarriages were frequently caused by corporal punishment and cane hold digging, he maintained.[71]

A modern study by Dr. Barry W. Higman confirms the impressions of Edward Long and William Taylor. Using multiple regression analysis to weigh the variables that affected the slave demography of Jamaica at the time of emancipation, Higman finds that whereas the slaves on small nonsugar properties tended to increase by natural means, those on sugar plantations with about 250 slaves had the highest mortality. Conversely, the birthrate was higher on small properties than it was on large sugar properties. By contrast with the pattern of mortality that varied from place to place, there was little significant variation in the birthrate. From 1817 to 1829 the island's slave population declined from 346,150 to 322,421, or an averge natural decrease of 0.47 percent per annum.[72]

Although the sex ratio among the blacks of Jamaica became balanced by 1820, the reverse tendency was characteristic of the whites. In the middle eighteenth century it was customary to employ married men as plantation managers and overseers. Their white wives supplied food, superintended the nurses and midwives, and saw that proper care was taken of pregnant and lying-in women. The Reverend James Ramsay deplored the tendency to replace the married manager by what he termed "a dissipated, careless, unfeeling young man, or a grovelling, lascivious, old batchelor (each with his half score of black or mulattoe pilfering harlots)."[73] By the early nineteenth century it was rare to find a white woman on a plantation. Almost every bookkeeper, overseer, or other persons in authority kept a black or mulatto mistress. The taking of black and mulatto concubines was not confined to single white men, for white masters are known to have had legitimate (white) children who mingled with their illegitimate (colored) offspring.[74]

Nonconformist missionaries testified to the sexual exploitation and violence committed against female blacks and mulattoes. The Reverend Peter Duncan, a Methodist missionary in Jamaica, told a select committee of the House of Lords that the proportion of white married men was very small, and that married whites were not generally allowed on plantations. Although it was considered a reproach for a white man to be married to a colored woman, illicit intercourse between whites and colored women was not regarded as any reproach at all. Duncan did not doubt that "Pagan Negresses" would prefer to sleep with their overseers to being flogged, but he was sure that "Religious Negressess" would not. In fact, he had known instances of Negresses resisting their overseers when it had almost cost them their lives. Confirming Duncan's testimony was that of the Reverend John Barry, another Methodist missionary in Jamaica. He believed it was very common for the owners or overseers of slaves to keep black and mulatto women in a state of concubinage on their respective properties; women were "subjected to Corporal Punishment for Non-compliance with the libidinous Desires of the Person in Authority on the Estate." Barry was informed by one man that when overseers and bookkeepers visited one another, which was common on Sunday, nothing was more common "than to have Women selected upon the Properties for the Purpose of sleeping with these Visitors." In a modern study, Lucille Mathurin Mair asserts that sexual exploitation and violence were inescapable features of the black woman's condition. "Until the last few years of slavery," she writes, "there was no redress against sexual attack for slave women in the courts."[75]

By taking concubines from the female slaves, the white men reduced the number of women available for mating with blacks. Few or none of the mulatto offspring of these unions were permitted to work in the field. Thus the cohabitation of white men with black and mulatto women contributed to the reduction of the effective labor force and interfered with the reproductive process. Nothing operated more severely on the minds of black women, wrote Dr. John Williamson, "than the improper connexions, imperiously formed by whites with negro women, to the injury of that negro man who considered her his own, and the rightful companion of his bed."[76]

Comparison of slave fertility in the United States and the British West Indies reveals significant differences. Stanley L. Engerman observes that in the United States in about 1830, the crude birthrate was about fifty per thousand of the population, whereas the Parliamentary registration reports for Jamaica indicate birthrates of about twenty-three per thousand. The birthrate in Jamaica was understated by an indeterminate quantity because infants who died were not always listed. Contemporaries commonly attributed the persistently low fertility in the West Indies to "the cultural and psychological shock of enslavement and movement to the New World, and as a response to the conditions of life: an unwillingness to bring offspring into such conditions. To accomplish this end, it has been claimed, there was frequent resort to abortion and infanticide."[77]

Planters commonly accused slave women of artifically bringing on abortions and miscarriages to be free to pursue their licentious sex lives. During her visit to Antigua in 1774, Janet Schaw learned of young black women who set out to lure white lovers and sometimes gave birth to mulattoes who were fit for neither the field nor any work. "Besides these wenches become licentious and insolent past all bearing," wrote Miss Schaw, "and as even a mulattoe child interrupts their pleasures and is troublesome, they have certain herbs and medicines, that free them from such an incumbrance, but which seldom fails to cut short their own lives, as well as that of their offspring. By this many of them perish every year."[78] Dr. Robert Thomas of Nevis attributed the decrease of the slaves, in part, to "the frequent abortions which Negro women designedly bring on themselves, either because a state of pregnancy in some measure puts a stop to their amorous pursuits for some time, or because they do not choose to be incumbered with the trouble of giving suck and of rearing their children." From whatever cause, miscarriages took a heavy toll. For example, Michael Craton's analysis of births and miscarriages on Worthy Park estate in Jamaica indicates the alarming rate of one miscarriage for every 4.6 births.[79]

That midwives administered abortifacients to pregnant blacks was the testimony of Sir Michael Clare, M.D., who practiced in Jamaica. He told the select committee of the House of Lords that in one case he saw the midwife administer the wild cassava, "which is a Drastic of the most violent Kind," to a young woman. He said he "showed the Midwife what she had been doing, by presenting to her the Foetus just as it passed off with the Cramp and Spasms." Women whose husbands had several wives were said to be motivated by jealousy to get an abortion so they would not have to give up that husband for a number of months.[80]

Some writers took note of abortions and infanticide motivated by the black woman's refusal to bring more slaves into the world. Sabrina Park, who was tried in Jamaica for the murder of her three-month-old child, complained to the court that she had worked enough for her master "and that she would not be plagued to raise the child . . . to work for white people." Dr. Williamson gave as a reason for induced abortion the slave woman's ill disposition toward her master. He wrote that abortion was frequently the event of pregnancy in black women. Moreover, its recurrence was certain unless regulations to prevent it were enforced. Dr. David Collins was perceptive of the slave woman's burdens and her reluctance to bear children when he wrote: "Upheld by no consolation, animated by no hope, her nine months of torment issue in the production of a being, doomed, like herself, to the rigours of eternal servitude, and aggravating, by its claims on maternal support, the weight of her own evils."[81]

Reluctance to bear children induced black women to nurse their babies for a long time. By abstaining from sexual intercourse during the long lactation period, slave mothers are thought to have achieved some control over the spacing of their children and thus prevented the birthrate from rising to the prevailing level of mortality. "Negroes are universally fond of suckling their children for a long time," wrote Dr. Collins. "If you permit them, they will extend it to the third year." He said they were motivated in this by habit, an idea of its necessity, the desire to be spared at their labor, and the wish to avoid another pregnancy. Dr. Thomas wrote that few black women weaned their children before the age of two years, "and few women ever breed as long as they continue to give suck." John Baillie, the Jamaica planter, said that besides the fee he gave mothers when they produced a child, he offered them two dollars if they would wean the child in twelve months. His records showed that not a single mother availed herself of that premium from 1808 to 1832. He explained their behavior by the indulgences allowed them during the time they suckled their children. Dr. James Thomson explained the late weaning was an African custom that had its origin in the mother's fear of being burdened with a second child before the first could manage without her continued attention. Mungo Park, the African explorer, confirmed Dr. Thomson's view that late weaning was an African custom. "The Negro women suckle their children until they are able to walk of themselves," he wrote. "Three years' nursing is not uncommon; and during this period the husband devotes his whole attention to his other wives."[82]

Differences in lactation periods were an influential cause of the disparate fertility patterns among the slave populations of the United States and the British West Indies. Herbert S. Klein and Stanley L. Engerman have explored these fertility differences. They point to the marked differences between rates of natural increase in the two slave societies, their differential dependence on the African slave trade until 1808, and the differential impact of African cultural influences. From both direct evidence and inferences drawn from patterns of spacing children, they find "that on the mainland of North America the breastfeeding interval was generally about one year, while in the West Indies it was typically at least two years." They attribute this in large measure to the fact that West Indians retained more elements of African culture than did the North American slaves. Long lactation and abstinence from sexual intercourse during the breast feeding were African cultural traits that were carried to the islands. These were strengthened by the physiological fact that lactation offers limited contraceptive protection.[83]

Besides lactation practices, contemporary and modern observers have attributed the low West Indian fertility to a combination of poor diet and the work routine on sugar plantations. Klein and Engerman note that a poor diet would have reduced the normal period of childbearing as well as cause greater spacing of children. The dual impact of a poor diet would be to increase infant deaths and reduce the number of potential children. Inadequate nutrition was an important factor in depressing the fertility of slave women, according to Richard S. Dunn. The female's nourishment affected the timing of her "adolescent growth spurt and menarche, the maintenance of regular menstrual function, the recovery of reproductive ability after childbirth, and the timing of menopause." Dunn's study of the slaves on the Mesopotamia sugar plantation in Jamaica reveals symptoms of impaired reproductive development: "delayed first births, long and irregular birth intervals, and early final births."[84] In their study of diet and disease in the antebellum South, Kenneth F. Kiple and Virginia Himmelsteib King find evidence to suggest that many slave children were in severe nutritional straits, in some instances even before birth. The same authors, in their study of deficiency diseases in the Caribbean, point out that "prolonged lactation substantially increased the risk of death by thiamine deficiency for many West Indian slave infants."[85]

Furthermore, diseases no doubt affected slave fertility and sterility as well as determined mortality on plantations. Michael Craton noted that such endemic diseases as syphilis, yaws, and elephantiasis, and such epidemic diseases as smallpox, measles, and scarlet fever "obviously increased the incidence of miscarriages and stillbirths, as well as reducing the ability or willingness to procreate."[86]

Conclusion

In the debate leading up to the act of 1807, the abolitionists urged the end of the slave trade as the only certain way to amend the treatment of slaves and secure their increase. In his pamphlet of 1788, Thomas Clarkson contended that it was in the power of the planters to do without fresh supplies of slaves from Africa and that prohibition of the trade would benefit both the planters and the slaves. To make his argument convincing, he presented a short history of twenty-six plantations in nine West Indian islands that had supported themselves independent of the slave trade.[87] William Wilberforce argued in a similar vein. He deplored the fact that, despite some notable exceptions, the mass of slave owners had adhered to "the system of working out their Slaves in a few years, and recruiting their gangs with imported Africans." He believed that abolition would give the death blow to this system. It would immediately become the "grand, constant, and incessant concern of every prudent man, both proprietor and manager" to attend to the preservation and increase of his slaves. Ruin would stare a man in the face, he believed, if he did not encourage family life and the reproduction of his labor force.[88]

James Stephen, on the other hand, was less sanguine regarding the possibility of achieving natural population growth. To achieve this goal, he wrote,

> a great diminution of labour, especially among the females, was essentially necessary; also a more liberal and expensive sustentation of the slaves in general, a more chargeable care of infants and invalids, and some other additions to the annual disbursements upon an estate, of which the produce at the same time was to be diminished.

Stephen came to advocate slave emancipation by the act of Parliament because he was convinced that the slave owners would not sacrifice their present gain by reducing labor and increasing subsistence in order to increase their labor force.[89]

It is the chief contention of this chapter that the British Caribbean plantocracy valued women as work units more than as breeding units. After an initial period when sugar planters made an effort to supply wives for their slaves, the patterns of reproduction and child care deteriorated as the planters turned more and more to the Atlantic slave trade to supply recruits to their plantations. The terrible waste of human life came to be questioned on grounds of self-interest, morality, and religion. By 1784 James Ramsay could no longer pass over in silence the harsh treatment of pregnant women and nursing mothers. His charges against the planters led to countercharges, Parliamentary investigations, amelioration measures, and abolition of the Atlantic slave trade. These and other measures were intended, in part, to encourage family life and lead to a self-generating slave labor force. Yet, as Dr. Lucille Mair has written, "no improvement in the treatment of women was discernible in the latter period of slavery: her condition in fact, may even have worsened." Sustained manual labor proved to be "inconsistent with the physical demands made on women by menstruation, pregnancy, lactation, infant and child care." The slave woman came to dominate the labor force. "She was not only a costly work-unit," writes Dr. Mair, "but she could hold the estate to ransom, by not working, or not breeding."[90] It can be argued that by not breeding, the slave women in the aggregate insured that the birthrate would not increase sufficiently to overtake the declining death rate. This is the key to the demographic failure.

9

Smallpox and slavery

Say, as this malady but once infests
The sons of Guinea, might not skill ingraft
(Thus the small-pox are happily convey'd)
This ailment early to thy Negro-train?

James Grainger, M.D., 1764[1]

This is the first of three chapters concerned with the health care system on West Indian slave plantations. This chapter takes up the dreaded plague of smallpox, its destruction of both white and black inhabitants, the great importance of preventive medicine in the form of variolation or inoculation and vaccination, and campaigns against smallpox in other New World colonies. Subsequent chapters will deal with slave hospitals and plantation medical practices.

Introduction

Smallpox or variola is an eruptive fever that was probably the deadliest of the early epidemic diseases of the Americas. It is an acute infectious virus disease characterized by vomiting, pain in the loins, fever, and eruptions that spread over the body; the eruptions are converted into pustules, which dry up into soft, yellow crusts that have a peculiar offensive odor. In the final stage the scabs fall off, leaving pitted scars or pock marks. Before Jenner's discovery of vaccination, smallpox reputedly killed, crippled, and disfigured one-tenth of all humans. The virulence of the disease varied according to conditions of poverty, overcrowding, migration of peoples and their microbes, as well as the ratio of immune to nonimmune inhabitants of a given community.

Smallpox was introduced into the West Indies in 1518–19, twenty-six years after the European discovery of America by Columbus, and contributed to the extermination of whole peoples. Further decimation of the Amerindians resulted when the disease reached Mexico in 1520 with troops from Spain. Although the northern Europeans brought smallpox to the Antilles in the seventeenth century, it was not until early in the following century that it became a deadly killer. Smallpox was slow to establish a foothold in the English West Indies until the late seventeenth century. Yellow fever was probably deadlier than smallpox, but it is of only peripheral interest to this study because its victims were chiefly Europeans. Although it is likely that smallpox was transmitted by immigrants from Europe, most accounts concern infected slaves from Africa. In March 1663 Captain Phillip Carteret arrived at Barbados in the *Speedwell* with a cargo of 155 men, 102 women, and 22 boys and girls. "The small-pox hitt unfortunately among them, distroyed [sic] many, rendered others unsaleable that had it in the harbor" and left others "very sickly." At this time high mortality was also reported from progressively severe diseases among the African slaves of St. Kitts and Nevis.[2] Captain Thomas Phillips of the *Hannibal* carried a cargo of slaves to Barbados in 1693–4. He wrote that "the Negroes are so incident to the small-pox, that few ships that carry them escape without it, and sometimes it makes vast havock and destruction among them." Though as many as a hundred were sick of it at a time, the *Hannibal* lost no more than a dozen slaves from smallpox.[3]

Epidemics raged in Barbados during King William's War from 1691 to 1698. As a result of the influx of soldiers as well as slaves, wrote John Oldmixon,

> the Island which before was reckoned to be the healthiest of all the Isles thereabouts, has ever since been very sickly, vast Number of Merchants, Captains of Ships, Planters, Labourers, and Negroes have been swept away by this [unidentified] Disease, and 'tis to be wished, they may have such Supplies of Men sent them, as they want for their Defence.

The epidemics, which probably included smallpox, were especially severe around Bridgetown.[4]

Jamaicans were seldom troubled with smallpox during the first thirty years of English occupation. Thomas Trapham, M.D., wrote in 1679 that the diseases of the island fell far short of those that infected the people of the mother country: "No small Pox or very rarely, saving sometimes brought from *Guinny* by Negroes, terrify or remark us; no Scurvy that almost universal contagion of our native Country is got here, or continued if brought; no depopulating Plague that ere I have heard of in the West Indies."[5] As with Barbados, the disease environment deteriorated during King William's War. George Reid wrote to Dr. Hans Sloane from Jamaica on 30 June 1690 that smallpox was raging among the islanders and had killed many.[6]

Variolation or inoculation

As in England and New England, smallpox epidemics became more frequent and destructive in the West Indies during the eighteenth century. The disease environments of northern Europe, tropical Africa, and the Caribbean were linked together more closely by shipping and trade, especially the growing trade in human chattels from Africa. Various remedies were used to prevent or cure smallpox. Robert Boyle, the chemist, recommended an infusion of fresh sheep's dung in white wine, given warm, a spoonful at a time every two or three hours. Calomel was thought to be effective in preventing infection. Sachets containing herbs to ward off smallpox were sold in London during the eighteenth century. We mentioned in Chapter 4 that Bishop Berkeley popularized the taking of tar-water for smallpox and other diseases. Tar was mixed with ordinary cold water, which was poured off and drunk in varying quantities after the tar had settled.[7] It is of interest that the island of Barbados was one source of green tar that oozed spontaneously out of the ground, giving off a disagreeable sulfur smell. It was said to be of singular service for "paralytic and nervous cases," as well as for curing cutaneous eruptions.[8] These and other remedies were mere palliatives or fetishes, however, in comparison with the immunity to be gained by inoculation and vaccination for smallpox.

Africans had knowledge of a practiced variolation before the spread of this form of immunization to Europe and America. It consisted of infecting a healthy individual with material taken from a patient who had a mild case of smallpox. Sometime between 1706 and 1716, Cotton Mather, the Puritan divine at Boston, learned from Onisemus, his black slave, that inoculation for smallpox was a relatively common practice in many parts of Africa. On 16 July 1721, at the time of an epidemic in Boston, Mather wrote in his *Diary*, "I have instructed our Physicians in the new Method used by the *Africans* and *Asiatics* to prevent and abate the Dangers of the Small-Pox, and infallibly to save the Lives of those that have wisely managed upon them."[9] Corroboration of Mather's story of African inoculation is found in the writings of the Reverend Benjamin Colman and Dr. Zabdiel Boylston, pioneer inoculator in Boston. Boylston wrote that the considerable number of Africans who lived in Boston "all agreed in *one* story; 'That abundance of poor Negro's die of the *Small Pox*, till they learn this Way; that People take the Juice of the *Small Pox*, and cut the Skin, and put in a drop; then by-'nd-by a little *Sick*, then few *Small Pox*; and no body dye of it: no body have *Small Pox* any more.' "[10]

The English learned of variolation from medical practitioners and others who lived in Constantinople. In 1717 Lady Mary Wortley Montagu, the wife of the British ambassador to Turkey, wrote to a friend in England that she intended to bring the usefulness of inoculation into common knowledge upon her return to England. Accordingly, in April 1721 she arranged to have her daughter inoculated in London with widely publicized success. In time, eminent physicians and surgeons came to support the practice of inoculation. Most prominent among them was Sir Hans Sloane, then president of the Royal Society and the most influential physician to the king. Smallpox inoculation spread from London to the provinces, and during the eighteenth century it was practiced on a massive scale.[11] Indeed, Dr. P. E. Razzell has marshaled much evidence to support his contention that inoculation against smallpox was an important cause of English population growth during the eighteenth century.[12]

Although no record has been found, variolation was probably introduced into the West Indies by African slaves. Sugar plantation owners were reported to be using this method to save their slaves in 1727, only six years after the first professional inoculation in England. Smallpox raged in Barbados in 1738, when it was said that inoculation was practiced with great success.[13] Josiah Martin, an absentee proprietor who lived at Watertown, Massachusetts, learned of a smallpox epidemic at Antigua. In a letter of 24 April 1738, he instructed his plantation manager in Antigua that if the smallpox should "spread so much as y[t] [that] my Negroes are in Danger of catching it, I w[oul]d have you make use of inoculation, it being ye only method of preserving them."[14] About a decade later Richard Mead, M.D., a leading London physician, learned of inoculation from a merchant in St. Kitts who employed a large number of slaves in the making of sugar. Mead wrote:

> In one year, when the small-pox raged with more than ordinary violence in the neighbouring islands, with his own hands, he inoculated three hundred of them, from five to thirty years of age, with such success, that not one of them died, though most of them were negroes. And whereas all the Americans suffer this distemper in a most terrible manner; yet experience shews, that it is much more dangerous, when it attacks the natives of Africa.[15]

At midcentury the Reverend Griffith Hughes, rector of St. Lucy's Parish in Barbados, wrote that the inhabitants were seldom free of smallpox in some part of the island or other: "However, since Inoculation hath been introduced among us, our Loss by that distemper hath hitherto been very small."[16]

"The Small Pox hath been among us these past two months or better, brought in by the French Pawpaw Guinea man," wrote Dr. Walter Tullideph of Antigua to his cousin in London on 23 February 1756. He went on to say that his foot boy had brought the smallpox from town, which had induced him to inoculate his gang of slaves.[17] Three months later Dr. Thomas Fraser, M.D., told of the smallpox epidemic and inoculation in Antigua in a long letter to Dr. Donald Monro of Jermyn Street, London. Dr. Fraser had delayed writing because his time had been entirely taken up in caring for smallpox patients. "The small-pox no sooner made its appearance here," he wrote, "than we immediately thought of inoculation; the success of which has been so remarkable among people of all ages, blacks as well as the other inhabitants, that the most obstinate were at last prevailed on to countenance this practice."[18]

The slaves who worked on the plantations of Antigua, and on whose lives the riches of the white inhabitants chiefly depended, had been very freely inoculated. From 270 to 300 slaves had, by direction of Dr. Fraser, been inoculated "with the loss of two out of the number, who had certainly the virus in them previous to the inoculation, as they sickened in two days after, and had perpetual intercourse with variolous people." Other medical practitioners had had similar success with Dr. Fraser.[19]

Inoculation was practiced with varying success on the two Tudway plantations in Antigua, where there were more than 500 slaves in the last quarter of the eighteenth century. Writing to the proprietor in England in March 1773, the plantation manager said that smallpox had infected slaves all over the island. Nearly a hundred of Tudway's slaves had been inoculated. One boy had been lost, and one or two other children were expected to die. The manager said it was remarkable that more people had died in Antigua after inoculation than ever was known, and particularly children, both whites and blacks.[20] Contrasted with the failure in this instance was the success of subsequent campaigns. The manager wrote in July 1789 that smallpox had been introduced into the island by some regimental recruits who had lately arrived from England. He explained that

> there are upwards of seventy of your Slaves who have not had this distemper, & We are now engaged in preparing them to receive it . . . We here entertain no apprehensions respecting the consequences of inoculation, and We never fail to get thro' it with the greatest success. You may rely that the utmost attention shall be paid to your Slaves, both with respect to their food & care of every sort, whilst they are under the effects of this distemper.

Preparations were being made by several proprietors who had as many or more slaves as the Tudways, "who will all of them undergo the operation at the same time."[21]

Inoculation gave way to vaccination on the Tudway properties between 1804 and 1809. In 1804 there were inoculated "seventy three little ones from a month to six years old & the six new Negroe men last purchased, making in the whole, seventy nine." Only one slave was lost, and he was a boy who was thought to have died of worms rather than smallpox. The doctors who performed the inoculation were paid nine shillings per slave, as compared with six shillings in former years.[22] In 1809 the plantation attorney reported, "The Vaccine innoculation has been introduced among us for some time, & is constantly performed on your little Negroes whenever we can produce good matter."[23]

Inoculation in Jamaica and England

Whether or not inoculation and vaccination were significant factors in reducing slave mortality in the British West Indies depends to a large extent on the incidence of smallpox and the success or failure of these preventive measures in the island of Jamaica. The estimated slave population of Jamaica increased form 45,000 in 1703 to 130,000 in 1754, and reached a peak of 346,150 in 1817, after which it declined to 311,070 at the time of slave emancipation in 1834. Jamaica was by far the most important sugar colony in the British West Indies, accounting for about 47 percent of the 666,024 black slaves in this group of colonies in 1834.[24]

According to Edward Long, the Jamaican planter-historian, smallpox was "one principal source of depopulation" among the slaves before inoculation came into general use, which he said was not long before the publication of his *History of Jamaica* in 1774. Regarding the slaves, he wrote:

> The small-pox has frequently made great ravage among them. Sometimes they have been landed with this disease upon them; and this has proved so fatal, that I have known seven in ten die of it, which is equal to seventy in a hundred, or fifty-six more than the computation made of those who die in England by this disorder taken in the natural way.

However, Long viewed the future optimistically: "The late method of inoculation, happily practised in this island, promises fair to put an end to such dreadful examples of mortality." One practitioner of his acquaintance had inoculated 1,500 blacks of all ages and habits of body and not one had died.[25]

The most detailed account of inoculation for smallpox came from Dr. John Quier, the leading plantation doctor in Jamaica. In three letters addressed to Dr. Donald Monro of London, he wrote concerning the subjects most fit for inoculation, the diet allowed to patients, preparative medicines and regimens used, insertion of variolous matter, appearance of the wound, treatment after the eruption, and other matters. Dr. Quier had 600 to 700 black and some white people regularly under his care. His first letter of 30 June 1770 had been written about the end of 1768 and beginning of 1769, after a severe smallpox epidemic. The smallpox began in the town and spread to the country. Dr. Quier wrote that he "first began to inoculate about the middle of March 1768, and by the end of the summer, near seven hundred negroes passed through the disease, under my care."[26]

In his second letter of 28 March 1773, he wrote that although he had inoculated again, nothing new was observed. In the third letter of 27 April 1774, Dr. Quier said he had had further opportunity to exercise this branch of medicine and the success had been the same as before. On this occasion he had inoculated 146 people. There were 120 children, of whom 50 were at the breast; "the rest were either new negroes, or people removed hither from other parts of the country since the preceding inoculation." Altogether over six years Dr. Quier inoculated at least 1,500 people who were with few exceptions blacks.[27]

Persons who were most hale and strong and thus most capable of bearing mercurial medicine and copious evacuations by purging were said to be best adapted for inoculation for smallpox. On the other hand, Dr. Quier said that caution should be exercised in inoculating those who were too young; those with great debility from old age, want of food, long diseases, and dropsy; those with acute diseases; and pregnant women. Many infants who were not more than a month old had been successfully inoculated by Dr. Quier, although he cautioned that much care and circumspection were needed to prevent accidents.[28]

The diet given the slaves during the process of inoculation was heavily weighted in favor of vegetable foodstuffs. These consisted of yams, cocos or eddoes, potatoes, plantains, and bananas. On the other hand, Dr. Quier said that all possible precautions should be taken to keep from the patients rum, herrings, salt fish, flesh of all kinds, salt, and the aromatics that were the natural produce of the island. Their drink was water, or a beverage made with water and sugar plus lime or lemon juice.[29] Dr. Quier tried various experiments with preparative medicines. He preferred calomel and emetic tartar, joined with some testaceous powder as recommended by Baron Dimsdale, a leading English authority on inoculation. Following this he used a purgative of jalap mixed with an equal quantity of cream of tartar. Although Dr. Quier did not favor the total omission of the mercurial medicine and purgatives, he administered them so as to weaken the patient as little as possible, and he took measures to support them with proper food. Moreover, the constant use of Peruvian bark in weakened patients, except during the time of the eruptive fever, succeeded.[30]

In inserting the variolous contagion, Dr. Quier made only the slightest scratch. He always took care to impregnate the incision well by wiping the point of the lancet on it and even by adding more matter if that appeared necessary. Quier used arm-to-arm inoculation, taking the matter warm from a subject present at the time. He said there was no danger of introducing too much of the contagion into the body. If the infection had not appeared by the fifth, sixth, or seventh day, he repeated the inoculation. This seldom happened, however, since he inoculated on both arms. He used no dressing on the incision, unless toward the end of the disease. A small dose of calomel and emetic tartar was given on the evening of the third day from the incision, and on the fourth day he commonly began to use a purging infusion. The bark was joined with a laxative infusion when eruptive symptoms appeared on the eighth or ninth day. After the eruption was over, Dr. Quier maintained that there were very few working slaves who could not pursue their usual occupations.[31]

Dr. Quier's work was praised by his colleague, Dr. Thomas Dancer, who wrote that he had "carried the practice of inoculation to a much greater length, than has been done by any of the boldest empirics in Europe. He has shewn that little preparation is necessary, or even much remission of labour; that hardly any age is an exception; that it is safe in pregnancy, that it may be performed without danger in intermittents, dropsy, yaws, and many other complaints."[32]

The Jamaican smallpox epidemic of 1768 came at a time when the art of inoculation was improved. According to Dr. Quier,

> inoculation had been frequently practised with success in this country, according to the methods formerly in use; and the extraordinary accounts which continually arrived here of the great improvements which that art had lately received in England, rendered people in general very much disposed to favour a practice which has so great a chance of securing their property, now in so much danger from the small-pox being epidemical, almost throughout the island.[33]

The new method was introduced by Dr. Gordon, who had recently returned from Europe. He had obligingly imparted to his acquaintance the particulars he had observed during the inoculation of his son in England by Daniel Sutton. Moreover, some copies of Baron Dimsdale's treatise on inoculation had been sent over by the agent for Jamaica, and the rules he laid down were generally followed by the practitioners in the colony. Though Dr. Quier disagreed with Dimsdale's rules regarding the preparation for inoculation and the treatment of natural smallpox, he wrote that "Dr. Dimsdale has described the phaemonena [sic] of this disease, from the insition to the compleat eruption, with great accuracy; I shall have therefore but little to say on that subject."[34]

Mass inoculation spread from England to the West Indies at a time of a smallpox epidemic in Jamaica and innovations in preparation, technique, and organization, which greatly reduced the cost of the operation. Robert Sutton, an apothecary in England, inoculated some 2,500 people by an "infallible" secret method he claimed to have discovered. His son Daniel and his assistants made the system famous throughout Europe and the Americas, and in 1764–6 they are reputed to have inoculated nearly 20,000 persons, all without a single death. Sutton later revealed that the secret remedies were calomel, tartar emetic, and jalap.[35] According to John N. Force, M.D., "the method of inoculation used by Sutton, Dimsdale, and their followers, i.e., thrusting a charged lancet between the epidermis and the true skin and withdrawing it, while pressing with the thumb above the wound, was as near our modern intradermal insertion as could be approximated without a hollow needle."[36] Dimsdale later wrote that the preparatory course of medicine and regimen was ill founded and that it was the practice to use a fresh infected thread in the incision without any bandage.[37]

Different views have been expressed regarding the extent to which inoculation was practiced in England and its effectiveness. P. E. Razzell, the demographic historian, says that inoculation appears to have been universally practiced in small towns and villages before the end of the eighteenth century and was making rapid headway in the large towns by the end of the century. He contends that inoculation against smallpox was dramatically effective in reducing mortality and that this was of profound significance for the demographic and economic history of England, Scotland, Ireland, and the United States.[38] On the other hand, C. W. Dixon, M.D., is of the opinion that inoculation did not master smallpox, as some historians suggest. He maintains that the artisans and the poor could not afford the time or the money to have their children inoculated. Support for Dixon is found in the work of Thomas McKeown, who argues that although there were many successes, there were also many failures in the form of fatal infections from inoculation, and that smallpox has been controlled by the surveillance and vaccination of contacts rather than by mass immunization.[39]

Although firsthand reports of inoculation in the West Indies are hard to come by, it may be surmised that the practice was widely adopted before the end of the eighteenth century. That Dr. Quier was not the only mass inoculator in Jamaica is clear from the medical ledger of Dr. Alexander Johnston, who lived in St. Ann's Parish on the north side of the island. In 1768 Dr. Johnston and his partner had 173 medical accounts with a total value of £3,240 6*s.* 3¾*d.* Jamaican currency. They ranged from single white persons and families to plantation accounts with as many as 345 slaves who were treated on an annual contract basis. The inoculation and smallpox accounts numbered sixty and amounted to £1,148 15*s.* 0*d.*, or 35.5 percent of the total. The entries with few exceptions were cryptically phrased, "To Account of Inoculation Account" or "To Account of Inoculation Account from Small Pox Book." Though no distinction is made between whites and blacks, it is unlikely that his practice departed very far from the island-wide ratio of about eleven blacks to one white. Dr. Johnston charged 12*s.* 6*d.* to inoculate a slave. At this rate he could have inoculated as many as 2,000 slaves in 1768.[40]

Other accounts of inoculation concern scattered plantations in Jamaica. Slaves were inoculated from time to time on York estate in Trelawny Parish. Here Dr. Samuel Curtin inoculated twenty-one blacks against smallpox at 12*s.* 6*d.* each in 1785, and the partnership of Curtin and Leckie was paid £66 5*s.* 0*d.* on 20 September 1792 "for preparing and Inoculating 106 Negroes for the Small Pox @ 12/6 ea."[41] On Trouthall estate in Clarendon Parish slaves were inoculated in 1782 and 1786.[42] Dr. James Chisholme, the proprietor of Trouthall and other estates, left the following instructions to his plantation manager at the time of his departure for Scotland in 1791: "The last time the Small pox was on any of the estates was in the year eighty five, at which time the negroes were all inoculated, but all those, that have been bought or have been born, since that time have not had the small pox. I wish that they may be all Inoculated as soon as the small pox comes into the Country."[43]

The Jamaican vaccine establishment

The chief difficulty with inoculation or variolation was the inherent danger of contracting a fatal case of smallpox. It was uncertain whether the disease would be mild or virulent. In the English colonies, where inoculation was widely practiced, the death rate ranged from one to six or seven per hundred. John Duffy contends that variolation had much in its favor in the eighteenth century, since smallpox was a horrible and highly contagious disease with "a case fatality rate that rarely ran less than ten per cent and was likely to average closer to twenty or thirty per cent."[44]

Edward Jenner launched a new era in the campaign against smallpox in 1798 when he published his famous book, *An Inquiry into the Causes and Effects of the Variolae Vaccinae.* Dr. Jenner had heard that people who had had cowpox, a disease of the udders of cows, were protected against smallpox. He carried out the first professional vaccination as a scientific experiment, showing that this mild disease could be passed on to other individuals. Cowpox vaccination, unlike smallpox inoculation, was never fatal and could be performed without infecting others. It conferred immunity for a limited number of years, however, whereas inoculation lasted a lifetime. The original material for vaccination, or lymph, was obtained from cowpox lesions on the udder of the cow, or from human cases.[45]

The dried lymph was first introduced into the West Indies from England. Lady Maria Nugent, wife of the lieutenant governor of Jamaica, wrote in her *Journal* on 9 November 1803, "A packet from England, with most comfortable letters, and a parcel containing more of the vaccine virus. Send for Dr. Clare, who immediately inoculated my little Louisa with it. God grant it may succeed!" After the first attempt failed, the operation was repeated a month later with apparent success.[46]

John Williamson, M.D., who practiced in the parish of St. Thomas in the Vale, told of his experience with vaccination. In the summer of 1803 he received some lymph from Dr. Weston of St. Ann's Parish and immediately vaccinated a child. When no inflammation followed, he inoculated the child successfully with variolous matter. "In that country," he explained, "extreme heat soon decomposed the vaccine lymph. To introduce it effectually, one or more children were sent to Dr Weston to establish infection; when they were brought back, to convey it to others in that quarter of the country; and thus communicated such blessing over the island." Dr. Weston was said to have taken great pains to publish "the observations he made in some of the newspapers, inviting the profession to accept of any assistance he could supply them with, by transmitting vaccine lymph in the most likely manner to preserve it, or by infecting any negroes that might be sent to him."[47] Writing in 1806, George Farquhar, M.D., said that the vaccine disease had been "diffused among many hundred negroes."[48]

Because of some early failures, the practice of vaccination was slow to be adopted in Jamaica. This was the opinion of Thomas Dancer, M.D., who wrote in 1809, "This would be matter of serious regret, were it not that variolous, or small-pox inoculation, under proper regulations, is nearly, if not wholly, as safe as vaccination; and in the latter, there is seldom any failure of uncertainty." Dancer was unable to explain why the "genuine vaccine matter, imported both from England and America, should so often produce a spurious and ineffective disease." At any event, great numbers of blacks and whites had contracted smallpox after being vaccinated.[49]

Dr. Dancer was not alone in his concern to get "genuine vaccine matter," for the speaker of the Assembly of Jamaica was instructed to appoint a committee "to consider of the best mode of procuring and keeping up a supply of vaccine matter in this island, and of securing to the public the benefit to be derived from substituting vaccination to inoculation for the small-pox." In its report of 30 November 1813, the committee submitted the following plan for a public vaccine establishment in Jamaica:

> That there be engrafted on the establishment of the public hospital in Kingston a vaccinating institution, under the government of the commissioners of the hospital appointed by law, and to be denominated the public vaccine establishment of Jamaica:
>
> That the physician and surgeon of the said hospital be the officers of the establishment, with power to employ a clerk or assistant:
>
> That the physician be denominated the director and register, and the surgeon the operator, of the establishment:
>
> That it be the duty of the director to superintend, and of the operator

> to perform, all the manual part of the practice of vaccination, and of the register to attend to the necessary correspondence in receiving and giving communications:
>
> That all subjects fit for vaccination, brought to the hospital, be so vaccinated *gratis*, on the stipulated conditions, that they appear at such stated times as shall be directed for examination, and to afford the means of supplying charges of vaccine lymph, and carefully preserve and deliver the dry crusts, which shall drop from the vaccine vesicles:
>
> That, as one of the principal objects of the establishment will be to afford the means of vaccine infection to medical practitioners in other parts of the island, all applications made to the register, either personally, or in any other way that shall put the establishment to no expence, be duly and carefully attended to, and charges of vaccine lymph be distributed to all who shall apply for them:
>
> That it be the further duty of the register to correspond with the national vaccine establishment in Leicester-square, in London, for the purpose of receiving and giving any communications respecting the progress of vaccination:
>
> That the register and operating surgeon do make a report annually to the house of assembly of the proceedings of the establishment:
>
> That for this duty, thus imposed upon them, an annual salary be granted, upon proof of the due performance thereof, to the physicians of the public hospital in Kingston, of 150*l.* and to the operating surgeon of 150*l.* with 50*l.* for a clerk or assistant.

After the report was read, the house agreed to carry out the plan for a vaccine establishment.[50]

Nearly two years passed before the first report of the Jamaican vaccine establishment was submitted by its director, Alexander MacLarty, M.D. He noted that the principal object of the establishment was "the preservation of the succession of vaccine matter for the public at large, as well as the medical practitioners." Accordingly, vaccine lymph had been distributed to most of the parishes in the island, as well as to the island of Curacao and the provinces of Caracas and Venezuela in South America. Only 122 persons had been vaccinated at the Kingston hospital, but it was expected that more would come forward because the popular prejudice against vaccination seemed to be rapidly losing ground.[51] In his subsequent reports, Dr. MacLarty was pleased to find more reasons for optimism. On 17 November 1818 the Assembly was informed that smallpox appeared to have become extinct, since not one case had occurred in any part of the island for nearly two years. Moreover, since the last report, thirty-four medical practitioners had been supplied with vaccine matter.[52] The demand for vaccine matter continued to grow during the following year, however, the report of 23 November 1819 was less optimistic than its predecessors. Dr. MacLarty lamented that many Jamaicans were still adverse to vaccination. "Some from prejudice," he wrote, "others from apathy, having had no recent cause of alarm, in consequence of the small-pox contagion having been for some time exterminated among us; hence a large proportion of our population has been left unprotected by either vaccine or variolous influence. Should therefore the dire contagion of small-pox be unfortunately introduced here, an extensive scene of distress may be anticipated."[53]

The dreaded event occurred some seven months later when a case of smallpox, "in its most loathsome and horrible form," was brought to Kingston from St. Jago de Cuba in the schooner *Aimable Theresa.* Great pains were taken to place the patient in a remote quarter of the hospital, to ventilate and fumigate his room, and to burn his bedding and clothing. Although the patient suffered a horrible death, the preventive measures proved successful and not one case of smallpox had occurred in the hospital or in any other part of the island when the report of 21 November 1821 was written.[54]

By far the most favorable report was the one submitted on 22 November 1821 by James Weir, M.D., who, upon the death of Alexander MacLarty, succeeded as director of the vaccine establishment.

> We have the greatest satisfaction in stating to your honourable house that since the last report of the director and surgeons of this establishment, small-pox has in Jamaica been totally unknown. This entire exemption from so dangerous and loathsome a malady, wont for ages past to produce such dreadful ravages, which for the last twelve months we have enjoyed, is in a great measure to be attributed to the increased confidence placed in that mild and certain preventive cow-pox; the prejudices against which, that have too generally prevailed, are now gradually giving way throughout the whole of this island, and more particularly in Kingston and its neighbourhood.

It was further stated that a correspondence had been opened with the National Vaccine Institution in London "by which the philanthropic views of the establishment here are likely to be very materially forwarded." Vaccination continued to be performed on all who were presented for the purpose, and numerous applications for supplies of fresh lymph and crusts were made by medical practitioners and private individuals from every quarter of the island.[55]

Probably to the great surprise of Dr. Weir, the vaccine establishment came under attack the day after he submitted his report. On 23 November 1821 a motion was made that the Assembly come to the following resolution: "that the public has not derived the benefit contemplated by the resolution of the 30th of November, 1813, for the support of the vaccine establishment in the city of Kingston, and that this house will no longer grant any money for the support of this establishment." Another motion was made to amend the resolution by striking out after the first word "that" and substituting the following words: "a committee be appointed to inquire how the vaccine establishment has been and is conducted, if any and what abuses exist, and how they may be remedied." The amended motion being approved, a committee was appointed and given "power to send for persons, papers, and records, and to examine all persons that come before them in the most solemn manner." Dr. Weir testified that upon becoming director in April 1821, he found there was no lymph on hand. He immediately entered into a correspondence with the director of the National Vaccine Institution in London, from whom he had since received several supplies of lymph. Hinton Spalding, M.D., said that he procured lymph from his brother practitioners rather than the Kingston vaccine institution. "The prejudice against taking the lymph from the institution arises," he said, "from the parties being unacquainted with the person from whom it has been taken." Michael Benignus Clare, M.D., testified that he considered a central establishment for vaccination highly useful in procuring a regular succession of the vaccine matter and also giving public sanction to vaccination.[56]

The final report of the vaccine establishment was submitted to the Assembly of Jamaica on 21 November 1822. It said that the practice of vaccination had been considerably extended in most parts of the island since the last report, and that public confidence in this mild protection from smallpox had greatly increased. Although one fatal case of smallpox had been reported in the parish of St. Elizabeth, the case had been isolated sufficiently to prevent other deaths. Fresh lymph had been supplied to all parts of the island by express couriers. Indeed, it was claimed that "innumberable lives amongst the negro population" had been saved "through the praiseworthy philanthropy of the legislature."[57]

Notwithstanding his favorable report, Dr. Weir and his assistants were paid for their services to 1 November 1822, at the same time that the Assembly passed a resolution that no further monies be voted to support the vaccine establishment.[58]

Though a causal nexus cannot be established, it is significant that in less than a decade after the vaccine establishment was closed, Jamaica had a smallpox epidemic of some virulence. The Reverend Peter Duncan, a Methodist missionary, wrote to his superiors in London from Kingston, Jamaica, on 11 July 1831:

> In this circuit we are still in the usual way. The raging of the small pox still prevents many of our people from attending the means of grace, and will seriously affect us in our temporal concerns. God has however been very meaningful to us both in this and the other circuit, notwithstanding the numerous cases of affliction we have not I believe lost twenty members by death throughout the city. This is but a small pro-

> portion, for I believe when the disease was at the worst, there was one week in which there were upwards of one hundred of the inhabitants committed [sic] to the dust.[59]

A few weeks later another missionary wrote from an outlying port town of Jamaica that the disease was making dreadful ravages in some parts of the island and thousands had died in a few weeks. Indeed, a most virulent kind of smallpox had thinned the population of Kingston and its neighborhood. He believed that a "holy and offended God" has seen fit to punish "a guilty and depraved people, for it is indescribable to what an awful extent, sin and iniquity of every kind, abound among every class of people in the island."[60]

Other campaigns against smallpox

Inoculation and vaccination were adopted in other parts of the Americas with considerable success. Although it was claimed that inoculation was practiced in Spanish America as early as 1722, it was not until the severe smallpox epidemics of 1765 and 1774 in Chile that large numbers of people were inoculated. Inoculation spread to other Spanish colonies, as did such preventive measures as isolation of the affected, the burning of sulfur, and the sprinkling of rooms with vinegar. Scattered accounts suggest that Spanish Americans responded positively to Edward Jenner's new technique of immunization. Jenner's work on the cowpox vaccine was published in Lima, Peru, in 1802, and three years later the first vaccine virus reached that city, having been brought across the mountains from Buenos Aires. One imaginative scheme to disseminate the new practice was a medical expedition that sailed from Spain in 1803. To have live vaccine, several boys who had never had smallpox were taken on board. During the long voyage they were vaccinated successively by the arm-to-arm method. This famous expedition visited ports in the Antilles, Mexico, Central America, and South America, sometimes vaccinating nearly a thousand persons in a week.[61]

As mentioned in Chapter 2, much of the improvement in Cuban medicine can be attributed to the talent and leadership of Tomás Romay y Chacón. He offered a prize to the person who successfully brought the vaccine to Cuba, demonstrated the safety and effectiveness of Jenner's discovery by vaccinating his own children, helped to establish a central vaccine board, and drew up a plan for the vaccination of new slaves at the port of Havana, as well as children in orphanages and every new baby within twelve days of birth. Moreover, Romay vaccinated the slaves on his own plantation and those of his relatives and distributed the vaccine to the towns, mills, and haciendas of the interior. Despite his heroic efforts, resistance to vaccination persisted not only among the ignorant and fanatical element of the population but also among some of the island's leading physicians. Preserving the vaccine virus was another persistent problem, as was maintaining government support and organization. Vaccination was most successful among privileged groups and the highly valued, high-risk populations of new slaves, immigrants, and students. Insufficient effort was directed toward the common people, however, especially in rural Cuba. Although the disease was partially contained, smallpox epidemics continued throughout the nineteenth century. Ross Danielson finds the root of failure in "an elitist, voluntaristic top-down approach to public health" that limited smallpox vaccination to certain sections of the Cuban population.[62]

The Spanish colony of Louisiana suffered several severe smallpox epidemics in the late eighteenth century that led to measures of isolation and immunization. The epidemic of 1778, which spread throughout the entire colony, was exceedingly fatal. The governor issued a decree to isolate all cases of infection by sending them to the other side of the Mississippi River where they were attended by physicians and, if children, accompanied by their parents. Another severe epidemic occurred in 1787 when the disease entered the colony in a cargo of slaves. The governor ordered the construction of two cottages or hospitals on the other side of the river: one for the isolation of infected blacks, the other for infected whites. Another cargo of infected slaves spread smallpox to the inhabitants of Louisiana in 1792, when the same measures of isolation were decreed. John Duffy writes that the epidemic of 1787 may have witnessed the first use of variolation or inoculation for smallpox in Louisiana. The success of inoculation in New Orleans weakened the opposition and encouraged the spread of the practice to outlying sections of the colony. New Orleans had a new weapon to fight smallpox when the infection spread to the city from a cargo of slaves in 1804. By this time many of the inhabitants had been vaccinated with a high degree of success.[63]

In Virginia smallpox epidemics occurred sporadically from the seventeenth to the late nineteenth century. Despite the appalling morbidity and mortality and the proven effectiveness of inoculation, Virginians with few exceptions believed that the procedure spread rather than prevented the disease. Indeed, an epidemic at Williamsburg in 1768 was blamed on a local inoculator whose house was burned by a mob. Anti-inoculation petitions were carried to the House of Burgesses, which passed an act in 1770 to regulate the practice. It imposed a fine of £1,000 on anyone who willfully imported any variolous or infectious matter with the intention of inoculating the inhabitants of Virginia. Only licensed practitioners were permitted to perform the operation, but magistrates might refuse to grant such licenses. The law was amended and made less severe in 1777, at a time when smallpox epidemics were more frequent and severe because of the movement of armies and the spread of pathogens during the Revolutionary War. But anti-inoculation sentiment continued strong down to the end of the eighteenth century. In fact, many Virginians who felt a need for immunization and could afford the expense went to inoculation hospitals in neighboring cities and states.[64]

Jenner's cowpox vaccine was introduced into the slave society of Virginia in circumstances that were in some ways similar to those prevailing in Cuba. In both societies slaves made up a large proportion of their populations, and planters and doctors who had these people under their care were confused about the merits and demerits of inoculation and vaccination. Both societies produced leaders who risked their reputation and property on the safety and efficacy of vaccination. We have seen that the Cuban leader was Tomás Romay y Chacón. In Virginia Thomas Jefferson was the first to introduce the vaccine virus, the first to vaccinate his family and slaves as well as those of his sons-in-law and neighbors, and a leader in preserving and perpetuating a pure virus and popularizing the knowledge of vaccination. "As a result of Jefferson's efforts," writes Todd L. Savitt, "vaccination became an established procedure in Virginia. By endorsing Jenner's technique, the President hastened its popular acceptance and thus indirectly helped to reduce the mortality from this dread disease."[65]

Conclusion

Notwithstanding the epidemic of 1831 in Jamaica, leading medical practitioners testified that the campaign against smallpox was generally successful in the British West Indies. Dr. David Collins of St. Vincent was particular in describing the process of inoculation "because it will frequently be undertaken by the proprietor of the estate, or the manager, to save the doctor's fee, for that which may safely be done without his assistance." In his judgment, Jenner's discovery was "the most valuable acquisition; the most complete and decisive, ever gained to medicine, since it was first cultivated as a science."[66] Inoculation had been adopted early in St. Vincent and neighboring islands, he said, and this process had been "continued with the greatest advantage, to the present day."[67]

Evidence points to the successful vaccination of slaves in British Guiana. Dr. Thomas Bell, who practiced medicine on the west coast of the Essequibo River, generally attended an average of 2,500 slaves. On 19 March 1824 he testified before a committee of the colonial assembly that he had "vaccinated all the slaves in my practice who had not had small pox, or been previously vaccinated; the number was upwards of 1200. For this some of my employers very liberally allowed me an extra gratuity. Vaccination is continued from time to time, so as effectually to guard against the small pox."[68] Sir John

Gladstone's plantation attorney wrote to Gladstone's son from Demerara on 16 June 1831, "I am glad to find that you intend sending out a supply of Vaccine Matter regularly – it may be the means of saving many lives. It appears by Letters received in the Colony that the Small Pox was raging in Glasgow in the beginning of May – the Vessels from the Clyde may bring it here."[69]

Dr. John Williamson was among the practitioners who sought by means of a vaccine establishment to provide an inexhaustible supply of lymph in Jamaica. He wrote that he "felt no hesitation in strenuously recommending to his friends the adoption of vaccination to prevent small-pox;" and, in his practice from 1801 until he left the island in 1812, "no circumstance occurred to raise a doubt in his mind of its efficacy."[70] In the second edition of *The Medical Assistant*, published in 1809, Dr. Thomas Dancer wrote that little needed to be said on the subject of smallpox since that disorder rarely appeared in the island because of inoculation, which was widely practiced and well understood.[71] Colin Chisholm, M.D., wrote in 1822 that whereas the settled islands in the British West Indies previously had been often visited by the smallpox, it had become very rare since the abolition of the slave trade and the introduction of vaccination.[72]

Writing in 1820, James Thomson, M.D., of Jamaica deemed it superfluous to describe the varieties of smallpox and the mode of treatment in that island.

> Happily for the human race this loathsome malady has been disarmed of all its terrors. Even the practice of inoculation renders it comparatively mild, and vaccination supersedes it entirely, except in some anomalous instances, which are of no authority in estimating the benefits of this blessed discovery. Formerly one subject in seven was supposed to die when the disease was produced in the natural way. By inoculation the mortality was reduced to one in nine hundred.[73]

Dr. Thomson found it "somewhat singular that the practice of inoculation against the small-pox has been known from the remotest ages in many parts of Africa even before the introduction of Mahometanism." He regretted that Europeans in the New World, who styled themselves enlightened, had not learned from their African slaves the art of inoculation at an early period and thus saved the lives of millions. "What a different aspect might the history of human affairs have presented at this time," he enquired in a speculative frame of mind, "had the practice of the discovery sooner become general?"[74]

Seconding Dr. Thomson was Sir Jacob Adolphus, M.D., deputy inspector of military hospitals in Jamaica. In a report of 26 October 1820, he wrote that although he had been often employed in vaccination, he had not seen a case of smallpox since 1804. He noted that before the abolition of the slave trade in 1808, smallpox had been "not unfrequently introduced into this Island in Slave Ships." He minimized the impact of abolition, however, observing that "the slave trade was carried on for some years after the first introduction of vaccination, during which time, as far as I can recollect, small pox was seldom observed and had become a mere sporadic disease, & I may add that this Island has been exempted from its ravages for nearly twenty years."[75]

From the evidence presented here, it can be argued that despite the recurrence of smallpox in the last years of slavery, the widespread practice of inoculation and vaccination reduced this most dreaded plague to a disease of minor consequence in the slave societies of the British Caribbean region. These immunization practices in all likelihood had a substantial impact in reducing the mortality of Afro-West Indian slaves.

10

Slave hospitals

> In the Fourth and Last Division, I make some observations on the food and clothing of Negroes; the sick houses where they are confined; and mention a few important medicines, for which succedaneums are not to be found in the islands, and which no plantation ought ever to be without.
>
> James Grainger, M.D., 1764[1]

The slave hospitals on sugar plantations played an important role in the health care system. In this chapter we look at such features of these hospitals as their siting, construction, interior arrangements, equipment, personnel, and the care and treatment of patients and prisoners. We look especially at the slave hospitals of Jamaica and British Guiana, and compare them with their counterparts in Cuba and the United States. Critical analysis reveals the strengths and weaknesses of slave hospitals.

Introduction

A hospital is a place that provides medical and/or surgical care and treatment for the sick and injured. Traditionally, hospitals have served as both medical schools for practitioners and resting places for patients under observation and treatment. In the Middle Ages hospitals were often constructed adjacent to monasteries, and members of religious orders devoted much of their time to nursing the sick. As Europe expanded overseas, new and often lethal disease environments were created as a result of war, migration, commerce, and natural disasters. Soldiers and sailors were the first to stimulate the building and staffing of hospitals in colonial territories. Military hospitals pioneered new medical knowledge and skill, as well as nursing and custodial procedures. Expanded and diversified hospital facilities were needed to accommodate European immigrants and African slaves. Hospital patients came to be segregated on the basis of race, class, sex, and age. They were also segregated according to the type of disease or accident – for example, surgical or medical cases, contagious or noncontagious cases, and somatic or psychological cases.

Hospitals may also be classified according to whether they are private or public institutions. Whereas public and church-related hospitals played a significant role in the treatment of slaves in the Catholic colonies in Latin America, the private plantation hospital was the preeminent institution in the tropical and subtropical colonies and the former colonies of Protestant European countries. In the British Caribbean colonies the public hospitals were devoted almost exclusively to the treatment of sick and injured Europeans and white Creoles. Jamaica affords an illustration of the antislave bias of the public hospitals. From 1774 to 1826, the Assembly of that island voted money to support army hospitals at Kingston and Spanish Town; marine and naval hospitals at Port Royal, Montego Bay, Savanna-la-mar, and Port Maria; three public baths or spas; and the public hospital at Kingston. In 1791 the staff of the Kingston hospital consisted of a part-time physician, two surgeons, two apothecaries, an assistant, and a white matron who was assisted by five women slaves. In December 1819 a committee of the Assembly recommended that three convalescent wards and twelve cells for "maniacal patients" be added to this hospital, which served only white patients and received most of the money voted in support of public health institutions.[2]

In his exhaustive search of the Kingston Vestry minutes, Edward Brathwaite finds that a "Slave Hospital" was established in 1779 and a "Negro Hospital" in 1812. A close inspection of the journals of the Assembly of Jamaica fails to turn up any record of financial support for these hospitals, however. It would thus appear that, apart from those who were prison or workhouse inmates, the slaves of Jamaica were seldom supplied with hospital and other medical services at public expense. Money was voted annually by the assembly to pay the salaries of doctors who attended the slaves in the jails and workhouses of the island. The workhouses were established in 1791, chiefly as places to confine runaway slaves. The prisoners were set to such productive labor as grinding corn on the treadmills or working in chain gangs on the roads.[3]

The eighteenth-century experience

Sick and injured slaves came to be treated in structures variously known as "sick houses," "hothouses," or "hospitals." Planters built these structures to meet various needs. Hospitals could be provided with the proper conveniences and attendants to care for the sick and indisposed, including medicines, surgical instruments, special diets, hygienic conditions, and personnel consisting of nurses, midwives, apothecaries, physicians, and surgeons. Separate wards might be provided for males and females, for lying-in women, and for patients with infectious diseases. Better supervision might be expected if the hospital was near the planter's or overseer's house. To prevent the spread of communicable diseases and to discourage slaves from feigning illness to avoid plantation labor, hospitals became places of confinement with barred windows, padlocked doors, and nurses who doubled as turnkeys to prevent patients from escaping. Indeed, hospitals were intended not only to improve the health of slaves, but also to serve as prisons for captured runaways and other offenders.

Though slave hospitals may go back to the seventeenth century, they do not appear in the plantation records known to the author until the middle eighteenth century. In his capacity as plantation attorney, Dr. Walter Tullideph of Antigua wrote to an absentee proprietor on 19 June 1749, "I have built a good Sick house at Winthorpes . . ."[4] The appraisement of Samuel Martin's Greencastle plantation in Antigua in 1769 includes "a Long hospital house of Lime and Stone" and "a large Yaws house of 4 Apartments and a Kitchen."[5] The inventory of William Belgrove's plantation in Barbados of 1755 contains "a Sick-House, and a proper Room to confine Negroes . . . £100."[6] John Pinney, a leading planter of Nevis, was somewhat amateurish in the medical care of his slaves, writes Richard Pares: "He had, of course, an hospital (fitted up in a former boiling-house) and a 'lying-in room' for serious cases, immediately under the manager's eye. He was very particular about keeping the sick negroes in the hospital and inspecting them there at least once a day, for if they were allowed to stay in their houses they would malinger – besides they would never get cured." Pinney also "enjoined the strictest caution about the use of lamps at night in the hospital, for negroes were notoriously careless with fire. But though the hospital was to be adequate, he did not much care for calling in the doctor."[7]

Special attention was given to sick houses by Dr. James Grainger in his *Essay on West-India Diseases* (1769). Not only should every plantation have a sick house, he said, but it should also have "a proper hut for the reception of yawey patients; this ought to be to leeward, and at some distance from the sick house, which should be built near the dwelling house, but leeward of it." Every sick house should have a chamber ventilator to windward and should receive some light from the roof. It should have a "necessary," which should be cleaned at least twice a day. It should also be furnished with a hearth and chimney. "Were I to give a model for a complete sick house," wrote Grainger, "it should consist of four detached chambers in a square form; in the centre should be a pump and bathing place; and the whole should be surrounded with a strong lemon or lime-hedge, with a gate to lock. Round the borders such herbs as are more commonly used in physic should be planted; and there should be a walk round the square for the convalescents." Of the four chambers, that to leeward should be appropriated to fevers, smallpox, etc.; that to windward for "chirurgical and common medical cases;" that on the right "for boiling drinks, victuals, &c. of the sick, and for lodging the nurse; with a little surgery;" and that on the left for the reception of patients with venereal diseases. Grainger wrote that the windward ward should have a piazza, and each ward a necessary and ventilator except the kitchen, which should be cooled by a window. "This plan would doubtless cost money," he admitted, "but if we must have slaves, our own interest would, me-thinks, teach us to take all imaginable care of them when they become sickly."[8]

Besides the white doctor, who was to make a weekly visit, Grainger's model hospital was to be staffed by a black doctor and a black nurse. He called for a "sensible Negroe" to be instructed "to bleed, give glysters, dress fresh wounds, spread plasters, and dress ulcers. This is of great consequence." Grainger complained that nurses were commonly so old that they could not take proper care of the sick. Instead, the nurse should be "strong, sensible, and sober. It is a most important office in a plantation," he wrote.[9]

By 1789 the treatment of slaves in health, sickness, and old age had become a concern to the British government. In that year the Privy Council committee put the following questions to witnesses: "What Care is taken of the Slaves in Sickness? Are there any Laws or Regulations for that Purpose? What Provision is made for them when old or disabled? Are their Masters obliged, in most Cases, to maintain them?" While admitting that there were no laws or regulations to oblige masters to care for the sick and aged, absentee proprietors testified that humanity and interest took the place of law. Planters from several islands testified that on most or all plantations there were hospitals for the sick, that each hospital had a black doctor or doctress and one or two black nurses, and that patients were supplied with medicine, nourishing food, and other comforts as directed by the white doctor.[10]

Governor Seton of St. Vincent, for example, testified in 1789 that on every plantation of any consequence, "there is a House allotted for the Reception of the Sick, and One or Two Nurses appointed to attend them. Medicines proper for their different Complaints are administered to them, under the Direction of the Physician; and Panado, Gruel, Sago, or other Food, supplied them by their Masters." Seton said that self-interest exclusive of any considerations of humanity motivated the planters to supply these services, which, although not established by law, was the common custom of the country.[11]

Voicing a minority opinion was James Tobin, a former planter of Nevis and St. Kitts. He testified before the Select Committee of the House of Commons on the Slave Trade in 1790 that many planters held that hospitals for the sick were "more detrimental than useful, as they are one means of increasing epidemical disorders, and on estates where a greater number of

Negroes are Creoles, the sick Negroes and lying-in women find themselves more at ease in their own houses, than in an hospital." Moreover, he said that it was not a general practice to have rooms in the hospital appropriated to the use of lying-in women.[12]

Critics of the planters gave a dismal picture of the treatment of sick slaves. The Reverend James Ramsay, who had firsthand experience with slavery in St. Kitts, said that although a surgeon was generally employed by the year to attend the sick slaves, some frugal planters trusted to their own skill. He wrote that the food of the sick was "often musty, indigestible horse beans, sometimes maize, flour, or rice; sometimes, as a dainty, brown biscuit. On some plantations, the manager is allowed to get, now-and-then, a fowl, or a kid to make soup for them. Sometimes the owner sends the manager a cask of wine, a few glasses of which are supposed to be for the use of the sick." Ramsay makes no mention of slave hospitals.[13] In his *Brief Account of the Island of Antigua* (1789), John Luffman wrote that every planter had a hospital or sick house "where the slaves as soon as infected with disorder, or having received hurt (the latter of which frequently happens in crop time), are sent." The hospitals that he saw were said to be "as bad you can well suppose, being not only destitute of almost every convenience, but filthy in the extreme, and the attendants generally such negroes as are nearly superannuated or unfit for active employment."[14]

Slaves often objected to being confined to hospitals when they were sick. Among other things, they were repelled by the stench and foul-tasting medicines and feared to go to a place where other slaves had died. In his testimony, Dr. Robert Thomas of Nevis said that he objected to allowing sick slaves to remain in their huts because, in that dispersed state, it was impossible for them to be cared for as constantly as when they were hospitalized. He was aware, however, that most of the "good and well-inclined negroes" shunned the hospital when they were ill, not wishing to be lodged under the same roof with those who were confined for misconduct. Thomas Cooper, a Unitarian missionary, thought that the slaves disliked being shut up in the hospital because it separated them from the kindness of their friends. They preferred being in their own houses, he said, even though in a miserable state.[15]

Laws and ordinances calling for suitable slave hospitals and lying-in wards were enacted in the 1790s. The detailed slave code enacted by the General Assembly of the Leeward Islands in 1798 contains clauses providing for hospitals and lying-in wards. A fine of a hundred pounds was imposed on masters who did not provide their slaves with "a commodious Hospital or Sick House, furnished with proper Conveniences for the Sick, and sufficient Number of Attendants." A penalty of twenty shillings was levied for failure by the master or some white person under his direction to "attend as often as may be requisite at the Hospital or Sick House, to see that the Sick are furnished with the Medicines that may be ordered for them by the said Practitioner or his Assistant, in the Manner so ordered, and also with such Diet as the said Practitioner or his Assistant shall reasonably direct to be given." In another clause the master was required to provide either a two-room house or accommodation in a lying-in section of the hospital for women in their first pregnancy. It was forbidden to give women heavy work during pregnancy or to subject them to punishment except for imprisonment. Another clause imposed a fine if sick and disabled slaves were not provided with ample food and necessaries.[16] Elsa Goveia, in her summary of the act of 1798, writes that its great weakness as a measure for providing legal and practical amelioration was that it completely lacked an effective executive principle and its enforcement was therefore difficult.[17]

By the Jamaica slave law of 1826, all sick or infirm slaves were to be clothed, housed, attended, and properly maintained by their owners, under a penalty of twenty pounds for every instance of neglect. Any sick or destitute slave who was found at large was to be taken to the workhouse and there maintained (but not worked) at the expense of the owner, until removed to his property.[18]

In the crown colony of Trinidad, slavery amelioration measures were proclaimed by the governor, who had absolute power from the conquest of the island in 1797 to the year 1801. On 30 June 1800 Governor Thomas Picton proclaimed an ordinance that required owners of slaves "to lodge, clothe, and maintain them sufficiently, as well in health, while able to work, as in time of sickness, age and infirmity." Article 13 of the ordinance provided: "There shall be on every plantation a hospital, proportioned to the number of its slaves, and one or more female attendants attached thereto. The Negro who from sickness is incapable of doing his duty shall there be lodged and attended until he is perfectly recovered; and here it is proper to observe that careful nursing is generally found the most efficacious remedy in Negro disorders." Moreover, the ordinance required the owner or manager of each plantation to "keep a hospital diary, on which he will note the date of admission and discharge, or decease of the slave; and on giving in the annual enumeration of the estate, he will make also an obituary report."[19]

That the moral suasion of Parliament may have led to private decisions to build slave hospitals and lying-in wards is suggested by three pieces of evidence for Jamaica. On Orange Valley estate in the parish of Trelawny the ruins of a two-story slave hospital of native stone construction still stand (Figure 10.1). The Latin inscription on the tablet over the door of this hospital translates into English as: "This hospital was built at the instance of H. N. Jarrett Esq., E. Earl being the architect and R. Harris the foreman, A.D. 1797. 'Not unmindful of the sick and wretched.' "[20]

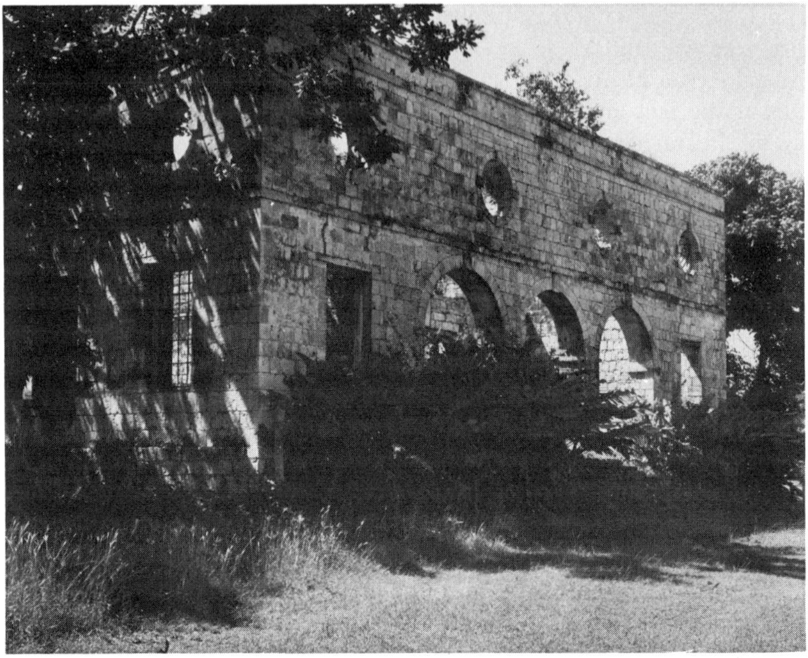

Figure 10.1. Orange Valley estate hospital, Jamaica. Photographed in 1974 by Mr. P. J. Hanbury Tenison of Good Hope estate.

The second piece of evidence is the "Plan of the Hospital for the sick Slaves upon Good Hope Estate the Property of John Tharp Esquire Situated in the Parish of Trelawny, 1798" (Figure 10.2). The building is still standing in a ruined state (Figure 10.3).[21] It is 82.6 feet long and 60 feet wide, with external stone walls 2 feet thick. The fifteen rooms on the first floor, each 12 feet high, consisted of a lobby, a medicine room, a room for the doctor in dangerous cases, three wards for women, kitchen for women, water closet for women, three wards for men, kitchen for men, water closet for men, passage to men's apartments, and passage to women's apartments. On the second floor, which was 10 feet high, there was a lobby for women, stairs to the women's apartments, a lobby for men, and stairs to the men's apartments. The other apartments on the second floor were precisely the same as those on the first floor. Two Quaker visitors from England visited the Tharp properties in 1837. They noted that Good Hope was the center of nine contiguous estates belonging to the Tharp family and comprising a population of 2,000 ex-slaves or apprentices. "The hospital," they wrote, "which is almost large enough for a county penitentiary, was originally built

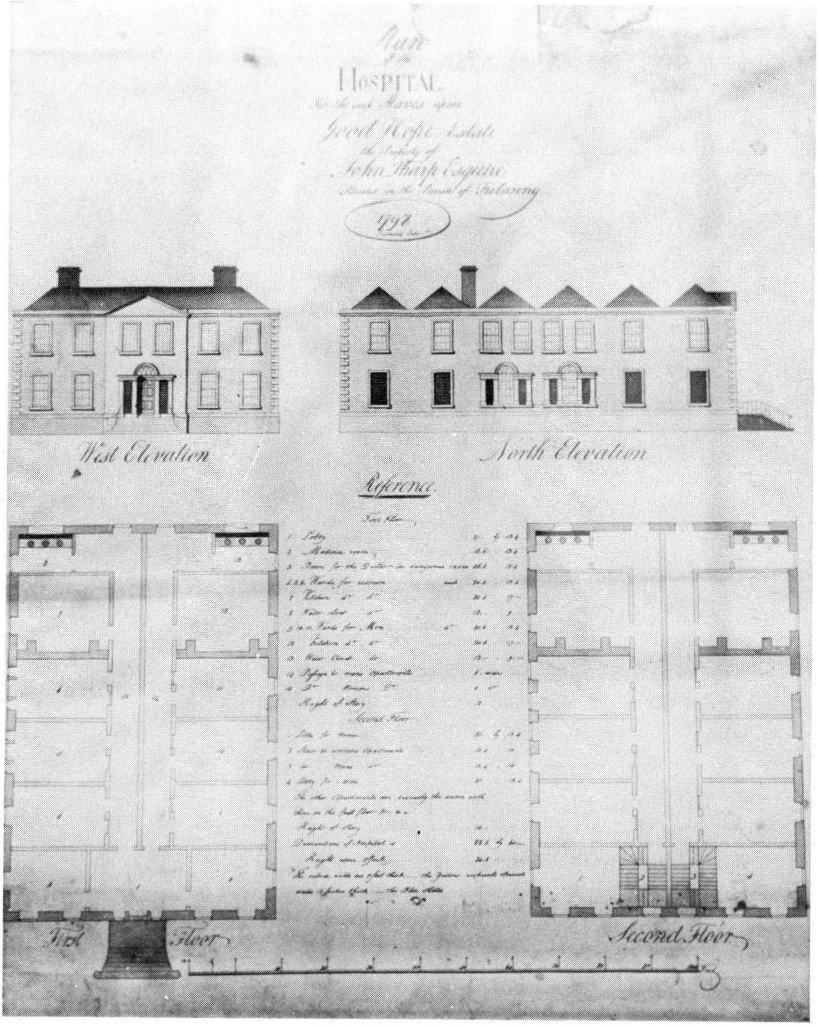

Figure 10.2. Plan of Good Hope estate hospital, Jamaica, 1798. Photographed by Mr. P. J. Hanbury Tenison of Good Hope estate.

for the joint purposes of a hospital and place of punishment for the nine estates; but is now appropriated as a hospital, school, and church."[22]

The third piece of evidence is a letter from one of the Scottish trustees of the estate of a deceased absentee proprietor of Jamaica to the manager of Dundee plantation in that island, saying, "I would not grudge being at

Figure 10.3. Good Hope estate hospital, Jamaica. Photographed in 1974 by Mr. P. J. Hanbury Tenison of Good Hope estate.

some expence for a Comfortable Room or two for lying-in Women, who are not well lodged in their own Houses. There used to be a Room in the Hothouse appropriated to them, but on my recollection it was subject to smoke. I do not know if one Child in Ten born on Dundee ever attained to Seven years old, surely therefore any attempt to alleviate this dreadful disease [tetanus] must command attention from every humane person."[23]

Practical rules for hospital management

The impelling motive to improve the condition of the slaves in the years prior to abolition in 1808 stemmed from the rise in the price of newly imported Africans and the planters' fear that Parliament would cut off their external supply. Certain doctors and planters drew on their extensive experience to write treatises for the instruction and guidance of their fellow planters. To Philip Gibbes, a Barbados proprietor, hospitals were needed for the preservation of the blacks. He wrote that he could not "too much lament the parsimony of the proprietors of plantations, who can behold a regular decrease of their negroes without attention to some of the most obvious means of preserving them." He urged that every plantation have a hospital equipped with a separate ward for each sick person and distinct apartments for the male and female convalescents. Gibbes said he knew from his own experience that the utility and comfort afforded by a hospital to sick slaves would soon repay the expense of building one. There should also be a proper room in the hospital for pregnant women to lie in. Fresh air and quiet were essential to the preservation of infants in the first month, and especially the first nine days, of their lives. The master who refused these comforts to his slaves, wrote Gibbes, "denies himself the satisfaction, which he would feel, as a good Christian, from the reflection, that he had fulfilled his duty, and as a worldly man, from the consideration that he has promoted his interest."[24]

One of the doctor-planters who claimed success in preserving the health and encouraging the breeding of slaves was Dr. David Collins of St. Vincent. In his *Practical Rules for the Management and Medical Treatment of Negro Slaves* (1803), he includes chapters "On the Sick" and "On the Hospital." Collins wrote that he was sorry to confess "that no part of negro management had been more neglected, or erroneously performed, than that which regards the treatment of the sick. I have seen many slaves, that were compelled to persevere at their work, who ought to have been in the hospital." In part, this was due to the impatience of the master to advance his work, but much more to the difficulty of "distinguishing real and affected illness." Even with slaves who were really sick there was still much to condemn, he said, "for, where negroes are labouring in the hospital under severe complaints, they are not commonly attended to as they ought to be." Collins also blamed the frequent neglect of the sick on the sorry condition of the hospital. "For the hospital being rather a disgusting scene, charged with unpleasant odours, and occupied by offensive objects, it is no wonder that men should neglect a duty, the performance of which is attended with painful emotions."[25]

Dr. Collins recommended that the hospital should be as near as possible to the dwelling place of the planter or his manager. Where the sick house was remote from the family dwelling, the slaves were overlooked and forgotten; they lingered in misery and pined in neglect, and if they recovered the planter could be assured it was nature that had carried them through the disorder. On the other hand, if the hospital was near the family, the slaves would be forced on their notice and would receive more careful attention. Indeed, he wished that the hospital were placed so "that not a sigh, nor a cough, nor a groan, should issue therefrom, without reaching the ears of those from whom relief ought to come, as, in that case, it will pretty certainly be administered."[26]

It was not enough to commit the care of sick slaves to the joint labors of the attendant doctor and the sick nurse or nurses. The master should realize that the doctor was not always present to see that his orders were carried out and that nurses were frequently ignorant or inattentive to the needs of the patients. Furthermore, Collins urged proprietors and managers to study medical books with practical precepts for the cure of tropical diseases. After a year's attention to the sick house with the example of the doctor and the aid of a few medical books, the planter of ordinary capacity might prescribe for the common disorders of his slaves, but by no means supersede the doctor who had been regularly educated to the profession. The planter who had some knowledge of medicine would, moreover, be able to distinguish between slaves who needed treatment and those who feigned illness to avoid plantation labor.[27]

Dr. Collins's plan for the hospital was no doubt ambitious. It was indispensable, he said, to have four separate apartments: "one for the male negroes, one for the female, a third for such as labour under dangerous diseases, requiring particular attention, and the fourth for the sick-nurses, who are to superintend them." The size of each of the apartments should be in proportion to the probable number of patients. The walls should be of stone and thick enough to preserve a constant temperature in the apartment throughout the day. Each apartment would be well ventilated. Each room should have a toilet. Beds could be separate or consist of platforms of boards about six and a half feet long. To keep the hospital clean, the floors should be sprinkled every morning, the boards of the bedplace scoured every week, and the walls and ceiling whitewashed with lime. Each patient was to receive a blanket. Bedpans were to be supplied to patients who were too weak to rise and also for dysenteric patients. In the nurse's room there should be a small closet "provided with tow, lint, basilicon, Turner's cerate, and powders of verdigrise, and blue vitriol, for the dressing of negro sores; and also of other common articles, of which she will stand, frequently, in need. Her apartment should be furnished with a chimney and fire-place, for the purpose of heating water, and for preparing sago, panada, or any other slops which may be ordered for the sick" (see Chapter 3).[28]

That infirm and superannuated women were usually selected by planters as hospital nurses was deplorable to Dr. Collins. Such women commonly lacked the strength and character to command the respect and obedience of the sick. Nursing was so important that the best black woman in the gang was not too good for the office, he believed. "Pains should be taken to instruct her in the use of the simples of the country, which she will soon acquire; the dressing of sores, and the doses of different purges and vomits." Having acquired such qualifications, the woman would be employed infinitely more advantageously as a nurse than as a fieldworker or in any other occupation.[29]

Rather surprisingly, Dr. Collins thought it was good policy to use the hospital as a prison. He cautioned that the windows should be fortified with bars or jalousies to prevent the escape of patients and inmates. In each of the apartments there should be a pair of stocks. These served the dual purpose of punishing the refractory and keeping patients with sores that were difficult to heal in a recumbent posture. Healthy slaves whose offenses were too light to be consigned to the dungeon should be put into the hospital. Dr. Collins regarded this as a suitable punishment, far superior to the whip and an effective substitute for it.[30]

Slave hospitals in Guyana

The Gladstone Papers give a mixed picture of slave hospitals in Demerara from 1816 to 1828. From the inventories of Sir John Gladstone's plantations in Demerara we learn that there was no hospital for the 175 slaves on Covenden plantation. For the 244 slaves on Vredestein and L'Incertitude, the hospital that rested on a brick foundation was 40 feet by 24 feet; on Mon Repos the 244 slaves had a hospital 52 feet long by 18 feet wide; on Vreeden Hoop, with 348 slaves, a new hospital was being erected in November 1825. It was 50 feet long by 32 feet wide, two stories high, and resting on brick pillars. Gladstone's plantation attorney wrote in September 1828 of "a sad continuance of sickness" on Success plantation, "but the mortality has been confined to useless Invalids & two young Children." He found the hospital much too small to accommodate the sick and had to put some of the patients in temporary quarters. Gladstone was told that "as soon as the Carpenters can be spared from the Negro houses, which require a great deal of work, we must erect a new Hospital."[31]

The reports of doctors give an idealized view of hospitals and the medical treatment of slaves in Demerara and Essequibo because they were solicited by the planters to strengthen their case in the debate on slavery. One lengthy report was submitted by Dr. Thomas Bell on 19 March 1824. As a medical practitioner with eight years of experience in Essequibo, he said he generally attended an average of 2,500 blacks, together with the "usual proportion of whites."[32]

> With respect to the hospital accommodation, the buildings erected for that purpose, are in general lofty, spacious and well ventilated. Some hospitals built within the last four or five years are finished in a style

> equal to a proprietor's dwelling-house; the window sashes hung on pullies to let up and down, the walls and ceilings painted, the apartments well arranged and neatly finished, built on brick pillars seven or eight feet from the ground, two stories high from the pillars, and some are three stories, with airy comfortable apartments in the upper story, for the lying-in women. One room is set apart for a pharmacy, and another for the residence of the head sick nurse, and as a store room for spare blankets, &c.
>
> Besides the lying-in rooms in the upper story, and the small apartments already mentioned, the hospital is generally divided into two or more wards for the reception of all cases except serious ulcers, and lacerated and contused wounds; these rooms are fitted out with platforms raised about 14 or 16 inches from the floor; which platforms are inclined planes of a very small degree of elevation, about 6½ feet in depth, and generally the whole length of one or more sides of the room; in these the patients' mattresses, blankets, &c. are placed, and they very completely answer the purposes of bedsteads, to which the platform is in many respects preferable.
>
> Two or more rooms are also set apart, and furnished with platforms and stocks for serious ulcers, punctures, lacerations and contusions from nails, splinters, &c.; rest and the horizontal position being absolutely necessary for the cure of the ulcers, and as a preventative of that fatal disease *tetanus*, so commonly the consequence of the above description of wounds. These stocks are merely intended to prevent the patients from retarding their recovery by walking about, and not observing the directions for keeping their legs in the horizontal position; this is done by medical advice, and not as a punishment to the parties, nor is it at all considered as a punishment or disgrace by the negroes themselves.[33]

Bell explained that the hospital contained other wooden stocks for slaves who were punished for transgressions. Although he questioned the wisdom of putting lawbreakers in the same hospital room with patients, he found that the former were so few in number and their incarceration was so short that separate stocks were quite unnecessary.[34]

Slave hospitals in Jamaica

Whether the slave hospitals of Jamaica were a boon or a bane to sick and injured slaves is not clear from extant records. Conflicting accounts of the efficacy of hospitals can be explained in part by the political contest over slavery, which pitted pro- against antislavery writers. Dr. William Sells, who practiced medicine among the slaves of Jamaica, reported favorably on slave hospitals. He told a committee of the Jamaica House of Assembly in 1815 that there was no plantation where a hospital was not provided. Hospitals were generally extensive, he said, under good regulation with respect to cleanliness and ventilation, and attended by a regularly bred practitioner. Dr. Sells said that the master supplied not only medicines, but also such special items as wine, rice, flour, sugar, and animal food.[35] According to H. T. De La Beche, a Jamaica sugar planter, "every estate has an hot-house, as the negroes are pleased to call it, which of course varies in dimensions and comforts in different places; they are in general perfectly well adapted to the purposes intended, and are regularly attended, by white medical men. Many of these buildings, that I have seen, were large, and properly divided into wards."[36] Bernard Martin Senior, a retired military officer who lived in Jamaica, wrote that on every property of any extent there was "a hospital, called the *hot-house*, for the reception of sick negroes, where great attention is paid to all who are really indisposed." A well-supplied medicine chest was kept in the overseer's house, and a white medical man was regularly paid for his attendance. Moreover, a careful black slave was excused from all work to give his or her whole attention daily at the hospital and nightly when necessary.[37]

Another group of writers included doctors and planters who, while defending slavery, saw reason to criticize the treatment of sick slaves. One of these critics was John Williamson, M.D., whose journal is an invaluable source on the history of slave medicine. Writing on 30 November 1798, he noted the "imperfect confused manner" that was adopted for the treatment of sick blacks in hothouses or hospitals. Despite serious deficiencies, he conceded that great pains were taken to promote the comfort and recovery of slaves who were dangerously ill. On 29 August 1799 Dr. Williamson wrote that although the subject had been often suggested, the legislature of Jamaica had "not interfered in the important matter of due attendance being given to the sick, and that their necessary comfort should be secured." About a year later he treated a slave at Prospect plantation where there was no suitable place for the sick. "The want of a hospital," he wrote, "under tolerable management, really puts it out of the power of any practitioner to get justice done to his prescriptions." Upon his visit to a hospital in August 1801, Dr. Williamson was disappointed to find that no provision had been made for hot and cold baths, which he considered one of the best remedies against diseases that resulted from suppressed perspiration. Moreover, baths contributed to the cleanliness of the patients, which was much neglected.[38]

Gilbert Mathison was a Jamaican proprietor who returned to the island after an extended absence to improve the lot of his slaves in the years after the abolition of the slave trade. He believed that the hospital establishment on many plantations required much improvement. It should be the duty of the overseer, he said, to take care that the sick were properly fed and attended to and the hospital kept very clean. The bookkeeper or overseer should attend in the hospital twice a day to see that medicines were properly administered and other wants properly supplied. "In cases of dangerous illness," wrote Mathison, "the overseer cannot be too often in the hospital." There should be a lying-in house where the midwife was always in attendance. There should be a hospital attached to the nursery where children who required medical attendance would be received. Finally, a separate hospital should be provided for blacks afflicted with the yaws.[39]

By far the most colorful and intimate view of hospitals in the era of slavery is in the journal of Matthew Gregory ("Monk") Lewis. Before leaving his Cornwall plantation in Jamaica in April 1816, Lewis ordered that "a new hospital for the lying-in women, and for those who might be seriously ill, should be built, and made as comfortable as possible; while the present one should be reserved for those whom the physicians might declare to be very slightly indisposed, or not ill at all." Furthermore, he ordered that the doors should be kept constantly locked and that the sexes be placed in separate chambers to prevent the hospital being made "a place of amusement by the lazy and lying, as is the case at present." Soon after Lewis returned to Jamaica in January 1818, the opening of the new hospital was made a festive occasion "to connect it as much as possible with pleasurable associations." The rooms were sprinkled with Madeira wine for good luck, and "the toast of 'Health to the new hospital, and shame to the old lazy house!' was drunk by the trustee, the doctoresses, the governors, &c." New clothes were then distributed, after which the blacks fell to dancing, singing, and drinking rum and sugar until the early hours of the sabbath.[40]

Lewis was concerned to prevent his slaves from feigning illness to avoid labor, but his rule was that no one was denied admittance. Even if no symptoms of illness were discovered, the slave was allowed one day to rest and take medicine. If the slave continued to insist that he was ill despite the doctor's opinion that he was shamming, he was "locked up in a room with others similarly circumstanced, where care is taken to supply him with food, water, physic, &c., and no restraint is imposed except that of not going out. Here he is suffered to remain unmolested as long as he pleases, and he is only allowed to leave the hospital upon his own declaration that he is well enough to go to work; when the door is opened, and he walks away unreproached and unpunished, however evident his deception may have been." Lewis said that before he adopted this rule he had thirty to forty-five patients daily, of whom not more than a dozen had anything the matter with them. After the regulation was in force the number of patients declined significantly.[41]

Like "Monk" Lewis, Thomas Roughley was much concerned with slaves who feigned illness to avoid labor. He believed that if they were not checked, the whole labor force of a plantation would present themselves for admittance to the hospital to avoid labor. They would strive to deceive even the wary, experienced overseer, prolonging their hospitalization by such means and irritating and keeping alive old sores. Slaves who had serious disorders were no doubt caught up with those who were believed to be feigning illness to "effect their lazy purpose of sitting down in the hospital." Roughley recommended that slaves suspected of feigning illness be given a large dose of some simple medicine and strictly confined to the hospital. "If no practising doctor is employed for the property," he wrote, "let them remain there for two or three days, and if nothing apparently ails them, send them to their work. If a doctor is employed, let him examine into their respective cases; if not found unwell, send them to their work again; and let a regular hothouse book be kept of what medicines are ordered and administered, when they are taken in, and when turned out." Roughley considered it the overseer's duty to do all in his power to free the hospital of its patients by restoring them "to renovated vigour and health."[42]

Conflicts frequently developed between doctors who sought to cure sick slaves and proprietors and overseers who believed that slaves took advantage of doctors and the hospital staff to feign illness and thus avoid work. The story of one such conflict was told by Benjamin McMahon, a bookkeeper on a coffee plantation in Jamaica. Believing that one of his slaves was pretending illness, the master resolved to "cure" him by administering six grains of tartar emetic. After several hours of retching, the slave died. The doctor arrived at the plantation shortly after the slave's death and inserted a note in the hospital book that the man had died from an overdose of tartar emetic. The proprietor then discharged the doctor, who retaliated by writing to the authorities in Kingston the circumstances of the death. An inquest was held, but the coroner and jurors, who were friends of the proprietor, returned a verdict, "Died by the visitation of God." A few weeks later the doctor was discharged from the practice of every plantation in the district. Furthermore, the proprietor sued the doctor for defamation of character and obtained a verdict "from a jury of planters like himself of one thousand pounds when poor Craig [the doctor] had not one thousand pence. The jury were quite exasperated at the idea of any white man daring to expose another, merely for being the cause of the death of a common negro. Craig was entirely ruined by this matter, and died not long after."[43]

Some slaves were treated in hospitals conducted by doctor-proprietors on a fee-paying basis. One Kingston doctor advertised that he had enlarged his infirmary where medical attendance and medicine would be given to "Wharf and Family Negroes, at 13*s.* 4*d.* each per annum, payable quarterly." Another doctor advertised that he would receive a few diseased slaves "(those with Coco-Bay and Yaws excepted)" at his pen, where they would be under his immediate supervision.[44]

Critics of hospital management

Highly critical of the treatment of sick slaves and the adequacy of the hospitals were certain men who lived in or visited the West Indies from about 1800 to 1834. Included among these critics of the planters and their peculiar institution were clergymen, missionaries, barristers, and overseers.

After his visit to the West Indies and particularly Jamaica, the Reverend Richard Bickell presented "a Real Picture of Slavery" upon returning to England in 1825. Having been on a great many plantations and seeing plenty of doctors, he said he never saw any flattering specimens of the boasted great care taken of sick slaves.

> Their hot-houses, or hospitals are, generally speaking, filthy receptacles; they are very happily styled hot-houses, for they are hot enough; as the hospital is, on most estates, a confined room, very often an earthen floor: in this, is a platform of boards, raised two or three feet high, like the soldier's guard-bed, on which the sick lie down in their own clothes, covered sometimes with a blanket, and sometimes not: on some large estates they have a superior kind of hospital, on a first floor, with better accommodations. The hot-house is often the place, where the Negroes are also confined in the stocks; so that it is both hospital and gaol.

Instead of making frequent visits, the doctor commonly visited the hospital once or twice a week, more frequently only once, unless on large estates. The "poor sick Negro" on the largest estates was "pretty sure of getting something from the master's table, but is not always so on small and poor properties, unless the overseer be very humane, and certainly there are many humane men among them."[45]

One of the most formidable critics of slavery was James Stephen, who was a barrister in St. Kitts before he returned to England to become a leader of the antislavery crusade. Stephen included a chapter in *The Slavery of the British West India Colonies Delineated*, in which he charged that sick slaves were treated with great harshness, neglect, and inhumanity. Stephen drew heavily from Dr. Collins's book on the medical treatment of slaves, both praising him for exposing evils and recommending improvements and criticizing him for defending colonial slavery as an institution fit to be upheld. Stephen praised Collins for calling attention to the fact that "poor patients have very little medical attention to compensate their painful confinement in the sick house." They were inadequately nursed by "a weakly old woman, unfit for ordinary labour," who was expected to attend all the patients, male and female, and with no assistance administer the medicines as well as keep the patients safely locked up and watch against their escape (see Chapter 3).[46]

On the other hand, Dr. Collins was criticized for his conciliatory and compromising maxims. Stephen thought Collins should have censured his fellow planters more for giving their sick inmates no allowance of food for their support. The fact that there were no bedsteads or bedding in the hospital was another deficiency Collins was charged with passing over without concern for the ease and comfort of the poor patients.[47] Stephen was most surprised that "the humane Dr. Collins should acquiesce in, and even approve the practice" of confining together in one building "the unoffending sick, the suspected imposters, and the convicts, so to call them, of their own dread tribunals." Stephen thought that the fear of infection might alone suffice to prevent these disparate groups from being confined in the hospital. He held out little hope that a separate building strong enough for the safe custody of the prisoners would be built. Not only would a prison be expensive to construct, he affirmed, but it would also require the constant time of at least a single slave or keeper. Indeed, the master key to the whole system was "the pinching, niggardly parsimony of which the master's profits, from sugar planting, and most commonly his escape from ruin, are felt by him to depend." Slaves were faced with the alternative of turning out for work in the field or reporting to the sick house. Stephen regarded this alternative, like many other severities, as a "necessary consequence of the cruel institution itself, while it is permitted to exist." Rather than being locked up in a narrow and loathsome prison, Stephen asked whether it would not be preferable for the sick or complaining black to be "allowed to retire to his own hut, to have there the society of his wife, children, and connections, to be cheered and nursed by their affectionate care while confined to his pallet; and to enjoy during convalescence, relaxation in the open air?"[48]

Because printed works on slavery are always more or less biased according to the authors' attitudes, it is fortunate that private manuscripts are extant to give a reasonably authentic account of the treatment of slaves. One such manuscript is a lengthy report from an agent on the management of his principal's plantations in the West Indies. In 1824 James Adam Gordon, an absentee proprietor who lived in England, sent John Johnson to inspect and report on his four sugar plantations and other properties in the islands of St. Kitts, Antigua, and St. Vincent. Altogether these properties contained 701 slaves.

During a visit that lasted from early February to late September 1824, Johnson lived chiefly in Antigua where two of Gordon's plantations were situated. On Sanderson's estate he observed that although the hospital and lying-in establishment were in a satisfactory state, they were still open to important improvements. "The Window Shutters were much decayed and admitted the Wind," he wrote, "many of the Beds were also wanting repair, and contrary to my expectations I observed that the rooms were not swept every morning, and were by no means clean." Johnson explained that one of the buildings of an old sugar works had been converted into a hospital on Sanderson's estate. His sketch of the hospital indicates it had few windows or doors on the two sides he chose to portray.[49]

Confining sick slaves to the hospital was no easy task. Johnson observed that the blacks had a great aversion to being kept in the "sick house" during their illness. If they could escape to their huts they would do so, "not unfrequently carrying disease among the healthy part of the Gang; and thereby occasionally aggravating their disorder by taking cold, or deviating from the regimen prescribed." To correct these faults, Johnson called for strict compliance with the rules and regulations of the hospital.[50]

Moreover, Johnson very much feared that many slaves had died from improper treatment or lack of attention in administering medicine by the sick nurse, who was an old slave and had little knowledge or aptitude for her office.

> The Doctor attends the Estate, sees the several patients, prescribes for them in the Sick-Book, which is afterwards forwarded to his Residence (unless it happens that Medicines are provided by the property) and the Messenger returns with several compounds, most frequently made up by his assistant – these are transferred by the Manager to the Sick Nurse who (not possessing a knowledge of Letters) as she receives her directions places each packet between her several fingers each of which it is presumed represents in her mind the patients to whom they are to be administered. Several circumstances affecting the safety of patients have passed under my own observation, but I have advanced sufficient in favor of the opinion that the Medicines should be on the Property, and if not administered by the Doctor, at least they should be prepared by him, and placed in such order on the spot as to preclude the possibility of an error.[51]

It was essential, Johnson asserted, that the doctor visit the hospital regularly twice a week and that the attorney or manager attend him in the hospital. Owing to ill health, the doctor had absented himself from Sanderson's estate for a considerable time and had entrusted the medical care of the slaves to an apothecary in the town of St. John's. The apothecary, in turn, had failed to visit the hospital, whereupon Johnson lost no time in appointing another person who had been very diligent in his attendance and attention to the sick and in whose ability he had great confidence.[52]

In his inspection of Lavington's estate in Antigua, Johnson found the hospital to be much too small and confined. He ordered it to be enlarged and put under the same regulations that had been drawn up for Sanderson's estate. Again, Johnson found that the doctor at Lavington's had not visited the hospital regularly twice a week and had neglected to record in the "sick book" the nature of the complaints of which patients had died. He forthwith transferred the medical attendance to the doctor who had been recently appointed to Sanderson's estate.[53]

Most shocking to Johnson's sensibility and respect for cleanliness and good order was the state of the hospital on Fairhall and Brebner estate in St. Vincent. He described the hospital as

> a wooden Structure of two compartments for the Males and Females of not more than 12 feet square each, rendered extremely dark by being surrounded by the other abovementioned buildings, and *extremely unhealthy* by the Horse Stable *being not only immediately attached to it, but directly to Windward of it.* This Circumstance I noticed in the presence of the Doctor as also the confined situation and dimensions of the Building, and the shameful accumulation of cobwebs which hung from the roof within reach of the hand – and, in short, the general dirty condition of the whole establishment.

Johnson forthwith ordered that the stable be removed and the hospital cleaned and whitewashed.[54]

Slave hospitals in Cuba and the United States

By contrast with Jamaica, where public health services were limited and sick slaves were seldom admitted to public hospitals, Cuba came to have wide-ranging health services in urban areas. The San Ambrosio military hospital in Havana was expanded to provide for a mixed group of patients, including wards for sick slaves and convicts and other wards for military officers and civilians and clergy of high rank. Moreover, Havana and other Cuban cities had specialty hospitals for women, slaves, convicts, the insane, and victims of leprosy. Nuns and friars administered numerous hospitals, while monasteries provided shelters for "the destitute, aged, and infirm – most of them old slaves and freedmen."[55]

Although some Cuban sugar and coffee plantations had hospitals for their slaves, it is doubtful whether these establishments compared in number and quality to those of Jamaica. The author has found few extant accounts of such hospitals. David Turnbull, British consul at Havana, visited several sugar plantations in the 1830s. On one property he observed a very large two-story stone building with strongly barred windows. He was told by the overseer that this "prison-like building" was the "infirmeria." It was evidently large enough to accommodate the whole population of 211 slaves on this plantation. Richard Henry Dana, Jr., the American writer, visited Cuba in 1859. On one sugar plantation he observed a row of stone buildings, comprising the storehouse, the penitentiary, the hospital, and the lying-in room. "The hospital and lying-in room are airy, well-ventilated, and suitable for their purposes," he wrote.[56]

In providing public health facilities for urban slaves and freedmen, the state of Virginia was perhaps more like Cuba than Jamaica. "Old slaves," according to Todd L. Savitt, "were fed, sheltered, clothed, and provided with medical care until their deaths, regardless of the length of their 'retirement.' " Slave owners who were unable to bear such charges were sometimes aided by city governments. Those who could pay took advantage of public and private hospitals, which were usually open to slaves as well as free blacks and whites. For example, two hospitals in Richmond admitted slaves at lower charges than those paid by whites, and a third hospital in that city was devoted entirely to the care of black slaves. When smallpox and cholera threatened all lives regardless of race or condition, slaves and freedmen were vaccinated free of charge and indigent blacks usually received free medical care in temporary hospitals called pesthouses.[57]

Plantation hospitals in the antebellum South ranged from one-room cabins or a room in the master's house to two-story stone structures with as many as six rooms or wards. Few large plantations in the sugar-growing region of Louisiana were without hospitals. One British journalist noted that the hospital he visited on a sugar plantation was in the charge of an old Negress and the patients were visited regularly by a doctor. "The naked rooms," he wrote, "contained several flock beds on rough stands, and five patients, three of whom were women . . . They were suffering from pneumonia and swellings of the glands of the neck; one man had fever." The visitor remarked that the patients sat listlessly on the beds, staring into space; "no books to amuse them, no conversation – nothing but their own dull thoughts, if they had any."[58]

Slave hospitals in Virginia varied from farm to farm and were probably less common than in the Deep South, where the labor force on cotton and rice plantations was generally larger than that on tobacco farms. In Mississippi some of the larger plantations had separate hospital buildings, but on small properties the sick blacks who needed careful attention were sometimes brought into the home of the master. In other cases, slaves were sent to hospitals that were built and maintained by doctors especially for sick slaves.[59] William Dosite Postell says that both planters and physicians strongly recommended that planters establish hospitals on their plantations. One planter advised his fellow planters as follows: "An hospital should be on each plantation, with proper nurses and apartments for lying-in women, for the men, and for a nursery; when any enter, not to leave the house until discharged."[60]

Postell observes that a clinic or pharmacy was frequently attached to the hospital. The equipment and instruments in the inventory of one pharmacy included "microscope and slides, nursing bottles, mortar and pestle, pharmaceutical scales, breast pumps, bleeding cups, feeding cups, liters, alcohol lamps, box of blue mass, and vapor-bath apparatus." An inventory of another pharmacy contained an itemized list of 166 separate medicinal items, plus one lot of dentist's tools, one box of pill molds, and three syringes. Other inventories contained such items as bathing tubs, cradles, bedpans, and injection pipes.[61]

By far the most famous slave hospital in Anglo-American history was on the rice plantation of Pierce Butler near the entrance of the Altamaha River on the coast of Georgia. In 1834 Butler married Frances Anne Kemble, an English actress who had been touring the U.S. theater circuit. In 1838–9 the Butlers with their two daughters took up residence on the Georgia estate. The journal "Fanny" Kemble kept during her residence on the plantation was published in 1863. The Butlers were divorced in 1849 and Fanny returned to the stage.

Fanny Kemble was drawn into the debate on American slavery after Harriet Beecher Stowe's famous novel, *Uncle Tom's Cabin*, was published in England in 1852. After reading several leading articles in *The Times* that criticized Mrs. Stowe's novel, Fanny was moved to reply in a long letter to the editor. The *Times* article referred to a slave hospital on a Georgia rice plantation that "consisted of three separate wards, all clean and well ventilated: one was for lying-in women who were invariably allowed a month's rest after their confinement." Fanny placed beside this picture that of the hospital or infirmary she found soon after taking up residence on her husband's plantation. The walls were mud and laths, and the dirt floor was damp from water dripping from holes in the roof. In the first room she entered only half of the windows were glazed; "these were almost as much obscured with dirt as the other windowless ones were darkened by the dingy shutters which the shivering inmates had closed in order to protect themselves from the cold." Most of the sick slaves "lay prostrate on the earth, without bedstead, bed, mattress, or pillow, with no covering but the clothes they had on and some filthy rags of blanket in which they endeavored to wrap themselves as they lay literally strewing the floor, so that there was hardly room to pass between them."[62]

Fanny decided to publish her *Journal* at a critical time in the Civil War when she found to her dismay that many of her British friends were siding with the South. Her *Journal* portrays the life of the slaves she lived with in much depth – often the depth of despair. She tells of not only the dirt, noise, stench, and suffering of the slaves in the hospitals on her husband's two plantations, but also the bad condition of the hospitals and patients on nearby hospitals she visited. She attributed the neglect and ill treatment of the slaves largely to absentee proprietorship, which gave a free hand to the cruel and capricious propensities of white overseers. Fanny Kemble's *Journal* had a wide and telling impact. It was reviewed in leading periodicals and parts of it were read aloud in the House of Commons. J. C. Furnas, author of the definitive biography of Fanny Kemble, claims that her *Journal* "was and is the best available firsthand account of America's black slavery."[63]

Conclusion

This chapter has been concerned chiefly with the private plantation hospitals that were intended to serve the needs of sick and injured slaves in the British Sugar Colonies. Certain pro-planter authors praised the hospital facilities on plantations. They maintained that the structures were lofty, spacious, well ventilated, and clean. They said that separate wards were provided for men and women, lying-in women, and patients with dangerous diseases. Patients were said to be attended on a regular basis by qualified doctors who diagnosed their diseases and prescribed suitable remedies with the assistance of black medical attendants. Critics of the planters and their slave system, on the other hand, pointed out numerous alleged defects in the hospital establishment. They claimed that the hospitals were commonly overcrowded, dirty, poorly ventilated, and charged with offensive odors; that patients were inadequately supplied with nourishing food, beds, blankets, and baths; that doctors and nurses were insufficiently qualified and attentive; and that there were confined in one structure the "unoffending" sick, the suspected imposters or slaves who shammed illness to avoid plantation labor, and captured runaways and other lawbreakers who were often put in stocks.

Both the protagonists and antagonists of the hospital establishment clearly overstated their cases in the highly charged political and moral atmosphere of the time. Yet it can be argued that considerable credence can be given to another group of writers – that is, doctors and planters who sought to preserve slavery by means of amelioration measures. Besides calling attention to obvious shortcomings, these writers urged fundamental reform in the laws and practices governing such matters as the structural characteristics and layout of hospitals, the maintenance of hygienic standards, and due attention to sick and injured slaves. They were concerned to prevent the slaves from feigning illness to avoid labor, at the same time that no legitimate patient was neglected. They were incensed by overseers who overruled doctors and ordered sick slaves to perform heavy plantation labor when it imperiled their survival. Some of these planter- and doctor-reformers were concerned that hospitals were used as prisons as well as for the needs of the sick and injured.

As with other problems taken up in this study, absentee proprietorship can be blamed for limiting the potential benefits of the hospital establishment. Attorneys and managers were inclined to ride roughshod over the doctors and sick slaves in their effort to maximize labor and the production of exportable stables. Had there been more resident proprietors, and especially proprietors' wives with the reforming zeal of Fanny Kemble, the hospital and its patients would have been managed and cared for in a more efficient and humane manner.

The neglect of the black medical attendants, and especially the nurses, was another serious defect in the hospital establishment. If they had been selected for their superior intelligence, health, and physique and properly trained, the black nurses would have been better able to hold the hospital together, enabling it to function as a viable organism.

Slaves were both attracted to and repelled by hospitals, finding them temporary refuges from hard labor and punishment on the one hand, and on the other hand prisons, pesthouses, and places to die apart from family and hearth. Chapter 11, which deals with plantation medical practice, is both complementary and supplementary to the concerns of this chapter.

11

Plantation medical practice

> The usual method of remunerating the medical man, if he be not attached to the property with a salary, is by paying him a dollar annually for every negro, whether sick or well, upon the estate which he attends; thus, if there be 300 negroes, he is paid 300 dollars, or 100*l.* currency per annum, for affording medical advice, the medicines being found by the proprietor. If the medical men form partnerships, and attend several properties, which is generally the case, their incomes become considerable.
>
> H. T. De La Beche, 1825[1]

In our investigation of plantation medical practice, we look at the doctors and other white and black people who treated slaves in the British Sugar Colonies. More specifically, we are concerned with the extent of practice, the frequency of visits to slave hospitals, methods of procuring and dispensing medicines, and doctors' compensation. Among other things, the chapter contains case studies of individual doctors and comparisons with plantation medical practices in other slave societies.

The "irregular" practitioners

West Indian medical practice in the age of slavery developed from a system dominated by urban-based doctors who mainly treated white patients on an individual basis to a system of both urban- and rural-based doctors, with the latter treating chiefly black patients who were attached to estates and plantations on an annual contract basis. The shift from a predominantly white, urban-based practice to one directed chiefly to slaves attached to agricultural units can be explained, in part, by the near-monoculture system of sugar production. As black slaves came to replace white indentured servants, African diseases compounded the already aggravated environment of Caribbean and European diseases. High mortality induced some planters to take measures to preserve the health of their slaves even when their colleagues were convinced that it was cheaper to buy newly imported Africans rather than to encourage family life and reproduction. Humanitarian pressure to ameliorate slavery, together with rising slave prices and the abolition of the Atlantic Slave trade, led to the expansion of plantation medical services in the late eighteenth and early nineteenth centuries. However, worsening economic conditions and the clash between the plantocracy and the anti-slavery movement may have contributed to deteriorating medical services in the decade before emancipation in 1834.

Although the treatment of slaves varied widely and was often brutal and harsh by modern standards, measures were taken to maintain a healthy force. One visitor to the West Indies no doubt exaggerated when he said that expense was never considered by the planter when the life and labor of his slaves were in jeopardy. He wrote that the grand and all-pervading principle of self-interest, independent of humanity, called upon the planter to endeavor to save the life and to render his slaves fit for the continuance of labor.[2]

The expansion of medical services involved not only white doctors and black medical assistants but also proprietors, managers, overseers, book-keepers, clergymen, wives, housekeepers, and others. When a prominent Jamaican built an infirmary and nursery for his slaves, his tutor recorded proudly in his diary, "Over the former I have the honor of being call'd Doctor in chief."[3] Dr. John Williamson said he knew of clergymen in remote areas of Jamaica who ministered to poor sick persons who were unable to obtain the services of medical men.[4] Samuel Martin, the Antigua planter, said that since his chief overseer knew little about the care of sick slaves, that office was exercised by his housekeeper. She was described as "tender hearted, but spirited, and really skillfull as well as conscientious in ye discharge of her whole duty, & is I believe a very virtuous good woman in all respects." Martin paid her £30 sterling per year and advised his son to continue to employ her in the event of his death "for the sake of my poor negroes, for whom I have a kind of paternal tenderness."[5] John Pinney of Nevis was one planter who dispensed with the services of doctors. After taking up residence at Bristol, he wrote to his plantation manager: "Avoid as much as possible the calling in of a Doctor to the Negroes; they are so exorbitant in their charges, it is impossible for an estate to support it. Simples, good nursing and kitchen physic are the only requisites to recover sick negroes; I was very successful in my practice, and have no doubt but you will be equally so."[6]

Humanitarian and economic pressures led planters not only to expand the medical establishment on plantations but also to learn the rudiments of medicine themselves. To further this objective, guide books were written for the better management and medical treatment of slaves. Dr. David Collins of St. Vincent advised proprietors and managers to direct a little of their attention to the science of medicine. He wrote his *Practical Rules* to help gentlemen qualify themselves to treat the common disorders of their slaves.[7] Similarly, Dr. Thomas Dancer wrote *The Medical Assistant; or Jamaica Practice of Physic: designed chiefly for the use of families and plantations*, saying that his chief objective was to supply laymen with enough medical knowledge to save lives, especially by treating acute diseases in situations too remote from the residence of physicians and surgeons.[8] Unfortunately, some frugal planters were said to "trust to their own skill and James's powder, and Ward's pill; and, then for the most part, a surgeon is only called in to pronounce them [patients] past recovery."[9]

Probably most often the health of slaves rested in the hands of the overseer or bookkeeper. On a day-to-day basis he superintended the planting and manufacturing concerns of the plantation, ordered the work to be done, and saw that it was duly executed. He not only directed the slaves in their labor but also supplied them, at least in part, with food, clothing, shelter, and medical services. In his *Jamaica Planter's Guide*, Thomas Roughley wrote that "an experienced, attentive overseer or book-keeper (as is usually the case) will perform cures in ordinary, simple cases, compound and administer the medicine to the afflicted and sick, with little necessity to call in the aid of the practising white doctor, except when danger threatens."[10] Robert Hibbert, author of another planter's guide, wrote that "as the hospital called the hot-house claims the constant attention of the overseer, he ought from practice to have acquired some knowledge of medicine, and to be a perfect master of the treatment proper for the negroes in the hospital."[11] John Baillie said that the overseer on his Jamaica plantation visited the hospital every morning after eating his breakfast. There he examined the patients individually and recorded their complaints in the hospital book. Baillie testified that "if it is a trivial Complaint – we are all more or less Doctors – we order them a Dose of Salts or Oil, or an Emetic: those are common things; a Negro who has the Superintendence of the Hospital administers them." On the other hand, if the complaint is serious, "then the Doctor is sent for; but the universal Practice is for the Doctor to visit the Estate Twice a Week. The Book is open to him, and he prescribes for the sick accordingly in that Book."[12]

Thomas Thistlewood was the exceptional overseer and planter who left a day-to-day account of his treatment of slaves. He was born and raised in Lincolnshire, attended school at Ackworth, and worked for a time on a farm at Tupholme, near Lincoln. On 5 February 1750 he embarked at London on the *Flying Flamborough* bound for Jamaica. Beginning as the overseer of a cattle ranch or pen, Thistlewood moved after a year to a small sugar plantation where he served as overseer. His successful climb up the plantation ladder included the purchase of a pen property and slaves who were hired out as jobbing gangs and the purchase with his partner of a sugar estate. During his long residence in Jamaica (he died in 1786), Thistlewood kept a daily journal as well as commonplace books and weather reports. Together with the journals and navigation books of his nephew John Thistlewood, who also lived in Jamaica, the Thistlewood Papers in the Lincolnshire Archives Office amount to ninety-two volumes.[13]

Thistlewood's interest in medicine antedated his going to Jamaica. Beginning on his first voyage to Jamaica he befriended the ship's surgeon, and throughout his long career in the island he had numerous doctor friends. He learned much by observing doctors treat slaves. For example, he "Saw a Negroe Man Tapp'd for ye Dropsy, about four gallons of Clear Water run from him; a very easy operation."[14] He read books on natural history and medicine, laboriously copying long extracts into his journals and commonplace books. On one occasion he copied the descriptions of numerous medicinal plants from *The Useful Family Herbal*, by John Hill, M.D. (2d ed., London, 1755), and on another the characters and abbreviations used in medicine, pharmacy, and chemistry.[15]

Thistlewood kept day-to-day records of sick and lame slaves, their ailments, whether or not the doctor was called in, and in some cases what medicines and other treatment were prescribed. Out of a total of eighty-nine slaves on Egypt plantation, the daily sick list varied from one or two to ten or twelve. Thistlewood must have had his hands full on 24 September 1751, when he cryptically recorded, "Many Sick," and again on 14 February 1752, when "Big Mimber, Old Sybil, George and Sampson [were] all laid up of ye Belly Ache; Little Mimber and Mirtilla of Pains; and Morris of a Swell'd Leg and Foot."[16] The doctor was called in to treat serious cases, as on 20 January 1751 when Thistlewood "Sent Juba for Dr Fairbairne to come to Phibbah again, for altho' yesterday he bled and laid a Blister on her yet her pain is nothing abated, but more Violent if any thing, and consequently worse." Eight days later Phibbah was said to be much better, but Sussex, Mary, and Acubah were all very ill.[17]

Though he lacked professional training, Thistlewood was widely read in medical lore and capable of practicing the rudiments of slave medicine and minor surgery. His journals show that his almost obsessive interest in collecting medical recipes began before he came to Jamaica and continued during his long residence on the island. Perhaps the outstanding feature of these recipes is the extent to which they incorporated medicinal plants from Jamaica and other New World territories.[18]

Grenada doctors and slaves

There were two methods of using the services of white doctors to treat slaves. One was called the fee or piecework system. Doctors were called only after the medical resources of the master and his black and white medical assistants had been exhausted, and it was believed that the patient could be saved only by professional treatment. Under this system the doctor's charges varied according to time, distance, number of visits, and severity of the illness. In other words, doctors made calls when they were sent for and received payment on a piecework basis. The other method, variously called the contract, salary, or practice-by-the-year system, bound the doctor by verbal agreement or written contract to visit the plantation hospital at regular intervals. There he saw the slaves on the sick list, diagnosed their ailments, and prescribed medicines, which were generally compounded and administered by black or white medical assistants. Besides their regular visits, doctors were expected to make "express" calls to treat cases of acute illness or accident. Doctors under contract were paid a fixed amount annually for each slave on the plantation, whether sick or healthy, old or young, male or female. Separate charges were made for surgical operations, midwifery, and other special services. Medicines were supplied by doctors in some cases, by proprietors in others.

Growth in both the number and size of plantations made it advantageous to adopt the contract or salary system of treating sick slaves. Dr. Collins condemned the practice of calling doctors occasionally on a case-by-case basis because emergencies that required such attendance occurred so frequently on every plantation during the year "as to render it either a very expensive or a very ineffectual mode of doing your business." Planters who let urgent illnesses go unattended to save the expense lost slaves who might have been saved if proper advice and remedies had been resorted to in time. Collins urged his fellow planters on grounds of both economy and conscience "never to think of employing a medical man by the job, instead of by the year." Not only was the latter system cheaper, but it also exonerated the planter from responsibility for treating acute cases of illness. Though Collins urged proprietors and managers to take pains to acquire knowledge necessary for the treatment of slaves, he cautioned them to consider themselves only as a supplement to the doctor to whom they should resort on the first appearance of difficulty.[19]

Grenada is the only island that kept records to show in some detail how slave medical practice was organized. The Grenada slave registration ledgers labeled "Increase and Decrease" supply, among other data, the names of plantations and their proprietors, number of slaves on each unit of ownership, parish of residence, increase by birth, decrease by death, manner of death, and names of the doctors who certified the death of each slave. Although it is not certain what type of medical practice was conducted, it is reasonable to assume that most estates and plantations had salaried medical practitioners who were compensated annually according to the number of slaves on each

Table 11.1. *Doctors and the slaves under their care in Grenada, 1820*

Doctors	Slaves on units of 1 to 49	Slaves on units of 50 or more	Slaves presumably under doctor's care	Number of accounts	Average slaves per account
Alexander Richard	18	1,703	1,721	13	132
George Macewan	36	1,641	1,677	12	140
John Bartlet	0	1,628	1,628	8	204
James Macewan	4	1,574	1,578	9	175
George Roberts	3	1,302	1,305	11	119
William Jardine	35	1,187	1,222	9	136
J. H. Kennedy	52	1,117	1,169	10	117
Alexander Duncan	36	1,127	1,163	10	116
James F. Romney	5	1,108	1,113	10	111
Murray and Brown	24	1,068	1,092	11	99
Robert Ross	82	1,000	1,082	8	135
John Fortune	114	782	896	10	90
Thomas Renwick	0	695	695	4	174
Cosens Johnstone	29	617	646	5	129
Duncan Blair	68	523	591	8	74
H. P. Palmer	72	511	583	8	73
G. T. Strahan	0	345	345	2	172
Thomas Murray	1	316	317	4	79
William Stephenson	30	270	300	4	75
F. Fleming	0	286	286	3	95
Thomas Duncan	0	282	282	1	282
Frederick Lornsworth	54	119	173	3	58
J. Hammond	14	86	100	2	50
P. Macnay	15	0	15	1	15
Total	692	19,287	19,979	166	Average 120

Total slaves in Grenada on 31 December 1820: 26,899

Source: Public Record Office, London, *Treasury* 71/273 (1820), Grenada Slave Registration Returns, Increase and Decrease.

cording to the number of slaves on each unit of ownership. Data for 1820 and 1830 have been summarized in Table 11.1 and 11.2.

The tables show that nearly the same number of slaves were presumably under the care of doctors in 1820 and 1830, but that the percentage of such

Table 11.2. *Doctors and the slaves under their care in Grenada, 1830*

Doctors	Slaves on units of 1 to 49	Slaves on units of 50 or more	Slaves presumably under doctor's care	Number of accounts	Average slaves per account
Blair and Gilland	185	2,467	2,652	24	111
Alexander Richard	117	2,142	2,259	23	98
James Macewan	50	2,185	2,235	14	160
A. H. Cuddy	233	1,912	2,145	35	61
Cosens Johnstone	21	2,023	2,044	14	146
W. F. Falconer	11	1,727	1,738	11	158
John Fortune	40	1,529	1,569	16	98
James F. Romney	54	1,321	1,375	15	92
Thomas Spence	57	1,016	1,073	12	89
James H. Reid	0	907	907	5	181
Robert Reith	11	665	676	6	113
James Patterson	2	545	547	5	109
George Macewan	140	265	405	17	24
M. Aquart	96	195	291	7	42
J. Fleming	18	154	172	2	86
William Stephenson	53	119	172	13	13
William Jardine	7	0	7	1	7
Total	1,095	19,172	20,267	220	Average 92
Total slaves in Grenada on 31 December 1830: 23,878					

Source: Public Record Office, London, *Treasury* 71/313 (1830), Grenada Slave Registration Returns, Increase and Decrease.

slaves to all slaves in Grenada increased during the decade from 74.2 to 84.9. In 1820 there were twenty-five doctors (including two in partnership) who certified the deaths on 166 plantations and other properties comprising 19,979 slaves. The average number of slaves per doctor was 799 and per account 120. But eleven of the twenty-five doctors had from 1,082 to 1,721 slaves presumably under their care, or in the aggregate 14,750 out of 19,979 (or 73.8 percent). In 1830 there were sixteen individual practitioners and two other doctors in partnership who certified the deaths of slaves. If the practice in other islands was followed, Grenada doctors who had extensive practices employed medical assistants. It is possible, therefore, that not all the doctors are listed in the registration returns. The eighteen doctors in the registration returns for 1830 certified the deaths on 220 plantations and other properties comprising 20,267 slaves. The average number of slaves per doctor was 1,126 and per account 92. Not only did the number of certifying doctors decline during the decade but also the practice of slave medicine became more concentrated. In 1830 there were eight individual practitioners and two doctors in partnership who had from 1,073 to 2,652 slaves presumably under their care, or in the aggregate 17,090 out of 20,267 (or 84.3 percent).

The number of accounts and the size of slave units served by doctors can be explained, in part, by geographical, demographic, and economic factors in Grenada. Doctors who lived in the town of St. George certified the deaths of a disproportionately large number of slaves belonging to small units of ownership, although this was more the case in 1830 than in 1820, when owners rather than doctors frequently certified the deaths of town slaves. Some town doctors also certified the deaths of slaves on plantations in the parish of St. George. In 1830 deaths were certified in both the town and parish by A. H. Cuddy, George Macewan, and William Stephenson; in the town only by John Fortune and William Jardine; and in the parish only by W. F. Falconer. A. H. Cuddy, for example, certified the deaths on ten units of from 1 to 9 slaves; four units of 10 to 19; five units of 20 to 49; and sixteen units of 50 or more. Of the sixteen units of 50 or more slaves, seven were from 50 to 99, and seven from 100 to 193. The medical practice on the island of Carriacou, which was under the government of Grenada, was virtually monopolized by the partnership of Blair and Gilland. They certified deaths on six units with from 1 to 9 slaves; five units of 10 to 49; three units of 50 to 99; four of 100 to 199; four of 200 to 299; and one each of 335 and 418 slaves. Doctors who practiced in parishes that produced minor staples tended to have many small accounts. Conversely, those who practiced in the sugar parishes had fewer accounts but more slaves on each unit of ownership.[20]

Doctors in the Leeward Islands and Barbados

On 9 August 1774 Samuel Martin of Antigua entered the following memorandum of agreement in his letter book:[21]

> This Day I agreed with Doc^{r} Jonas Blizzard to take Care of my Plantation Negroes as Doc^{r} at the rate of Six Shillings p. Head upon Condition of his Visiting twice every week in person, furnishing all necessary Medicines & doing the part of a Man Midwife upon all emergent Occasions & taking Care of my white People into the Bargain.
>
> Witness William Barnes

This agreement provided for the medical care of the 300 or more slaves on Martin's plantation, as well as looking after his white people and serving as a man-midwife. It states the frequency of the doctor's visits, gives the rate of payment, and makes him responsible for furnishing all necessary medicines. On the other hand, we do not know how extensive a practice Dr. Blizzard had and what agreements, if any, he made with other planters.

Slave medical practices in Antigua were described briefly by John Luffman in 1787. Sick slaves were visited by young doctors, he wrote, whose principals contracted with the owners of estates or their attorneys by the year. The common price per slave was 6*s.* currency, equal to 3*s.* 9*d.* sterling. Luffman said it was the business of these assistants to visit the hospitals on the estates that had been put under the care of their employers twice a week. The doctors were so poorly paid that Luffman thought it was "impossible for them to get the keep of one of their horses out of the undertakings although they should make use of the very cheapest drugs that can be procured, or if even only of medicinal simples, the growth of the island."[22]

In St. Kitts and Nevis the practice of slave medicine was both praised and criticized by contemporary writers. James Grainger, M.D., who both practiced and sought to improve the quality of slave medicine, wrote that no medical practitioner could do justice to a plantation who did not visit the sick twice a week, either himself or his assistant, or more often if necessary. A case book or diary should be kept in every sick house or hospital in which the doctor or his assistant should record the patient's name, when admitted and visited, the illness or disorder, symptoms and method of cure, and whether the patient was discharged or died. Planters should remember, warned Grainger, that those who presumed to prescribe to the sick without being qualified by study and experience must be murderers.[23]

The Reverend James Ramsay, a leading critic of the plantocracy, was both surgeon and Anglican clergyman in St. Kitts. When he took up his clerical duties in 1759, he found that there was no medical practitioner within many miles of him. Since his salary as a minister was inadequate to support his family and his neighbors pressed him to practice, he readily gave his medical advice and assistance to both blacks and whites.[24] Ramsay criticized the planters for paying doctors who were employed by the year only 14*d.* to 3*s.* per slave. He no doubt quoted salaries that prevailed before the planters were put on the defensive by the abolitionists. Defending the planters was James Tobin, a Bristol sugar merchant and former planter in Nevis and St. Kitts. Tobin asserted that doctors who were employed by the year to treat slaves received a constant allowance of 6*s.* per head. Moreover, he claimed that extra charges were made for night visits, amputations, midwifery, and inoculation, so that a doctor's income for treating a gang of 100 slaves might be reckoned at about £50 or £60 per year.[25] Dr. Robert Thomas, who had between 4,000 and 5,000 slaves in his medical practice in Nevis, testified before the privy Council committee in 1789 that surgeons were expected to attend slave hospitals once or twice a week at least, and daily if occasion required it. Most plantations were attended at 6*s.* per head for each Negro annually, with extra charges for surgical operations, midwifery, and night visits.[26]

Owing in part to Ramsay's criticisms and their impact on public opinion in England, fundamental changes were made in the slave laws of the Leeward Islands. By the law of 1798, slave owners were fined £100 if they did not provide their slaves with a "commodious" hospital, and of £50 if they failed to furnish regular medical assistance. The doctor was required to call at the plantation twice a week unless he was notified in writing that his services were not needed. An emergency supply of medicines, with written directions for their use, had to be left in each slave hospital, together with a register in which the treatment of every sick slave was recorded. The law required each doctor to submit a "sworn statement of the number of slaves who had died on each estate under his charge, giving the cause of death in each case and also an account of the treatment of sick slaves." Failure to submit this and other reports resulted in a fine of £100. Despite the effort to provide minimum standards for the slaves, the law of 1798 was weak because it lacked an efficient executive principle. Slave evidence was not admitted against free persons, and no official was specifically entrusted with enforcement of the law. Elsa Goveia, in her analysis of the law, writes that the position of the doctor was difficult, "since he was himself an employee of the planter on whom he would be forced to inform if he took his responsibilities to the slaves more seriously than his loyalty to an employer and fellow inhabitant." Faced with this conflict, doctors seldom, if ever, acted informally as guardians of the slaves.[27]

The compact and densely populated island of Barbados may have had enough medical practitioners to visit the sick slaves daily. Governor David Parry of Barbados testified before the Privy Council committee of 1789 that the plantations were constantly provided with an apothecary who was paid by the master annually and who generally visited the blacks every day, whether they were sick or well.[28] Doctors and other persons concerned with the slaves gave evidence before committees of the legislature of Barbados in 1818 and 1824. Though all the evidence favors the plantocracy and cannot be evaluated in the light of counterevidence, it may nevertheless reveal certain experiences of the individuals concerned. Apothecary Lewis Young, who had practiced for thirty years in the parish of St. Philip, said that he or his assistant visited the plantations in his practice daily, and in case of illness generally two or three times every day. Whenever he saw a necessity for it, he said he recommended to "the Owners and Overseers to call in the aid of a Physician or Surgeon (which is always readily attended to), who receive their fees from the Plantation, exclusive of my account for medicine and attendance as the Apothecary."[29] George Richards, M.D., testified that he practiced for about eight estates and other properties with a total population of about 2,500. He also had a general practice as physician and surgeon and visited many estates in that capacity. John E. Leacock, practitioner in physic and surgery, said that he had about thirty sugar plantations and many small places with a total of about 4,000 slaves under his care. He claimed that it was his habit to visit the plantations daily. Perhaps the largest medical practice in Barbados was that of Reynold C. Thomas, M.D., who was a physician, surgeon, and accoucheur. He testified that during the three years before 1824 his medical practice comprised about 10,000 slaves in the island.[30]

Doctor Jonathan Troup of Dominica

Dominica is a mountainous, well-watered island of 291 square miles situated between Guadeloupe and Martinique in the Lesser Antilles. Roseau, the capital, is on the southwest side of the island, and Prince Rupert's Bay on the northwest coast has a fine natural harbor. Because it was the scene of frequent military engagements during the Anglo-French wars, the island was sparsely populated and economically underdeveloped. The population of Dominica in 1787 consisted of 1,236 whites and 14,987 black slaves.[31]

An intimate view of the slave medical practice in Dominica is given in the diary of Dr. Jonathan Troup, which covers about ten months of his life on the island in 1789 and 1790. Troup, who held a M.A. degree from the University of Aberdeen, Scotland, came to Dominica at the invitation of Dr. Clarke, who was also from Aberdeen. Landing at Roseau on 11 May 1789, Troup was met by Dr. Fillan, who was described as "an excellent attentive practitioner generally beloved by the inhabitants." Dr. Clarke was then absent from the island. Troup learned that there were sixteen medical practitioners in Roseau, but that Dr. Fillan had two-thirds of all the practice in the town. Several days later Troup visited a hospital on a sugar plantation and saw the slaves "lying on tables like a Butcher's stall." Another shocking sight was one of Dr. Clarke's slaves with a "chain & collar of Iron round his Neck, the strong weight makes him bleed at Nose & Mouth."[32]

Together with Dr. John Carson from Galloway, Scotland, Troup began his medical practice in Dominica as assistant to Dr. Fillan. He treated blacks and whites, the latter individually and the former either by the case or as members of plantation gangs. For example, on Tuesday, 7 July 1789, he visited a black woman who was almost ready to be delivered of a child; on Friday he "went out of Town to visit a Negro of Mr Jardin's about 5–6 miles off;" and the following morning he visited Mr. Curry's estate. On Monday he visited Woodbridge estate where most of the complaints were small sores on the feet, and then on to Bath estate where he treated the "Negro boy Frank" who had "turned a skeleton with Diarrhoea & belly much swelled." The following Tuesday Dr. Troup visited four estates – Mr. Glennie's, Woodbridge, Mr. Cobham's, and Bath. At the first he treated a child with dysentery, at the second an old woman whose case of mal d'estomac or pica was better, at the third a slave woman who had been blistered, and at the fourth no special treatment.[33] Colds and rheumatism were the prevailing ailments when he visited Woodbridge and Bath estates on 11 August, and yaws cases were numerous when he visited these same estates on 3 September. Blacks who were treated apart from his plantation practice included a boy who was stung by a scorpion, a man who was inoculated against smallpox, a man with hydrophobia, and another man who had been scalded with boiling rum.[34] He treated a white boy who had passed a worm a foot long, another white boy who was inoculated against smallpox, a white man with gonorrhea, another white man with the dry bellyache, and a white woman who had a tooth extracted.[35]

In his treatment of blacks and whites, Dr. Troup resorted to the common practices of bleeding, purging, vomiting, blistering, and sweating. He prescribed such widely used medicines as tartar emetic, castor oil, jalap, rhubarb, Jesuits' bark or cinchona, anodyne pills, and James's powder. Table 11.3 shows the piecework charges he made for medicines and attendance on patients.

Dr. Troup prescribed medicines cautiously and differed fundamentally in this and other professional matters form his employer, Dr. Fillan. Troup accused Fillan of "pouring in Medicines" and especially overdosing his patients with mercury and Jesuit's bark. Fillan's small medical empire included an apothecary shop in Roseau. It was a meeting place for local practitioners who debated the respective merits of their potions, pills and prescriptions. Troup noted in his Diary that if he had his own practice he would have only a small list of medicines. He described Dr. Fillan and other local medical men as "Empirics" who learned only the simplest and most common things from experience "& they give themselves up to be Empirics because they don't understand the reasoning." They were said to have had only a smattering of liberal education. On the other hand, Troup prided himself for going beyond "vulgar" experience; "I always consult nature & from reason judge what will best assist her from my Knowledge of Anatomy & the Animal Oeconomy."[36]

Dr. Troup, however, was not without his own faults, which Fillan and other doctors and planters seized upon in retaliation against the young man's intellectual arrogance and eccentric avocations. Troup was accused of ne-

Table 11.3. *Dr. Troup's charges for medicines and attendance*

	£	s.	d.
Purge	0	4	6
Purging infusion	0	6	0
Blister	0	6	0
Cooling powder	0	6	0
Dose of rhubarb	0	6	0
Camphor	0	4	6
Vomit	0	4	6
Drawing tooth	0	8	3
Drawing teeth at night	0	16	6
6 Doses of bark	0	12	0
Opening large abscess	0	16	0
Extraordinary attendance for some days while in danger	0	3	6
Chamomile flowers for tea	0	6	0
Visit to New Town	0	12	0
Anodyne mixture	0	10	6
Purging draught for lady or gentleman	0	7	6
Medicines & dressing for negro's cut heel	1	13	0
Visit express to plantation of Monsr. Le Grand & bleeding Madame Le Grand	2	1	3
Visit in town express to Mr Webb	1	19	0

Source: The Diary of Dr. Jonathan Troup, Aberdeen University, MS 2070, f. 94.

glecting the practice of medicine, obstinately adhering to his own diagnosis and treatment of particular cases, being indolent, and secluding himself too much from society. In the tropical wonderland and manmade hell of Dominica, he gave nearly free rein to his instinct for idle curiosity. As an amateur anthropologist, he studied the blacks and mulattoes, their language, proverbs, dress, dance, and music. As an artist, he illustrated his diary with drawings of slaves, free mulattoes, birds, fish, insects, seashells, cloud formations, and other "curiosities." As a musician, he played the violin and took part in local musical performances.[37]

After being dismissed as Dr. Fillan's assistant, Dr. Troup set sail from Roseau in a small sloop on 18 December 1789. After "a tedious passage of two days & 2 nights in sailing 30 miles," he arrived at Prince Rupert's Bay.[38] There he applied to proprietors and attorneys for the medical practice on plantations and estates. He visited the slave hospitals on several estates at regular intervals, at the same time that his contract negotiations with proprietors and attorneys were pending. Negotiations were protracted because he insisted on a salary and other terms that were far out of line with customary practice. On 26 January 1790 he dined with Mr. Alleyn, who had seventy slaves on his own estate and was attorney for several other estates. Soon after the dinner Troup wrote the following letter to Alleyn:[39]

> Sir,
>
> You are very kind in giving me the Care of your own Estate, Baldwyn's & the two belong[g] to the late deceased Gov[r] Stewart. In return, as far as my abilities & knowledge extend, I shall exert myself for the preservation of the Negroes upon the above Estates: – but to do this with justice to them & satisfaction to myself I must have the best & freshest Medicines London can afford. Also it will be necessary to visit the Estates once a week but when Sickness and Accidents occur – to be ready day & night – I known very well the nature of Estates – Indeed very little at times is to be made from them – some years they will not pay the Medicines – I have some knowledge now of this Quarter, of the roads & distances to the above Estates – On the whole it will be impossible for me to attend the Estates in this Quarter under 20 Shillings P. Annum for Each Negroe – or if it shall be more agreeable to the Attorneys to pay so much p. visit or p. annum for visits & the price of Med[icine]s, I am perfectly satisfied – Upon any other conditions I am fully determined not to Practice on any of the Estates at Prince Ruperts.
>
> I am, &c. Your humble Obed[t] Serv[t]
>
> Jonathan Troup M. A.

The diary shows that Troup continued to refuse any other conditions. When a local planter advised him to gain the confidence of the people who employed him before making his price, Troup exclaimed, "I will not kill myself for nothing." The young doctor was burdened with debt, felt obliged to send money home to his poor parents, and hoped to return to Scotland in a few years with enough money to marry Miss Mary Ford. Troup suffered bouts of fever and stomach upsets and on one occasion was nearly killed by an earth slide while making the rounds of his practice on horseback. Frequent deaths among the white inhabitants of Dominica led him to observe, "Doctors and Managers of Estates die more than any set of people from their greater exposure on all occasions."[40] In the face of these risks and obligations, Troup obstinately adhered to his demands. He wrote in his diary on 14 February 1790, "Am fully determined not to practise here under 20 Sh[illings]. for each Negroe – Come what will – Tho' I should go to the last pitch of misery." Though direct evidence is lacking, it would appear that Dr. Troup lost his struggle to gain a medical practice in Dominica. After a gap from early April to early August, his diary ends abruptly on 9 August 1790 with a medical recipe and a drawing of two ships with the caption, "Our situation when we asked Assistance from French ship."[41]

Medical practice in Jamaica

Slave medicine in Jamaica, though organized in much the same way as in the Lesser Antilles, came under close scrutiny in the struggles that led to abolition and emancipation and became the focus of attention of defenders and critics of slavery. Before we turn to this critical literature, however, it will be well to survey the materials that shed light on the practice of slave medicine in Jamaica.

From the testimony and writings of doctors, planters, and other observers, some impression can be gained of the extent of practice, frequency of visits to slave hospitals, methods of procuring and dispensing medicines, doctors' compensation, and other aspects of medical practice in Jamaica. Three prominent Jamaican doctors testified before the Privy Council committee in 1789. Dr. John Quier said he had practiced in the parishes of St. John, St. Thomas in the Vale, and Clarendon for more than twenty-one years, and most of the time he had 4,000 to 5,000 slaves constantly under his care. During his practice of more than twenty-one years, Dr. James Chisholme said he had the care of at least 4,000 slaves annually, while Dr. Adam Anderson, whose practice in the island extended over twenty-eight years, had the physical care, with the help of a partner, of nearly 4,000 slaves annually.[42] John Stewart, the planter-author, noted that "a medical man, with only one assistant, has sometimes the practice of fifteen or more estates, which, with the smaller properties, may contain a population of about four thousand [slaves]." Even larger practices were reported by the Reverend Richard Bickell, who wrote that "in some parishes a surgeon and his assistant have perhaps, five or six thousand Negroes under their charge, (besides white and free persons); these living on thirty or forty different properties, some of them twelve or fifteen miles asunder."[43]

Whereas planters and their supporters contended that doctors visited the estates two or more times a week, other evidence points to an irregular pattern of attendance on slave hospitals. Sir Michael B. Clare, M.D., a leading practitioner in Jamaica, testified that it was the universal practice for the doctor to visit the estate twice a week.[44] William Burge, M.P. and agent for Jamaica, testified that "generally speaking, the medical men in the country reside in so central a situation, that they have an opportunity of visiting the estates, not merely once a week, as is supposed, but that there are few estates in which it is not required that, whether there are persons sick or not, the medical man should visit the estate, sometimes four and sometimes three times a week."[45]

One small piece of evidence that hospitals were visited two or more times a week is afforded by the hospital book of Harmony Hall estate in the parish of Trelawny, Jamaica (see Table 11.4). This book contains the dates of visits,

Table 11.4. *Extracts from the Harmony Hall Hospital Book, Trelawny Parish, Jamaica, 1822–6*

June 15th 1824

Jenny. To take 3 grains Calomel & 10 grains Jalap now & oil two hours after.
Kate. Vomit her now & oil two hours after.
Caroline. Apply a blister to the back.
Grace. To take a pill now & Salts two hours after.
Catherine. As before.
Joe. Apply a blister to the left Temple. To take Salts every other morning. Keep Goulard water to the eye.
Cecily. Vomit her now & in the Evening oil. To take at bed time 3 grains Calomel & 6 grains Jalap & oil to morrow.

June 22nd 1824

Henry. To take 5 grains Calomel, 15 Grains Jalap & 20 grains Cream Tartar now & Salts two hours after.
Bell. To take Salts.
Kate. As before.
Jacintha. To take a pill now & oil two hours after.

June 23rd 1824

Kate. To be vomited immediately and after the operation of the emetic to use the hot bath. When removed from the bath to give 5 grains Calomel, 4 grains Antimonial powder and 15 grains of Jalap in Syrup and in 2 hours after a dose of oil. Should she continue to breathe with difficulty, after the medicines have had their effect, to apply a blister to the chest and to give four times a day, 10 drops of paregoric and 20 drops of Vinegar of Squills in some of the Calabash Syrup.
Henry. 15 drops of the Elixir of Vitriol 3 times a day in a glass of an Infusion of Bitterwood.
Jacintha. As for Henry.

Source: Harmony Hall estate, Trelawny, Jamaica, *Hospital Book, 1822–1826*, Institute of Jamaica, Kingston, Jamaica.

the names of slave patients, and the prescriptions and instructions written by the doctor and initialed "J. H." Unfortunately, there are no data on the complaints, recovery, or characteristics of the patients. The book covers the period from 7 December 1822 to 4 February 1826, or approximately thirty-seven months. During this time a total of 412 visits were made by the doctor, or an average of slightly more than eleven per month. The number of visits ranged from a low of seven to a high of sixteen per month, however, and there is evidence of seasonal variation, with more visits made in the first eight months (average 12.2 per month) than the last four months (average 9.3 per month).[46]

Other data for ascertaining the frequency of hospital visits are contained in the journal of James Henry Archer, M.D., who practiced in the parish of St. Ann, Jamaica.[47] Archer made daily journal entries of his professional and personal activities, noting his visits to plantations, pens, and households, and in some cases the complaints and methods of treatment. An account book entry on 1 October 1828 shows that he had twenty-nine medical accounts that yielded an annual sum of £505 10*s*. 0*d*.[48] Of these accounts, thirteen were for plantations and pens in St. Ann's Parish, which he visited at varying intervals, probably on a contract basis. No uniform pattern of visitation is evident, however. Some estates were visited two or three days in a row or every other day, but more often the interval varied from a week to ten days, and in a few cases to several weeks or a month. Moreover, on a given day the number of estates visited ranged from one or two to five. The irregular pattern of visitation can be illustrated from the experience of December 1828. On 3 December Dr. Archer visited the estates of Rio Ho, Schwelenberg, Ardoch, Unity Valley, and Faith's Pen. These properties were visited again on 9 and 16 December. He visited Hopewell estate on 5 and 31 December, Retirement on 6 and 14, and Greenfield and Belmont on 6. Thus, five properties were visited three times during the month, two were visited twice, and two only once. Moreover, one property that Archer had visited the previous month was not visited.[49]

Why Dr. Archer was irregular in making the rounds of his practice can be surmised, in part, from a close reading of his journal. One possible explanation, for which supporting evidence is lacking, is that he shared his practice with a partner or employed a medical assistant. Other possible explanations, which are difficult to verify, are that he made more frequent visits to estates close to his home than to distant estates, and that he visited estates with large gangs of slaves more frequently than those with small gangs. It is interesting that Archer visited sugar plantations in the lowlands and other undesignated properties that he called his "Mountain Practice." Only one visit was made to his mountain practice in the six months before February 1829, after which they increased in subsequent months to four or five visits each month while his estate practice was constricted. White patients in the racist society of Jamaica commanded the lion's share of limited medical resources. Dr. Archer made frequent express calls to treat ailing whites. For example, he recorded in his journal on 30 October 1828: "Visited Mrs. Drew by Express – remained all day and night." He remained with Mrs. Drew without interruption until her death seven days later, attended her funeral the day after her death, and the next day had a severe headache after visiting two estate hospitals and returned home and went to bed. Frequent spells of sickness, time taken to manage his own pen property and slaves, extended periods away from his practice visiting relatives and celebrating holidays – these and other circumstances make it difficult to believe the planter-apologists who maintained that doctors made frequent and regular visits to slave hothouses.[50]

Medicines that had been supplied chiefly by doctors in the eighteenth century came to be the responsibility of proprietors and their attorneys in the last decades of slavery. John Baillie, the Jamaica planter, testified before the House of Lords select committee in 1832: "The Proprietor sends regularly to England for a Supply of Medicines, made out by a regular Practitioner." Baillie obtained the medicines for his plantation principally from Apothecaries Hall in Glasgow. They cost from £14 to £24 per year, and he said he had known medicines to cost as much as £60 on a large estate. Besides medicines, Baillie testified that he supplied his sick slaves with such special foods as mutton, oatmeal, rice, wheat flour, and Guinea corn, as well as sugar and port wine.[51]

Doctor John Williamson of Jamaica

John Williamson, M.D., was one medical professional whose long service and published works conferred honor on Jamaica. After receiving his diploma from the Royal College of Physicians at Edinburgh, he served for a time as surgeon to a Scottish regiment. He came to Jamaica in August 1798 under the patronage of the Earl of Harewood. He lived during the first four years on Williamsfield estate, the property of the Earl of Harewood, in the parish of St. Thomas in the Vale. He later lived in Spanish Town. Williamson's medical career in Jamaica extended over nearly fifteen years and included both a country and town practice. What is remarkable is that Williamson kept a journal of his practice, which he later edited and expanded into a two-volume work entitled *Medical and Miscellaneous Observations, Relative to the West India Islands* (1817). Among other things, he recorded the plantations he visited, the diseases he encountered, remedies prescribed and their effectiveness, interesting case histories, and suggestions for improving the treatment of black Jamaicans. He wrote that the purposes of his journal were "to shew, in a candid manner, the faulty and commendable measures pursued in a system peculiar to the West India islands." Young doctors were advised to keep medical memorandums of their practice to learn from their own experience and to share their experiences with others.[52]

Dr. Williamson entered into negotiations to join a medical partnership soon after his arrival in Jamaica. After a good deal of discussion, agreement was reached on the "premium" and other matters, and the articles of partnership for a period of seven years were concluded and executed. Meanwhile, Williamson began to make visits through his intended practice, observing that the humanity of proprietors and overseers to invalid slaves was very praiseworthy. He was later to find much ground for faulting the behavior of proprietors and especially overseers.[53]

Dr. Williamson said he began his practice with a strong sense of duty and a resolve to maintain conduct that would gain him esteem and the favorable opinion of his employers and colleagues. Soon he discovered that his charge demanded the utmost attention and industry. "The humanity of medical practitioners to their negro patients," he wrote, "is a duty which proper feeling calls upon them to discharge with scrupulous fidelity." Williamson's humanity was sorely tested by exposure to the elements, overcrowded and unsanitary hospitals, recalcitrant patients, hostile overseers, emergency night visits, fatigue, and the awareness that he practiced at the hazard of his life in the hostile disease environment of Jamaica. He observed that while in tropical climates all Europeans had to combat many things that were inimical to their health; it was "peculiarly the fate of medical practitioners to encounter duties which oblige them to be exposed at night, or urgent occasions of illness, when the sources of disease are more prevalent." He noted in his journal in December 1804 that remittent fever of a troublesome nature prevailed, and that only one of all the medical practitioners in the parish of St. Ann's was healthy and active.[54]

Dr. Williamson's *Medical and Miscellaneous Observations* contain such a wealth of information on plantation medical practice that only a few of them can be singled out for special mention. In October 1798 an epidemic ophthalmia was said to be "exceedingly troublesome, but, by plentiful evacuations, bleeding, and cathartics, the treatment was successful." Worms appeared to be a great source of disease in children and frequently in adults. In November of the same year the parish of St. Thomas in the Vale was unhealthy because of the prevalence of "remittents, fluxes, catarrhal, and pneumonic complaints." Cases of whooping cough were frequent that month; in February 1799 the "varicella, or chicken-pox, made its appearance on many properties." In March 1799 he wrote a long case history of Neptune, aged about seventeen, on Williamsfield estate, who was kicked by a powerful horse. Later in August of the same year he observed that "the yawy negroes on estates seemed to be in a very neglected state." Williamson treated blacks afflicted with worms, ulcers, yaws, diarrhea, dysentery, pneumonia, mal d'estomac, smallpox, fevers, putrid sore throat, tetanus, dropsy, and other diseases. He treated both blacks and whites, females and males, in his various capacities as physician, surgeon, man-midwife, and pharmacist.[55]

After making the rounds of his practice for a few months, Dr. Williamson became aware of the hardships and shortcomings of his profession. He incurred large expenses in acquiring medical books and instruments, as well as horses, carriages, and other appurtenances of his profession. Furthermore, his income, at least in the early months of his practice, was insufficient to support him at the level of his profession after paying living costs and the necessary expenses of his practice. It was doubly discouraging to find that, after incurring great risks and hardships, his claims for compensation were often ignored. He expressed his bitter feelings by copying the following jingle in his journal:

God and the Doctor we do both adore,
Just on the brink of danger, – not before
The danger o'er, both are alike requited,
God is forgotten, and the Doctor slighted.

Faced with an income that fell far short of expectations, the typical physician decided he must curry favor with proprietors, attorneys, and overseers and expand his practice by adding plantations. Success in this direction would confront him with a dilemma, however. Whereas his income would be greater, his ability to serve his expanded clientele and live up to his Hippocratic oath would be impaired. The consequence might well be an overextended practice with infrequent visits to slave hospitals and poor treatment.[56]

In his practice Dr. Williamson encountered managers and overseers who neglected the hothouse, being concerned to maximize labor even at the expense of the health and well-being of the slaves. He told of managers who wielded their power with an iron hand, indulging a cruel and tyrannizing disposition over the unhappy persons committed to their protection. Within a few months of the commencement of his practice, it became evident that the medical practice was unsatisfactory on estates and plantations. Rather than being the main object of attention, the sick department was in many instances managed in a careless manner. Williamson wrote that he often lamented that his "well considered prescriptions to subdue a chronic disease, and to restore an additional healthy labourer to his employer, were completely frustrated by the negligence of overseers." Because doctors were obliged to take on an extensive practice to support themselves, they could not remain on the estates to see their prescriptions administered properly. Instead, the medicines were administered by a bookkeeper under the direction of the overseer. But the bookkeeper was often so much engaged in other plantation duties "as to afford very little attention to chronic cases in the hot-house."[57]

To make his criticisms constructive, Dr. Williamson included a chapter in his book entitled "Thoughts on the Present Condition of Medical Practitioners on Estates and Plantations in Jamaica, in Towns and Cities: and the Means of Improvement in both these Departments." Again, he deplored the low salaries that made it necessary for plantation doctors to assume a more extensive practice than could be well attended to. To remedy this disadvantage, he recommended "that practitioners should be paid at the rate of ten shillings for each negro per annum; and that, in the lowlands, they should not be permitted to accept under their care more than four thousand negroes." Furthermore, doctors should be entitled to additional charges in cases of midwifery and when called out after hours to treat acute illnesses. Williamson urged the adoption of government regulations for licensing doctors. He recommended that qualified young doctors be placed first in mountain situations where the population was sparse. Moreover, he thought it "adviseable to limit such mountain practice to two thousand negroes; affording expectancy to those junior branches of the profession, that, by merit and industry, they might look forward to fill vacancies in the lowlands when they occurred."[58]

Another chapter in Dr. Williamson's book has the title "On the Medical Department, So Far as it Affects Attendance on Negroes, in Plantation Practice." Recollecting his experience as a regimental surgeon, Williamson said he believed that plantation medical services could be improved by applying certain practices that had proved beneficial in army hospitals. He urged that sick slaves be placed under the protection of public laws. Such laws should insure that doctors, rather than managers or overseers, be in control of slave hospitals. Each plantation should have one bookkeeper who directed his principal attention to the patients in the hothouse. He should be responsible for food and medical supplies and see that they were not misapplied or wasted. Each county in Jamaica should have a medical superintendent selected from among medical professionals who could afford to retire on the moderate salary that would be provided. The medical superintendents would be authorized "to testify for or against plantation practitioners, subjecting them for misconduct, to certain penalties in such cases." Williamson contended that the limitation of practice to 4,000 slaves would enable medical men "to make as many visits as any case can require; but it is adviseable to make occasional visits, to see that negroes, in sickness, have every care which humanity and duty to proprietors demand."[59]

Dr. Williamson was not sanguine that his "plan for the regulation of medical attendance in the West Indies" would be adopted. He anticipated that proprietors and their representatives in the colonies would object to it on the grounds that they would be "deprived of patronage, in the appointment of professional men to estates, of their own selection." Williamson must have realized that the plantocracy would surely resist any innovation that called for intervention between masters and slaves. Only in the crown colonies, which were subject to direct control from Whitehall, was there any possibility of intervention on behalf of the slaves.[60]

Medical practice in Cuba and the United States

Although the slaves on Cuban plantations were supplied with medical services, the limited data available indicate that these services were circumscribed and probably inferior in quality in comparison with those supplied the blacks in the British Caribbean colonies and the United States. Franklin W. Knight says that some estates had a part-time nurse or doctor who paid periodic visits for an agreed sum of money. An American doctor who visited Cuba in the 1840s estimated that a sugar plantation with 100 slaves spent two dollars per year for medical attendance on each slave and ten dollars for clothing and food. Mr. Moss of Liverpool, who had resided for many years in Cuba, submitted a written statement to the Board of Trade in 1830. "Medical attendance is by no means so good as in the British Colonies," he wrote, "and the very great facility of procuring fresh labourers, prevents the Cuba planters from introducing those ameliorating arrangements which, if expensive to the British planter, are still necessary to keep up the slave population, and thereby preserve the means for continuing cultivation."[61]

Structural differences in the economies and societies of the British West Indies and the American South influenced the scope and nature of medical services supplied to slaves. Compared to the West Indies, the southern economy and society extended over a vast territory, was more diversified by crop type and economic activity, and had a lower ratio of blacks to whites. Moreover, southern plantations tended to occupy more acres, were more dispersed, had a smaller labor force, and had more resident planters and their wives than their counterparts in the West Indies. As Richard H. Shryock points out, "The large plantation with a well-organized medical regime was an exceptional institution, save in certain rich areas." Slaves who contracted mild or common illnesses were generally treated by the planter, his wife, or overseer. Every plantation had its "doctor book" or manual, which told how to diagnose and treat common cases of illness or injury, and all planters professed some skill in the medical treatment of their slaves.[62]

Almost everyone in the South practiced medicine by 1850. "Planters, housewives, overseers, pharmacists, sectarians, quacks – all had a hand in the game," writes Shryock. Sick slaves on southern plantations were more likely than their island counterparts to be treated by planters, housewives, overseers, black nurses, and black foremen. Most masters and mistresses lived on their plantations, and those who were conscientious gave close personal attention to their ailing "people." When one South Carolina mistress met people who commented on her having so many slaves, she always told them, "It is the slaves who own me. Morning, noon, and night, I'm obliged to look after them, to doctor them, and attend to them in every way."[63]

Perhaps even more than their counterparts on the islands, white overseers in the South were charged with the medical treatment of slaves. They were expected to take charge of the hospital and have sufficient knowledge to administer medicines and perform minor surgery. On small properties the black nurse was frequently the "Doctress of the Plantation" who was held in esteem for her accumulated wisdom on practical medical matters. On large plantations the nurses were responsible for cleaning the bedding and utensils, cooking and serving food, dispensing medicine under the supervision of the doctor or overseer, caring for pregnant women and nursing mothers, and looking after babies and nursery children. Some plantations lacked white overseers and had absent masters and mistresses. They were often managed by black foremen who were successful in discharging their responsibilities for the medical care of the slaves.[64]

In Mississippi the normal planter is said to have "sent for the neighboring physician when his slaves suffered from such diseases as consumption, rheumatism, spasms, or pneumonia." Physicians were normally called upon by the plantation "to perform a range of tasks from extracting teeth to delivering babies, but mostly their work seems to have been that of dispensing medicines for routine but chronic complaints." In some cases, sick and injured slaves were taken to private hospitals that were established by certain doctors for the exclusive care of blacks.[65]

Southern doctors were paid on an annual contract basis as well as on a piecework or fee arrangement. Whereas the contract system became dominant in the plantation parishes of the West Indies, practice in the rural South was mixed and it tended to shift away from annual contracts. For one thing, the South had proportionately more small slave holders who in serious cases depended exclusively on doctors who treated illnesses on an individual basis. Since individual visits were often expensive, planters who had many slaves sought to economize by contracting with doctors to visit their slaves for a fixed sum annually, regardless of the number of visits and the amount of medicine required. Some doctors came to regard contract medicine as cheap and unprofessional, however, especially leading physicians. As Virginia's physicians developed local medical societies and later a statewide organization, the contract system came under attack. It was argued that the medical care of slaves would fail to measure up to the highest standards unless physicians were liberally compensated. Fee bills were drawn up that called on subscribing physicians to charge the amount set forth. "But," as Todd L. Savitt observes, "enough contract medicine persisted for angry doctors to continue their campaign against it through the 1850's."[66]

That white people who were conscientiously concerned with the welfare of blacks found their efforts frustrated by certain overseers is a common theme in the slavery literature of the South. One bone of contention was the white protector's willingness to hear and believe slaves who complained of illness and ill treatment, and the overseer's belief that such complaints were usually ingenuous and would interfere with the labor and discipline of the plantation. As the self-appointed protector of the slaves on her husband's plantations in Georgia, Fanny Kemble encountered almost insuperable obstacles in her repeated efforts to intercede on behalf of her "people." She was told of a former overseer who was renowned for the full income that was returned under his management, but who regarded sick slaves as "tools to be mended only if they can be made available again; if not to be flung by as useless, without farther expense of money, time, or trouble." She had a long conversation with the present overseer who complained of "the sham sicknesses of the slaves." He detailed "the most disgusting struggle which is going on the whole time, on the one hand to inflict, and on the other to evade oppression and injustice. With this sauce I ate my dinner, and truly it tasted bitter."[67]

Fanny Kemble told of pregnant women and nursing mothers who were assigned to heavy field labor within a few weeks of their confinement. On several occasions she was summoned to receive the petitions of "certain poor women in the family-way" who urged her to have their work lightened. After receiving one such petition she talked to the overseer who "seemed evidently annoyed at their having appealed to me; said that their work was not a bit too much for them, and that constantly, they were *shamming* themselves in the family-way in order to obtain a diminution of their labor." Fanny supposed that some of them did sham their pregnancy, "but again, it must be a hard matter for those who do not, not to obtain the mitigation of their toil which their condition requires." On another occasion an aggrieved woman came to see Fanny, accompanied by Old Sackey, who had been chief nurse in the slave hospital for many years. Old Sackey fully confirmed the other woman's account of "the terrible hardships the women underwent in being thus driven to labor before they had recovered from childbearing." Only three weeks were given to recover from confinement before the new mothers resumed hoe labor in the fields. Old Sackey claimed that so many women suffered from "falling of the womb and weakness of the back" that if the policy continued for very long the overseer would uttely destroy all the breeding women.[68]

Costs and benefits

Medical costs on slave plantations varied widely, depending on the incidence of disease and accidents, physicians' fees or contract rates, outlays for medicine, nursing, and midwifery, surgical charges, vaccination rates, hospital maintenance and amortization costs, and other variables. Eugene D. Genovese says that physicians' rates in the Cotton Belt varied but were never less than $1 per visit. Taking into account the general unhealthfulness of the Deep South and the prevalence of epidemics, together with the data yielded by contemporary sources, Genovese estimates that "the medical cost of slaveholding should not be calculated at less than three dollars per slave, including $2.50 or $2.75 for doctors' bills and the remainder for medical supplies and drugs." For Virginia from about 1830 to 1860, Savitt estimates the annual average medical cost at $3 to $4 per slave.[69]

As in the Cotton Belt and Virginia, medical costs varied widely in the British Sugar Colonies. In the testimony he gave to the select committee of the House of Lords in 1832, John Baillie detailed the costs of treating the 350 slaves on his sugar plantation in Jamaica. With respect to attendance of the doctor, he informed the committee:

> There are various Sums given; to some 6*s*. 8*d*., to some 7*s*. 6*d*. per Annum per Head, Old and Young, Male and Female, upon the whole of the Estate, whatever it may be; it depends upon the Situation the Doctor is placed in; if he has a long Journey to perform he is paid 7*s*. 6*d*., if a short Journey he is paid 6*s*. 8*d*. [total £116 per annum], I used to pay 7*s*. 6*d*.

The doctor charged extra for surgical operations (amputating a leg cost £5 6*s*. 8*d*.) and vaccination, which Baillie said amounted to 13*s*. 4*d*. for each slave vaccinated. When the black midwife found herself "embarrassed, the Medical Man is sent for, and he charges £5 6*s*. 8*d*. Currency for his Attendance." The cost of the medicine Baillie supplied varied from £8 or £10 to 24£ per year. Baillie neglected to say how much it cost to supply the midwife and nurses or to estimate the value of the slave hospital.[70]

Table 11.5 shows the estimated cost of providing medical care to the plantation slaves of Jamaica in about 1830. Besides the Parliamentary evidence submitted by John Baillie and others, data on medical costs have been derived from manuscript plantation records and printed works. Use has been made of the 6*s*. 8*d*. annual contract rate paid by John Baillie and also shown in several manuscript accounts. Estimated costs are believed to be on the high side for medicines and drugs, as well as for midwifery, surgery, vaccination, and other services. Bryan Edwards said that a plantation with 250 slaves should have a hospital valued at £300 Jamaica currency. A modern economic historian of Jamaica estimates that the average life of a house in about 1830 was forty years. Table 3.1 in Chapter 3 showed that there were fifty-one black medical attendants who served 2,990 slaves on the Tharp properties in Jamaica, or one medical attendant for every fifty-eight slaves. According to a modern economic historian, the yearly hiring rate for some

Table 11.5. *Estimated medical costs of slavery in Jamaica in about 1830: annual charges for 100 slaves (sterling values)*

Attendance of doctor[a]	£24
Medicines and drugs[b]	7
Midwifery, surgery, vaccination, etc.[c]	10
Hospital maintenance and amortization[d]	3
2 black nurses[e]	21
Total	£65
The sterling–dollar exchange rate for 1822–34 is £1 = $4.566	
65 × 4.566 = 296.79	
Medical cost per slave is $2.97	

Note: The Jamaica currency–sterling ratio of £1.4 to £1 is given in B. W. Higman, *Slave Population and Economy in Jamaica 1807–1834* (Cambridge, 1976), p. vii; the sterling–dollar ratio of £1 to $4.566 is given in L. E. Davies and J. R. T. Hughes, "A Dollar-Sterling Exchange, 1803–1895," *Economic History Review*, Vol. XIII (August 1960), p. 54.

[a]The 6*s*. 8*d*. contract rate is taken chiefly from John Baillie's testimony before the select committee of the House of Lords, and the Gale-Morant Papers at the University of Exeter Library.

[b]Outlays for medicines and drugs are taken chiefly from John Baillie's testimony and the Chisholme Mss. at the National Library of Scotland, Edinburgh.

Outlays for midwifery, surgery, vaccination, etc., are taken chiefly from John Baillie's testimony and the Gale-Morant Papers.

[d]Bryan Edwards, *History of the British Colonies in the West Indies* (New York, 1972), Vol. II, pp. 243–5; Gisela Eisner, *Jamaica, 1830–1930: A Study in Economic Growth* (Manchester, 1961), p. 30.

[e]See Table 3.1 in Chapter 3, and also Higman, *Slave Population and Economy in Jamaica*, p. 41.

tradesmen and domestics was generally £30 Jamaica currency. Because black medical attendants were generally older than most slaves and often physically impaired, this hiring rate has been halved to serve as a proxy for the opportunity cost of such slaves employed in plantation hospitals. To arrive at equivalent dollar values, Jamaica currency values have been converted to sterling at a ratio of £1.4 Jamaica currency to £1 sterling, and from sterling to dollar values at a ratio of £1 to $4.566.

The annual medical cost of nearly $3 for each plantation slave in Jamaica, as shown in Table 11.5, is low compared with estimates for the Cotton Belt and antebellum Virginia. The comparison is even more favorable to the South if the costs are confined to the doctor's attendance, medicines and drugs, midwifery, surgery, and vaccination. On this basis, the outlay per slave in Jamaica is $1.87, or only 62.3 percent of the minimum outlay of $3 in the antebellum South.

Testifying that the contract rate of $1 (equivalent to 6*s.* 8*d.*) was inadequate was Richard R. Madden, M.D., who practiced among the slaves of Jamaica. When he was asked by a select committee of the House of Commons if the typical medical man could satisfactorily perform his duties to the blacks, Madden replied:

> I do not think one medical man would be sufficient to attend on an estate that has perhaps 300 negroes; and perhaps that medical man may have the charge of a dozen properties with that number of negroes on each estate; if he was even so inclined he could not give sufficient attendance.

Moreover, Madden testified that hospital patients were generally supplied with a very poor diet of plantains or corn flour and were cared for by nurses who were usually old and infirm.[71]

Madden's criticisms were echoed by others. John Stewart claimed that a medical practice of as many as 4,000 slaves was far too extensive for two medical practitioners. Under such circumstances the hothouse, instead of being attended daily, could not be visited more often than twice or three times a week, especially on the more remote properties. "At the sickly period, therefore, strict medical attention to all the patients must become utterly impracticable, and the loss of many valuable slaves may ensue." Stewart deplored the fashion of throwing a vast medical practice into the hands of one man, to the injury of his brethren who were equally deserving.[72] Similarly, the Reverend Richard Bickell asserted that it was impossible for the doctor who had a vast practice to give much attention to his patients. Bickell ridiculed such a doctor who was said to have "his head full of calomel and jalap, which constitutes a great part of the *Pharmacopeia Jamaicensis.*" Such a "learned doctor" would merely walk into the room of the sick and destitute, ask a few questions, turn on his heel, and walk to the overseer's house to talk over the news of the day.[73]

Conclusion

The tendency for a few doctors to monopolize the practice of slave medicine was not the only shortcoming. From the data presented in this chapter, it can be argued that although the slaves on the typical sugar plantation were supplied with expanded medical services, authority was often so divided as to weaken the doctor's ability to carry out his professional duties. It was Dr. Williamson's belief, as noted in Chapter 10, that "an imperfect confused manner" had been adopted "for providing the sick negro suitably in a hot-house, or hospital."[74] Not only were many doctors overworked and underpaid, but they also lacked control of the hospitals and their attendants. Nurses and midwives commonly worked under the direct supervision of the planter or his overseer. When the planter was an absentee, his overseer was likely to regard the doctor as a meddling busybody who naively encouraged the slaves to pretend illness and rob the field gangs of potentially productive workers. Rather than consider themselves as only a supplement to the doctor, overseers and bookkeepers sometimes took it upon themselves to treat dangerous illnesses with fatal consequences. Overseers had the unenviable task of producing as much labor as possible at the same time that they were charged with protecting the health and well-being of the slaves. As Todd Savitt has observed, the overseer was "taskmaster, judge, and physician simultaneously – a tremendous and sometimes impossible responsibility."[75]

Pro-planter authors were arguably overgenerous in their praise of plantation medical practice and the white people who cared for the sick. They emphasized that white doctors were in the saddle much of the day on regular calls and frequently summoned on express calls at night, ministering to the sick and wounded, exposing themselves to dangerous diseases, and requiring phenomenal physical energy and will to make their rounds in the face of fatigue and frequent bouts of fever. At his best, the plantation practitioner was knowledgeable, skilled, considerate, and widely respected for his character and professional conduct. He was praised for being better educated, more attentive, more humane, and more worthy of respect than medical practitioners in Europe and North America. Similarly, planters and overseers were praised for supplying the sick with blankets, rice, oatmeal, flour, beef, and mutton, and exempting them from hard labor during the convalescent period.

Pro-planter authors were less inclined to emphasize the substantial role blacks and mulattoes played as medics. Although hospital patients saw white doctors, planters, and overseers at varying intervals, they were under the constant surveillance and care of black doctors, doctresses, and nurses. On small plantations the nurse frequently served as sick cook, midwife, and nursery attendant, as well as cleaning, bathing, and dosing the sick. On large plantations the head nurse or doctress commonly supervised a staff of cooks, midwives, nursery attendants, and sick nurses. Nurses frequently doubled as prison wardens. Some of them led lonely and isolated lives ministering to victims of the yaws. As suggested in Chapter 3, the informal practice of medicine by blacks, and especially women, as folk healers and nurses outside the hospitals may have exceeded in effectiveness all the health services provided by the white establishment on plantations.

Despite the obstacles they faced, plantation doctors did manage to reduce the sick list and save valuable lives. They inoculated and vaccinated against smallpox, performed minor surgery, and administered medicines to expel worms and treat other stomach and bowel disorders as well as respiratory ailments. They saw that their patients were provided with wholesome food, maintained high standards of cleanliness, provided commonsense counsel to planters, and eased their patients' fear, anxiety, and pain.

Not all the shortcomings of plantation medical practice can be attributed to the white and black medics. Given the prevailing theories of disease and methods of diagnosis and treatment, doctors literally hurried to their graves many patients who might have survived had they remained untreated.

Although it is not well documented, it is reasonable to believe that plantation medical practice deteriorated in the tumultuous times preceding slave emancipation in 1834. This period, extending over a decade or more, witnessed a series of external and internal shocks, including the decline of sugar prices and profits, growing planter indebtedness, slave unrest and insurrection, and conflict over the slavery question. Hope of gradual emancipation turned to despair as colonial governments either refused or only grudgingly carried out the amelioration laws and orders. In the end, after much soul searching, Parliament voted to emancipate the slaves throughout the British Empire.

12

Slavery and medicine

In the long and bitter debate on slavery, profound have been the essays on puberty, procreation, and the terms of child-bearing; registries have been dissected; figures have been heaped upon figures, returns have succeeded returns; Protectors transported across the Atlantic; learned actuaries employed on both sides; and to this day, the contest remains undecided, productive only of this unhappy result – that, to the West Indians, a drawn battle must always be defeat – to their adversaries victory.

William Burnley, 1833[1]

This final chapter first summarizes the demographic and economic history of slavery in the British West Indies. It then analyzes the demographic and economic situation and seeks to weigh the relative importance of the various factors. We investigate the practice of heroic medicine in the Sugar Colonies and assess the quality of health care supplied to the slaves. Finally we compare the demographic structure and health care systems under slavery and freedom and their chief consequences.

Slave population attrition

The primary goal of this study has been first to understand why the slave population of the British West Indies suffered a net natural decrease during the period 1680–1834, and second to ascertain the quality of health care provided the slaves. In seeking answer to the first question, I have looked at the macro disease environment and epidemiology of the Atlantic area and particularly the South Atlantic Systems, the planters' tendency to buy new slaves from Africa rather than to encourage reproduction, the role played by the Atlantic slave trade as a disease vector, the micro environment of the sugar plantation and its brutal labor system, the chief slave diseases and their incidence with special reference to nutrition-deficient diseases, and the problem of infertility. It is our task to show how these factors differed in their timing, duration, and significance, and how they interacted to produce one of the most oppressive slave systems in the Western Hemisphere.

Most basic to an understanding of the failure of the slave population to increase in the British Sugar Colonies were factors embedded in the complex of socioeconomic and political motives, organization, and conduct. As Sir Philip Sherlock points out:

> West Indian society was molded by three institutions; colonialism, the plantation system, and slavery . . . The old plantation system depended on a large, subservient labour force. The entry of Europe meant the entry of slavery, at first the enslavement of the Amerindian and his destruction, then the importation of white, indentured labour, and, finally, the importation of Africans as slaves . . . The system of production based on slave labour fostered habits of dependence and encouraged the acceptance of the owner class as a model of excellence, goodness, efficiency, and virtue; it engendered social divisions based not only on occupation but also on skin colour, and it led to self-distrust and even to self-contempt and self-rejection.[2]

From what is thought to have been a relatively mild form of slavery in the early decades of the sugar revolution, conditions became much harsher as planters turned to the combined and constant labor of gang slavery to compensate for declining soil fertility and the growth of weeds in the canefields. The fact that an annual supply of more than 5,000 African slaves was needed in Barbados to keep up the labor force after about 1680 points to a very high mortality. As Vincent T. Harlow noted, "It was cheaper to have them work out then die out."[3] John Oldmixon, the historian of the British Empire in America, wrote in 1708 that the planters of Barbados "are now forc'd to dung and plant every Year; insomuch that 100 Acres of Cane require almost double the Number of Hands they did formerly, while the Land retain'd its natural Vigour, which also then did not only bring forth certain Crops, but fewer Weeds too, the Weeds having been encreas'd by frequent Dunging."[4]

Douglas Hall says that slaves were purchased or reared because they provided agricultural and manufacturing power and services.[5] Their muscle and brain power was combined with power supplied by draft animals, windmills, water mills, and tide mills to make the production of sugar an energy-intensive and labor-intensive agro-industrial system without parallel. The sugar monoculture crowded out other land uses to such an extent that the islands became highly dependent on imported foodstuffs, draft animals, and building materials. We have seen that before the American War of Independence foodstuffs were imported chiefly from North America and that these calorie and protein inputs became precarious during the wars and hurricanes of the 1770s and 1780s. Writing in 1784, Edward Long urged the British government to permit free trade between the United States and the British Sugar Colonies. He contrasted the uncertainty of food imports from the British Isles with those from the United States "where, in such an extent of latitude and variety of climates, a general want of ability to afford the supply can hardly ever occur." Indeed, he affirmed that the granaries of the United States presented "immediate protection against famine: a protection which might not be in the power of Britain to give, notwithstanding her utmost despatch and exertion."[6]

Despite the restrictions imposed on trade between Yankees and Creoles after 1783, British sugar planters continued to import slaves from Africa. Lord Sheffield claimed that the British had such a decided superiority in the African trade that they were able to supply slaves to their colonies one-sixth cheaper than their French rivals could supply their own colonies.[7] That high profits were compatible with high slave mortality and short working-life expectancy was the opinion of knowledgeable observers. Lord Brougham maintained "that as long as a slave market exists, men find their profit in working out a certain number of their slaves, and supplying the blacks by purchase, rather than by breeding."[8] William Dickson, who observed slavery as secretary to the governor of Barbados, wrote that the period of "efficient, productive hard labour" fulfilled by slaves after they were purchased did "not exceed, or rather, in strictness, cannot be proved to equal SEVEN YEARS. I say, *after* they are bought, grown people being generally preferred, with a view to immediate labour."[9] Despite repeated warnings to treat newly imported slaves with care, many planters continued to purchase slaves at crop time and set them to work without proper seasoning.

As the Sugar Colonies approached a state of near-monoculture, planters generally calculated that it was "cheaper" to buy new slaves from Africa than to encourage family life and reproduction. But this inhumane calculation required that slaves be procurable when they were needed, in the quantities demanded, proportioned according to sex and age preference, and at prices low enough to yield profits from slave-grown staples. Moreover, the calculation required low slave maintenance costs in the form of food, clothing, shelter, and medical services. Dr. Robert Jackson, who had practiced medicine in Jamaica, gave testimony to the select committee of the House of Commons in 1790. He was asked "whether it was more the object of the overseers to work the slaves moderately, and keep up their numbers by breeding; or to work them out, increasing thereby the produce of the estate, and trusting for recruits to the Slave Market?" He replied, "The latter plan was more generally adopted, principally, I conceive, owing to this reason, that imported Slaves are fit for immediate labour – Slaves that are reared from childhood are liable to many accidents, and cannot make any return of labour for many years."[10] Another respondent to the same question was Captain Hall of the Royal Navy, who had lived for extended periods in Barbados and the Leeward Islands. "Breeding was by no means thought desirable," he testified, "as they rather thought it a misfortune to have pregnant women, or even young Slaves. They esteemed the charge of rearing a child to a state of manhood more troublesome, and greater, than the buying a Slave fit for work; and it was no uncommon thing for them to give away a child of two years old, as you would a puppy from a litter."[11]

The costs and benefits of a policy of amelioration were discussed with some care by Dr. David Collins, the St. Vincent doctor-planter. He admitted that such a policy would impose additional duties on the planter with respect to the care of his slaves. Moreover, greater expenses would be incurred, for he proposed "that the negroes should be fed and clothed more liberally than they now are, and be more indulged during their indisposition, whence an excess of expense, and an apparent decrease of income." If judiciously applied, however, these expenditures would, in fact, be an investment of capital. Slaves who were better treated would be "more robust of body, more alert and contented in mind, so that, performing more work, the gross income of the estate, far from being reduced, will necessarily experience a considerable increase." Not only would the gross income be greater, but also savings would result from more births and fewer deaths. Collins was aware that it would be difficult to adopt his reformed system of management on estates that were encumbered with debt. Furthermore, he cautioned absentee proprietors to "be less solicitous for the momentary increase of their income, than for the more solid improvement of their properties." Good management should not be judged exclusively by the criterion of monetary income; rather, under the new regime, a much more certain indication of good management would be "the scarcity of deaths, and the number of births."[12]

Dr. Collins's rational calculations and admonitions were largely ignored. As colonies of exploitation, the British sugar islands produced staple commodities for export markets and developed rigid systems of class and caste in which others did the toil and Europeans reaped the profits. The system of exploitation in the British West Indies was described by John Jeremie, an Englishman who served as first president of the royal court of St. Lucia from 1824 to 1830, as follows:

> Colonies were valuable in as much as they differed in productions from the nations to which they belonged; and as they exchanged all they produced, save the little required for their own consumption, for what is produced at home.
>
> This system has had its day, and those who have thriven under it are naturally inclined on recollecting its pecuniary advantages, or hearing of its profits but forgetting its loss, to overlook its evils. Under that system, every thing was forced; prices were forced, consignments in return were forced, labour forced, life forced; hence, high interest and usurious profits, rapid fortunes, rapid bankruptcies, smuggling, and perjury, producing excited passions, and rapid mortality; – thence also the iron collars and the

> whip; thence a decrease of population, and thence a continuation of the slave trade.

Jeremie went on to assert that the prejudice against color was erected upon this system until it became a political maxim that every individual who had African blood was "idle, worthless, and disaffected." "You deprive a man of every incentive to exertion but the *whip*," he exclaimed, "and then express surprise that he requires the *whip* to make him work!"[13]

In the age of the democratic revolution the British West Indies were dealt a scrics of blows by events that were both external and internal to the islands. First, the American Revolution, in conjunction with severe hurricanes, brought hunger and starvation in the short run and a less reliable and cheap source of foodstuffs in the long run. Second, slavery in the British Caribbean colonies was threatened by the successful slave revolt in the wealthy French colony of Saint Domingue and the establishment of the first black republic under the new name of Haiti. Third, the antislavery movement succeeded in its twin goals of legally abolishing the Atlantic slave trade in 1807 and then, after twenty-seven years, of emancipating all chattel slaves in the British Empire. Abolition of the slave trade was intended to induce planters to shift from anti-natalist to pro-natalist policies and to adopt other measures of amelioration. But the achievement of these reforms was made difficult by planter resistance and lax enforcement during the long wars against France and Napoleon. Fourth, the decline in sugar and coffee prices after 1815 further hindered efforts to ameliorate the condition of the slaves. Fifth, many Christian missionaries came to the islands in the last decade of slavery. Although they sought to draw a firm line btween the spiritual and the secular, they could not help but arouse political discontent among the slaves when they preached the doctrine of spiritual equality. Sixth, a series of slave insurrections were symptomatic of the internal conflicts between masters and slaves at a time of renewed debate on the question of emancipation in England.[14]

These external and internal shocks, in conjunction with persistent racism and oppression of the blacks, go far to explain the failure of amelioration of slavery in the British Sugar Colonies. By the last decade of slavery, island economies and governments were dominated by plantation attorneys and managers whose incomes and reputations depended on the volume of staples produced and exported. They bitterly resented any criticism of their mode of conducting plantations and governing the slaves under their jurisdiction, yet they made it difficult to confirm or deny the charges levied against them by their critics. Absentee proprietors who were induced by abolitionist propaganda to ameliorate the condition of their slaves were often thwarted by their attorneys and managers who disregarded the instructions received in letters from England and Scotland. The upshot of the conflict between masters and slaves, mother country and colonies, pro- and anti-abolitionists, absentees and residents, was Parliamentary action. At midnight on 31 July 1834, 770,270 slaves were emancipated in nineteen British colonies, of whom some 650,000 were inhabitants of thirteen Caribbean islands or groups of islands and the mainland colony of British Guiana. "Man now ceased to be the property of man," exclaimed the Reverend James Phillippo of Jamaica. "The former slaves were now to labour, not at the caprice of an absolute owner, enforced by the whip of an arbitrary and irresponsible task-master, but by settled rules."[15]

From this historical survey it is evident that the Sugar Colonies concentrated more and more resources on a few exportable staples and thus became dependent on a wide range of imports, including slave workers, and on exports to overseas markets. From admittedly sketchy information, West Indian slavery appears to have been relatively mild before and during the early phase of the mid-seventeenth-century sugar revolution. At this time plantation labor was shared with white indentured servants, locally grown foodstuffs were more plentiful than they became later, and, owing to such factors as a better balance of the sexes and a more benign disease environment, slave family life and reproduction met with some success. Beginning in the 1680s, at a time of relatively low slave prices, Barbadian planters shifted to anti-natalist policies. They calculated that it was cheaper to buy new workers than to bear the cost of breeding and raising slaves to working age in the colony. In their rage to push their estates, they imported proportionately more men than women and tended to put newly imported slaves in the labor force without adequate seasoning. The upshot was a rising death rate and a declining birthrate, owing to such factors as hard labor, cruel punishment, malnutrition, epidemics, and accidents.

In time, the curse of a slavery monoculture shifted from Barbados to other islands that provided a suitable environment for the production of sugar. The hazards attending the slaves of St. Kitts in the early eighteenth century were enumerated by the Reverend Robert Robertson, who was himself a planter. Two-fifths of the slaves imported from Africa died in the seasoning, whereas the mortality of the Creoles was annually one in fifteen. In dry years when local provisions were scarce, the loss was one in seven, and even higher in sickly seasons "and when the Small-Pox, which is almost as much dreaded in the Leeward Islands as the Pestilence in any Part of *Europe* happens to be imported, it is incredible what Havock it makes among the Blacks." On the other hand, Robertson said that little gain could be expected from the breeding of slaves. This was due to hard labor, venereal disease, infant mortality, "the little Work the Mother can do for three Months before and nine after the Birth, Midwifery, and some other Incidents, and the Maintenance of the Child for six or seven Years at a Peny *per Diem*." He observed that the increase by the births was not near so great as strangers to the colonies were apt to think. Notwithstanding that self-interest obliged the purchasers "to take all imaginable Care of the Salt-Water, that is, the newly imported Slaves, yet two Fifths of them, if not more, taking one importation with another, die in the Seasoning, which considering how the Affair is ordered, renders the Continuance of fresh Supplies absolutely necessary." Robertson estimated that the number of workers on a plantation of 150 slaves seldom exceeded 80 or 90. The rest were either too young or too old, or hindered by sickness, lameness, attendance on the white family, or had run away.[16] Had he possessed the insights of modern epidemiologists, Robertson would have deplored the concentration of people, plants, and animals in lowland tropical areas suited to cane sugar production, thus opening a Pandora's box of debilitating and lethal pathogens and their vectors to prey on the black and white inhabitants.

The impact of the Atlantic slave trade on the health and well-being of Caribbean slaves was enormous. Access to "cheap" laborers from Africa induced the planters to alter the ratio of the sexes, to regard female slaves more as work units than as breeding units, to shift land from food crops to sugarcane and thus depend on imported foodstuffs, and to increase the size and density of the plantation labor force and thus to spread infectious and epidemic disease. Access to cheap laborers increased the ratio of saltwater to Creole slaves, introduced black-related diseases to exacerbate the already noxious disease environment, brought to the islands debilitated and despondent Africans who had a one in three chance of surviving the seasoning, and commonly led to acute culture shock and resistance to harsh labor and punishment. Because of access to cheap labor from abroad, planters found themselves caught in a vicious circle of working out some of their slaves and replacing them with their newly imported brethren, rather than encouraging breeding. Compared with other societies in the New World, the Caribbean plantations stand out as the most destructive to life and limb.

As already discussed, the British West Indies were dealt a series of blows in the age of the democratic revolution that first brought the Atlantic slave trade to an end and then, after a generation or more, emancipated all slaves in the British Empire. Throughout the slavery era the wars between the great powers curtailed overseas trade and shipping and especially the trade in slaves across the Middle Passage. Because imported slaves were scarce and dear in wartime, planters were compelled by self-interest to take better care of their bondsmen. Wars also curtailed the import of foodstuffs, however, and in the event of hurricanes, devastated locally grown provisions. In a period of distress like the American War of Independence, this cutback led to widespread malnutrition and death. Whether the succession of shocks – American war, hurricanes, Haitian slave revolt, antislavery agitation – was sufficient to wean the planters from their "buy rather than breed" syndrome is hardly believable except for the slave owners in the island of Barbados.

By closing the Atlantic slave trade, the influx of diseased Africans was halted and attrition no longer resulted from the seasoning. Moreover, by shutting out cargoes of saltwater slaves, which had been mainly males, the sex ratio became better balanced because women tended to outlive men. In this situation it was to be expected that black women would be valued more highly as breeding units than as work units. But the continued attrition of the slave population on the sugar plantations, in combination with the growing proportion of women to men, pressured women to keep up the ranks of the field gangs. It was tragic that this conflict was resolved in favor of anti-natalist policies. Birthrates continued at abysmally low levels and, with the lone exception of Barbados, continued to lag behind the death rate. Thus a new vicious circle emerged whereby overworked and underfed women of childbearing age were unable or unwilling to bring new slaves into the world.

James Stephen stood apart from other antislavery leaders before passage of the abolition bill in doubting the simple formula that abolition would result in amelioration without outside intervention in relations between planters and slaves. In his seminal pamphlet, *The Crisis of the Sugar Colonies* (1802), he wrote: "I must here affirm a truth, of which though disputed by abolitionists, the owners of West India estates in general are but too conscious, 'that the present large profits of a successful sugar plantation could not be obtained, if the condition of the slaves were to be effectually improved.' " To Stephen, the only practicable foundation upon which to build the security of the Sugar Colonies "is that of meliorating the condition of the great mass of the people, and converting them from dangerous enemies into defenders, and this is only to be done by the exercise of the Legislative Authority of Parliament."[17]

As Stephen no doubt understood, the failure of amelioration was due in part to the growth of absentee proprietorship. We have seen that the interests of absentees and their attorneys and managers tended to diverge. Whereas the former tended to have a permanent interest in preserving their labor force, the latter were bent on maximizing production, commissions, and salaries by forcing slaves to make undue exertions in the cane fields and sugar works. The low life expectancy of white men in the tropics goes far to explain the large number of absentee proprietors. Whereas the absentees had managed to escape the scene of their former exertions and wealth getting, the attorneys and managers who remained behind were equally determined to get rich quick and thus be able to spend their remaining years in a more salubrious climate.

From the standpoint of both sexes and all age groups, the demographic failure of the Caribbean slave population can be explained in large measure by poor working and living conditions. As with the slaves in antebellum America, infectious and parasitic diseases were closely associated with work loads, fatigue, food, housing, clothing, sanitation, and interracial contacts. These factors combined in varying proportions with diseases transmitted through the slave trade and by contact with Europeans and North Americans to perpetuate low fertility and high mortality. More than other factors, what set the lives of Caribbean slaves apart from their brothers and sisters in the United States were their inordinate work loads and poor diets. Combined and constant labor, frequently extending beyond the traditional daylight hours, could not be sustained on the generally poor diets supplied to the slaves. Malnourished slaves were more susceptible to infectious diseases and suffered severely when they were infected. Had their labor been made lighter, the slaves would have had more time and energy to cultivate their provision grounds and raise small stock to sustain their families. In the final analysis, therefore, the slave labor regimen on Caribbean sugar plantations was the paramount cause of the demographic failure.

Heroic medicine in the West Indies

European doctors in the Sugar Colonies were at their best when they urged planters to enhance the life chances of their slaves by providing better diets, clothing, housing, and sanitation; tempering work loads and punishment; and taking care of pregnant women, mothers, and children. They were at their best when they made an effort to understand their black patients in a clinical sense and also the intimate union of medicine and magic in the minds of Afro-Caribbean slaves, the culture shock they suffered, and their suspicion and fear of white doctors and their medicines. They were at their best when they made an effort to learn the folk wisdom of the blacks, study their herbal remedies, and search out indigenous plants that have medicinal value. They were at their best when they combined the practice of medicine and surgery with scientific investigation and the publication of books concerned with tropical medicine and natural history. They were at their best when they were skeptical of fashionable theories of disease causation and sought to advance rational conceptual schemes adapted to the disease environment in the West Indies. They were at their best when they were alert to the baneful influence of certain medicines and limited their prescriptions to therapeutically effective drugs.

Very few, if any, medical men conformed to this ideal. One important source of error and malpractice was the humoral-climatic and miasmatic theory of medicine. It was widely believed that the underlying condition of disease was a morbid state or imbalance of the humors or vital fluids – that is, blood, phlegm, yellow bile, and black bile, which were the counterparts of earth, water, air, and fire. It was believed that the balance of the humors was upset when noxious miasmata were breathed in and mixed with the blood, or when sudden changes in temperature and moisture checked free perspiration and sweating. If a given humor was present in an excessive amount, it was believed that the illness should be treated by depletion – that is, bleeding, purging, blistering, or sweating; if deficient, the patient should be restored by means of proper diet and drugs. Moreover, the use of mineral and other chemical remedies was recommended to achieve a balance of the acids and alkalines in the body.[18]

Another source of error and malpractice was the search for one panacea for all human ailments. As John Duffy points out, "Calomel, bloodletting, and quinine were the main focal points of interest in this quest for a universal remedy. The first two, calomel and bloodletting, were aspects of the antiphlogistic treatment for ridding the body of excess humors; the latter, quinine, was derived from cinchona or Jesuit's bark, a wonder drug from the New World that had earlier been hailed as a miracle medicine." Actually, doctors prescribed many more therapeutically useless herbs and other substances to their patients than effective drugs. In his search of the first *United States Pharmacopoeia* (1820), Harry F. Dowling found only twenty active drugs. "Among these were three specifics for infections: quinine for malaria, mercury for syphilis, and ipecac for amebic dysentery. Other effective drugs were opium, belladonna, digitalis, and a few substances that either quieted the gastrointestinal tract or purged it." The medical world was far from static, however. Indeed, the first landmark in the modern therapeutic era dates from the early eighteenth-century practice of inoculating with smallpox to prevent that disease, followed by Jenner's cowpox vaccination of 1798, which did the same thing more safely.[19]

Extreme bleeding, vomiting, and purging, or heroic medicine, appear to have been widely practiced in the West Indies. Advocates of venesection or bloodletting claimed that it relieved pain, promoted relaxation and sleep, subdued fever and the force of the circulation, checked vomiting, and prevented hemorrhage. Although bloodletting came under attack in Europe and America and was seldom practiced during part of the nineteenth century, it experienced a revival during the first quarter of the twentieth century, but only for a few clinical conditions. Since the advent of new dietary and chemotherapeutic methods of treatment, bloodletting has been confined largely to the procurement of plasma for blood banks.[20]

Bloodletting reached its peak of popularity in Europe and America in the early nineteenth century, although it met with a mixed response by certain doctors in the British Sugar Colonies. In treating cases of pneumonia, Dr. James Thomson noted that in several instances within a sixty-hour period he had "taken away eighty ounces of blood from a robust negro and saved his life." Immediately after the first copious bleeding he administered a strong purge consisting of neutral salts with James's or antimonial powders. He warned, however, that after the second or third day bleeding became very dangerous and by many doctors was altogether interdicted. In the treatment of influenza patients, Dr. John Williamson cautioned doctors to exercise discretion and be aware that some blacks could not bear much, or perhaps any, bleeding. Dr. Thomas Dancer deplored the widespread use of the lancet and quoted with approval an author who asserted that if the disease of consumption had destroyed its thousands, the practice of bloodletting had destroyed its tens of thousands.[21]

Practitioners in the West Indies were not unlike their counterparts in North America and Europe in overdosing their patients with drugs. There is reason to believe that overdosing was carried to even greater lengths owing to both the belief that tropical diseases needed to be arrested quickly with strong remedies and the racist myth that blacks were less sensitive than whites to strong medicines. Dr. Collins voiced the latter belief in pungent language, pointing out that

> the most nauseous drugs, unless of the emetic tribe, seldom ruffle the stomachs of negroes, or dispose them to vomit. Bark they retain in almost any quantity, and their bowels resist the most drastic purges, without suffering much inconvenience. I have given, for the tape-worm, ten grains of calomel, and twenty-five of gamboge, to a constitution, which I had before found to be almost immoveable, without their occasioning one puke, or more than four or five motions of the belly.

Heavy doses of such active medicines as calomel, aloes, jalap, and the carthartic extract were required, as Dr. Williamson explained, "to produce their effects within a limited time; otherwise, the rapid advances of disease, where all efforts are no longer useful, will lead us to reflect on what few men can endure."[22]

If white doctors had a callous attitude toward their black patients' capacity to take medicines, it is not surprising that overseers and bookkeepers administered medicines to ailing blacks in a perfunctory manner. The anonymous author of the novel *Marly* recounted a conversation between George Marley, bookkeeper on Water Melon Valley estate in Jamaica, and another bookkeeper who was described as an illiterate "Old Dragoon" who had attended the sick in both military and slave hospitals. Not understanding the "whips and pot-hangers which they make in the book prescribing the doses of medicine," the Old Dragoon said he took "a look at the negro when he comes in, and if he seems very ill, ipecacuanha I know is the certain prescription. If not very ill, glauber salts or calomel according to the apparent case, of which I can easily judge; and if it be for jigars [chigoes], whereby their feet are very sore and proud flesh appears, then I know blue-stone is a certain thing." The Old Dragoon claimed that he had learned from long experience to weigh the vomit powder and calomel, and had fully mastered "the weights of salts, a man getting more than a woman, and children according to their ages; and I never yet was challenged for being wrong." He administered bark and wine for more stubborn illnesses. Except for castor oil, which the blacks made themselves, no other drugs were required or used by Jamaica doctors. Although Marly laughed at the Old Dragon's estimation of the medical profession, he thought it "very unjust to tax the whole body of medical gentlemen in the island, amongst whom there are many who would confer honour on any country."[23]

Overdosing with opium, mercury, and antimony was particularly destructive to the slaves. Opium and laudanum, which is a mixture of opium and alcohol, were the universal pain killers and sedatives of the age, However, they were addictive to the point of demoralization, they contained an active poison that killed quickly, and they induced withdrawal symptoms after very little use. Nevertheless, no other drug could compare with opium to relieve pain and induce sleep. By its liberal use Dr. Thomson believed he had saved his black patients many a miserable hour; "it is astonishing the relief they experience from it."[24]

Mercury, or quicksilver, was widely used in the treatment of syphilis, yaws, and leprosy. Its use was roundly condemned by Edward Long, the Jamaican planter-historian. Instead of curing the yaws, he found that mercurial preparations had the effect of rooting the disorder more in the system, resulting in the "joint evil" and dropsy. When Dr. Thomson arrived in Jamaica it was the practice to treat yaws with mercury. He soon perceived that although this mineral had a temporary influence in repelling the sores, it produced such lamentable consequences that he was induced "to look upon mercury as an exceedingly dangerous and destructive medicine in the treatment of yaws, and I abandoned its use in every case, and have no reason to regret my determination." By the time his book was published in 1820, Thomson affirmed that the use of mercury had been abandoned by most practitioners in Jamaica.[25]

Antimony is a metallic element that is hard, brittle, silver-white, and crystalline. It came into popular use in medicinal preparations in the seventeenth and eighteenth centuries. Physicians prescribed it as a diaphoretic and emetic for the treatment of fevers, cutaneous eruptions, gout, apoplexy, and other ailments. Among the antimonials, tartar emetic (antimony and potassium tartrate) was prescribed by physicians throughout the British Empire. By producing perspiration, nausea, and vomiting, tartar emetic was believed to create a mechanical or "shock" effect that checked fevers and other inflammatory diseases at the outset. As patent medicines, antimonials were retailed under such familiar labels as Dr. James's Fever Powder and Dr. Norris's Fever Drops. Since they destroyed many lives when used in an indiscriminate manner, antimonials came to be regarded as dangerous medicines. Today they are limited chiefly to the treatment of protozoal diseases.[26]

The quality of plantation health care

Not all medical practices and substances were harmful to slaves. To the baneful effects of heroic medicine must be opposed the beneficial results of inoculation, vaccination, quinine, and digitalis. In all likelihood limited gains came from the construction of sick houses and lying-in wards; the employment of black doctors, doctoresses, midwives, and nurses; the isolation of patients afflicted with yaws and leprosy; improvements in hygiene, especially in cutting the navel string of infants; the use of preventive medicines for worms; and better bandaging of sores and ulcers. Infants and young children were perhaps better cared for by the eve of emancipation. As a case in point, Sir Michael Clare testified that he personally attended the old nursery woman who administered a dose of worm medicine every Monday morning to the black children on the estates where he practiced. After the children were separated from their nursing mothers, they were put in charge of the "weaning woman" who had charge of preparing their meals and seeing that they ate them. The hospitals on the estates he attended were divided into men's and women's apartments. On many estates it was the custom to keep the children separate under the care of an old woman. Sick slaves were supplied with nourishing broths made from mutton, oatmeal, rice, Guinea corn, wheat flour, yams, and plantains. Hospitals were equipped with hot baths, which Sir Michael said were frequently ordered.[27]

Doctors and planters no doubt became more knowledgeable about the efficacy of different medicines. The "officinal," or shop medicines, wrote Dr. Dancer, were generally preferred over "the simples of the country" because their virtues and the manner of administering them were better understood. He believed that many of the simples had considerable efficacy, however, and could be substituted advantageously for the officinal ones. Dancer sought to extirpate quackery by publishing a medical manual designed to communicate the practical knowledge of tropical diseases to families and plantations. He reprinted a long article on quack or patent medicines, selecting from "the almost incalculable number of these vaunted remedies . . . such as are in more general use in this island." As noted, Dr. James's Fever Powder was an antimonial preparation used to treat fevers and other ailments. One packet of this preparation was said to retail at 2*s*. 6*d*., although it could not have cost the proprietor more than 2*d*. Other doctors became skeptical of the virtues of other widely used medicines. Dr. James Chisholme, for example, thought that the considerable charges his manager incurred for sarsaparilla for young slaves was wasted. Indeed, he claimed he had proved beyond contradiction that "a decoction of Sarsaparilla is of no more use in medicine than *ditch water* . . . and desire no more may be bought for me." On the other hand, he recommended a concoction of lignum-vitae as a "useful and powerful remedy for yawey blacks."[28]

Perhaps some gains in the health care of the blacks came from a better understanding of the nature and treatment of tropical diseases. European medical manuals, according to Dr. Dancer, were not well suited to the tropical climate of the West Indies, "where diseases put on a different aspect and character; where they commonly run a shorter course, and have a more fatal tendency; consequently requiring a treatment very different from that made use of in the same diseases elsewhere." John Stewart probably reflected the views of the Creole gentry when he wrote that

> perhaps the old experienced surgeon, who, by a long residence and extensive practice in the country, has acquired a thorough knowledge of the diseases incident to the climate, and the most successful mode of treatment, is a more desirable medical attendant than the regular bred young physician, just emerged from the cloisters of a college, and fortified with Greek, Latin and his diploma.

Similarly, Dr. Williamson was convinced that the various complaints of tropical climates required local knowledge and experience; he claimed that attentive observation and the facilities afforded by his medical journal had been eminently useful in his own practice.[29]

Foremost among the doctors who adapted their practice to the conditions of the West Indies was Dr. John Quier of Lluidas Vale, Jamaica. As a young practitioner on Worthy Park and other estates, Quier admitted to heroic practices including copious bleeding, savage purges consisting of mercurial calomel, jalap, and emetic tartar, and drastic doses of opium. After gaining experience, however, he realized that excessive purging and bleeding weakened and killed his patients. He was persuaded that, although his medications rarely cured, he could ameliorate symptoms, strengthen the patient's will to live, and provide care, cleanliness, fresh air, and decent food to encourage any natural tendency toward a cure. Whereas Quier continued to pay lip service to the conventional medical wisdom of his time, he more often came to prescribe "strengthening diets, emollients, cooling lotions, and analgesics such as the opiate laudanum." Like most of his medical colleagues, Quier owned slaves and identified with the planter class. He said he "always found proprietors and managers inclined to comply with his directions and recommendations of any thing that might be requisite and necessary for the comfort of the sick."[30]

Included among other Jamaican doctors whose careers in many ways paralleled that of Dr. Quier were William Wright, the two Francis Rigby Brodbelts, Fortunatus Dwarris, John Williamson, Benjamin Moseley, Thomas Dancer, James Maxwell, and James Thomson. Dr. Thomson stands out for his attack on mercury, his keen interest in the folk remedies of the blacks, and his use of local medicinal plants. Finding imported bark both expensive and adulterated in quality, he was induced to seek a substitute in the bark of the local quassia or bitterwood tree, which he used extensively to treat fevers and deranged action of the stomach and bowels. During a fatal epidemic of influenza he said he had dissected the bodies of forty or fifty black victims to obtain "a knowledge of the means requisite to stop its ravages." Thomson admitted he knew of no cure for the yaws. "There are many things celebrated as specifics which in reality have no virtues," he wrote, "and numerous histories of surprising cures, where nature ought to have had the merit. Such affections are too often incurable, and if we can prevent them from proceeding further we may be perfectly satisfied."[31]

The above-mentioned doctors notwithstanding, it is perhaps true that the European practitioners as a group had little positive impact on the health of their black patients. They lacked the authority and resources to alleviate the major medical problems of poverty, ignorance, poor nourishment, hard labor, and ill-regulated conditions of life. The white doctor often lacked authority to keep a slave in the hospital for treatment when the master or manager was convinced that the slave was feigning illness to avoid labor. The white doctor was both a technician and a colonizer who confronted a colonized and enslaved patient who was reluctant to entrust his life to a stranger. Slaves were generally alienated from colonial society and tended to fear and mistrust the white doctors who treated their illnesses. Lacking the ability to communicate and establish rapport with his patients, the white doctor could only practice plantation medicine as if he were a veterinarian. Slaves might be expected to resist the poisonous potions and pills that constituted the pharmacopoeia of European-trained doctors. Sir Michael Clare, M.D., a Jamaican practitioner, told of slaves objecting to coming to the hospital. He testified that the general cause of the objection was their dislike of medicine and medical treatment; "they do not like to be dosed with Medicine."[32] Medical practitioners in general received little credit from the blacks for their skill in the cure of yaws, said Dr. James Maxwell. Indeed, the blacks placed more faith in the primitive treatment of their African forefathers, which Dr. Maxwell thought to be "infinitely preferable to the practice of those who endeavour to cure yaws by the various preparations of mercury."[33] The struggle to prolong life and reduce misery on West Indian plantations was difficult because available knowledge was unsystematic and tools were rudimentary at best. The doctor almost always lost. "The good doctor was 'good'," as William H. Stewart observes, "because, lacking the ability to cure a specific ill, he gave 'care' to the whole patient and made him feel better, temporarily at least. He was a skillful, an artistic comforter."[34]

Black slave medics – whether attached to plantation hospitals or in informal practice – were often more effective in their cures than their white counterparts. As noted in Chapter 3, Afro-West Indian slaves depended on their own medical knowledge and art without much help from white professionals during the seventeenth and most of the eighteenth centuries. Rather than routinely purging, puking, and bleeding their patients, the black doctors administered herbs and roots that frequently contained curative properties. Even if their remedies did not cure, they did not kill as did opium, mercury, antimony, and venesection. Black medics were able to communicate with their patients in their native tongue, to make them feel better and thus speed recovery by caring for the whole patient.

The role of black medics on the plantations of the Sugar Colonies is difficult to reconstruct from written records. What we know is largely what has survived from accounts of slave hospitals and their black attendants. We do not know the nature and extent of black medical treatment of blacks outside the hospitals and of black self-care, which was hidden from white view. Indirect evidence that the African medical culture survived the Middle Passage is the substantial number of medicinal plants that are common to both African and Caribbean countries today.

Because women played a key role in the day-to-day medical practice of Africa in the era of the Atlantic slave trade, it is reasonable to assume that they continued to minister to the sick and wounded as plantation slaves. Sick nurses often combined supervisory, professional, and menial duties as they labored long hours in the slave hospitals. Whereas the white doctors and overseers visited the hospitals intermittently, black nurses provided sustained care of the sick and injured. They were more likely to be familiar with black-related diseases and cures than their white counterparts. They treated "their own kind," which probably gave them a more personal interest in effecting a cure. Although handicapped by age and frail health, black nurses often exhibited qualities of competence, patience, gentleness, and self-devotion that more than compensated for their physical limitations. Outside the hospitals women no doubt cared for their sick and injured family members and friends, but this aspect of plantation health care has gone unrecorded. More than any other contribution, the black medics comforted the sorrowing and invoked supernatural vengeance against oppressors, and thus strengthened their brothers' and sisters' defenses against the psychological assaults of slavery. In this way, their contribution to survival against racial oppression outweighed the health services provided by white doctors.

Though far removed in time and space, it is interesting that today black health professionals make up a disproportionate part of the medical and nursing staffs in the hospitals of the British National Health Service. It is ironic, as R. B. Davison writes, that many a white patient, previously riddled with racial prejudice, has, under the pressure of medical necessity, submitted to a surgical operation performed by a colored doctor and been "gratefully nursed back to health by a West Indian nurse."[35]

An epilogue

Some light can be shed on how medicine and living conditions affected the health of slaves if attention is directed to the nature and interaction of economic, demographic, and medical developments in the century following full slave emancipation in 1838. From an economic standpoint, the problem that faced imperial and colonial authorities at the time of emancipation was how to harmonize the interests of ex–masters and ex–slaves to preserve the plantation system. Factors that affected the successful resolution of this problem included the number and density of the population, availability of labor, proportion of land held in plantation units, land available for settlement by small holders, and profitability of sugar production in a wage economy. Generally speaking, the larger territories of Jamaica, Trinidad, and British Guiana had ample uncultivated and unpossessed lands that the freedmen could acquire to form a substantial peasantry. At the other extreme were the small, densely populated territories of Barbados and the Leeward Islands, which were largely taken up with sugar plantations. Here the freedmen found it difficult to make a living without working for wages on the plantations. In an intermediate position were the Windward Islands where the freedmen found alternatives to local wage labor by acquiring peasant holdings or emigrating to Trinidad and British Guiana where wages were higher.

If contemporary observers are to be believed, health conditions deteriorated in the decades following emancipation. Giving dramatic substance to this judgment was the cholera pandemic that struck in the 1850s. In Barbados, the cholera epidemic of 1854 reportedly killed 20,000, nearly all black or colored, from a population of some 140,000. In Jamaica, the cholera epidemic that broke out in October 1850 was estimated to have taken a toll of 25,000 to 30,000 lives. Smallpox raged for a time after the cholera subsided, to be followed by another outbreak of cholera in 1854. Taken together, the deaths from cholera and smallpox are estimated to have amounted to 31,300, nearly 8 percent of the estimated population of Jamaica in 1850.[36]

The epidemics called attention to the sad state of the island's public health facilities. Kingston, Jamaica, lacked proper drinking water and drainage. Its filthy hovels were unfit for human habitation. Other towns and villages also had no proper sanitation. The island's medical practitioners, who had numbered 200 in 1830, declined rapidly after emancipation. Their ranks were so depleted that only 87 remained by 1861, and of this number only 50 were said to be qualified. At the time of the first cholera epidemic, the British government sent Dr. Gavin Milroy to Jamaica to inspect and report on sanitary conditions and medical services. He found it painful to report that "thousands upon thousands" had died of the pestilence "unseen and unprescribed for by any medical man." He asserted that no class or section of the community had been more severely affected by the social changes that followed upon the Emancipation Act than the medical practitioners. Freedmen who had left the plantations in great numbers to take up peasant agriculture were unwilling or unable to pay for medical services. The upshot was, as Dr. Milroy described it, "an almost utter destitution, most dangerous to public welfare, of medical relief in most parts of the country." Decades passed before public health services were established adequate to control epidemic disease.[37]

The deplorable state of Jamaica's public health facilities after emancipation was also the concern of the Reverend Hope Masterton Waddell, the Presbyterian missionary. "Numerous *dispensaries* were required to supply the want of the old estate hospitals," he wrote. "Vaccination should have been enforced and made universal. The *estate villages*, the chief seats still [1843] of the labouring class, should have been opened, and purified, and brought under police regulations, and not suffered to continue, as in the former state, hot-beds of vice and disease."[38]

Although they escaped cholera, the blacks of Antigua were said to have experienced high mortality because of the decline of medical services. William G. Sewell, the *New York Times* correspondent who visited the British West Indies to report on the emancipation experiment, wrote that the planters of Antigua had made the life of a field laborer so distasteful to the freedmen "that the possession of half an acre, or the most meagre subsistence and independence, seem to him, in comparison with estate service, the very acme of luxurious enjoyment." Sewell claimed that through want of proper medical care, the agricultural population of Antigua had decreased at the rate of a half percent per year. Indeed, he asserted that mortality during the two decades of freedom was higher than it had been in the days of slavery. Sewell quoted an extract from an address made by the acting governor of Antigua to the local legislature. The governor believed that the high mortality, chiefly of infants and children, was "for the most part the result of neglect and want of medical attendance." He contrasted the days of slavery when hospitals and medical care were provided by the plantations with the present system of dispersed villages where the freedmen were either unwilling or unable to obtain medical assistance. Sewell noted that the eight or ten doctors of Antigua lived in the town of St. Johns "and that it is quite beyond the power of the peasant who lives five or ten miles off to pay for medical attendance and advice out of the four or five shillings that he may earn during the week."[39]

Demographic data, at least for Grenada and Jamaica, cast doubt on the proposition that, apart from epidemics, the health of the freedman deteriorated after emancipation. According to the census of 1851, the population of Grenada and the Grenadine was 32,671. Compared with the figure of 1844, which was 28,923, this was an increase of 3,748. John Davy, M.D., explained this increase, in part, by births exceeding deaths to the extent of 3,049, or about 1.5 percent per year, and partly by immigration.[40]

The population of Jamaica appears to have remained constant during the decade following emancipation, whereas the low rate of growth between 1844 and 1861 was due to the high death rate caused by severe epidemics. Gisela Eisner finds that the death rate, which is adjusted to allow for the underreporting of infant births and deaths during the registration periods, was 32.7 per thousand in 1817–29. The death rate began to decline in the middle 1830s and reached about 26 per thousand in 1861. The adjusted birthrate, on the other hand, which was 28.4 per thousand in 1817–29, began to rise during the 1830s and is estimated to have approached 40 per thousand by the middle 1840s. From a long-term standpoint, the death rate continued to fall. In the period 1881–1935, when vital statistics are reasonably reliable, it ranged from 18.26 to 26.89 per thousand (average 22.6). On the other hand, the birthrate, which in the same period ranged from 33.44 to 40.72 per thousand (average 37.4), appears to have stabilized. Infant mortality did not begin to fall definitely until the 1920's.[41]

The newly established peasantry of Jamaica exhibited a spirit of independence, pride, and industry by which a condition of rude comfort was achieved. Joseph John Gurney, a Quaker visitor, asserted that the personal comforts of the laboring population under freedom were multiplied tenfold. Not only were their dress and diet much better than they had been under slavery, he wrote, but the freedmen no longer suffered under the perpetual feeling of compulsion. Sewell attacked the myth of the lazy black, pointing out that the rural peasants lived comfortably and independently, owned houses and stock, paid taxes, polled votes, and built churches. The Reverend James Phillippo contended that the freedmen's cottages in the new villages that had been established throughout the island were "in all respects equal, and some of them superior, to the tenancies of labourers in the rural districts of England." The men were employed in both wage labor and improving their little freeholds; the women in culinary and other domestic duties. Phillippo believed that, if allowance was made for the influence of climate, no peasantry in the world displayed more cheerful and persevering industry.

To Douglas Hall, a modern authority, "it seems a safe conclusion that although in the 1850s the money incomes of most peasants and labourers were declining, there was no general poverty or destitution."[42]

Perhaps the most marked difference between slavery and freedom was in the condition of black women. In 1834, when everyone except children under six and the "aged, sick and runaways" were included in the labor force, as much as 82 percent of the slave population of Jamaica was listed as occupied. After emancipation, however, women generally abandoned field labor on plantations. They devoted their time to housekeeping, rearing families, and helping till peasant holdings and market the produce. According to the census of 1891, which was the first to classify occupations by sex, only 36.2 percent of all women of working age in Jamaica were occupied, compared with 81.6 percent of all men. Sewell, who visited all the British Caribbean colonies except British Guiana in 1859 and 1860, wrote, "It must be borne in mind that the effect of freedom was to abolish almost entirely the labor of women in the cane-fields." He found, for example, that women constituted half of the field laborers for whom compensation was paid by the British government to St. Vincent proprietors, but that after emancipation these women were engaged "in domestic and more congenial duties."[43]

Barbados, as we have seen, stands alone among the Sugar Colonies for the natural increase of its slave population in the decades before emancipation. In the aftermath of slavery it experienced remarkable growth in both its black and colored populations and its output of sugar. On his visit to Barbados in 1860, Sewell found the commerce of the island to be "much more extensive and much more flourishing under free labor than it was under slave labor." He thought it remarkable that there had been such a great increase since slavery of persons engaged in trade and craft work that the numbers engaged in field labor had declined from 81,000 in 1832 to only 22,000 in 1860. It was the adoption of a cheaper system of labor, Sewell believed, that enabled Barbados, with a diminished labor force and the same amount of land under cultivation, to produce more sugar than before the time of his visit. Although Sewell supplied no data on the demographic performance of different occupational groups, it seems likely that black traders and tradesmen experienced a higher rate of population growth than black fieldworkers.[44]

Modern economists of the English-speaking Caribbean territories find reason to believe that the societies dominated by plantation agriculture and staple export commodities tend toward a state of persistent underdevelopment by contrast with societies dominated by peasant agriculture, which have a potential for economic growth. Plantation societies are characterized by monocrop production, dependence on external produce markets and on imported capital and supplies, absentee ownership, rigid class lines, ethnic heterogeneity, and weak community structures. Most of the population is denied access to the means of production, especially land, which forces them to seek low-paid wage employment. The highly import-intensive pattern of consumption inhibits the development of a viable domestic agriculture geared to production for local and regional markets. George Beckford contends that although slavery has been formally abolished for about four generations, the basic structure of plantation society in the New World is much like it was during slavery. Indeed, he asserts, "the emergence of the vertically integrated corporate plantation enterprise has really served to preserve the character of the slave plantation system." He advances the hypothesis that the real dynamic for growth resides in the peasant sector but that its potential for growth has historically been stifled by the plantation sector in a number of ways.[45]

That demographic performance differs widely between plantation and peasant societies and sectors of the same society is the contention of Richard A. Lobdell. He has explored the relationship between economic structure and demographic performance in the administrative parishes of Jamaica during 1891–1935. He shows how the national income of Jamaica was divided into three broad sectors: plantation and/or staple exports, peasant and/or domestic agriculture, and nonagricultural production. Patterns of sectoral growth are analyzed and related to patterns of demographic performance for the island as a whole and for each parish. Lobdell's fundamental thesis is that the demographic performance of a parish was systematically influenced by the nature of its socioeconomic structure. The relationship between these structural features and demographic performance are set out in a formal economic–demographic model from which testable hypotheses are derived. "Multiple regression analysis of these data," writes Lobdell, "supports hypotheses which suggest that the cultivation of staple exports and/or the plantation organization of agriculture tend to increase parish mortality, to depress parish fertility and to encourage net in-migration." Conversely, the tests of his hypotheses suggest that parishes dominated by peasant organization of production had higher fertility and lower infant and general mortality than their plantation and/or staple export counterparts. He suggests that demographic performance be added to the list of variables influenced by staple export production and by plantation-organized economic activity. Lobdell's study points to sugar in its broad social and economic dimensions as the "sweet malefactor" during the eras of both slavery and freedom.[46]

In conclusion, it is evident that the health and longevity of AfroWest Indian slaves were related both directly and indirectly to their living conditions and the medical services they received. Despite popular prejudices, medicine was adapted to some degree to the requirements of a tropical environment. The gains that may have resulted from medical advances were largely negated, however, by the harsh conditions on the sugar plantations. Here was found the vicious circle of disease and racism, whereby the debility of blacks was often misconstrued by planters and doctors as racial characteristics of laziness and the shamming of illness. It was widely believed that slaves who failed to perform their quota of work deserved to be punished and deprived of food and other allowances, which, in turn, led to sickness and inability to perform assigned tasks. Perhaps the key to the question whether medical or environmental factors were most important to the health of slaves can be found in the early decades of freedom, at least for Jamaica. The growth of a free peasantry coincided with the retreat of the sugar monoculture and the establishment of a more balanced ecosystem. This was a period when, in the face of declining medical services, there was a rise in the birthrate and a fall in the death rate. Because the cholera epidemics were global in scope and their cause was not widely known until after their devastating effects were felt, it is doubtful whether their victims would have benefited if better medical services had been available. No doubt the greatest improvement accrued to black women who used their freedom to escape from field labor and devote their time to family life on peasant holdings. Before this brighter day dawned, though, sugar and slavery had taken a terrible toll of the black people of the West Indies. Frantz Fanon, who was born in Guadeloupe, became a doctor of medicine and a fighter and a voice for the wretched of the earth. In his *Black Skin, White Masks*, he declares: "Face to face with the white man, the Negro has a past to legitimate, a vengeance to exact."[47]

Notes

1. The disease environments and epidemiology

1. Thomas Jefferson to Caspar Wister, Washington, D.C., 21 July 1807, in T. J. Randolph, ed., *Memoir . . . of Thomas Jefferson* (Charlottesville, Va., 1829), Vol. IV, pp. 91–4; quoted in Richard Harrison Shryock, *Medicine and Society in America: 1660–1860* (Ithaca, N.Y.: Cornell University Press, 1960), p. 73.
2. Philip D. Curtin, "Epidemiology and the Slave Trade," *Political Science Quarterly*, Vol. LXXXIII, No. 2 (June 1968), p. 199; Eric Williams, *Capitalism and Slavery* (Chapel Hill: University of North Carolina Press, 1944), pp. 1–84.
3. Curtin, "Epidemiology and the Slave Trade," pp. 199–200; L. Dudley Stamp, *The Geography of Life and Death* (London: Collins, The Fontana Library, 1964), pp. 88–93; Ernest Rhys, ed., *The Travels of Mungo Park* (London: J. M. Dent, Everyman's Library, 1923), pp. 210–14, 220–1.
4. T. R. Malthus, *An Essay on Population*, 2 vols. (London: Everyman's Library, 1958), Vol. I, p. 91.
5. Curtin, "Epidemiology and the Slave Trade," pp. 193–5.
6. Ibid., pp. 196–8; William H. McNeill, *Plagues and Peoples* (Garden City, N.Y.: Anchor Books, 1977), pp. 5–6, 8–9; Stamp, *Geography of Life and Death*, pp. 13–16.
7. Curtin, "Epidemiology and the Slave Trade," pp. 193–6; McNeill, *Plagues and Peoples*, pp. 8–9, 176–99; D. J. P. Barker, *Practical Epidemiology* (London: Churchill Livingstone, 1973), pp. 1–9.
8. McNeill, *Plagues and Peoples*, pp. 5–6, 92–3; Robert William Fogel and Stanley L. Engerman, *Time on the Cross: The Economics of American Negro Slavery* (Boston: Little, Brown, 1974), pp. 107–9; J. R. Ward, "The Profitability of Sugar Planting in the British West Indies, 1650–1834," *The Economic History Review*, 2d series, Vol. XXXI, No. 2 (May 1978), pp. 197–213.
9. Alfred W. Crosby, Jr., *The Columbian Exchange: Biological and Cultural Consequences of 1492* (Westport, Conn.: Greenwood Publishing Co., 1972), pp. 3–34; Carlo M. Cipolla, *European Culture and Overseas Expansion* (Harmondsworth, Middlesex, England: Penguin Books, 1970), pp. 100–8.
10. P. M. Ashburn, *The Ranks of Death: A Medical History of the Conquest of America*

(New York: Coward McCann, 1947), pp. 14–18; Crosby, *Columbian Exchange*, pp. 20–1, 30–8; McNeill, *Plagues and Peoples*, pp. 176–8.

11. Sherburne F. Cook and Woodrow Borah, *Essays in Population History: Mexico and the Caribbean*, 3 vols. (Berkeley: University of California Press, 1971), Vol. I, p. 401; Carl Ortwin Sauer, *The Early Spanish Main* (Berkeley: University of California Press, 1966), p. 65.
12. D. A. Farnie, "The Commercial Empire of the Atlantic, 1607–1783," *The Economic History Review*, 2d series, Vol. XV, No. 2 (December 1962), pp. 209–11; Curtin, "Epidemiology and the Slave Trade," pp. 200–1.
13. Patrick Colquhoun, *A Treatise on the Wealth, Power, and Resources of the British Empire, in Every Quarter of the World* (London: printed for Joseph Mawman, Ludgate Street, 1814), pp. 318–19, 341.
14. Ibid., pp. 320, 337.
15. Ibid., pp. 319–20, 337.
16. Ibid., pp. 379–80.
17. J. F. Barham, *Considerations on the Abolition of Negro Slavery, and the Means of Practically Effecting it*, 3d ed. (London, 1824), pp. 78–83; Barry W. Higman, *Slave Population and Economy in Jamaica, 1807–1834* (Cambridge: Cambridge University Press, 1976), pp. 12–17.
18. Shryock, *Medicine and Society*, pp. 83–4; John Duffy, *Epidemics in Colonial America* (Baton Rouge: Louisiana State University Press, 1953), pp. 1–15; John Duffy, *The Healers: A History of American Medicine* (Urbana: University of Illinois Press, 1979), pp. 1–16.
19. Richard S. Dunn, *Sugar and Slaves: The Rise of the Planter Class in the English West Indies, 1624–1713* (Chapel Hill: University of North Carolina Press, 1972), pp. 300–1.
20. H. Harold Scott, *A History of Tropical Medicine*, 2 vols. (Baltimore: Williams & Wilkins, 1939), Vol. I, pp. 113–251; Francisco Guerra, "The Influence of Disease on Race, Logistics and Colonization in the Antilles," *Journal of Tropical Medicine and Hygiene*, Vol. LXIX (February 1966), pp. 23–35; Todd L. Savitt, *Medicine and Slavery: The Diseases and Health Care of Blacks in Antebellum Virginia* (Urbana: University of Illinois Press, 1978), pp. 17–35; Kenneth F. Kiple and Virginia Himmelsteib King, *Another Dimension to the Black Diaspora: Diet, Disease, and Racism* (Cambridge: Cambridge University Press, 1981), pp. 6–23.
21. Ashburn, *Ranks of Death*, pp. 125–6; McNeill, *Plagues and Peoples*, pp. 186–8; Crosby, *Columbian Exchange*, p. 208.
22. Ashburn, *Ranks of Death*, pp. 127–40; Scott, *History of Tropical Medicine*, Vol. I, pp. 279–453; Savitt, *Medicine and Slavery*, pp. 240–6; Kiple and King, *Black Diaspora*, pp. 31–49.
23. James D. Goodyear, "The Sugar Connection: A New Perspective on the History of Yellow Fever," *Bulletin of the History of Medicine*, Vol. 52, No. 1 (Spring 1978), pp. 5–21.
24. *Accounts and Papers (Parliamentary Papers)*, 1837–38, XL (417), p. 202: "Statistical Report of the Sickness, Mortality, and Invaliding among the Troops of the West Indies; Prepared from the Records of the Army Medical Department

and War-Office Returns. Presented to both Houses of Parliament by Command of her Majesty," prepared under the direction of Alexander M. Tulloch, major, and Henry Marshall, deputy inspector general of hospitals (cited hereafter as *West India Report*); George W. Roberts, *The Population of Jamaica* (Cambridge: Cambridge University Press, 1957), p. 165.

25. Curtin, "Epidemiology and the Slave Trade," see Table 1, p. 203, showing death rates per thousand among British military personnel who were recruited in the United Kingdom and serving overseas, 1817–36. See also Philip D. Curtin, *The Image of Africa: British Ideas and Action, 1780–1850*, 2 vols. (Madison: University of Wisconsin Press, 1964), Vol. I, pp. 58–87.
26. Tulloch and Marshall, *West India Report*, pp. 423–4; John MacPherson, *Caribbean Lands: A Geography of the West Indies* (London: Longmans, Green, 1964).
27. Tulloch and Marshall, *West India Report*, p. 424.
28. Ibid., pp. 425–6, 432.
29. Ibid., p. 429.
30. Ibid., pp. 426–30.
31. Ibid., pp. 431–2.
32. Ibid., pp. 432–4.
33. Ibid., pp. 459–60.
34. Roberts, *Population of Jamaica*, pp. 166–8, 172–5.
35. Tulloch and Marshall, *West India Report*, pp. 427, 432; *Accounts and Papers (Parliamentary Papers)*, 1840, XXX (135), pp. 146, 154; "Statistical Reports of the Sickness, Mortality, and Invaliding, Among the Troops in Western Africa, The Cape of Good Hope, and the Mauritius; Prepared from the Records of the Army Medical Department and War-Office Returns. Presented to both Houses of Parliament by Command of her Majesty," prepared under the direction of Alexander M. Tulloch, major, and Henry Marshall, deputy inspector general of hospitals; Roger Norman Buckley, *Slaves in Red Coats: The British West India Regiments, 1795–1815* (New Haven: Yale University Press, 1979), pp. vii–x, 2–7, 12–13, 20.
36. John P. Fox, Carrie E. Hall, and Lila R. Elvebach, *Epidemiology: Man and Disease* (London: The Macmillan, 1970), pp. v, 1–47, 75–97; Judith S. Mausner and Anita K. Bahn, *Epidemiology: An Introductory Text* (Philadelphia: W. B. Saunders, 1974), pp. 1–40; Barker, *Practical Epidemiology*, pp. 1–9, 52–5, 133–4.
37. Charles-E. A. Winslow, *The Conquest of Epidemic Disease: A Chapter in the History of Ideas* (New York: Hafner, 1967), pp. 56–67; Charles Singer and E. Ashworth Underwood, *A Short History of Medicine*, 2d ed. (New York: Oxford University Press, 1962), p. 16–66.
38. Winslow, *Epidemic Disease*, pp. 180–1.
39. Thomas Trapham, M.D., *A Discourse of the State of Health in the Island of Jamaica. With a provision therefore Calculated from the Air, the Place, and the Water: The Customs and Manner of Living; &c.* (London: printed for R. Boulter at the Turks Head in Cornhill over against the Royal Exchange, 1679). For a recent assessment of Trapham, see M. T. Ashcroft, M.D., "Tercentenary of the first

English book on tropical medicine, by Thomas Trapham of Jamaica," *British Medical Journal*, Vol. 2 (1979), pp. 475–7.

40. Trapham, *Discourse on Health*, pp. 17–38, 81–2.
41. Ibid., pp. 68–149; St. Julien R. Childs, "Sir George Baker and the Dry Belly-Ache," *Bulletin of the History of Medicine*, Vol. XLIV, No. 3 (May–June 1970), pp. 213–40.
42. Trapham, *Discourse on Health*, pp. 110–28.
43. Ibid., pp. 3, 17–18, 51, 56, 140–1; Ashcroft, "Thomas Trapham of Jamaica," p. 7.
44. Quoted in G. R. De Beer, *Sir Hans Sloane and the British Museum* (London: Oxford University Press, 1953), pp. 5–6, 25–6.
45. Sir Hans Sloane, M.D., *A Voyage to the Islands of Madera, Barbadoes, Nieves, S. Christophers and Jamaica, with the Natural History of the Herbs and Trees, Four-footed Beasts, Fishes, Birds, Insects, Reptiles &c. of the last of those Islands; to which is prefixed an Introduction, wherein is an Account of the Inhabitants, Air, Waters, Diseases, Trade &c. of that Place, with some Relations concerning the neighbouring Continent and Islands of America* (cited hereafter as *Natural History of Jamaica*), 2 vols. (London, 1707, 1725), Vol. I, Preface.
46. Ibid., Vol. I, Preface and Introduction, p. lxv.
47. Ibid., pp. xc, cxxxii–cxxxvi.
48. Quoted in De Beer, *Sir Hans Sloane*, p. 71.
49. Sloane, *Natural History of Jamaica*, Vol. I, pp. cxxvii, cxxxii–cxxxvi, cxli.
50. Ibid., pp. xxxi–lvii; E. St. John Brooks, *Sir Hans Sloane: The Great Collector and His Circle* (London: Batchworth Press, 1954), p. 70; De Beer, *Sir Hans Sloane*, p. 52.
51. William Hillary, M.D., *Observations on the Changes of the Air, and the Concomitant Epidemical Diseases in the Island of Barbadoes. To which is added a Treatise on the Putrid Bilious Fever, commonly called The Yellow Fever; and such other Diseases as are Indigenous or Endemial, in the West India Islands, or in the Torrid Zone. With Notes by Benjamin Rush, M.D.* (Philadelphia, 1811); Sir Leslie Stephen and Sir Sidney Lee, eds., *The Dictionary of National Biography* (London: Oxford University Press, 1917), Vol. IX, p. 880.
52. Hillary, *Epidemical Diseases*, pp. i–xiii. For studies of a similar nature, see George Cleghorn, *Observations on the Epidemical Diseases of Minorca* (London, 1779), which is discussed by Lester S. King, M.D., *The Medical World of the Eighteenth Century* (Chicago: University of Chicago Press, 1958), pp. 138–9; and the account of Dr. John Lining of Charleston, South Carolina, in Shryock, *Medicine and Society*, pp. 62–4, 78.
53. Hillary, *Epidemical Diseases*, pp. 32, 55, 81.
54. Ibid., pp. 16, 69, 70, 73.
55. Ibid., pp. 20–2, 25, 39, 87–8.
56. Ibid., pp. 21, 101–2, 105–13; King, *Medical World*, pp. 123–56.
57. Hillary, *Epidemical Diseases*, pp. 23, 86, 150.
58. James Lind, M.D., *An Essay on Diseases Incidental to Europeans in Hot Climates. With the Method of preventing their fatal Consequences*, 3d ed. (London: printed

for T. Becket, Corner of Adelphi, in the Strand, 1777); Louis Harry Roddis, *James Lind, Founder of Nautical Medicine* (New York: H. Schuman, 1950); Stephen and Lee, *Dictionary of National Biography*, Vol. XI, pp. 1150–1.

59. Lind, *Diseases in Hot Climates*, pp. 1–3, 141–3.
60. Ibid., pp. 11–15, 302–3.
61. Ibid., pp. 41–76, 278.
62. Ibid., pp. 126, 130–3, 219–29.
63. Ibid., pp. 150–1.
64. Robert Jackson, M.D., *A Sketch of the History and Cure of Contagious Fever* (London: printed for Burgess and Hill, Great Windmill Street, Haymarket, 1819), p. 121; Stephen and Lee, *Dictionary of National Biography*, Vol. X, pp. 542–3.
65. Ibid., pp. 229–30; King, *Medical World*, pp. 152–4.
66. Colin Chisholm, M.D., F.R.S., *A Manual of the Climate and Diseases, of Tropical Countries; in which a Practical View of the Statistical Pathology, and of the History and Treatment of the Diseases of those Countries, is attempted to be given: Calculated chiefly as a Guide to the Young Medical Practitioner on his first resorting to those Countries* (London: printed for Burgess and Hill, 1822), p. 18; Stephen and Lee, *Dictionary of National Biography*, Vol. IV, p. 261.
67. Ibid., pp. 19, 121.
68. King, *Medical World*, pp. 150–5, 270–83.
69. James Grainger, M.D., *An Essay on the More Common West-India Diseases; and the Remedies which that Country itself produces: To which are added, Some Hints on the Management, &c. of Negroes. The Second Edition. With Practical Notes, and a Linnaean Index, by William Wright, M.D., F.R.S.* (Edinburgh, 1802); Stephen and Lee, *Dictionary of National Biography*, 1890 ed., Vol. XXII, pp. 368–70.
70. Grainger, *West-India Diseases*, Advertisement, pp. v–viii, Preface, pp. i–iii.
71. Ibid., pp. ii, 7–21.
72. Ibid., pp. 21–67.
73. Ibid., pp. 68–87.
74. Ibid., pp.88–92.
75. [Dr. David Collins], *Practical Rules for the Management and Medical Treatment of Negro Slaves, in the Sugar Colonies. By a Professional Planter*, The Black Heritage Library Collection (Freeport, N.Y.: Books for Libraries Press, 1971), pp. 8–9; James Stephen, *The Slavery of the British West India Colonies Delineated* (New York: Kraus Reprint Co., 1969; first published 1824), Vol. I, pp. 432–3, note.
76. Collins, *Practical Rules*, p. 17.
77. Ibid., pp. 10, 17, 25–7, 183–90.
78. Ibid., pp. 199–202.
79. Ibid., pp. 200–3, 259–66.
80. Ibid., pp. 229–50.
81. Ibid., pp. 269–354.
82. Ibid., pp. 22.
83. John Williamson, M.D., *Medical and Miscellaneous Observations, Relative to the West India Islands*, 2 vols. (Edinburgh: printed by Alex. Smellie, Printer to the University, 1817).

84. Ibid., Vol. I, pp. vii–viii, 134, 393–4.
85. Ibid., Vol. I, pp. xiv–vx, 92, 134, 401; Vol. II, p. 63.
86. Ibid., Vol. I, pp. 81, 84, 90, 125, 149.
87. Ibid., Vol. I, pp. 185, 245.
88. Ibid., Vol. II, pp. 105–382.
89. James Thomson, M.D., *A Treatise on the Diseases of Negroes, As they Occur in the Island of Jamaica: With Observations on the Country Remedies* (Jamaica: printed by Alex. Aikman, 1820), pp. 1–11, 77, 105; The Jamaica Archives, Spanish Town, *Inventorys*, Vol. 137, ff. 94–6.
90. Ibid., pp. 13–14, 86–90, 129–31.
91. Singer and Underwood, *Short History of Medicine*, pp. 143–4, 147–51, 504; Shryock, *Medicine and Society*, pp. 51, 66–70, 168, n. 14; King, *Medical World*, pp. 139–47.
92. Thomson, *Treatise on Diseases of Negroes*, pp. 14–19, 28–34.
93. Ibid., pp. 1–11, 144–68.
94. Logan Clendening, M.D., *Source Book of Medical History* (New York: Dover Publications, 1960), p. 280.
95. Winslow, *Epidemic Diseases*, pp. 182–9.

2. The medical profession

1. Cynric R. Williams, *A Tour Through the Island of Jamaica, From the Western to the Eastern End, in the Year 1823*, 2d ed. (London, 1827), p. 134; Stanley L. Engerman and Eugene D. Genovese, eds., *Race and Slavery in the Western Hemisphere: Quantitative Studies*, copyright © 1975 by The Center for Advanced Study in the Behavioral Sciences, Stanford, California. Portions of "Mortality and the Medical Treatment of Slaves in the British West Indies," by Richard B. Sheridan, reprinted by permission of Princeton University Press.
2. Scottish Record Office, Edinburgh, *Cochrane MSS*, GD 237/106/5, Correspondence between Dr. John Cochrane, Kingston, Jamaica, and his brother Dr. William Cochrane, Edinburgh, 1714–48. Excerpts from this and other manuscripts are published by permission of Mr. James D. Galbraith, Deputy Keeper, Scottish Record Office, Edinburgh, Scotland.
3. Ibid., letter of 7 December 1714.
4. Ibid., letter dated London, 30 August 1715.
5. Ibid., letter dated Kingston, Jamaica, 24 June 1735.
6. Ibid., letter dated Kingston, Jamaica, 23 April 1737.
7. Ibid., letter to Dr. William Cochrane at Edinburgh, dated Kingston, Jamaica, 24 December 1743; John Cochrane is referred to as M.D. St. Andrews, 1744, of Jamaica; and William Cochrane, M.D. Rheims, 1712, and F.R.C.P. Edinburgh, in R. W. Innes Smith, *English Speaking Students of Medicine at the University of Leyden* (Edinburgh: Oliver and Boyd, 1932), p. 49.
8. Tobias Smollett, *The Adventures of Roderick Random* (New York: New American Library, 1964), pp. 225, 228–31.
9. *Memoirs of the Late William Wright, M.D., Fellow of the Royal Societies of London and Edinburgh*, etc. (Edinburgh, 1828), pp. 18–21.

10. University of Exeter Library, *Gale-Morant Papers*, MS. 1/d/3i, letter from Catharine Harding to Mr. Roberts at Wandsworth, England, dated Trelawny, Jamaica, 15 April 1778. I am indebted to Mr. D. W. Evans, Deputy Librarian, University of Exeter Library, for permission to quote extracts from the Gale-Morant Papers.
11. Scottish Record Office, Edinburgh, *Balfour-Melville Papers*, MS. GD 126, letter from Walter Train to John Whyte Melville at Bath, England, dated Melville Hall, Dominica, 4 January 1810.
12. West India Reference Library, Kingston, Jamaica, *Letter Books of Sir Jacob Adolphus, M.D.*, MS. 2, Vol. I, ff. 179–80; letter to Dr. Forbes, dated Kingston, 4 March 1820.
13. *The New Act of Assembly of the Island of Jamaica ... commonly called The New Consolidated Act*, December 1788 (London, 1789), p. 9.
14. Vere Langford Oliver, *The History of the Island of Antigua* (London, 1894–9), Vol. I, pp. xcviii–cix; *The Medical Register for the Year 1780* (London, 1780), p. 233.
15. John Poyer, *The History of Barbados*, etc. (London, 1808), n.p.
16. Richard B. Sheridan, *Sugar and Slavery: An Economic History of the British West Indies 1623–1775* (Baltimore: Johns Hopkins University Press, 1974), pp. 122–3, 124–8, 148–52, 208–10, 452–9.
17. Charles Shephard, *An Historical Account of the Island of St. Vincent* (London: Frank Cass, 1971), Appendix, pp. xlix–lviii.
18. *The Medical Register for the Year 1780* (London, 1780), pp. 221–3; Thomas Dancer, M.D., *A Short Dissertation on the Jamaica Bath Waters*, etc. (Kingston, Jamaica, 1784), pp. v–xvi.
19. Anon., "College of Physicians and Surgeons of Jamaica," *The Jamaica Physical Journal*, Vol. I (June 1834), pp. 377–8.
20. John Williamson, M.D., *Medical and Miscellaneous Observations, Relative to the West India Islands*, 2 vols. (Edinburgh, 1817), Vol. I, p. 190.
21. Charles Leslie, *A New History of Jamaica from the Earliest Accounts to the Taking of Porto Bello by Vice-Admiral Vernon* (London, 1740), p. 51.
22. William Beckford, *A Descriptive Account of the Island of Jamaica*, etc., 2 vols. (London, 1790), Vol. II, pp. 304–5.
23. Bryan Edwards, *The History, Civil and Commercial, of the British Colonies in the West Indies*, 2 vols. (Dublin, 1793), Vol. II, pp. 127–8.
24. Robert Renny, *An History of Jamaica*, etc. (London, 1807), p. 201.
25. Williamson, *Medical Observations*, Vol. II, p. 181.
26. J. Stewart, *A View of the Past and Present State of the Island of Jamaica* (Edinburgh, 1823), pp. 196–7.
27. *Accounts and Papers (Parliamentary Papers)*, 1832, Vol. 305, No. 127; "The Select Committee of the House of Lords Appointed to Inquire into the Laws and Usages of the several West India Colonies in relation to the Slave Population. Minutes of Evidence," Part II, p. 506, evidence of Barry.
28. Edward Long, *The History of Jamaica*, etc., 3 vols. (London, 1774), Vol. II, pp. 583–90. For another vivid description of quacks, see J. B. Moreton, *West India Customs and Manners*, etc. (London, 1793), pp. 18–20.

29. Long, *History of Jamaica*, Vol. II, pp. 591–3.
30. Williamson, *Medical Observations*, Vol. I, p. 239; Vol. II, pp. 179–82.
31. Gertrude Carmichael, *The History of the West Indian Islands of Trinidad and Tobago 1498–1900* (London: Alvin Redman, 1961), pp. 137–8, 400–4; see in particular Appendix XVIII, "Extract from a letter dated 1st December, 1815, from Governor Woodford to the Secretary of State," and Appendix XIX, "Extracts from a Proclamation forming the Medical Board, 20th December, 1814."
32. Anon., "Dr. John Baptiste Philip," *The Caribbean Medical Journal*, Vol. XXIX, Nos. 1–4 (1962), pp. 109–10.
33. Ibid., pp. 98–101; Edinburgh University Library, *MSS. Medical Matriculation Albums*, 1823–4, 1824–5, 1825–6, 1826–7; *List of the Graduates in Medicine in the University of Edinburgh from MDCCV to MDCCCLXVI* (Edinburgh: Neill & Company, 1867), p. 50. I am indebted to Dr. Carl Campbell, Senior Lecturer in History at the University of the West Indies, for supplying me with information about Dr. Philip.
34. *Journals of the Assembly of Jamaica*, Vol. XIV (Nov. and Dec. 1826), pp. 658–9, 662, 703, 707, 710, 717, 720–1, 758–60.
35. *The Kingston Chronicle and City Advertiser*, July 10, 1830, p. 3; other letters in this series appear in the issues of July 16, 23, 30, and August 6.
36. *The Jamaica Physical Journal*, Vol. I (January 1834), pp. 42–8; anon., "College of Physicians and Surgeons of Jamaica," *The Jamaica Physical Journal*, Vol. I (June 1834), pp. 377–8; Vol. II (May 1835), pp. 215–6.
37. Long, *History of Jamaica*, Vol. II, p. 594.
38. *Journals of the Assembly of Jamaica*, Vol. XIV (Nov. 21, 1826), p. 658; (Dec. 8, 1826), p. 696.
39. Robert H. Schomburgk, *The History of Barbados*, etc. (London: Frank Cass, 1971), pp. 111–6; Jean Bullen and Helen Livingston, "Of the State and Advancement of the College," in Frank J. Klingberg, ed., *Codrington Chronicle: An Experiment in Anglican Altruism on a Barbados Plantation, 1710–1834* (Berkeley: University of California Press, 1949), pp. 107–22; Long, *History of Jamaica*, Vol. II, pp. 591–4.
40. John Tate Lanning, *Academic Culture in the Spanish Colonies* (London: Oxford University Press, 1940), pp. 22–33, 93–111, 112–17.
41. Ross Danielson, *Cuban Medicine* (New Brunswick, N.J.: Transaction Books, 1979), pp. 21–5.
42. Ibid., pp. 21, 26–39, 42–67.
43. Todd L. Savitt, *Medicine and Slavery: The Diseases and Health Care of Blacks in Antebellum Virginia* (Urbana: University of Illinois Press, 1978), pp. 167–71; John Duffy, *The Healers: A History of American Medicine* (Urbana: University of Illinois Press, 1979), pp. 33, 69; Richard Harrison Shryock, *Medicine and Society in America: 1660–1860* (Ithaca, N.Y.: Cornell University Press, 1960), pp. 2–4, 9, 17; R. H. Shryock, "Medical Practice in the Old South," *The South Atlantic Quarterly*, Vol. XXIX, No. 2 (April 1930), pp. 166, 171–2.
44. Duffy, *The Healers*, pp. 33–4; Savitt, *Medicine and Slavery*, pp. 167–70; Shryock, *Medicine and Society*, pp. 5, 144–6.

45. Duffy, *The Healers*, pp. 69, 175–7, 291; Shryock, "Medical Practice in the Old South," pp. 171–2.
46. Shryock, "Medical Practice in the Old South," p. 166; Shryock, *Medicine and Society*, pp. 18–19.
47. Shryock, *Medicine and Society*, pp. 22–34; Duffy, *The Healers*, pp. 166–8.
48. Duffy, *The Healers*, pp. 167–70; Shryock, "Medical Practice in the Old South," pp. 166–70; Shryock, *Medicine and Society*, pp. 138–41.
49. Innes Smith, *English-Speaking Students at Leyden*, Introduction, pp. ix–xix; Charles Singer and E. Ashworth Underwood, *A Short History of Medicine*, 2d ed. (New York: Oxford University Press, 1962), pp. 147–50; Douglas Guthrie, *A History of Medicine* (London: Thomas Nelson, 1947), pp. 193, 220–1.
50. Innes Smith, *English-Speaking Students at Leyden*, pp. 2–249.
51. Guthrie, *History of Medicine*, pp. 225–31.
52. Anand Chidamber Chitnis, "The Edinburgh Professoriate 1790–1826 and the University's Contribution to Nineteenth Century British Society," unpublished Ph.D. dissertation, University of Edinburgh, March 1968, pp. 245–6.
53. J. Johnson, *A Guide for Gentlemen Studying Medicine at the University of Edinburgh* (London, 1792), pp. 4, 14, 24–8, 30–2.
54. Anand C. Chitnis, "Medical Education in Edinburgh, 1790–1826, and Some Victorian Social Consequences," *Medical History*, Vol. XVII (April 1973), pp. 173–85; John D. Comrie, *History of Scottish Medicine to 1860* (London: Bailliere, Tindell & Cox, 1927), pp. 196–8.
55. John Morgan, M.D., *A Discourse Upon the Institution of Medical Schools in America; Delivered at a Public Anniversary Commencement, held in the College of Philadelphia May 30 and 31, 1765* (Philadelphia, 1765), pp. 28–9.
56. Chitnis, "The Edinburgh Professoriate," pp. 19–20, 250, 253.
57. University of Edinburgh Library, *MSS. Medical Matriculation Albums, 1740–1830.*
58. *List of Graduates in Medicine, Edinburgh*, pp. 2–89.
59. Data on the doctors of Jamaica can be found in the Island Record Office, Spanish Town, *Inventorys* series.
60. *The Memoirs of James Stephen: Written by Himself for the Use of His Children*, edited with an introduction by Merle M. Bevington (London: Hogarth Press, 1954), pp. 41–2, 171–3.
61. Benjamin Moseley, M.D., *A Treatise on Tropical Diseases*, 2d ed. (London, 1789), pp. 103–5, 113–14.
62. William Hughes, *The American physitian; or a treatise on the roots, plants trees, shrubs, fruit, herbs, etc. growing in the English plantations in America* (London, 1672); see Jerome S. Handler, *A Guide to Source Materials for the Study of Barbados History 1627–1834* (Carbondale: Southern Illinois University Press, 1971), pp. 8–9.
63. Richard Towne, *A Treatise on the Diseases Most frequent in the West-Indies And herein more particularly of those which occur in Barbadoes* (London, 1726), pp. 3–5.

64. Henry Warren, *A Treatise concerning the malignant fever in Barbados and the neighboring islands: with an account of the seasons there, from the year 1734 to 1738* (London, 1741); Handler, *Guide to Barbados History*, pp. 24, 31.
65. Griffith Hughes, *The Natural History of Barbados*, etc. (London, 1750).
66. William Hillary, M.D., *Observations on the changes of the air and the concomitant epidemical diseases in the Island of Barbadoes*, etc., 2d ed. (London, 1766); this is an expanded version of his first edition of 1754. See also Handler, *Guide to Barbados History*, pp. 34, 35, 39.
67. William Sandiford, M.D., *An account of a late epidemical distemper, extracted from a letter addressed to Gedney Clarke, Esq.* (Barbados, 1771).
68. James Hendy, *An essay on glandular secretion; containing an experimental enquiry into the formation of pus* (London, 1775); an expanded version of this work was published in 1784, entitled *A treatise on the glandular disease of Barbadoes; proving it to be seated in the lymphatic system.* Hendy was "physician to His Majesty's naval hospital at Barbados and physician general to the militia of the island."
69. In 1785 John Rollo published a criticism of Hendy's treatise, entitled *Remarks on the disease lately described by Dr. Hendy under the appelation of the Glandular Disease of Barbados*, to which Hendy replied in 1789 with *A vindication of the opinions and facts, contained in a treatise on the Glandular Disease of Barbadoes.* See Handler, *Guide to Barbados History*, pp. 42, 43, 46–8, 53. John Rollo, *Observations on the diseases which appeared in the army of St. Lucia, in 1778 and 1779*, etc. (London, 1781); J. Rollo, *Observations on the means of preserving and restoring health in the West Indies* (London, 1783).
70. J. Bell, *An inquiry into the causes which produce, and the means of preventing diseases among British officers, soldiers, and others in the West Indies* (London, 1791).
71. Colin Chisholm, M.D., *An essay on the malignant pestilential fever introduced into the West India islands from Boullam, on the coast of Guinea, in 1793, 1794, 1795, 1796*, 2 vols. (London, 1801); C. Chisholm, *A Manual of the Climate and Diseases, of Tropical Countries*, etc. (London, 1822); J. Clark, *A treatise on the yellow fever, as it appeared in the island of Dominica, in the years 1793–1796*, etc. (London, 1797).
72. James Dottin Maycock, M.D., *Flora Barbadensis: a catalogue of plants, indigenous, naturalized, and cultivated in Barbados, to which is prefixed a geological description of the island* (London, 1830); see Handler, *Guide to Barbados History*, p. 83.
73. James Grainger, M.D., *An Essay on the More Common West-India Diseases; and the Remedies which that Country Itself Produces*, etc., 2d ed. (Edinburgh: Mundell & Son, 1802), pp. i–viii; Leslie Stephen and Sidney Lee, eds., *The Dictionary of National Biography* (cited hereafter as *DNB*) (New York: Macmillan, 1890), Vol. 22, pp. 368–9.
74. James Johnston Abraham, *Lettsom: His Life, Times, Friends and Descendants* (London: William Heinemann Medical Books, 1933), pp. 1–47.
75. Ibid., pp. 48–60.
76. Ibid., pp. 61–127, 150, 208, 276, 295–8.
77. Robert Thomas, *Medical Advice to the Inhabitants of Warm Climates, on the*

Domestic Treatment of all the Diseases Incidental Therein: With a Few Useful Hints to New Settlers, for the Preservation of Health, and the Prevention of Sickness. To the work are Prefixed, Some Observations on the proper Management of New Negroes, and the general Condition of Slaves in the Sugar Colonies (London, 1790), pp. ix–xx.

78. [Dr. David Collins], *Practical Rules for the Management and Medical Treatment of Negro Slaves, in the Sugar Colonies. By a Professional Planter* (reprint of the 1811 edition by Books for Libraries Press, Freeport, N.Y., 1971), pp. 7–9, 138.
79. Edward Bancroft, M.D., F.R.S., *An Essay on the Natural History of Guiana . . . with an account of the Religion, Manners, and Customs of several Tribes of its Indian Inhabitants* (London, 1769); Stephen and Lee, *DNB*, 1968 ed., Vol. I, pp. 1025–6.
80. John Hancock, M.D., *Observations on the Climate, Soil, and Productions of British Guiana, and on the Advantages of Emigration to and Colonizing the Interior of that Country: Together with Incidental Remarks on the Diseases, their treatment and Prevention; Founded on a Long Experience within the Tropics* (London: John Hatchard, 1835).
81. Henry Stubbe, M.D., "Observations made by a curious and learned person sailing from England to the Caribe Islands," *Philosophical Transactions of the Royal Society* No. 27 (1667); "An enlargement of the observations formerly published in No. 27, made and imparted by that learned and inquisitive Physician Dr. Stubbe," ibid., Nos. 36 and 37; see also "Henry Stubbe, M.D.," by L.B.F., in *Journal of the Institute of Jamaica*, Vol. I, pp. 360–1.
82. Thomas Trapham, M.D., *A Discourse of the State of Health in the Island of Jamaica. With a provision therefore Calculated from the Air, the Place, and the Water: The Customs and Manners of Living; &c.* (London, 1679), pp. 93, 123; M. T. Ashcroft, M.D., "Tercentenary of the first English book on tropical medicine, by Thomas Trapham of Jamaica," *British Medical Journal*, Vol. 2 (1979), pp. 475–7.
83. Stephen and Lee, *DNB*, 1897 ed., Vol. 52, pp. 379–80; K. E. Ingram, *Sources of Jamaican History 1655–1838: A Bibliographical Survey with Particular Reference to Manuscript Sources*, 2 vols. (Inter Documentation Company AG, Zug, Switzerland, 1976), Vol. II, pp. 916–26; G. R. de Beer, *Sir Hans Sloane and the British Museum* (London: Oxford University Press, 1953); E. St. John Brooks, *Sir Hans Sloane: The Great Collector and His Circle* (London: Batchworth Press, 1954); Raymond F. Stearns, *Science in the British Colonies of America* (Urbana: University of Illinois Press, 1970), pp. 236–43, 337–97.
84. Stephen and Lee, *DNB*, 1885 ed., Vol. 3, pp. 186–7; Frank Cundall, *The Press and Printers of Jamaica Prior to 1820* (Worcester, Mass.: American Antiquarian Society, 1916), pp. 45–7, 105; Ingram, *Sources of Jamaican History*, Vol. I, pp. 64–6; Vol. II, pp. 918–21.
85. Stephen and Lee, *DNB*, 1921–22 ed., Vol. IX, pp. 1319–20; Innes Smith, *English-Speaking Students at Leyden*, p. 121.
86. Ingram, *Sources of Jamaican History*, Vol. II, pp. 927–30.

87. Stephen and Lee, *DNB*, 1921–2 ed., Vol. III, p. 53; Innes Smith, *English-Speaking Students at Leyden*, p. 33.
88. Stephen and Lee, *DNB*, 1921–2 ed., Vol. II, p. 1367.
89. Ingram, *Sources of Jamaican History*, Vol. I, pp. 67–8.
90. William Fawcett and Alfred Barton Rendle, *Flora of Jamaica; Containing Descriptions of the Flowering Plants Known from the Island*, 6 vols. (London, 1914), Vol. III, Preface.
91. *Accounts and Papers (Parliamentary Papers)*, 1789, XXVI (646a): "Report of the Privy Council Committee on the Slave Trade," Part III, Jamaica Appendix, No. 8; Heinz Goerke, "The Life and Scientific Works of Dr. John Quier, Practitioner of Physic and Surgery, Jamaica: 1738–1822," *The West Indian Medical Journal*, Vol. V (1956), pp. 23–6; "Report of a Committee to Investigate the Unlawful Importation of Slaves," *Journals of the Assembly of Jamaica*, Vol. XII (20 December 1815), p. 806, evidence of Dr. Quier; Michael Craton and James Walvin, *A Jamaican Plantation: The History of Worthy Park 1670–1970* (Toronto: University of Toronto Press, 1970), pp. 1–4, 10, 88, 131–3, 145; Michael Craton, *Searching for the Invisible Man: Slaves and Plantation Life in Jamaica* (Cambridge, Mass.: Harvard University Press, 1978), pp. 128–30.
92. *Memoirs of the Late William Wright*, pp. 1–19.
93. *Ibid.*, pp. 23, 86, 90–2, 175, and Appendix; Williamson, *Medical Observations*, Vol. I, p. 70.
94. "A Sketch of the Life of the Late Thomas Dancer, M.D., Written by Himself," in his *The Medical Assistant*, 3d ed. (London, 1819), pp. xv–xx; Stephen and Lee, *DNB*, 1921–2 ed., Vol. V, pp. 463–4.
95. Frank Cundall, "Jamaica Worthies – Dr. Dancer," *Journal of the Institute of Jamaica* (February 1892), pp. 102 ff.; F. Cundall, *The Press and Printers of Jamaica*, pp. 27–31, 96, 98; Ingram, *Sources of Jamaican History*, Vol. I, pp. 65–6; Vol. II, pp. 939–40.
96. Thomas Dancer, M.D., *The Exposer Exposed, An Answer to Dr. Grant's Libellous Invective on the Conduct and Character of Dr. Dancer* (Kingston, 1805), p. 6.
97. Cundall, *The Press and Printers of Jamaica*, pp. 29–31; Lowell J. Ragatz, *A Guide for the Study of British Caribbean History, 1763–1834* (Washington, D.C., 1932), pp. 196, 290, 372–3; *Journals of the Assembly of Jamaica*, Vol. IX (27 November 1793), p. 247.
98. M. T. Ashcroft, M.D., "Publish and Perish: A Fatal Medical Controversy," *Journal of the Royal College of Physicians of London*, Vol. 13, No. 4 (October 1979), pp. 227–30.
99. Ragatz, *Guide for British Caribbean History*, pp. 371–6; Edward Nathaniel Bancroft, M.D., *Essay on the Disease called Yellow Fever, with Observations concerning Febrile Contagion, Typhus Fever, Dysentery, and the Plague* (London, 1811, with a "Sequel" to the same, London, 1817); Stephen and Lee, *DNB*, 1969 ed., Vol. I, pp. 1026–7.
100. Regatz, *Guide for British Caribbean History*, pp. 371–6.
101. Stephen and Lee, *DNB*, 1921–2 ed., Vol XIII, pp. 1071–2; Innes Smith, *English-Speaking Students at Leyden*, p. 165.

102. James Thomson, M.D., *A Treatise on the Diseases of Negroes, As they Occur in the Island of Jamaica, with Observations on the Country Remedies* (Jamaica, 1820), pp. 1–11, 112, 143–68; Todd Lee Savitt, "Sound Minds and Sound Bodies: The Diseases and Health Care of Blacks in Ante-Bellum Virginia," 2 vols., unpublished Ph.D. dissertation, University of Virginia, Charlottesville, May 1975, Vol. I, p. 8.
103. Long, *History of Jamaica*, Vol. II, pp. 594–5.
104. Collins, *Practical Rules*, pp. 199–200.

3. African and Afro-West Indian Medicine

1. R. R. Madden, M.D., *A Twelve Month Residence in the West Indies, During the Transition from Slavery to Apprenticeship*, etc. (London, 1835), p. 66. I am indebted to Michael T. Ashcroft, M.D., for valuable suggestions and the loan of source materials for the writing of this chapter.
2. Orlando Patterson, *The Sociology of Slavery: An Analysis of the Origins, Development and Structure of Negro Slave Society in Jamaica* (London: MacGibbon & Kee, 1967), pp. 182–5.
3. Michael Gelfand, *Medicine and Custom in Africa* (Edinburgh: E. & S. Livingstone, 1964), pp. 22–3; John S. Mbiti, *African Religions and Philosophy* (London: Heinemann, 1969), pp. 166–78.
4. Thomas M. Winterbottom, M.D., *Account of the Native Africans in the Neighbourhood of Sierra Leone; To which is added, An Account of the Present State of Medicine Among Them*, 2 vols. (London, 1803), Vol. I, pp. 251–9; Vol. II, pp. 10–12.
5. George Way Harley, *Native African Medicine, With Special Reference to its Practice in the Mano Tribe of Liberia* (London: Frank Cass, 1970), pp. 5–8, 11, 15–16, 31–2; M. J. Field, *Religion and Medicine of the Ga People* (London: Oxford University Press, 1961), pp. 130–1.
6. Harley, *Native African Medicine*, pp. 5, 38–40, 193.
7. Ibid., pp. 20–1, 27–30; Field, *Religion and Medicine*, pp. 128–35; Gelfand, *Medicine and Custom*, pp. 34–7.
8. D. Maier, "Nineteenth-Century Asante Medical Practices," *Comparative Studies in Society and History*, Vol. 21, No. 1 (January 1970), pp. 63–81. I am indebted to Dr. Howard Johnson for bringing this reference to my attention.
9. T. E. Bowdich, *Mission from Cape Coast to Ashantee* (London, 1819), p. 306; quoted in ibid.
10. Maier, "Asante Medical Practices," pp. 68–71.
11. W. Bosman, *A New and Accurate Description of the Coast of Guinea* (London, 1705), pp. 221, 224; quoted in ibid.
12. H. Tedlie, "Materia Medica and Diseases," in T. Bowdich, ed., *Mission from Cape Coast to Ashantee*, p. 374; Maier, "Asante Medical Practices," pp. 66–8.
13. Edward Long, *The History of Jamaica*, etc., 3 vols. (London: Frank Cass, 1970; first published 1774), Vol. II, p. 381.
14. Sir Edward Evans-Pritchard, *Witchcraft, Oracles and Magic among the Azande* (Oxford: Clarendon Press, 1937), pp. 9, 202–30, 435. For a penetrating analysis

of primitive medicine and its cultural setting, see Erwin H. Ackerknecht, "Problems of Primitive Medicine," *Bulletin of the History of Medicine*, Vol. XI, No. 5 (May 1942), pp. 503–21.

15. G. B. Marini Bettolo, "Present Aspects of the Use of Plants in Traditional Medicine," *Journal of Ethno-Pharmacology*, Vol. 2, No. 1 (March 1980), pp. 5–7; Dan N. Lantum, "The Knowledge of Medicinal Plants in Africa Today," ibid., pp. 9–17; James U. Oguakwa, "Plants Used in Traditional Medicine in West Africa," ibid., pp. 29–31.
16. Madden, *Twelve Month Residence*, pp. 104–9.
17. Patterson, *Sociology of Slavery*, pp. 185–6, 188; Field, *Religion and Medicine*, p. 137.
18. *Accounts and Papers (Parliamentary Papers)*, 1789, XXVI (646a): "Report of the Privy Council Committee on the Slave Trade" (cited hereafter as *Privy Council Report*), Part IV, Jamaica, Answers to questions 22, 23, 24, 25 and 26 by Stephen Fuller, Edward Long, and Dr. James Chisholme; Madden, *Twelve Month Residence*, p. 106.
19. Martha Warren Beckwith, *Black Roadways: A Study of Jamaican Folk Life* (Chapel Hill: University of North Carolina Press, 1929), p. 107.
20. Thomas Atwood, *The History of the Island of Dominica* (London, 1791), pp. 268–72.
21. Patterson, *Sociology of Slavery*, p. 192.
22. 1 Geo. III, c. 22; Act 24 of 1760, clause X, *Acts of Assembly* (1769), Vol. I, p. 55; quoted by Edward Brathwaite, *The Development of Creole Society in Jamaica 1770–1820* (Oxford: Clarendon Press, 1971), p. 162.
23. Madden, *Twelve Month Residence*, p. 101; Brathwaite, *Creole Society*, pp. 162–3; Michael H. Beaubrun, "Psychiatric Education for the Caribbean," *The West Indian Medical Journal*, Vol. 15, No. 1 (March 1966), pp. 60–1.
24. Patterson, *Sociology of Slavery*, pp. 186–9; Beckwith, *Black Roadways*, pp. 142–58; Joseph J. Williams, *Psychic Phenomena of Jamaica* (New York: Dial Press, 1934), p. 59; Monica Schuler, "Myalism and the African Religious Tradition in Jamaica," in Margaret E. Crahan and Franklin W. Knight, eds., *Africa and the Caribbean: The Legacies of a Link* (Baltimore, Md.: Johns Hopkins University Press, 1979), pp. 65–79.
25. Martha Warren Beckwith, *Notes on Jamaican Ethnobotany* (Poughkeepsie, N.Y.: Vassar College Press, 1927), pp. 5–33; Morris Steggerda, "Plants of Jamaica Used by Natives for Medicinal Purposes," *American Anthropologist*, Vol. 31, No. 3 (July–Sept. 1929), pp. 431–4; G. R. Asprey and Phyllis Thornton, "Medicinal Plants of Jamaica," *The West Indian Medical Journal*, Parts 1–4, Vol. 2 (June 1953), pp. 233–52; Vol. 3, No. 1 (March 1954), pp. 17–41; Vol. 4, No. 2 (June 1955), pp. 69–82, 145–68.
26. George E. Simpson, "Folk Medicine in Trinidad," *Journal of American Folklore*, Vol. 75, No. 298 (Oct.–Dec. 1962), pp. 326–40; G. E. Simpson, *Religious Cults of the Caribbean: Trinidad, Jamaica, and Haiti* (Rio Piedras, P.R.: Institute of Caribbean Studies, University of Puerto Rico, 1970), pp. 11–139; Melville J. Herskovits and Frances S. Herskovits, *Trinidad Village* (New York: Alfred A. Knopf, 1947), pp. 321–39.

27. Sir Hans Sloane, *A Voyage to the Islands of Madera, Barbados, Nieves, S. Christophers and Jamaica*, etc., 2 vols. (London, 1707–25), Vol. I, p. liv.
28. Ibid., Vol. I, pp. liii–lv, cxli.
29. British Library, *Additional MS.* 12,419, Vol. II, f. 90: James Knight, *MS. History of Jamaica*, ca. 1746.
30. *Privy Council Report*, 1789, XXVI (646a), pt. III, reply of Mr. Spooner to queries 22, 23, 24; quoted in Bernard Marshall, "Society and Economy in the British Windward Islands, 1763–1823," unpublished Ph.D. dissertation, University of the West Indies, Jamaica, 1972, p. 409.
31. *Memoirs of the Late William Wright, M.D.*, etc. (Edinburgh, 1828), pp. 308–10.
32. James Thomson, M.D., *A Treatise on the Diseases of Negroes, As They Occur in the Island of Jamaica, with Observations on the Country Remedies* (Jamaica, 1820), pp. 1–2, 8–11, 112, 143–68.
33. This quotation is from the opening paragraph of Chap. 4, "Medicine and Colonialism," in Frantz Fanon's *A Dying Colonialism* (New York: Grove Press, 1967), pp. 121–45, which discusses perceptively the cultural barriers that impeded European doctors in treating patients in colonial countries.
34. Thomson, *Diseases of Negroes*, pp. 8–10.
35. Matthew Gregory Lewis, *Journal of a West India Proprietor 1815–17*, edited with an Introduction by Mona Wilson (Boston: Houghton Mifflin, 1929), pp. 123–4, 128.
36. Sir Philip H. Manson-Bahr, *Manson's Tropical Diseases: A Manual of the Diseases of Warm Climates* (London: Cassell, 1954), pp. 599–601; Kenneth R. Hill, "Non-Specific Factors in the Epidemiology of Yaws," *The West Indian Medical Journal*, Vol. 2, No. 3 (1953), pp. 155–83.
37. Manson-Bahr, *Manson's Tropical Diseases*, pp. 604–17; Charles Wilcocks, *Health and Disease in the Tropics* (London: Oxford University Press, 1950), pp. 82–4; *Memoirs of William Wright*, pp. 400–13; John Williamson, M.D., *Medical and Miscellaneous Observations, Relative to the West India Islands*, 2 vols. (Edinburgh, 1817), Vol. II, pp. 141–61.
38. *Memoirs of William Wright*, p. 399.
39. Williamson, *Medical Observations*, Vol. II, pp. 141–2.
40. Ibid., Vol. I, p. 88.
41. Ibid., Vol. II, pp. 142–3.
42. *Memoirs of William Wright*, p. 411; James Maxwell, M.D., *Observations on Yaws, And its Influence in Originating Leprosy: Also Observations on Acute Traumatic Tetanus and Tetanus Infantum* (Edinburgh, 1839), p. 36.
43. Maxwell, *Observations on Yaws*, pp. viii–ix, 23, 36, 43–8.
44. William Hillary, M.D., *Observations on the Changes of the Air, and the Concomitant Epidemical Diseases in the Island of Barbados* (Philadelphia, 1811), pp. 246–7.
45. Knight, *MS. History of Jamaica*, Vol. II, ff. 89–90.
46. J. Stewart, *A View of the Past and Present State of the Island of Jamaica* (Edinburgh, 1823), p. 312.
47. Edinburgh University Library, *Joseph Black's Correspondence*, Vol. I, ff. 58–64: A. J. Alexander to Prof. Joseph Black, dated Bacolet, Grenada, 21 April 1773.

I am indebted to Dr. J. T. D. Hall, Sub-Librarian, Special Collections, Edinburgh University Library, for permission to quote extracts from this manuscript.

48. Bryan Edwards, *The History, Civil and Commercial, of the British Colonies in the West Indies*, 2 vols. (Dublin, 1793), Vol. II, pp. 64, 128; Maxwell, *Observations on Yaws*, pp. 22–3, 37; R. Hoeppli, M.D., *Parasitic Diseases in Africa and the Western Hemisphere: Early Documentation and Transmission by the Slave Trade* (Basel: Verlag für Recht und Gesellschaft, 1969), pp. 85–93.
49. Benjamin Moseley, M.D., *Medical Tracts. 3. On the Yaws*, 2d ed. (London, 1804), pp. 187–8.
50. *Memoirs of William Wright*, p. 410.
51. Gilbert Mathison, *Notices Respecting Jamaica in 1808, 1809, 1810* (London, 1811), pp. 43–4.
52. H. A. Alford Nicholls, M.D., *Report on Yaws in Tobago, Grenada, St. Vincent, St. Lucia, and the Leeward Islands* (London: His Majesty's Stationery Office, 1894), pp. 11–14.
53. Letter to the author from Dr. M. T. Ashcroft, dated Jamaica, 15 August 1977. See also M. T. Ashcroft, A. E. Urquhart, and G. H. K. Gentle, "Treponemal Serological Tests in Jamaican School Children," *Transactions of the Royal Society of Tropical Medicine and Hygiene*, Vol. 59, No. 6 (1965), pp. 649–56.
54. Thomson, *Diseases of Negroes*, p. 10.
55. National Library of Scotland, Edinburgh, *Chisholme Papers*, MS. 5476, f. 14; *Letter Books of James Chisholme 1793–1812*, James Chisholme to James Craggs in Jamaica, dated Bath, 2 November 1793. I am indebted to Mr. P. M. Cadell, Keeper of Manuscripts, National Library of Scotland, for permission to quote extracts from this and other manuscripts.
56. [Dr. David Collins], *Practical Rules for the Management and Medical Treatment of Negro Slaves, in the Sugar Colonies. By a Professional Planter* (Freeport, N.Y.: Books for Libraries Press, 1971; first published 1803), pp. 212–13.
57. Alexander Barclay, *A Practical View of the Present State of Slavery in the West Indies*, etc. (London, 1826), p. 321.
58. George Pinckard, M.D., *Notes on the West Indies*, etc. 3 vols. (Westport, Conn.: Negro Universities Press, 1970; first published 1806), Vol. I, pp. 388–9.
59. Rev. James Ramsay, *An Essay on the Treatment and Conversion of African Slaves in the British Sugar Colonies* (London, 1784), p. 244; Barclay, *Practical View of Slavery*, p. 322.
60. J. Harry Bennett, *Bondsmen and Bishops: Slavery and Apprnticeship on the Codrington Plantations of Barbados, 1710–1838* (Berkeley: University of California Press, 1958), pp. 41–2.
61. *Privy Council Report*, 1789, XXVI (646a), pt. III, evidence of Mr. Laing of Dominica.
62. Lewis, *West India Proprietor*, p. 142.
63. Mrs. A. C. Carmichael, *Domestic Manners and Society Conditions of the White, Coloured, and Negro Population of the West Indies*, 2 vols. (Westport, Conn.: Negro Universities Press, 1969; first published 1833), Vol. II, pp. 199–200.
64. *Accounts and Papers (Parliamentary Papers)*, 1836, XV (605), p. 62: "Report from

the Select Committee on Negro Apprenticeship in the Colonies," evidence of Dr. Madden.

65. Collins, *Practical Rules*, p. 222.
66. Thomas Roughley, *The Jamaica Planter's Guide*, etc. (London, 1823), p. 91.
67. Williamson, *Medical Observations*, Vol. I, pp. 237–8.
68. Lucille Mathurin Mair, "A Historical Study of Women in Jamaica from 1655 to 1844," unpublished Ph.D. dissertation, University of the West Indies, Jamaica, October 1974, pp. 314–20.
69. G. F. Asprey and Phyllis Thornton, "Medicinal Plants of Jamaica," *The West India Medical Journal*, Part I, Vol. 2 (June 1953), pp. 233–52; Long, *History of Jamaica*, Vol. III, pp. 788–9.
70. Beckwith, *Jamaican Ethnobotany*, pp. 8–9; Leonard Barrett, "The Portrait of a Jamaican Healer: African Medical Lore in the Caribbean," *Caribbean Quarterly*, Vol. 19, No. 3 (September 1973), pp. 6–19.
71. A. J. Oakes and M. P. Morris, "The West Indian Weedwoman of the United States Virgin Islands," *Bulletin of the History of Medicine*, Vol. XXXII, No. 2 (March–April 1958), pp. 164–70.
72. Todd L. Savitt, *Medicine and Slavery: The Diseases and Health Care of Blacks in Antebellum Virginia* (Urbana: University of Illinois Press, 1978), pp. 149–50, 171–84; John Duffy, "Medical Practice in the Ante-bellum South," *Journal of Southern History*, Vol. XXV (February 1959), pp. 53–72.
73. Eugene D. Genovese, *Roll, Jordan, Roll: The World the Slaves Made* (New York: Random House, 1974), pp. 223–8; W. E. B. Du Bois, *The Souls of Black Folk* (New York, 1964; first published 1903), p. 144; quoted in ibid.

4. The Guinea surgeons

1. Thomas Winterbottom, M.D., *An Account of the Native Africans in the Neighbourhood of Sierra Leone; To Which is Added, An Account of the Present state of Medicine among them*, 2 vols. (London, 1803), Vol. II, p. 43.
2. Philip D. Curtin, *The Atlantic Slave Trade: A Census* (Madison: University of Wisconsin Press, 1969), pp. 88–9; Robert William Fogel and Stanley L. Engerman, *Time on the Cross: The Economics of American Negro Slavery* (Boston: Little, Brown, 1974), Vol. I, p. 14; Vol. II, pp. 27–32; see also Fogel and Engerman, "Recent Findings in the Study of Slave Demography and Family Structure," *Sociology and Social Research*, Vol. 63, No. 3 (1979), pp. 566–89; Stanley L. Engerman, "Some Economic and Demographic Comparisons of Slavery in the United States and the British West Indies," *The Economic History Review*, 2d series, Vol. XXIX, No. 2 (May 1976), pp. 258–75; Michael Craton, *Sinews of Empire: A Short History of British Slavery* (Garden City, N.Y.: Anchor Books, 1974), pp. 187–99; Richard B. Sheridan, "Africa and the Caribbean in the Atlantic Slave Trade," *The American Historical Review*, Vol. 77, No. 1 (February 1972), pp. 15–35.
3. Stanley L. Engerman and Eugene D. Genovese, eds., *Race and Slavery in the Western Hemisphere: Quantitative Studies*, copyright © 1975 by The Center for Advanced Study in the Behavioral Sciences, Stanford, California; portions of

"Mortality and the Medical Treatment of Slaves in the British West Indies," by Richard B. Sheridan, reprinted by permission of Princeton University Press.

4. Richard Ligon, *A True and Exact History of the Island of Barbadoes*, etc. (London: Frank Cass, 1970; reprinted from 1673 ed.), pp. 37–8, 43–4, 46; Richard Blome, *A Description of Jamaica* (London, 1672), p. 86.
5. J. Harry Bennett, "Cary Helyar, Merchant and Planter of Seventeenth-Century Jamaica," *The William and Mary Quarterly*, 3d series, Vol. XXI, No. 1 (January 1964), pp. 68–9.
6. Richard B. Sheridan, *Sugar and Slavery: An Economic History of the British West Indies 1623–1775* (Baltimore, Md.: Johns Hopkins University Press, 1974), pp. 241–5; Elsa V. Goveia, *Slave Society in the British Leeward Islands at the End of the Eighteenth Century* (New Haven, Conn.: Yale University Press, 1965), pp. 117–35.
7. Richard Pares, *Merchants and Planters, The Economic History Review Supplement No. 4* (Cambridge: Cambridge University Press, 1960), pp. 39–40.
8. Sheridan, *Sugar and Slavery*, pp. 251–3.
9. Curtin, *Atlantic Slave Trade*, pp. 13, 268.
10. J. E. Inikori, "Measuring the Atlantic Slave Trade: An Assessment of Curtin and Anstey," *The Journal of African History*, Vol. 7 (1976), pp. 197–223; J. F. Ade Ajayi and J. E. Inikori, "An Account of Research on the Slave Trade in Nigeria," in Ajayi and Inikori, eds., *The African Slave Trade from the Fifteenth to the Nineteenth Century* (Paris: UNESCO, 1979), p. 248; Robert Stein, "Measuring the French Slave Trade, 1713–1792/3," *Journal of African History*, Vol. XIX, No. 4 (1978), pp. 515–21; D. Eltis, "The Direction and Fluctuation of the Transatlantic Slave Trade, 1821–1843: A Revision of the 1845 Parliamentary Paper," in Henry A. Gemery and Jan S. Hogendorn, eds., *The Uncommon Market: Essays in the Economic History of the Atlantic Slave Trade* (New York: Academic Press, 1979), pp. 289–91; James A. Rawley, *The Transatlantic Slave Trade: A History* (New York: W. W. Norton, 1981), pp. 427–9; Paul E. Lovejoy, "The Volume of the Atlantic Slave Trade: A Synthesis," *Journal of African History*, Vol. 23, No. 4 (1982), pp. 473–501.
11. Curtin, *Atlantic Slave Trade*, pp. 13, 268.
12. Public Record Office, London, *Colonial Office* 137/38, Hh 3, 4: Appendix to a memorial from Stephen Fuller, agent for Jamaica, to the Board of Trade, 30 January 1778; *Accounts and Papers (Parliamentary Papers)*, 1801–1802: "An Account of all Vessels which arrived in the British West Indies from Africa with Slaves, 1796–1800," *Journals of the Assembly of Jamaica*, Vol. XII (23 November 1815), p. 825.
13. Bryan Edwards, *The History, Civil and Commercial, of the British Colonies in the West Indies*, 2 vols. (London, 1801), Vol. II, pp. 70–92; R. B. LePage, "An Historical Introduction to Jamaican Creole," in R. B. LePage, ed., *Creole Language Studies* (London, 1960), pp. 74–6; Orlando Patterson, *The Sociology of Slavery: An Analysis of the Origins, Development and Structure of Negro Slave Society in Jamaica* (London: MacGibbon and Kee, 1967), pp. 113–44.
14. Eric Williams, *Capitalism and Slavery* (Chapel Hill: University of North Car-

olina Press, 1944), pp. 51–2, 65–84, 98–107; R. B. Sheridan, "The Commercial and Financial Organization of the British Slave Trade, 1750–1807," *The Economic History Review*, Vol. XI, No. 2 (December 1958), pp. 249–63.

15. Quoted in Elizabeth Donnan, ed., *Documents Illustrative of the History of the Slave Trade to America*, 4 vols. (New York: Octagon Books, 1965), Vol. II, p. 273.
16. Edward Long, *The History of Jamaica*, etc., 3 vols. (London, 1774), Vol. II, p. 491.
17. Herbert S. Klein and Stanley L. Engerman, "Slave Mortality on British Ships 1791–1797," in Roger Anstey and P. E. H. Hair, eds., *Liverpool, the African Slave Trade, and Abolition: Essays to Illustrate Current Knowledge and Research* (Bristol: Western Printing Services, 1976), pp. 116–17.
18. *Accounts and Papers (Parliamentary Papers)*, 1789, XXVI (646a): "Report of the Lords of the Committee of Council for Trade and Plantations on the Slave Trade" (cited hereafter as *Privy Council Report*); *Accounts and Papers (Parliamentary Papers)*, 1790–1791, XXIX (698): "Minutes of Evidence: Select Committee of the House of Commons on the Slave Trade" (cited hereafter as *House of Commons Report*).
19. *Privy Council Report*, 1789, XXVI (646a), Part I.
20. Ibid., Part I, evidence of Young.
21. Ernest Rhys, ed., *The Travels of Mungo Park* (London: J. M. Dent, 1923), p. 220.
22. Ibid., pp. 18, 221–6.
23. Quoted in Donnan, *Documents of the Slave Trade*, Vol. II, pp. 278–82; Walter Rodney, *West Africa and the Atlantic Slave Trade. The Historical Association of Tanzania Paper No. 2* (Nairobi, Kenya: East African Publishing House, 1967), pp. 1–16.
24. Klein and Engerman, "Slave Mortality on British Ships," pp. 116–17.
25. Rodney, *West Africa and the Slave Trade*, pp. 9–16.
26. *Privy Council Report*, 1789, Part I, evidence of Poplett and Heatley.
27. Herbert S. Klein, *The Middle Passage: Comparative Studies in the Atlantic Slave Trade* (Princeton, N.J.: Princeton University Press, 1978), Table 7.4, p. 149.
28. David Richardson, "West African Consumption Patterns and Their Influence on the Eighteenth-Century English Slave Trade," in Gemery and Hogendorn, eds., *The Uncommon Market*, pp. 303–30.
29. J. E. Inikori, "The Import of Firearms into West Africa 1750–1807: A Quantitative Analysis," *The Journal of African History*, Vol. XVIII, No. 3 (1977), pp. 339–68; Richard L. Roberts, "Production and Reproduction of Warrior States: Segu Bambara and Segu Tokolor, c. 1712–1890," *The International Journal of African Historical Studies*, Vol. 13, No. 3 (1980), pp. 389–419.
30. Marion Johnson, "The Atlantic slave trade and the economy of West Africa," in Anstey and Hair, eds., *Liverpool and the Slave Trade*, pp. 14–38; B. K. Drake, "The Liverpool-African voyage, c. 1790–1807: commercial problems," in ibid., pp. 126–56; A. G. Hopkins, *An Economic History of West Africa* (New York: Columbia University Press, 1973), pp. 87–112; J. D. Fage, "Slav-

ery and the slave trade in the context of West African history," *Journal of African History*, Vol. X (1969), pp. 393–404; Joseph C. Miller, "Some Aspects of the Commercial Organization of Slaving at Luanda, Angola – 1760–1830," in Gemery and Hogendorn, eds., *The Uncommon Market*, pp. 77–106; Mahdi Adamu, "The Delivery of Slaves from the Central Sudan to the Bight of Benin in the Eighteenth and Nineteenth Centuries," in ibid., pp. 163–180; Patrick Manning, "The Slave Trade in the Bight of Benin, 1640–1890," in ibid., pp. 107–41; Martin Klein and Paul E. Lovejoy, "Slavery in West Africa," in ibid., pp. 181–212; Paul E. Lovejoy and Jan S. Hogendorn, "The Patterns of Slave Marketing," in ibid., pp. 213–35; Ralph A. Austen, "Slavery among Coastal Middlemen: The Duala of Cameroon," in Suzanne Miers and Igor Kopytoff, eds., *Slavery in Africa: Historical and Anthropological Perspectives* (Madison: University of Wisconsin Press, 1977), pp. 305–33; Philip D. Curtin, *Economic Change in Precolonial Africa: Senegambia in the Era of the Slave Trade* (Madison: University of Wisconsin Press, 1975); Rawley, *Transatlantic Slave Trade*, pp. 247–81.

31. Adamu, "Delivery of Slaves," in Gemery and Hogendorn, eds., *The Uncommon Market*, pp. 166–9.
32. Johnson, "Economy of West Africa," in Anstey and Hair, eds., *Liverpool and the Slave Trade*, pp. 27–9.
33. Igor Kopytoff and Suzanne Miers, "African 'Slavery' as an Institution of Marginality," in Miers and Kopytoff, eds., *Slavery in Africa*, pp. 3–14, 51, 56–62, 65–9; for a critique of the Kopytoff and Miers thesis, see James L. Watson, "Slavery as an Institution: Open and Closed Systems," in James L. Watson, ed., *Asian and African Systems of Slavery* (Berkeley: University of California Press, 1980), pp. 1–15.
34. Jack Goody, "Slavery in Time and Space," in Watson, ed., *Asian and African Slavery*, pp. 37–8, 42.
35. For studies that minimize the impact of the slave trade, see J. D. Fage, *A History of West Africa: An Introductory Survey* (Cambridge: Cambridge University Press, 1969), pp. 84–9; Roger Anstey, *The Atlantic Slave Trade and British Abolition 1760–1810* (Atlantic Highlands, N.J.: Humanities Press, 1975), pp. 58–88.
36. Henry A. Gemery and Jan S. Hogendorn, "The Economic Costs of West African Participation in the Atlantic Slave Trade: A Preliminary Sampling for the Eighteenth Century," in Gemery and Hogendorn, eds., *The Uncommon Market*, pp. 6, 143–61. See also J. E. Inikori, "Market Structure and the Profits of the British African Trade in the Late Eighteenth Century," *Journal of Economic History*, Vol. XLI, No. 4 (December 1981), pp. 745–76; Walter Rodney, *How Europe Underdeveloped Africa* (London: Bogle-L'Ouverture Publications, 1972); W. Rodney, *A History of the Upper Guinea Coast 1545–1800* (Oxford: Oxford University Press, 1970); W. Rodney, "African Slavery and Other Forms of Social Oppression on the Upper Guinea Coast in the Context of the Atlantic Slave Trade," *Journal of African History*, Vol. VII, No. 3 (1966), pp. 431–43; G. N. Uzoigwe, "The Slave Trade and African Societies," *Trans-*

actions of the Historical Society of Ghana, Vol. XIV, No. 2 (December 1973), pp. 187–212.

37. Joseph C. Miller, "Mortality in the Atlantic Slave Trade: Statistical Evidence on Causality," *Journal of Interdisciplinary History*, Vol. XI, No. 3 (Winter 1981), pp. 385–423.
38. Charles Singer and E. Ashworth Underwood, *A Short History of Medicine*, 2d ed. (New York: Oxford University Press, 1962), pp. 185–9; Philip D. Curtin, "Epidemiology and the Slave Trade," *Political Science Quarterly*, Vol. LXXXIII, No. 2 (June 1968), pp. 190–216.
39. T. Aubrey, M.D., *The Sea-Surgeon, Or the Guinea Man's Vade Mecum. In which is laid down, The Method of curing such Diseases as usually happen Abroad, especially on the Coast of Guinea; with the best way of treating Negroes, both in Health and in Sickness. Written for the Use of young Sea Surgeons* (London, 1729), pp. 134–5.
40. *House of Commons Report*, 1790, pp. 28–30; W. N. Boog Watson, M.D., "The Guinea Trade and Some of Its Surgeons (with special reference to the Royal College of Surgeons of Edinburgh)," *Journal of the Royal College of Surgeons of Edinburgh*, Vol. 14, No. 3 (May 1969), pp. 207–8. I am indebted to A. H. B. Masson, M.D., for calling my attention to this article.
41. "An Act to Regulate the Carrying of Slaves, 28 Geo. III, c. 54," printed in Donnan, *Documents of the Slave Trade*, Vol. II, pp. 582–9.
42. Christopher Lloyd, *The Navy and the Slave Trade* (London: Longmans, Green, 1949), pp. 3–11.
43. Alexander Falconbridge, *An Account of the Slave Trade on the Coast of Africa* (London, 1788), p. 28.
44. Edinburgh University Library, *Letters of Archibald Dalziel* [sic], Dk. 7. 52., Archibald Dalzel to Mr. Andrew Dalzel, dated London, 4 March 1763, f. 5. I am grateful to Mr. Charles Finlayson, Keeper of the Manuscripts at Edinburgh University, for calling my attention to these letters.
45. Tobias Smollett, *The Adventures of Roderick Random* (New York: New American Library, 1964), p. 46.
46. Ibid., pp. 51, 94–8, 108–10.
47. I. A. Akinjogbin, "Archibald Dalzel: Slave Trader and Historian of Dahomey," *Journal of African History*, Vol. VII, No. 1 (1966), pp. 67–77; J. A. Nixon, "Health and Sickness in the Slave Trade," Appendix to Chap. XI, in C. Northcote Parkinson, ed., *The Trade Winds: A Study of British Overseas Trade during the French Wars 1793–1815* (London: Allen & Unwin, 1948), pp. 274–5.
48. *House of Commons Report*, 1790, pp. 561, 573–4, evidence of Wilson.
49. Rhys, *Travels of Mungo Park*, pp. 275–7.
50. Boog Watson, "Guinea Trade and Its Surgeons," pp. 209–10; Christopher Lloyd, ed., *The Health of Seamen: Selections from the Works of Dr. James Lind, Sir Gilbert Blane and Dr. Thomas Trotter* (London: Navy Records Society, 1965), pp. 214–15.
51. Thomas Clarkson, *History of the Rise, Progress and Accomplishment of the Abolition*

of the African Slave Trade (London: John W. Parker, 1839), pp. 331–2; Boog Watson, "Guinea Trade and Its Surgeons," p. 208.

52. Clarkson, *History of Slave Trade*, pp. 207–9.
53. Nixon, "Health and Sickness in the Slave Trade," p. 276; Boog Watson, "Guinea Trade and Its Surgeons," pp. 208–9.
54. Aubrey, *The Sea-Surgeon*, pp. 132–3.
55. P.R.O. London, *Rogers Papers*, *Chancery* C. 107/5, Box No. 2, No. 25, William Dineley, surgeon of the ship *Recovery*, to James Rogers in Bristol, dated Bananas Island, 3 March 1791. I am indebted to Mr. David Richardson for calling my attention to these letters.
56. Ibid., same to same, 10 September 1791.
57. Ibid., Box No. 2, No. 18, Captain John Goodrich of the ship *Sarah* to James Rogers in Bristol, dated Bembia, 4 February 1790.
58. *House of Commons Report*, 1790, pp. 96–100, evidence of Trotter.
59. Aubrey, *The Sea-Surgeon*, pp. 118–19; Donnan, *Documents of the Slave Trade*, Vol. II, pp. 404–5.
60. Falconbridge, *Account of Slave Trade*, pp. 17–18.
61. Quoted by J. A. Nixon, "Health and Sickness in the Slave Trade," p. 275.
62. P.R.O. London, *Rogers Papers*, *Chancery* C. 107/14, Box No. 2, No. 21, Captain William Woodville Jun. of the ship *Rodney* to Messrs. James Rogers and Company in Bristol, dated Bannee [sic Bonny Island], 16 May 1791.
63. Aubrey, *The Sea-Surgeon*, p. 102.
64. Darold D. Wax, "A Philadelphia Surgeon on a Slaving Voyage to Africa, 1749–1751," *The Pennsylvania Magazine of History and Biography*, Vol. XCII, No. 4 (October 1968), p. 490.
65. *Privy Council Report*, 1789, Part II, evidence of Anderson.
66. Ibid., evidence of Norris.
67. *House of Commons Report*, 1790, p. 590, evidence of Falconbridge.
68. Sir H. Harold Scott, M.D., "The Influence of the Slave-Trade in the Spread of Tropical Disease," *Transactions of the Royal Society of Tropical Medicine and Hygiene*, Vol. XXXVII, No. 3 (December 1943), pp. 169–88; Frederick F. Cartwright, "Disease and the Exploration of Africa," Chap. 6 of his *Disease and History* (New York: Mentor Books, 1972), pp. 135–62.
69. Alexander Bryson, M.D., *Report on the Climate and Principal Diseases of the African Station* (London, 1847), quoted in R. Hoeppli, M.D., *Parasitic Diseases in Africa and the Western Hemisphere: Early Documentation and Transmission by the Slave Trade* (Basel: Verlag für Recht und Gesellschaft Ag, 1969), p. 64.
70. John Barbot, *A Description of the coasts of North and South Guinea and of Ethiopia Inferior, vulgarly called Angola*, etc., in Awnsham Churchill, ed., *A Collection of Voyages and Travels* (London, 1732), Vol. V, p. 118.
71. Bryson, *Report of African Station*, in Hoeppli, ed., *Parasitic Diseases*, p. 64.
72. Ibid., pp. 62–4.
73. Donnan, *Documents of Slave Trade*, Vol. I, pp. 392–410.
74. *Privy Council Report*, 1789, Part II, evidence of Anderson.
75. *House of Commons Report*, 1790, pp. 562–3, 575, 579, evidence of Wilson.

76. Ibid., pp. 590–1, evidence of Falconbridge.
77. Ibid., pp. 158, evidence of Morley.
78. Aubrey, *The Sea-Surgeon*, p. 107.
79. Barbot, *Description of Guinea*, p. 277.
80. Aubrey, *The Sea-Surgeon*, p. 107.
81. Alexander Campbell Fraser, ed., *The Works of George Berkeley, D.D.* (Oxford: Clarendon Press, 1871), Vol. III, pp. 476–7.
82. Rhys, *Travels of Mungo Park*, p. 118; Winterbottom, *Account of Native Africans*, Vol. II, pp. 135–6.
83. I am indebted to M. T. Ashcroft, M.D., and Dr. Roderick McDonald for supplying this and other slave cargo advertisements.
84. Donnan, *Documents of Slave Trade*, Vol. II, p. 282.
85. Winterbottom, *Account of Native Africans*, Vol. II, p. 129.
86. James Grainger, M.D., *An Essay on the More Common West-India Diseases; and the Remedies which that Country itself Produces*, etc. (Edinburgh 1802), pp. 77–9.
87. E. N. Chamberlain, "The Influence of the Slave Trade on Liverpool Medicine," *Fourteenth International Congress of the History of Medicine* (Rome and Salerno, 1954), pp. 768–73.
88. Aubrey, *The Sea-Surgeon*, pp. 126–8.
89. Falconbridge, *Account of Slave Trade*, p. 29.
90. Aubrey, *The Sea-Surgeon*, pp. 110–26; Hoeppli, *Parasitic Diseases*, pp. 85–93.
91. Winterbottom, *Account of Native Africans*, Vol. II, pp. 26–8.
92. *Privy Council Report*, 1789, Part II, evidence of Dalzel.
93. "An Act to Regulate the Carrying of Slaves, 28 Geo III, c. 54," printed in Donnan, *Documents of Slave Trade*, Vol. II, pp. 582–9.
94. *Accounts and Papers (Parliamentary Papers)*, 1789, XXIX (632), pp. 1–5: "Extracts from Journals of the Surgeons employed in Ships trading to the Coast of Africa, since the 1st of August 1788 ... which relate to the Slaves during the Time they were on Board the Ships, 16th June 1789."
95. Boog Watson, "Guinea Trade and Its Surgeons," pp. 210–13; J. A. Nixon, "Health and Sickness," pp. 136–8.
96. Chamberlain, "Slave Trade and Liverpool Medicine," pp. 770–3.
97. Gomer Williams, *History of the Liverpool Privateers and Letters of Marque with an Account of the Liverpool Slave Trade* (London and Liverpool, 1897), p. 680.
98. K. G. Davies, *The Royal African Company* (London: Longmans, 1957), p. 292; Anstey, *Atlantic Slave Trade*, pp. 31, 414–15.
99. Johannes Postma, "Mortality in the Dutch Slave Trade, 1675–1795," in Gemery and Hogendorn, eds., *The Uncommon Market*, pp. 239–60; Herbert S. Klein and Stanley L. Engerman, "A Note on Mortality in the French Slave Trade in the Eighteenth Century," in ibid., pp. 261–72.
100. Klein and Engerman, "Slave Mortality on British Ships 1791–1797," in Anstey and Hair, eds., *Liverpool and the Slave Trade*, pp. 113–25; Klein, *Middle Passage*, pp. 64–5, 160–3, 173–4, 196, 199, 229–41.
101. *The Parliamentary Register* (London, 1788), Vol. XXIII, pp. 606–7; Anstey, *Atlantic Slave Trade*, pp. 30–1.

102. Klein, *Middle Passage*, pp. 120–2, 145, 174.
103. Ibid., pp. 157–8; Rawley, *Transatlantic Slave Trade*, pp. 301–3. I am indebted to Dr. Rawley for permitting me to read his book at the manuscript stage.
104. Klein, *Middle Passage*, p. 162; Rawley, *Transatlantic Slave Trade*, pp. 304–6; Postma, "Mortality in Dutch Slave Trade," pp. 239–46.
105. James Jones to Lord Hawkesbury, 26 July 1788, quoted in Donnan, *Documents of Slave Trade*, Vol. II, pp. 589–92.
106. Klein, *Middle Passage*, p. 162; see also Joseph C. Miller, "Mortality in the Atlantic Slave Trade," *Journal of Interdisciplinary History*, Vol. XI, No. 3 (Winter 1981), pp. 385–423.
107. *Second Report of the Committee of the House of Assembly of Jamaica*, 12 November 1788, printed in *Privy Council Report*, 1789, Part III, Jamaica Appendix.
108. Walter Rodney, *How Europe Underdeveloped Africa* (London: Bogle-L'Ouverture Publications, 1972), pp. 104–5.

5. Slaves and plantations

1. Copy of Circular Despatch No. 1, from Lord Goderich to the Governors of British Guiana, Trinidad, St. Lucia, Mauritius, and the Cape of Good Hope, accompanying the General Order in Council of 1831; in *Food and Other Maintenance and Allowances, Under the Apprenticeship System; Extracted from the Appendix to a Report Recently Published by the Committee of the London Anti-Slavery Society* (London, 1838), p. 16.
2. Sidney W. Mintz, Foreward to Ramiro Guerra y Sanchez, *Sugar and Society in the Caribbean: An Economic History of Cuban Agriculture* (New Haven, Conn.: Yale University Press, 1964), p. xiv.
3. Joseph A. Schumpeter, *The Theory of Economic Development* (Cambridge, Mass.: Harvard University Press, 1934).
4. Richard B. Sheridan, *Sugar and Slavery: An Economic History of the British West Indies 1623–1775* (Baltimore, Md.: Johns Hopkins University Press, 1974), pp. 97–122.
5. Rev. Hope Masterton Waddell, *Twenty-Nine Years in the West Indies and Central Africa: A Review of Missionary Work and Adventure 1829–1858*, 2d ed. (London: reprinted by Frank Cass, 1970), pp. 20–1.
6. Ibid., pp. 21–2.
7. Richard B. Sheridan, "Simon Taylor, Sugar Tycoon of Jamaica, 1740–1813," *Agricultural History*, Vol. XLV, No. 4 (October 1971), pp. 287–8.
8. Sheridan, *Sugar and Slavery*, pp. 257–9, 372–4, 377–81.
9. Jay R. Mandel, *The Roots of Black Poverty: The Southern Plantation Economy after the Civil War* (Durham, N.C.: Duke University Press, 1978), pp. 12–15.
10. Elsa V. Goveia, *Slave Society in the British Leeward Islands at the End of the Eighteenth Century* (New Haven, Conn.: Yale University Press, 1965), pp. vii–viii, 318–20.
11. Eugene D. Genovese, "The Treatment of Slaves in Different Countries: Problems in the Applications of the Comparative Method," in Laura Foner and

Eugene D. Genovese, eds., *Slavery in the New World: A Reader in Comparative History* (Englewood Cliffs, N.J.: Prentice-Hall, 1969), pp. 202–10.

12. Herbert S. Klein, *The Middle Passage: Comparative Studies in the Atlantic Slave Trade* (Princeton, N.J.: Princeton University Press, 1978), pp. 155–6.
13. [Dr. David Collins], *Practical Rules for the Management and Medical Treatment of Negro Slaves in the Sugar Colonies. By a Professional Planter* (Freeport, N.Y.: Books for Libraries Press, 1971; first published 1803), p. 132.
14. William Beckford, *Remarks Upon the Situation of Negroes in Jamaica, Impartially Made From a Local Experience of Nearly Thirteen Years in that Island* (London, 1788), pp. 13–14.
15. W. J. Gardner, *A History of Jamaica*, etc. (London, 1909), p. 165; Edward Brathwaite, *The Development of Creole Society in Jamaica 1770–1820* (Oxford: Clarendon Press, 1971), pp. 6, 281.
16. The act of 5 May 1732 was apparently the only quarantine act passed during the slavery era. It was entitled "An act to prevent the landing or keeping of negroes infected with small-pox in any of the three towns of St. Catherine, Port-Royal, and Kingston." Enforcement of this act was generally lax. See *Journals of the Assembly of Jamaica*, Vol. III, 29 April to 6 May 1732, pp. 85–90.
17. David L. Chandler, "Health Conditions in the Slave Trade of Colonial New Granada," in Robert B. Toplin, ed., *Slavery and Race Relations in Latin America* (Westport, Conn.: Greenwood Press, 1974), pp. 51–67.
18. Goveia, *Slave Society*, p. 124; see also Svend E. Green-Pedersen, "Slave Demography in the Danish West Indies and the Abolition of the Danish Slave Trade," in David Eltis and James Walvin, eds., *The Abolition of the Atlantic Slave Trade: Origins and Effects in Europe, Africa, and the Americas* (Madison: University of Wisconsin Press, 1981), pp. 231–57; Richard B. Sheridan, "Slave Demography in the British West Indies and the Abolition of the Slave Trade," in ibid., pp. 259–85.
19. Charles Leslie, *History of Jamaica*, etc. (London, 1740), p. 328; British Library, *Additional MS.* 12,405, f. 357: Papers of C. E. Long.
20. William Beckford, *A Descriptive Account of the Island of Jamaica*, 2 vols. (London, 1790), Vol. II, p. 342.
21. J. Harry Bennett, *Bondsmen and Bishops: Slavery and Apprenticeship on the Codrington Plantations of Barbados, 1710–1838* (Berkeley: University of California Publications in History, Vol. 62, 1958), pp. 54, 60–1, 95.
22. *Accounts and Papers (Parliamentary Papers)*, 1789, XXVI (646a), Part 3, Jamaica, Nos. 7, 8: "Report of the Lords of the Committee of Council for Trade and Plantations on the Slave Trade" (cited hereafter as *Privy Council Report*), evidence of Doctors Anderson and Quier.
23. James Grainger, M.D., *An Essay on the More Common West-India Diseases*, etc. (Edinburgh, 1802; 1st ed. London, 1764), pp. i–ii, 7–14.
24. Collins, *Practical Rules*, pp. 44–74.
25. Beckford, *Remarks on Negroes*, pp. 6–7, 16, 20–34.
26. Clement Caines, *Letters on the Cultivation of the Otaheite Cane*, etc. (London,

1801), pp. 251–67; George W. Roberts, *The Population of Jamaica* (Cambridge: Cambridge University Press, 1957), pp. 223–5.

27. Collins, *Practical Rules*, pp. 104–8.
28. *Letter Book of Nathaniel Phillips* (microfilm copy in the library, University of the West Indies, Mona, Jamaica), Letter No. 11,484 from Nathaniel Phillips to Thomas Barritt, overseer in Jamaica, dated London, 7 July 1790. I am indebted to Dr. Roderick McDonald for this reference.
29. Bryan Edwards, *The History, Civil and Commercial, of the British Colonies in the West Indies*, 2 vols. (Dublin: Luke White, 1793), Vol. II, p. 118; Collins, *Practical Rules*, p. 54.
30. Edwards, *History of West Indies*, Vol. II, p. 148; *Privy Council Report*, Part 3, report of Mr. Reeves, law clerk, on the slave laws of the British West India colonies.
31. George Pinckard, M.D., *Notes on the West Indies*, etc., 3 vols. (Westport, Conn.: Negro Universities Press, 1970; first published 1806), Vol. II, pp. 113–14.
32. Robert Renny, *An History of Jamaica*, etc. (London, 1807), p. 179.
33. See the discussion of foot and leg ailments in Chapter 7.
34. Samuel Martin, *An Essay on Plantership*, etc. (London, 1773), pp. 10–11.
35. Collins, *Practical Rules*, p. 116.
36. *Privy Council Report*, Part I, Barbados, letter from Governor David Parry to Lord Sydney, dated Barbados, 18 August 1788.
37. J. Stewart, *A View of the Past and Present State of the Island of Jamaica; with Remarks on the Moral and Physical Condition of the Slaves* (Edinburgh, 1823), pp. 266–7. For modern accounts of slave housing and clothing in Jamaica, see Orlando Patterson, *The Sociology of Slavery: An Analysis of the Origins, Development and Structure of Negro Society in Jamaica* (London: MacGibbon & Kee, 1967), pp. 54–6, 83, 222–3; Brathwaite, *Creole Society*, pp. 232–6.
38. Bennett, *Bondsmen and Bishops*, pp. 32–3.
39. Jerome S. Handler and Frederick W. Lange, *Plantation Slavery in Barbados: An Archaeological and Historical Investigation* (Cambridge, Mass.: Harvard University Press, 1978), pp. 46, 51–6, 95–7.
40. B. W. Higman, "Household Structure and Fertility on Jamaican Slave Plantations: A Nineteenth-century Example," *Population Studies*, Vol. 27, No. 3 (November 1972), pp. 540–3.
41. Robert W. Fogel and Stanley L. Engerman, *Time on the Cross: The Economics of American Negro Slavery*, 2 vols. (Boston: Little, Brown, 1974), Vol. I, pp. 116–17.
42. [Philip Gibbes], *Instructions for the Treatment of Negroes*, etc. (London, 1797), pp. 2–3.
43. Matthew Gregory Lewis, *Journal of a West India Proprietor 1815–17*, edited with an Introduction by Mona Wilson (Boston: Houghton Mifflin, 1929), pp. 95–6.
44. Rev. James M. Phillippo, *Jamaica; Its Past and Present State* (Westport, Conn.: Negro Universities Press, 1970; first published 1843), pp. 216–17.
45. Renny, *History of Jamaica*, p. 178.

46. *J. Johnson MS., Reports relating to Mr. Gordon's Estate in the West Indies, 1824*, Part III, ff. 7–8, 16–22, Microfilm no. 203, Beinecke Lesser Antilles Collection, The Burke Library, Hamilton College, Clinton, New York. I am indebted to Mr. Frank K. Lorenz, Reference Librarian at The Burke Library, for making this microfilm available.
47. Ibid., Part III, ff. 8–9.
48. Ibid., Part II, ff. 9, 24.
49. Collins, *Practical Rules*, pp. 116–27.
50. Ward Barrett, "Caribbean Sugar-Production Standards in the Seventeenth and Eighteenth Centuries," in John Parker, ed., *Merchants and Scholars: Essays in the History of Exploration and Trade collected in memory of James Ford Bell* (Minneapolis: University of Minnesota Press, 1965), pp. 164–5.
51. Michael Craton, *Searching for the Invisible Man: Slaves and Plantation Life in Jamaica* (Cambridge, Mass.: Harvard University Press, 1978), Fig. 26, p. 141.
52. Collins, *Practical Rules*, p. 168.
53. Joseph Sturge and Thomas Harvey, *The West Indies in 1837, Being the Journal of a Visit to Antigua, Montserrat, Dominica, St. Lucia, Barbados, and Jamaica* (London: Frank Cass, 1968), p. lxxvii.
54. Somerset County Record Office, Taunton, *Tudway Papers*: "Journal of the Work and Transactions of Parham New Work" plantation in Antigua, the property of John Paine Tudway of Wells, County Somerset, England.
55. John Luffman, *A Brief Account of the Island of Antigua*, etc. (London, 1789), printed in Vere Langford Oliver, *The History of the Island of Antigua*, etc., 3 vols. (London, 1894–9), Vol. I, p. cxxxiii.
56. Martin, *Essay on Plantership*, pp. 6–7; Collins, *Practical Rules*, p. 151.
57. Collins, *Practical Rules*, pp. 151, 156; Beckford, *Remarks Upon Negroes*, p. 33.
58. Goveia, *Slave Society*, p. 318.
59. Edward Long, *The History of Jamaica*, etc., 3 vols. (London, 1774), Vol. I, pp. 377, 386; Douglas Hall, *Free Jamaica 1838–1865: An Economic History* (New Haven, Conn.: Yale University Press, 1959), p. 82; B. W. Higman, *Slave Population and Economy in Jamaica 1807–1834* (Cambridge: Cambridge University Press, 1976), pp. 12–13.
60. Beckford, *Account of Jamaica*, Vol. II, p. 366; Douglas Hall, "Absentee-Proprietorship in the British West Indies, to about 1850," *The Jamaican Historical Review*, Vol. 4 (1964), pp. 15–35; Lowell Joseph Ragatz, *The Fall of the Planter Class in the British Caribbean, 1763–1833* (New York: Octagon Books, 1963), pp. 54–6.
61. Beckford, *Account of Jamaica*, Vol. II, pp. 364–5.
62. Ibid., p. 368.
63. Collins, *Practical Rules*, pp. 15–18.

6. Labor, diet, and punishment

1. William Dickson, LLD., *Mitigation of Slavery*, etc. (London: Longman, 1814), Part II, p. 316. I am indebted to Stanley L. Engerman, Barry W. Higman, and John R. Ward for helpful suggestions in preparing this chapter.

2. [Philip Gibbes], *Instructions for the Treatment of Negroes*, etc. (London, 1797), p. 74.
3. *A Letter from Capt. J. S. Smith to the Rev*[d] *Mr Mill on the State of the Negro Slaves* (London, 1786), p. 42.
4. Rev. James Ramsay, *An Essay on the Treatment and Conversion of African Slaves in the British Sugar Colonies* (London, 1784), p. 119; [James Stephen], *The Crisis of the Sugar Colonies*, etc. (London, 1802), pp. 10–11.
5. J. B. Moreton, *West India Customs and Manners*, etc. (London, 1793), p. 88.
6. *Accounts and Papers (Parliamentary Papers)*, 1831–32, XX (721): "Report from the Select Committee on the Extinction of Slavery throughout the British Dominions. With Minutes of Evidence, Appendix and Index" (cited hereafter as *Report on Slavery*, 1832), pp. 13–15, 43, 45, evidence of Taylor; Barry W. Higman, *Slave Population and Economy in Jamaica, 1807–1834* (Cambridge: Cambridge University Press, 1976), pp. 105–15, 118–38.
7. John Davy, M.D., F.R.S., *The West Indies Before and Since Slave Emancipation* (London, 1854), pp. 116, 134; Janet Schaw, *Journal of a Lady of Quality*, etc., edited by Evangeline and Charles M. Andrews (New Haven, Conn.: Yale University Press, 1921), pp. 127–8.
8. Ramsay, *Essay on African Slaves*, pp. 69–73. For grass picking in Jamaica, see Moreton, *West India Customs and Manners*, pp. 146–8.
9. Michael Scott, *Tom Cringle's Log* (London: J. M. Dent, 1938), pp. 118–19.
10. Richard B. Sheridan, *Sugar and Slavery: An Economic History of the British West Indies 1623–1775* (Baltimore, Md.: Johns Hopkins University Press, 1974), pp. 112–18.
11. *Report on Slavery*, 1832, pp. 332–4, evidence of Scott.
12. Ibid., pp. 523–5, evidence of Wildman.
13. Gilbert Mathison, *Notices Respecting Jamaica, in 1808, 1809, 1810* (London, 1811), p. 35.
14. Rev. Hope Masterton Waddell, *Twenty-Nine Years in the West Indies and Central Africa: A Review of Missionary Work and Adventure 1829–1858* (London: Frank Cass, 1970; first published 1863), pp. 21–2.
15. Robert William Fogel, *Without Consent or Contract: The Rise and Fall of American Slavery*. I am indebted to Professor Fogel for permission to quote this extract from his forthcoming book.
16. James Stephen, *The Slavery of the British West India Colonies Delineated*, etc., 2 vols. (London: Saunders and Benning, 1824, 1830), Vol. II, pp. 184–91.
17. Lowell Joseph Ragatz, *The Fall of the Planter Class in the British Caribbean, 1763–1833* (New York: Octagon Books, 1963), pp. 142–3; Edward Brathwaite, *The Development of Creole Society in Jamaica* (Oxford: Clarendon Press, 1971), pp. 68–73.
18. Thomas Southey, *Chronological History of the West Indies*, 3 vols. (London: Frank Cass, 1968), Vol. II, p. 426.
19. Public Record Office, London, *Colonial Office* 28/57.
20. P.R.O. London, *C.O.* 137/71; letter from Gov. Sir Basil Keith to Earl of Dartmouth, 18 January 1776.

21. Ibid., *C.O.* 137/71, address of the Assembly of Jamaica to Gov. Keith, 24 October 1776.
22. Ibid., *C.O.* 137/71, address of the Assembly of Jamaica to Gov. Keith.
23. Bodleian Library, Oxford, *Barham Papers, MSS. Clarendon Dep.* C 357, Bund. 1, letter from William Smalling to Sir Joseph Foster Barham, 10 July 1777.
24. British Library, *Additional MS.* 41,348, Vol. III, f. 189, *Letter Book of Colonel Samuel Martin of Antigua.*
25. Ibid., ff. 197, 221, 222, 270.
26. Somerset Record Office, Taunton, *Tudway Papers*, DD/TD, c/2209; letter from Main Swete Walrond to Clement Tudway, Antigua, 28 March 1776; ibid., letter from same to same, 18 April 1776.
27. Ibid., letter from Francis Farley to Clement Tudway, Antigua, 27 October 1777; ibid., letter from Main Swete Walrond to Clement Tudway, Antigua, 9 December 1778.
28. Ibid., letter from Walrond to Tudway, 29 September 1779; Vere Langford Oliver, *The History of the Island of Antigua*, etc., 3 vols. (London, 1894–9), Vol. I, p. cxxiv; Southey, *Chronological History*, Vol. II, p. 459; Rev. Thomas Coke, *A History of the West Indies*, etc., 3 vols. (London, 1810), Vol. II, p. 429.
29. P.R.O. London, *C.O.* 152/57, letter of 17 March 1788; and *C.O.* 152/58, letter of 17 June 1778; Elsa V. Goveia, *Slave Society in the British Leeward Islands at the End of the Eighteenth Century* (New Haven, Conn.: Yale University Press, 1965), pp. 4–14.
30. Douglas Hall, *Free Jamaica 1838–1865: An Economic History* (New Haven, Conn.: Yale University Press, 1959), pp. 164–5; John H. Parry, "Plantation and Provision ground: An historical sketch of the introduction of food crops into Jamaica," *Revista de Historia de America* (Mexico), Numero 39, Junio de 1955, pp. 15–18; Sidney W. Mintz and Douglas G. Hall, "The Origins of the Jamaican Internal Marketing System," *Yale University Publications in Anthropology No. 57* (New Haven, Conn., 1960); Orlando Patterson, *The Sociology of Slavery: An Analysis of the Origins, Development and Structure of Negro Slave Society in Jamaica* (London: MacGibbon & Kee, 1967), pp. 216–30.
31. P.R.O. London, *C.O.* 138/28; letter no. 80 of 20 October 1780; *The Gentleman's Magazine*, 1780, pp. 619–23.
32. National Library of Scotland, Edinburgh, *Charles Steuart Papers, MS.* 5032, ff. 57d–58, letter from Charles Ruddach to Charles Steuart in Jamaica, 30 October 1780; *Annual Register*, 1780, pp. 292–4; 1781, pp. 35–6.
33. *Accounts and Papers (Parliamentary Papers)*, 1789, XXVI (646a): "Report of the Privy Council Committee on the Slave Trade" (cited hereafter as *Privy Council Report*, 1789), Part 3, Barbados, A. No. 15.
34. *Annual Register*, 1780, pp. 295–6; 1781, pp. 30–3; *Gentleman's Magazine, Supplement for 1780*, pp. 619–23; 1781, p. 43.
35. *Annual Register*, 1780, p. 295.
36. P.R.O. London, *C.O.* 138/29, letter from Gov. Dalling to Lord Germaine, no. 110.
37. John Ehrman, *The Younger Pitt: The Years of Acclaim* (London: Constable, 1969),

pp. 332–8; *Tudway Papers*, letter to Clement Tudway at Wells, county Somerset, 29 April 1784.

38. *Gentleman's Magazine*, October 1784, p. 789.
39. *Second Report of the Committee of the House of Assembly of the Island of Jamaica*, 12 November 1788, printed in the *Privy Council Report*, 1789, Part 3, Jamaica Appendix.
40. *Gentleman's Magazine, Supplement for 1785*, p. 1034; *Second Report of Committee of Assembly of Jamaica*, 1788.
41. *Gentleman's Magazine*, October 1785, p. 825; November 1785, p. 912; February 1785, p. 171.
42. Ibid., November 1786, pp. 987–8, December 1786, p. 1083; *Annual Register*, 1786, p. 214.
43. Dickson, *Mitigation of Slavery*, p. 431.
44. *Second Report of Committee of Assembly of Jamaica*, 1788.
45. Mr. Wynne, *Notes on the two Reports, from the Committee of the Hon. Assembly of Jamaica*, of 16 October and 12 November 1788 (no date), pp. 40–2, quoted in Dickson, *Mitigation of Slavery*, pp. 313–16. Drawing on local printed sources, Dr. Brathwaite estimates that between 15,000 and 24,000 slaves perished of famine or of disease contracted by scarcity and unwholesome diet (*Creole Society in Jamaica*, pp. 85–6).
46. Hector McNeill, *Observations on the Treatment of Negroes in the Island of Jamaica* (London, 1788), p. 39.
47. *Privy Council Report*, 1789, XXVI (646a), Part 3, Antigua, evidence of Athill.
48. *Journals of the Assembly of Jamaica* (cited hereafter as *J.A.J.*), Vol. X, pp. 315–16.
49. Ibid., Vol. XII, p. 792; Derrick B. Jelliffe, M.D., *Child Nutrition in Developing Countries*, Office of War on Hunger, Agency for International Development, Washington, D.C., 1969, pp. 5, 16–18.
50. *J.A.J.*, Vol. XII, pp. 792–3; David MacPherson, *Annals of Commerce*, 4 vols. (London, 1805), Vol. III, pp. 725–6; *Food Composition Tables for Use in the English-Speaking Caribbean*, compiled by the Caribbean Food and Nutrition Institute, 1973, pp. 5, 44; Richard N. Bean, "Food Imports into the British West Indies: 1680–1845," in Vera Rubin and Arthur Tuden, eds., *Comparative Perspective on Slavery in New World Plantation Societies* (New York Academy of Sciences, 1977), p. 587.
51. *Accounts and Papers (Parliamentary Papers)*, 1836, XV (605): "Report from the Select Committee on Negro Apprenticeship in the Colonies," evidence of Burge, Oldham, Jones.
52. *Privy Council Report*, 1789, Part 3, Barbados, evidence of Nicholls; *Accounts and Papers (Parliamentary Papers)*, 1790, XXIX (698): "Minutes of Evidence: Select Committee of the House of Commons on the Slave Trade" (cited hereafter as *House of Commons Report*, 1790), p. 108, evidence of Terry.
53. Bean, "Food Imports into the British West Indies," p. 587.
54. J. Stewart, *A View of the Past and Present State of the Island of Jamaica* (Edinburgh, 1823), pp. 267–8.

55. William Beckford, *A Descriptive Account of the Island of Jamaica*, 2 vols. (London, 1790), Vol. I, pp. 256–7; Edward Long, *The History of Jamaica*, etc., 3 vols. (London, 1774), Vol. II, p. 492.
56. Bryan Edwards, *The History, Civil and Commercial, of the British Colonies in the West Indies*, 2 vols. (Dublin, 1793), Vol. II, pp. 122–5, 133.
57. Mintz and Hall, "Origins of Internal Marketing System," p. 11; Patterson, *Sociology of Slavery*, pp. 216–22; Parry, "Plantation and Provision Ground," pp. 1–2, 11–12, 16–20.
58. Edwards, *History of West Indies*, Vol. II, pp. 145–6, 158; *J.A.J.*, Vol. X, p. 562; *The Consolidated Slave Law, Passed December 22, 1826* (Jamaica, 1827), pp. 3–4.
59. *Report on Slavery*, 1832, pp. 25–6, evidence of Taylor; Benjamin McMahon, *Jamaica Plantership*, etc. (London, 1839), pp. 143–5; *Accounts and Papers (Parliamentary Papers)*, 1832, Vol. 305, No. 127, Part I, p. 475: "The Select Committee of the House of Lords Appointed to Inquire into the Laws and Usages of the several West India Colonies in relation to the Slave Population. Minutes of Evidence," evidence of Barry.
60. *Report on Slavery*, 1832, pp. 25, 110–11, evidence of Taylor and Duncan.
61. Thomas Cooper, *Facts Illustrative of the Condition of the Negro Slaves in Jamaica* (London, 1824), pp. 1–8.
62. Quoted in F. R. Augier et al., *The Making of the West Indies* (Trinidad: Longman Caribbean, 1970), p. 141.
63. *Report on Slavery*, 1832, p. 68, evidence of Barry; Parry, "Plantation and Provision Ground," pp. 11–12.
64. Edwards, *History of West Indies*, Vol. II, pp. 124–5.
65. Mathison, *Notices Respecting Jamaica*, pp. v–vi, 30–4.
66. Gisela Eisner, *Jamaica, 1830–1930: A Study in Economic Growth* (Manchester: Manchester University Press, 1961), pp. 9–12.
67. *Food Composition Tables for Use in the Caribbean*, pp. 7–15.
68. Robert Dirks, "Resource Fluctuations and Competitive Transformations in West Indian Slave Societies," in Charles D. Laughlin, Jr., and Ivan A. Brady, eds., *Extinction and Survival in Human Populations* (New York: Columbia University Press, 1978), pp. 137–9. Estimates of food allowances that appear in the printed works of partisan planter-authors are highly suspect. Kenneth F. Kiple and Virginia H. Kiple have drawn on these works and calculated an average daily intake of 3,000 calories by the slaves in the West Indies in their article, "Deficiency Diseases in the Caribbean," *Journal of Interdisciplinary History*, Vol. XI, No. 2 (Autumn 1980), pp. 199–201.
69. *The Fourth World Food Survey* (Rome: Food and Agriculture Organization, 1977), pp. 16–19, 78–9; *Feeding of Workers in Developing Countries* (Rome: FAO, 1976), pp. 1–14, 61–2; Robert W. Fogel and Stanley L. Engerman, *Time on the Cross: The Economics of American Negro Slavery*, 2 vols. (Boston: Little, Brown, 1974), Vol. I, pp. 109–15, Vol. II, pp. 90–9. For a critique of Fogel and Engerman's work, see Richard Sutch, "The Care and Feeding of Slaves," in Paul A. David et al., eds., *Reckoning with Slavery: A Critical Study in the Quan-*

titative History of American Negro Slavery (New York: Oxford University Press, 1976), pp. 231–301. See also Sam Bowers Hilliard, *Hog Meat and Hoecake: Food Supply in the Old South, 1840–1860* (Carbondale: Southern Illinois University Press, 1972), pp. 55–69, 104–5, 182–5.

70. Stephen, *Slavery Delineated*, Vol. I, Appendix III, p. 465; Goveia, *Slave Society*, pp. 195–200.
71. Stephen, *Slavery Delineated*, Vol. I, Appendix III, pp. 464–8; Michael Craton, "Hobbesian or Panglossian? The Two Extremes of Slave Conditions in the British Caribbean, 1783 to 1834," *William and Mary Quarterly*, 3d series, Vol. XXXV, No. 2 (April 1978), pp. 324–56.
72. Dirks, "Resource Fluctuations," pp. 141–2.
73. Sir William Young, *The West-India Common-Place Book*, etc. (London, 1807), pp. 98, 201–2.
74. John Williamson, M.D., *Medical and Miscellaneous Observations, Relative to the West India Islands*, 2 vols. (Edinburgh, 1817), Vol. I, p. 59.
75. Dirks, "Resource Fluctuations," pp. 160–77.
76. Dickson, *Mitigation of Slavery*, p. 312; J. Harry Bennett, *Bondsmen and Bishops: Slavery and Apprenticeship on the Codrington Plantations of Barbados, 1710–1838* (Berkeley: University of California Publications in History, Vol. 62, 1958), p. 101; Gibbes, *Instructions for Treatment of Negroes*, pp. 1–48, 84–5, 121–3, 131–2.
77. *Privy Council Report*, 1789, evidence of Parry; Bennett, *Bondsmen and Bishops*, p. 101.
78. Joseph Sturge and Thomas Harvey, *The West Indies in 1837, Being the Journal of a Visit to Antigua, Montserrat, Dominica, St. Lucia, Barbados, and Jamaica, Undertaken for the Purpose of Ascertaining the Actual Condition of the Negro Population of those Islands* (London: Frank Cass, 1968), pp. 152–3; John Davy, M.D., F.R.S., *The West Indies Before and Since Slave Emancipation*, etc. (London, 1854), pp. 112, 126–8. For an explanation of why Barbados achieved a self-reproducing labor supply when Jamaica did not, see R. Keith Aufhauser, "Profitability of Slavery in the British Caribbean," *Journal of Interdisciplinary History*, Vol. V, No. 1 (Summer 1974), pp. 45–67.
79. Davy, *West Indies*, pp. 123–30.
80. Letter from Mr. F. Clarke to the Rev. Anthony Hamilton, secretary of the Society for the Propagation of the Gospel, no date, quoted in F. W. N. Bayley, *Four Years' Residence in the West Indies*, etc. (London, 1830), pp. 136–7.
81. Jerome S. Handler and Frederick W. Lange, *Plantation Slavery in Barbados: An Archaeological and Historical Investigation* (Cambridge, Mass.: Harvard University Press, 1978), pp. 86–9; J. R. Ward, "The Profitability of Sugar Planting in the British West Indies, 1650–1834," *The Economic History Review*, 2d series, Vol. XXXI, No. 2 (May 1978), pp. 202–3.
82. *House of Commons Report*, 1790, pp. 103–4, evidence of Byam.
83. [Dr. David Collins], *Practical Rules for the Management and Medical Treatment of Negro Slaves, in the Sugar Colonies. By a Professional Planter* (Freeport, N.Y.: Books for Libraries Press, 1971; first published 1803), pp. 74–103.

84. Ibid., pp. 79–80; Gabriel Debien, "La Nourriture des Esclaves sur les Plantations des Antilles Francaises aux XVIIe et XVIIIe Siecles," *Caribbean Studies*, Vol. 4, No. 2 (July 1964), p. 25.
85. Patterson, *Sociology of Slavery*, pp. 260–83.
86. Dirks, "Resource Fluctuations," pp. 154–6.
87. Goveia, *Slave Society*, pp. 156–8, 163, 168, 173, 179, 184; Elsa V. Goveia, "The West Indian Slave Laws of the Eighteenth Century," *Revista de Ciencias Sociales*, Vol. 4, No. 1 (1960), pp. 83–92; Roderick A. McDonald, " 'Goods and Chattles': The Economy of Slaves on Sugar Plantations in Jamaica and Louisiana," unpublished Ph.D. dissertation, University of Kansas, February 1981, pp. 75–88.
88. Bryan Edwards, *An Historical Survey of the French Colony in the Island of St. Domingo* (London, 1797), p. 11.
89. British Library, *Additional MS.* 12,418, Vol. II, f. 87; James Knight, *MS. History of Jamaica.*
90. *Privy Council Report*, 1789, Part 3, St. Kitts, evidence of Ramsay; Schaw, *Journal of a Lady of Quality*, p. 127.
91. *House of Commons Report*, 1790, p. 329, evidence of Nicholls.
92. Eric Williams, *From Columbus to Castro: The History of the Caribbean 1492–1969* (London: Andre Deutsch, 1970), p. 299. I am indebted to Dr. Stanley L. Engerman for calling my attention to this reference.
93. Edwards, *History of West Indies*, Vol. II, pp. 150–4; [Bernard Martin Senior], *Jamaica, As It Was, As It Is, And As It May Be*, etc. (New York: Negro Universities Press, 1969; first published 1835), pp. 145–6.
94. Matthew Gregory Lewis, *Journal of a West India Proprietor 1815–17* (Boston: Houghton Mifflin, 1929), pp. 119, 136, 162, 284–5; Gibbes, *Treatment of Negroes*, pp. 71–3, 108–14; Benjamin McMahon, *Jamaica Plantership*, etc. (London, 1839), pp. 57–8.
95. *Report on Slavery*, 1832, pp. 480–1, evidence of Shand.
96. Ibid., pp. 23–4, 539, evidence of Wildman and Taylor.
97. Stephen, *Crisis of Sugar Colonies*, p. 123; Collins, *Practical Rules*, pp. 78–9.

7. Morbidity and mortality

1. Thomas Joseph Pettigrew, *Memoirs of the Life and Writings of the late John Coakley Lettsom, M.D., F.R.S. With a Selection of his Correspondence*, 3 vols. (London, 1817), Vol. II, pp. 433–4; letter from Dr. Benjamin Rush to Dr. J. C. Lettsom in London, dated Philadelphia, 21 April 1788.
2. Bryan Edwards, *The History, Civil and Commercial, of the British Colonies in the West Indies*, 2 vols. (Dublin, 1793), Vol. II, p. 134.
3. J. Stewart, *A View of the Past and Present State of the Island of Jamaica* (Edinburgh, 1823), p. 301.
4. J. H. Buchner, *The Moravians in Jamaica. History of the Mission of the United Brethren's Church to the Negroes in the Island of Jamaica, From the Year 1754 to 1854* (Freeport, N.Y.: Books for Libraries Press, 1971; first published 1854), p. 15.

5. [Dr. David Collins], *Practical Rules for the Management and Medical Treatment of Negro Slaves in the Sugar Colonies. By a Professional Planter* (Freeport, N.Y.: Books for Libraries Press, 1971; first published 1803), p. 200.
6. Peter H. Wood, *Black Majority: Negroes in Colonial South Carolina from 1670 through the Stono Rebellion* (New York: Alfred A. Knopf, 1974), pp. 90–1.
7. John Williamson, M.D., *Medical and Miscellaneous Observations, Relative to the West India Islands*, 2 vols. (Edinburgh, 1817), Vol. I, p. 258.
8. James Thomson, M.D., *A Treatise on the Diseases of Negroes, As they Occur in the Island of Jamaica*, etc. (Jamaica, 1820), pp. 13–14.
9. Todd L. Savitt, *Medicine and Slavery: The Diseases and Health Care of Blacks in Antebellum Virginia* (Urbana: University of Illinois Press, 1978), pp. 17–47; Kenneth F. Kiple and Virginia Himmelsteib King, *Another Dimension to the Black Diaspora: Diet, Disease, and Racism* (Cambridge: Cambridge University Press, 1981), pp. 4–28.
10. Eric Williams, *Capitalism and Slavery* (Chapel Hill: University of North Carolina Press, 1944), pp. 19–20.
11. Savitt, *Medicine and Slavery*, pp. 41–7.
12. Dr. George Farquhar, "An Account of the Climate and Diseases of Jamaica," *The Philadelphia Medical Museum*, Vol. I (1805), pp. 183–5.
13. Collins, *Practical Rules*, p. 203.
14. Hector McNeill, *Observations on the Treatment of Negroes in the Island of Jamaica* (London, 1788), p. 44.
15. B. W. Higman, *Slave Population and Economy in Jamaica, 1807–1834* (Cambridge: Cambridge University Press, 1976), p. 111.
16. *Accounts and Papers (Parliamentary Papers)*, 1789, XXVI (646a): "Report of the Privy Council Committee on the Slave Trade" (cited hereafter as *Privy Council Report*), Part III, Jamaica Appendix, No. 6, evidence of Chisholme.
17. Stanley L. Engerman, "Some Economic and Demographic Comparisons of Slavery in the United States and the British West Indies," *Economic History Review*, 2d series, Vol. XXIX, No. 2 (May 1976), p. 272.
18. Edwards, *History of West Indies*, Vol. II, pp. 120, 131.
19. Higman, *Slave Population in Jamaica*, pp. 101–12, 118–38, 202.
20. *Privy Council Report*, 1789, XXVI (646a), Part III, Jamaica Appendix, No. 8, evidence of Quier.
21. Cumberland County Record Office, Carlisle, *Senhouse Papers. Joseph Senhouse Memoirs*, Vol. 3, f. 60.
22. Ibid., ff. 17–18, 20, 60.
23. James Grainger, M.D., *An Essay on the More Common West-India Diseases*, etc. (Edinburgh, 1802), pp. 78, 84.
24. Williamson, *Medical Observations*, Vol. I, pp. 72, 81, 90, 106, 140, 181.
25. Sir Hans Sloane, *A Voyage to the Islands of Madera, Barbadoes, Nieves, St. Christophers, and Jamaica*, etc., 2 vols. (London, 1707, 1725), Vol. I, p. lvii.
26. Ibid.
27. Lincolnshire Archives Office, Lincoln, *Monson Papers. MS* 31/2, No. 2, f. 234, *Thomas Thistlewood's Journal 1751–52*; J. R. Ward, "A Planter and His

Slaves in Eighteenth-Century Jamaica," in T. C. Smout, ed., *The Search for Wealth and Stability: Essays in Economic and Social History presented to M. W. Flinn* (London: Macmillan, 1979), pp. 1–19; O. A. Sherrard, *Freedom from Fear: The Slave and His Emancipation* (London: Bodley Head, 1959), pp. 85–94.

28. *Accounts and Papers (Parliamentary Papers)*, 1790/1, XXXIV (745), pp. 64, 68: "Select Committee of the House of Commons on the Slave Trade" (cited hereafter as *House of Commons Report*), evidence of Ross.
29. Farquhar, "Account of Climate and Diseases of Jamaica," pp. 175–7.
30. Ibid., pp. 177–81.
31. Matthew Gregory Lewis, *Journal of a West India Proprietor* (Boston: Houghton Mifflin, 1929), pp. 176–7.
32. Collins, *Practical Rules*, p. 379; Thomson, *Treatise on Diseases of Negroes*, pp. 103–10.
33. Collins, *Practical Rules*, pp. 345–6.
34. National Library of Scotland, Edinburgh, *Chisholme Papers. MS.* 5477, f. 45, *Letterbook of William Chisholme*: letter to James Craggs in Clarendon, Jamaica, dated London, 5 August 1801.
35. Grainger, *Essay on West-India Diseases*, pp. 21–2.
36. Collins, *Practical Rules*, pp. 345–8.
37. Savitt, *Medicine and Slavery*, pp. 85–6; *Accounts and Papers (Parliamentary Papers)*, 1832, Vol. 305, No. 127: "The Select Committee of the House of Lords Appointed to Inquire into the Laws and Usages of the Several West India Colonies in relation to the Slave Population. Minutes of Evidence," Part I, pp. 54, 63, 66, 147, evidence of Baillie.
38. Calculated from *Parliamentary Papers*, 1833, 26 (530), pp. 473–7; ibid., 1845, 51, by Barry W. Higman, in "The Slave Population of the British Caribbean: Some Nineteenth Century Variations," in Samuel Proctor, ed., *Eighteenth-Century Florida and the Caribbean* (Gainesville: University Presses of Florida, 1976), pp. 67–70.
39. Ibid., pp. 60–7.
40. B. W. Higman, "Slave Population and Economy in Jamaica at the Time of Emancipation," unpublished Ph.D. dissertation, University of the West Indies, Mona, Jamaica, 1970, p. 181; B. W. Higman, "Slavery and the Development of Demographic Theory in the Age of the Industrial Revolution," in James Walvin, ed., *Slavery and British Society 1776–1846* (Baton Rouge: Louisiana State University Press, 1982), pp. 164–94; George W. Roberts, "A Life Table for a West Indian Slave Population," *Population Studies*, Vol. V, No. 3 (1952), pp. 238–42; G. W. Roberts, *The Population of Jamaica* (Cambridge: Cambridge University Press, 1957), pp. 174–6.
41. Philip D. Curtin, *The Atlantic Slave Trade: A Census* (Madison: University of Wisconsin Press, 1969), p. 29; Higman, *Slave Population in Jamaica*, pp. 134–5.
42. University of Exeter Library, *Gale-Morant Papers*, 3/c, 3/e/3, Lists of Slaves on York Estate, Jamaica, 1 January 1778 and 1 January 1829; Higman, *Slave*

Population in Jamaica, pp. 80–98; Michael Craton, *Searching for the Invisible Man: Slaves and Plantation Life in Jamaica* (Cambridge, Mass.: Harvard University Press, 1978), pp. 60–118. I am indebted to Mr. D. W. Evans, Deputy Librarian, University of Exeter Library, for permission to quote extracts from the Gale-Morant Papers.

43. Higman, "Slave Populations of the British Caribbean," p. 69; Higman, *Slave Population in Jamaica*, pp. 110–12, 118–38, 202; Public Record Office, London, *Treasury* 71/264 (1817), Grenada Slave Registration Return, Increase and Decrease.
44. Charles Shephard, *An Historical Account of the Island of Saint Vincent* (London, 1831), pp. 212, 215.
45. Engerman, "Economic and Demographic Comparisons," pp. 269–72.
46. Benjamin Moseley, M.D., *A Treatise on Tropical Diseases* (London, 1789), p. 517.
47. Farquhar, "Account of Climate and Diseases of Jamaica," p. 185.
48. Higman, *Slave Population in Jamaica*, p. 113.
49. *Privy Council Report*, 1789, XXVI (646a), Part III, Jamaica Appendix, No. 8, evidence of Quier.
50. *House of Commons Report*, 1790/1, XXXIV (745), p. 209, evidence of Castles.
51. Alexander Barclay, *A Practical View of the Present State of Slavery in the West Indies*, etc. (London, 1826), pp. 344–5.
52. Somerset Record Office, Taunton, *Tudway Papers. MS.* DD/6d, Acc. c/2290, Box 11, letter from John Gray to Clement Tudway at Wells, dated Antigua, 6 June 1791.
53. E. F. Patrice Jelliffe, "Nutritional Status of Infants and Pre-School Children," *West Indian Medical Journal*, Vol. XX, No. 3 (September 1971), pp. 145–9.
54. Williamson, *Medical Observations*, Vol. I, p. 284.
55. Higman, *Slave Population in Jamaica*, p. 114.
56. See Chapter 6.
57. British Library, *Additional MS.* 12,418, Vol. II, f. 89, J. Knight, *MS. History of Jamaica*, 1742.
58. *Journals of the Assembly of Jamaica*, Vol. XI (10 July 1805), p. 316: "Representation of the Assembly to Lieut-General George Nugent."
59. National Library of Scotland, Edinburgh, *Cochrane Papers. MS.* 2267, f. 54, letter from Thomas Cochrane to Admiral Sir Thomas Cochrane, dated Trinidad, 21 August 1821.
60. Nevin S. Scrimshaw, "Interactions of Malnutrition and Infection: Advances in Understanding," in Robert E. Olson, ed., *Protein-Calorie Malnutrition* (New York: Academic Press, 1975), pp. 363–4; R. E. Chandra and P. M. Newberne, *Nutrition, Immunity, and Infection: Mechanisms of Interaction* (New York: Plenum Press, 1977), pp. 41–7, 67.
61. Derrick B. Jelliffe, M.D., ed., *Child Health in the Tropics: A Practical Handbook for Medical and Para-Medical Personnel* (Baltimore: Williams & Wilkins, 1968), pp. 7–8, 47–9; D. B. Jelliffe, *Child Nutrition in Developing Countries: A Handbook for Fieldworkers* (Washington, D.C.: U.S. Government Printing Office, 1969),

pp. 8–9; Donald S. McLaren, M.D., *Nutrition and Its Disorders*, 3d ed. (Edinburgh: Churchill Livingstone, 1981), pp. 105–11; Erik Eckholm and Frank Record, *The Two Faces of Malnutrition* (Washington, D.C.: Worldwatch Institute, 1976), pp. 10–11, 14–18.

62. Jerome S. Handler and Robert S. Corruccini, "Plantation Slave Life in Barbados: Evidence from a Physical Anthropological and Historical-Archaeological Analysis." I am indebted to Dr. Handler for sending me a copy of this paper. For the published version of this paper, see Robert S. Corruccini, Jerome S. Handler, Robert J. Mutaw, and Frederick W. Lange, "Osteology of a Slave Burial Population from Barbados, West Indies," *American Journal of Physical Anthropology*, Vol. 58 (1982), pp. 443–59; Jerome S. Handler and Robert S. Corruccini, "Plantation Slave Life in Barbados: A Physical Anthropological Analysis," *Journal of Interdisciplinary History*, Vol. XIV, No. 1 (Summer 1983), pp. 65–90.

63. Robert W. Fogel and Stanley L. Engerman, "Recent Findings in the Study of Slave Demography and Family Structure," *Sociology and Social Research*, Vol. 63, No. 3 (1979), pp. 569–74; B. W. Higman, "Growth in Afro-Caribbean Slave Populations," *American Journal of Physical Anthropology*, 2d series, Vol. 50, No. 3 (March 1979), pp. 393–5; Gerald C. Friedman, "The Heights of Slaves in Trinidad," *Social Science History*, Vol. 6, No. 4 (Fall 1982), pp. 482–515.

64. M. T. Ashcroft and P. Desai, "Ethnic differences in growth potential of children of African, Indian, Chinese and European origin," *Transactions of the Royal Society of Tropical Medicine and Hygiene*, Vol. 70, Nos. 5/6 (1976), pp. 433–8; Higman, "Afro-Caribbean Slave Populations," pp. 383–5.

65. M. T. Ashcroft and H. G. Lovell, "Heights and Weights of Jamaica Children of Various Racial Origins," *Tropical and Geographical Medicine*, Vol. 16 (1964), pp. 346–53; M. T. Ashcroft, P. Heneage, and H. G. Lovell, "Heights and Weights of Jamaican Schoolchildren of Various Ethnic Groups," *American Journal of Physical Anthropology*, Vol. 24, No. 1 (January 1966), pp. 35–44.

66. Ashcroft and Desai, "Ethnic differences in growth potential," pp. 433–8; M. T. Ashcroft, R. Bell, and C. C. Nicholson, "Anthropometric Measurement of Guyanese Schoolchildren of African and East Indian Racial Origins," *Tropical and Geographical Medicine*, Vol. 20 (1968), pp. 159–71.

67. M. T. Ashcroft, I. C. Buchanan, and H. G. Lovell, "Heights and Weights of Primary Schoolchildren in St. Christopher-Nevis-Anguilla, West Indies," *The Journal of Tropical Medicine and Hygiene*, Vol. 68, No. 11 (November 1965), pp. 277–83.

68. R. J. Gourlay and M. T. Ashcroft, "Heights and Weights of Bermudian School-Children of African and European Origins," *The West Indian Medical Journal*, Vol. XVIII, No. 1 (March 1969), pp. 40–5.

69. Kenneth F. Kiple and Virginia H. Kiple, "Slave Child Mortality: Some Nutritional Answers to a Perennial Puzzle," *Journal of Social History*, Vol. 10, No. 3 (March 1977), pp. 284–309; Kiple and King, *Black Diaspora*, pp. 5, 9, 11, 17, 55, 91–4, 98, 111–13, 132.

70. Kiple and Kiple, "Slave Child Mortality," pp. 287–309.
71. Kenneth F. Kiple and Virginia H. Kiple, "Deficiency Diseases in the Caribbean," *Journal of Interdisciplinary History*, Vol. XI, No. 2 (Autumn 1980), pp. 197–205; Kiple and King, *Black Diaspora*, pp. 36–8, 58, 60.
72. Higman, *Slave Population in Jamaica*, pp. 114–15.
73. *House of Commons Report*, 1790, XXIX (698), p. 250, evidence of Thomas.
74. *Journals of the Assembly of Jamaica*, Vol. XII, p. 807: "Report from the Committee on the Registration Bill," 17 November 1815, evidence of Sells. See also Williamson, *Medical Observations*, Vol. II, pp. 107–37.
75. Michael Craton, "Death, Disease and Medicine on Jamaican Slave Plantations: the Example of Worthy Park, 1767–1838," *Histoire Sociale – Social History*, Vol. II, No. 18 (November 1976), pp. 237–55; Higman, *Slave Population in Jamaica*, pp. 57–63, 67–8, 102–3, 109–15, 142.
76. Charles Wilcocks and Philip Manson-Bahr, *Manson's Tropical Diseases* (Baltimore, 1972), pp. 543–8; Sir MacFarlane Burnet and David O. White, *Natural History of Infectious Disease*, 4th ed. (Cambridge: Cambridge University Press, 1972), pp. 44–6.
77. Grainger, *Essay on West-India Diseases*, pp. 33–9; Collins, *Practical Rules*, pp. 247–58; Benjamin Moseley, M.D., *Observations on the Dysentery of the West-Indies with a new and successful Manner of treating it*, 2d ed. (London, 1781), pp. 15–18.
78. Logan Clendening, M.D., *Source Book of Medical History* (New York: Dover Publications, 1960), pp. 530–9; Savitt, *Medicine and Slavery*, pp. 131, 142–5.
79. Richard Towne, *A Treatise of the Diseases Most Frequent in the West-Indies* (London, 1726), pp. 10–11; Grainger, *Essay on West-India Diseases*, pp. 45–8.
80. Collins, *Practical Rules*, pp. 159–60; James Stephen, *The Slavery of the British West India Colonies Delineated*, etc., 2 vols. (London, 1824, 1830), Vol. II, pp. 70–1; Richard S. Dunn, "A Tale of Two Plantations: Slave Life at Mesopotamia in Jamaica and Mount Airy in Virginia, 1799 to 1828," *William and Mary Quarterly*, 3d series, Vol. XXXIV, No. 1 (January 1977), p. 62.
81. Collins, *Practical Rules*, pp. 306–9.
82. For an extract from William Withering's *An Account of the Foxglove and Some of Its Medical Uses* (London, 1785), see Clendening, *Source Book of Medical History*, pp. 421–8; Williamson, *Medical Observations*, Vol. I, pp. 213, 225, 240, 248, 402–4; Thomson, *Treatise on Diseases of Negroes*, pp. 26, 126.
83. Stewart, *View of Jamaica*, pp. 305–6.
84. Williamson, *Medical Observations*, Vol. I, pp. 54, 407; Thomson, *Treatise on Diseases of Negroes*, pp. 19–20.
85. L. Dudley Stamp, *The Geography of Life and Death* (London: Collins, Fontana Library, 1965), pp. 55–6; Williamson, *Medical Observations*, Vol. I, pp. 183, 407; Vol. II, pp. 106–37; Stewart, *View of Jamaica*, pp. 305–6; Thomson, *Treatise on Diseases of Negroes*, pp. 28–33.
86. Kiple and King, *Black Diaspora*, pp. 77, 136–7; Savitt, *Medicine and Slavery*, pp. 55–6; P.R.O. London, *Treasury* 71/314 (1830); 71/316 (1831), Grenada Slave Registration Returns.

87. Collins, *Practical Rules*, p. 259.
88. Ibid., pp. 262–85.
89. Dr. John Quier, "Account of the Measles in Jamaica," in John Quier et al., eds., *Letters and Essays on the Small-Pox and Inoculation, Measles, Dry Belly-Ache*, etc. (London, 1778), pp. 113–23.
90. Stewart, *View of Jamaica*, p. 303; Grainger, *Essay on West-India Diseases*, p. 75; Collins, *Practical Rules*, p. 354.
91. J. Walter Beck, Ph.D., and Elizabeth Barrett-Connor, M.D., *Medical Parasitology* (St. Louis: C. V. Mosby, 1971), p. 81; Savitt, *Medicine and Slavery*, pp. 63–6, 68–9, 89–90; Kiple and King, *Black Diaspora*, pp. 113–14.
92. Beck and Barrett-Connor, *Medical Parasitology*, pp. 85–99.
93. Ibid., p. 121; Collins, *Practical Rules*, pp. 340–2.
94. Frederick J. Wright and James P. Baird, *Tropical Diseases*, 4th ed. (Edinburgh: Churchill Livingstone, 1972), pp. 97–8; Collins, *Practical Rules*, pp. 342–5.
95. Grainger, *Essay on West-India Diseases*, pp. 26–9; Collins, *Practical Rules*, pp. 336–40; Williamson, *Medical Observations*, Vol. I, p. 79.
96. Savitt, *Medicine and Slavery*, pp. 69–71; Sir Philip H. Manson-Bahr, *Manson's Tropical Diseases: A Manual of the Diseases of Warm Climates* (London: Cassell, 1954), pp. 801–13; R. Hoeppli, M.D., *Parasitic Diseases in Africa and the Western Hemisphere: Early Documentation and Transmission by the Slave Trade* (Basel, Switzerland: Verlag für Recht and Gesellschaft, 1969), pp. 113–24.
97. Stewart, *View of Jamaica*, p. 307; Thomson, *Treatise on Diseases of Negroes*, pp. 44–6; Collins, *Practical Rules*, p. 295; Thomas Dancer, M.D., *The Medical Assistant, or Jamaica Practice of Physic*, 2d ed. (Jamaica, 1809), p. 174; James Maxwell, M.D., "Pathological Inquiry into the Nature of Cachexia Africana," *The Jamaica Physical Journal*, Vol. II (Nov.–Dec. 1835), pp. 413, 428.
98. Williamson, *Medical Observations*, Vol. II, p. 269; Thomson, *Treatise on Diseases of Negroes*, p. 46; Maxwell, "Inquiry into Cachexia Africana," pp. 409–35.
99. Kiple and King, *Black Diaspora*, pp. 119–22; John M. Hunter, "Geophagy in Africa and in the United States: A Culture-Nutrition Hypothesis," *Geographical Review*, Vol. 63, No. 2 (April 1973), pp. 170–95; Donald E. Vermeer, "Geophagy Among the Ewe of Ghana," *Ethnology*, Vol. 10 (1971), pp. 56–72; Edwin S. Bronstein and Jerry Dollar, "Pica in Pregnancy," *Journal of the Medical Association of Georgia*, Vol. 63 (1974), pp. 332–5; Robert W. Twyman, "The Clay Eater: A New Look at an Old Southern Enigma," *Journal of Southern History*, Vol. 37 (1971), pp. 439–48.
100. *Privy Council Report*, 1789, XXVI (646a), Part III, evidence of the legislature of Grenada; Dancer, *Medical Assistant*, p. 176; Collins, *Practical Rules*, p. 294; Williamson, *Medical Observations*, Vol. II, p. 264.
101. *Privy Council Report*, 1789, XXVI (646a), Part III, Jamaica Appendix, No. 2; Maxwell, "Inquiry into Cachexia Africana," p. 417; Williamson, *Medical Observations*, Vol. I, pp. 174–5; Thomson, *Treatise on Diseases of Negroes*, p. 44.
102. Maxwell, "Inquiry into Cachexia Africana," pp. 417–20; Williamson, *Medical Observations*, Vol. II, pp. 265–9; Stewart, *View of Jamaica*, p. 307; Thomson, *Treatise on Diseases of Negroes*, pp. 45–7; Collins, *Practical Rules*, pp. 295–300.

For a modern discussion of hookworm and other diseases in the West Indies, see M. T. Ashcroft, M.D., "A history and general survey of the helminth and protozoal infections of the West Indies," *Annals of Tropical Medicine and Parasitology*, Vol. 59, No. 4 (December 1965), pp. 478–93.

8. The problem of reproduction

1. [David Collins], *Practical Rules for the Management and Medical Treatment of Negro Slaves in the Sugar Colonies. By a Professional Planter* (Freeport, N.Y.: Books for Libraries Press, 1971; first published 1803), p. 382.
2. Richard Ligon, *A True and Exact History of the Island of Barbadoes*, etc. (London: Frank Cass, 1970; reprinted from 1673 edition), pp. 46–8.
3. Sir Hans Sloane, *A Voyage to the Islands of Madera, Barbadoes, Nieves, St. Christophers, and Jamaica*, 2 vols. (London, 1707, 1725), Vol. I, pp. cxlvii, xlviii, lii.
4. George W. Roberts, *The Population of Jamaica* (Cambridge: Cambridge University Press, 1957), pp. 223–6.
5. Morgan Godwyn, *The Negro's and Indian's Advocate, Suing for Their Admission into the Church*, etc. (London, 1680), p. 84.
6. Michael Craton, *Sinews of Empire: A Short History of British Slavery* (Garden City, N.Y.: Doubleday, 1974), pp. 197–8.
7. [Edward Trelawny], *An Essay Concerning Slavery*, etc. (London, 1746), pp. 35–6.
8. Edward Long, *The History of Jamaica*, etc., 3 vols. (London, 1774), Vol. II, pp. 435–6.
9. James Grainger, M.D., *An Essay on the More Common West-India Diseases*, etc. (Edinburgh, 1802), p. 8.
10. Richard S. Dunn, "A Tale of Two Plantations: Slave Life at Mesopotamia in Jamaica and Mount Airy in Virginia, 1799 to 1828," *The William and Mary Quarterly*, 3d series, Vol. XXXIV, No. 1 (January 1977), pp. 61–2; Kenneth F. Kiple and Virginia Himmelsteib King, *Another Dimension to the Black Diaspora: Diet, Disease, and Racism* (Cambridge: Cambridge University Press, 1981), pp. 96–116.
11. Grainger, *Essay on West-India Diseases*, p. 18.
12. University of Aberdeen, Scotland, MSS. and Archives Section, *MS.* 2070, *The Diary of Dr. Jonathan Troup 1788–1790*, f. 29.
13. Lucille Mathurin Mair, "A Historical Study of Women in Jamaica from 1655 to 1844," unpublished Ph.D. dissertation, University of the West Indies, Mona, Jamaica, October 1974, pp. 313–16.
14. Ibid., p. 313.
15. James Ramsay, M.A., *An Essay on the Treatment and Conversion of African Slaves in the British Sugar Colonies* (London, 1784), pp. 88–90.
16. [James Tobin], *Cursory Remarks Upon the Reverend Mr. Ramsay's Essay on the Treatment and Conversion of African Slaves in the Sugar Colonies. By a Friend of the West India Colonies, and their Inhabitants* (London, 1785), pp. 75–80.
17. *Accounts and Papers (Parliamentary Papers)*, 1789, XXVI (646a): "Report of the

Privy Council Committee on the Slave Trade" (cited hereafter as *Privy Council Report*), Part III, evidence of Ramsay.

18. *Accounts and Papers (Parliamentary Papers)*, 1790, XXIX (698): "Minutes of Evidence: Select Committee of the House of Commons on the Slave Trade" (cited hereafter as *House of Commons Report*), pp. 261–2, evidence of Tobin.
19. Ibid., p. 261, evidence of Tobin.
20. Ibid., pp. 207–8, evidence of Dr. Castles.
21. Ibid., p. 252, evidence of Dr. Thomas.
22. Ibid., pp. 300–1, evidence of Kerby.
23. *Privy Council Report*, Part III, 1788, evidence of Matthew.
24. *House of Commons Report*, 1791, p. 89, evidence of Coor.
25. Ibid., p. 58, evidence of Dr. Jackson.
26. Lincolnshire Archives Office, Lincoln, *Journals of Thomas Thistlewood, Monson MS.* 3/86: "Richard Beckford's Instructions to his Plantation Attorneys in Jamaica, 1754."
27. J. Harry Bennett, Jr., *Bondsmen and Bishops: Slavery and Apprenticeship on the Codrington Plantations of Barbados, 1710–1838* (Berkeley: University of California Press, 1958), pp. 91–5.
28. [Philip Gibbes], *Instructions for the Treatment of Negroes, &c. &c. &c.* (London, 1786; reprinted with additions 1797), pp. iv, 128–30; see Jerome S. Handler, *A Guide to Source Materials for the Study of Barbados History 1627–1834* (Carbondale: Southern Illinois University Press, 1971), pp. 49–50, 57–8.
29. [Gibbes], *Instructions for the Treatment of Negroes*, pp. 81–103, 120–6; David Lowenthal, "The Population of Barbados," *Social and Economic Studies*, Vol. 6 (1957), pp. 445–501.
30. Bryan Edwards, *The History, Civil and Commercial, of the British Colonies in the West Indies*, 2 vols. (Dublin, 1793), Vol. II, p. 166.
31. *Journals of the Assembly of Jamaica*, Vol. X (5 November 1799), pp. 320–1.
32. Orlando Patterson, *The Sociology of Slavery: An Analysis of the Origins, Development and Structure of Negro Slave Society in Jamaica* (London: MacGibbon and Kee, 1967), pp. 73–9.
33. A summary of this law is given in Bernard Martin Senior, *Jamaica, As It Was, As It Is, And As It May Be*, etc. (New York: Negro Universities Press, 1969; first published 1835), pp. 140–58.
34. Roberts, *Population of Jamaica*, pp. 242–3. For discussions of slave family life and reproduction, see Elsa V. Goveia, *Slave Society in the British Leeward Islands at the End of the Eighteenth Century* (New Haven, Conn.: Yale University Press, 1965), pp. 234–8; Patterson, *Sociology of Slavery*, pp. 9, 167; M. G. Smith, *West Indian Family Structure* (Seattle, 1962), pp. 12, 263; B. W. Higman, "Household Structure and Fertility on Jamaican Slave Plantations: A Nineteenth-century Example," *Population Studies*, Vol. 27, No. 3 (November 1973), pp. 527–50; B. W. Higman, "The Slave Family and Household in the British West Indies, 1800–1834," *Journal of Interdisciplinary History*, Vol. VI, No. 2 (Autumn 1975), pp. 261–87.
35. Gilbert Mathison, *Notices Respecting Jamaica, in 1808, 1809, 1810* (London, 1811), pp. 27–30, 89–92.

36. Department of Manuscripts, the library, University College, Bangor, Wales, and the library, University of the West Indies, Mona, Jamaica (microfilm), *Penrhyn Castle Papers, MS.* 1361, letter from Rowland William Fearon to Lord Penrhyn, dated Clarendon, Jamaica, 26 January 1805. I am indebted to Ms. Janet Douglas Pennant for granting permission to publish excerpts from the Penrhyn Papers.
37. Ibid., *MS.* 1467, letter from Samuel Jeffries to Lord Penrhyn, dated King's Valley Estate, Westmoreland, Jamaica, 20 April 1807.
38. Ibid., *MS.* 1477, letter from David Ewart to Lord Penrhyn, dated King's Valley Estate, 6 August 1807.
39. Ibid., *MS.* 1527, letter from J. Shand to George H. Dawkins Pennant, dated Spanish Town, Jamaica, 26 October 1814.
40. The library, University of the West Indies, Mona, Jamaica (microfilm), *Records of Duckenfield Hall Estate, St. Thomas in the East, Jamaica*, letter from John Kelly, attorney, to Jacob Franks at Molesworth near London, 7 September 1810. I am indebted to Dr. Roderick McDonald for this extract.
41. Matthew Gregory Lewis, *Journal of a West India Proprietor 1815–17*, edited with an introduction by Mona Wilson (Boston: Houghton Mifflin, 1929), pp. 86–7, 106–9, 194–5.
42. Ibid., pp. 76, 268–9, 314–15.
43. The Bodleian Library, Oxford, *Barham Papers, MS. Clarendon Dep.* c. 358, Bundle 1, letters from John R. Webb to J. Foster Barham, dated St. Elizabeth and Westmoreland, Jamaica, 10 April and 16 June 1809. I am indebted to Lord Clarendon for granting permission to quote excerpts from the Barham Papers.
44. Ibid., letters from Webb to Barham, dated St. Elizabeth and Westmoreland, 5 September 1810 and 14 September 1811.
45. Ibid., letters from Webb to Barham, ST. Elizabeth, 2 September 1812; and James Colquhoun Grant and J. R. Webb to Barham, Westmoreland, 19 October 1812.
46. Dunn, "A Tale of Two Plantations," pp. 32–41.
47. Ibid., pp. 59–64.
48. *Privy Council Report*, 1789, Part III, Jamaica, evidence of Messrs. Fuller, Long, and Chisholme; Part III, Jamaica appendix, evidence of Quier.
49. J. Stewart, *A View of the Past and Present State of the Island of Jamaica* (Edinburgh, 1823), pp. 303–7.
50. *Privy Council Report*, 1789, Part III, evidence of Parry; Robert Hibbert, Jr., *Hints to the Young Jamaica Sugar Planter* (London, 1825), p. 14; Somerset Record Office, Taunton, *Tudway Papers*, DD/TD, c/2209, John Gray to Clement Tudway at Wells, dated Antigua, 6 June 1791.
51. Public Record Office, London, *Treasury* 71/274 (1820), and T71/313 (1830), Grenada Slave Registration Returns, Increase and Decrease; Jeffrey P. Koplan, "Slave Mortality in Nineteenth-Century Grenada," *Social Science History*, Vol. 7, No. 3 (Summer 1983), pp. 311–20.
52. Ibid. For the diseases, births, and mortality of slave children in the American South, see William D. Postell, "Births and Mortality Rates Among Slave Infants

on Southern Plantations," *Pediatrics*, Vol. 10 (1952), p. 538; Kenneth F. and Virginia H. Kiple, "Slave Child Mortality: Some Nutritional Answers to a Perennial Puzzle," *Journal of Social History*, Vol. 10, No. 3 (March 1977), pp. 284–309.

53. *Privy Council Report*, 1789, Part III, evidence of Spooner.
54. *House of Commons Report*, 1790, XXIX (698), pp. 208–11, 308, evidence of Dalrymple and Castles.
55. Barry W. Higman, "The Slave Population of the British Caribbean: Some Nineteenth-Century Variations," in Samuel Proctor, ed., *Eighteenth-Century Florida and the Caribbean* (Gainesville: University Presses of Florida, 1976), p. 69.
56. *Privy Council Report*, 1789, Part III, Jamaica Appendix, No. 7, evidence of Anderson; James Thomson, M.D., *A Treatise on the Diseases of Negroes, As They Occur in the Island of Jamaica* (Jamaica, 1820), p. 119.
57. *Privy Council Report*, 1788, Part III, evidence of the Council and Assembly of St. Kitts.
58. Ibid., 1789, Part III, Jamaica Appendix, No. 7, evidence of Anderson.
59. Ibid., 1789, Part III, Jamaica Appendix, No. 6, evidence of Chisholme; Ralph Spaeth, M.D., "Tetanus," *Encyclopedia Britannica* (Chicago, 1955), Vol. 21, pp. 978A–9.
60. Collins, *Practical Rules*, p. 138.
61. Lewis, *Journal of a West India Proprietor*, p. 269.
62. Alexander Barclay, *A Practical View of the Present State of Slavery in the West Indies* (London, 1826), p. 344.
63. James Maxwell, M.D., *Observations on Yaws, And its Influence in Originating Leprosy: Also Observations on Acute Traumatic Tetanus and Tetanus Infantum* (Edinburgh, 1839), pp. 121–2, 128–9.
64. Letter to the author from Michael T. Ashcroft, M.D., dated Medical Research Council Laboratories, Mona, Jamaica, 15 May 1975.
65. John Williamson, M.D., *Medical and Miscellaneous Observations, Relative to the West India Islands*, 2 vols. (Edinburgh, 1817), Vol. II, pp. 197–211; Collins, *Practical Rules*, pp. 135–50; Thomson, *Treatise on Diseases of Negroes*, pp. 110–22.
66. Mair, "Historical Study of Women," pp. 295–304; Michael Craton and James Walvin, *A Jamaican Plantation: The History of Worthy Park 1670–1970* (Toronto: University of Toronto Press, 1970), p. 138; Michael Craton, "Jamaican Slave Mortality: Fresh Light from Worthy Park, Longville and the Tharp Estates," *The Journal of Caribbean History*, Vol. 3 (November 1971), pp. 1–27; Patterson, *Sociology of Slavery*, p. 157.
67. Patterson, *Sociology of Slavery*, p. 98.
68. University of Exeter Library, Exeter, *Gale-Morant Papers*, 3/c, 3/c/1, 3/c/14, 3/d/3, "Lists of Slaves on York Estate, Jamaica," 1 January 1778, 9 May 1782, 1 January 1820, 1 January 1829.
69. Michael Craton, *Searching for the Invisible Man: Slaves and Plantation Life in Jamaica* (Cambridge, Mass.: Harvard University Press, 1978), pp. 142–3; B.

W. Higman, *Slave Population and Economy in Jamaica, 1807–1834* (Cambridge: Cambridge University Press, 1976), p. 208; Mair, "Historical Study of Women," p. 295.

70. Long, *History of Jamaica*, Vol. II, pp. 437–9.
71. *Accounts and Papers (Parliamentary Papers)*, 1831–2, XX (721): "Report from the Select Committee of the House of Commons on the Extinction of Slavery throughout the British Dominions. With Minutes of Evidence, Appendix and Index," pp. 27–8, 43–5, evidence of Taylor; Mair, "Historical Study of Women," pp. 306–25.
72. Barry W. Higman, "Slave Population and Economy in Jamaica at the time of Emancipation," unpublished Ph.D. dissertation, University of the West Indies, Mona, Jamaica, 1970, pp. 80–97, 100–28.
73. Ramsay, *Essay on African Slaves*, p. 83.
74. Patterson, *Sociology of Slavery*, pp. 41–2.
75. *Accounts and Papers (Parliamentary Papers)*, 1832, Vol. 305, No. 127; "The Select Committee of the House of Lords Appointed to Inquire into the Laws and Usages of the several West India Colonies in relation to the Slave Population. Minutes of Evidence" (cited hereafter as *House of Lords Report*), Part I, pp. 497–8, 501, 513–14, 516–17, 531, 534, 640, 698, evidence of Barry and Duncan; Mair, "Historical Study of Women," pp. 347–51.
76. Williamson, *Medical Observations*, Vol. II, pp. 200–1; Roberts, *Population of Jamaica*, pp. 229–32; Patterson, *Sociology of Slavery*, p. 108.
77. Stanley L. Engerman, "Some Economic and Demographic Comparisons of Slavery in the United States and the British West Indies," *The Economic History Review*, 2d series, Vol. XXIX, No. 2 (May 1976), pp. 270–2; Edward Brathwaite, *The Development of Creole Society in Jamaica 1770–1820* (Oxford: Clarendon Press, 1971), p. 206.
78. Janet Schaw, *Journal of a Lady of Quality: Being the Narrative of a Journey from Scotland to the West Indies, North Carolina, and Portugal, in the Years 1774 to 1776*, edited by Evangeline Walker Andrews, in collaboration with Charles McLean Andrews (New Haven, Conn.: Yale University Press, 1923), pp. 112–13.
79. *House of Commons Report*, 1790, XXIX (698), p. 252, evidence of Thomas; Craton, *Invisible Man*, p. 87. For other contemporary and modern accounts of abortion, see Long, *History of Jamaica*, Vol. II, p. 436; Edwards, *History of West Indies*, Vol. II, pp. 135–6; H. T. De La Beche, *Notes on the Present Condition of the Negroes in Jamaica* (London, 1825), p. 18; Roberts, *Population of Jamaica*, p. 226; Craton and Walvin, *A Jamaican Plantation*, p. 134.
80. *House of Lords Report*, 1832, Part I, pp. 274–5, evidence of Clare.
81. *The Jamaica Journal*, Vol. I, No. 43, extracts from the case of Sabrina Park as quoted in Patterson, *Sociology of Slavery*, pp. 106–7; Williamson, *Medical Observations*, Vol. II, p. 200; Collins, *Practical Rules*, pp. 134–5, 384.
82. Collins, *Practical Rules*, p. 146; *House of Commons Report*, 1790, XXIX (698), p. 252, evidence of Thomas; *House of Lords Report*, 1832, Part I, p. 51, evidence of Baillie; Thomson, *Treatise on Diseases of Negroes*, p. 116; Ernest Rhys, ed., *The Travels of Mungo Park* (London: J. M. Dent, 1923), p. 203.

83. Herbert S. Klein and Stanley L. Engerman, "Fertility Differentials between Slaves in the United States and the British West Indies: A Note on Lactation Practices and Their Possible Implications," *William and Mary Quarterly*, 3d series, Vol. XXXV, No. 2 (April 1978), pp. 357–74.
84. Ibid., pp. 366–7, 370–1; Dunn, "A Tale of Two Plantations," pp. 62–3.
85. Kiple and King, *Black Diaspora*, pp. 96–104; Kenneth F. Kiple and Virginia H. Kiple, "Deficiency Diseases in the Caribbean," *Journal of Interdisciplinary History*, Vol. XI, No. 2 (Autumn 1980), pp. 211–15; Kiple and Kiple, "Slave Child Mortality," pp. 284–309.
86. Craton, *Invisible Man*, p. 99.
87. Thomas Clarkson, *An Essay on the Impolicy of the African Slave Trade* (London, 1788), pp. 82–9.
88. William Wilberforce, *A Letter on the Abolition of the Slave Trade, Addressed to the Freeholders and other Inhabitants of Yorkshire* (London, 1807), pp. 243–4.
89. James Stephen, *The Slavery of the British West India Colonies Delineated*, etc. 2 vols. (New York: Kraus Reprint Co., 1969; first published 1824, 1830), Vol. II, pp. 404–5.
90. Mair, "Historical Study of Women," pp. 287–311, 343, 349.

9. Smallpox and slavery

1. James Grainger, M.D., *The Sugar Cane: A Poem*, in Dr. Samuel Johnson, ed., *The Works of the English Poets, From Chaucer to Cowper* (London, 1810), Vol. 14, p. 507. I am indebted to Barry Higman and Jeoffrey Koplan, M.D., for supplying data and making helpful suggestions in the writing of this chapter.
2. Public Record Office, London, *Colonial Office* 1/18, f. 39; quoted in Carl and Roberta Bridenbaugh, *No Peace Beyond the Line: The English in the Caribbean 1624–1690* (New York: Oxford University Press, 1972), p. 246, n. 25.
3. Thomas Phillips, "A Journal of a Voyage made in the Hannibal of London, 1693–1694," quoted in Elizabeth Donnan, ed., *Documents Illustrative of the Slave Trade to America* (New York: Octagon Books, 1965), Vol. I, p. 409.
4. [John Oldmixon], *The British Empire in America, Containing the History of the Discovery, Settlement, Progress and State of the British Colonies on the Continent and Islands of America* (London, 1741; reprinted by Augustus M. Kelly Publishers, New York, 1969), Vol. II, p. 117.
5. Thomas Trapham, M.D., *A Discourse of the State of Health in the Island of Jamaica*, etc. (London, 1679), p. 68.
6. British Library, London, *Sloane MS*. 4036, original letters of Sir H. Sloane, Vol. I, 1681–97, f. 87.
7. Genevieve Miller, *The Adoption of Inoculation for Smallpox in England and France* (Philadelphia: University of Pennsylvania Press, 1957), pp. 40–1; Philip D. Curtin, "Epidemiology and the Slave Trade," *Political Science Quarterly*, Vol. LXXXIII, No. 2 (June 1968), pp. 190–216.
8. Carlisle Record Office, Carlisle, England, *Senhouse Papers*: "Recollections of William Senhouse, Surveyor-General of Barbados and the Leeward Islands, 1770–1787," f. 104.

9. *Diary of Cotton Mather* (New York: Frederick Ungar, 1957), Vol. I, pp. 631–2; Otho T. Beall, Jr., and Richard H. Shryock, *Cotton Mather: First Significant Figure in American Medicine* (Baltimore: Johns Hopkins University Press, 1954), pp. 98–9; John B. Blake, *Public Health in the Town of Boston 1630–1822* (Cambridge, Mass.: Harvard University Press, 1959), p. 54; John Duffy, *Epidemics in Colonial America* (Baton Rouge: Louisiana State University Press, 1953), pp. 16–111.
10. Dr. Zabdiel Boylston, *Some Account of what is said of Innoculating or Transplanting the Small Pox*, etc. (Boston, 1721), p. 9; Benjamin Colman, *Some Observations on the New Method of Receiving the Small-Pox by Ingrafting or Inoculating* (Boston, 1721), pp. 1–5.
11. Miller, *Inoculation for Smallpox*, pp. 24–32, 55, 80–90; C. W. Dixon, M.D., *Smallpox* (London: J. & A. Churchill, 1962), pp. 219–25, 239–48.
12. P. E. Razzell, "Population Change in Eighteenth Century England: A Re-Appraisal," *The Economic History Review*, Vol. XVIII, No. 2 (August 1965), pp. 134–5; P. E. Razzell, *The Conquest of Smallpox: The Impact of Inoculation on Smallpox Mortality in Eighteenth Century Britain* (Firlie, Sussex: Caliban Books, 1977).
13. Philip Rose, *An Essay on the Small-Pox, Whether Natural or Inoculated*, 2d ed. (London, 1727), p. 85; Robert H. Schomburgk, *The History of Barbados* (London, 1848; reprinted by Frank Cass, 1971), p. 85.
14. British Library, London, *Martin Papers*, Vol. VIII, Part II, *Add. MS*, 41,352(II), f. 155; Josiah Martin to Barry Anderson in Antigua, Water Town, Massachusetts, 24 April 1738.
15. Richard Mead, M.D., *A Discourse on the Small-Pox and Measles* (London, 1748), pp. 50, 90.
16. Rev. Griffith Hughes, M.A., F.R.S., *The Natural History of Barbados* (London, 1750), p. 39.
17. *Tullideph Letter Books*, Vol. II, Dr. Walter Tullideph to Dr. Walter Sydserfe in London, Antigua, 23 February 1756.
18. John Quier, "A Letter on the Small-Pox and Inoculation," in [J. Quier et al.], *Letters and Essays on the Small-Pox and Inoculation, Measles, Dry Belly-Ache*, etc. (London, 1778), pp. 105–7: Thomas Fraser, M.D., to Dr. D. Monro of Jermyn Street, London, Antigua, 22 May 1756.
19. Ibid., p. 107.
20. Somerset Record Office, Taunton, England, *Tudway Papers* DD/TD, c/2209, Box 11; Main Swete Walrond to Clement Tudway at Wells, Antigua, 6 March 1773.
21. Ibid., John Gray to Clement Tudway, Antigua, 21 July 1789.
22. Ibid., Samuel Eliot to Clement Tudway, Antigua, 29 February 1804; ibid., *Plantation Accounts*, 1782, f. 30; 1785, f. 24; 1790, f. 23; 1791, f. 22; 1794, f. 21; 1798, f. 18; 1804, f. 13; 1807, f. 5; 1811, f. 7; 1827, f. 6.
23. Ibid., George W. Ottley to John Paine Tudway at Wells, Antigua, 1 February 1809.
24. George W. Roberts, *The Population of Jamaica* (Cambridge: Cambridge Uni-

versity Press, 1957), pp. 36–42; George R. Mellor, *British Imperial Trusteeship 1783–1850* (London: Faber & Faber, 1951), p. 442.

25. Edward Long, *The History of Jamaica*, etc., 3 vols. (London, 1774), Vol. II, pp. 276, 434; Duffy, *Epidemics in Colonial America*, p. 35.
26. Quier, "Letter on the Small-Pox and Inoculation," pp. 1–9. For the medical and scientific career of Dr. John Quier, see Heinz Goerke, "The Life and Scientific Works of Dr. John Quier, Practitioner of Physic and Surgery, Jamaica: 1738–1822," *West Indian Medical Journal*, Vol. 5, No. 23 (1956), pp. 23–7; Michael Craton, *Searching for the Invisible Man: Slaves and Plantation Life in Jamaica* (Cambridge, Mass.: Harvard University Press, 1978), pp. 259–64.
27. Quier, "Letter on the Small-Pox and Inoculation," pp. 56, 63, 64, 101.
28. Ibid., pp. 10–17, 56.
29. Ibid., pp. 20–1.
30. Ibid., pp. 22–6.
31. Ibid., pp. 27–41.
32. Thomas Dancer, M.D., *The Medical Assistant, Or Jamaica Practice of Physic. Designed Chiefly for the Use of Families and Plantations*, 2d ed. (St. Jago de la Vega, Jamaica, 1809), p. 156.
33. Quier, "Letter on the Small-Pox and Inoculation," p. 6.
34. Ibid., pp. 7–8, 33.
35. John N. Force, M.D., "Daniel Sutton and the Revival of Variolation," *University of California Publications in Public Health*, Vol. I, No. 7 (21 April 1931), pp. 323–35.
36. Ibid., p. 332; Dixon, *Smallpox*, pp. 243–4.
37. Baron T. Dimsdale, *Tracts on Inoculation written and published at St. Petersburg in the Year 1768 ... With Additional Observations*, etc. (London, 1781), pp. 241–6.
38. Razzell, "Population Change in England," pp. 317–21.
39. Dixon, *Smallpox*, p. 247; Thomas McKeown, *The Modern Rise of Population* (New York: Academic Press, 1976), pp. 11–13, 107–9.
40. The Historical Society of Pennsylvania, Philadelphia, *Powel Papers, Afro-Americana* 2328: *Dr. Alexander Johnston's Ledger, 1768–1774*, ff. 1–282. I am indebted to The Historical Society of Pennsylvania for granting permission to reproduce materials from Dr. Alexander Johnson's Ledger.
41. University of Exeter, Exeter, England, *Gale-Morant Papers*, 3/c/1, 3/e/6: York Estate Accounts for 1785; York Estate General Accounts, 1792. I am indebted to Mr. D. W. Evans, Deputy Librarian, University of Exeter Library, for permission to quote extracts from the Gale-Morant Papers.
42. National Library of Scotland, Edinburgh, *Chisholme Papers*, MS. 5479, ff. 39, 96, 98: "Ledger of Trout Hall Estate and William Chisholme, 1775–1806."
43. Ibid., *MS*. 5484, f. 18: "Notebook of James Chisholme."
44. John Duffy, ed., *The Rudolph Matas History of Medicine in Louisiana* (Baton Rouge: Louisiana State University Press, 1958), Vol. I, p. 203.
45. Dixon, *Smallpox*, pp. 249, 260, 276–7, 286; Charles Singer and E. A. Underwood, *A Short History of Medicine*, 2d ed. (London: Oxford University Press, 1962), pp. 188, 190, 200–2, 213.

46. *Lady Nugent's Journal of Her Residence in Jamaica from 1801 to 1805*, a new and revised edition by Philip Wright (Kingston: Institute of Jamaica, 1966), pp. 181, 185.
47. John Williamson, M.D., *Medical and Miscellaneous Observations, Relative to the West India Islands* (Edinburgh, 1817), Vol. II, pp. 165–71, 213.
48. George Farquhar, M.D., "Observations on the Vaccine," *The Philadelphia Museum*, Vol. II (1806), pp. 315–16.
49. Dancer, *The Medical Assistant*, pp. 155–6.
50. *Journals of the Assembly of Jamaica*, 30 November 1813, Vol. XII, pp. 552–3; Edward Brathwaite, *The Development of Creole Society in Jamaica 1770–1820* (Oxford: Clarendon Press, 1971), pp. 282–3.
51. *Journals of the Assembly of Jamaica*, 31 October 1815, Vol. XII, pp. 694–5.
52. Ibid., 17 November 1818, Vol. XIII, p. 241.
53. Ibid., 23 November 1819, Vol. XIII, p. 351.
54. Ibid., 21 November 1820, Vol. XIII, p. 469.
55. Ibid., 22 November 1821, Vol. XIII, p. 615.
56. Ibid., 23 November 1821, Vol. XIII, pp. 619–20, 628–30.
57. Ibid., 21 November 1822, Vol. XIV, p. 67.
58. Ibid., 17 December 1822, Vol. XIV, p. 144.
59. The Library, School of Oriental and African Studies, London, *Methodist Missionary Society Papers* 130, No. 172: Rev. Peter Duncan to The General Secretaries of the Wesleyan Methodist Missionary Society, 77 Hatton Garden, London, Kingston, Jamaica, 8 August 1831. I am indebted to the Librarian, Methodist Church Overseas Division, London, for granting permission to quote excerpts from the Methodist Missionary Society Papers.
60. Ibid., *M.M.S.* 130, No. 182: Rev. Henry Bleby to same, dated Lucea, Jamaica, 17 August 1831.
61. John Tate Lanning, *Academic Culture in the Spanish Colonies* (London: Oxford University Press, 1940), pp. 119–24.
62. Ross Danielson, *Cuban Medicine* (New Brunswick, N.J.: Transaction Books, 1979), pp. 51–8.
63. Duffy, *History of Medicine in Louisiana*, Vol. I, pp. 198–217.
64. Wyndham B. Blanton, M.D., *Medicine in Virginia in the Eighteenth Century* (Richmond, Va.: Garrett & Massie, 1931), pp. 60–5, 284–7.
65. Todd L. Savitt, *Medicine and Slavery: The Diseases and Health Care of Blacks in Antebellum Virginia* (Urbana: University of Illinois Press, 1978), pp. 221–2, 293–7; Blanton, *Medicine in Virginia in the Eighteenth Century*, pp. 192–6.
66. [Dr. David Collins], *Practical Rules for the Management and Medical Treatment of Negro Slaves in the Sugar Colonies* (London, 1811; reprinted by Books for Libraries Press, Freeport, N.Y.: 1971), pp. 280–3.
67. Ibid., p. 274.
68. Alexander M'Donnell, *Considerations on Negro Slavery. With Authentic Reports, Illustrative of the Actual Condition of the Negroes in Demerara* (London: Longmans, 1824), pp. 179, 183.
69. Flintshire County Record Office, Hawarden, North Wales, *The John Gladstone*

Papers, Box CH 20: John McLean to Robertson Gladstone, Demerara, 16 June 1831.

70. Williamson, *Medical Observations*, Vol. II, p. 168.
71. Dancer, *The Medical Assistant*, p. 155.
72. Colin Chisholm, M.D., F.R.S., *A Manual of the Climate and Diseases of Tropical Countries*, etc. (London, 1822), p. 18.
73. James Thomson, M.D., *A Treatise on the Diseases of Negroes, As They Occur in the Island of Jamaica*, etc. (Jamaica: Alex. Aikman, 1820), p. 69.
74. Ibid., pp. 69–70.
75. West India Reference Library, Kingston, Jamaica, *Letter Books of Sir Jacob Adolphus, M.D., MS.* 2, Vol. 1, ff. 242–3: "Report to the Army Medical Board," enclosed in Jacob Adolphus's letter to Sir James McGrigor, Kingston, 26 October 1820.

10. Slave hospitals

1. James Grainger, M.D., *An Essay on the More Common West-India Diseases*, etc., 2d ed. (Edinburgh, 1802; first published 1764), p. v.
2. *Journals of the Assembly of Jamaica*, Vol. VIII, 18 February 1791, p. 634; ibid., Vol. XIII, 8 December 1819, p. 381; Edward Brathwaite, *The Development of Creole Society in Jamaica 1770–1820* (Oxford: Clarendon Press, 1971), pp. 128, 284–91.
3. Brathwaite, *Creole Society in Jamaica*, pp. 128, 290.
4. *Letter Books of Dr. Walter Tullideph of Antigua and Scotland*, Vol. II: Tullideph to George Thomas, deputy governor of Pennsylvania, 19 June 1749.
5. British Library, London, *Martin Papers, Additional MS.* 41,350, Vol. V, ff. 68–70: "A Fair Estimate of Samuel Martin's Plantation in New Division in Antigua, 1768."
6. William Belgrove, *A Treatise upon Husbandry or Planting* (Boston, 1755), p. 40.
7. Richard Pares, *A West-India Fortune* (London: Longmans, Green, 1950), p. 128.
8. Grainger, *Essay on West-India Diseases*, pp. 90–1.
9. Ibid., p. 91.
10. *Accounts and Papers (Parliamentary Papers)*, 1789, XXVI (646): "Report of the Privy Council Committee on the Slave Trade" (cited hereafter as *Privy Council Report*), Part 1, evidence of Parry; ibid., XXVI (646a), Part 3, evidence of Spooner, Matthew, Robinson, Laing, Bruce, Gillon, and Fraser.
11. Ibid., XXVI (646a), Part 3, evidence of Seton, Orde, and Hutchinson.
12. *Accounts and Papers (Parliamentary Papers)*, 1790, XXIX (698), p. 273: "Minutes of Evidence: Select Committee of the House of Commons on the Slave Trade" (cited hereafter as *House of Commons Report*), evidence of Tobin.
13. Rev. James Ramsay, *An Essay on the Treatment and Conversion of African Slaves in the British Sugar Colonies* (London, 1784), pp. 82–3.
14. John Luffman, *Brief Account of the Island of Antigua*, etc. (London, 1789), reprinted in Verre Langford Oliver, *The History of the Island of Antigua*, 3 vols. (London, 1894–9), Vol. I, p. cxxxiii.

15. *House of Commons Report*, 1790, XXIX (698), pp. 255–9, evidence of Thomas; Thomas Cooper, *Facts Illustrative of the Condition of the Slaves in Jamaica* (London, 1824), p. 27.
16. *Accounts and Papers (Parliamentary Papers)*, 1798–9, XLVIII (967a), pp. 1, 45: President Robert Thomson to the Duke of Portland, secretary of state, St. Kitts, 22 June 1798, enclosing Leeward Islands Act No. 36 of 1798: "An Act more effectually to provide for the Support and to extend certain Regulations for the Protection of Slaves; to promote and encourage their Increase, and generally to meliorate their condition, clause XXX." See also clauses XXXI, XXXIII, XXXV, XXXVII, and XXXVIII, which are summarized in Elsa V. Goveia, *Slave Society in the British Leeward Islands at the End of the Eighteenth Century* (New Haven, Conn.: Yale University Press, 1965), pp. 194–6.
17. Goveia, *Slave Society*, pp. 191–202.
18. [Bernard Martin Senior], *Jamaica, As it Was, As it Is, and As it May be*, etc. (New York: Negro Universities Press, 1969; first printed 1835), p. 143.
19. "Ordinance of the Governor, Lieut.-Colonel Thomas Picton, proclaimed June 30th, 1800," reprinted in Appendix VIII, Gertrude Carmichael, *The History of the West Indian Islands of Trinidad and Tobago 1498–1900* (London: Alvin Redman, 1961), pp. 379–83.
20. Philip Wright, *Monumental Inscriptions of Jamaica* (London: Society of Genealogists, 1966), p. 262.
21. Cambridge County Record Office, *Tharp Papers*, R.55.7.121.16: "Plan of the Hospital for Sick Slaves upon the Good Hope Estate, etc." I am indebted to Mr. P. J. Hanbury Tenison for providing me with photographs of the hospital on Orange Valley estate and the plan and photograph of the hospital on Good Hope estate.
22. Joseph Sturge and Thomas Harvey, *The West Indies in 1837: Being the Journal of a Visit to Antigua, Montserrat, Dominica, St. Lucia, Barbados, and Jamaica*, etc. (London: Frank Cass, 1968), pp. 220–1.
23. Scottish Public Record Office, Edinburgh, GD 241/189/1, *Letter Books of the Cargen Trustees*, Vol. I: Cargen Trustees to David Hood in Jamaica, Edinburgh, 21 June 1797.
24. [Philip Gibbes], *Instructions for the Treatment of Negroes*, etc. (London, 1797), pp. 92–4.
25. [Dr. David Collins], *Practical Rules for the Management and Medical Treatment of Negro Slaves in the Sugar Colonies*, etc. (Freeport, N.Y.: Books for Libraries Press, 1971; first published 1803), pp. 203–4, 218.
26. Ibid., pp. 217–19.
27. Ibid., pp. 204–6, 226.
28. Ibid., pp. 217, 220–1.
29. Ibid., p. 222.
30. Ibid., pp. 220–9.
31. Flintshire County Record Office, Hawarden, North Wales, *John Gladstone's Papers*, loose bundles of plantation documents, especially the "Papers relating to the Fileen estates in Demerara," which contain the letter from Frederick Cort to John Gladstone, Demerara, 6 September 1828.

32. Alexander McDonnell, *Considerations on Negro Slavery. With Authentic Reports on the Negroes in Demerara* (London: Longmans, 1824), pp. 177–9.
33. Ibid., pp. 179–80.
34. Ibid., pp. 180–2.
35. William Sells, *Remarks on the Condition of the Slaves in the Island of Jamaica* (London, 1823), pp. 14–15.
36. H. T. De La Beche, *Notes on the Present Condition of the Negroes in Jamaica* (London, 1825), pp. 13, 25.
37. Senior, *Jamaica As it Was*, p. 59.
38. John Williamson, M.D., *Medical and Miscellaneous Observations, Relative to the West India Islands*, 2 vols. (Edinburgh, 1817), Vol. I, pp. 54–5, 88–9, 116, 156, 187, 189.
39. Gilbert Mathison, *Notices Respecting Jamaica, in 1808, 1809, 1810* (London, 1811), pp. 42–5, 92–3, 107–9.
40. Matthew Gregory Lewis, *Journal of a West India Proprietor 1815–17* (Boston: Houghton Mifflin, 1929), pp. 194, 285–6.
41. Ibid., pp. 316–17.
42. Thomas Roughley, *The Jamaica Planter's Guide*, etc. (London, 1823), pp. 93–5.
43. Benjamin McMahon, *Jamaica Plantership*, etc. (London, 1839), pp. 23–9, 192–4.
44. *The Kingston Chronicle and City Advertiser*, February 3, 1830, p. 1; February 24, 1830, p. 1.
45. Rev. Richard Bickell, *The West Indies As They Are; Or a Real Picture of Slavery: But More Particularly as it Exists in the Island of Jamaica* (London, 1825), p. 52.
46. James Stephen, *The Slavery of the British West India Colonies Delineated*, 2 vols. (New York: Kraus Reprint Co., 1969; first published 1824, 1830), Vol. II, pp. 365–6.
47. Ibid., pp. 238, 369, 370.
48. Ibid., pp. 363–4, 368.
49. *J. Johnson MS., Reports relating to Mr. Gordon's Estate in the West Indies, 1824*, Part II, f. 6, Beinecke Lesser Antilles Collection, The Burke Library, Hamilton College, Clinton, New York.
50. Ibid., Part II, f. 7.
51. Ibid., Part II, ff. 7–8.
52. Ibid., Part II, f. 8.
53. Ibid., Part II, ff. 22–3.
54. Ibid., Part III, ff. 5–6.
55. Ross Danielson, *Cuban Medicine* (New Brunswick, N.J.: Transaction Books, 1979), pp. 26–33, 61–5.
56. David Turnbull, *Travels in the West. Cuba: with Notices of Porto Rico, and the Slave Trade* (New York: Negro Universities Press, 1969; first published 1840), pp. 283–4; Richard Henry Dana, Jr., *To Cuba and Back*, edited and with an introduction by C. Harvey Gardiner (Carbondale: Southern Illinois University Press, 1966; first published 1859), p. 69.

57. Todd L. Savitt, *Medicine and Slavery: The Diseases and Health Care of Blacks in Antebellum Virginia* (Urbana: University of Illinois Press, 1978), pp. 192–3, 202, 223, 234.
58. J. Carlyle Sitterson, *Sugar Country: The Cane Sugar Industry in the South, 1753–1950* (Lexington: University of Kentucky Press, 1953), p. 95; William Howard Russell, *My Diary North and South*, 2 vols. (London: Bradbury and Evans, 1863), Vol. I, pp. 373–4.
59. Savitt, *Medicine and Slavery*, pp. 162–3; Kenneth F. Kiple and Virginia Himmelsteib King, *Another Dimension to the Black Diaspora: Diet, Disease, and Racism* (Cambridge: Cambridge University Press, 1981), pp. 168–9; Charles S. Sydnor, *Slavery in Mississippi* (Baton Rouge: Louisiana State University Press, 1966), pp. 51–3.
60. William Dosite Postell, *The Health of Slaves on Southern Plantations* (Gloucester, Mass.: Peter Smith, 1970), p. 129, quoting R. King, Jr., "On the Management of the Butler Estate . . .," *Southern Agriculturist*, Vol. I (1828), p. 527.
61. Postell, *Health of Slaves*, pp. 132–4.
62. Frances Anne Kemble, *Journal of a Residence on a Georgian Plantation in 1838–1839* (Chicago: Afro-Am Press, 1969; first published 1863), pp. 299, 311, 313, 316–8.
63. Ibid., pp. 32–5, 37–40, 56, 63, 73, 82, 121, 149, 214–16; J. C. Furnas, *Fanny Kemble: Leading Lady of the Nineteenth-Century Stage* (New York: Dial Press, 1982), pp. 388–405.

11. Plantation medical practice

1. H. T. De La Beche, *Notes on the Present Condition of Negroes in Jamaica* (London, 1825), p. 25; Stanley L. Engerman and Eugene D. Genovese, eds., *Race and Slavery in the Western Hemisphere: Quantitative Studies*, copyright © 1975 by The Center for Advanced Study in the Behavioral Sciences, Stanford, California. Portions of "Mortality and Medical Treatment of Slaves in the British West Indies," by Richard B. Sheridan, reprinted by permission of Princeton University Press.
2. F. W. N. Bayley, *Four Years' Residence in the West Indies* (London, 1830), p. 93.
3. O. F. Christie, ed., *The Diary of the Revd. William Jones 1777–1821, Curate and Vicar of Broxbourne and the Hamlet of Hoddesdon 1781–1821* (London: Bretano's, 1929), p. 34.
4. John Williamson, M.D., *Medical and Miscellaneous Observations, Relative to the West India Islands*, 2 vols. (Edinburgh, 1817), Vol. I, p. xii.
5. British Library, *Additional MS*. 41,346, Vol. I, ff. 208–9, *Letter Books of Colonel Samuel Martin of Antigua and England*, letter to Samuel Martin, Jr., in London, dated Antigua, 14 June 1758.
6. University of Bristol, Bristol, England, *Pinney Papers, Business Letter-book, 1779–1784*, f. 318; quoted in C. M. MacInnes, *Bristol: A Gateway of Empire* (New York: Augustus M. Kelly, 1968), p. 212.
7. [Dr. David Collins], *Practical Rules for the Management and Medical Treatment of Negro Slaves, in the Sugar Colonies. By a Professional Planter* (Freeport, N.Y.: Books for Libraries Press, 1971; first published 1803), pp. 207–8.

8. Thomas Dancer, M.D., *The Medical Assistant: Or Jamaica Practice of Physic: designed chiefly for the use of families and plantations* (Kingston, Jamaica, 1801), Preface.
9. Rev. James Ramsay, M.A., *An Essay on the Treatment and Conversion of African Slaves in the British Sugar Colonies* (London, 1784), p. 82.
10. Thomas Roughley, *The Jamaica Planter's Guide*, etc. (London, 1823), pp. 92–3.
11. Robert Hibbert, Jr., *Hints to the Young Jamaica Sugar Planter* (London, 1825), pp. 14–15.
12. *Accounts and Papers (Parliamentary Papers)*, 1832, Vol. 305, No. 127, Part II, p. 63: "The Select Committee of the House of Lords Appointed to Inquire into the Laws and Usages of the several West India Colonies in relation to the Slave Population. Minutes of Evidence" (cited hereafter as *House of Lords Report*), evidence of Baillie.
13. Lincolnshire Archives Office, Lincoln, *Monson MS.* 31/1, ff. 1–74, *Thomas Thistlewood's Journal 1748–50*. I am indebted to Lord and Lady Monson for permission to quote extracts from the Thistlewood Papers. For accounts of Thistlewood, see J. R. Ward, "A Planter and His Slaves in Eighteenth-Century Jamaica," in T. C. Smout, ed., *The Search for Wealth and Stability: Essays in Economic and Social History presented to M. W. Flinn* (London: Macmillan, 1979), pp. 1–19; and O. A. Sherrard, *Freedom from Fear: The Slave and His Emancipation* (London: Bodley Head, 1959), pp. 85–94.
14. *Monson MS.* 31/2, f. 152, *Thomas Thistlewood's Journal 1751–52*.
15. Ibid., f. 195; *Monson MS.* 31/74, f. 198, *Thomas Thistlewood's Commonplace Book*.
16. *Monson MS.* 31/2, f. 224, *Journal 1741–52*; ibid., 31/3, f. 39, *Journal 1752–54*.
17. *Monson MS.* 31/2, ff. 12, 17, *Journal 1751–52*.
18. *Monson MS.* 31/74; Thistlewood recorded eighty-eight "Receipts for a Physic" in this journal.
19. Collins, *Practical Rules*, pp. 208–11.
20. Public Record Office, London, *Treasury* 71/273 (1820), 71/313 (1830): Grenada Slave Registration Returns, Increase and Decrease.
21. B. L. *Add. MS.* 41,351, Vol. VI, f. 3, *Martin Papers*, 9 August 1774.
22. John Luffman, *Brief Account of the Island of Antigua*, etc. (London, 1789), reprinted in Vere L. Oliver, *The History of the Island of Antigua*, etc., 3 vols. (London, 1894–9), Vol. I, p. cxxxiii.
23. James Grainger, M.D., *An Essay on the More Common West-India Diseases*, etc. (Edinburgh, 1802), pp. 90–1.
24. Rev. James Ramsay, *A Reply to the Personal Invectives and Objections contained in Two Answers, Published by certain Anonymous Persons, to An Essay on the Treatment and Conversion of African Slaves, in the British Sugar Colonies, by James Ramsay* (London, 1785), pp. 15–20.
25. James Tobin, *Cursory Remarks upon the Reverend Mr. Ramsay's Essay on the Treatment of African Slaves* (London, 1785), pp. 68–9.
26. *Accounts and Papers (Parliamentary Papers)*, 1790, XXIX (698): "Minutes of

Evidence: Select Committee of the House of Commons on the Slave Trade," pp. 246–7, evidence of Thomas.

27. *Accounts and Papers (Parliamentary Papers)*, 1798/9, XLVIII (967a), pp. 1–49, President Robert Thomson to the Duke of Portland, secretary of state, dated St. Kitts, 22 June 1798, enclosing Leeward Islands Act, No. 36, of 1798: "An Act more effectually to provide for the Support and to extend certain Regulations for the Protection of Slaves; to promote and encourage their Increase, and generally to meliorate their condition," clauses XIX, XXIV, XXVIII, XXIX, XXX, XXXI, XXXIII, XXXV, and XXXVI. This law is summarized and analyzed in Elsa V. Goveia, *Slave Society in the British Leeward Islands, at the End of the Eighteenth Century* (New Haven, Conn.: Yale University Press, 1965), pp. 191–8.
28. *Accounts and Papers (Parliamentary Papers)*, 1789, XXVI (646a): "Report of the Privy Council Committee on the Slave Trade," Part 3, Barbados, evidence of Parry.
29. *The Report from a Select Committee of the House of Assembly Appointed to Inquire into the Origin, Causes, and Progress, of the Late Insurrection* (Barbadoes and London, 1818), Appendix, pp. 54–5.
30. *A Report of a Committee of the Council of Barbadoes, Appointed to Inquire into the Actual Condition of the Slaves in this Island*, etc. (London, 1824), Appendix, pp. 120–3.
31. Thomas Atwood, *The History of the Island of Dominica* (London, 1791), pp. iii–v; Noel Deerr, *The History of Sugar* (London, 1950), Vol. II, p. 279.
32. University of Aberdeen, Scotland, MSS and Archives Section, *MS. 2070, The Diary of Dr. Jonathan Troup 1788–1790*, ff. 11–14. I am indebted to Mr. Colin A. McLaren, Archivist and Keeper of Manuscripts, Aberdeen University Library, for permission to quote extracts from this manuscript.
33. Ibid., ff. 11, 25–7.
34. Ibid., ff. 15, 16, 41, 70, 77.
35. Ibid., ff. 51, 68, 90, 104.
36. Ibid., ff. 59, 66, 68, 71, 77–9, 82, 104.
37. Ibid., ff. 38, 56, 59.
38. Ibid., ff. 27–8, 35, 107, 139–40, 145.
39. Ibid., f. 150.
40. Ibid., ff. 30, 159, 160, 166, 171.
41. Ibid., f. 160.
42. *Privy Council Report*, Part 3, Jamaica Appendix, evidence of Quier, Chisholme, and Anderson.
43. J. Stewart, *A View of the Past and Present State of the Island of Jamaica* (Edinburgh, 1823), pp. 195–6; Rev. Richard Bickell, *The West Indies as They Are; Or a Real Picture of Slavery: But More Particularly as It Exists in the Island of Jamaica* (London, 1825), p. 52.
44. *House of Lords Report*, 1832, Part II, Minutes of Evidence, p. 63, evidence of Clare.
45. *Accounts and Papers (Parliamentary Papers)*, 1836, XV (605), p. 274: "Report

from the Select Committee on Negro Apprenticeship in the Colonies," Minutes of Evidence, evidence of Burge.

46. Harmony Hall estate, Trelawny, Jamaica, *Hospital Book, 1822–1826*, Institute of Jamaica, Kingston, Jamaica. I am indebted to Ms. Carmen Latty for the extracts from this hospital book.
47. British Library, *Additional MS.* 33,294, *Journal of Dr. James Henry Archer of Jamaica, 1828–1841*, ff. 38, 197.
48. British Library, *Add. MS.* 27,970, *Capt. Archer's Memoranda, Accounts, etc.*, f. 219.
49. British Library, *Add. MS.* 33,294, *Journal of J. H. Archer*, ff. 22–3.
50. Ibid., ff. 11, 13, 17–21, 23, 26, 27, 34, 40–1, 49.
51. *House of Lords Report*, 1832, Part II, Minutes of Evidence, p. 63, evidence of Baillie.
52. Williamson, *Medical Observations*, Vol. I, pp. i–xix, 76, 134, 249–53.
53. Ibid., Vol. I, pp. 47–9.
54. Ibid., Vol. I, p. 243; Vol. II, p. 178.
55. Ibid., Vol. I, pp. 52–99.
56. Ibid., Vol. I, pp. 189, 224, 251–3.
57. Ibid., Vol. I, pp. 55, 64–5, 93, 120–2, 134, 190, 191, 249, 251, 273; Vol. II, pp. 8–9, 177–93.
58. Ibid., Vol. II, pp. 177–83.
59. Ibid., Vol. II, pp. 187–91.
60. Ibid., Vol. II, pp. 191–3.
61. Franklin W. Knight, *Slave Society in Cuba during the Nineteenth Century* (Madison: University of Wisconsin Press, 1970), p. 70; John G. F. Wurdemann, *Notes on Cuba* (New York: Arno Press, 1971; first published 1844), p. 152; *Accounts and Papers (Parliamentary Papers)*, 1830–1, Vol. IX, p. 52: "Statements, Calculations, and Explanations Submitted to the Board of Trade, Relating to the Commercial, Financial, and Political State of the British West India Colonies," evidence of Moss.
62. Richard H. Shryock, "Medical Practice in the Old South," *The South Atlantic Quarterly*, Vol. XXIX, No. 2 (April 1930), p. 174; William Dosite Postell, *The Health of Slaves on Southern Plantations* (Gloucester, Mass.: Peter Smith, 1970), pp. 54–8.
63. Shryock, "Medical Practice in South," p. 171; *Weeks Collection*: Rachel O'-Connor to David Weeks, 4 August 1831; and same to Mary C. Weeks, 1 September 1833, quoted in Kenneth M. Stampp, *The Peculiar Institution: Slavery in the Ante-Bellum South* (New York: Vintage Books, 1964), p. 314.
64. Robert William Fogel and Stanley L. Engerman, *Time on the Cross: The Economics of American Negro Slavery* (Boston: Little, Brown, 1974), pp. 117–26; Kenneth F. Kiple and Virginia Himmelsteib King, *Another Dimension to the Black Diaspora: Diet, Disease, and Racism* (Cambridge: Cambridge University Press, 1981), pp. 165, 168; Stampp, *Peculiar Institution*, pp. 315–16; Postell, *Health of Slaves*, pp. 52–4, 63–5.
65. Charles S. Sydnor, *Slavery in Mississippi* (Baton Rouge: Louisiana State University Press, 1966), pp. 51–3; Kiple and King, *Black Diaspora*, p. 167.

66. Todd L. Savitt, *Medicine and Slavery: The Diseases and Health Care of Blacks in Antebellum Virginia* (Urbana: University of Illinois Press, 1978), pp. 198–200; Shryock, "Medical Practice in South," pp. 172–3.
67. Frances Anne Kemble, *Journal of a Residence on a Georgian Plantation in 1838–1839* (Chicago: Afro-Am Press, 1969; first published 1864), pp. 34–5, 49–50, 56.
68. Ibid., pp. 56, 135–6, 182–3, 245, 251, 261–2, 272.
69. Eugene D. Genovese, "The Medical and Insurance Costs of Slaveholding in the Cotton Belt," *The Journal of Negro History*, Vol. XLV, No. 3 (July 1960), pp. 152–5; Savitt, *Medicine and Slavery*, pp. 194–6.
70. *House of Lords Report*, 1832, Part I, pp. 63–5, evidence of Baillie.
71. *Accounts and Papers (Parliamentary Papers)*, 1836, XV (605), pp. 62–3: "Report from the Select Committee on Negro Apprenticeship in the Colonies. Minutes of Evidence," evidence of Madden.
72. Stewart, *View of Jamaica*, pp. 195–8.
73. Bickell, *The West Indies as They Are*, p. 52.
74. Williamson, *Medical Observations*, Vol. I, pp. 54–5.
75. Savitt, Medicine and Slavery, p. 156.

12. Slavery and medicine

1. William H. Burnley, *Opinions on Slavery and Emancipation in 1823; Referred to in a Recent Debate in the House of Commons. . .for the Extinction of Slavery* (London, 1833), pp. x–xiv.
2. Sir Philip Sherlock, "The West Indian Experience," in Samuel Proctor, ed., *Eighteenth-Century Florida and the Caribbean* (Gainesville: University Presses of Florida, 1976), pp. 44–9.
3. Vincent T. Harlow, *A History of Barbados 1625–1685* (Oxford: Oxford University Press, 1926), pp. 323–4.
4. John Oldmixon, *The British Empire in America*, etc., 2 vols. (London, 1708), Vol. II, pp. 140–1.
5. Douglas Hall, "Slaves and Slavery in the British West Indies," *Social and Economic Studies*, Vol. 11, No. 4 (December 1962), pp. 308–9.
6. [Edward Long], *A Free and Candid Review*, etc. (London, 1784), pp. 68–70.
7. Lord Sheffield, *Observations on the Commerce of the American States*, etc. (London, 1784), p. 160.
8. Henry Brougham, *An Inquiry into the Colonial Policy of the European Powers*, 2 vols. (Edinburgh, 1803), Vol. II, p. 469.
9. William Dickson, *The Mitigation of Slavery*, etc. (London, 1814), p. 205.
10. *Accounts and Papers (Parliamentary Papers)*, 1790, XXIX (698), p. 58: "Minutes of Evidence: Select Committee of the House of Commons on the Slave Trade," evidence of Jackson.
11. Ibid., p. 101, evidence of Hall.
12. [Dr. David Collins], *Practical Rules for the Management and Medical Treatment of Negro Slaves, in the Sugar Colonies. By a Professional Planter* (Freeport, N.Y.: Books for Libraries Press, 1971; first published 1803), pp. 6–18.

13. John Jeremie, *Four Essays on Colonial Slavery* (London, 1831), pp. 31, 55, 57; Franklin W. Knight, *The Caribbean: The Genesis of a Fragmented Nationalism* (New York: Oxford University Press, 1978), pp. 56–62.
14. Eric Williams, *Capitalism and Slavery* (Chapel Hill: University of North Carolina Press, 1944), pp. 108–25, 147–53, 178–212; Mary Turner, *Slaves and Missionaries: The Disintegration of Jamaican Slave Society, 1787–1834* (Urbana: University of Illinois Press, 1982); Michael Craton, *Testing the Chains: Resistance to Slavery in the British West Indies* (Ithaca, N.Y.: Cornell University Press, 1982).
15. Rev. James M. Phillippo, *Jamaica: Its Past and Present State* (Westport, Conn.: Negro Universities Press, 1970; first published 1843), pp. 170–1.
16. [Robert Robertson], *A Detection of the State and Situation of the Present Sugar Planters of Barbados and the Leeward Islands*, etc. (London, 1732), pp. 41–5; Rev. Robert Robertson, *A Letter to the Right Reverend The Lord Bishop of London* (London, 1730), p. 11. I am indebted to Dr. D. Barry Gaspar for this citation.
17. [James Stephen], *The Crisis of the Sugar Colonies; or an Enquiry into the Objects and Probable Effects of the French Expedition to the West Indies*, etc. (London, 1802), pp. 122–4, 150.
18. Richard H. Shryock, *Medicine and Society in America: 1660–1860* (Ithaca, N.Y.: Cornell University Press, 1960), pp. 17–18, 50–1.
19. John Duffy, "Medical Practice in the Ante Bellum South," *The Journal of Southern History*, Vol. XXV, No. 1 (February 1959), pp. 53–72; Harry F. Dowling, M.D., "The Impact of New Discoveries on Medical Practice: Advances in the Diagnosis and Treatment of the Infectious Diseases," in Lester S. King, M.D., ed., *Mainstreams of Medicine: Essays on the Social and Intellectual Context of Medical Practice* (Austin: University of Texas Press, 1971), pp. 108–22.
20. Guenter B. Risse, "The Renaissance of Bloodletting: A Chapter in Modern Therapeutics," *Journal of the History of Medicine and Allied Sciences*, Vol. XXXIV, No. 1 (January 1979), pp. 3–22; Lester S. King, "The Bloodletting Controversy: A Study in the Scientific Method," *Bulletin of the History of Medicine*, Vol. XXXV, No. 1 (Jan.–Feb. 1961), pp. 1–13.
21. James Thomson, M.D., *A Treatise on the Diseases of Negroes, As they Occur in the Island of Jamaica: With Observations on the Country Remedies* (Jamaica, 1820), pp. 21–2; John Williamson, M.D., *Medical and Miscellaneous Observations, Relative to the West India Islands*, 2 vols. (Edinburgh, 1817), Vol. II, pp. 134–5; Thomas Dancer, M.D., *The Medical Assistant, Or Jamaica Practice of Physic. Designed Chiefly for the Use of Families and Plantations*, 3d ed. (St. Jago De La Vega, Jamaica, 1819), p. 148, note.
22. Collins, *Practical Rules*, pp. 200–1; Williamson, *Medical Observations*, Vol. I, p. 170.
23. Anon., *Marly: Or, A Planter's Life in Jamaica* (Glasgow: Richard Griffin, 1828), pp. 160–2.
24. Thomson, *Treatise on Diseases of Negroes*, p. 38; Michael Craton, "Death, Disease and Medicine on Jamaican Slave Plantations: the Example of Worthy Park, 1767–1838," *Histoire Sociale – Social History*, Vol. II, No. 18 (November 1976),

pp. 250–1; Norman Taylor, *Plant Drugs that Changed the World* (New York: Dodd, Mead, 1965), pp. 207–18.

25. Edward Long, *The History of Jamaica*, etc., 3 vols. (London, 1774), Vol. II, pp. 433–4; Thomson, *Treatise on Diseases of Negroes*, pp. 44, 126. For a discussion of mercury poisoning, see Alfred W. Crosby, Jr., *The Columbian Exchange: Biological and Cultural Consequences of 1492* (Westport, Conn.: Greenwood, 1972), p. 153.
26. John S. Haller, Jr., "The Use and Abuse of Tartar Emetic in the 19th Century Materia Medica," *Bulletin of the History of Medicine*, Vol. 49, No. 2 (Summer 1975), pp. 235–57.
27. *Accounts and Papers (Parliamentary Papers)*, 1832, Vol. 305, No. 127, Part II, p. 265: "The Select Committee of the House of Lords Appointed to Inquire into the Laws and Usages of the several West India Colonies in relation to the Slave Population. Minutes of Evidence," evidence of Clare.
28. Dancer, *The Medical Assistant*, 2d ed., 1809, pp. 419–32; National Library of Scotland, Edinburgh, *Chisholme Papers, MS.* 5476, *Letter Book of James Chisholme 1793–1812*, letter to William Anderson of Jamaica, dated Portland Place, London, 2 November 1808.
29. Dancer, *The Medical Assistant*, 2d ed., 1809, p. ix; [John Stewart], *An Account of Jamaica and Its Inhabitants* (London, 1808), pp. 145–6; Williamson, *Medical Observations*, Vol. I, p. 401.
30. Craton, "Death, Disease and Medicine," pp. 251–5; *Journals of the Assembly of Jamaica*, Vol. XII, pp. 805–6: "Report from the Committee on the Registration Bill," 17 November 1815.
31. Thomson, *Treatise on Diseases of Negroes*, pp. 28–30, 76, 141–2, 148–50.
32. "House of Lords Select Committee," 1832, Vol. 305, No. 127, Part II, p. 264, evidence of Clare.
33. James Maxwell, M.D., *Observations on Yaws, And Its Influence in Originating Leprosy; Also Observations on Acute Traumatic Tetanus and Tetanus Infantum* (Edinburgh, 1839), pp. 43–8; Frantz Fanon, "Medicine and Colonialism," chap. 4 of his *A Dying Colonialism* (New York: Grove Press, 1965), pp. 121–45.
34. William H. Stewart, "Health – the Next Fifty Years," in William R. Ewald, Jr., ed., *Environment and Policy: The Next Fifty Years* (Bloomington: Indiana University Press, 1968), p. 107.
35. R. B. Davison, *Commonwealth Immigrants* (London: Oxford University Press, 1964), pp. 44–5.
36. William G. Sewell, *The Ordeal of Free Labor in the British West Indies* (New York: Harper and Brothers, 1861), p. 60; Gisela Eisner, *Jamaica, 1830–1930: A Study in Economic Growth* (Manchester: Manchester University Press, 1961), p. 136; L. Dudley Stamp, *The Geography of Life and Death* (London: Collins, 1964), pp. 26–36.
37. *Accounts and Papers (Parliamentary Papers)*, 1852–3, LXVII (76): "Report on the Sugar Growing Colonies," letter from Gavin Milroy, M.D., medical inspector, to Sir Charles Edward Grey, governor of Jamaica, 31 March 1851. For Dr. Milroy's "Report on the Cholera Epidemic," see *Parliamentary Papers*, 1854, XLIII (235), Cholera (Jamaica); Eisner, *Jamaica, 1830–1930*, pp. 165–6.

38. Rev. Hope Masterton Waddell, *Twenty-Nine Years in the West Indies and Central Africa: A Review of Missionary Work and Adventure 1829–1858* (London: Frank Cass, 1970; first published 1863), pp. 202–3.
39. Sewell, *Ordeal of Free Labor*, pp. 154–6; Eric Williams, *From Columbus to Castro: The History of the Caribbean 1492–1969* (London: Andre Deutsch, 1970), pp. 328–46; Douglas Hall, *Five of the Leewards 1834–1870: The major problems of the post-emancipation period in Antigua, Barbuda, Montserrat, Nevis and St. Kitts* (Barbados: Caribbean Universities Press, 1971), pp. 32–58.
40. John Davy, M.D., F.R.S., *The West Indies Before and Since Slave Emancipation*, etc. (London, 1854), p. 213.
41. Eisner, *Jamaica, 1830–1930*, pp. 133–8; George W. Roberts, *The Population of Jamaica* (Cambridge: Cambridge University Press, 1957), pp. 247–64.
42. Joseph John Gurney, *A Winter in the West Indies*, etc., 2d ed. (London, 1840), pp. 182–3; Sewell, *Ordeal of Free Labor*, pp. 195–9; Phillippo, *Jamaica: Its Past and Present State*, pp. 220–38; Douglas Hall, *Free Jamaica 1838–1865: An Economic History* (New Haven, Conn.: Yale University Press, 1959), pp. 180–1; Woodville K. Marshall, "Notes on Peasant Development in the West Indies since 1838," *Social and Economic Studies*, Vol. 17, No. 3 (September 1968), pp. 252–63; Philip D. Curtin, *Two Jamaicas: The Role of Ideas in a Tropical Colony 1830–1864* (Cambridge, Mass.: Harvard University Press, 1955), pp. 101–21.
43. Eisner, *Jamaica, 1830–1930*, pp. 157–8; Sewell, *Ordeal of Free Labor*, p. 79; F. R. Augier, D. G. Hall, S. C. Gordon, and M. Record, *The Making of the West Indies* (London: Longman Caribbean, 1970), p. 188.
44. Sewell, *Ordeal of Free Labor*, pp. 59–61.
45. George L. Beckford, *Persistent Poverty: Underdevelopment in Plantation Economies of the Third World* (New York: Oxford University Press, 1972), pp. 16–29, 48, 64, 224.
46. Richard A. Lobdell, "Economic Structure and Demographic Performance in Jamaica, 1891–1935," unpublished Ph.D. dissertation, McGill University, Montreal, Canada, October 1975; see his Abstract and pp. 18–20, 25–6, 45–60, 201–4.
47. Frantz Fanon, *Black Skin, White Masks* (New York: Grove Press, 1967), p. 225.

Bibliography

1. Manuscripts

Edinburgh University Library

Joseph Black's Correspondence
Archibald's Dalzel's Correspondence
Alston's Materia Medica or A History of Drugs
Medical Matriculation Albums

Scottish Record Office, Edinburgh

Balfour-Melville Manuscripts
Cargen Trustees Letter Book
Cochrane Papers
Dr. Walter Tullideph's Letter and Account Books

National Library of Scotland, Edinburgh

Robertson-MacDonald Letters
Chisholme Manuscripts

University Library, King's College, Aberdeen

The Diary of Dr. Jonathan Troup 1788–1790

Lincolnshire Archives Office, Lincoln

Monson Manuscripts: Journals of Thomas Thistlewood of Jamaica

Carlisle Record Office, Carlisle

The Senhouse Papers 1762–1831

The Library, University of Exeter

Gale-Morant Papers 1731–1925

Bibliography

Somerset Record Office, Taunton

Tudway Papers
Dickinson of Kingsweston Manuscripts

County Record Office, Shire Hall, Castle Hill, Cambridge

Tharp Collection

Bodleian Library, Oxford

Clarendon Manuscripts: Barham Papers

Flintshire Record Office, Hawarden, North Wales

John Gladstone Manuscripts

Department of Manuscripts, British Library

Martin Papers
Sloane Manuscripts
Long Manuscripts
Journal of Dr. James Henry Archer, Jamaica

Public Record Office, London

Treasury 71 Series, Slave Registration Returns
Colonial Office despatches and reports for the British West Indian Colonies

University of the West Indies, Mona, Jamaica

Penrhyn Castle Manuscripts, relating to Jamaica, 1709–1834 (microfilm; original at the University College of North Wales, Bangor)
Nathaniel Phillips Papers, ca. 1759–1813 (microfilm; original at the National Library of Wales, Slebech Collection)

Island Record Office, Spanish Town, Jamaica

Inventorys Series (personal property inventories)

Institute of Jamaica, Kingston

Harmony Hall Estate, Trelawny, Hospital Book, 1823–6
Letter Books of Sir Jacob Adolphus, M.D.
Newspaper collections

The Historical Society of Pennsylvania, Philadelphia

Powel Papers: Dr. Alexander Johnston's Ledger, Jamaica, 1769–1774

The Burke Library, Hamilton and Kirkland Colleges, Clinton, New York

J. Johnson Manuscript, Reports Relating to Mr. Gordon's Estates in the West Indies, 1824

2. Official publications

British Parliamentary Papers

1789, XXVI (646a), Report from Privy Council Committee on the Slave Trade; with the minutes of evidence

1790–1, XXIX (698), Report from Select Committee of the House of Commons on the Slave Trade; with the minutes of evidence

1807, XVIII (435), Report from Select Committee of the House of Commons on the Commercial State of the West India Colonies; with the minutes of evidence

1831–2, XX (721), Report from Select Committee of the House of Commons on the Extinction of Slavery throughout the British Dominions; with the minutes of evidence

1832, 305 (127), House of Lords, Report from Select Committee on the State of the West India Colonies; with the minutes of evidence

1836, XV (605), Report from Select Committee of the House of Commons on Negro Apprenticeship in the Colonies; with the minutes of evidence

1837–8, XL (417), Statistical Report of the Sickness, Mortality, and Invaliding among the Troops of the West Indies. Prepared under the direction of Alexander M. Tulloch, Major, and Henry Marshall, Deputy Inspector General of Hospitals

Jamaica

Jamaica, House of Assembly, Journals

Jamaica, House of Assembly, Votes

Laws of Jamaica

3. Unpublished theses and dissertations

Chitnis, Anand Chidamber, "The Edinburgh Professoriate 1790–1826, and the University's Contribution to Nineteenth Century British Society," Ph.D. dissertation, University of Edinburgh, 1968.

Higman, Barry W., "Slave Population and Economy in Jamaica at the Time of Emancipation," Ph.D. dissertation, University of the West Indies, Mona, Jamaica, 1970.

Lobdell, Richard A., "Economic Structure and Demographic Performance in Jamaica, 1891–1935," Ph.D. dissertation, McGill University, Montreal, Canada, 1975.

McDonald, Roderick A., " 'Goods and Chattels': The Economy of Slaves on Sugar Plantations in Jamaica and Louisiana," Ph.D. dissertation, University of Kansas, Lawrence, 1981.

Mair, Lucille Mathurin, "A Historical Study of Women in Jamaica from 1655 to 1844," Ph.D. dissertation, University of the West Indies, Mona, Jamaica, 1974.

Savitt, Todd Lee, "Sound Minds and Sound Bodies: The Diseases and Health Care of Blacks in Ante-Bellum Virginia," Ph.D. dissertation, University of Virginia, 1975.

4. Books and articles published before 1850

Anon., "College of Physicians and Surgeons of Jamaica," *The Jamaica Physical Journal* 1(1834), 377; 2(1835), 215–16.

Anon., *Memoirs of the Late William Wright, M.D., Fellow of the Royal Societies of London and Edinburgh, etc.* (Edinburgh, 1828).

Aubrey, Thomas, *The Sea-Surgeon, Or the Guinea Man's Vade Mecum* (London, 1729).

Barclay, Alexander, *A Practical View of the Present State of Slavery in the West Indies* (London, 1826).

Beckford, William, *Remarks upon the Situation of the Negroes in Jamaica* (London, 1788).

A Descriptive Account of the Island of Jamaica (London, 1790).

Chisholm, Colin, *A Manual of the Climate and Diseases of Tropical Countries* (London, 1822).

[Collins, David], *Practical Rules for the Management and Medical Treatment of Negro Slaves in the Sugar Colonies* (London, 1803).

Cooper, Thomas, *Facts Illustrative of the Condition of the Slaves in Jamaica* (London, 1824).

Dancer, Thomas, *A Short Dissertation on the Jamaica Bath Waters* (Jamaica, 1784).

The Medical Assistant, Or Jamaica Practice of Physic. Designed Chiefly for the Use of Families and Plantations, 2d ed. (Jamaica, 1809).

De la Beche, H. T., *Notes on the Present Condition of the Negroes in Jamaica* (London, 1825).

Dickson, William, *The Mitigation of Slavery* (London, 1814).

Edwards, Bryan, *The History, Civil and Commercial, of the British Colonies in the West Indies* (London, 1793).

Falconbridge, Alexander, *An Account of the Slave Trade on the Coast of Africa* (London, 1788).

Farquhar, George, "An Account of the Climate and Diseases of Jamaica," *The Philadelphia Medical Museum* 1(1805), 183–5.

[Gibbes, Philip], *Instructions for the Treatment of Negroes* (London, 1797).

Grainger, James, *An Essay on the More Common West-India Diseases; and the Remedies which that Country Itself Produces: to which are added, some hints on the Management, &c. of Negroes*, 2d ed. (Edinburgh, 1802).

Hancock, John, *Observations on the Climate, Soil, and Production of British Guiana . . . : Together with Incidental Remarks on the Diseases, their Treatment and Prevention* (London, 1835).

"Observations on Tetanus Infantum, or Lock-jaw of Infants," *Edinburgh Medical and Surgical Journal* 35(1831), 343–7.

Hillary, William, *Observations on the Changes of the Air, and the Concomitant Epidemical Diseases in the Island of Barbadoes* (Philadelphia, 1811).

Jackson, Robert, *A Sketch of the History and Cure of Contagious Fever* (London, 1819).

Johnson, J., *A Guide for Gentlemen Studying Medicine at the University of Edinburgh* (London, 1792).

Lascelles, Edwin, et al., *Instructions for the Management of a Plantation in Barbadoes, and for the Treatment of Negroes* (London, 1786).

Lewis, Matthew Gregory, *Journal of a West India Proprietor, kept during a residence in the island of Jamaica* (London, 1834).

Lind, James, *An Essay on Diseases Incidental to Europeans in Hot Climates*, 3d ed. (London, 1777).

Long, Edward, *The History of Jamaica* (London, 1774).

McMahon, Benjamin, *Jamaica Plantership* (London, 1839).

McNeill, Hector, *Observations on the Treatment of Negroes in the Island of Jamaica* (London, 1788).

Martin, Samuel, *An Essay on Plantership* (London, 1773).

Mason, David, "A descriptive account of Framboesia or Yaws," *Edinburgh Medical and Surgical Journal* 35(1831), 52–66.

Mathison, Gilbert, *Notices Respecting Jamaica, in 1808, 1809, 1810* (London, 1811).

Maxwell, James, *Observations on Yaws, and Its Influence in Originating Leprosy: Also Observations on Acute Traumatic Tetanus and Tetanus Infantum* (Edinburgh, 1839).

"Pathological Inquiry into the Nature of Cachexia Africa," *The Jamaica Physical Journal* 2(1835), 409–35.

Mead, Richard, *A Discourse on the Small-Pox and Measles*, 3d ed. (Edinburgh, 1763).

Moseley, Benjamin, *Observations on the Dysentery of the West-Indies with a new and successful Manner of treating it*, 2d ed. (London, 1781).

A Treatise on Tropical Diseases, 2d ed. (London, 1789).

Park, Mungo, *The Travels of Mungo Park* (London, 1799).

Phillippo, James M., *Jamaica: Its Past and Present State* (London, 1843).

Quier, John, et al., *Letters and Essays on the Small-Pox and Inoculation, the Measles, the Dry Belly-Ache, the Yellow, and Remitting and Intermitting Fevers of the West Indies* (London, 1778).

Ramsay, James, *An Essay on the Treatment and Conversion of African Slaves in the British Sugar Colonies* (London, 1784).

Roughley, Thomas, *The Jamaica Planter's Guide* (London, 1823).

Sells, William, *Remarks on the Condition of the Slaves in the Island of Jamaica* (London, 1823).

Sloane, Hans, *A Voyage to the Islands of Madera, Barbadoes, Nieves, S. Christophers and Jamaica, with . . . an Account of the Inhabitants, Air, Waters, Diseases, Trade &c* (London, 1707, 1725).

Smollett, Tobias, *The Adventures of Roderick Random* (London, 1748).

Stephen, James, *The Slavery of the British West India Colonies Delineated* (London, 1824, 1830).

Stewart, J., *A View of the Past and Present State of the Island of Jamaica; with Remarks on the Moral and Physical Condition of the Slaves, and on the Abolition of Slavery in the Colonies* (Edinburgh, 1823).

Thomas, Robert, *Medical Advice to the Inhabitants of Warm Climates . . . To the work are Prefixed, Some Observations on the proper Management of New Negroes, and the general Condition of Slaves in the Sugar Colonies* (London, 1790).

Thomson, James, *A Treatise on the Diseases of Negroes, as they Occur in the Island of Jamaica: with Observations on the Country Remedies* (Jamaica, 1820).

Tobin, James, *Cursory Remarks upon the Reverend Mr. Ramsay's Essay on the Treatment of African Slaves* (London, 1785).

Towne, Richard, *A Treatise on the Diseases Most frequent in the West-Indies and herein more particularly of those which occur in Barbadoes* (London, 1726).

Trapham, Thomas, *A Discourse of the State of Health in the Island of Jamaica* (London, 1679).

Williamson, John, *Medical and Miscellaneous Observations, Relative to the West India Islands* (Edinburgh, 1817).

Winterbottom, Thomas M., *Account of the Native Africans in the Neighbourhood of Sierra Leone; To which is added, An Account of the Present State of Medicine Among Them* (London, 1803).

5. Books and articles published in 1850 and thereafter

Anstey, Roger, *The Atlantic Slave Trade and British Abolition 1760–1810* (Atlantic Highlands, N.J., 1975).

Ashburn, P. M., *The Ranks of Death: A Medical History of the Conquest of America* (New York, 1947).

Ashcroft, Michael T., "A history and general survey of the helminth and protozoal infections of the West Indies," *Annals of Tropical Medicine and Parasitology* 59(1965), 478–93.

"Tercentenary of the first English book on tropical medicine, by Thomas Trapham of Jamaica," *British Medical Journal* 2(1979), 475–7.

Ashcroft, Michael T., et al., "Treponemal Serological Tests in Jamaican School Children," *Transactions of the Royal Society of Tropical Medicine and Hygiene* 59(1965), 649–56.

"Ethnic differences in growth potential of children of African, Indian, Chinese and European origin," *Transactions of the Royal Society of Tropical Medicine and Hygiene* 70(1976), 433–8.

Augelli, John P., "The Rimland–Mainland Concept of Culture Areas in Middle America," *Annals of the Association of American Geographers* 52(1962), 119–29.

Augier, F. R., D. G. Hall, S. C. Gordon, and M. Record, *The Making of the West Indies* (London, 1970).

Barrett, Leonard, "The Portrait of a Jamaican Healer: African Medical Lore in the Caribbean," *Caribbean Quarterly* 19(1973), 6–19.

Beckford, George L., *Persistent Poverty: Underdevelopment in plantation economies of the Third World* (New York, 1972).

Beckwith, Martha Warren, *Notes on Jamaican Ethnobotany* (Poughkeepsie, N.Y., 1927).

Black Roadways: A Study of Jamaican Folk Life (Chapel Hill, N.C., 1929).

Bennett, J. Harry, *Bondsmen and Bishops: Slavery and Apprenticeship on the Codrington Plantations of Barbados, 1710–1838* (Berkeley, Cal., 1958).

Brathwaite, Edward, *The Development of Creole Society in Jamaica 1770–1820* (Oxford, 1971).

Bridenbaugh, Carl, and Roberta Bridenbaugh, *No Peace Beyond the Line: The English in the Caribbean 1624–1690* (New York, 1972).

Chitnis, Anand C., "Medical Education in Edinburgh, 1790–1826, and some Victorian Social Consequences," *Medical History* 17(1973), 173–85.

Cipolla, Carlo M., *The Economic History of World Population* (Harmondsworth, England, 1962).

Clendening, Logan, *Source Book of Medical History* (New York, 1960).

Comrie, John D., *History of Scottish Medicine to 1860* (London, 1927).

Craton, Michael, *Sinews of Empire: A Short History of British Slavery* (Garden City, N.Y., 1974).

Searching for the Invisible Man: Slaves and Plantation Life in Jamaica (Cambridge, Mass., 1978).

"Jamaican Slave Mortality: Fresh Light from Worthy Park, Longville and the Tharp Estates," *The Journal of Caribbean History* 3(1971), 1–27.

"Death, Disease and Medicine on Jamaican Slave Plantations: the Example of Worthy Park, 1767–1838," *Histoire Sociale – Social History* 18(1976), 237–55.

Testing the Chains: Resistance to Slavery in the British West Indies (Ithaca, N.Y., 1982).

Craton, Michael, and James Walvin, *A Jamaican Plantation: The History of Worthy Park 1670–1970* (Toronto, 1970).

Crosby, Alfred W., Jr., *The Columbian Exchange: Biological and Cultural Consequences of 1492* (Westport, Conn., 1972).

Cundall, Frank, *The Press and Printers of Jamaica Prior to 1820* (Worcester, Mass., 1916).

Curtin, Philip, D., *Two Jamaicas. The Role of Ideas in a Tropical Colony, 1830–1865* (Cambridge, Mass., 1955).

The Atlantic Slave Trade: A Census (Madison, Wis., 1969).

"Epidemiology and the Slave Trade," *Political Science Quarterly* 83(1968), 190–216.

Danielson, Ross, *Cuban Medicine* (New Brunswick, N.J., 1979).

Davis, David Brion, *The Problem of Slavery in the Age of Revolution* (Ithaca, N.Y., 1975).

Davy, John, *The West Indies Before and Since Slave Emancipation* (London, 1854).

Debien, Gabriel, "La Nourriture des Esclaves sur les Plantations des Antilles Francaises aux XVIIe et XVIIIe Siecles," *Caribbean Studies* 4(1964), 3–27.

Dirks, Robert, "Resource Fluctuations and Competitive Transformations in West Indian Slave Societies," in Charles E. Laughlin, Jr., and Ivan A. Brady, eds., *Extinction and Survival in Human Populations* (New York, 1978).

Donnan, Elizabeth, ed., *Documents Illustrative of the History of the Slave Trade to America* (New York, 1965).

Drescher, Seymour, *Econocide: British Slavery in the Era of Abolition* (Pittsburgh, 1977).

Duffy, John, *Epidemics in Colonial America* (Baton Rouge, La., 1953).

The Healers: A History of American Medicine (Urbana, Ill., 1979).

Dunn, Richard S., *Sugar and Slaves: The Rise of the Planter Class in the English West Indies, 1624–1713* (Chapel Hill, N.C., 1972).

"A Tale of Two Plantations: Slave Life at Mesopotamia in Jamaica and Mount Airy in Virginia, 1799 to 1828," *William and Mary Quarterly*, 3d series 34(1977), 32–65.

Eisner, Gisela, *Jamaica, 1830–1930: A Study in Economic Growth* (Manchester, 1961).

Eltis, David, and James Walvin with the collaboration of Svend E. Green-Pedersen, *The Abolition of the Atlantic Slave Trade: Origins and Effects in Europe, Africa, and the Americas* (Madison, Wis., 1981).

Engerman, Stanley L., "Some Economic and Demographic Comparisons of Slavery in the United States and the British West Indies," *Economic History Review*, 2d series 29(1976), 258–75.

Engerman, Stanley L., and Eugene D. Genovese, eds., *Race and Slavery in the Western Hemisphere: Quantitative Studies* (Princeton, N.J., 1975).

Fanon, Frantz, *A Dying Colonialism* (New York, 1965).

Black Skin, White Masks (New York, 1967).

Fogel, Robert William, *Without Consent or Contract: The Rise and Fall of American Slavery* (forthcoming).

Fogel, Robert William, and Stanley L. Engerman, *Time on the Cross: The Economics of American Negro Slavery* (Boston, 1974).

"Recent Findings in the Study of Slave Demography and Family Structure," *Sociology and Social Research* 63(1979), 569–74.
Galenson, David W., *White Servitude in Colonial America: An Economic Analysis* (Cambridge, 1981).
"The Slave Trade to the English West Indies, 1673–1724," *Economic History Review*, 3d series 32(1979), 241–9.
Gaspar, David Barry, *Slave Resistance and Social Control in Antigua, 1632–1764* (forthcoming).
Gelfand, Michael, *Medicine and Custom in Africa* (Edinburgh, 1964).
Gemery, Henry A., and Jan S. Hogendorn, *The Uncommon Market: Essays in the Economic History of the Atlantic Slave Trade* (New York, 1979).
Genovese, Eugene D., *Roll, Jordan, Roll: The World the Slaves Made* (New York, 1974).
Goerke, Heinz, "The Life and Scientific Works of Dr. John Quier, Practitioner of Physic and Surgery, Jamaica: 1738–1822," *West Indian Medical Journal* 5(1956), 23–6.
Goveia, Elsa V., *Slave Society in the British Leeward Islands at the End of the Eighteenth Century* (New Haven, Conn., 1965).
Green, William A., *British Slave Emancipation: The Sugar Colonies and the Great Experiment 1830–1865* (Oxford, 1976).
Green-Pedersen, Svend E., "Slave Demography in the Danish West Indies and the Abolition of the Danish Slave Trade," in David Eltis and James Walvin, eds., *The Abolition of the Atlantic Slave Trade: Origins and Effects in Europe, Africa, and the Americas* (Madison, Wisc., 1981), pp. 231–57.
Greene, Jack P., "Society and Economy in the British Caribbean during the Seventeenth and Eighteenth Centuries," *American Historical Review* 79(1974), 1499–1517.
Guthrie, Douglas, *A History of Medicine* (London, 1947).
Hall, Douglas, *Free Jamaica 1838–1865: An Economic History* (New Haven, Conn., 1959).
"Slaves and Slavery in the British West Indies," *Social and Economic Studies* 11(1962), 305–18.
"Absentee-Proprietorship in the British West Indies, to about 1850," *The Jamaican Historical Review* 4(1964), 15–35.
Handler, Jerome S., and Robert S. Corruccini, "Plantation Slave Life in Barbados: A Physical Anthropological Analysis," *Journal of Interdisciplinary History* 14(1983), 65–90.
Handler, Jerome S., Frederick W. Lange, and Robert V. Riordan, *Plantation Slavery in Barbados: An Archaeological and Historical Investigation* (Cambridge, Mass., 1978).
Harley, George Way, *Native African Medicine, With Special Reference to its Practice in the Mano Tribe of Liberia* (London, 1970).
Herskovits, Melville J., *The Myth of the Negro Past* (Boston, 1958).
Higman, Barry W., *Slave Population and Economy in Jamaica, 1807–1834* (Cambridge, 1976).
"Household Structure and Fertility on Jamaican Slave Plantations: A Nineteenth-century Example," *Population Studies* 27(1973), 527–50.
"The Slave Family and Household in the British West Indies, 1800–1834," *Journal of Interdisciplinary History* 6(1975), 261–87.
"The Slave Population of the British Caribbean: Some Nineteenth-Century Var-

iations," in Samuel Proctor, ed., *Eighteenth-Century Florida and the Caribbean* (Gainesville, 1976), pp. 60–70.
"Growth in Afro-Caribbean Slave Populations," *American Journal of Physical Anthropology*, 2d series 50(1979), 373–85.
Hoeppi, R., *Parasitic Diseases in Africa and the Western Hemisphere: Early Documentation and Transmission by the Slave Trade* (Basel, Switzerland, 1969).
Hollingsworth, T. H., *Historical Demography* (London, 1969).
Hopkins, A. G., *An Economic History of West Africa* (New York, 1973).
Hudson, Robert P., *Disease and Its Control: The Shaping of Modern Thought* (Westport, Conn., 1983).
Hughes, Thomas P., *Medicine in Virginia, 1607–1699* (Williamsburg, Va., 1957).
Hunter, John M., "Geophagy in Africa and in the United States: A Culture-Nutrition Hypothesis," *Geographical Review* 63(1973), 170–95.
Ingram, K. E., *Sources of Jamaican History 1655–1838* (Zug, Switzerland, 1976).
Inikori, J. E., "Measuring the Atlantic Slave Trade: An Assessment of Curtin and Anstey," *Journal of African History* 7(1976), 197–223.
Jakobsson, Stiv, *Am I Not a Man and a Brother? British Missions and the Abolition of the Slave Trade and Slavery in West Africa and the West Indies 1786–1838* (Uppsala, Sweden, 1972).
Jordan, Winthrop D., *White Over Black: American Attitudes toward the Negro, 1550–1812* (Chapel Hill, N.C., 1968).
King, Lester S., *The Medical World of the Eighteenth Century* (Chicago, 1958).
Kiple, Kenneth F., and Virginia Himmelsteib King, *Another Dimension to the Black Diaspora: Diet, Disease, and Racism* (Cambridge, 1981).
Kiple, Kenneth F., and Virginia H. Kiple, "Slave Child Mortality: Some Nutritional Answers to a Perennial Puzzle," *Journal of Social History* 10(1977), 284–309.
"Deficiency Diseases in the Caribbean," *Journal of Interdisciplinary History* 11(1980), 197–205.
Klein, Herbert S., *The Middle Passage: Comparative Studies in the Atlantic Slave Trade* (Princeton, N.J., 1978).
Klein, Herbert S., and Stanley L. Engerman, "Fertility Differentials between Slaves in the United States and the British West Indies: A Note on Lactation Practices and Their Possible Implications," *William and Mary Quarterly*, 3d series 35(1978), 357–74.
Knight, Franklin W., *The Caribbean: The Genesis of a Fragmented Nationalism* (New York, 1978).
Koplan, Jeffrey, P., "Slave Mortality in Nineteenth-Century Grenada," *Social Science History* 7(1983), 311–20.
Kulikoff, Allan, "A 'Prolifick' People: Black Population Growth in the Chesapeake Colonies, 1700–1790," *Southern Studies* 16(1977), 391–428.
Littlefield, Daniel C., *Rice and Slaves: Ethnicity and the Slave Trade in Colonial South Carolina* (Baton Rouge, La., 1981).
McKeown, Thomas, *The Modern Rise of Population* (New York, 1976).
McNeill, William H., *Plagues and Peoples* (Garden City, N.Y., 1977).
Maier, D., "Nineteenth-Century Asante Medical Practices," *Comparative Studies in Society and History* 21(1979), 63–81.
Major, Ralph Hermon, *A History of Medicine* (Springfield, Ill., 1954).
Menard, Russell R., "The Maryland Slave Population, 1658 to 1730: A Demographic Profile of Blacks in Four Countries," *William and Mary Quarterly*, 3d series 32(1975), 29–54.

Miller, Genevieve, *The Adoption of Inoculation for Smallpox in England and France* (Philadelphia, 1957).
Mintz, Sidney W., "Time, Sugar, and Sweetness," *Marxist Perspectives* 2(1979–80), 56–73.
Mintz, Sidney W., and Douglas G. Hall, "The Origins of the Jamaican Internal Marketing System," *Yale University Publications in Anthropology No. 57* (New Haven, 1960).
Mintz, Sidney W., and Richard Price, *An Anthropological Approach to the Afro-American Past: A Caribbean Perspective* (Philadelphia, 1976).
Pares, Richard, *A West-India Fortune* (London, 1950).
Merchants and Planters, Economic History Review Supplement, No. 4 (1960).
Parry, John H., "Plantation and Provision Ground: An historical sketch of the introduction of food crops into Jamaica," *Revista de Historia de America* (Mexico), Numero 39(Junio de 1955), 1–20.
Patterson, Orlando, *The Sociology of Slavery: An Analysis of the Origins, Development and Structure of Negro Slave Society in Jamaica* (London, 1967).
Slavery and Social Death: A Comparative Study (Cambridge, Mass., 1982).
Postell, William Dosite, *The Health of Slaves on Southern Plantations* (Gloucester, Mass., 1970).
Ragatz, Lowell J., *A Guide for the Study of British Caribbean History, 1763–1834* (Washington, D.C., 1932).
The Fall of the Planter Class in the British Caribbean, 1763–1833: A Study in Social and Economic History (New York, 1963).
Rawley, James A., *The Transatlantic Slave Trade: A History* (New York, 1981).
Razzell, Peter, *The Conquest of Smallpox: The Impact of Inoculation on Smallpox Mortality in Eighteenth Century Britain* (Firle, Sussex, 1977).
Roberts, George W., *The Population of Jamaica* (Cambridge, 1957).
"A Life Table for a West Indian Slave Population," *Population Studies* 5(1952), 238–42.
Rodney, Walter, *A History of the Upper Guinea Coast 1545–1800* (Oxford, 1970).
West Africa and the Atlantic Slave Trade (Nairobi, Kenya, 1967).
How Europe Underdeveloped Africa (London, 1972).
Rubin, Vera, and Arthur Tuden, eds., *Comparative Perspectives on Slavery in New World Plantation Societies* (New York, 1977).
Sauer, Carl Ortwin, *The Early Spanish Main* (Berkeley, Cal., 1966).
Savitt, Todd L., *Medicine and Slavery: The Diseases and Health Care of Blacks in Antebellum Virginia* (Urbana, Ill., 1978).
Scott, H. Harold, *A History of Tropical Medicine* (Baltimore, 1939).
"The Influence of the Slave-Trade in the Spread of Tropical Diseases," *Transactions of the Royal Society of Tropical Medicine and Hygiene* 37(1943), 169–88.
Sheridan, Richard B., *Sugar and Slavery: An Economic History of the British West Indies 1623–1775* (Baltimore, 1974).
"Africa and the Caribbean in the Atlantic Slave Trade," *American Historical Review* 77(1972), 15–35.
"Mortality and the Medical Treatment of Slaves in the British West Indies," in Stanley L. Engerman and Eugene D. Genovese, eds., *Race and Slavery in the Western Hemisphere: Quantitative Studies* (Princeton, N.J., 1976), 285–310.
" 'Sweet Malefactor': The Social Costs of Slavery and Sugar in Jamaica and Cuba, 1807–54," *Economic History Review*, 2d series 29(1976), 236–57.
"The Crisis of Slave Subsistence in the British West Indies during and after the

American Revolution," *William and Mary Quarterly*, 3d series 33(1976), 615–41.
"The Guinea Surgeons on the Middle Passage: The Provision of Medical Services in the British Slave Trade," *International Journal of African Historical Studies* 14(1982), 601–25.
Shryock, Richard H., *Medicine and Society in America: 1660–1860* (Ithaca, N.Y., 1960).
Simpson, George E., "Folk Medicine in Trinidad," *Journal of American Folklore* 75(1962), 326–40.
Singer, Charles, and E. Ashworth Underwood, *A Short History of Medicine*, 2d ed. (New York, 1962).
Stemp, L. Dudley, *The Geography of Life and Death* (London, 1964).
Turner, Mary, *Slaves and Missionaries: The Disintegration of Jamaican Slave Society, 1787–1834* (Urbana, Ill., 1982).
Walvin, James, ed., *Slavery and British Society 1776–1846* (Baton Rouge, La., 1982).
Ward, J. R., "The Profitability of Sugar Planting in the British West Indies, 1650–1834," *Economic History Review*, 2d series 31(1978), 197–213.
Whitten, David O., "Medical Care of Slaves: Louisiana Sugar Region and South Carolina Rice District," *Southern Studies* 16(1977), 153–80.
Wilcocks, Charles, *Health and Disease in the Tropics* (London, 1950).
Wilcocks, Charles, and Philip Manson-Bahr, *Manson's Tropical Diseases* (Baltimore, 1972).
Williams, Eric, *Capitalism and Slavery* (Chapel Hill, N.C., 1944).
From Columbus to Castro: The History of the Caribbean 1492–1969 (London, 1970).
Winslow, Charles-E. A., *The Conquest of Epidemic Disease: A Chapter in the History of Ideas* (New York, 1967).
Wood, Peter H., *Black Majority: Negroes in Colonial South Carolina from 1670 through the Stono Rebellion* (New York, 1974).
Wrigley, E. A., *Population and History* (New York, 1969).

Index